Texts in Theoretical Computer Science
An EATCS Series

T0189805

Erich Grädel · Phokion G. Kolaitis · Leonid Libkin
Maarten Marx · Joel Spencer · Moshe Y. Vardi
Yde Venema · Scott Weinstein

Finite Model Theory and Its Applications

With 35 Figures and 2 Tables

 Springer

Authors

Erich Grädel
Mathematical Foundations
of Computer Science
RWTH Aachen
graedel@informatik.rwth-aachen.de

Phokion G. Kolaitis
IBM Almaden Research Center
kolaitis@almaden.ibm.com
and
Univ. of California at Santa Cruz
kolaitis@cs.ucsc.edu

Leonid Libkin
Univ. of Edinburgh
libkin@inf.ed.ac.uk

Maarten Marx
ISLA, Universiteit van Amsterdam
marx@science.uva.nl

Joel Spencer
Courant Institute
spencer@cims.nyu.edu

Moshe Y. Vardi
Rice University
vardi@cs.rice.edu

Yde Venema
Universiteit van Amsterdam
yde@science.uva.nl

Scott Weinstein
Univ. of Pennsylvania
weinstein@cis.upenn.edu

Series Editors

Prof. Dr. Wilfried Brauer
Institut für Informatik der TUM
Boltzmannstr. 3
85748 Garching, Germany
brauer@informatik.tu-muenchen.de

Prof. Dr. Juraj Hromkovič
ETH Zentrum
Department of Computer Science
Swiss Federal Institute of Technology
8092 Zürich, Switzerland
juraj.hromkovic@inf.ethz.ch

Prof. Dr. Grzegorz Rozenberg
Leiden Institute of Advanced
Computer Science
University of Leiden
Niels Bohrweg 1
2333 CA Leiden, The Netherlands
rozenber@liacs.nl

Prof. Dr. Arto Salomaa
Turku Centre of
Computer Science
Lemminkäisenkatu 14 A
20520 Turku, Finland
asalomaa@utu.fi

ACM Computing Classification (1998): F.4.1, F.1.3, H.2.3, I.2.4, I.2.8

ISSN 1862-4499
ISBN 978-3-642-43860-8 Springer Berlin Heidelberg New York

Springer is a part of Springer Science+Business Media
springer.com

© Springer-Verlag Berlin Heidelberg 2007
Softcover re-print of the Hardcover 1st edition 2007

Cover Design: KünkelLopka, Heidelberg
Typesetting: by the authors
Production: Integra Software Services Pvt. Ltd., Pondicherry, India

Printed on acid-free paper   45/3100/Integra   5 4 3 2 1 0

Preface

Finite model theory, as understood here, is an area of mathematical logic that has developed in close connection with applications to computer science, in particular the theory of computational complexity and database theory. One of the fundamental insights of mathematical logic is that our understanding of mathematical phenomena is enriched by elevating the languages we use to describe mathematical structures to objects of explicit study. If mathematics is the science of patterns, then the media through which we discern patterns, as well as the structures in which we discern them, command our attention. It is this aspect of logic which is most prominent in model theory, "the branch of mathematical logic which deals with the relation between a formal language and its interpretations". No wonder, then, that mathematical logic, and finite model theory in particular, should find manifold applications in computer science: from specifying programs to querying databases, computer science is rife with phenomena whose understanding requires close attention to the interaction between language and structure.

This volume gives a broad overview of some central themes of finite model theory: expressive power, descriptive complexity, and zero–one laws, together with selected applications to database theory and artificial intelligence, especially constraint databases and constraint satisfaction problems. The final chapter provides a concise modern introduction to modal logic, which emphasizes the continuity in spirit and technique with finite model theory. Chapters 2–7 are extensively revised and updated versions of tutorials presented at the University of Pennsylvania on April 12–15, 1999, under the sponsorship of Penn's Institute for Research in Cognitive Science (IRCS) and the Center for Discrete Mathematics and Theoretical Computer Science (DIMACS) at Rutgers University. We would like to express our gratitude to DIMACS and IRCS for their support, which made these tutorials possible. The tutorials were presented to a diverse audience of computer scientists, linguists, logicians, mathematicians, and philosophers, and the chapters of the book retain the broad accessibility and wide appeal of the tutorials. The introductory chapter highlights common themes among the tutorials that follow.

This volume is not meant to be a textbook on finite model theory. There are three such texts currently available. *Finite Model Theory*, by Ebbinghaus and Flum, and *Elements of Finite Model Theory*, by Libkin, provide general coverage of the field, while *Descriptive Complexity*, by Immerman, focuses on the connection between finite model theory and computational-complexity theory. Rather, this volume aims at highlighting applications of finite model theory, emphasizing "the unusual effectiveness of logic in computer science".

December 18, 2006   Moshe Y. Vardi
                                                     Scott Weinstein

Contents

Authors

Erich Grädel
Mathematical Foundations
of Computer Science
RWTH Aachen
52056 Aachen, Germany
graedel@informatik.
rwth-aachen.de

Phokion G. Kolaitis
IBM Almaden Research Center
Computer Science Principles
and Methodologies
650 Harry Road
San Jose, CA 95120-6099, USA
kolaitis@almaden.ibm.com
and
Computer Science Dept.
Univ. of California at Santa Cruz
CA 95064, USA
kolaitis@cs.ucsc.edu

Leonid Libkin
School of Informatics
Univ. of Edinburgh
Edinburgh, EH8 9LE
UK
libkin@inf.ed.ac.uk

Maarten Marx
ISLA, Universiteit van Amsterdam
The Netherlands
marx@science.uva.nl

Joel Spencer
Courant Institute
251 Mercer Street
New York, NY 10012, USA
spencer@cims.nyu.edu

Moshe Y. Vardi
Dept. of Computer Science
Rice University
Mail Stop 132
6100 S. Main Street
Houston, TX 77005-1892, USA
vardi@cs.rice.edu

Yde Venema
Inst. for Logic, Language and
Computation
Universiteit van Amsterdam
Plantage Muidergracht 24
1018 TV Amsterdam
The Netherlands
yde@science.uva.nl

Scott Weinstein
Dept. of Philosophy
Univ. of Pennsylvania
Philadelphia, PA 19104, USA
weinstein@cis.upenn.edu

1

Unifying Themes in Finite Model Theory

Scott Weinstein

One of the fundamental insights of mathematical logic is that our understanding of mathematical phenomena is enriched by elevating the languages we use to describe mathematical structures to objects of explicit study. If mathematics is the science of pattern, then the media through which we discern patterns, as well as the structures in which we discern them, command our attention. It is this aspect of logic which is most prominent in model theory, "the branch of mathematical logic which deals with the relation between a formal language and its interpretations" [21]. No wonder, then, that mathematical logic, in general, and finite model theory, the specialization of model theory to finite structures, in particular, should find manifold applications in computer science: from specifying programs to querying databases, computer science is rife with phenomena whose understanding requires close attention to the interaction between language and structure.

As with most branches of mathematics, the growth of mathematical logic may be seen as fueled by its applications. The very birth of set theory was occasioned by Cantor's investigations in real analysis, on subjects themselves motivated by developments in nineteenth-century physics; and the study of subsets of the real line has remained the source of some of the deepest results of contemporary set theory. At the same time, model theory has matured through the development of ever deeper applications to algebra. The interplay between language and structure, characteristic of logic, may be discerned in all these developments. From the focus on definability hierarchies in descriptive set theory, to the classification of structures up to elementary equivalence in classical model theory, logic seeks order in the universe of mathematics through the medium of formal languages.

As noted, finite model theory too has grown with its applications, in this instance not to analysis or algebra, but to combinatorics and computer science. Beginning with connections to automata theory, finite model theory has developed through a broader and broader range of applications to problems in graph theory, complexity theory, database theory, computer-aided verification, and artificial intelligence. And though its applications have demanded the development of new techniques, which have given the subject a distinctive character as compared to classical model theory, the fundamental focus on organizing and understanding phenomena through attention to the relation between language and structure remains prominent. Indeed, the detailed investigation of definability hierarchies and classifications of finite structures up to equivalence relations coarser than elementary equivalence, which are defined in terms of a wide variety of fragments of first-order, second-order, fixed-point, and infinitary logics, is a hallmark of finite model theory. The remaining sections of this chapter will highlight common themes among the chapters to follow.

1.1 Definability Theory

The volume begins with a chapter by Phokion Kolaitis, "On the expressive power of logics on finite models", which surveys major topics in the theory of definability in the context of finite structures. "The theory of definability is the branch of logic which studies the complexity of concepts by looking at the grammatical complexity of their definitions." [3]. This characterization indicates that the theory of definability has two main aspects:

- to establish a classification of concepts in terms of definitional complexity
- to establish that such classification is in some way informative about the intrinsic or intuitive "complexity" of the concepts thus classified.

Chapter 2 provides an extended treatment of both these aspects of definability theory, which reappear throughout the volume as important themes in finite model theory and its applications.

1.1.1 Classification of Concepts in Terms of Definitional Complexity

In the context of finite model theory, the "concepts" with which we are concerned are queries on classes of finite relational structures. Chapter 2 provides precise definitions of these notions; for the purposes of introduction, let us focus on Boolean queries on a particular set of finite undirected graphs as follows. Let G_n be the collection of undirected graphs with vertex set $[n]$ $(= \{1, \ldots, n\})$, and let $G = \bigcup_n G_n$. Thus, each $G \in G$ has a vertex set $V^G = [n]$, for some n, and an irreflexive and symmetric edge relation $E^G \subseteq [n] \times [n]$. A Boolean query Q on G is just an isomorphism-closed subset of G, that is, $Q \subseteq G$ is a Boolean query if and only if, for all $G, H \in G$,

$$G \cong H \implies (G \in Q \Leftrightarrow H \in Q).$$

Logical languages provide a natural means for classifying Boolean queries. A logical language L consists of a set of L-sentences, S_L, and an L-satisfaction relation $\models_L$. In the current setting, we may understand $\models_L$ as a relation between graphs $G \in \mathsf{G}$ and sentences $\varphi \in S_L$: $G \models_L \varphi$, if and only if G satisfies the condition expressed by φ. A fundamental notion is the Boolean query, $\varphi[\mathsf{G}]$, defined by an L-sentence, φ:

$$\varphi[\mathsf{G}] = \{G \in \mathsf{G} \mid G \models_L \varphi\}.$$

A Boolean query Q on G is L-definable if and only if there is an L-sentence φ with $Q = \varphi[\mathsf{G}]$.

Let us look at some examples. Consider the following Boolean queries:

Size$_n$ the set of graphs of size n;
Diam$_n$ the set of graphs of diameter $\leq n$;
Color$_k$ the set of k-colorable graphs;
Conn the set of connected graphs;
Card$_X$ the set of graphs of size n for some $n \in X \subseteq \mathsf{N}$.

The first two queries are defined by first-order sentences σ_n and δ_n, respectively, for each n; for example, the query Size$_2$ is defined by the first-order sentence σ_2,

$$\exists x \exists y (x \neq y) \wedge \neg \exists x \exists y \exists z (x \neq y \wedge x \neq z \wedge y \neq z),$$

and the query Diam$_2$ is defined by the first-order sentence δ_2,

$$\forall x \forall y (x = y \vee Exy \vee \exists z (Exz \wedge Ezy)).$$

For each k, the third query is defined by a sentence χ_k of existential monadic second-order logic, that is, the fragment of second-order logic consisting of sentences all of whose second-order quantifiers are existential, bind monadic predicate symbols, and do not occur within the scope of any first-order quantifier or truth-functional connective; for example, Color$_2$ is defined by the sentence χ_2,

$$\exists Z \forall x \forall y (Exy \rightarrow (Zx \leftrightarrow \neg Zy)).$$

The next query is defined by a sentence γ of $L_{\omega_1 \omega}$, the infinitary logic obtained by adding the operations of countable conjunction and countable disjunction to first-order logic, as follows:

$$\bigvee_{n \in \mathsf{N}} \delta_n.$$

Note that in general, γ expresses the condition that a graph has bounded diameter – over G, this condition coincides with connectedness. Finally, for each $X \subset \mathsf{N}$, the query Card$_X$ is defined by a sentence κ_X of $L_{\omega_1 \omega}$ as follows:

$$\bigvee_{n \in X} \sigma_n.$$

Now, broadly speaking, definability theory provides techniques for determining whether or not given queries, or collections of queries, are definable in a specified logic L, and attempts to extract useful information about queries from the fact that they are L-definable. For example, Chap. 2 develops tools to show that neither Color_k nor Conn is first-order definable, and thus stronger logics are needed to express such basic combinatorial properties.

1.1.2 What More Do We Know When We Know a Concept Is L-Definable?

This, of course, depends on L. One striking feature of finite model theory has been that it has drawn attention to the fact that a great deal of interesting information about Boolean queries *can* be extracted from the fact that they are definable in familiar logical languages, and, perhaps even more striking, it has highlighted the importance of some natural, though hitherto neglected, fragments of well-studied languages, such as the finite variable fragments of first-order logic and infinitary logic discussed below.

Before we proceed to explore this aspect of definability theory in the context of finite model theory, let us reflect for a moment on a paradigmatic example of extracting information from the fact that a set is definable in a certain way: the celebrated result of Cantor concerning the cardinality of closed sets of real numbers. Recall that a closed set can be defined as the complement of a countable union of open intervals with rational endpoints (which implies, in modern parlance, that a closed set is $\mathbf{\Pi}_1^0$). Note that we may infer from this definability characterization that there are only $2^{\aleph_0}$ closed sets of reals, while there are $2^{(2^{\aleph_0})}$ sets of reals altogether. Cantor showed that closed sets satisfy a very strong dichotomy with respect to their cardinalities: every infinite closed set is either countable or of cardinality $2^{\aleph_0}$, that is, there is no closed set witnessing a cardinality strictly between $\aleph_0$ and $2^{\aleph_0}$. On the basis of his success with closed sets, Cantor was motivated to formulate the Continuum Hypothesis (CH): the conjecture that all infinite sets of reals satisfy this strong cardinality dichotomy. In 1963, Cohen established that if Zermelo–Fraenkel set theory with the Axiom of Choice (ZFC) is consistent, then it is consistent with the statement that there is an infinite set of reals whose cardinality is neither $\aleph_0$ nor $2^{\aleph_0}$, that is, ZFC $+\neg$CH is consistent relative to ZFC. Thus, Cantor's result shows how it is possible to gain significant structural information about a concept from the knowledge that it admits a "simple" enough definition. In what Moshovakis describes as "one of the first important results of descriptive set theory" [52], Suslin generalized Cantor's solution of the continuum problem from closed sets to analytic sets, that is, projections of closed sets ($\mathbf{\Sigma}_1^1$ sets). Indeed, he showed that every uncountable analytic set contains a nonempty perfect set, as Cantor had established for closed sets. Further generalization of this property to sets whose definitional complexity is greater, even to co-analytic sets, is not possible on the basis of ZFC.

Finite model theory provides a rich collection of phenomena which illustrate this paradigm of wresting structural information about concepts from definability conditions. Let us begin with an example from asymptotic combinatorics which touches on topics dealt with in detail in Chaps. 2 and 4. Let Q be a Boolean query on G. Recall that $\mathrm{card}(\mathsf{G}_n) = 2^{\binom{n}{2}}$. The density μ_n of Q at G_n is defined as follows:

$$\mu_n(Q) = \mathrm{card}(Q \cap \mathsf{G}_n) \cdot 2^{-\binom{n}{2}}.$$

The limit density $\mu(Q) = \lim_{n \longrightarrow \infty} \mu_n(Q)$ may or may not exist, depending on the query Q. For example, if $X \subseteq \mathsf{N}$ is finite or cofinite, then $\mu(\mathrm{Card}_X)$ is 0 or 1, respectively, whereas $\mu(\mathrm{Card}_X)$ is undefined if X is infinite and coinfinite. Thus, definability in $L_{\omega_1\omega}$ does not guarantee that a query has a limit density. Indeed, for every graph $G \in \mathsf{G}$, the query

Isom_G the set of graphs isomorphic to G

is definable by a single first-order sentence ι_G; for example, the graph G with $V^G = \{1, 2\}$ and $E^G = \{\langle 1, 2 \rangle, \langle 2, 1 \rangle\}$ is defined, up to isomorphism, by the first-order sentence

$$\kappa_2 \wedge \forall x \forall y (Exy \leftrightarrow x \neq y).$$

It follows that for each query Q, the $L_{\omega_1\omega}$ sentence

$$\bigvee_{G \in Q} \iota_G$$

defines Q. Thus, no information flows from the fact that a query is $L_{\omega_1\omega}$-definable, in particular, no information about the limit density of Conn is forthcoming from its definability in $L_{\omega_1\omega}$. (Note that the expressive power of $L_{\omega_1\omega}$ is limited on the collection of all finite and infinite structures; indeed, from cardinality considerations, there is an ordinal α such that the isomorphism type of $\langle \alpha, < \rangle$ cannot be characterized by a sentence of $L_{\omega_1\omega}$.) Perhaps we can find another source for such information.

Let us consider the query Diam_2. How can we compute its density at G_n? It will be useful to think of this in probabilistic terms. The density of a query Q at G_n is just the probability of the event $Q \cap \mathsf{G}_n$ with respect to the uniform measure on G_n, that is, the measure u with $\mathsf{u}(\{G\}) = 2^{-\binom{n}{2}}$, for each $G \in \mathsf{G}_n$. The measure u may be thought of as follows: for each pair of vertices $1 \leq i < j \leq n$, we flip a fair coin to determine whether or not there is an edge between i and j. This point of view facilitates the computation of a useful approximation to the density of Diam_2. For a fixed pair of distinct vertices i and j, the probability that a distinct vertex k is a neighbor of both i and j is $1/4$. Therefore, the probability that none of the $n - 2$ vertices distinct from i and j is a neighbor of them both is $(3/4)^{(n-2)}$. It is now easy to see that the probability that some pair of vertices lacks a common neighbor is bounded by $\binom{n}{2} \cdot (3/4)^{(n-2)}$. It follows at once that

$$\mu_n(\mathrm{Diam}_2) \geq 1 - \binom{n}{2} \cdot \left(\frac{3}{4}\right)^{(n-2)}.$$

But,

$$\lim_{n \to \infty} \binom{n}{2} \cdot \left(\frac{3}{4}\right)^{(n-2)} = 0.$$

Therefore, $\mu(\mathrm{Diam}_2) = 1$. Note that $\mathrm{Diam}_2 \subseteq \mathrm{Conn}$ (cast logically, δ_2 implies γ), and thus, $\mu(\mathrm{Conn}) = 1$. We shall see that this is no isolated phenomenon, but rather one instance of a beautiful dichotomy revealed by definability theory.

As observed above, there are continuum-many queries whose limit density is undefined; moreover, it is not hard to see that for every real number $r \in [0,1]$, there is a query with limit density r. A noteworthy dichotomy is enshrined in the following definition. A logic L satisfies the 0–1 law with respect to the uniform measure on G if and only if, for all L-definable queries Q,

$$\mu(Q) = 0 \text{ or } \mu(Q) = 1.$$

A 0–1 law codifies important structural information about L-definable queries and provides a useful tool for establishing that specific queries are not L-definable; for example, none of the queries Card_X, for X infinite and coinfinite, is L-definable if L satisfies the 0–1 law. It is remarkable that some natural logics satisfy the 0–1 law. The first such result is due to Glebskii et al. [28] and, independently, to Fagin [26], who established that first-order logic satisfies the 0–1 law with respect to the uniform measure. A brief look at an argument for this result will be instructive.

The query Diam_2 is an *extension property* – it requires that every pair of vertices share a common neighbor. A generalization of this is the (m,n)-extension property: this requires that for every pair of disjoint sets of vertices $\{x_1, \ldots, x_m\}$ and $\{y_1, \ldots, y_n\}$, there is a vertex z which is a neighbor of all the x_i and none of the y_j. It is easy to see that this condition is expressible by a first-order sentence $\eta_{m,n}$ (with $m + n + 1$ variables), and that, just as the limit density of Diam_2 is 1, so too $\mu(\eta_{m,n}[\mathsf{G}]) = 1$, for all m, n with $m + n > 0$. Let η_k be the conjunction $\eta_{m,n}$ with $k = m + n + 1$. Each η_k is a first-order sentence with k variables expressing a query with limit density 1; moreover, for all $l \leq k$, η_k implies η_l. Therefore, by the Compactness Theorem for first-order logic, the set of sentences $\Gamma = \{\eta_k \mid k > 1\}$ is consistent. To complete the argument, it suffices to show that for every first-order sentence φ, there is a k such that η_k implies φ, or η_k implies $\neg\varphi$; indeed, if η_k implies φ, then $\mu(\varphi[\mathsf{G}]) = 1$, and if η_k implies $\neg\varphi$, then $\mu(\varphi[\mathsf{G}]) = 0$. Now, Γ has no finite models, and is $\aleph_0$-categorical, that is, any two countable models of Γ are isomorphic (the back-and-forth argument, used by Cantor to prove that the rational numbers are, up to isomorphism, the unique countable dense linear order without endpoints, may be deployed here; compare Chap. 4). It follows at once, via the Löwenheim–Skolem Theorem, that Γ axiomatizes a complete first-order theory. From this, another application of the Compactness Theorem for first-order logic yields the conclusion that for every first-order sentence φ, there is a k such that η_k implies φ, or η_k implies $\neg\varphi$. Can we say, for a given first-order sentence φ, how large a k is required? Kolaitis and Vardi [48] showed that the answer to this question leads to a significant extension of the 0–1 law to a rich fragment of infinitary logic.

1.1.3 Logics with Finitely Many Variables

For each $k \geq 1$, FO^k is the fragment of first-order logic consisting of exactly those formulas all of whose variables, both free and bound, are among $x_1, \ldots, x_k$. To understand the effect of this restriction, it is useful to observe that variables may be reused within such sentences, so that, for example, the queries Diam_k are all FO^3-definable. Here is a sentence of FO^3 that defines Diam_3:

$$\forall x_1 \forall x_2 (\; x_1 = x_2 \vee E x_1 x_2 \vee$$
$$\exists x_3 (E x_1 x_3 \wedge E x_3 x_2) \vee$$
$$\exists x_3 (E x_1 x_3 \wedge \exists x_1 (E x_3 x_1 \wedge E x_1 x_2))).$$

We have already noted that the logic $L_{\omega_1 \omega}$ is too powerful to be of interest in the context of finite model theory, since every query is definable in this logic. The logic $L^k_{\omega_1 \omega}$ is the fragment of $L_{\omega_1 \omega}$ consisting of exactly those formulas all of whose variables, both free and bound, are among $x_1, \ldots, x_k$; $L^\omega_{\omega_1 \omega} = \bigcup_k L^k_{\omega_1 \omega}$. In light of the FO^3-definability of Diam_k, observe that Conn is $L^3_{\omega_1 \omega}$-definable. Indeed, as discussed in Chap. 2, all queries definable in the fixed-point logics **LFP**, **IFP**, and **PFP**, which provide means for definition of relations by recursion, for example the transitive closure of the edge relation, are $L^\omega_{\omega_1 \omega}$-definable (note that, in general, these inclusions fail on collections of finite and infinite structures; for example, the notion of well-foundedness is **LFP**-definable on the class of all directed graphs, but is not even definable in the powerful infinitary logic $L_{\infty \omega}$ discussed below).

Kolaitis and Vardi established that the 0–1 law holds for $L^\omega_{\omega_1 \omega}$ with respect to the uniform measures on G_n. In particular, they showed that for every $k > 1$, η_k axiomatizes a complete $L^k_{\omega_1 \omega}$ theory. Thus, even though $L^\omega_{\omega_1 \omega}$ has expressive power sufficient to encompass various forms of recursion, it retains some of the structural simplicity of first-order logic; indeed, every $L^\omega_{\omega_1 \omega}$-definable query or its complement is implied by a first-order definable query of limit density 1 (the analogy with Suslin's generalization of the theorem of Cantor mentioned above is irresistible). This result gave a coherent explanation for earlier work on 0–1 laws for fixed-point logics (see [14, 47]), and thereby highlighted the important role that finite-variable logics can play in definability theory over finite structures. Hella, Kolaitis, and Luosto [41] further illuminated the situation by showing that FO and $L^\omega_{\omega_1 \omega}$ are *almost everywhere equivalent* with respect to the uniform measure, that is, there is a set $\mathcal{C} \subseteq \mathsf{G}$ of limit density one such that FO and $L^\omega_{\omega_1 \omega}$ define exactly the same collection of queries over $\mathcal{C}$ (even including non-Boolean queries). Dawar [22], Grohe [33], and Otto [54] are valuable sources of information about the finite model theory of finite-variable logics. The following chapters offer many other compelling illustrations of the use of definability theory to yield insight into a wide range of mathematical and computational phenomena. Before exploring some of these examples, let us look at some other important notions from definability theory which receive extended treatment in Chap. 2.

1.1.4 Distinguishing Structures: L-Equivalence and Comparison Games

One approach to the question whether a query Q is definable in a logic L is to ask whether Q distinguishes between graphs which are indistinguishable from the point of view of L. Two graphs G and H are L-equivalent ($G \equiv_L H$), that is, indistinguishable from the point of view of L, if and only if, for every L-definable query Q,

$$G \in Q \iff H \in Q.$$

Clearly, a query Q must be closed under L-equivalence if it is L-definable.

When L is first-order logic, L-equivalence is the notion of elementary equivalence familiar from classical model theory. The classification of infinite structures up to elementary equivalence plays a central role in classical model theory and in its applications to algebra and analysis. On the other hand, as observed above, elementary equivalence coincides with isomorphism on G (and on the class of finite structures in general), so the foregoing necessary condition is deprived of direct application to definability over G with respect to any logic extending FO. This suggests that analysis of L-equivalence for logics L weaker than, or orthogonal to, first-order logic may be of paramount importance in the context of finite model theory. Indeed, this is the case. Let us approach the matter from the point of view of combinatorial comparison games between graphs.

Suppose we want to compare (finite or countably infinite) graphs G and H with the object of determining whether or not they are isomorphic. One way of doing so (inspired by the celebrated Cantor "back-and-forth" argument mentioned above) would be to play the following game. The game has two players, Spoiler and Duplicator; the equipment for the game consists of "boards" corresponding to the graphs G and H and pebbles $a_1, a_2, \ldots$ and $b_1, b_2, \ldots$. The game is organized into rounds $r_1, r_2, \ldots$. At each round r_i the Spoiler plays first and picks one of the pair of pebbles a_i or b_i to play onto a vertex of G or H, respectively; the Duplicator then plays the remaining pebble of the pair onto a vertex of the structure into which the Spoiler did not play. This completes the round. Let v_i (and w_i) be the vertex of G (and of H, respectively) pebbled at round i, let G_i and H_i be the subgraphs of G and H induced by $\{v_1, \ldots, v_i\}$ and $\{w_1, \ldots, w_i\}$, respectively, and let $R_i = \{\langle v_j, w_j \rangle \mid 1 \le j \le i\}$. The Duplicator loses the game at round r_i if the relation R_i fails to be the graph of an isomorphism from G_i onto H_i. The Duplicator wins the game if she does not lose at any round. The Duplicator has a winning strategy for the game if she has a method of play which results in a win for her no matter how the Spoiler plays. In this case, we say that G is partially isomorphic to H ($G \cong_p H$).

It is easy to see that the Duplicator has a winning strategy for this game played on finite or countably infinite graphs G and H if and only if G is isomorphic to H. Indeed, if I is an isomorphism from G onto H, and the Spoiler pebbles the vertex v in G at some round, then the Duplicator will guarantee a win by pebbling $I(v)$ in H (and similarly, if the Spoiler plays onto w in H, then the Duplicator answers by playing onto $I^{-1}(w)$ in G). On the other hand, suppose the Duplicator has a winning strategy for the game played on G and H. Then, she can win against the following strategy of Spoiler. The Spoiler can enumerate the vertices of G as $s_0, s_1, \ldots$ and the vertices of H as $t_0, t_1, \ldots$. Now the Spoiler plays according to the following strategy. For $i \geq 0$, at round r_{2i+1} he places the pebble a_{2i+1} on s_i and at round r_{2i+2} he places the pebble b_{2i+2} on t_i. The Duplicator now answers the Spoiler's moves according to her winning strategy. It follows at once that the relation $R = \bigcup_{i \in \mathbb{N}} R_i$ is the graph of an isomorphism from G onto H. So, if G and H are countable, and $G \cong_p H$, then $G \cong H$. Carol Karp [46] established an interesting connection between partial isomorphism and logical definability: arbitrary graphs G and H are partially isomorphic if and only if they are $L_{\infty\omega}$-equivalent ($L_{\infty\omega}$ strengthens $L_{\omega_1\omega}$ by allowing conjunctions over arbitrary, not necessarily countable, sets of formulas).

Various modifications of this game, which deprive the players of some of their access to resources, or alter the winning condition, or add rules that restrict legitimate play, lead to useful characterizations of equivalence for much weaker languages. Let us consider some examples of these.

First, we might restrict the number of pebble pairs that are available for the game, and allow players to replay pebbles that they have played earlier in the game. If the Duplicator has a winning strategy for the foregoing game played on G and H when the equipment consists of only k pairs of pebbles, we say that G is k-partially isomorphic to H ($G \cong_p^k H$). This variant is discussed at length in Chap. 2 where a proof sketch of Barwise's result [9] that for all G and H, $G \cong_p^k H$ if and only if G is $L_{\infty\omega}^k$-equivalent to H is presented. We have already seen one application of this result to definability over G: it is easy to see that for all $G, H \in \mathbf{G}$, if $G \models \eta_k$ and $H \models \eta_k$, then G is k-partially isomorphic to H; it follows at once from Barwise's result that for every $L_{\infty\omega}^k$ sentence φ, η_k implies φ, or η_k implies $\neg\varphi$, which is the key step in Kolaitis and Vardi's proof of the 0–1 law for $L_{\infty\omega}^k$.

Second, we might restrict the length of play, so the Duplicator need only successfully respond to the Spoiler's moves through some fixed finite number n of rounds in order to win. This is called the n-round Ehrenfeucht–Fraïssé (E–F) game. As discussed in Chap. 2, these games give a characterization of definability in a hierarchy of fragments of first-order logic; in particular, the Duplicator has a winning strategy for the n-round E–F game played on G and H if and only if G and H are FO_n-equivalent, where FO_n is the fragment of first-order logic consisting of all sentences of quantifier rank bounded by n. This is the key to using logical indistinguishability to establish that queries are not first-order definable over G despite the fact that first-order indistinguishability coincides with isomorphism over G. In order to show that a query Q is not first-order definable, it suffices to show that for every n there are FO_n-equivalent G and H with $G \in Q$ and $H \notin Q$. Chapter 2 includes several examples of this technique, among them the queries Conn and $Color_k$ mentioned earlier.

Third, we might require that beyond the first round, the Spoiler play onto a vertex that is adjacent to some vertex which has been pebbled at an earlier round. The single-pebble variant of the game thus restricted characterizes the relation of bisimilarity between vertex-colored directed graphs. Johan van Benthem first introduced this relation and recognized its significance in connection with the study of Kripke models for modal logic [11, 12]; the notion was rediscovered in the context of analyzing the "behavioral equivalence" of transition systems [42, 57]. Chapter 7 elucidates the fundamental importance of bisimilarity invariance in explaining various nice features of modal logic.

Fourth, we might require that the Spoiler always play onto a vertex of G. In this case, by virtue of the asymmetry of play, a win for Duplicator in the resulting game no longer characterizes an equivalence relation between graphs, but rather a preorder. In particular, the Duplicator has a winning strategy for this variant of the game if and only if every existential sentence of $L_{\infty\omega}$ which is true in G is also true in H. If, in addition, we relax the winning condition to require only that at the end of each round r_i the relation R_i is the graph of a homomorphism from G to H, then the Duplicator has a winning strategy if and only if every positive existential sentence of $L_{\infty\omega}$ that is true in G is also true in H. This last variant, in combination with the resource restriction on the number of pebbles discussed above, characterizes the positive existential fragment of $L_{\infty\omega}^\omega$. This fragment is of particular interest from the perspective of database theory, since it suffices to express every Datalog-definable query; several applications of this definability result are discussed in Chaps. 2 and 6.

1.1.5 Random Graphs and 0–1 Laws

Joel Spencer's chapter, "Logic and random structures" (Chap. 4), gives an exposition of a 0–1 law for first-order logic he and Saharon Shelah discovered [62], and related phenomena in the theory of random graphs. From the perspective of this theory, the uniform distribution on finite graphs considered above is an instance of a far more general scenario developed by Erdős and Renyi in [24]. From this perspective, one considers a sequence of finite probability spaces (G_n, μ_n^p), where the measure μ_n^p is determined by an "edge probability" p_n which is a function of n; the uniform distribution is just the special case where $p_n = .5$ for all n. Let us write $\mu^p(Q)$ for the limit probability of the query Q with respect to the sequence of measures μ_n^p, that is,

$$\mu^p(Q) = \lim_{n \longrightarrow \infty} \mu_n^p(Q \cap G_n).$$

In this context, combinatorists have discovered that threshold phenomena arise, that is, there are queries Q and functions p with the property that for all q, if $q \ll p$, then $\mu^q(Q) = 0$, and if $p \ll q$, then $\mu^q(Q) = 1$. (Here, $p \ll q$ if and only if $\lim_{n \longrightarrow \infty} p_n/q_n = 0$.) One class of cases which arose naturally in the study of threshold phenomena is the edge probabilities $p(\alpha)_n = n^{-\alpha}$, for some real $\alpha \in (0,1)$. Spencer observed that among the many queries analyzed by graph theorists, none possessed a threshold of the form $n^{-\alpha}$ for $\alpha \in (0,1)$ and irrational. Shelah and Spencer discovered a definability result that provided an explanation for these threshold phenomena. They showed that for all $\alpha \in (0,1)$, if α is irrational, then first-order logic satisfies the 0–1 law with respect to $(\mathsf{G}_n, \mu_n^{p(\alpha)})$, that is, for every first-order definable query Q,

$$\mu^{p(\alpha)}(Q) = 0 \text{ or } \mu^{p(\alpha)}(Q) = 1.$$

This is an outstanding example of how definability considerations can provide insight through systematization of apparently disparate combinatorial facts. Further investigations of the complete theories $T^\alpha = \{\varphi \in \mathrm{FO} \mid \mu^{p(\alpha)}(\varphi[\mathsf{G}]) = 1\}$ have revealed interesting connections with classical model theory (see [8, 51]). This aspect of definability theory has also been prominent in computer science, as well as in combinatorics.

1.1.6 Constraint Satisfaction Problems

In Chap. 6 of the volume, "A logical approach to constraint satisfaction", Kolaitis and Vardi survey some applications of definability theory to the study of constraint satisfaction problems, a subject that is important in several areas of computer science, including artificial intelligence, database theory, and operations research. For example, the k-colorability problem for graphs may be formulated as a constraint satisfaction problem. Given a graph (V, E), we may think of its vertices as *variables*. We ask whether there is an assignment of k colors $c_1, \ldots, c_k$, one to each variable, so as to satisfy the constraint that adjacent variables are assigned distinct colors. Feder and Vardi [27] made the following important observation that advanced the understanding of the computational complexity of constraint satisfaction problems: they noted that all such problems may be formulated as homomorphism problems on suitable relational structures (in general, these relational structures will not be graphs). For a simple example using graphs, recall that a homomorphism h from $G = (V, E)$ to $H = (V', E')$ is a map satisfying the condition

$$Eab \Rightarrow E'h(a)h(b), \text{ for all } a, b \in V.$$

A graph G is k-colorable if and only if there is a homomorphism from G into K_k, the complete graph on k vertices (thought of as the colors $c_1, \ldots, c_k$) – the constraint that adjacent "variables" are assigned distinct colors by any homomorphism is enforced by the irreflexivity of the edge relation in K_k.

In general, a constraint satisfaction problem can be formulated as a homomorphism problem: given two classes of relational structures $\mathcal{A}$ and $\mathcal{B}$, the constraint satisfaction problem $CSP(\mathcal{A}, \mathcal{B})$ asks, for each pair of structures $A \in \mathcal{A}$ and $B \in \mathcal{B}$, whether or not there is a homomorphism from A to B. Insofar as the homomorphism problem in general is NP-complete, the search for "islands of tractability", that is, collections of structures $\mathcal{A}$ and $\mathcal{B}$ such that $CSP(\mathcal{A}, \mathcal{B})$ can be computed in polynomial time, is of interest.

Two cases which have been studied intensively are nonuniform and uniform constraint satisfaction problems. The case in which $\mathcal{B}$ is a singleton, $\{B\}$, and $\mathcal{A}$ is $\mathcal{U}$, the collection of all finite structures, is called the non-uniform constraint satisfaction problem with template B – $CSP(B)$ for short; on the other hand, the constraint problem $CSP(\mathcal{A}, \mathcal{U})$ is called the uniform constraint satisfaction problem with input $\mathcal{A}$. To illustrate this terminology by the above example, for each k, the k-colorability problem is the nonuniform constraint satisfaction problem $CSP(K_k)$. This is a suggestive example. Recall that the 2-colorability problem is solvable in polynomial time, while the k-colorability problem is NP-complete, for each $k \geq 3$. Recall too (see [50]) that if $P \neq NP$, then there are problems in NP which are neither NP-complete nor in P. Could it be that nonuniform constraint satisfaction problems are so special that they would exhibit the following remarkable dichotomy?

F–V   For every template B, $CSP(B)$ is either in P or is NP-complete.

This is the well-known Feder–Vardi Dichotomy Conjecture, which was articulated in [27] as a generalization of a theorem of Schaefer [61] that established the dichotomy for the case of templates B with a two-element domain (called *Boolean templates*). Indeed, Schaefer showed that it can be decided in polynomial time whether or not $CSP(B)$ is NP-complete for any Boolean template B. Subsequent investigations have established that the Dichotomy Conjecture holds for other classes of templates. Generalizing the example of k-colorability, Hell and Nešetřil [40] showed that for all templates B which are undirected graphs, if B is bipartite, then $CSP(B)$ is in P, while if B is not bipartite, then $CSP(B)$ is NP-complete. Building on a group-theoretic approach initiated in [27], Bulatov extended Schaefer's dichotomy to $CSP(B)$ for all three element templates B [17]. In their chapter, Kolaitis and Vardi explore definability frameworks for understanding some of the known results concerning the conjectured dichotomy. They also show how definability theory illuminates the study of uniform constraint satisfaction problems.

1.2 Descriptive Complexity

In the preceding section, we have traced the theme of definability as a source of structural information as it arises in several settings throughout the volume. Let us turn our attention to another major theme, the relation between definability and computational complexity. This is the focus of Erich Grädel's chapter on "Finite model theory and descriptive complexity" (Chap. 3).

1.2.1 Satisfaction

Let us look again at the definition of a query Q being definable by a sentence φ of a logic L :

$$\varphi \text{ defines } Q \text{ if and only if } \forall G \in \mathsf{G}(G \models_L \varphi \Leftrightarrow G \in Q).$$

If we think of queries as combinatorial problems, it is natural to ask whether we can obtain information about the computational complexity of a problem from the fact that it is definable in one language or another. This question focuses attention on the complexity of the satisfaction relation itself, (also known as the model-checking problem). Vardi [68] formulated three notions of complexity associated with the satisfaction relation for L (relative to a collection of finite structures $\mathcal{C}$). The first, called the *combined complexity* of L is just the complexity of the satisfaction relation itself, viewed as a binary relation on strings encoding structures in $\mathcal{C}$ on the one hand, and sentences of L on the other. The second, called the *data complexity* of L, is the complexity of the decision problems associated with L-definable queries Q over $\mathcal{C}$. The third, called the *expression complexity* of L, is the complexity of the decision problems associated with the L-theories $\mathrm{Th}_L(G)$ of finite structures G in $\mathcal{C}$, where

$$\mathrm{Th}_L(G) = \{\varphi \in L \mid G \models_L \varphi\}.$$

The study of these notions is rooted in the great developments in logic in the 1930s. In the first work which rigorously defined the notion of satisfaction, "On the concept of truth in formalized languages," [65], Tarski famously resolved a basic question concerning expression complexity in the context of infinite structures, and in descriptive terms at that: he showed that the first-order theory of the structure $\mathsf{N} = \langle N, 0, +, \times \rangle$ is not arithmetically definable, that is, there is no first-order formula $\theta(x)$ in the language of arithmetic such that for all $i \in N$,

$$\mathsf{N} \models \varphi(i) \Leftrightarrow \mathsf{N} \models \chi_i,$$

where χ_i is the sentence in the first-order language of arithmetic with code i. Subsequent work by Kleene and Post revealed the intimate connection between arithmetic definability and complexity as measured by Turing degrees, thereby transforming Tarski's undefinability result into a lower bound on recursion-theoretic complexity. Moreover, Tarski's definition of satisfaction itself exhibited that the first-order theory of N could be defined by both an existential and a universal sentence in the second-order language of arithmetic. Again, later work by Kleene yielded a "computational" interpretation of this descriptive result – the first-order theory of N is hyperarithmetical.

Chapter 3 presents a comprehensive overview of results concerning combined, data, and expression complexity in the context of finite model theory. One theme that runs through the chapter is the role of combinatorial games in analyzing the combined complexity of many logics, among them first-order logic and various fixed-point logics, including the modal μ-calculus, a natural fixed-point extension of propositional modal logic with applications ranging from hardware verification to analysis of hybrid systems. The chapter begins with an incisive analysis of the complexity of first-order logic using the technique of model-checking games $\mathcal{G}(A, \varphi)$ in which a Verifier and a Falsifier compete, and Verifier has a winning strategy just in case $A \models \varphi$. In the case of first-order logic, the model-checking games are positional and have a finite game graph. The strategy problem for such games in general, "does Player I have a winning strategy for the game from position p?", can be solved in linear time. Analysis of an alternating algorithm for the first-order model-checking game yields the following information: the combined complexity of FO is PSPACE-complete, while the combined complexity of FO^k is PTIME-complete – yet another source of interest in the finite-variable fragments. Moreover, PSPACE-completeness follows from the fact that the satisfiability problem for quantified Boolean formulas is easily reduced to the first-order theory of the unary structure $A = \langle \{0, 1\}, \{0\} \rangle$, from which it follows at once that the expression complexity of FO is also PSPACE-complete. On the other hand, the data complexity of FO is in deterministic LOGSPACE. This gap between expression complexity and data complexity obtains for many well-known logics.

When we turn from first-order to second-order logic, the situation is quite different. For example, the data complexity of the monadic existential fragment of second-order logic (mon-ESO) is NP-complete, that is, every mon-ESO-definable query is in NP, and some such queries, for example, 3-colorability, are NP-hard. On the other hand, as discussed in Chap. 2, there are PTIME queries on G, for example, connectivity, which are not mon-ESO-definable. This suggests that definability theory could be used to illuminate differences in complexity which are not easily characterized in terms of computational resources – a good example of this is the result of Ajtai and Fagin that undirected reachability is mon-ESO-definable, while directed reachability is not [4] (recently, Reingold has established that undirected reachability is in DLOGSPACE, whereas directed reachability is a paradigmatic NLOGSPACE-complete problem [58] – separating these two complexity classes remains an outstanding open question). On the other hand, it is also interesting when definability of queries in well-understood logics coincides with resource complexity classes, from at least two points of view: first, the logical language could then be used as a transparent specification language for queries in the class, and second, methods of logic could be deployed in complexity-theoretic investigations.

A logic L *captures* a complexity class K on a collection of structures $\mathcal{C}$ if and only if, for every query Q over $\mathcal{C}$,

$$Q \text{ is } L\text{-definable} \Leftrightarrow Q \in \mathsf{K}.$$

In 1970, Fagin [25] showed that the existential fragment of second-order logic captures the complexity class NP over the class of all finite structures (see

Chap. 3 for discussion and a proof). Fagin's result launched an active search for characterizations of other complexity classes in logical terms. Since the natural specification of many combinatorial problems is given by an existential second-order sentence, Fagin's Theorem provides a convenient tool for recognizing that problems are in NP. From the point of view of specification languages for database queries, it would be most useful to find logics that capture complexity classes below NP. Though Fagin's Theorem extends easily to show that full second-order logic captures the polynomial-time hierarchy, PH, over arbitrary finite structures, thus far no logic has been identified that captures a complexity class presumed to be strictly contained in NP over the collection of all finite structures. On the other hand, much has been learned about logics that capture such complexity classes over particular collections of finite structures. Indeed, the first capturing result was of just this kind. In 1960, Büchi [16] showed that mon-ESO captures the collection of regular languages over the class of string structures, that is, structures of the form $\langle [n], S, \overline{P} \rangle$, where S is the usual successor relation on $[n]$ and $\overline{P}$ is a finite sequence of unary predicates; it is worth noting that over string structures, all of monadic second-order logic is no more expressive than its existential fragment (see [63] and [32] for extended treatments of connections between logic and automata theory). Chapter 3 shows how other fragments of second-order logic yield characterizations of complexity classes over ordered finite structures, that is, structures which interpret a distinguished binary relation as a linear order on the universe. These include Grädel's results that second-order Horn logic (and its existential fragment) captures polynomial time on ordered finite structures and that second-order Krom logic (and its existential fragment) captures nondeterministic logarithmic space on ordered finite structures.

An especially active area of investigation in descriptive complexity theory is the analysis of logics with fixed-point operators that allow for defining queries by induction. The clarification of the nature of inductive definitions was a task undertaken by the pioneers of modern logic. Indeed, among Frege's great contributions in *Die Grundlagen der Arithmetik* was the analysis of one of the simplest fixed-point operators, which allows definition of the ancestral of a relation (now called transitive closure), in the universal fragment of second-order logic: a is an E-ancestor of b ($\mathrm{tc}xy(Exy)ab$) if and only if

$$\forall R((\forall x \forall y(Exy \to Rxy) \wedge \forall z((Rxy \wedge Ezx) \to Rzy)) \to Rab).$$

From the point of view of descriptive complexity, transitive closures appear to be quite weak compared with universal second-order quantification. Immerman [43] showed that the extension of first-order logic with the transitive-closure operator (TC) captures NLOGSPACE over the class of ordered finite structures, while, by Fagin's Theorem, the universal fragment of second-order logic captures co-NP, which has been conjectured to properly include NLOGSPACE. If transitive closure is applied only to single-valued relations, one obtains, as an extension of first-order logic, deterministic transitive-closure logic (DTC), which captures DLOGSPACE over the class of ordered finite structures [43]. In this instance, the descriptive separation, DTC $\neq$ TC, over the class of all finite structures was established by Grädel and McColm [31], whereas the separation on ordered finite structures is equivalent to the unresolved complexity-theoretic question: is DLOGSPACE distinct from NLOGSPACE?

Richer fixed-point logics yield characterizations of PTIME and PSPACE over ordered finite structures. Chapters 2 and 3 contain detailed developments of logical and complexity-theoretic results concerning the least fixed-point (LFP), inflationary fixed-point (IFP), and partial fixed-point (PFP) extensions of first-order logic, including proofs that LFP captures PTIME over ordered finite structures [43, 68], that PFP captures PSPACE over ordered finite structures [1, 68], and that LFP = IFP over arbitrary finite structures [39] (indeed, Kreutzer established that LFP = IFP over arbitrary, not just finite, structures [49]). In contrast to the aforementioned descriptive separation of TC and DTC, and in spite of the fact that LFP and PFP do not capture PTIME and PSPACE over finite graphs without an ordering, Abiteboul and Vianu [2] established that there are PFP-definable queries on finite graphs which are not LFP-definable, if and only if PSPACE is distinct from PTIME, a striking result which solved an open problem posed by Chandra [20].

As noted earlier, the fixed-point logics LFP, IFP, and PFP are all fragments of $L^\omega_{\infty\omega}$ with respect to definability over the class of finite structures, and consequently they lack the means to express any nontrivial cardinality queries on finite graphs. The extension of IFP with counting quantifiers (IFP+C) yields a logic that captures PTIME over wider classes of finite structures; for example, Grohe established that IFP+C captures PTIME on the class of planar graphs (in fact, on any class of structures whose Gaifman graphs are of bounded genus) [34, 35] and on any class of structures of bounded tree-width [36]. On the other hand, Cai, Fürer, and Immerman established that IFP+C does not capture PTIME over the class of all finite graphs [18]. It is natural to ask: is there a logic that captures PTIME on the class of all finite graphs?

1.2.2 What Is a Logic for PTIME?

In order to sensibly address the preceding question, we need to refine the notion of a logic capturing a complexity class – otherwise, for all we have said about logics in the abstract, we might be tempted to answer that the collection of PTIME queries itself is a logic that captures PTIME. Chandra and Harel [19] introduced the notion of an effectively enumerable query complexity class and posed the question of whether the PTIME-computable queries are effectively enumerable; Gurevich [38] introduced the closely related notion of a logic for PTIME (see also [23] and [53] for further discussion of logics for complexity classes). In order to explain this notion, we need to focus closely on the satisfaction relation. Recall that a logic L is a pair consisting of a set of sentences S_L and a satisfaction relation $\models_L$. We say that L is uniformly contained in PTIME on a collection of finite structures $\mathcal{C}$ if and only if S_L and $\models_L$ are decidable, and there are effectively computable functions m and t such that for every $\varphi \in S_L$, $m(\varphi)$ is a deterministic Turing machine which decides $Q(\varphi) \cap \mathcal{C}$ in time $n^{t(\varphi)}$. Note that SO-Horn, LFP, and IFP are uniformly contained in PTIME on the collection of all finite structures. A logic L effectively captures PTIME on $\mathcal{C}$ if and only if L is uniformly contained in PTIME on $\mathcal{C}$ and every PTIME query on $\mathcal{C}$ is L-definable. In this sense, a logic for PTIME embodies a query language which can be compiled into machine code with explicit bounds on running time, and which expresses every PTIME query. (The notion of "effectively capturing" can easily be extended to other resource complexity classes; for example, in the obvious sense, Fagin's Theorem establishes that ESO effectively captures NP.)

Insofar as we have placed only quite abstract requirements on a logic L effectively capturing PTIME, the question naturally arises whether the collection T_p of n^k-clocked Turing machines, for all $k \in \mathbb{N}$, itself might not be such a logic, where the associated satisfaction relation is just acceptance. The problem with this suggestion is that the "queries" definable in this logic are not necessarily queries, that is, they are not in general isomorphism-invariant. One way of overcoming this obstacle would be to preprocess input graphs so that a fixed representative of each isomorphism type of structure would be presented to a clocked machine. Given an equivalence relation $\sim$ on G, we say $f : \mathsf{G} \longrightarrow \mathsf{G}$ is a $\sim$-canon if and only if, for all $G, H \in \mathsf{G}$, $G \sim f(G)$ and if $G \sim H$, then $f(G) = f(H)$. Given a Turing machine M which computes an isomorphism canon, we could "compose" M with each of the machines $M' \in T_p$ and thereby arrive at a logic which captures PTIME on G; if, moreover, M ran in polynomial time in the length of its input, this would yield a logic that effectively captures PTIME on G. The existence of a polynomial-time-computable isomorphism canon for graphs is a major open problem in complexity theory. It is well known that if P = NP, then there is a polynomial-time-computable isomorphism canon for finite graphs, though it is unknown whether the existence of such a canon would imply that P = NP [5]. It follows at once that if there is no logic that effectively captures PTIME on G, then there is no polynomial-time-computable isomorphism canon for graphs, and hence P $\neq$ NP. (Indeed, if P = NP, then existential second-order logic is a logic for P. This follows from Fagin's Theorem and the "polynomially uniform" completeness of typical NP-complete problems.) On the other hand, if there is a polynomial-time-computable $\sim$-canon for a class of graphs $\mathcal{C}$, then there is a logic L that effectively captures $\sim$-invariant PTIME on $\mathcal{C}$, that is, a logic which is uniformly contained in PTIME and expresses all and only the PTIME-computable queries on $\mathcal{C}$ which are closed under $\sim$. In some cases, such as Grohe's capturing results for IFP+C cited above, there is a "familiar" logic that does the capturing. Another example of this phenomenon is Otto's result [55] that bisimulation-invariant PTIME is uniformly captured by the multidimensional μ-calculus (see Chap. 3 and references there).

1.3 Finite Model Theory and Infinite Structures

The concluding section of Chap. 3 surveys several areas where the perspective of descriptive complexity theory has been extended to the study of certain classes of infinite structures. Such extension requires, at minimum, that the structures in question be finitely presentable and that the satisfaction relation be computable when restricted to the given setting (structures and language). One active research direction here is the study of automatic structures, that is, structures whose universe and relations are regular sets of strings. Automatic structures have nice closure properties from the point of view of definability theory; for example, all first-order-definable relations on such structures are regular, and so the expansion of an automatic structure by first-order-definable relations is itself automatic, a property not shared, for example, by recursively presented structures.

Another research direction where the point of view of descriptive complexity is extended to infinite structures is the study of metafinite structures, which were introduced by Grädel and Gurevich in [30]. A paradigmatic example of such structures is edge-weighted graphs. Here one has a finite graph and a numerical structure, such as the ring Z or the ordered field R, and a function which assigns weights in the numerical structure to edges in the graph. Such two-sorted structures arise naturally in several areas of computer science, including database theory, optimization theory, and complexity theory. A hallmark of metafinite model theory is the simplicity of the languages deployed to describe these hybrid structures. In particular, there is no quantification allowed over the numerical structure, indeed, no variables which admit assignment from the numerical domain. The only access to the numerical structure is via weight terms that assign numerical values to tuples from the nonnumerical sort, and terms which combine these by use of operations on the numerical universe. Following [30], Chap. 3 shows how the notion of a generalized spectrum admits two extensions to the context of metafinite structures (one allowing projection of weight functions, in addition to projection of relations on the finite structure). In the context of arithmetical structures (those whose numerical part consists of the standard model of arithmetic with additional polynomial-time-computable multiset operations) with "small weights", the more restricted notion of a generalized spectrum captures NP, whereas on arithmetical structures in general, the wider notion captures the class of all recursively enumerable relations. Chapter 3 concludes with a proof of the result, due to Grädel and Meer, that in the case of metafinite structures whose numerical part is the real ordered field extended with constants for all real numbers, the wide notion of a metafinite spectrum captures NP_R, the collection of nondeterministic polynomial-time-acceptable relations on the reals in the Blum–Schub–Smale model of computation over the reals [15].

A third area which involves a blend of finite and classical model theory is the study of "Embedded finite models and constraint databases", the subject of Leonid Libkin's chapter (Chap. 5). In the context of geographical information systems, the management of spatio-temporal data, bioinformatics, and numerous other database application areas, it is useful to look at relational data over infinite sets which may themselves be endowed with additional structure. The approach via constraint databases, pioneered by Kanellakis *et al.* [45], where, for example, geographical regions are stored as logical formulas that define them, via coordinatization, over the real ordered field R or the real ordered group, has proven to be fruitful. In this context, new definability questions arise; for example, can one define topological connectivity of (definable) spatial regions? As discussed in Chap. 5, the work of Grumbach and Su [37] revealed that many definability questions of this kind could be reduced to definability questions about *embedded finite structures*, that is, finite structures whose domain is drawn from some ambient infinite structure such as the real ordered field. For example, if G is a finite graph whose vertices are real numbers, then the expansion $A = \langle R, E^G \rangle$ of R is an embedded finite model with "active domain" the set of nonisolated vertices of G. Now, it can be shown that there is a first-order formula $\varphi(x, y)$ such that the region in R^2 defined by φ in A is topologically connected, if and only if G is a connected graph. Thus, if topological connectivity of definable planar regions were first-order-definable in R, then connectivity of embedded finite graphs would also be definable over $\{\langle R, E \rangle \mid E \subset_{\text{fin}} R^2\}$. This is exactly the point at which embedded finite model theory comes into play in offering a variety of techniques to answer definability questions of the latter sort. One of the main thrusts of embedded finite model theory is to establish "collapse results", which reduce questions about definability over embedded finite structures to questions about definability over finite structures. It turns out that general model-theoretic conditions on the ambient infinite structure are of paramount importance in determining the extent to which such collapse results obtain. Chapter 5 provides a detailed account of such phenomena. These phenomena provide considerable evidence that infinite structures which are well-behaved from the point of view of definability theory in the infinite are similarly tame with respect to embedded finite structures. For example, Benedikt *et al.* [10] have shown that if M is an o-minimal structure and Q is an order-generic query on finite structures A embedded in M, which is first-order definable over $\langle M, A \rangle$, then Q is first-order definable (with order) over finite structures A; the real ordered field is a paradigmatic o-minimal structure, and recent work in model theory has established the o-minimality of various of its extensions [66, 70]. Baldwin and Benedikt [7] have shown, more generally, that the same collapse obtains for any M which lacks the *independence property*, a condition familiar from stability theory. Chapter 5 reveals deep connections between the independence property and definability over embedded finite models.

1.4 Tame Fragments and Tame Classes

The book concludes with a concise, modern introduction to modal logic, "Local variations on a loose theme: modal logic and decidability", by Maarten Marx and Yde Venema (a comprehensive treatment in this spirit can be found in [13]). Modal logics have numerous applications to computer science, ranging from specification of hybrid systems to knowledge representation, and these applications rest on the delicate balance between the expressive power of modal languages and their good algorithmic properties. The chapter provides an incisive analysis of this balance (other useful discussions include [29, 69]).

Propositional modal languages can be viewed, via the Kripke modeling, as vehicles for expressing unary queries over labeled transition systems, that is, structures whose universe consists of a collection of states equipped with binary "accessibility" relations and unary labels. When viewed in this way, a propositional modal sentence φ, such as

$$P \to \Box(\neg P \wedge \Diamond P),$$

can be translated into a first-order formula φ° with one free variable,

$$P(x) \to \forall y(Rxy \to (\neg P(y) \wedge \exists x(Ryx \wedge P(x)))),$$

so that, for any Kripke model $M = \langle U^M, R^M, P^M \rangle$ and any $s \in U^M$,

$$M, s \Vdash \varphi \Leftrightarrow M \models \varphi^\circ[s].$$

For example, if M is the structure with

$$U^M = \{1, 2, 3\}, R^M = \{\langle 1, 1 \rangle, \langle 1, 2 \rangle, \langle 2, 3 \rangle, \langle 3, 2 \rangle\}, P^M = \{1, 3\},$$

then φ° defines the set $\{2, 3\}$ in M. It is easy to check that for any basic modal sentence φ, φ° is in the the two-variable fragment of first-order logic, and all quantifiers in φ° are relativized to the collection of states directly accessible from a given state. The collection of translations of modal sentences is called the modal fragment of first-order logic.

Chapter 7 emphasizes that bisimulation invariance is the fundamental property of the modal fragment of first-order logic. As mentioned above, bisimilarity can be characterized in terms of a simple one-pebble comparison game. Kripke structures M and M' with states $s \in M$ and $s' \in M'$ are bisimilar if and only if the Duplicator has a winning strategy in the following game. Initially, pebbles are placed on the distinguished states s and s'. At each round of play, the Spoiler chooses one of the pebbles and moves it to a state accessible from the state on which it lies. The Duplicator must move the other pebble in like fashion, and to a state which is labeled identically to the state onto which Spoiler has moved. The game ends with a win for the Spoiler if the Duplicator cannot thus move at some round. Otherwise, the Duplicator wins the (perhaps infinite) play of the game.

It is easy to check that every formula in the modal fragment is bisimulation invariant; that is, if M, s is bisimilar to M', s' then

$$M \models \varphi^{\circ}[s] \Leftrightarrow M' \models \varphi^{\circ}[s'],$$

for every modal sentence φ. The authors show that by "unraveling" a Kripke structure M at a state s one can create a tree model M' (that is, $\langle U', R^{M'} \rangle$ is a directed tree) that is bisimilar to M at s (the unraveling consists of collecting all finite walks in M starting at s and ordering them by immediate extension). Thus, any bisimulation-invariant language has the "tree model" property. The authors refer to this as the looseness property of modal logic, and identify it as one of the sources of the good algorithmic behavior of modal logics. They observe that this is not the entire story, and note that modal logics also exhibit some interesting locality properties that also partly account for the relatively low complexity of their satisfiability and model-checking problems. Indeed, since there are continuum-many bisimulation-invariant queries even on finite labeled transition systems, the tree model property could not be the complete account for the computational tameness of the modal fragment. The authors identify two locality properties that are important in explaining the behavior of modal logic. The first is related to the Hanf and Gaifman locality of first-order logic as discussed in Chap. 2 (note that modal depth equates to quantifier depth in the modal fragment); the second is related to the fact that the modal fragment is contained in FO^2.

The connection between bisimilarity invariance and modal definability is intimate – Johan van Benthem established [11, 12] a preservation theorem for the modal fragment: every bisimulation-invariant first-order formula is equivalent to a formula in the modal fragment. Eric Rosen [59] showed that this preservation theorem persists to the class of finite structures; that is, if a formula of first-order logic is preserved under bisimulation over the collection of finite Kripke structures, then it is equivalent, over finite Kripke structures, to a formula in the modal fragment. This result provides evidence that the modal fragment is tame not only from an algorithmic point of view, but also from the point of view of finite model theory. How so? Several well-known preservation theorems from classical model theory fail when relativized to finite structures. For example, Tait [64] showed that the Łoś–Tarski existential preservation theorem does not persist to the class of finite structures – there is a first-order sentence that is preserved under extensions relative to the collection of finite structures, but is not equivalent over finite structures to an existential sentence. An even more telling example in the current context is the failure of a preservation theorem for the two-variable fragment of first-order logic to persist to the class of finite structures. A query is 2-invariant if and only if it is closed under $L^2_{\infty\omega}$ equivalence. Immerman and Kozen [44] showed that if a query is 2-invariant and first-order definable, then it is expressible by a sentence of FO^2. This result does not persist to the finite case; for example, the collection of finite linear orderings is 2-invariant and FO^3-definable with respect to the collection of finite structures, but is not FO^2-definable over finite structures. So the modal fragment is in some sense tamer than the two-variable fragment with respect to model theory over the class of finite structures. Otto [56] has proved a generalization of Rosen's preservation result which gives yet more evidence that the tameness of modal finite model theory is connected to the relativization of quantification in the modal fragment. He established that any formula of FO^2 that is invariant under *guarded bisimulations* with respect to the class of finite structures is equivalent, over finite structures, to a formula in the guarded fragment of FO^2. Chapter 7 explains how the guarded fragment of first-order logic is a natural extension of the modal fragment and discusses aspects of its good algorithmic behavior. Rossman [60] recently established that the homomorphism preservation theorem persists to finite structures, that is, if a first-order definable query is closed under homomorphisms with respect to the class of finite structures, then it is equivalent over finite structures to a positive existential sentence. So, in the sense to hand, the positive existential fragment of first-order logic is also "tame" for finite model theory. It is worth noting that some fragments that are ill-behaved with respect to the collection of all finite structures may be tame with respect to interesting subclasses. Though the existential preservation theorem fails over the collection of all finite structures, Atserias, Dawar, and Grohe [6] have shown that it holds with respect to classes of finite structures of bounded degree and bounded tree-width. To echo a motto proposed by Hrushovski ("model theory = geography of tame mathematics" [67]), a geography of tame fragments and tame classes may yield some insight into finite model theory.

Acknowledgments

I am grateful to Phokion G. Kolaitis for many corrections and suggestions which substantially improved this chapter. This work was supported in part by NSF grant CCR-9820899. Part of this work was done while I was visiting the Isaac Newton Institute for Mathematical Sciences, during a Special Programme on Logic and Algorithms.

References

1. S. Abiteboul and V. Vianu. Datalog extensions for database queries and updates. *Journal of Computer and System Sciences*, 43:62–124, 1991.
2. S. Abiteboul and V. Vianu. Generic computation and its complexity. In *STOC*, pages 209–219. ACM, 1991.
3. J. W. Addison. Tarski's theory of definability: common themes in descriptive set theory, recursive function theory, classical pure logic, and finite-universe logic. *Annals of Pure and Applied Logic*, 126:77–92, 2004.
4. M. Ajtai and R. Fagin. Reachability is harder for directed than for undirected finite graphs. *Journal of Symbolic Logic*, 55:113–150, 1990.

5. V. Arvind and J. Torán. Isomorphism testing: Perspective and open problems. *Bulletin of the EATCS*, 86:66–84, 2005.

6. A. Atserias, A. Dawar, and M. Grohe. Preservation under extensions on well-behaved finite structures. In L. Caires, G. F. Italiano, L. Monteiro, C. Palamidessi, and M. Yung, editors, *ICALP*, Lecture Notes in Computer Science, volume 3580, pages 1437–1449. Springer, 2005.

7. J. Baldwin and M. Benedikt. Stability theory, permutations of indiscernibles, and embedded finite models. *Transactions of the American Mathematical Society*, 352:4937–4969, 2000.

8. J. Baldwin and S. Shelah. Randomness and semi-genericity. *Transactions of the American Mathematical Society*, 349:1359–1376, 1997.

9. J. Barwise. On Moschovakis closure ordinals. *Journal of Symbolic Logic*, 42: 292–296, 1977.

10. M. Benedikt, G. Dong, L. Libkin, and L. Wong. Relational expressive power of constraint query languages. *Journal of the ACM*, 45(1):1–34, 1998.

11. J. van Benthem. *Modal Correspondence Theory*. PhD thesis, Mathematisch Instituut & Instituut voor Grondslagenonderzoek, University of Amsterdam, 1976.

12. J. van Benthem. *Modal Logic and Classical Logic*. Bibliopolis, 1983.

13. P. Blackburn, M. de Rijke, and Y. Venema. *Modal Logic*. Cambridge University Press, 2002.

14. A. Blass, Y. Gurevich, and D. Kozen. A zero–one law for logic with a fixed-point operator. *Information and Control*, 67(1-3):70–90, 1985.

15. L. Blum, M. Shub, and S. Smale. On a theory of computation over the real numbers; np completeness, recursive functions and universal machines (extended abstract). In *FOCS*, pages 387–397. IEEE Computer Society, 1988.

16. J. R. Büchi. Weak second-order arithmetic and finite automata. *Zeitschrift für Mathematische Logik und Grundlagen der Mathematik*, 6:66–92, 1960.

17. A. A. Bulatov. A dichotomy theorem for constraints on a three-element set. In *FOCS*, pages 649–658. IEEE Computer Society, 2002.

18. J-y. Cai, M. Fürer, and N. Immerman. An optimal lower bound on the number of variables for graph identification. In *FOCS*, pages 612–617. IEEE Computer Society, 1989.

19. A. Chandra and D. Harel. Structure and complexity of relational queries. *Journal of Computer and System Sciences*, 25:99–128, 1982.

20. A. K. Chandra. Theory of database queries. In *PODS*, pages 1–9. ACM, 1988.

21. C. C. Chang and H. J. Keisler. *Model Theory*. North-Holland, 1990.

22. A. Dawar. Finite models and finitely many variables. In D. Niwinski and R. Maron, editors, *Logic, Algebra and Computer Science*, Banach Center Publications, volume 46, pages 93–117. Polish Academy of Sciences, 1999.

23. A. Dawar. Generalized quantifiers and logical reducibilities. *Journal of Logic and Computation*, 5(2):213–226, 1995.

24. P. Erdös and A. Rényi. On the evolution of random graphs. *Public Mathematical Institute of Hungary Academy of Sciences*, 5:17–61, 1960.

25. R. Fagin. Generalized first-order spectra and polynomial-time recognizable sets. In R. M. Karp, editor, *Complexity of Computation, SIAM-AMS Proceedings*, volume 7, pages 43–73, 1974.

26. R. Fagin. Probabilities on finite models. *Journal of Symbolic Logic*, 41(1):50–58, March 1976.

27. T. Feder and M. Y. Vardi. The computational structure of monotone monadic SNP and constraint satisfaction: a study through datalog and group theory. *SIAM Journal on Computing*, 28:57–104, 1998.

28. Y. Glebskii, D. Kogan, M. Liogon'kii, and V. Talanov. Range and degree of realizability of formulas in the restricted predicate calculus. *Cybernetics*, 5:142–154, 1969.

29. E. Grädel. Why are modal logics so robustly decidable? *Bulletin of the EATCS*, 68:90–103, 1999.

30. E. Grädel and Y. Gurevich. Metafinite model theory. *Information and Computation*, 140:26–81, 1998.

31. E. Grädel and G. L. McColm. Hierarchies in transitive closure logic, stratified datalog and infinitary logic. *Annals of Pure and Applied Logic*, 77:166–199, 1996.

32. E. Grädel, W. Thomas, and T. Wilke, editors. *Automata, Logics, and Infinite Games: A Guide to Current Research*, Lecture Notes in Computer Science, volume 2500, Springer, 2002.

33. M. Grohe. Finite variable logics in descriptive complexity theory. *Bulletin of Symbolic Logic*, 4:345–398, 1998.

34. M. Grohe. Fixed-point logics on planar graphs. In *LICS*, pages 6–15. IEEE Computer Society, 1998.

35. M. Grohe. Isomorphism testing for embeddable graphs through definability. In *STOC*, pages 63–72. ACM, 2000.

36. M. Grohe and J. Mariño. Definability and descriptive complexity on databases of bounded tree-width. In C. Beeri and P. Buneman, editors, *ICDT*, Lecture Notes in Computer Science, volume 1540, pages 70–82. Springer, 1999.

37. S. Grumbach and J. Su. Queries with arithmetical constraints. *Theoretical Computer Science*, 173(1):151–181, 1997.

38. Y. Gurevich. Logic and the challenge of computer science. In E. Börger, editor, *Current Trends in Theoretical Computer Science*, pages 1–57. Computer Science Press, 1988.

39. Y. Gurevich and S. Shelah. Fixed-point extensions of first-order logic. *Annals of Pure and Applied Logic*, 32:265–180, 1986.

40. P. Hell and J. Nešetřil. On the complexity of H-coloring. *Journal of Combinatorial Theory-Series B*, 48:92–110, 1990.

41. L. Hella, Ph. G. Kolaitis, and K. Luosto. Almost everywhere equivalence of logics in finite model theory. *The Bulletin of Symbolic Logic*, 2(4):422–443, 1996.

42. M. Hennessy and R. Milner. Algebraic laws for nondeterminism and concurrency. *Journal of the ACM*, 32(1):137–161, 1985.

43. N. Immerman. Relational queries computable in polynomial time. *Information and Control*, 68:86–104, 1986.

44. N. Immerman and D. Kozen. Definability with bounded number of bound variables. *Information and Computation*, 83:121–139, 1989.

45. P. C. Kanellakis, G. M. Kuper, and P. Z. Revesz. Constraint query languages. In *PODS*, pages 299–313. ACM, 1990.

46. C. Karp. Finite quantifier equivalence. In J. W. Addison, L. Henkin, and A. Tarski, editors, *The Theory of Models*, pages 407–412. North-Holland, 1965.

47. Ph. G. Kolaitis and M. Y. Vardi. The decision problem for the probabilities of higher-order properties. In *STOC*, pages 425–435. ACM, 1987.

48. Ph. G. Kolaitis and M. Y. Vardi. Infinitary logics and 0–1 laws. *Information and Computation*, 98(2):258–294, 1992.
49. S. Kreutzer. Expressive equivalence of least and inflationary fixed-point logic. *Annals of Pure and Applied Logic*, 130(1–3):61–78, 2004.
50. R. E. Ladner. On the structure of polynomial time reducibility. *Journal of the ACM*, 22(1):155–171, 1975.
51. M. C. Laskowski. A simpler axiomatization of the Shelah–Spencer almost sure theories. *Israel Journal of Mathematics*, to appear.
52. Y. N. Moschovakis. *Descriptive Set Theory*. North-Holland, 1980.
53. A. Nash, J. B. Remmel, and V. Vianu. Ptime queries revisited. In T. Eiter and L. Libkin, editors, *ICDT*, Lecture Notes in Computer Science, volume 3363, pages 274–288. Springer, 2005.
54. M. Otto. *Bounded Variable Logics and Counting*. Springer, 1997.
55. M. Otto. Bisimulation-invariant ptime and higher-dimensional μ-calculus. *Theoretical Computer Science*, 224(1-2):237–265, 1999.
56. M. Otto. Modal and guarded characterisation theorems over finite transition systems. *Annals of Pure and Applied Logic*, 130:173–205, 2004.
57. D. Park. Concurrency and automata on infinite sequences. In P. Deussen, editor, *Theoretical Computer Science*, Lecture Notes in Computer Science, volume 104, pages 167–183. Springer, 1981.
58. O. Reingold. Undirected st-connectivity in log-space. In H. N. Gabow and R. Fagin, editors, *STOC*, pages 376–385. ACM, 2005.
59. E. Rosen. Modal logic over finite structures. *Journal of Logic, Language and Information*, 6(4):427–439, 1997.
60. B. Rossman. Existential positive types and preservation under homomorphisms. In *LICS*, pages 467–476. IEEE Computer Society, 2005.
61. T. J. Schaefer. The complexity of satisfiability problems. In *STOC*, pages 216–226. ACM, 1978.
62. S. Shelah and J. Spencer. Zero–one laws for sparse random graphs. *Journal of the American Mathematical Society*, 1:97–115, 1988.
63. H. Straubing. *Finite Automata, Formal Logic, and Circuit Complexity*. Birkhäuser, 1994.
64. W. Tait. A counterexample to a conjecture of Scott and Suppes. *Journal of Symbolic Logic*, 24(1):15–16, 1959.
65. A. Tarski. The concept of truth in formalized languages. In *Logic, Semantics, Metamathematics*, pages 152–278. Clarendon Press, Oxford, 1956.
66. L. van den Dries. *Tame Topology and o-Minimal Structures*. Cambridge University Press, 1998.
67. L. van den Dries. Classical model theory of fields. In D. Haskell, A. Pillay, and C. Steinhorn, editors, *Model Theory, Algebra, and Geometry*, pages 37–52. Cambridge University Press, 2000.
68. M. Y. Vardi. The complexity of relational query languages. In *STOC*, pages 137–146. ACM, 1982.
69. M. Y. Vardi. Why is modal logic so robustly decidable? In N. Immerman and Ph. G. Kolaitis, editors, *Descriptive Complexity and Finite Models*, volume 31 of *DIMACS Series in Discrete Mathematics and Theoretical Computer Science*, pages 149–184. American Mathematical Society, 1996.
70. A. J. Wilkie. Model completeness results for expansions of the ordered field of real numbers by restricted pfaffian functions and the exponential function. *Journal of the American Mathematical Society*, 9:1051–1094, 1996.

2

On the Expressive Power of Logics on Finite Models

Phokion G. Kolaitis

2.1 Introduction

Finite model theory can be succinctly described as the study of logics on classes of finite structures. In addition to first-order logic, various other logics have been explored in the context of finite model theory, including fragments of second-order logic, logics with fixed-point operators, infinitary logics, and logics with generalized quantifiers. Some typical classes of finite structures on which these logics have been investigated are the class of all finite graphs, the class of all finite ordered graphs, the class of all finite planar graphs, the class of all finite strings, and the class of all finite trees.

Finite model theory provides a conceptual and methodological framework for exploring the connections between logic and several key areas of computer science, such as database theory, computational complexity, and computer-aided verification. This is perhaps the primary motivation for developing finite model theory. As its development progressed, however, it became clear that finite model theory was an area of research that deserved to be studied in its own right. While the traditional focus of mathematical logic has been on fixed infinite structures or on classes of finite and infinite structures, it has turned out that new phenomena emerge when one focuses on classes of finite structures. These phenomena give finite model theory its own distinctive character and set it apart from other areas of mathematical logic.

There are three main areas of research in finite model theory: the study of the expressive power of logics on finite structures; the study of the connections between logic and computational complexity, an area which is also known as descriptive complexity; and the study of the connections between logic and asymptotic probabilities. The first of these three areas is the focus of the present chapter.

2.2 Basic Concepts

A *vocabulary* is a finite set $\sigma = \{R_1, \ldots, R_m, c_1, \ldots, c_s\}$ of relation symbols of specified arities, and constant symbols. A σ-*structure* is a tuple $\mathbf{A} = (A, R_1^{\mathbf{A}}, \ldots, R_m^{\mathbf{A}}, c_1^{\mathbf{A}}, \ldots, c_s^{\mathbf{A}})$ such that A is a nonempty set, called the *universe* of $\mathbf{A}$, each $R_i^{\mathbf{A}}$ is a relation on A such that $\text{arity}(R_i^{\mathbf{A}}) = \text{arity}(R_i)$, $1 \leq i \leq m$, and each $c_j^{\mathbf{A}}$ is a distinguished element of A, $1 \leq j \leq s$. A *finite* σ-*structure* is a σ-structure $\mathbf{A}$ whose universe A is a finite set. In what follows, we shall assume that the universe of every finite structure is an initial segment $\{1, \ldots, n\}$ of the integers. If the vocabulary is understood from the context, we shall simply use the terms "structure" and "finite structure". Also, whenever no confusion arises and in order to simplify the notation, we shall use the same symbol for both a relation (constant) symbol and the relation (distinguished element) interpreting it on a structure.

Let us assume that $\mathbf{A} = (A, R_1^{\mathbf{A}}, \ldots, R_m^{\mathbf{A}}, c_1^{\mathbf{A}}, \ldots, c_s^{\mathbf{A}})$ and $\mathbf{B} = (B, R_1^{\mathbf{B}}, \ldots, R_m^{\mathbf{B}}, c_1^{\mathbf{B}}, \ldots, c_s^{\mathbf{B}})$ are two σ-structures. An *isomorphism* between $\mathbf{A}$ and $\mathbf{B}$ is a mapping $h : A \to B$ that satisfies the following conditions:

- h is a one-to-one and onto function.
- For every constant symbol c_j, $1 \leq j \leq s$, we have that $h(c_j^{\mathbf{A}}) = c_j^{\mathbf{B}}$.
- For every relation symbol R_i, $1 \leq i \leq m$, of arity t and for every t-tuple $(a_1, \ldots, a_t)$ from A, we have that $R_i^{\mathbf{A}}(a_1, \ldots, a_t)$ if and only if $R_i^{\mathbf{B}}(h(a_1), \ldots, h(a_t))$.

A structure $\mathbf{B} = (B, R_1^{\mathbf{B}}, \ldots, R_m^{\mathbf{B}}, c_1^{\mathbf{B}}, \ldots, c_s^{\mathbf{B}})$ is a *substructure* of $\mathbf{A}$ if $B \subseteq A$, each $R_i^{\mathbf{B}}$ is the restriction of $R_i^{\mathbf{A}}$ to B (which means that $R_i^{\mathbf{B}} = R_i^{\mathbf{A}} \cap B^t$, where t is the arity of R_i), $1 \leq i \leq m$, and $c_j^{\mathbf{B}} = c_j^{\mathbf{A}}$, $1 \leq j \leq s$. If $\mathbf{A}$ is a σ-structure and D is a subset of A, then the *substructure of* $\mathbf{A}$ *generated by* D is the structure $\mathbf{A} \upharpoonright D$ having the set $D \cup \{c_1^{\mathbf{A}}, \ldots, c_s^{\mathbf{A}}\}$ as its universe and having the restrictions of the relations $R_i^{\mathbf{A}}$ on $D \cup \{c_1^{\mathbf{A}}, \ldots, c_s^{\mathbf{A}}\}$ as its relations.

A *partial isomorphism from* $\mathbf{A}$ *to* $\mathbf{B}$ is an isomorphism from a substructure of $\mathbf{A}$ to a substructure of $\mathbf{B}$. From the preceding definitions, it follows that every partial isomorphism from $\mathbf{A}$ to $\mathbf{B}$ must map each constant $c_j^{\mathbf{A}}$ of $\mathbf{A}$ to the constant $c_j^{\mathbf{B}}$, $1 \leq j \leq s$.

The following examples illustrate some of these concepts. A *directed graph* is a structure $\mathbf{G} = (V, E)$, where E is a binary relation on V. An *undirected graph* or, simply, a *graph* is a structure $\mathbf{G} = (V, E)$ such that E is a binary symmetric relation on V without self-loops. The subgraph of $\mathbf{G}$ induced by a set D of nodes is precisely the substructure of $\mathbf{G}$ generated by D. A *directed graph with two distinguished nodes s and t* is a structure $\mathbf{G} = (V, E, s, t)$. An *ordered directed graph* is a structure $\mathbf{G} = (V, E, \leq)$, where E is a binary relation on V and $\leq$ is a linear order on V. A *k-colored directed graph* is a structure $\mathbf{G} = (V, E, P_1, \ldots, P_k)$, where E is a binary relation on V and each P_i is a unary relation on V consisting of all nodes of color i, $1 \leq i \leq k$. Finally, a *binary string* of length n can be thought of as a structure $\mathbf{S} = (\{1, 2, \ldots, n\}, P)$, where P is a unary relation on $\{1, \ldots, n\}$

such that $i \in P$ if and only if the ith bit of the string is equal to 1, where $1 \leq i \leq n$. For instance, the string 10001 can be identified with the finite structure $(\{1, 2, 3, 4, 5\}, \{1, 5\})$.

The concept of a *query*, which originated in database theory, is one of the most fundamental concepts in finite model theory. We now give a precise definition and present several examples.

Definition 2.2.1. *Let σ be a vocabulary and k a positive integer.*

- *A class of σ-structures is a collection $\mathcal{C}$ of σ-structures that is closed under isomorphisms, which means that if $\mathbf{A} \in \mathcal{C}$ and $\mathbf{B}$ is a structure that is isomorphic to $\mathbf{A}$, then $\mathbf{B} \in \mathcal{C}$.*
- *A k-ary query on a class $\mathcal{C}$ is a mapping Q with domain $\mathcal{C}$ and such that*
  - *$Q(\mathbf{A})$ is a k-ary relation on $\mathbf{A}$, for $\mathbf{A} \in \mathcal{C}$;*
  - *Q is preserved under isomorphisms, which means that if $h : \mathbf{A} \to \mathbf{B}$ is an isomorphism, then $Q(\mathbf{B}) = h(Q(\mathbf{A}))$.*
- *A Boolean query on a class $\mathcal{C}$ is a mapping $Q : \mathcal{C} \to \{0, 1\}$ that is preserved under isomorphisms, i.e., if $\mathbf{A}$ is isomorphic to $\mathbf{B}$, then $Q(\mathbf{A}) = Q(\mathbf{B})$. Consequently, Q can be identified with the subclass $\mathcal{C}' = \{\mathbf{A} \in \mathcal{C} : Q(\mathbf{A}) = 1\}$ of $\mathcal{C}$.*

Example 2.2.2. Consider the following queries on graphs $\mathbf{G} = (V, E)$.

- The TRANSITIVE CLOSURE query TC is the binary query such that

$$TC(\mathbf{G}) = \{(a, b) \in V^2 : \text{there is a path from } a \text{ to } b\}.$$

- The 2-DISJOINT PATHS query is the 4-ary query $2DP$ such that

$$2DP(\mathbf{G}) = \{(a, b, c, d) \in V^4 : \text{there are two node-disjoint paths from } a \text{ to } b \text{ and from } c \text{ to } d\}.$$

- The ARTICULATION POINT query is the unary query AP such that

$$AP(\mathbf{G}) = \{a \in V : a \text{ is an articulation point of } \mathbf{G}\}.$$

- The EVEN CARDINALITY query $EVEN$ is the Boolean query such that

$$EVEN(\mathbf{G}) = \begin{cases} 1 \text{ if } \mathbf{G} \text{ has an even number of nodes} \\ 0 \text{ otherwise.} \end{cases}$$

- The CONNECTIVITY query CN is the Boolean query such that

$$CN(\mathbf{G}) = \begin{cases} 1 \text{ if } \mathbf{G} \text{ is connected} \\ 0 \text{ otherwise.} \end{cases}$$

- The Boolean queries EULERIAN, ACYCLICITY, k-COLORABILITY, and HAMILTONIAN PATH are defined in an analogous way.

Queries are mathematical objects that formalize the concept of a "property" of structures and of elements of structures. This formalization makes it possible to define and study what it means for such a "property" to be expressible in some logic. In other words, we shall use logic as a *specification language* of "properties" of structures and of elements of structures.

Definition 2.2.3. *Let L be a logic and C a class of σ-structures.*

- *A k-ary query Q on C is L-definable if there is an L-formula $\varphi(x_1, \ldots, x_k)$ with $x_1, \ldots, x_k$ as free variables and such that for every $\mathbf{A} \in C$,*

$$Q(\mathbf{A}) = \{(a_1, \ldots, a_k) \in A^k : \mathbf{A} \models \varphi(a_1, \ldots, a_k)\}.$$

- *A Boolean query Q on C is L-definable if there is an L-sentence ψ such that for every $\mathbf{A} \in C$,*

$$Q(\mathbf{A}) = 1 \iff \mathbf{A} \models \psi.$$

- *$L(C)$ denotes the collection of all L-definable queries on C.*

Two remarks are in order now. First, it should be emphasized that the concept of an L-definable query Q on a class C of σ-structures is a concept of *uniform definability*. This means that the same L-formula serves as a specification of the query on every structure in C, which is entirely analogous to the requirement that an algorithm for a problem must produce the correct answer on every instance of the problem. Along these lines, note that if a query Q is L-definable on C and C' is a subclass of C, then the restriction of Q on C' is also L-definable using the formula that defines it on C. Second, the concept of an L-definable query on a class C makes sense for an arbitrary class of σ-structures, which may very well consist of both finite and infinite structures, or only infinite structures, or only finite structures. In particular, this concept contains the following important cases as special cases:

1. C is the class S of all (finite and infinite) σ-structures. This is the primary case of uniform definability studied in classical model theory.
2. C consists of a single infinite structure $\mathbf{A}$ (and all its isomorphic copies). This is the case of *local definability* on a fixed structure. The two primary examples are the structure $\mathbf{N} = (N, +, \times)$ of arithmetic and the structure $\mathbf{R} = (R, +, \times)$ of analysis, where N is the set of all natural numbers and R is the set of all real numbers.
3. C is the class $\mathcal{F}$ of finite σ-structures. As stated earlier, this means that $\mathcal{F}$ consists of all σ-structures with universe $\{1, \ldots, n\}$ for some positive integer n. This is the primary case of uniform definability studied in finite model theory.

We now present several examples of queries that are definable in first-order logic or in fragments of second-order logic. We assume familiarity with the syntax and semantics of first-order logic and second-order logic (see [20] for the precise definitions). Informally, first-order logic FO over a vocabulary σ has (first-order) variables that are interpreted by elements of the structure at hand; has atomic formulas of the form $s_1 = s_2$ and $R_i(s_1, \ldots, s_t)$, where R_i is a relation symbol and each s_j is a variable or a constant symbol; has the standard propositional connectives $\neg$, $\vee$, $\wedge$, $\rightarrow$; and, finally, has first-order quantifiers $\forall x$ and $\exists x$, for each variable x, that range over elements of the universe of the structure at hand.

Example 2.2.4. The following queries are first-order definable on the class of all (finite or infinite) graphs.

- The Boolean query "the graph **G** has an isolated node" is definable by the first-order formula

$$(\exists x)(\forall y)(\neg E(x, y)).$$

- The unary query "the node x has at least two distinct neighbors" is definable by the first-order formula

$$(\exists y)(\exists z)(\neg(y = z) \wedge E(x, y) \wedge E(x, z)).$$

Similarly, for each fixed k, the Boolean query "**G** is a k-regular graph" (i.e., each node has exactly k neighbors) is first-order definable.
- The binary query "there is a path of length 2 from x to y" is definable by the first-order formula

$$(\exists z)(\neg(x = z) \wedge \neg(y = z) \wedge E(x, z) \wedge E(z, y)).$$

The syntax of second-order logic SO is obtained by augmenting the syntax of first-order logic with second-order variables $X, Y, \ldots$ and second-order quantifiers $\exists X, \exists Y, \ldots, \forall X, \forall Y, \ldots$ that are interpreted by relations of fixed arities over the universe of the structure at hand. *Existential second-order logic* ESO and *universal second-order logic* USO are the syntactically simplest fragments of second-order logic. Specifically, ESO consists of all second-order formulas of the form

$$(\exists S_1) \cdots (\exists S_m)\varphi(\overline{x}, S_1, \ldots, S_m),$$

where each S_i is a second-order variable, $1 \le i \le m$, and $\varphi(\overline{x}, S_1, \ldots, S_m)$ is a first-order formula. In a dual manner, USO consists of all second-order formulas of the form

$$(\forall S_1) \cdots (\forall S_m)\varphi(\overline{x}, S_1, \ldots, S_m),$$

where each S_i is a second-order variable, $1 \le i \le m$, and $\varphi(\overline{x}, S_1, \ldots, S_m)$ is a first-order formula. *Monadic second-order logic* MSO is the fragment of second-order logic consisting of all second-order formulas in which every second-order quantifier is applied to a unary second-order variable, which means that all second-order quantifiers in the formula range over subsets of the universes of structures. *Existential monadic second-order logic* consists of all formulas that are both ESO formulas and monadic second-order formulas. Similarly, *universal monadic second-order logic* consists of all formulas that are both USO formulas and monadic second-order formulas.

Example 2.2.5. The following queries are definable in existential monadic second-order logic on the class of all (finite or infinite) graphs:

1. The Boolean query DISCONNECTIVITY is definable by the formula

$$(\exists S)((\exists x)S(x) \wedge (\exists y)\neg S(y) \wedge (\forall z)(\forall w)(S(z) \wedge \neg S(w) \rightarrow \neg E(z,w))).$$

   Intuitively, this sentence asserts that there are two disjoint, nonempty sets of nodes with no edge between them.

2. The Boolean query 2-COLORABILITY is definable by the formula

$$(\exists R)(\forall x)(\forall y)(E(x,y) \rightarrow (R(x) \leftrightarrow \neg R(y))).$$

   Intuitively, the two colors are encoded by R and the complement of R.

3. For every $k \geq 3$, the Boolean query k-COLORABILITY is definable by a formula of existential monadic second-order logic with $k - 1$ existential monadic quantifiers. The formula is similar to the one above used to define 2-COLORABILITY: each of the $k - 1$ monadic second-order variables encodes a different color, while the kth color is encoded by the complement of the union of these $k - 1$ colors. Indeed, the reader may verify that $\lceil \log k \rceil$ existential monadic quantifiers suffice.

Example 2.2.6. The WELL-FOUNDEDNESS Boolean query is definable on the class of all linear orders $(V, \leq)$ by the following formula of universal monadic second-order logic:

$$(\forall S)((\exists x)S(x) \rightarrow (\exists y)(S(y) \wedge (\forall z)(S(z) \rightarrow y \leq z))).$$

Example 2.2.7. The Boolean query HAMILTONIAN PATH is definable on the class of all finite graphs $G = (V, E)$ by an existential second-order formula that asserts that

$$(\exists T)(\text{``T is a linear order on V''}) \wedge$$
$$(\forall x)(\forall y)(\text{``y is the successor of x in T''} \rightarrow E(x,y))),$$

where T is a second-order variable of arity 2. In the above formula, the properties "T is a linear order on V" and "y is the successor of x in T" are clearly expressible in first-order logic.

Example 2.2.8. The Boolean query RIGIDITY (i.e., given a graph $\mathbf{G} = (V, E)$, is the identity function its only automorphism?) is definable on the class of all finite graphs by a universal second-order formula that asserts that

$$(\forall S)(\text{``S encodes an automorphism of $\mathbf{G}$''} \rightarrow (\forall x)S(x,x)),$$

where S is a binary relation symbol.

The expressive power of a logic L on a class $\mathcal{C}$ of finite structures is measured by the collection $L(\mathcal{C})$ of L-definable queries on $\mathcal{C}$. As a general rule, the expressive power of a logic L is *context-dependent*, that is to say, $L(\mathcal{C})$ depends on the class $\mathcal{C}$ on which the logic L is studied. For instance, first-order logic has very high expressive power on the structure $\mathbf{N} = (N, +, \times)$ of arithmetic, since every recursively enumerable relation is first-order definable on $\mathbf{N}$. In contrast, first-order logic has limited expressive power on the class of all (finite or infinite) graphs, since properties as basic as CONNECTIVITY and ACYCLICITY are not first-order definable. First-order logic has limited expressive power on the class of all finite graphs as well. In particular, none of the following queries is first-order definable on finite graphs: EVEN CARDINALITY; CONNECTIVITY; ACYCLICITY; PLANARITY; EULERIAN; k-COLORABILITY, for every fixed $k \geq 2$; and HAMILTONIAN PATH. Actually, it is fair to say that *no* property of finite graphs that requires recursion is first-order definable.

The central question about the expressive power of a logic L on a class $\mathcal{C}$ of structures is to determine which queries on $\mathcal{C}$ are L-definable and which are not. Clearly, to show that a query Q on $\mathcal{C}$ is L-definable, it suffices to find some L-formula that defines it on every structure in $\mathcal{C}$. In contrast, showing that Q is *not* L-definable is in principle a more challenging task, since it entails showing that *no* formula of L defines the property. In many respects, this is analogous to the difference between establishing upper and lower bounds on the computational complexity of an algorithmic problem. For this reason, much of the investigation of the expressive power of a logic centers on the development of techniques for showing that queries are not definable in that logic.

There are three main tools for investigating the expressive power of first-order logic:

- the *Compactness Theorem*;
- the method of *ultraproducts*;
- the method of *Ehrenfeucht–Fraïssé games*.

The Compactness Theorem and the method of ultraproducts are direct and effective tools for analyzing the expressive power of first-order logic on the class of all (finite or infinite) structures over a given vocabulary. To illustrate this point, let us recall the standard proof that CONNECTIVITY is not first-order definable on the class of all graphs. Towards obtaining a contradiction, assume that there is a first-order sentence ψ such that for every graph $\mathbf{G} = (V, E)$ we have that $\mathbf{G} \models \psi$ if and only if $\mathbf{G}$ is connected. Let c', d' be two constant symbols and, for every $n \geq 1$, let φ_n be a first-order sentence asserting that there is no path of length n from c to d. Then every finite subset of the set

$$T = \{\varphi_n : n \geq 1\} \cup \{\psi\}$$

has a model (for instance, a sufficiently long path with c and d as its endpoints). Consequently, the Compactness Theorem implies that T has a model $\mathbf{G} = (V, E, c, d)$. This, however, gives rise to a contradiction. Indeed, on the one hand, $\mathbf{G}$ is connected, since $\mathbf{G} \models \psi$; in particular, there is a path from (the distinguished element interpreting) c to (the distinguished element interpreting) d in $\mathbf{G}$. On the other hand, however, there is no path from c to d in $\mathbf{G}$, since $\mathbf{G} \models \varphi_n$, for every $n \geq 1$.

Although the above proof establishes that CONNECTIVITY is not first-order definable on the class of all graphs, it does *not* establish that this property is not first-order definable on the class of all finite graphs. The reason is that the model of T guaranteed to exist by the Compactness Theorem need not be finite. In general, it may very well be the case that every finite subset of a set T of first-order sentences has a finite model, but that T itself has only infinite models. Therefore, a proof that uses the Compactness Theorem to show that a query is not first-order definable on all structures does not automatically translate to a proof that the query is not first-order definable on all finite structures. Similar obstacles arise when using the method of ultraproducts. While it is still possible to use the Compactness Theorem and the method of ultraproducts to study the expressive power of first-order logic on finite structures [29], the use of these tools is often somewhat cumbersome or not intuitive. In contrast, the method of Ehrenfeucht–Fraïssé games is a tool that has been successfully applied to the study of first-order logic in finite model theory. Furthermore, it is a flexible and extendible tool, since variants of Ehrenfeucht–Fraïssé games can be formulated and used to study the expressive power of logics that are stronger than first-order logic and do not possess the Compactness Theorem.

2.3 Ehrenfeucht–Fraïssé Games for First-Order Logic

This section is devoted to a presentation of the Ehrenfeucht–Fraïssé games and their applications to the analysis of the expressive power of first-order logic on finite structures.

Definition 2.3.1. *Let r be a positive integer, σ a vocabulary, and $\mathbf{A}$ and $\mathbf{B}$ two σ-structures.*

The r-move Ehrenfeucht–Fraïssé game on $\mathbf{A}$ and $\mathbf{B}$ is played between two players, called the Spoiler *and the* Duplicator, *according to the following rules.*

Each run of the game has r moves. In each move, the Spoiler plays first and picks an element from the universe A of $\mathbf{A}$ or from the universe B of $\mathbf{B}$; the Duplicator then responds by picking an element from the universe of the other structure (i.e., if the Spoiler has picked an element from A, then the Duplicator picks an element from B, and vice versa). Let $a_i \in A$ and $b_i \in B$ be the two elements picked by the Spoiler and the Duplicator in their ith move, $1 \leq i \leq r$.

- *The* Duplicator *wins the run $(a_1, b_1), \ldots, (a_r, b_r)$ if the mapping*

$$a_i \mapsto b_i, \ 1 \leq i \leq r, \ and \ c_i^{\mathbf{A}} \mapsto c_j^{\mathbf{B}}, \ 1 \leq j \leq s,$$

is a partial isomorphism from **A** *to* **B**, *which means that it is an iso-morphism between the substructure* **A** $\restriction \{a_1, \ldots, a_r\}$ *of* **A** *generated by* $\{a_1, \ldots, a_r\}$ *and the substructure* **B** $\restriction \{b_1, \ldots, b_r\}$ *of* **B** *generated by* $\{b_1, \ldots, b_r\}$. *Otherwise,* the Spoiler wins the run $(a_1, b_1), \ldots, (a_r, b_r)$.

- *The* Duplicator wins the r-move Ehrenfeucht–Fraïssé game on **A** and **B** *if the Duplicator can win every run of the game, i.e., if (s)he has a* winning strategy *for the Ehrenfeucht–Fraïssé game. Otherwise, the* Spoiler wins the r-move Ehrenfeucht–Fraïssé game on **A** and **B**.
- *We write* **A** $\sim_r$ **B** *to denote that the Duplicator wins the r-move Ehrenfeucht–Fraïssé game on* **A** *and* **B**.

A typical run of the r-move Ehrenfeucht–Fraïssé game on **A** *and* **B** *is depicted in Fig. 2.1.*

The next proposition follows immediately from Definition 2.3.1.

Proposition 2.3.2. $\sim_r$ *is an equivalence relation on the class S of all σ-structures.*

Example 2.3.3. Let **A** and **B** be the graphs depicted in Fig. 2.2. Then

- **A** $\sim_2$ **B**, i.e., the Duplicator wins the 2-move Ehrenfeucht–Fraïssé game on **A**, **B**;
- **A** $\not\sim_3$ **B**, i.e., the Spoiler wins the 3-move Ehrenfeucht–Fraïssé game on **A**, **B**.

$$\begin{array}{c} \text{Spoiler} \quad a_1 \in A \;\; b_2 \in B \;\; b_3 \in B \;\ldots\; a_r \in A \\ \updownarrow \qquad \updownarrow \qquad \updownarrow \qquad \ldots \updownarrow \\ \text{Duplicator } b_1 \in B \;\; a_2 \in A \;\; a_3 \in A \;\ldots\; b_r \in B \end{array}$$

Fig. 2.1. A typical run of the r-move Ehrenfeucht–Fraïssé game

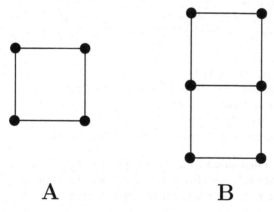

A   **B**

Fig. 2.2. A difference between the 2-move and the 3-move Ehrenfeucht–Fraïssé game

The Duplicator can win the 2-move game by playing in such a way that there is an edge between a_1 and a_2 if and only if there is an edge between b_1 and b_2. In contrast, the Spoiler can win the 3-move game by picking three elements in **B** with no edge between any two of them.

Note that the description of a winning strategy for the Duplicator in the Ehrenfeucht–Fraïssé game, as presented in Definition 2.3.1, is rather informal. The concept of a winning strategy for the Duplicator can be made precise, however, in terms of families of partial isomorphisms with appropriate extension properties.

Definition 2.3.4. *Let r be a positive integer. A winning strategy for the Duplicator in the r-move Ehrenfeucht–Fraïssé game on* **A** *and* **B** *is a sequence $I_0, I_1, \ldots, I_r$ of nonempty sets of partial isomorphisms from* **A** *to* **B** *such that*

- *The sequence $I_0, I_1, \ldots, I_r$ has the* forth *property: For every $i < r$, every $f \in I_i$, and every $a \in A$, there is a $g \in I_{i+1}$ such that $a \in \mathrm{dom}(g)$ and $f \subseteq g$.*
- *The sequence $I_0, I_1, \ldots, I_r$ has the* back *property: For every $i < r$, every $f \in I_i$, and every $b \in B$, there is a $g \in I_{i+1}$ such that $b \in \mathrm{rng}(g)$ and $f \subseteq g$.*

In effect, the forth property provides the Duplicator with a good move when the Spoiler picks an element of **A**, while the back property provides the Duplicator with a good move when the Spoiler picks an element of **B**.

The key feature of Ehrenfeucht–Fraïssé games is that they capture the combinatorial content of first-order quantification; for this reason, Ehrenfeucht–Fraïssé games can be used to characterize definability in first-order logic on an arbitrary class of σ-structures. To describe the precise connection between first-order logic and Ehrenfeucht–Fraïssé games, we need to bring into the picture a well-known concept from mathematical logic.

Definition 2.3.5. *Let φ be a first-order formula over a vocabulary σ. The quantifier rank of φ, denoted by $\mathrm{qr}(\varphi)$, is the depth of quantifier nesting in φ. More formally, $\mathrm{qr}(\varphi)$ is defined by the following induction on the construction of φ:*

- *If φ is atomic, then $\mathrm{qr}(\varphi) = 0$.*
- *If φ is of the form $\neg\psi$, then $\mathrm{qr}(\varphi) = \mathrm{qr}(\psi)$.*
- *If φ is of the form $\psi_1 \wedge \psi_2$ or of the form $\psi_1 \vee \psi_2$, then $\mathrm{qr}(\varphi) = \max\{\mathrm{qr}(\psi_1), \mathrm{qr}(\psi_2)\}$.*
- *If φ is of the form $\exists x\psi$ or of the form $\forall x\psi$, then $\mathrm{qr}(\varphi) = \mathrm{qr}(\psi) + 1$.*

Note that if a first-order formula is in prenex normal form, then its quantifier rank is equal to the number of the quantifiers in its prefix. For instance, if φ is $(\forall x)(\forall y)(\exists z)\theta$, where θ is quantifier-free, then $\mathrm{qr}(\varphi) = 3$. In contrast, if φ

is $(\exists x)E(x,x) \vee (\exists y)(\forall z)\neg E(y,z)$, then $\mathrm{qr}(\varphi) = 2$. Note also that if $\mathrm{qr}(\varphi) = r$, then for every $r' > r$ there is a first-order formula ψ such that $\mathrm{qr}(\psi) = r'$ and φ is logically equivalent to ψ.

Definition 2.3.6. *Let r be a positive integer, and let $\mathbf{A}$ and $\mathbf{B}$ be two σ-structures. We write $\mathbf{A} \equiv_r \mathbf{B}$ to denote that $\mathbf{A}$ and $\mathbf{B}$ satisfy the same first-order sentences of quantifier rank r.*

Proposition 2.3.7. $\equiv_r$ *is an equivalence relation on the class $\mathcal{S}$ of all σ-structures.*

Note that the equivalence relation $\equiv_r$ is defined using purely logical concepts. The main technical result of this section asserts that $\equiv_r$ coincides with the equivalence relation $\sim_r$, which was defined using purely combinatorial concepts.

Theorem 2.3.8. [19, 27] *Let r be a positive integer, and let $\mathbf{A}$ and $\mathbf{B}$ be two σ-structures. Then the following statements are equivalent:*

1. $\mathbf{A} \equiv_r \mathbf{B}$, *i.e., $\mathbf{A}$ and $\mathbf{B}$ satisfy the same first-order sentences of quantifier rank r.*
2. $\mathbf{A} \sim_r \mathbf{B}$, *i.e., the Duplicator wins the r-move Ehrenfeucht–Fraïssé game on $\mathbf{A}$ and $\mathbf{B}$.*

Moreover, the following are true:

- $\equiv_r$ *has finitely many equivalence classes.*
- *Each $\equiv_r$-equivalence class is definable by a first-order sentence of quantifier rank r.*

Example 2.3.9. Before embarking on the proof of Theorem 2.3.8, let us briefly revisit Example 2.3.3. As seen in that example, the Spoiler wins the 3-move Ehrenfeucht–Fraïssé game on the structures $\mathbf{A}$ and $\mathbf{B}$ shown in Fig. 2.2. Therefore, Theorem 2.3.8 tells that there is a first-order sentence of quantifier rank 3 that is satisfied by one of the two structures, but not by the other. Indeed, if φ is the sentence

$$\exists x \exists y \exists z (x \neq y \wedge x \neq z \wedge y \neq z \wedge \neg E(x,y) \wedge \neg E(x,z) \wedge \neg E(y,z)),$$

then $\mathbf{B} \models \varphi$, but $\mathbf{A} \not\models \varphi$. Note also that this sentence yields a strategy for the Spoiler to win the 3-move Ehrenfeucht–Fraïssé game on $\mathbf{A}$ and $\mathbf{B}$: the Spoiler picks three elements b_1, b_2, b_3 from B such that $\mathbf{B}, b_1, b_2, b_3 \models (x \neq y \wedge x \neq z \wedge y \neq z \wedge \neg E(x,y) \wedge \neg E(x,z) \wedge \neg E(y,z))$. Another sentence witnessing that $\mathbf{A} \not\equiv_3 \mathbf{B}$ is the sentence

$$(\forall x)(\forall y)(\exists z)(x \neq y \wedge \neg E(x,y) \rightarrow E(x,z) \wedge E(y,z)),$$

which is true on $\mathbf{A}$, but is false on $\mathbf{B}$. In turn, this sentence yields another strategy for the Spoiler to win the 3-move Ehrenfeucht–Fraïssé game on $\mathbf{A}$:

$$\text{Spoiler} \quad b_1 \in B \; b_2 \in B \; a_3 \in A$$
$$\updownarrow \qquad \updownarrow \qquad \updownarrow$$
$$\text{Duplicator } a_1 \in A \; a_2 \in A \; b_3 \in B.$$

The Spoiler first picks two elements b_1, b_2 from B such that $\mathbf{B}, b_1, b_2 \models x \neq y \wedge \neg E(x, y) \wedge \forall z \neg (E(x, z) \wedge E(y, z))$. After the Duplicator has picked elements a_1, a_2 from A, the Spoiler picks an element a_3 from A such that $\mathbf{A}, a_1, a_2, a_3 \models x \neq y \wedge \neg E(x, y) \rightarrow E(x, z) \wedge E(y, z)$; the Duplicator is unable to respond to this move in such a way that a partial isomorphism is maintained.

We now proceed with the proof of Theorem 2.3.8. One part of this theorem has a relatively straightforward proof.

Theorem 2.3.10. *Let r be a positive integer. If $\mathbf{A}$ and $\mathbf{B}$ are two σ-structures such that the Duplicator wins the r-move Ehrenfeucht–Fraïssé game on $\mathbf{A}$ and $\mathbf{B}$, then every first-order sentence of quantifier rank r that is true on $\mathbf{A}$ is also true on $\mathbf{B}$. Consequently, if $\mathbf{A} \sim_r \mathbf{B}$, then $\mathbf{A} \equiv_r \mathbf{B}$.*

Proof. We proceed by induction on the quantifier rank of formulas. Assume that the result holds for all formulas of quantifier rank r over an arbitrary vocabulary. We have to show that if φ is a formula of quantifier rank $r + 1$ and $\mathbf{A}, \mathbf{B}$ are two σ-structures such that $\mathbf{A} \sim_{r+1} \mathbf{B}$ and $\mathbf{A} \models \varphi$, then $\mathbf{B} \models \varphi$. The interesting cases are the ones in which φ is of the form $\exists x \psi$ or of the form $\forall x \psi$.

Assume that φ is of the form $\exists x \psi$, which implies that $\mathrm{qr}(\psi) = r$. We have to show that $\mathbf{B} \models \exists x \psi$. Since $\mathbf{A} \models \varphi$, there is an element $a \in A$ such that $\mathbf{A}, a \models \psi$. Let c be a new constant symbol and let $\psi[x/c]$ be the first-order sentence obtained from ψ by replacing every free occurrence of the variable x by c. Clearly, $\psi[x/c]$ is a sentence of quantifier rank r over the vocabulary $\sigma \cup \{c\}$. Now view the above element $a \in A$ as the first move of the Spoiler in a run of the $(r + 1)$-move Ehrenfeucht–Fraïssé game on $\mathbf{A}$ and $\mathbf{B}$. Let $b \in B$ be the response of the Duplicator in this game played according to the Duplicator's winning strategy. Therefore, the Duplicator wins the r-move Ehrenfeucht–Fraïssé game on $(\mathbf{A}, a)$ and $(\mathbf{B}, b)$ viewed as structures over the vocabulary $\sigma \cup \{c\}$ (and thus, a and b are distinguished elements interpreting the constant c). Moreover, $(\mathbf{A}, a) \models \psi[x/c]$, so the induction hypothesis implies that $(\mathbf{B}, b) \models \psi[x/c])$, which, in turn, implies that $\mathbf{B} \models \exists x \psi$.

Next, assume that φ is of the form $\forall x \psi$, which again implies that $\mathrm{qr}(\psi) = r$. We have to show that $\mathbf{B} \models \forall x \psi$. Let b be an arbitrary element of B. View this element as the first move of the Spoiler in a run of the $(r + 1)$-move

Ehrenfeucht–Fraïssé game on $\mathbf{A}$ and $\mathbf{B}$. Let $a \in A$ be the response of the Duplicator in this game played according to the Duplicator's winning strategy. Therefore, the Duplicator wins the r-move Ehrenfeucht–Fraïssé game on $(\mathbf{A}, a)$ and $(\mathbf{B}, b)$ viewed as structures over the vocabulary $\sigma \cup \{c\}$, where, as in the previous case, c is a new constant symbol. Since $\mathbf{A} \models \forall x \psi$, we have that $(\mathbf{A}, a) \models \psi[x/c]$. Consequently, the induction hypothesis implies that $(\mathbf{B}, b) \models \psi[x/c]$. $\square$

To prove the remaining parts of Theorem 2.3.8, we need to first introduce the concept of an (m, r)-type, $0 \le m \le r$, and establish some basic properties of this concept. The definition of an (m, r)-type is by backward induction on m.

Definition 2.3.11. *Assume that σ is a vocabulary, r is a positive integer, and $x_1, \ldots, x_r$ are variables of first-order logic.*

- *An (r, r)-type is a conjunction of atomic or negated atomic formulas over the vocabulary σ such that every variable occurring in this conjunction is one of the variables $x_1, \ldots, x_r$ and, for every atomic formula θ over σ with variables among $x_1, \ldots, x_r$, either θ or $\neg\theta$ occurs as a conjunct.*
- *Assume that the concept of an $(m + 1, r)$-type has been defined, where $0 \le m \le r - 1$. An (m, r)-type is an expression of the form*

$$\bigwedge \{\exists x_{m+1} \varphi : \varphi \text{ is an } (m + 1, r)\text{-type in } S\} \wedge$$

$$\bigwedge \{\forall x_{m+1} \neg\varphi : \varphi \text{ is an } (m + 1, r)\text{-type not in } S\},$$

where S is a subset of the set of all $(m + 1, r)$-types.

Lemma 2.3.12. *Let σ be a vocabulary, r a positive integer, and m an integer such that $0 \le m \le r$.*

- *Every (m, r)-type is a first-order formula over the vocabulary σ such that its free variables are among $x_1, \ldots, x_m$ and its quantifier rank is $r - m$.*
- *There are only finitely many distinct (m, r)-types.*
- *For every σ-structure $\mathbf{A}$ and every sequence $a_1, \ldots, a_m$ of elements of A, there is exactly one (m, r)-type φ such that $\mathbf{A}, a_1, \ldots, a_m \models \varphi$.*

Proof. We use backward induction on m. Since σ consists of finitely many relation and constant symbols, there are finitely many atomic and negated atomic formulas over σ with variables among $x_1, \ldots, x_r$. It follows that every (r, r)-type is a finite conjunction of such formulas and, thus, is a first-order formula of quantifier rank 0. Moreover, every sequence $a_1, \ldots, a_m$ of elements from the universe of a structure $\mathbf{A}$ satisfies a unique (r, r)-type, namely the conjunction of all atomic and negated atomic formulas over σ that are satisfied by this tuple.

Assume that the properties of the lemma hold for $(m + 1, r)$-types. In particular, the set of all $(m+1, r)$-types is finite, and hence it has finitely many subsets, which implies that there are finitely many (m, r)-types. Moreover, the defining expression of an (m, r)-type is a first-order formula of quantifier rank $r - m$, since each $(m + 1, r)$-type is a first-order formula of quantifier rank $r - (m+1) = r - m - 1$. Finally, assume that $\mathbf{A}$ is a σ-structure and $a_1, \ldots, a_m$ is a sequence of elements from A. Let S^* be the set of all $(m + 1, r)$-types φ such that $\mathbf{A}, a_1, \ldots, a_m \models \exists x_{m+1} \varphi$. Then $\mathbf{A}, a_1, \ldots, a_m$ satisfies the (m, r)-type determined by S^*, i.e., the formula

$$\bigwedge \{\exists x_{m+1} \varphi : \varphi \in S^*\} \wedge \bigwedge \{\forall x_{m+1} \neg \varphi : \varphi \notin S^*\},$$

where φ ranges over all (m, r)-types. Moreover, if $\mathbf{A}, a_1, \ldots, a_m$ satisfies some other (m, r)-type determined by a set S, then it is easy to see that $S = S^*$, and so $\mathbf{A}, a_1, \ldots, a_m$ satisfies a unique (m, r)-type. $\square$

Definition 2.3.13. *Let σ be a vocabulary, r a positive integer, m an integer such that $0 \leq m \leq r$, $\mathbf{A}$ a σ-structure, and $a_1, \ldots, a_m$ a sequence of elements from the universe of $\mathbf{A}$.*

We write $\varphi_r^{\mathbf{A}, a_1, \ldots, a_m}$ to denote the unique (m, r)-type satisfied by $\mathbf{A}, a_1, \ldots, a_m$. In particular, when $m = 0$, we write $\varphi_r^{\mathbf{A}}$ to denote the unique $(0, r)$-type satisfied by $\mathbf{A}$.

According to Lemma 2.3.12, each expression $\varphi_r^{\mathbf{A}, a_1, \ldots, a_m}$ is a first-order formula of quantifier rank $r - m$ with free variables among $x_1, \ldots, x_m$. In particular, each $\varphi_r^{\mathbf{A}}$ is a first-order sentence of quantifier rank r. It should be pointed out that the assumption that the vocabulary σ consists of finitely many relation and constant symbols was critical in showing that each (m, r)-type is a first-order formula and also that, for each m and each r with $0 \leq m \leq r$, there are finitely many distinct (m, r)-types. We are now ready to complete the proof of Theorem 2.3.8 and also to establish that $\varphi_r^{\mathbf{A}}$ defines the $\equiv_r$-equivalence class of $\mathbf{A}$.

Theorem 2.3.14. *Let r be a positive integer, let $\mathbf{A}$ and $\mathbf{B}$ be two σ-structures, and let $\varphi_r^{\mathbf{A}}$ be the unique $(0, r)$-type satisfied by $\mathbf{A}$. Then the following statements are equivalent:*

1. *$\mathbf{A} \equiv_r \mathbf{B}$, i.e., $\mathbf{A}$ and $\mathbf{B}$ satisfy the same first-order sentences of quantifier rank r.*
2. *$\mathbf{B} \models \varphi_r^{\mathbf{A}}$.*
3. *$\mathbf{A} \sim_r \mathbf{B}$, i.e., the Duplicator wins the r-move Ehrenfeucht–Fraïssé game on $\mathbf{A}$ and $\mathbf{B}$.*

Proof. The implication $(1) \Rightarrow (2)$ follows from the definitions and the fact that $\varphi_r^{\mathbf{A}}$ is satisfied by $\mathbf{A}$ and has quantifier rank r. The implication $(3) \Rightarrow (1)$ was established in Theorem 2.3.10. Consequently, it remains to prove the implication $(2) \Rightarrow (3)$.

Assume that $\mathbf{B} \models \varphi_r^{\mathbf{A}}$. We describe a winning strategy for the Duplicator in the r-move Ehrenfeucht–Fraïssé game on $\mathbf{A}$ and $\mathbf{B}$. The key property of the

Duplicator's strategy is that, for every run of the game and for every integer m with $0 \leq m \leq r$, if $a_1, \ldots, a_m$ and $b_1, \ldots, b_m$ are the elements of $\mathbf{A}$ and $\mathbf{B}$ played in the first m moves of that run, then $\mathbf{A}, a_1, \ldots, a_m$ and $\mathbf{B}, b_1, \ldots, b_m$ satisfy the same (m, r)-type.

Assume first that the Spoiler begins by playing an element a_1 from A. Let $\varphi_r^{\mathbf{A}, a_1}$ be the unique $(1, r)$-type satisfied by $\mathbf{A}, a_1$. Hence, the sentence $\exists x_1 \varphi_r^{\mathbf{A}, a_1}$ is a conjunct of $\varphi_r^{\mathbf{A}}$, which implies that $\mathbf{B} \models \exists x_1 \varphi_r^{\mathbf{A}, a_1}$. Let b_1 be an element of B such that $\mathbf{B}, b_1 \models \varphi_r^{\mathbf{A}, a_1}$. This element b_1 is the Duplicator's response to the Spoiler's first move. Assume then that the Spoiler begins by playing an element b_1 from B. Let $\varphi_r^{\mathbf{B}, b_1}$ be the unique $(1, r)$-type satisfied by $\mathbf{B}, b_1$. We claim that $\mathbf{A} \models \exists x_1 \varphi_r^{\mathbf{B}, b_1}$. Otherwise, we would have $\mathbf{A} \models \forall x_1 \neg \varphi_r^{\mathbf{B}, b_1}$, which implies that $\forall x_1 \neg \varphi_r^{\mathbf{B}, b_1}$ is a conjunct of $\varphi_r^{\mathbf{A}}$. Consequently, $\mathbf{B} \models \forall x_1 \neg \varphi_r^{\mathbf{B}, b_1}$, which contradicts the fact that $\mathbf{B}, b_1 \models \varphi_r^{\mathbf{B}, b_1}$.

By continuing to play in this way, the Duplicator ensures that at the end of the run the sequences $a_1, \ldots, a_r$ and $b_1, \ldots, b_r$ are such that $\mathbf{A}, a_1, \ldots, a_r$ and $\mathbf{A}, b_1, \ldots, b_r$ satisfy the same (r, r)-type, i.e., the same atomic and negated atomic formulas. This implies that the mapping $a_i \mapsto b_i$, $1 \leq i \leq r$, is a partial isomorphism. $\square$

The first application of the preceding results is a characterization of first-order definability on arbitrary classes of structures.

Theorem 2.3.15. *Let σ be a vocabulary, $\mathcal{C}$ a class of σ-structures, and Q a Boolean query on $\mathcal{C}$. Then the following statements are equivalent:*

1. *Q is first-order definable on $\mathcal{C}$.*
2. *There is a positive integer r such that, for every structure $\mathbf{A} \in \mathcal{C}$ and every structure $\mathbf{B} \in \mathcal{C}$, if $Q(\mathbf{A}) = 1$ and the Duplicator wins the r-move Ehrenfeucht–Fraïssé game on $\mathbf{A}$ and $\mathbf{B}$, then $Q(\mathbf{B}) = 1$.*

Proof. The implication $(1) \Rightarrow (2)$ is an immediate consequence of Theorem 2.3.10. For the other direction, assume that such a positive integer r exists. Let S be the set of all $(0, r)$-types of structures $\mathbf{A}$ in $\mathcal{C}$ such that $Q(\mathbf{A}) = 1$. Lemma 2.3.12 implies that S is a finite set, and hence the disjunction

$$\bigvee \{\varphi_r^{\mathbf{A}} : \mathbf{A} \in \mathcal{C} \text{ and } Q(\mathbf{A}) = 1\}$$

is a first-order sentence, which we denote by φ. We now claim that φ defines the query Q on $\mathcal{C}$. If $\mathbf{B}$ is a structure in $\mathcal{C}$ such that $Q(\mathbf{B}) = 1$, then its $(0, r)$-type $\varphi_r^{\mathbf{B}}$ is one of the disjuncts of φ, and so $\mathbf{B} \models \varphi$. Conversely, if $\mathbf{B}$ is a structure in $\mathcal{C}$ such that $\mathbf{B} \models \varphi$, then there is a structure $\mathbf{A}$ in $\mathcal{C}$ such that $Q(\mathbf{A}) = 1$ and $\mathbf{B} \models \varphi_r^{\mathbf{A}}$. Theorem 2.3.14 implies that the Duplicator wins the r-move Ehrenfeucht–Fraïssé game on $\mathbf{A}$ and $\mathbf{B}$, and hence $Q(\mathbf{B}) = 1$. $\square$

Theorem 2.3.15 gives rise to a combinatorial method for studying first-order definability and obtaining lower bounds on the expressive power of first-order logic on arbitrary classes of structures.

Method 2.3.16 The Method of Ehrenfeucht–Fraïssé Games for FO. Let σ be a vocabulary, $\mathcal{C}$ a class of σ-structures, and Q a Boolean query on $\mathcal{C}$.

Soundness. To show that Q is *not* first-order definable on $\mathcal{C}$, it suffices to show that for every positive integer r there are structures $\mathbf{A}_r$ and $\mathbf{B}_r$ in $\mathcal{C}$ such that
- $Q(\mathbf{A}_r) = 1$ and $Q(\mathbf{B}_r) = 0$;
- the Duplicator wins the r-move Ehrenfeucht–Fraïssé game on $\mathbf{A}$ and $\mathbf{B}$.

Completeness. This method is also *complete*; that is, if Q is *not* first-order definable on $\mathcal{C}$, then for every positive integer r such structures $\mathbf{A}_r$ and $\mathbf{B}_r$ exist.

Note that the soundness of the method of Ehrenfeucht–Fraïssé games follows from Theorem 2.3.10, which is the easier part of establishing that the two equivalence relations $\sim_r$ and $\equiv_r$ coincide. In contrast, the proof of the completeness of the method requires Theorem 2.3.14. We now illustrate this method with two easy applications.

Proposition 2.3.17. *The* EVEN CARDINALITY *query is not first-order definable on the class of all finite graphs.*

Proof. For every $n \geq 1$, let $\overline{\mathbf{K}}_n$ be the totally disconnected graph with n nodes (Fig. 2.3). It is obvious that, for every $r \geq 1$, every $m \geq r$, and every $n \geq r$, the Duplicator wins the r-move Ehrenfeucht–Fraïssé game on $\overline{\mathbf{K}_m}$ and $\overline{\mathbf{K}}_n$. Thus, we can apply the method of Ehrenfeucht–Fraïssé games using the structures $\overline{\mathbf{K}_m}$ with $m \geq r$ an even number and $\overline{\mathbf{K}}_n$ with $n \geq r$ an odd number. $\square$

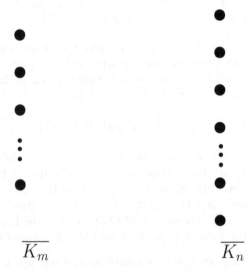

$$\overline{K_m} \qquad\qquad \overline{K_n}$$

Fig. 2.3. EVEN CARDINALITY is not first-order definable on finite graphs

Proposition 2.3.18. *The* Eulerian *query is not first-order definable on the class of all finite graphs.*

Proof. By definition, a graph is Eulerian if there is a closed walk that traverses each edge exactly once. Euler showed that this property holds if and only if every node has even degree, i.e., an even number of neighbors. For every $n \geq 1$, let $\mathbf{A}_n$ be the graph depicted in Fig. 2.4. Clearly, $\mathbf{A}_n$ is Eulerian if and only if n is an even number. Moreover, for every $n \geq r$, the Duplicator wins the r-move Ehrenfeucht–Fraïssé game on $\mathbf{A}_n$ and $\mathbf{A}_{n+1}$. Thus, we can apply the method of Ehrenfeucht–Fraïssé games using the structures $\mathbf{A}_{2n}$ and $\mathbf{A}_{2n+1}$ with $2n \geq r$. $\square$

As seen earlier, the method of Ehrenfeucht–Fraïssé games is complete, which implies that if a query Q is not first-order definable on a class $\mathcal{C}$ of structures, then in principle this can be established using the method of Ehrenfeucht–Fraïssé games. In practice, however, the following technical difficulties may arise when one attempts to apply this method to concrete queries:

- How does one find, for every $r \geq 1$, structures $\mathbf{A}_r$ and $\mathbf{B}_r$ in $\mathcal{C}$ such that $Q(\mathbf{A}_r) = 1$, $Q(\mathbf{B}_r) = 0$, and the Duplicator wins the r-move Ehrenfeucht–Fraïssé game on $\mathbf{A}_r$ and $\mathbf{B}_r$?
- After such candidate structures $\mathbf{A}_r$ and $\mathbf{B}_r$ have been identified, how does one show rigorously that $\mathbf{A}_r \sim_r \mathbf{B}_r$?

As a general rule, both these tasks can be challenging. Nonetheless, they can be eased by pursuing the following two approaches.

- Whenever possible, analyze the $\sim_r$-equivalence classes, $r \geq 1$, of the structures in $\mathcal{C}$ and obtain explicit descriptions of them.
- Find general *sufficient* conditions for the Duplicator to win the r-move Ehrenfeucht–Fraïssé game, and thus build a "library" of winning strategies for the Duplicator in this game.

The class $\mathcal{L}$ of all finite linear orders provides an interesting, albeit rather rare, case in which it is possible to analyze the $\sim_r$-equivalence classes, $r \geq 1$.

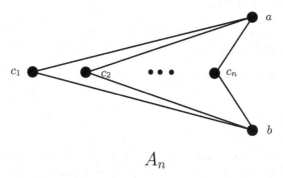

A_n

Fig. 2.4. Eulerian is not first-order definable on finite graphs

$$\mathbf{L}_6 : \ 1 \leq 2 \leq 3 \leq 4 \leq 5 \leq 6$$
$$\mathbf{L}_7 : \ 1 \leq 2 \leq 3 \leq 4 \leq 5 \leq 6 \leq 7$$
$$\mathbf{L}_8 : \ 1 \leq 2 \leq 3 \leq 4 \leq 5 \leq 6 \leq 7 \leq 8$$

Fig. 2.5. $\mathbf{L}_6 \not\sim_3 \mathbf{L}_7$, but $\mathbf{L}_7 \sim_3 \mathbf{L}_8$

Before presenting the full analysis, we give a motivating example. For every $n \geq 1$, we let $\mathbf{L}_n = (\{1, \ldots, n\}, \leq)$ be the standard linear order on $\{1, \ldots, n\}$.

Example 2.3.19. The following are true for the 3-move Ehrenfeucht–Fraïssé game (Fig. 2.5).

- The Spoiler wins the 3-move Ehrenfeucht–Fraïssé game on $\mathbf{L}_6$ and $\mathbf{L}_7$.
- The Duplicator wins the 3-move Ehrenfeucht–Fraïssé game on $\mathbf{L}_7$ and $\mathbf{L}_8$.

The Spoiler can win the 3-move Ehrenfeucht–Fraïssé game on $\mathbf{L}_6$ and $\mathbf{L}_7$ by playing as follows. The first move of the Spoiler is element 4 in $\mathbf{L}_7$. In order to avoid losing in the next move, the Duplicator has to play either element 4 in $\mathbf{L}_6$ or element 3 in $\mathbf{L}_6$. If the Duplicator plays 4 in $\mathbf{L}_6$, then the Spoiler plays element 6 in $\mathbf{L}_7$. At this point, the Duplicator must play either element 5 in $\mathbf{L}_6$ or element 6 in $\mathbf{L}_6$. In the first case, the Spoiler wins the run by playing element 5 in $\mathbf{L}_7$; in the second case, the Spoiler wins the run by playing element 7 in $\mathbf{L}_7$. An essentially symmetric argument shows that the Spoiler can win if the first move of the Duplicator is element 3 in $\mathbf{L}_6$.

In contrast, consider the 3-move Ehrenfeucht–Fraïssé game on $\mathbf{L}_7$ and $\mathbf{L}_8$, and suppose that the Spoiler plays element 4 in $\mathbf{L}_8$. In this case, the Duplicator responds by playing element 4 in $\mathbf{L}_7$. If the Spoiler plays element 6 in $\mathbf{L}_8$, then the Duplicator plays element 6 in $\mathbf{L}_7$, and after this can easily maintain a partial isomorphism no matter what the third move of the Spoiler is. Similarly, if the second move of the Spoiler is element 7 in $\mathbf{L}_8$, then the second move of the Duplicator is element 6 in $\mathbf{L}_7$. We leave it to the reader to fill in the remaining cases and verify that the Duplicator wins the 3-move Ehrenfeucht–Fraïssé game on $\mathbf{L}_7$ and $\mathbf{L}_8$.

We are now ready to describe the analysis of $\sim_r$, $r \geq 1$, on finite linear orders and derive Example 2.3.19 as a special case.

Theorem 2.3.20. *Let r, m, and n be positive integers. The following are equivalent:*

- $\mathbf{L}_m \sim_r \mathbf{L}_n$.
- $(m = n)$ or $(m \geq 2^r - 1$ and $n \geq 2^r - 1)$.

Proof. (Hint) If c is an element of the linear order $\mathbf{L}_n$, then $\mathbf{L}_n^{>c}$ denotes the linear order with universe $\{d : c < d \leq n\}$ and, similarly, $\mathbf{L}_n^{<c}$ denotes the

linear order with universe $\{d : 1 \leq d < c\}$. It is easy to see that, for every positive integer s, we have that $\mathbf{L}_m \sim_{s+1} \mathbf{L}_n$ if and only if the following two conditions hold:

1. For every $a \in \mathbf{L}_m$, there is a $b \in L_n$ such that $\mathbf{L}_m^{>a} \sim_s \mathbf{L}_n^{>b}$ and $\mathbf{L}_m^{<a} \sim_s \mathbf{L}_n^{<b}$.
2. For every $b \in \mathbf{L}_n$, there is an $a \in \mathbf{L}_m$ such that $\mathbf{L}_m^{>a} \sim_s \mathbf{L}_n^{>b}$ and $\mathbf{L}_m^{<a} \sim_s \mathbf{L}_n^{<b}$.

The required result can then be derived from the above fact using induction on $\min(m, n)$. $\square$

Corollary 2.3.21. *The* EVEN CARDINALITY *query is not first-order definable on the class $\mathcal{L}$ of all finite linear orders.*

Proof. Apply the method of Ehrenfeucht–Fraïssé games using the linear orders $\mathbf{L}_{2m}$ and $\mathbf{L}_{2m+1}$ with $m \geq 2^r - 1$. $\square$

As indicated earlier, the class of finite linear orders provides a rather rare example of a class of structures for which a complete analysis of the $\equiv_r$-equivalence classes, $r \geq 1$, has been obtained. Over the years, however, researchers have succeeded in identifying general sufficient conditions for the Duplicator to win the r-move Ehrenfeucht–Fraïssé game. These conditions give "off-the-shelf" winning strategies for the Duplicator and thus facilitate the application of the method of Ehrenfeucht–Fraïssé games. In what follows, we shall present such a useful and widely applicable sufficient condition discovered by Fagin, Stockmeyer, and Vardi [25], who built on earlier work by Hanf [36]. Additional useful sufficient conditions for the Duplicator to win the Ehrenfeucht–Fraïssé game have been found by Schwentick [59], Arora and Fagin [6], and others (see [24] for a survey). Underlying this work is Gaifman's Theorem [28], which, intuitively, asserts that first-order logic can express *local* properties only. Although we shall not discuss or use Gaifman's Theorem here, we shall introduce the fundamental concept of *neighborhood*, which plays a key role in both Gaifman's work and the work on sufficient conditions for the Duplicator to win the Ehrenfeucht–Fraïssé game.

Definition 2.3.22. *Let $\mathbf{A} = (A, R_1^{\mathbf{A}}, \ldots, R_m^{\mathbf{A}}, c_1^{\mathbf{A}}, \ldots, c_s^{\mathbf{A}})$ be a σ-structure, let a be an element of A, and let d be a positive integer.*

- *The* Gaifman graph *$\mathbf{G_A} = (A, E_{\mathbf{A}})$ of $\mathbf{A}$ is the undirected graph having the elements of A as nodes and an edge relation $E_{\mathbf{A}}$ defined as follows: there is an edge $E_{\mathbf{A}}(b, c)$ between two elements b and c of A if there is a relation $R_i^{\mathbf{A}}$, $1 \leq i \leq m$, and a tuple $(t_1, \ldots, t_s) \in R_i^{\mathbf{A}}$ such that b and c are among $t_1, \ldots, t_s$.*
- *The* neighborhood *$N(a, d)$ of a of radius d is the set of all nodes whose distance in the Gaifman graph $\mathbf{G_A}$ from a or from one of the constants*

$c_1^{\mathbf{A}}, \ldots, c_s^{\mathbf{A}}$ is less than d. More formally, $N(a, d)$ is defined by the following induction on d:

$$N(a, 1) = \{a, c_1^{\mathbf{A}}, \ldots, c_s^{\mathbf{A}}\}.$$
$$N(a, d + 1) = N(a, d) \cup \{c \in A : \text{there is } a \, b \in N(a, d) \text{ such that } E_{\mathbf{A}}(b, c)\}.$$

The following examples reveal that the neighborhood of an element can vary widely.

Example 2.3.23. Let $n \geq 1$ and $d \geq 2$ be positive integers.

- If $\mathbf{L}_n = (L_n, \leq)$ is a linear order with n elements, then $N(a, d) = L_n$, for every $a \in L_n$.
- If $\mathbf{K}_n = (K_n, E)$ is a clique with n nodes, then $N(a, d) = K_n$, for every $a \in K_n$.
- If $\overline{\mathbf{K}}_n = (\overline{K}_n, E)$ is a totally disconnected graph with n nodes, then $N(a, d) = \{a\}$, for every $a \in \overline{K}_n$.
- If $\mathbf{C}_n = (C_n, E)$ is a (directed or undirected) cycle C_n with n nodes and $d \leq n/2$, then the subgraph $\mathbf{G}_{\mathbf{C}_n} \upharpoonright N(a, d)$ of the Gaifman graph $\mathbf{G}_{\mathbf{C}_n}$ induced by $N(a, d)$ is an undirected path with $2d - 1$ nodes having a as its midpoint.

Definition 2.3.24. *Let* $\mathbf{A} = (A, R_1^{\mathbf{A}}, \ldots, R_m^{\mathbf{A}}, c_1^{\mathbf{A}}, \ldots, c_s^{\mathbf{A}})$ *be a σ-structure, let a be an element of A, and let d be a positive integer.*

- $(\mathbf{A}, a)$ *denotes the expansion of* $\mathbf{A}$ *obtained by augmenting it with a as a distinguished element interpreting a new constant.*
- $(\mathbf{A}, a) \upharpoonright N(a, d)$ *denotes the substructure of* $(\mathbf{A}, a)$ *generated by $N(a, d)$.*
- *The d-type of a is the isomorphism type of the structure* $(\mathbf{A}, a) \upharpoonright N(a, d)$.

Note that the universe of $(\mathbf{A}, a) \upharpoonright N(a, d)$ is $N(a, d)$, since $N(a, d)$ contains $a, c_1^{\mathbf{A}}, \ldots, c_s^{\mathbf{A}}$ as members. Moreover, if $\mathbf{B} = (B, R_1^{\mathbf{B}}, \ldots, R_m^{\mathbf{B}}, c_1^{\mathbf{B}}, \ldots, c_s^{\mathbf{B}})$ is a σ-structure and b is an element of B, then a and b have the same d-type precisely when there is a one-to-one and onto mapping $h : N(a, d) \to N(b, d)$ such that $h(a) = b$, $h(c_i^{\mathbf{A}}) = c_i^{\mathbf{B}}$, $1 \leq i \leq s$, and for every relation symbol R_i of arity t, $1 \leq i \leq m$, and every t-tuple $(a_1, \ldots, a_t)$ from $N(a, d)$, we have that $R_i^{\mathbf{A}}(a_1, \ldots, a_t)$ if and only if $R_i^{\mathbf{B}}(h(a_1), \ldots, h(a_t))$.

Definition 2.3.25. *Assume that d is a positive integer, σ is a vocabulary, and $\mathbf{A}$ and $\mathbf{B}$ are two σ-structures. We say that $\mathbf{A}$ and $\mathbf{B}$ are d-equivalent if for every d-type τ they have the same number of elements of d-type τ.*

Clearly, d-equivalence is an equivalence relation on the class S of all σ-structures. The next result, due to Fagin, Stockmeyer and Vardi [25], asserts that if d is larger than r by a sufficient amount, then d-equivalence is actually a refinement of $\equiv_r$-equivalence.

Theorem 2.3.26. *For every positive integer r and for every positive integer $d \geq 3^{r-1}$, if $\mathbf{A}$ is d-equivalent to $\mathbf{B}$, then $\mathbf{A} \equiv_r \mathbf{B}$.*

Proof. (Hint) Assume that $\mathbf{A}$ is d-equivalent to $\mathbf{B}$, where $d \geq 3^{r-1}$. We can show that the Duplicator wins the r-move Ehrenfeucht–Fraïssé game on $\mathbf{A}$ and $\mathbf{B}$ by maintaining a partial isomorphism between not only the elements of $\mathbf{A}$ and $\mathbf{B}$ played thus far, but also between neighborhoods of these points of sufficiently large radius. Specifically, by induction on $j \leq r$, it can be shown that the Duplicator can win the r-move Ehrenfeucht–Fraïssé game via a winning strategy that has the following property, called the *j-matching condition*: If $a_1, \ldots, a_j$ and $b_1, \ldots, b_j$ are the elements of $\mathbf{A}$ and $\mathbf{B}$ played in the first j moves of a run, then $\mathbf{A} \restriction \cup_{i=1}^{j} N(a_i, 3^{r-j})$ is isomorphic to $\mathbf{B} \restriction \cup_{i=1}^{j} N(b_i, 3^{r-j})$ via an isomorphism that maps a_i to b_i, for $1 \leq i \leq j$.

Note that the Duplicator can ensure that the 1-matching condition holds as follows. If the Spoiler plays an element a_1 in A (or an element b_1 in B), then, by d-equivalence, there is an element b_1 in B (or an element a_1 in A) such that a_1 and b_1 have the same d-type, which implies that $\mathbf{A} \restriction N(a_1, 3^{r-1})$ is isomorphic to $\mathbf{B} \restriction N(b_1, 3^{r-1})$ via an isomorphism that maps a_1 to b_1. The inductive step from j to $j+1$ uses d-equivalence combined with a counting argument to the effect that the Duplicator can always find at least one element with the same d-type as the last element played by the Spoiler, but not contained in the union of neighborhoods of radius $3^{r-(j+1)}$ of the elements played so far. □

Theorem 2.3.26 gives rise to a new method for studying first-order definability.

Method 2.3.27 Let σ be a vocabulary, $\mathcal{C}$ a class of σ-structures, and Q a Boolean query on $\mathcal{C}$. To show that Q is *not* first-order definable on $\mathcal{C}$, it suffices to show that, for every positive integer r, there are structures $\mathbf{A}_r$ and $\mathbf{B}_r$ in $\mathcal{C}$ such that

- $Q(\mathbf{A}_r) = 1$ and $Q(\mathbf{B}_r) = 0$.
- $\mathbf{A}_r$ is d-equivalent to $\mathbf{B}_r$ for some $d \geq 3^r$.

Although, by Theorem 2.3.26, this method is sound, it is not complete. For instance, it cannot be used to analyze first-order definability on the class $\mathcal{L}$ of all finite linear orders, since, for all positive integers d, m, and n, the linear order $\mathbf{L}_m$ is d-equivalent to the linear order $\mathbf{L}_n$ if and only if $m = n$. In particular, this method cannot be used to show that EVEN CARDINALITY is not first-order definable on finite linear orders. Nonetheless, whenever applicable, Method 2.3.27 is usually technically simpler than Method 2.3.16, since it replaces the task of proving that the Duplicator wins the r-move Ehrenfeucht–Fraïssé game with the task of analyzing and counting d-types. Moreover, the analysis of d-types often provides a clue for finding candidate structures $\mathbf{A}_r$ and $\mathbf{B}_r$. In the remainder of this section, we present several applications of Method 2.3.27 to finite model theory.

Proposition 2.3.28. *The CONNECTIVITY query is not first-order definable on finite graphs.*

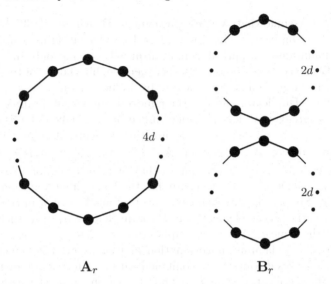

$\mathbf{A}_r$ $\mathbf{B}_r$

Fig. 2.6. CONNECTIVITY is not first-order definable on finite graphs

Proof. For every r and every $d \geq 3^{r-1}$, let $\mathbf{A}_r$ be a cycle with $4d$ nodes and let $\mathbf{B}_r$ be the union of two disjoint cycles each with $2d$ nodes, as depicted in Fig. 2.6. Clearly, each d-type in $\mathbf{A}_r$ or in $\mathbf{B}_r$ is a path with $2d - 1$ nodes. Moreover, $\mathbf{A}_r$ is d-equivalent to $\mathbf{B}_r$, since each structure contains exactly $4d$ points of this d-type. $\square$

Proposition 2.3.29. *The* 2-COLORABILITY *query is not first-order definable on finite graphs.*

Proof. For every r, let $d = 3^{r-1}$, and let $\mathbf{A}_r$ be a cycle with $6d$ nodes and let $\mathbf{B}_d$ be the union of two disjoint cycles each with $3d$ nodes, as depicted in Fig. 2.7. Clearly, $\mathbf{A}_r$ is 2-colorable, but $\mathbf{B}_r$ is not, since $\mathbf{A}_r$ is an even cycle, while $\mathbf{B}_r$ contains an odd cycle. Moreover, $\mathbf{A}_r$ is d-equivalent to $\mathbf{B}_r$. $\square$

Proposition 2.3.30. *The* ACYCLICITY *query is not first-order definable on finite graphs.*

Proof. Let $\mathbf{A}_r$ and $\mathbf{B}_r$ be the two structures depicted in Fig. 2.8 Clearly, $\mathbf{A}_r$ is acyclic, $\mathbf{B}_r$ contains a cycle, and $\mathbf{A}_r$ is d-equivalent to $\mathbf{B}_r$. $\square$

Exercise 2.3.31. Show that the following queries are not first-order definable on the class of all finite graphs:

- k-COLORABILITY, for every fixed $k \geq 3$;
- PLANARITY;
- RIGIDITY.

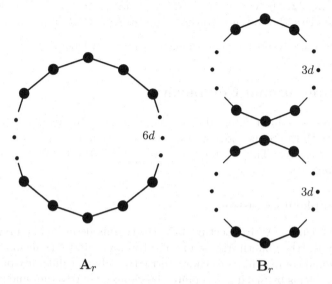

$\mathbf{A}_r$ $\mathbf{B}_r$

Fig. 2.7. 2-Colorability is not first-order definable on finite graphs

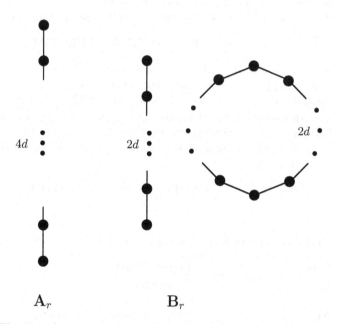

$\mathbf{A}_r$ $\mathbf{B}_r$

Fig. 2.8. Acyclicity is not first-order definable on finite graphs

Exercise 2.3.32. Show that the CONNECTIVITY query is not first-order definable on the class $\mathcal{O}$ of all finite ordered graphs $\mathbf{G} = (V, E, \leq)$.

Hint. Use the analysis of $\equiv_r$-equivalence on linear orders.

2.4 Computational Complexity

This section is a brief interlude on computational complexity and a first encounter with the connections between computational complexity and logics on finite structures. These connections are explored in depth in Chap. 3 of this volume.

2.4.1 Complexity Classes

In his 1993 Turing Award Lecture [37], Hartmanis described computational complexity as "the quantitative study of solvability". Indeed, the main goal of computational complexity is to characterize the inherent difficulty of solvable decision problems by placing them into classes according to the time resources or space resources required to solve them in some model of computation, which is usually either the (deterministic) Turing machine or the nondeterministic Turing machine. The following major complexity classes will be of interest to us here; their precise definitions can be found in [55].

It is well known and easy to show that the following containments hold:

$$L \subseteq P \subseteq NP \subseteq PSPACE \subseteq EXPTIME \subseteq NEXPTIME.$$

It is also conjectured and widely believed that each of the above containments is a proper one, but proving this remains the central open problem in the field of computational complexity to date. It has been established, however, that if there is an exponential gap in the amount of the resource (space or time) used in defining two complexity classes, then one is properly contained in the other. These results, which are known as space and time *hierarchy* theorems (see [55]), imply that

$$L \subsetneq PSPACE, \quad P \subsetneq EXPTIME, \quad NP \subsetneq NEXPTIME.$$

Table 2.1. Some major computational complexity classes

Class	Resource bound
L	Logarithmic space
P	Polynomial time
NP	Nondeterministic polynomial time
PSPACE	Polynomial space
EXPTIME	Exponential time
NEXPTIME	Nondeterministic exponential time

A possible approach to separating two complexity classes is to show that there is a structural property possessed by one class but not by the other. Clearly, each of the deterministic classes L, P, PSPACE, and EXPTIME is closed under complements. In contrast, the class NP of all problems solvable by a nondeterministic polynomial-time bounded Turing machine is not known to be closed under complements. Thus, the question "is NP = coNP?" constitutes another major open problem in the field of computational complexity. The same state of affairs holds true for the class NEXPTIME.

Each of the aforementioned complexity classes contains problems that are *complete* for the class, i.e., problems that embody the intrinsic computational difficulty of the class at hand. More precisely, let C be a complexity class and Q a decision problem. We say that Q is *C-complete* if Q is in C and Q is *C-hard*, i.e., for every $Q' \in C$, there is a "suitable" many–one reduction f of Q' to Q, so that for every input x,

$$x \in Q' \Longleftrightarrow f(x) \in Q.$$

If C is the class P of all polynomial-time solvable problems, then "suitable" means that f is computable in logarithmic space. For NP and all other larger classes, "suitable" means that f is computable in polynomial time. Representative natural NP-complete problems include Boolean satisfiability (SAT), 3-COLORABILITY, and HAMILTONIAN PATH (see [30]). The prototypical PSPACE-complete problem is QBF, the satisfiability problem for quantified Boolean formulas [63].

2.4.2 The Complexity of Logic

Vardi [67] singled out certain fundamental decision problems that arise from the analysis of the satisfaction relation between sentences of a logic L and finite structures.

Definition 2.4.1. [67] *Let L be a logic.*

- *The* combined complexity *of L is the following decision problem: given a finite structure $\mathbf{A}$ and an L-sentence ψ, does $\mathbf{A} \models \psi$?*
- *The* data complexity *of L is the family of the following decision problems Q_ψ, one for each fixed L-sentence ψ: given a finite structure $\mathbf{A}$, does $\mathbf{A} \models \psi$?*
- *The* expression complexity *of L is the family of the following decision problems $Q_{\mathbf{A}}$, one for each fixed finite structure $\mathbf{A}$: given an L-sentence ψ, does $\mathbf{A} \models \psi$?*

The combined-complexity problem for L is also known as the *model-checking* problem for L. In this problem, the input consists of both a finite structure and an L-sentence. The data complexity and the expression complexity are the restricted cases of the combined-complexity problem in which the L-sentence is kept fixed or the finite structure is kept fixed, respectively. Note that the data complexity and the expression complexity are not single decision problems, but families of decision problems. The next definition provides a way to "measure" the computational complexity of these families of decision problems.

Definition 2.4.2. [67] *Let L be a logic and C a complexity class.*

- The data complexity of L is in C *if for each L-sentence ψ, the decision problem Q_ψ is in C.*
- The data complexity of L is C-complete *if it is in C and there is at least one L-sentence ψ such that the decision problem Q_ψ is C-complete.*
- The expression complexity of L is in C *if for each finite structure $\mathbf{A}$, the decision problem $Q_\mathbf{A}$ is in C.*
- The expression complexity of L is C-complete *if it is in C and there is at least one finite structure $\mathbf{A}$ such that the decision problem $Q_\mathbf{A}$ is C-complete.*

The next result pinpoints the data complexity, expression complexity, and combined complexity of first-order logic.

Theorem 2.4.3. *The following hold for first-order logic* FO.

- *The data complexity of* FO *is in* L.
- *The expression complexity of* FO *is* PSPACE-*complete*
- *The combined complexity of* FO *is* PSPACE-*complete.*

Proof. (*Hint*) For simplicity, assume that ψ is a first-order sentence in prenex normal form. Given a finite structure $\mathbf{A}$, one can check whether $\mathbf{A} \models \psi$ by examining each possible instantiation of quantifiers in ψ one at a time (this requires logarithmic space), while keeping track of the number of them in binary with the aid of a counter. Since there are polynomially many such instantiations, only logarithmically many cells are used to keep track of the counter, so the entire computation requires $O(\log(|A|)$ space, where $|A|$ is the cardinality of the universe of $\mathbf{A}$.

If the sentence ψ is part of the input, then the above computation can be carried out in a space bounded by a polynomial in $|A|$, so the combined complexity of FO is in PSPACE. Finally, the expression complexity of FO is PSPACE-complete (and hence the combined complexity of FO is PSPACE-complete as well) because, for every fixed finite structure $\mathbf{A}$ with at least two distinct elements, the satisfiability problem QBF for quantified Boolean formulas is easily reducible to the expression complexity problem $Q_\mathbf{A}$. $\square$

Theorem 2.4.3 shows that an exponential gap exists between the data complexity of first-order logic and the expression complexity of first-order logic, and that the expression complexity of first-order logic is as hard as the combined complexity of first-order logic. As pointed out by Vardi [67], this phenomenon is also encountered in several other logics studied in finite model theory.

The r-move Ehrenfeucht–Fraïssé game gives rise to the natural decision problem of determining the winner of this game. In fact, there are two versions of this problem, one in which the number of moves is fixed and one in which the number of moves is part of the input. The next two results identify the computational complexity of these problems.

Proposition 2.4.4. *Let r be a fixed positive integer. The following problem is in* L *and, hence, also in* P*: given two finite structures* **A** *and* **B***, does the Duplicator win the r-move Ehrenfeucht–Fraïssé game on* **A** *and* **B***?*

Proof. By Theorem 2.3.8, for each fixed r, there are finitely many $\equiv_r$-classes and each such class is first-order definable; moreover, the proof of Lemma 2.3.12 provides an explicit construction of the first-order formulas that define the $\equiv_r$-equivalence classes. The conclusion now follows from the fact that, by Theorem 2.4.3, the data complexity of FO is in L. □

Pezzoli [56] established that if the number of moves is part of the input, then determining the winner of the r-move Ehrenfeucht–Fraïssé game is a much harder task.

Theorem 2.4.5. *The following problem is* PSPACE*-complete: given a positive integer $r \geq 1$ and two finite structures* **A** *and* **B***, does the Duplicator win the r-move Ehrenfeucht–Fraïssé game on* **A** *and* **B***?*

This result is proved via a reduction from QBF that entails the construction of rather complicated combinatorial gadgets. It should be pointed out that, unlike many other decision problems in which integers are part of the input, here the computational complexity remains the same (the problem is PSPACE-complete) irrespective of whether the number r of moves is given in unary or in binary. The reason is that if r is bigger than $\max\{|A|, |B|\}$, then r can be replaced by $\max\{|A|, |B|\}$; moreover, this quantity is given in unary, since at least $\max\{|A|, |B|\}$ bits are needed to encode **A** and **B**.

As shown in Sect. 2.3, first-order logic has severely limited expressive power on finite graphs. In particular, none of the queries DISCONNECTIVITY, k-COLORABILITY, for $k \geq 2$, and HAMILTONIAN PATH is first-order definable on the class of all finite graphs. Recall also that these queries are easily expressible in existential second-order logic ESO, one of the two syntactically simplest fragments of second-order logic. This increase in expressive power, however, is accompanied by an increase in complexity.

Proposition 2.4.6. *The data complexity of* ESO *is* NP*-complete.*

Proof. Let Ψ be a fixed ESO-sentence $(\exists S_1) \cdots (\exists S_m)\varphi(S_1, \ldots, S_m)$, where $\varphi(S_1, \ldots, S_m)$ is a first-order sentence. Given a finite structure **A**, one can check that $\mathbf{A} \models \Psi$ by first "guessing" relations $S_1', \ldots, S_m'$ on A and then verifying that $(\mathbf{A}, S'_1, \ldots, S'_m) \models \varphi(S_1, \ldots, S_m)$. This computation can be carried out in nondeterministic polynomial time, since the size of the relations guessed is polynomial in $|A|$ and the data complexity of first-order logic is in P. Consequently, the data complexity of ESO is in NP.

Since 3-COLORABILITY is definable by a monadic ESO-sentence and it is an NP-complete problem, it follows that the data complexity of monadic ESO is NP-complete; hence, the data complexity of ESO is also NP-complete. □

Vardi [67] has shown that both the expression complexity of ESO and the combined complexity of ESO are NEXPTIME-complete; this is another instance of the exponential-gap phenomenon between the data complexity and the expression (and combined) complexity of a logic.

The link between the data complexity of ESO and NP turns out to be much stronger. The exact connection is provided by the following result, which has become known as Fagin's Theorem and constitutes the prototypical result of descriptive complexity.

Theorem 2.4.7. [21] *The following are equivalent for a Boolean query Q on the class $\mathcal{F}$ of all finite σ-structures:*

- *Q is in NP.*
- *Q is ESO-definable on $\mathcal{F}$.*

In other words, NP $=$ ESO on $\mathcal{F}$.

Fagin's Theorem asserts that, in a precise sense, ESO *captures* NP on the class of all finite structures and, thus, provides a logic-based and machine-independent characterization of NP. Moreover, it makes it possible to reformulate the "NP $\overset{?}{=}$ coNP" question in terms of logic alone.

Corollary 2.4.8. *The following statements are equivalent:*

- NP *is closed under complements (in other words, NP $=$ coNP).*
- ESO *is closed under complements on the class $\mathcal{F}$ of all finite structures (in other words, ESO[$\mathcal{F}$] $=$ USO[$\mathcal{F}$]).*
- 3-COLORABILITY *is USO-definable on the class of all finite graphs.*
- HAMILTONIAN PATH *is USO-definable on the class of all finite graphs.*

Proof. The result follows from Fagin's Theorem (Theorem 2.4.7) and the NP-completeness of 3-COLORABILITY and HAMILTONIAN PATH. □

2.5 Ehrenfeucht–Fraïssé Games for Existential Second-Order Logic

In this section, we consider certain extensions of the Ehrenfeucht–Fraïssé games that are powerful enough to characterize definability in existential second-order logic.

Definition 2.5.1. *Let $s_1, \ldots, s_k, r$ be positive integers, let σ be a vocabulary, and let* **A**, **B** *be two σ-structures. The $(\langle s_1, \ldots, s_k \rangle, r)$ Ehrenfeucht–Fraïssé game on* **A** *and* **B** *is played according to the following rules. In a run of the game:*

- *The Spoiler picks relations $S_1, \ldots, S_k$ of arities $s_1, \ldots, s_k$ on* **A**.
- *The Duplicator picks relations $S_1', \ldots, S_k'$ of arities $s_1, \ldots, s_k$ on* **B**.
- *After this, the two players engage in a run of the r-move Ehrenfeucht–Fraïssé game on the expanded structures $(\mathbf{A}, S_1, \ldots, S_k)$ and $(\mathbf{B}, S_1', \ldots, S_k')$.*
- *Let $(a_1, b_1), \ldots, (a_r, b_r)$ be the elements of $A \times B$ picked by the two players in their r moves. The Duplicator wins this run if the mapping*

$$a_i \mapsto b_i, \ 1 \leq i \leq r, \ and \ c_i^{\mathbf{A}} \mapsto c_j^{\mathbf{B}}, \ 1 \leq j \leq s,$$

  is a partial isomorphism, that is, an isomorphism between the substructure $(\mathbf{A}, S_1, \ldots, S_k) \restriction \{a_1, \ldots, a_r\}$ of $(\mathbf{A}, S_1, \ldots, S_k)$ generated by $\{a_1, \ldots, a_r\}$ and the substructure $(\mathbf{B}, S_1', \ldots, S_k') \restriction \{b_1, \ldots, b_r\}$ of $(\mathbf{B}, S_1', \ldots, S_k')$ generated by $\{b_1, \ldots, b_r\}$. Otherwise, the Spoiler wins the run.
- *The Duplicator wins the $(\langle s_1, \ldots, s_k \rangle, r)$ game on* **A** *and* **B** *if the Duplicator can win every run of the game, i.e., if (s)he has a winning strategy for this game. Otherwise, the Spoiler wins the $(\langle s_1, \ldots, s_k \rangle, r)$-Ehrenfeucht–Fraïssé game on* **A** *and* **B**.

Using Theorem 2.3.8 and the semantics of existential second-order logic, it is quite straightforward to establish the following result.

Proposition 2.5.2. *Let Ψ be an ESO-sentence of the form $(\exists P_1) \cdots (\exists P_k)\psi$, where each P_i is a relation symbol of arity s_i and ψ is a first-order sentence of quantifier rank r. If* $\mathbf{A} \models \Psi$ *and the Duplicator wins the $(\langle s_1, \ldots, s_k \rangle, r)$ Ehrenfeucht–Fraïssé game on* **A** *and* **B**, *then* $\mathbf{B} \models \Psi$.

In turn, this result gives rise to a combinatorial method for establishing limitations on the expressive power of existential second-order logic on arbitrary classes of structures. Moreover, it is not hard to show that the method is complete as well.

Method 2.5.3 The Method of Ehrenfeucht–Fraïssé Games for ESO.
Let σ be a vocabulary, $\mathcal{C}$ a class of σ-structures, and Q a Boolean query on $\mathcal{C}$.

Soundness. To show that Q is *not* ESO-definable on $\mathcal{C}$, it suffices to show that for every sequence of positive integers $s_1, \ldots, s_k, r$, there are structures **A** and **B** in $\mathcal{C}$ such that
- $Q(\mathbf{A}) = 1$ and $Q(\mathbf{B}) = 0$;
- the Duplicator wins the $(\langle s_1, \ldots, s_k \rangle, r)$ Ehrenfeucht–Fraïssé game on **A** *and* **B**.

Completeness. This method is also *complete*, i.e., if Q is not ESO-definable on $\mathcal{C}$, then for every sequence $s_1, \ldots, s_k, r$ of positive integers, such structures $\mathbf{A}$ and $\mathbf{B}$ exist.

Corollary 2.4.8 and Method 2.5.3 imply that the NP $\overset{?}{=}$ coNP question is equivalent to a problem about combinatorial games.

Corollary 2.5.4. *The following statements are equivalent:*

- NP $\neq$ coNP;
- *For every* $s_1, \ldots, s_k, r$, *there are finite graphs* $\mathbf{G}$ *and* $\mathbf{H}$ *such that*
  - $\mathbf{G}$ *is not* 3-COLORABLE *and* $\mathbf{H}$ *is* 3-COLORABLE;
  - *the Duplicator wins the* $(\langle s_1, \ldots, s_k \rangle, r)$ *Ehrenfeucht–Fraïssé game on* $\mathbf{G}$ *and* $\mathbf{H}$.

Although $(\langle s_1, \ldots, s_k \rangle, r)$ Ehrenfeucht–Fraïssé games yield a sound and complete method for studying ESO-definability (and thus potentially leading to the separation of NP from coNP), so far this approach has had rather limited success. The reason is that formidable combinatorial difficulties arise in implementing this method when one of the integers s_i is bigger than 1, that is, when dealing with ESO-formulas in which at least one of the existentially quantified second-order variables has an arity bigger than 1. Nonetheless, this method has made it possible to obtain lower bounds for definability in monadic ESO, which is the fragment of existential second-order logic that can be analyzed using $(\langle 1, 1, \ldots, 1 \rangle, r)$ Ehrenfeucht–Fraïssé games.

In certain cases, the study of ESO-definability can be made easier using a variant of the $(\langle s_1, \ldots, s_k \rangle, r)$ Ehrenfeucht–Fraïssé games that has become known as *Ajtai–Fagin games*. In what follows in this section, we present the intuition behind the Ajtai–Fagin games and highlight some of their applications to the study of definability in monadic ESO. The first observation is that, when the method of Ehrenfeucht–Fraïssé games or one of their variants is used to show that a particular query is not definable in a certain logic, one can expand the scope of the game and view the selection of the structures $\mathbf{A}$ and $\mathbf{B}$ as being part of the Duplicator's moves. Now, one of the main difficulties with the $(\langle s_1, \ldots, s_k \rangle, r)$ Ehrenfeucht–Fraïssé games is that in effect the Duplicator has to select the structure $\mathbf{B}$ *before* the Spoiler has picked relations $S_1, \ldots, S_k$ on $\mathbf{A}$. To make the Duplicator's task easier, Ajtai and Fagin [4] introduced a variant of the $(\langle s_1, \ldots, s_k \rangle, r)$ Ehrenfeucht–Fraïssé games in which the Duplicator selects the structure $\mathbf{B}$ *after* the Spoiler has picked relations $S_1, \ldots, S_k$ on $\mathbf{A}$. The next definition introduces the Ajtai–Fagin games for monadic ESO; it can be easily extended to games for the full ESO with notational modifications only.

Definition 2.5.5. *Let* $\mathcal{C}$ *be a class of* σ-*structures*, Q *a Boolean query on* $\mathcal{C}$, *and* k, r *two positive integers. The* (k, r) *Ajtai–Fagin game for* Q *on* $\mathcal{C}$ *is played according to the following rules. In a run of the game:*

- *The Duplicator picks a structure $\mathbf{A} \in \mathcal{C}$ such that $Q(\mathbf{A}) = 1$.*
- *The Spoiler picks k unary relations $S_1, \ldots, S_k$ on $\mathbf{A}$ (i.e., k subsets of A).*
- *The Duplicator picks a structure $\mathbf{B} \in \mathcal{C}$ such that $Q(\mathbf{B}) = 0$ and then picks k unary relations $S'_1, \ldots, S'_k$ on $\mathbf{B}$ (i.e., k subsets of B).*
- *After this, the two players engage in a run of the r-move Ehrenfeucht–Fraïssé game on the expanded structures $(\mathbf{A}, S_1, \ldots, S_k)$ and $(\mathbf{B}, S'_1, \ldots, S'_k)$.*

The winning conditions are as in Definition 2.5.1.

Note that another difference between the Ajtai–Fagin games and the Ehrenfeucht–Fraïssé games considered earlier is that each Ajtai–Fagin game is defined with respect to a particular Boolean query, i.e., the query itself is one of the parameters of the game. The Ajtai–Fagin games give rise to the following method for investigating definability in monadic ESO.

Method 2.5.6 The Method of Ajtai–Fagin Games for monadic ESO. Let σ be a vocabulary, $\mathcal{C}$ a class of σ-structures, and Q a Boolean query on $\mathcal{C}$.

Soundness. To show that Q is *not* monadic ESO-definable on $\mathcal{C}$, it suffices to show that for every k and every r, the Duplicator wins the (k, r) Ajtai–Fagin game for Q on $\mathcal{C}$.

Completeness. This method is also *complete*, i.e., if Q is *not* monadic ESO-definable on $\mathcal{C}$, then for every k and every r, the Duplicator wins the (k, r) Ajtai–Fagin game for Q on $\mathcal{C}$.

Fagin [22] showed that the CONNECTIVITY query is not monadic ESO-definable on the class of all finite graphs, using Ehrenfeucht–Fraïssé games for monadic ESO. Later on, Fagin, Stockmeyer and Vardi [25] obtained a much simpler proof of this result using Ajtai–Fagin games for monadic ESO and Theorem 2.3.26 about d-equivalence.

Theorem 2.5.7. *The CONNECTIVITY query is not monadic ESO-definable on the class of all finite graphs.*

Proof. (Sketch) We shall show that, for every positive integer k and every positive integer r, the Duplicator wins the (k, r) Ajtai–Fagin game for CONNECTIVITY on the class of all finite graphs.

Suppose that k is a positive integer, $\mathbf{A} = (A, E)$ is an undirected cycle, and $S_1, \ldots, S_k$ are unary relations on A. For every node $b \in A$, we define the *color* of b to be the Boolean vector $c(b) = (c_1, \ldots, c_k)$ such that if $b \in S_i$, then $c_i = 1$; otherwise, $c_i = 0$. Note that the number of colors depends only on k. Moreover, it is easy to see that, for every $d \geq 1$ and every $a \in A$, the neighborhood $N(a, d)$ of a in $(\mathbf{A}, S_1, \ldots, S_k)$ consists of $2d - 1$ points whose distance from a in $\mathbf{A}$ is at most d, and is completely determined by the colors of these points (this, of course, hinges on the fact that each S_i is a unary relation on A). Consequently, the number of different d-types depends only on k and d (and not on the cardinality $|A|$ of A).

Using these facts, we can show that the Duplicator wins the (k, r) Ajtai–Fagin game for CONNECTIVITY on the class of all finite graphs by playing according to the following strategy:

- The Duplicator picks a large enough cycle $\mathbf{A}$ such that, for all unary relations $S_1, \ldots, S_k$ on A, there are at least $4d$ points with the same d-type in $(\mathbf{A}, S_1, \ldots, S_k)$, where $d = 3^{r-1}$.
- After the Spoiler picks unary relations $S_1, \ldots, S_k$ on A, there are two nodes a_p and a_q in A that have the same d-type and are such that $N(a_p, 2d) \cap N(a_q, 2d) = \emptyset$.
- The Duplicator constructs $\mathbf{B} = \mathbf{B}_0 \oplus \mathbf{B}_1$, consisting of two disjoint cycles $\mathbf{B}_0$ and $\mathbf{B}_1$ constructed as follows:
  - The Duplicator disconnects $\mathbf{A}$ by "pinching" it at a_p, a_q.
  - The Duplicator creates $\mathbf{B}_0$ by joining a_p and a_{q+1} in the first component.
  - The Duplicator creates $\mathbf{B}_1$ by joining a_{p+1} and a_q in the second component.
- Finally, the Duplicator picks the same unary relations $S_1, \ldots, S_k$ in $\mathbf{B}$ as the ones picked by the Spoiler on $\mathbf{A}$.

Note that the structures $(\mathbf{A}, S_1, \ldots, S_k)$ and $(\mathbf{B}, S_1, \ldots, S_k)$ are d-equivalent, as it is not too hard to verify that each node in A has the same d-type as its "clone" in B. Consequently, the Duplicator wins the r-move Ehrenfeucht–Fraïssé game on these structures. $\square$

Since the DISCONNECTIVITY query is monadic ESO-definable on the class of all finite graphs, we obtain the following separation between monadic ESO and monadic USO on finite graphs.

Corollary 2.5.8. *Monadic ESO is not closed under complements on the class of all finite graphs.*

It should be pointed out that Theorem 2.5.7 and Corollary 2.5.8 do not have any implications for the NP $\overset{?}{=}$ coNP problem, because CONNECTIVITY is a polynomial-time-computable query and monadic ESO cannot express all NP queries. Any breakthroughs towards the separation of NP from coNP using combinatorial games will entail proving limitations on the expressive power of existential second-order formulas in which the existentially quantified second-order variables have an arity bigger than one. So far, however, the successes of combinatorial games have been essentially limited to monadic existential second-order logic. In particular, the following test problem is open.

Problem 2.5.9. Show that there is a Boolean query Q on finite graphs such that

- Q is in NP (and hence Q is ESO-definable);
- Q is not binary ESO-definable, i.e., Q is not definable by any ESO-sentence $(\exists P_1) \cdots (\exists P_k)\psi$, where each P_i is a binary relation symbol.

Nonetheless, combinatorial games have been successfully used to establish limitations on the expressive power of monadic ESO over the class of finite graphs with "built-in" predicates, such as a *successor* relation [16] or a *total order* [59]. Such results are viewed as the first stepping stone towards analyzing definability in binary existential second-order logic.

Theorem 2.5.10. *The* CONNECTIVITY *query is not monadic* ESO-*definable on the class of finite structures with successor, i.e., finite structures of the form* $\mathbf{G} = (V, E, \mathrm{Suc})$, *where* E *is a binary relation on* V *and* Suc *is the graph of a successor function on* V.

Theorem 2.5.11. *The* CONNECTIVITY *query is not monadic* ESO-*definable on the class of finite ordered graphs, i.e., finite structures of the form* $\mathbf{G} = (V, E, \leq)$, *where* E *is a binary relation on* V *and* $\leq$ *is a linear order on* V.

2.6 Logics with Fixed-Point Operators

In Sect. 2.3, we used Ehrenfeucht–Fraïssé games to establish that first-order logic has severely limited expressive power on the class $\mathcal{G}$ of all finite graphs; in particular, first-order logic fails to express such basic polynomial-time computable queries as TRANSITIVE CLOSURE, ACYCLICITY, 2-COLORABILITY, EULERIAN, and PLANARITY. Several different mechanisms can be used to augment the syntax of first-order logic, so that the resulting logic has strictly higher expressive power on finite structures. We have already seen that second-order quantification is such a mechanism. In fact, Fagin's Theorem (Theorem 2.4.7) calibrates the exact gain in expressive power that is achieved when only existential second-order quantification in prefix form is allowed; moreover, it implies that, unless P = NP, even the syntactically simplest fragments of second-order logic can express queries that are not polynomial-time computable.

As mentioned earlier, the limited expressive power of first-order logic on finite graphs can be interpreted as an inability to express *recursion*. This realization suggests that higher expressive power can also be achieved by augmenting the syntax of first-order logic with mechanisms that embody recursion. Perhaps the most natural such mechanism is to use fixed points of operators that describe recursive specifications; this approach has been used fruitfully in many different areas of computer science, including computability theory, logic programming, and the denotational semantics of programming languages. As a motivating example, let us consider the *factorial* function $f(n)$, $n \geq 0$, which is usually defined inductively as

$$\left|\begin{array}{l} f(0) = 1 \\ f(n) = nf(n-1). \end{array}\right.$$

Alternatively, the factorial function can be defined as a fixed point of the recursive specification

$$f = \lambda n.(n = 0 \to 1 \,\square\, nf(n-1)).$$

Observe that the building blocks of the above recursive specification are operations on functions, such as definition by cases and multiplication. Here, we are interested in developing a formalism for specifying queries recursively. The key idea is to describe recursive specifications using formulas of first-order logic and then to augment the syntax of first-order logic with fixed points of such specifications. Before making this idea precise, we need to develop the basics of fixed-point theory.

2.6.1 Operators and Fixed Points

Let A be a set and k a positive integer. A k-ary *operator* on A is a mapping $\Phi : \mathcal{P}(A^k) \to \mathcal{P}(A^k)$, where $\mathcal{P}(A^k)$ is the power set of A^k (that is, the set of all k-ary relations on the universe A of $\mathbf{A}$).

A k-ary relation P is a *fixed point* of the operator Φ if $P = \Phi(P)$. Thus, every fixed point of Φ satisfies the recursive specification

$$(x_1, \ldots, x_k) \in P \iff (x_1, \ldots, x_k) \in \Phi(P).$$

An operator may have no fixed points whatsoever or it may have more than one fixed point. For instance, the unary operator $\Phi(P) = \overline{P}$, where $\overline{P}$ is the complement of P, has no fixed points. In contrast, let Φ be a binary operator such that if $\mathbf{G} = (V, E)$ is a graph and P is a binary relation on V, then

$$\Phi(P) = \{(a, b) : \mathbf{G} \models E(a, b) \vee P(a, b) \vee (\exists z)(E(a, z) \wedge P(z, b))\}.$$

This operator may have several fixed points, since every transitive relation P containing the edge relation is a fixed point of it.

A k-ary relation P^* is the *least fixed point* of Φ if P^* is a fixed point of Φ and, for every fixed point P of Φ, we have that $P^* \subseteq P$. We write $\mathbf{lfp}(\Phi)$ to denote the least fixed point of Φ (if it exists). For instance, if Φ is the above binary operator on graphs $\mathbf{G} = (V, E)$, then $\mathbf{lfp}(\Phi)$ is the transitive closure of the relation E. The property of having a least fixed point is shared by every operator that is *monotone*; furthermore, the least fixed point of a monotone operator can be obtained by iterating the operator. We now spell out these concepts and facts in precise terms.

Definition 2.6.1. *Let* $\Phi : \mathcal{P}(A^k) \to \mathcal{P}(A^k)$ *be a* k-*ary operator on a set* A.

- *The* finite stages Φ^n, $n \geq 1$, *of* Φ *are defined by the induction*

$$\left| \begin{array}{ll} \Phi^1 & = \Phi(\emptyset) \\ \Phi^{n+1} & = \Phi(\bigcup_{m=1}^n \Phi^m). \end{array} \right.$$

In general, for every ordinal α, the stage Φ^α of Φ is defined by the transfinite induction

$$\Phi^\alpha = \Phi(\textstyle\bigcup_{\beta<\alpha} \Phi^\beta).$$

We write $\Phi^\infty = \bigcup_\alpha \Phi^\alpha$ for the union of all stages of Φ.
- *The operator Φ is* monotone, *if for every two k-ary relations P_1, P_2 on A such that $P_1 \subseteq P_2$, we have that $\Phi(P_1) \subseteq \Phi(P_2)$.*

The next result, which is known as the Knaster–Tarski Theorem, describes the fundamental properties of monotone operators.

Theorem 2.6.2. [43, 64] *Let Φ be a monotone k-ary operator on a set A.*

- *The sequence of stages of Φ is monotone, that is, if $\alpha < \beta$, then $\Phi^\alpha \subseteq \Phi^\beta$. Consequently, for every ordinal α, we have that $\Phi^{\alpha+1} = \Phi(\Phi^\alpha)$.*
- *Φ has a least fixed point $\mathbf{lfp}(\Phi)$.*
- *There is an ordinal $\gamma < |A^k|^+$, where $|A^k|^+$ is the smallest cardinal greater than the cardinal $|A^k|$ of A^k, such that*

$$\mathbf{lfp}(\Phi) = \Phi^\infty = \Phi^\gamma = \Phi^\delta, \text{ for every } \delta > \gamma.$$

In particular, if A is a finite set, then there is an integer $s \leq |A|^k$ such that

$$\mathbf{lfp}(\Phi) = \Phi^\infty = \Phi^s = \Phi^\delta, \text{ for every } \delta > s.$$

- *The least fixed point of Φ is equal to the intersection of all fixed points of Φ.*

Proof. Since Φ is monotone, it is easy to show by transfinite induction that the sequence of stages is also monotone, that is, if $\alpha < \beta$, then $\Phi^\alpha \subseteq \Phi^\beta$. Since each Φ^α is a k-ary relation on A, it has at most $|A^k|$ elements. It follows that there must exist an ordinal $\gamma < |A^k|^+$ such that $\Phi^\gamma = \Phi^{\gamma+1}$. Consequently, Φ^γ is a fixed point of Φ, and also $\Phi^\infty = \Phi^\gamma = \Phi^\delta$, for every $\delta > \gamma$. Moreover, using the monotonicity of Φ again, it is easy to show by transfinite induction that if P is a fixed point of Φ, then $\Phi^\alpha \subseteq P$, for every α. Consequently, Φ^γ is the least fixed point $\mathbf{lfp}(\Phi)$ of Φ, and also the intersection of all of its fixed points. $\square$

Definition 2.6.3. *Let Φ be a monotone k-ary operator on a set A. The* closure ordinal *of Φ, denoted by $\mathrm{cl}(\Phi)$, is the smallest ordinal γ such that $\Phi^\gamma = \bigcup_{\beta<\gamma} \Phi^\beta$.*
Note that if A is a finite set, then $\mathrm{cl}(\Phi)$ is a positive integer.

Let Φ be a k-ary operator on a set A. A k-ary relation P^* is the *greatest fixed point* of Φ if P^* is a fixed point of Φ and, for every fixed point P of Φ, we have that $P \subseteq P^*$. We write $\mathbf{gfp}(\Phi)$ to denote the greatest fixed point of Φ (if it exists). Every monotone operator has a greatest fixed point that can be obtained via an iteration that is *dual* to the iteration used to obtain the least fixed point of the operator. Specifically, the *dual stages* Φ_α of Φ, where α is an ordinal, are defined by the transfinite induction

$$\left|\begin{array}{l} \Phi_1 = \Phi(A^k) \\ \Phi_\alpha = \Phi(\bigcap_{\beta<\alpha} \Phi_\beta). \end{array}\right.$$

We also write $\Phi_\infty = \bigcap_\alpha \Phi_\alpha$ for the intersection of all dual stages of Φ. If Φ is monotone, then its greatest fixed point $\mathbf{gfp}(\Phi)$ is equal to Φ_∞ and also equal to the union of all fixed points of Φ. Moreover, there is an ordinal $\gamma < |A^k|^+$ such that

$$\mathbf{gfp}(\Phi) = \Phi_\infty = \Phi_\gamma = \Phi_\delta, \text{ for every } \delta > \gamma.$$

The duality relationship between the least fixed point and the greatest fixed point of a monotone k-ary operator Φ can also be seen by considering the *dual* operator $\breve{\Phi}$ of Φ, where $\breve{\Phi}(P) = \overline{\Phi(\overline{P})}$ and $\overline{P} = A^k - P$ is the complement of P. If Φ is a monotone operator, then so is its dual $\breve{\Phi}$. Moreover, using transfinite induction, it is easy to show that $\breve{\Phi}^\alpha = \overline{\Phi_\alpha}$, for every ordinal α. Consequently, $\mathbf{gfp}(\Phi) = \overline{\mathbf{lfp}(\breve{\Phi})}$. Similarly, it is easy to show that $\mathbf{lfp}(\Phi) = \overline{\mathbf{gfp}(\breve{\Phi})}$.

As an example of an operator with interesting greatest fixed points, let Φ be a binary operator such that if $\mathbf{G} = (V, E)$ is a graph and P is a binary relation on V, then

$$\Phi(P) = \{(a,b) : \mathbf{G} \models (\forall a')(E(a,a') \rightarrow (\exists b')(E(b,b') \wedge P(a',b'))) \wedge$$
$$(\forall b')(E(b,b') \rightarrow (\exists a')(E(a,a') \wedge P(a',b')))\}.$$

The greatest fixed point $\mathbf{gfp}(\Phi)$ of Φ is the greatest *bisimulation* relation on $\mathbf{G} = (V, E)$; the concept of bisimulation plays an important role in modal logic [66] and also in the semantics of concurrent processes [53]. The same example can also be used to illustrate the concept of the dual operator $\breve{\Phi}$ of Φ, which in this case is defined by

$$\breve{\Phi}(P) = \{(a,b) : \mathbf{G} \models (\exists a')(E(a,a') \wedge (\forall b')(E(b,b') \rightarrow P(a',b'))) \wedge$$
$$(\exists b')(E(b,b') \wedge (\forall a')(E(a,a') \rightarrow P(a',b')))\}.$$

In what follows, we shall focus on operators that are definable using formulas of some logical formalism. Let σ be a vocabulary, S a k-ary relation symbol not in σ, and $\varphi(x_1, \ldots, x_k, S)$ a formula of some logic over the vocabulary $\sigma \cup \{S\}$ with free variables among $x_1, \ldots, x_k$. On every σ-structure $\mathbf{A}$, the formula $\varphi(x_1, \ldots, x_k, S)$ gives rise to a k-ary operator $\Phi : \mathcal{P}(A^k) \rightarrow \mathcal{P}(A^k)$ such that if P is a k-ary relation on A, then

$$\Phi(P) = \{(a_1, \ldots, a_k) : \mathbf{A} \models \varphi(a_1, \ldots, a_k, P)\}.$$

For instance, both the operator whose least fixed point is the transitive closure of the edge relation E of a graph $\mathbf{G} = (V, E)$ and the operator whose greatest fixed point is the greatest bisimulation relation on $\mathbf{G} = (V, E)$ are definable using first-order formulas. In what follows, we shall use the terms "the least fixed point of a formula" and "the greatest fixed point of a formula" for the least fixed point and the greatest fixed point, respectively, of the operator associated with the formula. Similarly, we shall use the term "the closure ordinal of a formula" for the closure ordinal of the operator associated with the formula, and we shall denote it by $cl(\varphi)$.

Operators also arise from formulas with *parameters*. Specifically, assume that σ is a vocabulary, $S_1, S_2, \ldots, S_m$ are relation symbols not in σ, and $\varphi(x_1, \ldots, x_k, y_1, \ldots, y_n, S_1, \ldots, S_m)$ is a formula of some logic over the vocabulary $\sigma \cup \{S_1, \ldots, S_m\}$ with free variables among $x_1, \ldots, x_k, y_1, \ldots, y_n$. Assume also that the arity of the relation symbol S_i is equal to k. For every σ-structure $\mathbf{A}$, every sequence $b_1, \ldots, b_n$ of elements from the universe A of $\mathbf{A}$, and every sequence $T_1, \ldots, T_{i-1}, T_{i+1}, \ldots, T_m$ of relations on A whose arities match those of $S_1, \ldots, S_{i-1}, S_{i+1}, \ldots, S_m$, the formula φ gives rise to a k-ary operator $\Phi : \mathcal{P}(A^k) \to \mathcal{P}(A^k)$ such that

$$\Phi(P) = \{\mathbf{a} : \mathbf{A} \models \varphi(\mathbf{a}, \mathbf{b}, T_1, \ldots, T_{i-1}, P, T_{i+1}, \ldots, T_m)\},$$

where $\mathbf{a} = (a_1, \ldots, a_k)$ and $\mathbf{b} = (b_1, \ldots, b_n)$. Note that operators with parameters can also be thought of as operators (without parameters) on structures expanded with the given parameters.

As an example, let $\varphi(x_1, y_1, S)$ be the first-order formula $E(y_1, x_1) \vee (\exists z)(S(z) \wedge E(z, x_1))$, in which y_1 is a parameter. If $\mathbf{G} = (V, E)$ is a graph and a is a node in V, then this formula gives rise to a unary operator Φ such that

$$\Phi(P) = \{b : \mathbf{G} \models E(a, b) \vee (\exists z)(P(z) \wedge E(z, b))\}.$$

The least fixed point $\mathbf{lfp}(\Phi)$ then consists of all nodes b in V that are reachable from a. Similarly, let $\varphi(x_1, y_1, S_1, S_2)$ be the first-order formula $E(y_1, x_1) \vee (\exists z)(S_1(z) \wedge S_2(z) \wedge E(z, x_1))$, in which y_1 and S_2 are parameters. If $\mathbf{G} = (V, E)$ is a graph, a is a node in V, and T is a subset of V, then this formula gives rise to a unary operator Φ such that

$$\Phi(P) = \{b : \mathbf{G} \models E(a, b) \vee (\exists z)(P(z) \wedge T(z) \wedge E(z, b))\}.$$

The least-fixed point $\mathbf{lfp}(\Phi)$ then consists of all nodes b in V that are reachable from a via a path in which every intermediate node is in T.

It is easy to see that if $\varphi(x_1, \ldots, x_k, S)$ is an arbitrary first-order formula over the vocabulary $\sigma \cup \{S\}$, then, for every $n \geq 1$, there is a first-order formula $\varphi^n(x_1, \ldots, x_k)$ over the vocabulary σ such that it defines the nth stage Φ^n of the operator Φ associated with $\varphi(x_1, \ldots, x_k, S)$ on every σ-structure $\mathbf{A}$. Consequently, if $\varphi(x_1, \ldots, x_k, S)$ is a first-order formula such that the associated operator Φ is monotone on every finite σ-structure, then for every finite σ-structure $\mathbf{A}$, there is an integer s such that the least fixed point $\mathbf{lfp}(\Phi)$ of Φ is definable by $\varphi^s(x_1, \ldots, x_k)$ on $\mathbf{A}$. In general, however, this integer depends on $\mathbf{A}$, and there may be no integer s such that $\varphi^s(x_1, \ldots, x_k)$ defines the least fixed point $\mathbf{lfp}(\Phi)$ of Φ on every finite σ-structure, because $\mathbf{lfp}(\Phi)$ may not be first-order definable. For instance, if $\varphi(x, y, S)$ is the formula $E(x, y) \lor (\exists z)(E(x, z) \land S(z, y))$, then the least fixed point $\mathbf{lfp}(\Phi)$ is the transitive closure of E; moreover, for every $n \geq 1$, $\varphi^n(x, y)$ is a first-order formula asserting that there is a path of length at most n from x to y. This formula defines the transitive closure of E on every finite graph of diameter at most n, but, as we have seen earlier, there is no first-order formula that defines the transitive closure of E on every finite graph.

2.6.2 Least Fixed-Point Logic

We now examine how to augment the syntax of first-order logic with least fixed points and greatest fixed points of operators definable by logical formulas. Since we want our operators to be monotone, it is natural to focus on formulas that give rise to monotone operators.

Let σ be a vocabulary, $\mathcal{C}$ a class of σ-structures, and $\varphi(x_1, \ldots, x_k, S)$ a formula of some logic over the vocabulary $\sigma \cup \{S\}$, where S is a k-ary relation symbol and the free variables of φ are among $x_1, \ldots, x_k$. We say that $\varphi(x_1, \ldots, x_k, S)$ is *monotone on* $\mathcal{C}$ if, for every structure $\mathbf{A} \in \mathcal{C}$, the operator Φ associated with $\varphi(x_1, \ldots, x_k, S)$ is monotone. More generally, let $\varphi(x_1, \ldots, x_k, y_1, \ldots, y_n, S, S_1, \ldots, S_m)$ be a formula of some logic over the vocabulary $\sigma \cup \{S, S_1, \ldots, S_m\}$, where S is a k-ary relation symbol and the free variables of φ are among $x_1, \ldots, x_k, y_1, \ldots, y_n$. We say that $\varphi(x_1, \ldots, x_k, y_1, \ldots, y_n, S, S_1, \ldots, S_m)$ is *monotone on* $\mathcal{C}$ if, for every structure $\mathbf{A} \in \mathcal{C}$, every sequence $b_1, \ldots, b_n$ of elements from the universe A of $\mathbf{A}$, and every sequence $T_1, \ldots, T_m$ of relations on A whose arities match those of $S_1, \ldots, S_m$, the operator Φ associated with the formula $\varphi(x_1, \ldots, x_k, y_1, \ldots, y_n, S, S_1, \ldots, S_m)$ and the parameters $b_1 \ldots, b_n, T_1, \ldots, T_m$ is monotone.

So, it is tempting to consider augmenting the syntax of first-order logic with the least fixed points and the greatest fixed points of first-order formulas that are monotone on the class $\mathcal{F}$ of all finite σ-structures. Serious difficulties arise in doing so, however. Specifically, it is known that there is no algorithm for testing whether a given first-order formula is monotone on $\mathcal{F}$ [5]. Consequently, if the syntax of first-order logic is augmented with the least fixed points of first-order formulas that are monotone on $\mathcal{F}$, then the resulting logic does not have an effective syntax. One way to bypass this obstacle is to restrict attention to *positive* formulas, since positivity is a syntactic property of formulas that implies monotonicity and is easily checkable. More precisely, let $\varphi(S)$ be a first-order formula over a vocabulary containing a k-ary relation symbol S. We say that $\varphi(S)$ is *positive in* S if every occurrence of S in $\varphi(S)$ is within an even number of negations. Equivalently, a first-order formula $\varphi(S)$ is positive in S if and only if, after all occurrences of the negation symbol in $\varphi(S)$ are "pushed inside", no occurrence of S is negated in the resulting formula. It is easy to verify that if $\varphi(x_1, \ldots, x_k, S)$ is positive in S and the free variables of $\varphi(x_1, \ldots, x_k, S)$ are among $x_1, \ldots, x_k$, then it is monotone on the class $\mathcal{S}$ of all σ-structures (finite and infinite). Moreover, there is a linear-time algorithm for testing whether a given first-order formula is positive. At this point, it is also worth recalling a classical result in mathematical logic to the effect that if a first-order formula is monotone on the class $\mathcal{S}$ of all σ-structures (finite and infinite), then it is logically equivalent to a positive first-order formula. Thus, positivity is a syntactic property of first-order formulas that, up to logical equivalence, exhausts the semantic property of monotonicity of first-order formulas on $\mathcal{S}$.

In view of the above, we shall augment the syntax of first-order logic with the least fixed point and the greatest fixed point of operators definable by positive first-order formulas. However, in order to obtain a logic whose syntax is closed under the formation rules used, we shall close the syntax under applications of the operations of first-order logic (that is, Boolean connectives and first-order quantification) and also under applications of least fixed points and greatest fixed points of positive formulas, where, as with first-order logic, a formula $\varphi(S)$ of the extended formalism is positive in a relation symbol S if every occurrence of S in $\varphi(S)$ is within an even number of negations. The resulting logic is *least fixed-point logic* LFP, whose precise syntax and semantics are given in the next definition.

Definition 2.6.4. *Let σ be a vocabulary and let $S_1, \ldots, S_n, \ldots$ be a sequence of relation symbols such that for every $m \geq 1$, this sequence contains infinitely many relation symbols of arity m.*

LFP Syntax. *The collection of* LFP-*formulas over σ is defined inductively as follows:*

- *Every atomic formula θ over $\sigma \cup \{S_1, \ldots, S_n, \ldots\}$ is an* LFP-*formula. The set* free(θ) *is the union of the set of all first-order variables occurring in θ and the set of all relation symbols S_i occurring in θ.*
- *If φ and ψ are* LFP-*formulas, then so are $\neg\varphi$, $\varphi \wedge \psi$, $\varphi \vee \psi$. Moreover,* free$(\neg\varphi) = $ free(φ), *and* free$(\varphi \wedge \psi) = $ free$(\varphi \vee \psi) = $ free$(\varphi) \cup $ free(ψ).
- *If φ is an* LFP-*formula and x is a first-order variable, then $\exists x \varphi$ and $\forall x \varphi$ are* LFP-*formulas. Moreover,* free$(\exists x \varphi) = $ free$(\forall x \varphi) = $ free$(\varphi) \setminus \{x\}$.
- *Assume that φ is an* LFP-*formula, S_i is a k-ary relation symbol in* free(φ) *which is* positive *in φ (that is, every occurrence of S_i in φ is within an even number of negation symbols), $\mathbf{x} = (x_1, \ldots, x_k)$ is a k-tuple of first-order variables each of which is in* free(φ), *and $\mathbf{u} = (u_1, \ldots, u_k)$ is a k-tuple of first-order variables not occurring in φ. Then the expressions $[\mathbf{lfp}\ S_i \mathbf{x}.\varphi](\mathbf{u})$ and $[\mathbf{gfp}\ S_i \mathbf{x}.\varphi](\mathbf{u})$ are* LFP-*formulas. Moreover,* free$([\mathbf{lfp}\ S_i \mathbf{x}.\varphi](\mathbf{u})) = $ free$([\mathbf{gfp}\ S_i \mathbf{x}.\varphi](\mathbf{u})) = ($free$(\varphi) \setminus \{x_1, \ldots, x_k, S_i\}) \cup \{u_1, \ldots, u_k\}$.*
  Notation. *If φ is such that S_i is the only relation symbol from $S_1, \ldots, S_n, \ldots$ that occurs free in φ and all free first-order variables*

of φ are among $\mathbf{x} = (x_1, \ldots, x_k)$, *then we shall often write* $\varphi^\infty(\mathbf{u})$ *instead of* $[\mathbf{lfp}\ S_i\mathbf{x}.\varphi](\mathbf{u})$.

LFP Semantics. *The semantics of least fixed-point logic is defined by a straightforward induction on the construction of LFP-formulas. For instance, the semantics of* $[\mathbf{lfp}\ S_i\mathbf{x}.\varphi](\mathbf{u})$ *is the least fixed point of the operator associated with* φ *on a* σ*-structure* $\mathbf{A}$ *and parameters from* $\mathbf{A}$ *corresponding to the first-order variables and relation symbols in* $\mathrm{free}([\mathbf{lfp}\ S_i\mathbf{x}.\varphi](\mathbf{u}))$. *Specifically, assume that* φ *is an LFP-formula such that* $\mathrm{free}(\varphi) \subseteq \{x_1, \ldots, x_k, y_1, \ldots, y_n, S_1, \ldots, S_m\}$ *and* S_i *is a* k*-ary relation symbol that is positive in* φ. *Write* $\mathbf{x} = (x_1, \ldots, x_k)$ *and* $\mathbf{y} = (y_1, \ldots, y_n)$. *Let* $\mathbf{A}$ *be a* σ*-structure,* $\mathbf{a}$ *a* k*-tuple from* A, $\mathbf{b}$ *an* n*-tuple from* A, *and* $T_1, \ldots, T_{i-1}, T_{i+1}, \ldots, T_m$ *relations on* A *whose arities match those of the relation symbols* $S_1, \ldots, S_{i-1}, S_{i+1}, \ldots S_m$. *Then* $\mathbf{A}, \mathbf{a} \models [\mathbf{lfp}\ S_i\mathbf{x}.\varphi](\mathbf{u})$ *if* $\mathbf{a} \in \mathbf{lfp}(\Phi)$, *where* Φ *is the* k*-ary operator on* A *such that*

$$\Phi(P) = \{\mathbf{a} \in A^k : \mathbf{A} \models \varphi(\mathbf{a}, \mathbf{b}, T_1, \ldots, T_{i-1}, P, T_{i+1}, \ldots, T_m)\}.$$

Similarly, the semantics of $[\mathbf{gfp}\ S_i\mathbf{x}.\varphi](\mathbf{u})$ *is the greatest fixed point of the operator associated with* φ *on a* σ*-structure* $\mathbf{A}$ *and parameters from* $\mathbf{A}$ *corresponding to the first-order variables and relation symbols in* $\mathrm{free}([\mathbf{gfp}\ S_i\mathbf{x}.\varphi](\mathbf{u}))$.

As an example, if $\varphi(x_1, y_1, S_1, S_2)$ is the first-order formula $E(y_1, x_1) \vee (\exists z)(S_1(z) \wedge S_2(z) \wedge E(z, x_1))$, then for every graph $\mathbf{G} = (V, E)$, every node a in V, and every subset T of V, the LFP-formula $[\mathbf{lfp}\ S_1(x_1).\varphi](u)$ defines the set of nodes u reachable from a via a path in which every intermediate node is in T.

The syntax of least fixed-point logic LFP, as presented in Definition 2.6.4, allows arbitrary nesting of least fixed points and greatest fixed points, as well as interleaving of least and greatest fixed points with the operations of first-order logic. Although the full syntax of LFP will be used in other chapters in this volume, in the remainder of this chapter we shall focus on LFP_1, which is one of the syntactically simplest and most well-studied fragments of LFP. Informally, LFP_1 is the extension of first-order logic obtained by augmenting the syntax of first-order logic with the least fixed points of positive formulas (without parameters) and then closing under conjunctions, disjunctions, and existential and universal first-order quantification. The precise definition of LFP_1 follows.

Definition 2.6.5. *Let* σ *be a vocabulary. The collection of* LFP_1*-formulas over* σ *is defined inductively as follows:*

- *Every first-order formula over* σ *is an* LFP_1*-formula over* σ.
- *If* k *is a positive integer,* S *is a* k*-ary relation symbol not in* σ, $\varphi(x_1, \ldots, x_k, S)$ *is a first-order formula over the vocabulary* $\sigma \cup \{S\}$ *that*

is positive in S, and $u_1, \ldots, u_k$ are first-order variables, then the expression $[\mathbf{lfp}\ S\mathbf{x}.\varphi](\mathbf{u})$ *is an* LFP$_1$-*formula, where* $\mathbf{x} = (x_1, \ldots, x_k)$ *and* $\mathbf{u} = (u_1, \ldots, u_k)$. *Since* $\varphi(x_1, \ldots, x_k, S)$ *contains no parameters, we shall use the expression* $\varphi^\infty(u_1 \ldots, u_k)$ *to denote the formula* $[\mathbf{lfp}\ S\mathbf{x}.\varphi](\mathbf{u})$ *in what follows.*

- *If ϕ and ψ are* LFP$_1$-*formulas over σ, then $\phi \wedge \psi$ and $\phi \vee \psi$ are* LFP$_1$-*formulas over σ.*
- *If ψ is an* LFP$_1$-*formula over σ and x is a first-order variable, then $\exists x\psi$ and $\forall x\psi$ are* LFP$_1$-*formulas over σ.*

Since every LFP$_1$-*formula is an* LFP-*formula, the semantics of* LFP$_1$ *is inherited from the semantics of* LFP.

The study of LFP$_1$-definable relations on fixed infinite structures is the focus of Moschovakis's monograph *Elementary Induction on Abstract Structures* [54], where they are called *inductive* relations. It should also be pointed out that in Immerman's book *Descriptive Complexity* [40], LFP is denoted by FO(LFP) (the closure of FO under least fixed points) and LFP$_1$ is denoted by LFP(FO) (least fixed points of first-order formulas).

Note that LFP$_1$-formulas are closed under the positive operations of first-order logic, but they are not closed under negation. Consequently, for every class $\mathcal{C}$ of σ-structures, it is an interesting problem to determine whether or not the collection of LFP$_1$-definable queries on $\mathcal{C}$ is closed under complements. In what follows, we shall explore the expressive power of LFP$_1$ on the class $\mathcal{F}$ of all finite σ-structures and we shall also study the complementation problem for LFP$_1$-definable queries on $\mathcal{F}$. We begin by presenting several examples that illustrate the expressive power of LFP$_1$ on finite structures.

Example 2.6.6. TRANSITIVE CLOSURE and CONNECTIVITY. Let $\varphi(x, y, S)$ be the existential and positive in S first-order formula

$$E(x, y) \vee (\exists z)(E(x, z) \wedge S(z, y)).$$

As seen earlier, $\varphi^\infty(x, y)$ defines the TRANSITIVE CLOSURE query TC on the class of all graphs $\mathbf{G} = (V, E)$. Thus, TC is an example of a query that is LFP$_1$-definable, but not FO-definable. Note that for every graph $\mathbf{G} = (V, E)$ (finite or infinite), we have that $\mathrm{cl}(\varphi) \leq \omega$.

Observe that the LFP$_1$-formula $(\forall x)(\forall y)\varphi^\infty(x, y)$ defines the CONNECTIVITY query CN on the class of all graphs; this gives another example of a query that is LFP$_1$-definable, but not FO-definable.

If $\psi(x, y, S)$ is the existential and positive in S first-order formula

$$E(x, y) \vee (\exists z)(S(x, z) \wedge S(z, y)),$$

then $\psi^\infty(x, y)$ is an LFP$_1$-formula that also defines the TRANSITIVE CLOSURE query TC on the class of all graphs. Although $\varphi(x, y, S)$ and $\psi(x, y, S)$ have the same least fixed points, their stages behave differently. Specifically, for every $n \geq 1$, the nth stage $\varphi^n(x, y)$ defines all pairs of nodes that are connected via a path of length at most n, while the nth stage $\psi^n(x, y)$ defines all pairs of nodes that are connected via a path of length at most 2^n. Thus, on a finite structure $\mathbf{A}$, we have that $\mathrm{cl}(\varphi) \leq |A|$, while $\mathrm{cl}(\psi) \leq \log(|A|)$.

Example 2.6.7. PATH SYSTEMS. Let σ be a vocabulary consisting of a unary relation symbol and a ternary relation symbol. Thus, a σ-structure is a structure of the form $\mathbf{S} = (F, A, R)$, where A is a subset of F and R is a ternary relation on F. Such structures can be thought of as encoding *proof systems* in which F is a set of *formulas*, A is a set of *axioms*, and R is a ternary *rule of inference*, such as modus ponens or resolution (that is, $R(f, g, h)$ means that f can be derived from g and h using the rule R). In this framework, a formula $f \in F$ is a *theorem* of S if either f is one of the axioms in A or it can be derived from other previously derived theorems g and h of $\mathbf{S}$ using the rule of inference R.

The following unary query, called PATH SYSTEM, arises naturally now: given a finite σ-structure $\mathbf{S} = (F, A, R)$ and a formula $f \in F$, is f a theorem of S? The computational complexity of this query was investigated by Cook [13], who showed that it is P-complete under logarithmic space reductions. In fact, this was the first problem shown to be complete for polynomial-time computability, and its discovery gave rise to the theory of P-completeness (see [32]).

Using Ehrenfeucht–Fraïssé games, it can be proved that PATH SYSTEMS is not FO-definable. It is easy to see, however, that PATH SYSTEMS is LFP$_1$-definable. Indeed, if $\varphi(x, T)$ is the existential and positive in T first-order formula

$$A(x) \vee (\exists y)(\exists z)(T(y) \wedge T(z) \wedge R(x, y, z)),$$

then PATH SYSTEMS is definable by the least fixed point $\varphi^\infty(x)$ of $\varphi(x, T)$.

Example 2.6.8. ACYCLICITY. Let $\psi(x, S)$ be the universal and positive in S first-order formula

$$(\forall y)(E(y, x) \to S(y)).$$

Let $\mathbf{G} = (V, E)$ be a directed graph. Clearly, the first stage $\psi^1(x)$ defines the set of all nodes x of in-degree equal to 0. Similarly, the second stage $\psi^2(x)$ defines the set of all nodes x that either have an in-degree equal to 0 or have the property that if y is a node such that $E(y, x)$, then y has an in-degree equal to 0. By continuing this analysis for all stages $\psi^n(x)$, $n \geq 1$, it can be seen that, on every finite directed graph $\mathbf{G} = (V, E)$, the least fixed point $\psi^\infty(x)$ defines the set of all nodes in V such that "no path down from x leads to a cycle", that is, the set of all nodes x such that there is no sequence of nodes $y_1, \ldots, y_m$ such that $E(y_1, x)$, $E(y_2, y_1)$, $\ldots$, $E(y_m, y_{m-1})$ and such that y_m is a node on a cycle of $\mathbf{G}$. It follows that ACYCLICITY is an LFP$_1$-definable query, since it is definable by the LFP$_1$-formula $(\forall x)\psi^\infty(x)$.

Although our main focus is on finite structures, it is worth pointing out that on every directed graph $\mathbf{G} = (V, E)$ (finite or infinite), the least fixed point $\psi^\infty(x)$ of $\psi(x, S)$ defines the *well-founded part* of E, that is the set of all nodes x in V such that there is no infinite descending E-chain $E(y_1, x)$, $E(y_{m+1}, y_m)$, $m \geq 1$. For finite directed graphs, of course, the well-founded part of E is the set of all nodes x such that no path down from x leads to a cycle. It should also be pointed out that the closure ordinal of the formula $\psi(x, S)$ can be arbitrarily large. Indeed, if $\mathbf{G} = (V, E)$ is a well-ordering of rank α, then $\mathrm{cl}(\psi) = \alpha$.

Example 2.6.9. GEOGRAPHY. Every finite directed graph $\mathbf{G} = (V, E)$ gives rise to a two-person game played according to the following rules: Player I and Player II take turns to pick nodes in V; if a is the last node picked, then the player whose turn is next must pick a node b such that $E(a, b)$, or else this player loses. This abstracts a game played between two children in which they take turns to write down the name of a city whose first letter is the same as the last letter of the city written down in the previous step of the game.

Consider now the following unary query, called GEOGRAPHY: given a finite directed graph $\mathbf{G} = (V, E)$ and a node v in V, is v a winning position for Player I? It is well known that this query is P-complete (see [32]); moreover, using Ehrenfeucht–Fraïssé games, it can be shown that it is not FO-definable. It is easy to see, however, that GEOGRAPHY is LFP$_1$-definable. Indeed, if $\varphi(x, S)$ is the universal-existential and positive in S first-order formula

$$(\forall y) \neg E(x, y) \vee (\forall y)(E(x, y) \to (\exists z)(E(y, z) \wedge S(z))),$$

then on every directed graph $\mathbf{G} = (V, E)$, the least fixed point $\varphi^\infty(x)$ of $\varphi(x, S)$ defines the set of all winning positions for Player I.

As a by-product of Theorem 2.6.2 and Examples 2.6.7 and 2.6.9, we can determine the data complexity of LFP and of LFP$_1$.

Proposition 2.6.10. *The data complexity of* LFP *is* P-*complete; the data complexity of* LFP$_1$ *is* P-*complete as well.*

Proof. (Sketch) Given a finite σ-structure, the least fixed points and the greatest fixed points of LFP-formulas can be evaluated by iterating the stages of the associated operator a polynomial number of times in the size of the given structure. Moreover, each step in the iteration amounts to evaluating a first-order formula on the structure obtained by expanding the given σ-structure with the current stage of the operator. Thus, each step in the iteration can be carried out in a time bounded by a polynomial in the size of the given σ-structure, since by Theorem 2.4.3, the data complexity of FO is in P. It follows that the data complexity of LFP (and, a fortiori, of LFP$_1$) is in P. Since LFP$_1$ can express P-complete queries, such as PATH SYSTEMS and GEOGRAPHY, it follows that the data complexity of LFP$_1$ (and, a fortiori, of LFP) is P-complete. $\square$

It is also known that the expression complexity and the combined complexity of LFP and of LFP$_1$ are EXPTIME-complete [67]; this is yet another instance of the exponential-gap phenomenon between the data complexity and the expression (and combined) complexity of a logic.

Let σ be a vocabulary containing at least one relation symbol of arity 2 or higher, and let $\mathcal{F}$ be the class of all finite σ-structures. Although LFP can express P-complete queries on $\mathcal{F}$, it cannot express every polynomial-time-computable query on $\mathcal{F}$. Indeed, in the next section we shall show that LFP cannot express *counting* queries, such as Even Cardinality. Thus, the following proper containments hold on $\mathcal{F}$:

$$\mathrm{FO}(\mathcal{F}) \subset \mathrm{LFP}(\mathcal{F}) \subset \mathrm{P}.$$

Immerman [38, 39] and Vardi [67], however, showed that LFP can express all polynomial-time-computable queries on classes of *ordered* finite structures, that is, on classes of finite structures in which one of the relations is a linear order on the universe of the structure.

Theorem 2.6.11. [38, 39, 67] . *Let $\mathcal{C}$ be a class of ordered finite structures. The following are equivalent for a query Q on $\mathcal{C}$.*

- *Q is polynomial-time computable.*
- *Q is LFP-definable on $\mathcal{C}$.*

In other words, $\mathrm{P}(\mathcal{C}) = \mathrm{LFP}(\mathcal{C})$.

So far, we have focused on recursive specifications of single queries. In many areas of computer science, however, it is quite common to specify objects recursively using *mutual recursion*, that is, the object of interest is defined together with several other auxiliary objects via a simultaneous recursive specification. In what follows, we formalize the mechanism of mutual recursion for queries and explore its basic properties.

Definition 2.6.12. *Let A be a set.*

- *A* system *of operators on a A is a finite sequence $(\Phi_1, \ldots, \Phi_m)$ of mappings*

$$\Phi_i : \mathcal{P}(A^{k_1}) \times \cdots \times \mathcal{P}(A^{k_m}) \to \mathcal{P}(A^{k_i}), \quad 1 \le i \le m.$$

- *A sequence $(P_1, \ldots, P_m)$ of relations on A is a* fixed point *of the system $(\Phi_1, \ldots, \Phi_m)$ if $P_i \subseteq A^{k_i}$, for $1 \le i \le m$, and $(\Phi_1(P_1), \ldots, \Phi_m(P_m)) = (P_1, \ldots, P_m)$.*
- *A sequence $(P_1, \ldots, P_m)$ of relations on A is the* least fixed point *of the system $(\Phi_1, \ldots, \Phi_m)$ if it is a fixed point of $(\Phi_1, \ldots, \Phi_m)$ and, for every fixed point $(P'_1, \ldots, P'_m)$ of $(\Phi_1, \ldots, \Phi_m)$, we have that $P_i \subseteq P'_i$, for $1 \le i \le m$. We write $\mathbf{lfp}(\Phi_1, \ldots, \Phi_m)$ to denote the least fixed point of $(\Phi_1, \ldots, \Phi_m)$, if it exists.*
- *A system $(\Phi_1, \ldots, \Phi_m)$ is* monotone *if, for every two sequences $(P_1, \ldots, P_m)$, $(P'_1, \ldots, P'_m)$ of relations on A such that $P_i \subseteq P'_i \subseteq A^{k_i}$, $1 \le i \le m$, we have that $\Phi_i(P_1, \ldots, P_m) \subseteq \Phi_i(P'_1, \ldots, P'_m)$, for $1 \le i \le m$.*

- *The (finite) stages $(\Phi_1^n, \ldots, \Phi_m^n)$, $n \geq 1$, of the system $(\Phi_1, \ldots, \Phi_m)$ are defined by the following simultaneous induction:*

$$\left|\begin{array}{ll} \Phi_i^1 & = \Phi_i(\emptyset, \ldots, \emptyset), \quad 1 \leq i \leq m \\ \Phi_i^{n+1} & = \Phi_i(\Phi_1^n, \ldots, \Phi_m^n), \, 1 \leq i \leq m. \end{array}\right.$$

In general, for every ordinal α, the stage $(\Phi_1^\alpha, \ldots, \Phi_m^\alpha)$ is defined by the simultaneous transfinite induction

$$\Phi_i^\alpha = \Phi_i(\bigcup_{\beta < \alpha} \Phi_1^\beta, \ldots, \bigcup_{\beta < \alpha} \Phi_m^\beta), 1 \leq i \leq m.$$

We write $(\Phi_1^\infty, \ldots, \Phi_m^\infty) = (\bigcup_\alpha \Phi_1^\alpha, \ldots, \bigcup_\alpha \Phi_m^\alpha)$ for the union of the stages.

Using simultaneous transfinite induction, it is easy to verify that the Knaster–Tarski Theorem (Theorem 2.6.2) extends to monotone systems of operators.

Theorem 2.6.13. *Let A be a set, and $(\Phi_1, \ldots, \Phi_m)$ a monotone system of operators on A.*

- *$(\Phi_1, \ldots, \Phi_m)$ has a least fixed point $\mathbf{lfp}(\Phi_1, \ldots, \Phi_m)$.*
- *There is an ordinal γ such that for every $\delta > \gamma$,*

$$\mathbf{lfp}(\Phi_1, \ldots, \Phi_m) = (\Phi_1^\infty, \ldots, \Phi_m^\infty) = (\Phi_1^\gamma, \ldots, \Phi_m^\gamma) = (\Phi_1^\delta, \ldots, \Phi_m^\delta).$$

If A is a finite set, then there is an integer $s \leq \prod_{i=1}^m |A|^{k_i}$ such that for every $\delta > s$,

$$\mathbf{lfp}(\Phi_1, \ldots, \Phi_m) = (\Phi_1^\infty, \ldots, \Phi_m^\infty) = (\Phi_1^s, \ldots, \Phi_m^s) = (\Phi_1^\delta, \ldots, \Phi_m^\delta).$$

- *The least fixed point $\mathbf{lfp}(\Phi_1, \ldots, \Phi_m)$ of $(\Phi_1, \ldots, \Phi_m)$ is equal to the (coordinatewise) intersection of all fixed points of $(\Phi_1, \ldots, \Phi_m)$.*

Definition 2.6.14. *Let $(\Phi_1, \ldots, \Phi_m)$ be a monotone system of operators on A. The closure ordinal of this system, denoted by $\mathrm{cl}(\Phi_1, \ldots, \Phi_m)$, is the smallest ordinal γ such that*

$$(\Phi_1^\gamma, \ldots, \Phi_m^\gamma) = (\bigcup_{\beta < \gamma} \Phi_1^\beta, \ldots, \bigcup_{\beta < \gamma} \Phi_m^\beta).$$

We now consider systems of operators arising from first-order formulas.

Definition 2.6.15. *Let σ be a vocabulary.*

- *A system of first-order formulas is a sequence*

$$(\varphi_1(\mathbf{x}_1, S_1, \ldots, S_m), \ldots, \varphi_m(\mathbf{x}_m, S_1, \ldots, S_m))$$

of first-order formulas over the vocabulary $\sigma \cup \{S_1, \ldots, S_m\}$ such that each $\mathbf{x}_i$ is a sequence of variables whose length is equal to the arity of the relation symbol S_i, $1 \leq i \leq m$. (Of course, some of the relation symbols $S_1, \ldots, S_m$ may not occur in the formula φ_i.)

- If $\mathbf{A}$ *is a σ-structure, then a system of first-order formulas as defined above gives rise to a system $(\Phi_1, \ldots, \Phi_m)$ of operators on A such that for every $i \leq m$,*

$$\Phi_i(P_1, \ldots, P_m) = \{\mathbf{a}_i : \mathbf{A} \models \varphi_i(\mathbf{a}_i, P_1, \ldots, P_m)\}.$$

- *Let $(\varphi_1(\mathbf{x}_1, S_1, \ldots, S_m), \ldots, \varphi_m(\mathbf{x}_m, S_1, \ldots, S_m))$ be a system of first-order formulas, each of which is positive in $S_1, \ldots, S_m$. We write $(\varphi_1^\infty, \ldots, \varphi_m^\infty)$ for the least fixed point of the monotone system associated with this system of positive first-order formulas. Similarly, we write $\mathrm{cl}(\varphi_1, \ldots, \varphi_m)$ for the closure ordinal of this system.*

Example 2.6.16. EVEN PATH and ODD PATH. Let $\varphi_1(x, y, S_1, S_2)$ be the positive first-order formula

$$E(x, y) \vee (\exists z)(E(x, z) \wedge S_2(z, y)),$$

and let $\varphi_2(x, y, S_1, S_2)$ be the positive first-order formula

$$(\exists z)(E(x, z) \wedge S_1(z, y)).$$

Consider the least fixed point $(\varphi_1^\infty, \varphi_2^\infty)$ of the system consisting of these two formulas. It is easy to see that φ_1^∞ defines the ODD PATH query OP on graphs and φ_2^∞ defines the EVEN PATH query EP on graphs, where, for every graph $\mathbf{G} = (V, E)$,

$$OP(\mathbf{G}) = \{(a, b) \in V^2 : \text{there is a path of odd length from } a \text{ to } b\}$$
$$EP(\mathbf{G}) = \{(a, b) \in V^2 : \text{there is a path of even length from } a \text{ to } b\}.$$

The next result asserts that least fixed points of systems of positive first-order formulas have the same expressive power as LFP_1-formulas. Moreover, it asserts that systems consisting of positive existential and positive universal first-order formulas are as powerful as systems of arbitrary positive first-order formulas.

Theorem 2.6.17. *Let σ be a vocabulary, let $\mathcal{C}$ be a class of σ-structures each of which has at least two elements in its universe, and let Q be a query on $\mathcal{C}$. Then the following statements are equivalent:*

1. *Q is LFP_1-definable on $\mathcal{C}$.*
2. *There is a system $(\varphi_1(\mathbf{x}_1, S_1, \ldots, S_m), \ldots, \varphi_m(\mathbf{x}_m, S_1, \ldots, S_m))$ of positive first-order formulas such that φ_m^∞ defines Q on $\mathcal{C}$ and each $\varphi_i(\mathbf{x}_i, S_1, \ldots, S_m)$ is either a positive existential first-order formula or a positive universal first-order formula, $1 \leq i \leq m$.*
3. *There is a system $(\varphi_1(\mathbf{x}_1, S_1, \ldots, S_m), \ldots, \varphi_m(\mathbf{x}_m, S_1, \ldots, S_m))$ of positive first-order formulas such that φ_m^∞ defines Q on $\mathcal{C}$.*

Proof. (Sketch) Since the direction (2) $\Rightarrow$ (3) is trivial, it suffices to establish the directions (1) $\Rightarrow$ (2) and (3) $\Rightarrow$ (1). The proof of (1) $\Rightarrow$ (2) is by induction on the construction of LFP$_1$-formulas. For concreteness, suppose that we are given the LFP$_1$-formula $(\exists y)\varphi^\infty(x, y)$, where $\varphi(x, y, S)$ is a first-order formula of the form $(\forall z)(\exists w)\theta(x, y, z, w, S)$ that is positive in S, and where $\theta(x, y, z, w, S)$ a quantifier-free formula and S a binary relation symbol. Consider the system

$$(\varphi_1(x, y, z, S_1, S_2, S_3), \varphi_2(x, y, S_1, S_2, S_3), \varphi_3(x, S_1, S_2, S_3)),$$

where

$$\varphi_1(x, y, z, S_1, S_2, S_3) \equiv (\exists w)\theta(x, y, z, w, S_2)$$
$$\varphi_2(x, y, S_1, S_2, S_3) \equiv (\forall z)S_1(x, y, z)$$
$$\varphi_3(x, S_1, S_2, S_3) \equiv (\exists y)S_2(x, y),$$

and where S_1 is a ternary relation symbol, S_2 a binary one, and S_3 a unary one. By transfinite induction on the stages and using the monotonicity of the formulas, it is not hard to verify that the given LFP$_1$-formula $(\exists y)\varphi^\infty(x, y)$ is logically equivalent to $\varphi_3^\infty(x)$.

The other steps of this direction are quite similar. For instance, suppose we are given the LFP$_1$-formula $\varphi^\infty(x, y) \wedge \psi^\infty(x, y)$, where $\varphi(x, y, S)$ and $\psi(x, y, S)$ are first-order formulas that are positive in S. By the induction hypothesis, we may assume that there are systems $(\varphi_1, \ldots, \varphi_m)$ and $(\psi_1, \ldots, \psi_s)$ of positive existential and positive universal first-order formulas such that $\varphi^\infty(x, y)$ is logically equivalent to $\varphi_m^\infty(x, y)$ and $\psi^\infty(x, y)$ is logically equivalent to $\psi_s^\infty(x, y)$. Suppose that the relation variables in the first system are $S_1, \ldots, S_m$ and in the second system $T_1, \ldots, T_s$. Consider the system

$$(\varphi_1, \ldots, \varphi_m, \psi_1, \ldots, \psi_s, \chi),$$

where χ is the formula $S_m(x, y) \wedge T_s(x, y)$. Then the given LFP$_1$-formula $\varphi^\infty(x, y) \wedge \psi^\infty(x, y)$ is logically equivalent to $\chi^\infty(x, y)$.

We now focus on the direction (3) $\Rightarrow$ (1). Again, for concreteness, suppose we are given the system $(\varphi_1(x, S_1, S_2), \varphi_2(y, z, S_1, S_2))$, where φ_1 and φ_2 are first-order formulas that are positive in S_1, S_2, and where S_1 is a unary relation symbol, and S_2 is a binary relation symbol. Let S be a 5-ary relation symbol and let $\varphi(u, v, x, y, z, S)$ be the first-order formula

$$(u \neq v \wedge \varphi_1(x, T_1, T_2)) \vee (u = v \wedge \varphi_2(y, z, T_1, T_2)),$$

which is positive in S, and where

$$T_1 = \{x' : (\exists u')(\exists v')(u' \neq v' \wedge S(u', v', x', u', u'))\}$$
$$T_2 = \{(y', z') : (\exists u')S(u', u', u', y', z')\}.$$

By induction on the stages and using the monotonicity of the formulas, one can verify that for every ordinal α, we have that $\varphi_1^\alpha(x)$ is logically equivalent to $(\exists u)(\exists v)((u \neq v) \wedge \varphi_1^\alpha(u, v, x, u, u))$, while at the same time $\varphi_2^\alpha(y, z)$ is logically equivalent to $(\exists u)(\varphi^\alpha(u, u, u, y, z)$. It follows that $\varphi_1^\infty(x)$ is logically equivalent to $(\exists u)(\exists v)((u \neq v) \wedge \varphi^\infty(u, v, x, u, u))$ and $\varphi_2^\infty(y, z)$ is logically equivalent to $(\exists u)\varphi^\infty(u, u, u, y, z)$. $\square$

Several remarks are in order now. In Moschovakis's book [54], the equivalence between statements (1) and (2) is attributed to P. Aczel (in an unpublished note); the same monograph contains a detailed proof of the direction (3) $\Rightarrow$ (1), which is often called the Simultaneous Induction Lemma.

Theorem 2.6.17 is a basic and extremely useful result about the expressive power of least fixed-point logic LFP$_1$. It shows that, although on the face of it from Definition 2.6.5 the syntax of LFP$_1$ is quite restricted, LFP$_1$ is robust enough to simulate least fixed points of systems of positive first-order formulas. It also facilitates the task of showing that a query is LFP$_1$-definable, because quite often it is easier to define a query by mutual recursion using a system of positive first-order formulas. Furthermore, the equivalence between statements (1) and (2) in Theorem 2.6.17 reveals that no hierarchy of progressively more expressive sublogics of LFP$_1$ arises when one restricts the length of quantifier alternation in the formulas occurring in systems. Thus, there are just two main sublogics of least fixed-point logic obtained by imposing restrictions on the quantification pattern: ELFP$_1$ and ULFP$_1$. The former is the sublogic of LFP$_1$ determined by systems of positive existential first-order formulas, while the latter is the sublogic of LFP$_1$ determined by systems of positive universal first-order formulas. In what follows, we shall consider certain fragments of ELFP$_1$ that have played an important role in database theory.

2.6.3 Datalog and Datalog($\neq$)

Datalog can be succinctly described as the data sublanguage of logic programming. More formally, a *Datalog program* π is a finite set of function-free, $\neq$-free, and negation-free *rules* of the form

$$t_0 :- t_1, \ldots, t_m,$$

where each t_i is an atomic formula $R(x_1, \ldots, x_n)$ for some n-ary relation symbol, $n \geq 1$; in addition, t_0 may be a 0-ary relation symbol standing for "true". The expression t_0 is the *the head* of the rule, and the expression $t_1, \ldots, t_m$ is the *body* of the rule. The relation symbols that occur in the heads of the rules of a given Datalog program π are usually called the *intensional database* predicates (IDBs) of π, and all others are the *extensional database* predicates (EDBs) of π. One of the IDBs is designated as the *goal* of π. Note that IDBs may occur in the bodies of rules and, thus, a Datalog program can be viewed as a simultaneous recursive specification of the IDBs. Given a set of relations for the EDBs of π, each IDB is originally instantiated to the empty relation and then the rules of the Datalog program are applied repeatedly until no new tuples are added to the IDBs. An application of a rule entails adding to the IDB in the head of the rule all tuples that satisfy the head of the rule. This is an informal description of the "bottom-up" evaluation of a Datalog program, and it provides the *procedural semantics* of that program. Alternatively, a Datalog program can be given *declarative semantics* using least fixed points of a recursive specification (see [1, 65] for precise definitions). The query defined by a Datalog program π is the query whose value on a structure **A** is the value of the goal of π with the relations of **A** as EDBs of π. If the goal of π is 0-ary, then π defines a Boolean query.

Example 2.6.18. TRANSITIVE CLOSURE revisited. Consider the following Datalog program having E as its only EDB and S as its only IDB:

$$\left| \begin{array}{l} S(x,y) : - E(x,y) \\ S(x,y) : - E(x,z), S(z,y) \end{array} \right.$$

This program defines the TRANSITIVE CLOSURE query. Note that the TRANSITIVE CLOSURE query is also definable by the following Datalog program:

$$\left| \begin{array}{l} S(x,y) : - E(x,y) \\ S(x,y) : - S(x,z), S(z,y) \end{array} \right.$$

Example 2.6.19. PATH SYSTEMS revisited. Consider the following Datalog program having A and R as its EDBs and T as its only IDB:

$$\left| \begin{array}{l} T(x) : - A(x) \\ T(x) : - T(y), T(z), R(x,y,z) \end{array} \right.$$

This program defines the PATH SYSTEMS query.

Note that Example 2.6.19 reveals that the data complexity of Datalog is P-complete, that is, it is the same as that of the full LFP, even though Datalog is a small fragment of it.

Example 2.6.20. NON-2-COLORABILITY. Consider the following Datalog program having E as its only EDB, O and Q as its IDBs, and Q as its 0-ary goal predicate:

$$\left| \begin{array}{ll} O(x,y) : - E(x,y) \\ O(x,y) : - E(x,z), E(z,w), O(w,y) \\ Q \qquad : - O(x,x) \end{array} \right.$$

In this program, O defines the set of pairs of nodes connected via a path of odd length. Consequently, Q defines the set of all graphs that contain a cycle of odd length, that is, the set of all graphs that are not 2-colorable.

As seen earlier in Example 2.6.6, the TRANSITIVE CLOSURE query is definable as the least fixed point of an existential and positive in S first-order formula. Similarly, as seen in Example 2.6.7, the PATH SYSTEMS query is definable as the least fixed point of an existential and positive in T first-order formula. Moreover, these formulas are $\neq$-free and negation-free (that is, they are also positive in E). In the other direction, the NON-2-COLORABILITY query is definable by the formula $(\exists x)\varphi^\infty(x, x)$, where $\varphi(x, y, O)$ is the following existential first-order formula that is positive in O and E, and also $\neq$-free:

$$E(x, y) \vee (\exists z)(\exists w)(E(x, z) \wedge E(z, w) \wedge O(w, y)).$$

Chandra and Harel [12] were the first to point out that these connections are not accidental.

Proposition 2.6.21. [12] *Let C be a class of structures and Q a query on C. The following statements are then equivalent:*

- *Q is definable on C by a Datalog program.*
- *Q is definable on C by φ_m^∞ for some system $(\varphi_1, \ldots, \varphi_m)$ of first-order formulas such that each φ_i is of the form $(\exists \mathbf{z}_i)\psi_i$ and ψ_i is a conjunction of atomic formulas.*

Proof. (Hint) Every rule of a Datalog program gives rise to a formula of a system of the required form. Specifically, the body of the rule is first rewritten as a conjunction of the atomic formulas occurring in it; after this, the variables occurring in the body, but not in the head of the rule, are existentially quantified out. Conversely, every formula in such a system can be viewed as a rule of a Datalog program. $\square$

Although Datalog can express P-complete queries, it is strictly less expressive than LFP_1. As we shall see next, some of the limitations of Datalog are consequences of *preservation* properties possessed by Datalog queries.

Definition 2.6.22. *Let σ be a vocabulary.*

- *A homomorphism $h : \mathbf{A} \to \mathbf{B}$ between two σ-structures $\mathbf{A}$ and $\mathbf{B}$ is a mapping h from the universe A of $\mathbf{A}$ to the universe B of $\mathbf{B}$ with the following properties:*
  - *for every constant symbol c in σ, we have that $h(c^{\mathbf{A}}) = c^{\mathbf{B}}$;*
  - *for every relation symbol R in σ and every tuple $\mathbf{a}$ from A, if $\mathbf{a} \in R^{\mathbf{A}}$, then $h(\mathbf{a}) \in R^{\mathbf{B}}$.*
- *Let Q be a k-ary query on a class C of σ-structures. We say that Q is preserved under homomorphisms if, for every two structures $\mathbf{A}$, $\mathbf{B}$ in C, every homomorphism $h : \mathbf{A} \to \mathbf{B}$, and every k-tuple $\mathbf{a}$ from A, if $\mathbf{a} \in Q(\mathbf{A})$, then $h(\mathbf{a}) \in Q(\mathbf{B})$.*
- *Let Q be a Boolean query on a class C of σ-structures. We say that Q is preserved under homomorphisms if, for every two structures $\mathbf{A}$, $\mathbf{B}$ in C such that there is a homomorphism from $\mathbf{A}$ to $\mathbf{B}$, if $\mathbf{A} \models Q$, then $\mathbf{B} \models Q$.*

Proposition 2.6.23. *Let σ be a vocabulary. Every Datalog-definable query is preserved under homomorphisms on the class S of all σ-structures.*

Proof. (Sketch) Proposition 2.6.21 implies that the system of operators associated with a Datalog program is definable by first-order formulas that are positive in every relation symbol occurring in them and also are $\neq$-free. Using this fact and induction on the stages of the system, it is easy to show that each stage of the system is preserved under homomorphisms on S. $\square$

Consider the existential first-order sentence $(\exists x)(\exists y)(x \neq y)$ asserting that there are at least two distinct elements in the universe. An immediate consequence of Proposition 2.6.23 is that this sentence is *not* equivalent to any Datalog sentence, because it is not preserved under homomorphisms.

Datalog($\neq$) is the extension of Datalog in which $\neq$ is allowed in the rules. The next example illustrates the syntax of Datalog($\neq$).

Example 2.6.24. NODE-AVOIDING PATH. Let Q be the following query on graphs: given a graph $\mathbf{G} = (V, E)$ and three nodes a, b, c, is there a path from a to b that avoids c?

This query is definable by the following Datalog($\neq$)-program:

$$T(x, y, w) : -\ E(x, y) \wedge w \neq x \wedge w \neq y$$
$$T(x, y, w) : -\ E(x, z) \wedge T(z, y, w) \wedge w \neq x.$$

It is easy to see that Q is not preserved under homomorphisms and, consequently, it is not expressible in Datalog.

Note that the above query is also definable by the least fixed point of the existential and positive in T first-order formula

$$(E(x, y) \wedge w \neq x \wedge w \neq y) \vee (\exists z)(E(x, z) \wedge T(z, y, w) \wedge w \neq x).$$

This is an instance of a more general result that is analogous to Proposition 2.6.21. Specifically, a query Q is definable on a class C by a Datalog($\neq$) program if and only if Q is definable on C by φ_m^∞ for some system $(\varphi_1, \ldots, \varphi_m)$ of first-order formulas such that each φ_i is of the form $(\exists \mathbf{z}_i)\psi_i$ and ψ is a conjunction of atomic formulas and inequalities $\neq$.

We now present an example of a query on undirected graphs that is definable by a Datalog($\neq$) program, but proving this fact requires some machinery from graph theory.

Example 2.6.25. The EVEN SIMPLE PATH query asks: given a graph $\mathbf{G} = (V, E)$ and two nodes a, b, is there a simple path of even length from a to b?

Using some results of Fortune, Hopcroft, and Wyllie [26] about the GRAPH HOMEOMORPHISM PROBLEM, it can be shown that EVEN SIMPLE PATH on directed graphs is an NP-complete problem. In contrast, there is a polynomial-time algorithm for EVEN SIMPLE PATH when the inputs are undirected graphs. Moreover, in an unpublished note, Yannakakis showed that the following Datalog($\neq$) program with Q as its goal defines the EVEN SIMPLE PATH query on undirected graphs:

$$\left|\begin{array}{ll} T(x,y,w) :- E(x,y) \wedge w \neq x \wedge w \neq y \\ T(x,y,w) :- E(x,z) \wedge T(z,y,w) \wedge w \neq x \\ P(x,y) \quad\; :- E(x,y) \\ P(x,y) \quad\; :- Q(x,w), E(w,y), T(x,w,y) \\ Q(x,y) \quad\; :- P(x,w), E(w,y), T(x,w,y). \end{array}\right.$$

The correctness of this program is established by proving the following on undirected graphs:

- T defines the NODE-AVOIDING PATH query.
- P defines the ODD SIMPLE PATH query (that is, "is there a simple path of odd length from a to b?").
- Q defines the EVEN SIMPLE PATH query.

The proof proceeds by induction on the stages of the above Datalog($\neq$) program and makes use of Menger's Theorem, a well-known result in graph theory which asserts that if an undirected graph $G = (V, E)$ and two nodes a, b have the property that every two paths from a to b intersect at some intermediate node, then there is a node c different from a and b such that all paths from a to b intersect at c (Menger's Theorem is a special case of the Max Flow–Min Cut Theorem; see [18]).

A *one-to-one homomorphism* between two σ-structures $\mathbf{A}$ and $\mathbf{B}$ is a homomorphism $h : \mathbf{A} \to \mathbf{B}$ that is also a one-to-one mapping from A to B. The next result is proved along the lines of the proof of Proposition 2.6.23.

Proposition 2.6.26. *Every Datalog($\neq$)-definable query is preserved under one-to-one homomorphisms on the class $\mathcal{S}$ of all σ-structures.*

Consider the universal first-order sentence $(\forall x)(\forall y)(x \neq y \to E(x,y))$, which asserts that $\mathbf{G} = (V, E)$ is a complete graph. Since this sentence is not preserved under one-to-one homomorphisms, it is not equivalent to any Datalog($\neq$) sentence. Thus, on the class $\mathcal{G}$ of all finite graphs, Datalog($\neq$) is strictly more expressive than Datalog, but strictly less expressive than LFP$_1$.

Another difference between Datalog($\neq$) and LFP$_1$ has to do with closure ordinals on infinite structures. As seen earlier in Example 2.6.8, there are positive universal first-order formulas whose closure ordinal can be arbitrarily large on infinite structures. In contrast, it is not hard to prove that, on every infinite structure, the closure ordinal of every of Datalog($\neq$) program is at most ω. This follows from the fact that existential quantification distributes over an infinite union, that is, $(\exists x)(\bigcup_{n=1}^{\infty} P_n)$ is logically equivalent to $\bigcup_{n=1}^{\infty} (\exists x) P_n$.

2.6.4 The Complementation Problem for LFP$_1$ and a Normal Form for LFP

The *structure of arithmetic* is the structure $\mathbf{N} = (N, +, \times)$, where N is the set of all natural numbers, and $+$ and $\times$ are ternary relations for the graphs of the addition and multiplication functions on the natural numbers. The expressive power of LFP$_1$ on $\mathbf{N} = (N, +, \times)$ was first studied by Kleene [42] and Spector [62], who established the following important result, known as the Kleene–Spector Theorem (see [54]).

Theorem 2.6.27. *Let* $\mathbf{N} = (N, +, \times)$ *be the structure of arithmetic.*

- LFP$_1(\mathbf{N})$ = USO$(\mathbf{N})$, *that is, a relation* $R \subseteq N^k$ *is* LFP$_1$*-definable on* $\mathbf{N}$ *if and only if it is definable on* $\mathbf{N}$ *by a universal second-order formula.*
- LFP$_1(\mathbf{N})$ *is not closed under complements.*

Several remarks are now in order, so that the Kleene–Spector Theorem be put into the right perspective. First, if σ is a vocabulary and $\mathbf{A}$ is an arbitrary σ-structure, then LFP$_1(\mathbf{A}) \subseteq$ USO$(\mathbf{A})$. The reason for this is that if $\varphi(\mathbf{x}, S)$ is a first-order formula that is positive in S over the vocabulary $\sigma \cup \{S\}$, then it is easy to see that the least fixed point $\varphi^\infty(\mathbf{x})$ is definable on $\mathbf{A}$ by the USO-formula

$$(\forall S)((\forall \mathbf{z})(\varphi(\mathbf{z}, S) \leftrightarrow S(\mathbf{z}))) \rightarrow S(\mathbf{x})),$$

which asserts that $\mathbf{x}$ belongs to every fixed point of φ. Indeed, this formula defines the least fixed point of $\varphi(\mathbf{x}, S)$, because, as seen in Theorem 2.6.2, the least fixed point of a monotone operator is the intersection of all its fixed points. If $\mathbf{A}$ is an arbitrary infinite σ-structure, then LFP$_1(\mathbf{A})$ may be properly contained in USO$(\mathbf{A})$; for instance, this is the case for the structure $\mathbf{Q} = (Q, <)$, where Q is the set of rational numbers and $<$ is the standard linear order on Q. In contrast, the Kleene–Spector Theorem asserts that the LFP$_1$-definable relations coincide with the USO-definable ones on the structure $\mathbf{N} = (N, +, \times)$ of arithmetic; thus, this result provides a "constructive" characterization of universal second-order logic on $\mathbf{N}$. Moschovakis [54] has shown that the Kleene–Spector Theorem actually extends to countable structures $\mathbf{A}$ possessing a first-order *coding machinery* for finite sequences, that is, countable structures in which finite sequences of arbitrary length can be encoded by individual elements and decoded in a first-order-definable way. Moreover, on such countable structures $\mathbf{A}$ there is a binary USO-definable relation whose projections are exactly all unary USO-definable relations (such relations are called *universal* USO-definable relations). Using this fact and a diagonalization argument, it can be shown that the USO-definable relations on such structures $\mathbf{A}$ are not closed under complements. In particular, the LFP$_1$-definable relations on $\mathbf{N}$ are not closed under complements.

Chandra and Harel [10] initiated the study of LFP on finite structures; moreover, motivated by the Kleene–Spector Theorem, they conjectured that the LFP$_1$-definable queries on the class $\mathcal{G}$ of all finite graphs were *not* closed under complements. This conjecture, however, was refuted by Immerman [38, 39], who showed that if $\mathcal{C}$ is an arbitrary class of finite structures, then $\mathrm{LFP}_1(\mathcal{C})$ is closed under complements. In what follows, we shall outline a proof of this result and, in the process of doing so, we shall present some other fundamental properties of LFP_1.

Definition 2.6.28. *Let σ be a vocabulary.*

- *Let $\varphi(x_1, \ldots, x_k, S)$ be a first-order formula that is positive in S over the vocabulary $\sigma \cup \{S\}$. For every σ-structure $\mathbf{A}$ and every k-tuple $\mathbf{a} \in A^k$, we write*

$$|\mathbf{a}|_\varphi = \begin{cases} \min\{\alpha : \mathbf{A} \models \varphi^\alpha(\mathbf{a})\} & \text{if } \mathbf{A} \models \varphi^\infty(\mathbf{a}) \\ \infty & \text{if } \mathbf{A} \models \neg\varphi^\infty(\mathbf{a}) \end{cases}$$

- *Let $\varphi(\mathbf{x}, S)$ be a first-order formula that is positive in S over $\sigma \cup \{S\}$ and let $\psi(\mathbf{y}, T)$ be a first-order formula that is positive in T over $\sigma \cup \{T\}$. The* stage comparison queries *$\preceq^*_{\varphi,\psi}$ and $\prec^*_{\varphi,\psi}$ associated with the formulas $\varphi(\mathbf{x}, S)$ and $\psi(\mathbf{y}, T)$ are the queries such that for every σ-structure $\mathbf{A}$,*

$$\mathbf{a} \preceq^*_{\varphi,\psi} \mathbf{b} \iff \varphi^\infty(\mathbf{a}) \wedge (|\mathbf{a}|_\varphi \leq |\mathbf{b}|_\psi)$$

$$\mathbf{a} \prec^*_{\varphi,\psi} \mathbf{b} \iff |\mathbf{a}|_\varphi < |\mathbf{b}|_\psi.$$

Note that if $\mathbf{a} \prec^*_{\varphi,\psi} \mathbf{b}$, then $|\mathbf{a}|_\varphi < \infty$ and, thus, $\mathbf{a} \in \varphi^\infty$.

- *We write $\preceq^*_\varphi$ and $\prec_\varphi$ for the queries $\preceq^*_{\varphi,\varphi}$ and $\prec_{\varphi,\varphi}$, respectively.*

The next two examples illustrate the meaning of the stage comparison queries $\preceq^*_\varphi$ and $\prec_\varphi$ for concrete formulas φ.

Example 2.6.29. Let $\mathbf{G} = (V, E)$ be a graph and let $\varphi(x, y, S)$ be the formula

$$E(x, y) \vee (\exists z)(E(x, z) \wedge S(z, y)),$$

whose least fixed point defines the transitive closure of E. A moment's reflection reveals that $\preceq^*_\varphi$ is the *distance query* on graphs. More precisely, $(a, a') \preceq^*_\varphi (b, b')$ holds if and only if there is a path from a to a' and either there is no path from b to b' or the length of the shortest path from a to a' is at most equal to the length of the shortest path from b to b'.

Example 2.6.30. As in Examples 2.6.7 and 2.6.19, assume that a proof system is encoded by a structure $\mathbf{S} = (F, A, R)$, where F is a set of formulas, A is a set of axioms, and R is a ternary rule of inference. Let $\psi(x, T)$ be the formula

$$A(x) \vee (\exists y)(\exists z)(T(y) \wedge T(z) \wedge R(x, y, z)),$$

whose least fixed point defines the set of all theorems of this proof system. Then the stage comparison queries $\preceq^*_\psi$ and $\prec^*_\psi$ compare lengths of derivations of theorems of $\mathbf{S}$. In particular, $f \prec^*_\psi g$ holds if and only if f is a theorem of $\mathbf{S}$ and either g is not a theorem of $\mathbf{S}$ or f has a derivation in the proof system $\mathbf{S}$ that is shorter than any derivation of g.

Theorem 2.6.31. (The Stage Comparison Theorem [54].) *Let σ be a vocabulary. If $\varphi(\mathbf{x}, S)$ and $\psi(\mathbf{y}, T)$ are positive first-order formulas, then the stage comparison queries $\preceq^*_{\varphi,\psi}$ and $\prec^*_{\varphi,\psi}$ are LFP_1-definable on the class of all σ-structures.*

Proof. (Hint) The stage comparison queries satisfy the equivalences

$$\mathbf{x} \preceq^*_{\varphi,\psi} \mathbf{y} \iff \Phi^{|\mathbf{y}|_\psi}(\mathbf{x}) \iff \Phi(\mathbf{x}, \{\mathbf{x}' : |\mathbf{x}'|_\varphi < |\mathbf{y}|_\psi\})$$
$$\mathbf{x} \prec^*_{\varphi,\psi} \mathbf{y} \iff \neg\Psi^{|\mathbf{x}|_\varphi}(\mathbf{y}) \iff \neg\Psi(\mathbf{y}, \{\mathbf{y}' : |\mathbf{y}'|_\psi < |\mathbf{x}|_\varphi\}).$$

Note that if $\mathbf{x} \in \varphi^\infty$, then, for every $\mathbf{y}'$, we have that $|\mathbf{y}'|_\psi < |\mathbf{x}|_\varphi$ holds if and only if $\neg(\mathbf{x} \preceq^*_{\varphi,\psi} \mathbf{y}')$. It follows that the stage comparison queries satisfy the following recursive specifications:

$$\mathbf{x} \preceq^*_{\varphi,\psi} \mathbf{y} \iff \varphi(\mathbf{x}, \{\mathbf{x}' : \mathbf{x}' \prec^*_{\varphi,\psi} \mathbf{y}\})$$
$$\mathbf{x} \prec^*_{\varphi,\psi} \mathbf{y} \iff \neg\psi(\mathbf{y}, \{\mathbf{y}' : \neg (\mathbf{x} \preceq^*_{\varphi,\psi} \mathbf{y}')\}).$$

This motivates us to consider the system $(\chi_1(x, y, S_1, S_2), \chi_2(x, y, S_1, S_2))$ of the first-order formulas

$$\chi_1(x, y, S_1, S_2) \equiv \varphi(\mathbf{x}, \{\mathbf{x}' : S_2(\mathbf{x}', \mathbf{y})\})$$
$$\chi_2(x, y, S_1, S_2) \equiv \neg\psi(\mathbf{y}, \{\mathbf{y}' : \neg S_1(\mathbf{x}, \mathbf{y}')\}).$$

Note that these formulas are positive in both S_1 and S_2, and thus their system has a least fixed point $(\chi_1^\infty, \chi_2^\infty)$. Using transfinite induction, it can be shown that χ_1^∞ defines $\preceq^*_{\varphi,\psi}$, and that χ_2^∞ defines $\prec^*_{\varphi,\psi}$. □

While the Stage Comparison Theorem is a result about the class of all structures, the next theorem is rather special to classes of finite structures.

Theorem 2.6.32. (The Complementation Theorem for LFP_1 [38, 39].) *Let σ be a vocabulary. If $\mathcal{C}$ is a class of finite σ-structures, then $\mathrm{LFP}_1(\mathcal{C})$ is closed under complements.*

Proof. (Sketch) It suffices to show that if $\varphi(\mathbf{x}, S)$ is a first-order formula that is positive in S over the vocabulary $\sigma \cup \{S\}$, then the complement $\neg\varphi^\infty$ is LFP_1-definable on $\mathcal{C}$.

Let Max_φ be the query that, given a σ-structure $\mathbf{A}$, returns the set of all tuples $\mathbf{a}$ in φ^∞ on $\mathbf{A}$ such that, for every $\mathbf{b} \in \varphi^\infty$ on $\mathbf{A}$, we have that $|\mathbf{b}|_\varphi \leq |\mathbf{a}|_\varphi$. In other words, $\mathrm{Max}_\varphi(\mathbf{A})$ consists of all tuples from $\mathbf{A}$ that enter the "last" stage of the evaluation of φ^∞ on $\mathbf{A}$. Note that if $\mathbf{A}$ is an infinite structure, then $\mathrm{Max}_\varphi(\mathbf{A})$ may be empty, because there may be no "last" stage in the evaluation of φ (this happens precisely when the closure ordinal $\mathrm{cl}\varphi$ on $\mathbf{A}$ is a limit ordinal). For instance, this is the case when $\mathbf{G} = (V, E)$ is a graph of infinite diameter and $\varphi(x, y, S)$ is the formula whose least fixed point defines the transitive closure of the edge relation E. In contrast, if $\mathbf{A}$ is a finite structure, then $\mathrm{Max}_\varphi(\mathbf{A}) \neq \emptyset$ (unless $\varphi^\infty = \emptyset$ on $\mathbf{A}$).

We shall now show that Max_φ is LFP_1-definable on the class of all finite σ-structures. Note that Max_φ satisfies the equivalence

$$\mathbf{a} \in \text{Max}_\varphi(\mathbf{A}) \iff \mathbf{A} \models (\mathbf{a} \in \varphi^\infty) \wedge (\forall \mathbf{b})(|\mathbf{a}|_\varphi < |\mathbf{b}|_\varphi \to |\mathbf{a}|_\varphi + 1 < |\mathbf{b}|_\varphi).$$

It is easy to find a positive first-order formula ψ such that, on finite structures, ψ simulates φ with a "one-step" delay, that is, for every tuple $\mathbf{c} \in \varphi^\infty$, we have that $\mathbf{c}$ enters ψ^∞ exactly one stage after the stage where it enters φ^∞. Using stage comparison queries, the above equivalence can be rewritten as

$$\mathbf{a} \in \text{Max}_\varphi(\mathbf{A}) \iff \mathbf{A} \models (\mathbf{a} \in \varphi^\infty) \wedge (\forall \mathbf{b})((\mathbf{b} \preceq^*_\varphi \mathbf{a}) \vee (\mathbf{a} \prec^*_{\psi,\varphi} \mathbf{b})).$$

The Stage Comparison Theorem (Theorem 2.6.31) immediately implies that Max_φ is LFP_1-definable on the class of all finite σ-structures.

It is now easy to show that the complement $\neg\varphi^\infty$ is LFP_1-definable on the class of all finite σ-structures. Indeed, if $\mathbf{A}$ is a finite σ-structure, then

$$\mathbf{A} \models \neg\varphi^\infty(\mathbf{a}) \iff \mathbf{A} \models (\exists \mathbf{y})(\mathbf{y} \in \text{Max}_\varphi \wedge \mathbf{y} \prec^*_\varphi \mathbf{a}). \quad \square$$

With some extra work and using the ideas in the proof of Theorem 2.6.32, it is possible to establish the following *normal form* for least fixed-point logic LFP on classes of finite structures.

Theorem 2.6.33. [38, 39] *If σ is a vocabulary and $\mathcal{C}$ is a class of finite σ-structures, then every LFP-definable query on $\mathcal{C}$ is LFP_1-definable on $\mathcal{C}$. Consequently, $\text{LFP}(\mathcal{C}) = \text{LFP}_1(\mathcal{C})$.*

Informally, this result asserts that on finite structures the nesting of least fixed points, greatest fixed points, and negations can be eliminated and reduced to a single formation of the least fixed point of a positive first-order formula combined with the positive operations of first-order logic (disjunction, conjunction, and universal and existential quantification).

2.6.5 Partial Fixed-Point Logic

The fundamental idea behind least fixed-point logic LFP is that recursive specifications involving positive first-order formulas can be given meaningful fixed point semantics, because, by the Knaster-Tarski Theorem (Theorem 2.6.2), every positive first-order formula has a least fixed point. Can more powerful logics be obtained by giving fixed point semantics to specifications involving arbitrary (not just positive) first-order formulas? There are two main motivations behind this question, which we now describe briefly.

Recall that on every class of finite structures, least fixed-point logic is at least as expressive as first-order logic, but it is no more expressive than polynomial-time computability. In particular, on the class of all finite structures, LFP cannot express every polynomial-time-computable query, even though it can express P-complete queries. As discussed at length in Chap. 3 of this volume, one of the outstanding open problems in finite model theory is whether or not there is *a logic that captures* P on the class of all finite structures. This has motivated the study of fixed-point logics that are at least as expressive as least fixed-point logic, but are still within the realm of polynomial-time computability on finite structures. One such logic is *inflationary fixed-point logic* IFP, which, however, was shown by Gurevich and Shelah [35] to have the same expressive power as LFP on classes of finite structures (see Chap. 3 for the precise definitions of IFP and a presentation of some of its main properties on finite structures).

The second motivation for studying logics with more powerful fixed point mechanisms has to do with the problem of finding logics that can express queries in higher computational-complexity classes, beyond P and NP. The most prominent logic in this family is *partial fixed-point logic*, whose main features we shall describe in the remainder of this section.

Let $\Phi : \mathcal{P}(A^k) \to \mathcal{P}(A^k)$ be an arbitrary (not necessarily monotone) k-ary operator on a finite set A. As seen earlier, the finite stages Φ^n, $n \geq 1$, of Φ are defined by the induction

$$\left| \begin{aligned} \Phi^1 &= \Phi(\emptyset) \\ \Phi^{n+1} &= \Phi(\Phi^n). \end{aligned} \right.$$

If Φ is not monotone, then the sequence Φ^n, $n \geq 1$, need not be an increasing one. Nonetheless, since A is a finite set and each Φ_n is a k-ary relation on A, there must exist two positive integers m and m' such that $m < m'$ and $\Phi^m = \Phi^{m'}$. Let m' be the smallest integer greater than m having this property. If $m' = m + 1$, then Φ^m is actually a fixed point of Φ, and thus the sequence of stages of Φ converges to this fixed point. If, however, $m' > m + 1$, then the sequence of stages of Φ cycles without ever reaching a fixed point of Φ. This state of affairs motivates us to use the concept of the *partial fixed point* of an operator Φ.

Definition 2.6.34. *Let* $\Phi : \mathcal{P}(A^k) \to \mathcal{P}(A^k)$ *be an arbitrary (not necessarily monotone) k-ary operator on a finite set A. The* partial fixed point **pfp**(Φ) *of Φ is a stage Φ^m such that $\Phi^m = \Phi^{m+1}$, if such a stage exists, or the empty relation $\emptyset$ otherwise.*

If **A** *is a finite structure and Φ is the operator associated with some formula $\varphi(x_1, \ldots, x_k, S)$ on* **A***, then the* partial fixed point **pfp**(φ) *of $\varphi(x_1, \ldots, x_k, S)$ is the partial fixed point* **pfp**(Φ) *of Φ.*

Abiteboul and Vianu [2] introduced *partial fixed-point logic* PFP on finite structures, which is the extension of first-order logic obtained by augmenting the syntax and the semantics with partial fixed points of formulas.

Definition 2.6.35. *Let σ be a vocabulary.*

- *The collection of* PFP-*formulas over σ is defined inductively by adding the following rule to the rules for the syntax of first-order logic. Assume that φ is a* PFP-*formula, S is a k-ary relation symbol in* free(φ), $\mathbf{x} = (x_1, \ldots, x_k)$ *is a k-tuple of first-order variables each of which is in* free(φ), *and $\mathbf{u} = (u_1, \ldots, u_k)$ is a k-tuple of first-order variables not occurring in φ. Then the expression* $[\mathbf{pfp}\ S.\varphi](\mathbf{u})$ *is a* PFP-*formula; moreover,* free($[\mathbf{pfp}\ S.S](\mathbf{u})$) = free($\varphi$) $\setminus \{x_1 \ldots, x_k, S\}$.

- *If $\mathbf{A}$ is a finite σ-structure, and $\mathbf{a}$ is a k-tuple from $\mathbf{A}$, then $\mathbf{A}, \mathbf{a} \models$* $[\mathbf{pfp}\ S.\varphi](\mathbf{u})$ *if $\mathbf{a} \in \mathbf{pfp}(\Phi)$, where Φ is the operator associated with φ on $\mathbf{A}$.*

Clearly, if $\varphi(x_1, \ldots, x_k, S)$ is a formula that is positive in S, then the partial fixed point $\mathbf{pfp}(\varphi)$ of φ is equal to its least fixed point $\mathbf{lfp}(\varphi)$. It follows that on finite structures, partial fixed-point logic PFP is at least as expressive as least fixed-point logic LFP. More precisely, if $\mathcal{C}$ is a class of finite structures, then

$$\text{LFP}(\mathcal{C}) \subseteq \text{PFP}(\mathcal{C}).$$

Let $\varphi(x_1, \ldots, x_k, S)$ be an arbitrary first-order formula over the vocabulary $\sigma \cup \{S\}$, where S is a k-ary relation symbol. It is easy to see that, on every finite structure $\mathbf{A}$, the partial fixed point $\mathbf{pfp}(\varphi)$ can be evaluated in polynomial space. To do this, one has to compute in succession the stages Φ^n of the operator Φ associated with $\varphi(x_1, \ldots, x_k, S)$, while at the same time maintaining a counter that stores in binary the number n of the current stage. At any given time in this computation, a polynomial amount of space is used to store the current stage Φ^n, to compute the next stage Φ^{n+1}, and to test whether $\Phi^{n+1} = \Phi^n$. If $\Phi^{n+1} = \Phi^n$, then the computation terminates and returns Φ^n as the value of the partial fixed point $\mathbf{pfp}(\varphi)$ of $\varphi(x_1, \ldots, x_k, S)$ on $\mathbf{A}$. Otherwise, Φ^n is replaced by Φ^{n+1} and the counter is incremented by one. If at some point the value of the counter exceeds $2^{|A|^k}$ (which is the total number of k-ary relations on A), then the computation terminates and returns the empty relation $\emptyset$ as the value of the partial fixed point $\mathbf{pfp}(\varphi)$ of $\varphi(x_1, \ldots, x_k, S)$ on $\mathbf{A}$. Thus, on every class $\mathcal{C}$ of finite structures, we have that

$$\text{LFP}(\mathcal{C}) \subseteq \text{PFP}(\mathcal{C}) \subseteq \text{PSPACE}.$$

The next example shows that PFP can actually express PSPACE-complete queries.

Example 2.6.36. GENERALIZED PATH SYSTEMS. Let σ be a vocabulary consisting of a unary relation symbol and a ternary relation symbol. As in Example 2.6.7, a σ-structure is of the form $\mathbf{S} = (F, A, R)$, where A is a subset of F and R is a ternary relation on F; moreover, such a structure can be interpreted as consisting of a set F of formulas, a set A of axioms, and a ternary rule of inference R. Let $\varphi(x, T)$ be the following existential first-order formula over the vocabulary $\sigma \cup \{T\}$:

$$A(x) \vee (\exists y)(\exists z)(T(y) \wedge \neg T(z) \wedge R(x, y, z)).$$

Intuitively, a fixed point of this formula can be viewed as a recursive specification of a nonmonotonic proof system in which a formula x is a *theorem* of the system if it is an axiom in A or it can be derived from the rule of inference R using a theorem y of the proof system and a nontheorem z of the proof system.

Let $\mathbf{pfp}(\varphi)$ be the partial fixed point of the formula $\varphi(x, T)$. Grohe [33] showed that evaluating $\mathbf{pfp}(\varphi)$ on finite σ-structures is a PSPACE-complete problem. It follows that, unless P = PSPACE, the partial fixed point $\mathbf{pfp}(\varphi)$ cannot be evaluated in polynomial time and, a fortiori, it cannot be expressed in LFP.

The preceding remarks and Example 2.6.36 imply the following result concerning the data complexity of PFP.

Proposition 2.6.37. *The data complexity of* PFP *is* PSPACE-*complete.*

Let σ be a vocabulary containing at least one relation symbol of arity 2 or higher, and let $\mathcal{F}$ be the class of all finite σ-structures. Although PFP can express P-complete queries on $\mathcal{F}$, it cannot express every polynomial-time computable query on $\mathcal{F}$. Indeed, in the next section we shall show that the expressive power of PFP on $\mathcal{F}$ has limitations that are similar to those of LFP on $\mathcal{F}$, namely, PFP cannot express *counting* queries, such as EVEN CARDINALITY. Thus, the following proper containment holds on $\mathcal{F}$:

$$\text{PFP}(\mathcal{F}) \subset \text{PSPACE}.$$

The state of affairs, however, is different on classes of ordered finite structures.

Theorem 2.6.38. [2, 67]. *Let $\mathcal{C}$ be a class of ordered finite structures. The following are equivalent for a query Q on $\mathcal{C}$:*

- *Q is polynomial-space computable.*
- *Q is PFP-definable on $\mathcal{C}$.*

In other words, PSPACE$(\mathcal{C})$ = PFP$(\mathcal{C})$.

Chapter 3 contains a proof of the above theorem. Here, we discuss briefly the history of this result and state who should be credited with the various parts of the work. Chandra and Harel [11] introduced and studied a logic called RQL, which is an extension of first-order logic FO with recursion embodied in the form of WHILE looping. Vardi [67] proved that on classes of ordered finite structures, a query is polynomial-space computable if and only if it is RQL-definable. Later on, Abiteboul and Vianu [2] introduced partial fixed-point logic PFP and showed that on classes of finite structures, RQL has the same expressive power as PFP. From these results, it follows that PSPACE $=$ PFP on every class $\mathcal{C}$ of ordered finite structures.

In this section, we have shown that on the class $\mathcal{F}$ of all finite σ-structures, LFP can express P-complete problems and PFP can express PSPACE-complete problems. At the same time, we have asserted that these logics cannot express such basic counting properties as EVEN CARDINALITY on $\mathcal{F}$, but have given no proof of this fact. This will be done in the next section, where we shall bring into the picture a family of infinitary logics with finitely many variables, shall introduce new combinatorial games for analyzing their expressive power, and shall apply the methodology of games to derive lower bounds for expressibility in fixed-point logics and in infinitary logics with finitely many variables.

2.7 Infinitary Logics with Finitely Many Variables

The syntax of the logics that we have encountered thus far is finitary. Mathematical logicians, however, have also investigated in depth logics whose syntax has infinitary constructs. Such logics can be obtained by augmenting the syntax of first-order logic with disjunctions and conjunctions over infinite sets of formulas, with infinite strings of quantifiers, or with both these types of constructs. Moreover, different families of infinitary logics can be obtained by imposing cardinality restrictions on the size of the infinitary constructs allowed (see [17, 41]). The infinitary logic $L_{\infty\omega}$ is the most powerful among all logics with infinitary connectives and with finite strings of quantifiers. In addition to the rules of first-order logic, the syntax of $L_{\infty\omega}$ has the following two rules:

- If Φ is an arbitrary set of $L_{\infty\omega}$-formulas, then the infinitary disjunction $\bigvee \Phi$ is also an $L_{\infty\omega}$-formula.
- If Φ is an arbitrary set of $L_{\infty\omega}$-formulas, then the infinitary conjunction $\bigwedge \Phi$ is also an $L_{\infty\omega}$-formula.

The infinitary formulas $\bigvee \Phi$ and $\bigwedge \Phi$ have straightforward semantics. For instance, if Φ is a set of $L_{\infty\omega}$-sentences and $\mathbf{A}$ is a structure, then $\mathbf{A} \models \bigvee \Phi$ if and only if there is at least one $L_{\infty\omega}$-sentence φ in Φ such that $\mathbf{A} \models \varphi$.

Although $L_{\infty\omega}$ can make interesting distinctions on infinite structures, it turns out that this logic is too powerful on classes of finite structures to be of any use. Specifically, it is easy to see that *every* Boolean query Q on the class $\mathcal{F}$ of all finite σ-structures is $L_{\infty\omega}$-definable. For every finite structure $\mathbf{A}$, let $\psi_{\mathbf{A}}$ be a first-order sentence that defines $\mathbf{A}$ up to isomorphism; such a sentence asserts that there are precisely as many elements as the cardinality of the universe A of $\mathbf{A}$, and states which tuples are in the relations of $\mathbf{A}$ and which are not. Since Boolean queries are closed under isomorphisms, Q is definable by the $L_{\infty\omega}$-sentence $\bigvee_{\{\mathbf{A}:Q(\mathbf{A})=1\}} \psi_{\mathbf{A}}$. Note that Q is also definable by the $L_{\infty\omega}$-sentence $\bigwedge_{\{\mathbf{A}:Q(\mathbf{A})=0\}} \neg\psi_{\mathbf{A}}$. Thus, every query on the class $\mathcal{F}$

of all finite σ-structures can be defined by both a countable disjunction of first-order formulas and a countable conjunction of first-order formulas.

2.7.1 The Infinitary Logic $L^{\omega}_{\infty\omega}$

In general, $L_{\infty\omega}$-formulas may have an infinite number of distinct variables. Barwise [8] introduced a family of fragments of $L_{\infty\omega}$ in which there is a finite upper bound on the number of distinct variables in each formula.

Definition 2.7.1. *Let σ be a vocabulary.*

- *For every positive integer k, we write FO^k to denote the collection of all first-order formulas over σ with at most k distinct variables.*
- *For every positive integer k, the k-variable infinitary logic $L^k_{\infty\omega}$ is the collection of all $L_{\infty\omega}$-formulas over σ with at most k distinct variables.*
- *The finite-variable infinitary logic $L^{\omega}_{\infty\omega}$ is the collection of all $L_{\infty\omega}$-formulas over σ with finitely many variables, that is,*

$$L^{\omega}_{\infty\omega} = \bigcup_{k \geq 1} L^k_{\infty\omega}.$$

Note that, although each $L^k_{\infty\omega}$-formula has at most k distinct variables, there is no restriction on the number of occurrences of each variable in the formula. In particular, even FO^k-formulas may be of unbounded quantifier rank. In many cases, this makes it possible to define interesting properties by judiciously reusing the available variables, in spite of the limited supply of distinct variables. To illustrate this point, for every positive integer m, let θ_m be a first-order sentence asserting that there are at least m elements in the universe of the structure. It can be shown that on the class $\mathcal{G}$ of all finite graphs, θ_m is *not* equivalent to any first-order sentence with fewer than m variables. In contrast, it is easy to see that on the class $\mathcal{L}$ of all finite linear orders, θ_m is equivalent to a sentence of FO^2. For instance, θ_4 is equivalent to the FO^2-sentence

$$(\exists x)(\exists y)[y < x \wedge (\exists x)(x < y \wedge (\exists y)(y < x))].$$

It follows that $L^2_{\infty\omega}$ can define arbitrary cardinalities on $\mathcal{L}$, since, for every set S of integers, we have that

$$n \in S \Longleftrightarrow L_n \models \bigvee_{m \in S} (\theta_m \wedge \neg\theta_{m+1}).$$

In particular, the EVEN CARDINALITY query is $L^2_{\infty\omega}$-definable on $\mathcal{L}$.

The original motivation behind the introduction of finite-variable infinitary logics was to study inductive definability on fixed infinite structures. Indeed, Barwise [8] used the infinitary logics $L^k_{\infty\omega}$, $k \geq 1$, as a tool to solve an open problem concerning the closure ordinals of positive first-order formulas on fixed infinite structures. Since the 1980s, however, these logics have found many uses and applications in finite model theory, where they have become quite indispensable in the study of fixed-point logics. The main reason for this is that on classes of finite structures, $L_{\infty\omega}^{\omega}$ subsumes the fixed-point logics LFP and PFP that we encountered earlier. Moreover, definability in the infinitary logics $L_{\infty\omega}^{k}$, $k \geq 1$, can be characterized in terms of certain combinatorial games in a manner analogous to the characterization of first-order definability in terms of Ehrenfeucht–Fraïssé games.

Before spelling out the connection between fixed-point logics and $L_{\infty\omega}^{\omega}$ in more precise terms, we present a relevant example. Let $\varphi^{n}(x, y)$ be the first-order formula

$$(\exists z_1)\ldots(\exists z_{n-1})(E(x, z_1) \wedge \ldots \wedge E(z_{n-1}, y)),$$

which defines the query "there is a path of length n from x to y", $n \geq 1$. At first sight, it appears that this query cannot be expressed with fewer than $n + 1$ variables, since, in addition to the variables x and y, another $n - 1$ variables seem to be needed in order to describe the intermediate nodes on a path of length n from x to y. It turns out, however, that just three variables, x, y, and z, suffice to express this query; the third variable z can be repeatedly reused in such a way that it ranges over the intermediate points on a path from x to y. Specifically, it can be shown by induction on n that each formula $\varphi^{n}(x, y)$ is equivalent to an FO^{3}-formula $\psi^{n}(x, y)$ whose variables are among x, y, and z. First, $\psi^{1}(x, y)$ is equivalent to the atomic formula $E(x, y)$. Assume now that $\varphi^{n}(x, y)$ is equivalent to an FO^{3}-formula $\psi^{n}(x, y)$ whose variables are x, y, and z. Then $\varphi^{n+1}(x, y)$ is equivalent to the FO^{3}-formula

$$(\exists z)[E(x, z) \wedge (\exists x)(z = x \wedge \psi^{n}(x, y))],$$

whose variables are x, y, and z. Consequently, the CONNECTIVITY query is $L_{\infty\omega}^{3}$-definable by the sentence

$$(\forall x)(\forall y)(\bigvee_{n \geq 1} \psi^{n}(x, y)).$$

The preceding construction can be extended and applied to the stages of every first-order-definable operator; this makes it possible to show that the stages of every first-order-definable operator are definable by an $L_{\infty\omega}^{k}$-formula for some positive integer k that depends only on the formula defining the operator and not on the particular level of the stage. A detailed proof of the next result can be found in [46, 49]

Theorem 2.7.2. *Assume that σ is a vocabulary, S is a m-ary relation symbol not in σ, and $\varphi(x_1, \ldots, x_m, S)$ is a first-order formula over the vocabulary $\sigma \cup \{S\}$ such that the number of variables (free and bound) of $\varphi(x_1, \ldots, x_m, S)$ is equal to k.*

- *For every positive integer $n \geq 1$, there is an FO^{k}-formula $\varphi^{n}(x_1, \ldots, x_m)$ that defines the nth stage Φ^{n} of the operator Φ associated with the formula $\varphi(x_1, \ldots, x_m, S)$ on every σ-structure.*

- *The partial fixed point* $\mathbf{pfp}(\varphi)$ *of* $\varphi(x_1, \ldots, x_m, S)$ *is* $L^k_{\infty\omega}$*-definable on the class of all finite* σ*-structures.*

Consequently, if $\mathcal{C}$ *is a class of finite* σ*-structures, then*

$$\mathrm{LFP}(\mathcal{C}) \subseteq \mathrm{PFP}(\mathcal{C}) \subseteq L^\omega_{\infty\omega}(\mathcal{C}).$$

For arbitrary first-order formulas $\varphi(x_1, \ldots, x_m, S)$, only the finite stages of the associated operator were defined earlier. Recall, however, that if $\varphi(x_1, \ldots, x_m, S)$ is a positive first-order formula, we have actually defined the stages Φ^α of the associated operator Φ for an arbitrary ordinal α (Definition 2.6.1). It can be shown that each such stage Φ^α is definable by an $L^k_{\infty\omega}$-formula, where k is the number of variables (free and bound) in $\varphi(x_1, \ldots, x_m, S)$. It is not true, however, that every LFP-definable query on the class $\mathcal{S}$ of all σ-structures is $L^\omega_{\infty\omega}$-definable. For instance, the WELL-FOUNDEDNESS query is LFP-definable on $\mathcal{S}$, but it is not $L_{\infty\omega}$-definable on $\mathcal{S}$ (see [17]); consequently, this query is not $L^\omega_{\infty\omega}$-definable either. Intuitively, $L^\omega_{\infty\omega}$ cannot subsume LFP on the class $\mathcal{S}$ of all σ-structures, because the closure ordinals of positive first-order formulas can be arbitrarily large and so the least fixed point of a positive formula cannot be obtained by taking the disjunction over the formulas defining the stages of the formula (this would require taking a disjunction over a proper class, which is not allowed in the syntax of $L_{\infty\omega}$). It is true, however, that if $\mathcal{C}$ is a class of σ-structures of bounded cardinality (that is, there is a cardinal number λ such that the universe of each structure in $\mathcal{C}$ has cardinality at most λ), then $\mathrm{LFP}(\mathcal{C}) \subseteq L^\omega_{\infty\omega}(\mathcal{C})$.

2.7.2 Pebble Games and $L^\omega_{\infty\omega}$-Definability

The finite-variable infinitary logic $L^\omega_{\infty\omega}$ can be used as a tool in studying fixed-point logics on finite structures. In particular, certain structural properties of $L^\omega_{\infty\omega}$ are inherited by the fixed-point logics LFP and PFP. Moreover, lower bounds for definability in $L^\omega_{\infty\omega}$ yield immediately similar results for definability in LFP and PFP. The advantage of $L^\omega_{\infty\omega}$ over LFP and PFP is that, for every positive integer k, definability in $L^\omega_{\infty\omega}$ can be characterized in terms of combinatorial k-*pebble games*, which we introduce next.

Definition 2.7.3. *Let* k *be a positive integer,* σ *a vocabulary, and* **A** *and* **B** *two* σ*-structures.*

The k-*pebble game on* **A** *and* **B** *is played between two players, called the* Spoiler *and the* Duplicator, *each of whom has* k *pebbles that are labeled* $1, \ldots, k$. *In each move, the Spoiler selects one of the two structures and either places a pebble that is not currently used on an element of the chosen structure or removes a pebble from an element of the chosen structure. The Duplicator responds by either placing the pebble with the same label on an element of the other structure or by removing the pebble with the same label from an element of the other structure.*

Assume that at some point in time during the game, r pebbles have been placed on each structure, where $1 \leq r \leq k$, and let $(a_i, b_i) \in A \times B$, $1 \leq i \leq r$, be the pairs of elements of $\mathbf{A}$ and $\mathbf{B}$ such that the label of the pebble on a_i is the same as the label of the pebble on b_i. The Spoiler wins the k-pebble game on $\mathbf{A}$ and $\mathbf{B}$ at this point in time if the mapping $a_i \mapsto b_i$, $1 \leq i \leq r$, is not an isomorphism between the substructures of $\mathbf{A}$ and $\mathbf{B}$ generated by $\{a_1, \ldots, a_r\}$ and $\{b_1, \ldots, b_r\}$, respectively.

The Duplicator wins the k-pebble game on $\mathbf{A}$ and $\mathbf{B}$ if the above never happens, which means that the Duplicator has a winning strategy that allows him to continue playing "forever" by maintaining a partial isomorphism at every point in time.

The above description of a winning strategy for the Duplicator in the k-pebble game is rather informal. The concept of a winning strategy can be made precise, however, in terms of families of partial isomorphisms with appropriate closure and extension properties. Recall that a partial isomorphism from a σ-structure $\mathbf{A}$ to a σ-structure $\mathbf{B}$ is an isomorphism from a substructure of $\mathbf{A}$ to a substructure of $\mathbf{B}$. In particular, every partial isomorphism from $\mathbf{A}$ to $\mathbf{B}$ must map each constant $c_j^{\mathbf{A}}$ of $\mathbf{A}$ to the constant $c_j^{\mathbf{B}}$ of $\mathbf{B}$, $1 \leq j \leq s$, where s is the number of distinct constant symbols in σ. Thus, when viewed as a set of ordered pairs, each partial isomorphism from $\mathbf{A}$ to $\mathbf{B}$ must contain all pairs $(c_j^{\mathbf{A}}, c_j^{\mathbf{B}})$, $1 \leq j \leq s$.

Definition 2.7.4. *A winning strategy for the Duplicator in the k-pebble game on $\mathbf{A}$ and $\mathbf{B}$ is a nonempty family $\mathcal{I}$ of partial isomorphisms from $\mathbf{A}$ to $\mathbf{B}$ with the following properties:*

1. *If $f \in \mathcal{I}$, then $|f - \{(c_1^{\mathbf{A}}, c_1^{\mathbf{B}}), \ldots, (c_s^{\mathbf{A}}, c_s^{\mathbf{B}})\}| \leq k$.*
2. *$\mathcal{I}$ is closed under subfunctions:*
   If $g \in \mathcal{I}$ and f is a function such that $\{(c_1^{\mathbf{A}}, c_1^{\mathbf{B}}), \ldots, (c_s^{\mathbf{A}}, c_s^{\mathbf{B}})\} \subseteq f \subseteq g$, then $f \in \mathcal{I}$.
3. *$\mathcal{I}$ has the forth property up to k:*
   If $f \in \mathcal{I}$ and $|f - \{(c_1^{\mathbf{A}}, c_1^{\mathbf{B}}), \ldots, (c_s^{\mathbf{A}}, c_s^{\mathbf{B}})\}| < k$, then for every $a \in A$, there is a $g \in \mathcal{I}$ such that $f \subseteq g$ and $a \in \mathrm{dom}(g)$.
4. *$\mathcal{I}$ has the back property up to k:*
   If $f \in \mathcal{I}$ and $|f - \{(c_1^{\mathbf{A}}, c_1^{\mathbf{B}}), \ldots, (c_s^{\mathbf{A}}, c_s^{\mathbf{B}})\}| < k$, then for every $b \in B$, there is a $g \in \mathcal{I}$ such that $f \subseteq g$ and $b \in \mathrm{rng}(g)$.

Intuitively, the second condition provides the Duplicator with a "good" move when the Spoiler removes a pebble from an element of $\mathbf{A}$ or $\mathbf{B}$, while the last two conditions provide the Duplicator with "good" moves when the Spoiler places a pebble on an element of $\mathbf{A}$ or of $\mathbf{B}$.

Several properties of the k-pebble game follow easily from the definitions. For instance, if $k' \geq k$ and the Spoiler wins the k-pebble game on $\mathbf{A}$ and $\mathbf{B}$, then the Spoiler also wins the k'-pebble game on $\mathbf{A}$ and $\mathbf{B}$. Moreover, for every $k \geq 1$, the relation "the Duplicator wins the k-pebble game on $\mathbf{A}$ and $\mathbf{B}$" is an equivalence relation on the class $\mathcal{S}$ of all σ-structures.

The following examples illustrate k-pebble games on concrete finite structures.

Example 2.7.5. For every $m \geq 1$, let $\mathbf{K}_m$ be the m-clique, that is, the complete graph with m nodes. It is quite clear that for every $k \geq 1$,

- the Duplicator wins the k-pebble game on $\mathbf{K}_k$ and $\mathbf{K}_{k+1}$;
- the Spoiler wins the $(k+1)$-pebble game on $\mathbf{K}_k$ and $\mathbf{K}_{k+1}$.

The case $k = 4$ is illustrated in Fig. 2.9.

Note that the same state of affairs holds for the Ehrenfeucht–Fraïssé game on cliques: the Duplicator wins the k-move Ehrenfeucht–Fraïssé game on $\mathbf{K}_k$ and $\mathbf{K}_{k+1}$, but the Spoiler wins the $(k+1)$-move Ehrenfeucht–Fraïssé game on $\mathbf{K}_k$ and $\mathbf{K}_{k+1}$.

Example 2.7.6. For every $m \geq 1$, let $\mathbf{L}_m$ be the linear order with m elements.

It is easy to see that for all positive integers m and n with $m < n$, the Spoiler wins the 2-pebble game on $\mathbf{L}_m$ and $\mathbf{L}_n$. In the first two moves, the Spoiler places his two pebbles on the two smallest elements of $\mathbf{L}_n$; it is then in the best interests of the Duplicator to place his two pebbles on the two smallest elements of L_m. In his next two moves, the Spoiler moves the pebble from the smallest element of $\mathbf{L}_n$ and places it on the third smallest element of $\mathbf{L}_n$; the Duplicator has to follow suit with similar moves on $\mathbf{L}_m$. By continuing playing in this way, the Spoiler forces the placement of pebbles with the same label on progressively bigger elements of the two linear orders. Since $m < n$, eventually the Duplicator "runs out of elements" in $\mathbf{L}_m$ and cannot duplicate the move of the Spoiler.

In view of Theorem 2.3.20, this example shows a dramatic difference between the pebble games and the Ehrenfeucht–Fraïssé games, since for every r and for all sufficiently large m and n, the Duplicator wins the r-move Ehrenfeucht–Fraïssé game on $\mathbf{L}_m$ and $\mathbf{L}_n$.

Example 2.7.7. For every $m \geq 3$, let $\mathbf{A}_m$ be a directed cycle with $2m$ nodes and let $\mathbf{B}_m$ be the union of two disjoint directed cycles, each with m nodes, as depicted in Fig. 2.10.

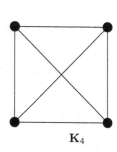

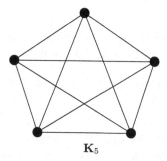

$\mathbf{K}_4$ $\qquad\qquad\qquad$ $\mathbf{K}_5$

Fig. 2.9. Graphs illustrating the 4-pebble game and the 5-pebble game

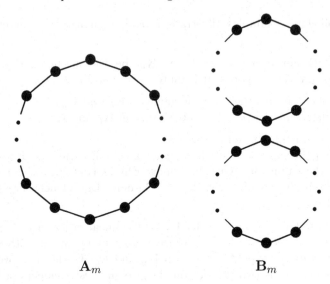

$$\mathbf{A}_m \qquad\qquad \mathbf{B}_m$$

Fig. 2.10. The Spoiler wins the 3-pebble game on $\mathbf{A}_m$ and $\mathbf{B}_m$

It is easy to see that for every $m \geq 3$, the Spoiler wins the 3-pebble game on $\mathbf{A}_m$ and $\mathbf{B}_m$. In the first two moves, the Spoiler places his first pebble on a node in the top cycle of $\mathbf{B}_m$ and his second pebble on a node in the bottom cycle of $\mathbf{B}_m$; thus, the Duplicator has to respond by placing his first two pebbles on elements of $\mathbf{A}_m$ (presumably as far apart as possible). From this point on, the Spoiler keeps his first pebble fixed in the top cycle, but uses his second and third pebbles to force a walk along edges of the bottom cycle, in the same way as the Spoiler moved from smaller to bigger elements in Example 2.7.6. Eventually, the three pebbles of the Duplicator are lined up along adjacent nodes in $\mathbf{A}_m$, but this does not hold for the pebbles of the Spoiler in $\mathbf{B}_m$.

This example should be contrasted with the fact that, as implied by the proof of Proposition 2.3.28, for every $r \geq 1$ and for all sufficiently large values of m, the Duplicator wins the r-move Ehrenfeucht–Fraïssé game on $\mathbf{A}_m$ and $\mathbf{B}_m$.

We are now ready to present the connection between k-pebble games and definability in the k-variable infinitary logics $\mathrm{L}^k_{\infty\omega}$, $k \geq 1$.

Definition 2.7.8. *Let k be a positive integer, and let $\mathbf{A}$ and $\mathbf{B}$ be two σ-structures.*

- *We say that $\mathbf{A}$ is $\mathrm{L}^k_{\infty\omega}$-equivalent to $\mathbf{B}$, denoted by $\mathbf{A} \equiv^k_{\infty\omega} \mathbf{B}$, if $\mathbf{A}$ and $\mathbf{B}$ satisfy the same $\mathrm{L}^k_{\infty\omega}$-sentences.*
- *We write $\mathbf{A} \equiv^k_{\omega\omega} \mathbf{B}$ to denote that $\mathbf{A}$ and $\mathbf{B}$ satisfy the same FO^k-sentences.*

- Let $a_1, \ldots, a_r$ be a sequence of elements from A and let $b_1, \ldots, b_r$ be a sequence of elements from B, for some $r \le k$. We say that $(\mathbf{A}, a_1, \ldots, a_r)$ is $L_{\infty\omega}^k$-equivalent to $(\mathbf{B}, b_1, \ldots, b_r)$ if, for every $L_{\infty\omega}^k$-formula $\varphi(v_1, \ldots, v_r)$ with free variables among $v_1, \ldots, v_r$, we have that

$$\mathbf{A} \models \varphi(v_1/a_1, \ldots, v_r/a_r) \iff \mathbf{B} \models \varphi(v_1/a_1, \ldots, v_r/b_r).$$

We write $(\mathbf{A}, a_1, \ldots, a_r) \equiv_{\infty\omega}^k (\mathbf{B}, b_1, \ldots, b_r)$ to denote that $(\mathbf{A}, a_1, \ldots, a_r)$ is $L_{\infty\omega}^k$-equivalent to $(\mathbf{B}, b_1, \ldots, b_r)$.

Clearly, $\equiv_{\infty\omega}^k$ is an equivalence relation on the class $\mathcal{S}$ of all σ-structures, which we call $L_{\infty\omega}^k$-*equivalence*. The next result asserts that $L_{\infty\omega}^k$-equivalence coincides with the equivalence relation that arises from the k-pebble game. Here, we shall only outline the main ideas of the proof; complete details can be found in [46].

Theorem 2.7.9. [8, 38] *Let k be a positive integer, and let $\mathbf{A}$ and $\mathbf{B}$ be two σ-structures. The following statements are then equivalent:*

- $\mathbf{A} \equiv_{\infty\omega}^k \mathbf{B}$.
- *The Duplicator wins the k-pebble game on $\mathbf{A}$ and $\mathbf{B}$.*

Moreover, if $\mathbf{A}$ and $\mathbf{B}$ are finite, then the above statements are also equivalent to

- $\mathbf{A} \equiv_{\omega\omega}^k \mathbf{B}$.

Proof. (Outline) Assume first that $\mathbf{A}$ and $\mathbf{B}$ are two σ-structures such that $\mathbf{A} \equiv_{\infty\omega}^k \mathbf{B}$. We have to show that there is a family $\mathcal{I}$ of partial isomorphisms on $\mathbf{A}$ and $\mathbf{B}$ that provides a winning strategy for Player II in the k-pebble game, as described in Definition 2.7.4.

We take $\mathcal{I}$ to be the family of all partial isomorphisms f between $\mathbf{A}$ and $\mathbf{B}$ such that the following hold:

- $|f - \{(c_1^{\mathbf{A}}, c_1^{\mathbf{B}}), \ldots, (c_1^{\mathbf{A}}, c_s^{\mathbf{B}})\}| \le k$.
- If $a_1, \ldots, a_r$ are elements in the domain of f other than the elements $c_1^{\mathbf{A}}, \ldots, c_s^{\mathbf{A}}$ interpreting the constant symbols, and $b_1 = f(a_1), \ldots, b_r = f(a_r)$ are their images under f, then $(\mathbf{A}, a_1, \ldots, a_r) \equiv_{\infty\omega}^k (\mathbf{B}, b_1, \ldots, b_r)$.

To show that $\mathcal{I}$ is a winning strategy for the Duplicator, first note that $\mathcal{I}$ is nonempty, because $\mathbf{A} \equiv_{\infty\omega}^k \mathbf{B}$, and thus the function f with $f(c_j^{\mathbf{A}}) = c_j^{\mathbf{B}}$, $1 \le j \le s$, is a member of $\mathcal{I}$ (if σ has no constant symbols, then $\mathcal{I}$ contains the empty partial isomorphism). Moreover, $\mathcal{I}$ is clearly closed under subfunctions. To show that $\mathcal{I}$ has the forth property up to k, it suffices to show that for all $r < k$, if we have two sequences of distinct elements $a_1, \ldots, a_r$ in A and $b_1, \ldots, b_r$ in B such that

$$(\mathbf{A}, a_1, \ldots, a_r) \equiv_{\infty\omega}^k (\mathbf{B}, b_1, \ldots, b_r),$$

then, for every element a in A that is different from $a_1, \ldots, a_r$, there is an element b in B that is different from $b_1, \ldots, b_r$ and is such that

$$(\mathbf{A}, a_1, \ldots, a_r, a) \equiv_{\infty\omega}^{k} (\mathbf{B}, b_1, \ldots, b_r, b).$$

Assume that no such $b \in B$ exists for a certain $a \in A$. Then, for every $b \in B$ that is different from $b_1, \ldots, b_r$, there is an $\mathrm{L}_{\infty\omega}^{k}$-formula $\psi_b(v_1, \ldots, v_r, v)$ such that

$$(\mathbf{A}, a_1, \ldots, a_r, a) \models \psi_b(v_1, \ldots, v_r, v)$$

and

$$(\mathbf{B}, b_1, \ldots, b_r, b) \not\models \psi_b(v_1, \ldots, v_r, v).$$

Hence,

$$(\mathbf{A}, a_1, \ldots, a_r) \models (\exists v) \left((v_1 \neq v) \wedge \cdots \wedge (v_r \neq v) \wedge \bigwedge_{b \in B} \psi_b(v_1, \ldots, v_r, v) \right),$$

and, at the same time,

$$(\mathbf{B}, b_1, \ldots, b_r) \not\models (\exists v) \left((v_1 \neq v) \wedge \cdots \wedge (v_r \neq v) \wedge \bigwedge_{b \in B} \psi_b(v_1, \ldots, v_m, v) \right).$$

But this is a contradiction, since

$$(\exists v) \left((v_1 \neq v) \wedge \cdots \wedge (v_m \neq v) \wedge \bigwedge_{b \in B} \psi_b(v_1, \ldots, v_m, v) \right)$$

is an $\mathrm{L}_{\infty\omega}^{k}$-formula and $(\mathbf{A}, a_1, \ldots, a_r) \equiv_{\infty\omega}^{k} (\mathbf{B}, b_1, \ldots, b_r)$. The back property up to k is established in an analogous manner, using an infinitary conjunction over elements of A. Note that if $\mathbf{A}$ and $\mathbf{B}$ are finite σ-structures, then these conjunctions are actually finitary. Using this observation, we can mimic the preceding argument with $\equiv_{\omega\omega}^{k}$ in place of $\equiv_{\infty\omega}^{k}$ in the definition of the winning strategy $\mathcal{I}$. It follows that if $\mathbf{A}$ and $\mathbf{B}$ are finite σ-structures satisfying the same FO^k-sentences, then the Duplicator wins the k-pebble game on $\mathbf{A}$ and $\mathbf{B}$.

Conversely, let $\mathcal{I}$ be a winning strategy for the Duplicator in the k-pebble game on $\mathbf{A}$ and $\mathbf{B}$. We have to show that $\mathbf{A}$ and $\mathbf{B}$ satisfy the same $\mathrm{L}_{\infty\omega}^{k}$-sentences. This is a consequence of the following stronger statement, which can be proved by induction on the construction of $\mathrm{L}_{\infty\omega}^{k}$-formulas using the closure and extension properties of $\mathcal{I}$:

If $\psi(v_1, \ldots, v_r)$ is an $\mathrm{L}_{\infty\omega}^{k}$-formula whose variables are among $v_1, \ldots, v_k$ and whose free variables are among $v_1, \ldots, v_r$, then for all $f \in \mathcal{I}$ and for all (not necessarily distinct) elements $a_1, \ldots, a_r$ from the domain of f, we have

$$\mathbf{A} \models \psi(v_1/a_1, \ldots, v_r/a_r) \iff \mathbf{B} \models \psi(v_1/f(a_1), \ldots, v_m/f(a_r)).$$

□

As a consequence of Theorem 2.7.9, we obtain a characterization of $\mathrm{L}_{\infty\omega}^{\omega}$-definability on classes of finite structures.

Corollary 2.7.10. *Let σ be a vocabulary, $\mathcal{C}$ a class of finite σ-structures, and Q a Boolean query on $\mathcal{C}$. The following statements are then equivalent:*

1. *Q is $L^{\omega}_{\infty\omega}$-definable on $\mathcal{C}$.*
2. *There is a positive integer k such that, for every structure $\mathbf{A} \in \mathcal{C}$ and every structure $\mathbf{B} \in \mathcal{C}$, if $Q(\mathbf{A}) = 1$ and the Duplicator wins the k-pebble game on $\mathbf{A}$ and $\mathbf{B}$, then $Q(\mathbf{B}) = 1$.*

Proof. If Q is $L^{\omega}_{\infty\omega}$-definable on $\mathcal{C}$, then there is a positive integer k such that Q is definable on $\mathcal{C}$ by some $L^{k}_{\infty\omega}$-sentence θ. Theorem 2.7.9 implies that if $\mathbf{A}$ and $\mathbf{B}$ are structures in $\mathcal{C}$ such that $Q(\mathbf{A}) = 1$ and the Duplicator wins the k-pebble game on $\mathbf{A}$ and $\mathbf{B}$, then $\mathbf{B} \models \theta$, and hence $Q(\mathbf{B}) = 1$. Note that the assumption that $\mathcal{C}$ consists of finite structures has not been used in this direction.

For the other direction, assume that k is a positive integer with the property that if $\mathbf{A}$ and $\mathbf{B}$ are structures in $\mathcal{C}$ such that $Q(\mathbf{A}) = 1$ and the Duplicator wins the k-pebble game on $\mathbf{A}$ and $\mathbf{B}$, then $Q(\mathbf{B}) = 1$. For every structure $\mathbf{A} \in \mathcal{C}$, let $\Psi_{\mathbf{A}}$ be the set of all FO^k-sentences ψ such that $\mathbf{A} \models \psi$. Note that $\Psi_{\mathbf{A}}$ is actually a countable set, because there are countably many first-order formulas; consequently, $\bigwedge \Psi_{\mathbf{A}}$ is an $L^{k}_{\infty\omega}$-sentence. Let $\mathbf{A}_1, \ldots, \mathbf{A}_n, \ldots$ be a list of representatives of all isomorphism types of structures $\mathbf{A}$ in $\mathcal{C}$, with $Q(\mathbf{A}) = 1$. Such a list is countable, since there are countably many non-isomorphic finite structures. Using Theorem 2.7.9, it is easy to see that the $L^{k}_{\infty\omega}$-sentence $\bigvee \{\bigwedge \Psi_{\mathbf{A}_n} : n \geq 1\}$ defines the query Q on $\mathcal{C}$. $\square$

Method 2.7.11. The Method of k-Pebble Games for $L^{\omega}_{\infty\omega}$. Let σ be a vocabulary, $\mathcal{C}$ a class of finite σ-structures, and Q a Boolean query on $\mathcal{C}$.

Soundness. To show that Q is *not* $L^{\omega}_{\infty\omega}$-definable on $\mathcal{C}$, it suffices to show that for every positive integer k, there are structures $\mathbf{A}_k$ and $\mathbf{B}_k$ in $\mathcal{C}$ such that
- $Q(\mathbf{A}_k) = 1$ and $Q(\mathbf{B}_k) = 0$;
- the Duplicator wins the k-pebble game on $\mathbf{A}_k$ and $\mathbf{B}_k$.

Completeness. This method is also complete, that is, if Q is *not* $L^{\omega}_{\infty\omega}$-definable on $\mathcal{C}$, then for every positive integer k, such structures $\mathbf{A}_k$ and $\mathbf{B}_k$ exist.

We note that the above method is sound for arbitrary classes of σ-structures, not just classes of finite σ-structures. Moreover, it can be shown that it is complete for classes of σ-structures of bounded cardinality. We now present some applications of this method.

Proposition 2.7.12. *Let $\mathcal{G}$ be the class of all finite graphs.*

- *The* EVEN CARDINALITY *query is not $L^{\omega}_{\infty\omega}$-definable on $\mathcal{G}$. Consequently, the* EVEN CARDINALITY *query is neither* LFP-*definable nor* PFP-*definable on $\mathcal{G}$.*

- *For every $k \geq 1$, the query "does the graph contain a $(k+1)$-clique?" is not $\mathrm{L}_{\infty\omega}^{k}$-definable on $\mathcal{G}$.*

Proof. This is an immediate consequence of Example 2.7.5, Theorem 2.7.10, and Theorem 2.7.2. □

Proposition 2.7.13. [16] *The query* HAMILTONIAN PATH *is not* $\mathrm{L}_{\infty\omega}^{\omega}$-*definable on the class $\mathcal{G}$ of all finite graphs. Consequently, the query* HAMILTONIAN PATH *is neither* LFP-*definable nor* PFP-*definable on $\mathcal{G}$.*

Proof. For every $m \geq 1$ and every $n \geq 1$, let $\overline{\mathbf{K}}_m \times \mathbf{C}_n$ be the product graph of the totally disconnected m-node graph $\overline{\mathbf{K}}_m$ with the n-node cycle $\mathbf{C}_n$, as depicted in Fig. 2.11.

It is easy to see that $\overline{\mathbf{K}}_m \times \mathbf{C}_n$ has a HAMILTONIAN PATH if and only if $m \leq n$. This holds because, in order to visit two nodes of $\overline{\mathbf{K}}_m$ by traveling along edges of $\overline{\mathbf{K}}_m \times \mathbf{C}_n$, one has to visit a node of $\mathbf{C}_n$. Moreover, it is quite clear that for every $k \geq 1$, the Duplicator wins the k-pebble game on $\overline{\mathbf{K}}_k \times \mathbf{C}_k$ and $\overline{\mathbf{K}}_{k+1} \times \mathbf{C}_k$. Since $\overline{\mathbf{K}}_k \times \mathbf{C}_k$ has a HAMILTONIAN PATH, but $\overline{\mathbf{K}}_{k+1} \times \mathbf{C}_k$ does not, the conclusions follow immediately from Theorems 2.7.10, and 2.7.2. □

As an exercise, we invite the reader to apply Method 2.7.11 and show that the PERFECT MATCHING query is not $\mathrm{L}_{\infty\omega}^{\omega}$-definable on $\mathcal{G}$. Note that, using the same method, Dawar [14] showed that 3-COLORABILITY is not $\mathrm{L}_{\infty\omega}^{\omega}$-definable on $\mathcal{G}$. This is a technically difficult result that requires the construction of complicated graphs $\mathbf{A}_k$ and $\mathbf{B}_k$, $k \geq 1$, such that $\mathbf{A}_k$ is

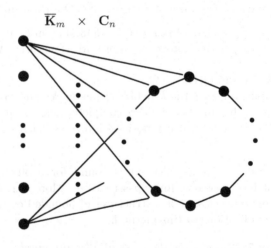

$$\overline{\mathbf{K}}_m \quad \times \quad \mathbf{C}_n$$

Fig. 2.11. HAMILTONIAN PATH is not $\mathrm{L}_{\infty\omega}^{\omega}$-definable

3-colorable, **B** is not 3-colorable, and the Duplicator wins the k-pebble game on $\mathbf{A}_k$ and $\mathbf{B}_k$. In contrast, 2-COLORABILITY is $L^\omega_{\infty\omega}$-definable on $\mathcal{G}$; in fact, it is $L^4_{\infty\omega}$-definable, since NON-2-COLORABILITY is definable by a Datalog program with at most four variables in each rule, as shown in Example 2.6.20.

It should be pointed out that, although Method 2.7.11 can be used to establish limitations on the expressive power of LFP and PFP on the class $\mathcal{G}$ of all finite graphs, this method cannot be used to establish such results on the class $\mathcal{O}$ of all finite ordered graphs. The reason for this is that *every* query on $\mathcal{O}$ is $L^2_{\infty\omega}$-definable, since the isomorphism type of every ordered finite structure is definable by an FO^2-sentence (this is an extension of the fact that FO^2 can express every fixed finite cardinality on linear orders). In particular, HAMILTONIAN PATH and 3-COLORABILITY are $L^2_{\infty\omega}$-expressible on $\mathcal{O}$. Consequently, Method 2.7.11 cannot be used to establish limitations on the expressive power of LFP and PFP on the class $\mathcal{O}$ of all ordered finite graphs; this is not surprising, since, as stated in Theorems 2.6.11 and 2.6.38, LFP captures PTIME and PFP captures PSPACE on $\mathcal{O}$.

Up to this point, k-pebble games have been used to establish mainly *negative* results, that is, lower bounds for definability in $L^\omega_{\infty\omega}$ and, a fortiori, lower bounds for definability in LFP and in PFP. These games, however, can also be used to establish *positive* results in the form of structural properties of $L^\omega_{\infty\omega}$, which, in many cases, are inherited by LFP and PFP. Moreover, k-pebble games can be used to unveil certain deeper connections between LFP and $L^\omega_{\infty\omega}$. As will be seen in the remainder of this section, all these results involve an in-depth study of the family of the equivalence relations $\equiv^k_{\infty\omega}$, $k \geq 1$, using k-pebble games.

2.7.3 0–1 Laws for $L^\omega_{\infty\omega}$

A major direction of research in finite model theory has focused on the study of the asymptotic probabilities of queries on classes of finite structures. This is the topic of Chap. 4 of this volume. Here, we present a brief overview of 0–1 laws for the infinitary logic $L^\omega_{\infty\omega}$.

Definition 2.7.14. *Let σ be a vocabulary, $\mathcal{C}$ a class of finite σ-structures, and Q a Boolean query on $\mathcal{C}$.*

- *For every $n \geq 1$, we write $\mathcal{C}_n$ to denote the subclass of $\mathcal{C}$ consisting of all structures $\mathbf{A}$ in $\mathcal{C}$ with universe $\{1, \ldots, n\}$.*
- *For every $n \geq 1$, let μ_n be a probability measure on $\mathcal{C}_n$.*
  - *We write $\mu_n(Q)$ to denote the probability of the query Q on $\mathcal{C}_n$ with respect to the measure μ_n, $n \geq 1$.*
  - *The asymptotic probability $\mu(Q)$ of the query Q with respect to the family of measures μ_n, $n > 1$, is defined as*

$$\mu(Q) = \lim_{n\to\infty} \mu_n(Q),$$

provided the limit exists.

Of all measures on classes of finite structures, the *uniform measure* is the most well-studied one. More precisely, if C is a class of finite σ-structures and Q is a Boolean query on C, then the value $\mu_n(Q)$ of the uniform measure is equal to the fraction of structures in C_n that satisfy the query Q, $n \geq 1$. Combinatorialists have studied in depth the asymptotic probabilities of queries on finite graphs with respect to the uniform measure. For instance, it is well known that $\mu(4\text{-REGULAR}) = 0$, $\mu(2\text{-COLORABILITY}) = 0$, and $\mu(\text{HAMILTONIAN PATH}) = 1$. Note, however, that $\mu(\text{EVEN CARDINALITY})$ does *not* exist, since we have that $\mu_{2n}(\text{EVEN CARDINALITY}) = 1$ and $\mu_{2n+1}(\text{EVEN CARDINALITY}) = 0$.

In the late 1960s and early 1970s, researchers raised the question of whether there was a connection between the definability of a query Q in some logic and its asymptotic probability with respect to a given measure. The next definition captures a case in which such a connection exists, and it is tight.

Definition 2.7.15. *Let L be a logic, let σ be a vocabulary consisting of relation symbols only, let C be a class of finite σ-structures, and let μ_n, $n \geq 1$, be a family of measures on C_n.*

We say that L has a 0–1 law on C with respect to μ_n, $n \geq 1$, if for every $\mathcal{L}$-definable query Q on C, we have that $\mu(Q) = 0$ or $\mu(Q) = 1$.

Note that the presence of constant symbols causes a failure of the 0–1 law for first-order logic with respect to the uniform measure. Indeed, if σ is a vocabulary containing a constant symbol c and a unary relation symbol P, then it is quite easy to verity that $\mu(P(c)) = 1/2$. This explains why, in Definition 2.7.15, it was assumed that the vocabulary consists of relation symbols only.

Over the years, there has been an extensive investigation of 0–1 laws for various logics with respect to the uniform measure on classes of finite σ-structures and, in particular, on the class $\mathcal{F}$ of all finite σ-structures. This investigation started with the independent discovery by Glebskii et al. [31] and Fagin [23] that first-order logic FO has a 0–1 law with respect to the uniform on the class $\mathcal{F}$ of all finite σ-structures. After this, Blass, Gurevich, and Kozen [9] showed that least fixed-point logic LFP has a 0–1 law with respect to the uniform measure on $\mathcal{F}$, and Kolaitis and Vardi [44] showed that partial fixed-point logic PFP has a 0–1 law with respect to the uniform measure on $\mathcal{F}$. These 0–1 laws for progressively more expressive logics turned out to be special cases of the 0–1 law for the infinitary logic $L^\omega_{\infty\omega}$ with respect to the uniform measure on $\mathcal{F}$, a result established by Kolaitis and Vardi [46].

Theorem 2.7.16. *Let σ be a vocabulary consisting of relation symbols only. The finite-variable infinitary logic $L^\omega_{\infty\omega}$ then has a 0–1 law with respect to the uniform measure on the class $\mathcal{F}$ of all finite σ-structures.*

Proof. (Hint) For every $k \geq 1$, let θ_k be the conjunction of all *extension axioms* for σ with at most k variables, that is, the conjunction of all FO^k-sentences that assert that every substructure with fewer than k elements has an extension to a substructure with k elements. Fagin [23] showed that $\mu(\theta_k) = 1$, where μ_n is the uniform measure on $\mathcal{F}_n$, $n \geq 1$. Let $\mathbf{A}_k$ be a model of θ_k, and let $[\mathbf{A}_k]_{\equiv^k_{\infty\omega}} = \{\mathbf{B} \in \mathcal{F} : \mathbf{A}_k \equiv^k_{\infty\omega} \mathbf{B}\}$ be the $\equiv^k_{\infty\omega}$-equivalence class of $\mathbf{A}_k$. Using the characterization of $\equiv^k_{\infty\omega}$ via k-pebble games in Theorem 2.7.9, it can be shown that $[\mathbf{A}_k]_{\equiv^k_{\infty\omega}} = \{\mathbf{B} \in \mathcal{F} : \mathbf{B} \models \theta_k\}$. Consequently, $\mu([\mathbf{A}_k]_{\equiv^k_{\infty\omega}}) = 1$, which easily implies that the 0–1 law holds for the k-variable infinitary logic $L^k_{\infty\omega}$. $\square$

Since the asymptotic probability of the EVEN CARDINALITY query does not exist, Theorem 2.7.16 gives another proof that EVEN CARDINALITY is not $L^\omega_{\infty\omega}$-definable on the class $\mathcal{F}$ of all finite σ-structures.

The next result characterizes when a 0–1 law holds for the k-variable infinitary logics $L^k_{\infty\omega}$, $k \geq 1$, on a class of finite structures with respect to an arbitrary measure.

Theorem 2.7.17. *Let σ be a vocabulary consisting of relation symbols only, let $\mathcal{C}$ a class of finite σ-structures, and let μ_n be a measure on $\mathcal{C}_n$, $n \geq 1$. Then, for every positive integer k, the following two statements are equivalent:*

1. *The k-variable infinitary logic $L^k_{\infty\omega}$ has a 0–1 law with respect to μ_n, $n \geq 1$, on $\mathcal{C}$.*
2. *There is an equivalence class D of $\equiv^k_{\infty\omega}$ on $\mathcal{C}$ such that $\mu(D) = 1$.*

In effect, Theorem 2.7.17 reveals that $L^k_{\infty\omega}$ has a 0–1 law if and only if there is a "giant" $L^k_{\infty\omega}$-equivalence class; all other $L^k_{\infty\omega}$-equivalence classes must have an asymptotic probability equal to 0. Moreover, the existence of a 0–1 law for $L^k_{\infty\omega}$ can be established using k-pebble games.

As described in Chap. 4, Shelah and Spencer [61] investigated 0–1 laws for first-order logic FO on the class $\mathcal{G}$ of all finite graphs under nonuniform measures on $\mathcal{G}_n$ of the form $p(n) = n^{-\alpha}$, where α is a fixed real number. Their main finding was that for all real $\alpha \in (0, 1)$, FO has a 0–1 law on $\mathcal{G}$ with respect to the measures $p(n) = n^{-\alpha}$ if and only if α is an irrational number. It follows that if $\alpha \in (0, 1)$ is rational, then the 0–1 law fails for the finite-variable infinitary logic $L^\omega_{\infty\omega}$ on $\mathcal{G}$ with respect to the measures $p(n) = n^{-\alpha}$. Moreover, McArthur [52] showed that the 0–1 law also fails for $L^\omega_{\infty\omega}$ on $\mathcal{G}$ with respect to the measures $p(n) = n^{-\alpha}$ when $\alpha \in (0, 1)$ is irrational. Thus, the 0–1 law fails for $L^\omega_{\infty\omega}$ on $\mathcal{G}$ with respect to every measure of the form $p(n) = n^{-\alpha}$, where $0 < \alpha < 1$.

2.7.4 Definability and Complexity of $L^k_{\infty\omega}$-Equivalence

If L is a logic and σ is a vocabulary, then two σ-structures $\mathbf{A}$ and $\mathbf{B}$ are *L-equivalent* if they satisfy the same *L*-sentences. The concept of *L*-equivalence gives rise to the following decision problem: given two finite σ-structures $\mathbf{A}$ and $\mathbf{B}$, are they *L*-equivalent? Strictly speaking, this decision problem is not a query on finite structures, since, according to

Definition 2.2.1, queries take single structures, not pairs of structures, as inputs. It is easy, however, to view this decision problem as a query on an expanded vocabulary $\sigma_1 + \sigma_2$ that consists of two disjoint copies of the relation and constant symbols in the vocabulary σ together with two unary predicates D_1 and D_2. Using the vocabulary $\sigma_1 + \sigma_2$, a pair (A, B) of two σ-structures $\mathbf{A}$ and $\mathbf{B}$ is identified with a single $\sigma_1 + \sigma_2$-structure $\mathbf{A} + \mathbf{B}$ defined as follows: the universe of $\mathbf{A} + \mathbf{B}$ is the union $A \cup B$ of the universes of $\mathbf{A}$ and $\mathbf{B}$, the relation symbol D_1 is interpreted by the universe A of $\mathbf{A}$, the relation symbol D_2 is interpreted by the universe B of $\mathbf{B}$, and the remaining relation and constant symbols of $\sigma_1 + \sigma_2$ are interpreted by the corresponding relations and constants of $\mathbf{A}$ and $\mathbf{B}$. This encoding makes it possible to formally view queries on pairs of σ-structures as queries on single $\sigma_1 + \sigma_2$-structures.

Note that FO-equivalence coincides with the ISOMORPHISM PROBLEM, since the isomorphism type of every finite σ-structure is FO-definable; as a result, FO-equivalence is not FO-definable. The same line of reasoning shows that $L^\omega_{\infty\omega}$-equivalence is not $L^\omega_{\infty\omega}$-definable. In what follows, we shall investigate the logical definability and computational complexity of $L^k_{\infty\omega}$-equivalence, $k \geq 1$.

Using Theorem 2.7.9 and the infinitary syntax of $L^k_{\infty\omega}$, it is easy to see that $L^k_{\infty\omega}$-equivalence is $L^k_{\infty\omega}$-definable, $k \geq 1$. Indeed, as in the proof of Theorem 2.7.10, for every finite σ-structure $\mathbf{A}$, let $\Psi_\mathbf{A}$ be the conjunction of all FO^k-sentences satisfied by $\mathbf{A}$; clearly, $\Psi_\mathbf{A}$ is an $L^k_{\infty\omega}$-sentence. Note that for every $L^k_{\infty\omega}$-sentence Ψ, there are $L^k_{\infty\omega}$-sentences Ψ^1 and Ψ^2 over $\sigma_1 + \sigma_2$ such that for all σ-structures $\mathbf{A}$ and $\mathbf{B}$, the following hold:

- $\mathbf{A} + \mathbf{B} \models \Psi^1$ if and only if $\mathbf{A} \models \Psi$.
- $\mathbf{A} + \mathbf{B} \models \Psi^2$ if and only if $\mathbf{B} \models \Psi$.

Finally, let $\mathbf{A}_1, \ldots, \mathbf{A}_n, \ldots$ be a list of representatives of all isomorphism types of finite σ-structures. Then $L^k_{\infty\omega}$-equivalence on σ is definable by the $L^k_{\infty\omega}$-sentence

$$\bigvee \{ (\Psi^1_{\mathbf{A}_i} \wedge \Psi^2_{\mathbf{A}_i}) : i \geq 1 \}.$$

The preceding construction shows that $L^k_{\infty\omega}$ is powerful enough to express its own equivalence, but provides no information about the computational complexity of $L^k_{\infty\omega}$-equivalence. Nonetheless, the characterization of $L^k_{\infty\omega}$-equivalence in terms of k-pebble games can be used to show that $L^k_{\infty\omega}$-equivalence is LFP-definable and, thus, it is also polynomial-time computable. This result, whose proof is outlined next, was obtained by Dawar, Lindell and Weinstein [15] and by Kolaitis and Vardi [45] independently.

Proposition 2.7.18. *Let σ be a vocabulary and k a positive integer. There is then a positive first-order formula $\varphi(x_1, \ldots, x_k, y_1, \ldots, y_k, S)$ over the vocabulary $\sigma_1 + \sigma_2$ such that the least fixed point $\varphi^\infty(x_1, \ldots, x_k, y_1, \ldots, y_k)$*

of this formula defines the query "given two σ-structures $\mathbf{A}$, $\mathbf{B}$ *and two* k*-tuples* $(a_1 \ldots, a_k) \in A^k$ *and* $(b_1, \ldots, b_k) \in B^k$, *is* $(\mathbf{A}, a_1, \ldots, a_k) \not\equiv^k_{\infty\omega}$ $(\mathbf{B}, b_1 \ldots, b_k)$?"

Consequently, for each $k \geq 2$, $\mathrm{L}^k_{\infty\omega}$-*equivalence is* LFP-*definable.*

Proof. From the proof of Theorem 2.7.9, it follows that $(\mathbf{A}, a_1, \ldots, a_k) \not\equiv^k_{\infty\omega}$ $(\mathbf{A}, b_1 \ldots, b_k)$ if and only if the Spoiler wins the k-pebble game on $\mathbf{A}$ and $\mathbf{B}$ starting with the *configuration* $(a_1, \ldots, a_k, b_1, \ldots, b_k)$, that is, the Spoiler wins the k-pebble game when the game begins with pebbles of the same label placed on a_i and b_i, $i = 1, \ldots, k$. The latter statement is definable by the least fixed point φ^∞ of a positive first-order formula $\varphi(x_1, \ldots, x_k, y_1, \ldots, y_k, S)$ over the vocabulary $\sigma_1 + \sigma_2$ with a total of $2k$ distinct variables, which, intuitively, asserts that the Spoiler wins in the initial configuration or in the "next" move of the game. More precisely, $\varphi(x_1, \ldots, x_k, y_1, \ldots, y_k, S)$ is the formula

$$\chi(x_1, \ldots, x_k, y_1, \ldots, y_k) \vee (\vee_{i=1}^k \psi_i(x_1, \ldots, x_k, y_1, \ldots, y_k, S)),$$

where

- χ is a quantifier-free formula stating that $x_i \in D_1$, $y_i \in D_2$, for $i = 1, \ldots, k$, and the substructures generated by $\{x_1, \ldots, x_k\}$ and $\{y_1, \ldots, y_k\}$ are not isomorphic;
- ψ_i is the formula

$$(\exists x_i \in D_1)(\forall y_i \in D_2)S(x_1, \ldots, x_k, y_1, \ldots, y_k)\vee$$

$$(\exists y_i \in D_2)(\forall x_i \in D_1)S(x_1, \ldots, x_k, y_1, \ldots, y_k). \ \square$$

Proposition 2.7.18 implies that for every $k \geq 2$, $\mathrm{L}^k_{\infty\omega}$-equivalence is in P. Grohe [34] established the following matching lower bound for the computational complexity of $\mathrm{L}^k_{\infty\omega}$-equivalence.

Theorem 2.7.19. *Let* σ *be a vocabulary containing at least one binary relation symbol. For each positive integer* $k \geq 2$, *the following problem is* P-*complete: given two finite* σ-*structures* $\mathbf{A}$ *and* $\mathbf{B}$, *does the Duplicator win the* k-*pebble game on* $\mathbf{A}$ *and* $\mathbf{B}$?

Consequently, for each $k \geq 2$, $\mathrm{L}^k_{\infty\omega}$-*equivalence is* P-*complete.*

This result can be proved via an intricate reduction from the MONOTONE CIRCUIT VALUE PROBLEM. Note that it provides a sharp contrast between the k-pebble game and the r-move Ehrenfeucht–Fraïssé game, since, by Theorem 2.4.4, for each fixed $r \geq 1$, determining the winner in the r-move Ehrenfeucht–Fraïssé game is solvable in logarithmic space (and, hence, it is unlikely to be P-complete). Note that if the number k of pebbles is also part of the input, then determining the winner in the k-pebble game is solvable in exponential time. It has been conjectured, but has not been proved, that this upper bound is tight, which means that the following query is EXPTIME-complete:

given a positive integer k and two finite σ-structures $\mathbf{A}$ and $\mathbf{B}$, does the Duplicator win the k-pebble game on $\mathbf{A}$ and $\mathbf{B}$? This would complement Theorem 2.4.5 to the effect that, when the number r of moves is part of the input, determining the winner in the r-move Ehrenfeucht–Fraïssé game is a PSPACE-complete problem.

For every finite σ-structure $\mathbf{B}$, let $[\mathbf{B}]^k_{\infty\omega}$ be the $L^k_{\infty\omega}$-equivalence class of $\mathbf{B}$ on finite σ-structures, that is,

$$[\mathbf{B}]^k_{\infty\omega} = \{\mathbf{A} \in \mathcal{F} : \mathbf{A} \equiv^k_{\infty\omega} \mathbf{B}\}.$$

Clearly, $[\mathbf{B}]^k_{\infty\omega}$ can also be viewed as a Boolean query $Q^k_{\mathbf{B}}$ on the class $\mathcal{F}$ of all finite σ-structures: given a finite σ-structure $\mathbf{A}$, is $\mathbf{A} \equiv^k_{\infty\omega} \mathbf{B}$? For every finite σ-structure $\mathbf{B}$ and every k-tuple $\mathbf{b}$ from B, we can also consider the related k-ary query $Q^k_{\mathbf{B},\mathbf{b}}$ on $\mathcal{F}$ such that, given a finite σ-structure $\mathbf{A}$, we have that

$$Q^k_{\mathbf{B},\mathbf{b}}(\mathbf{A}) = \{\mathbf{a} \in A^k : (\mathbf{A}, \mathbf{a}) \equiv^k_{\infty\omega} (\mathbf{B}, \mathbf{b})\}.$$

Theorem 2.7.9 implies that the query $Q^k_{\mathbf{B}}$ is definable by the $L^k_{\infty\omega}$-sentence $\bigwedge \Psi_{\mathbf{B}}$, where, as earlier, $\Psi_{\mathbf{B}}$ is the set of all FO^k-sentences satisfied by $\mathbf{B}$. Similarly, each query $Q^k_{\mathbf{B},\mathbf{b}}$ is $L^k_{\infty\omega}$-definable as well. Dawar, Lindell, and Weinstein [15] established a much stronger result by showing that all queries $Q^k_{\mathbf{B}}$ and $Q^k_{\mathbf{B},\mathbf{b}}$ are actually FO^k-definable. This was achieved via a careful adaptation to $L^k_{\infty\omega}$ of Scott's theorem [60] to the effect that the isomorphism type of every countable structure is definable in the infinitary logic $L_{\omega_1\omega}$. Here, we outline a different proof, which was given in [49]. As a stepping stone, we first establish the following result.

Proposition 2.7.20. *Let $\mathbf{B}$ be a finite σ-structure and let $\mathbf{b}_1, \ldots, \mathbf{b}_l$ be an enumeration of all k-tuples from $\mathbf{B}$. For every positive integer k, there is a system $\mathsf{S}_{\mathbf{B}} = (\varphi_{\mathbf{B},\mathbf{b}_i}(x_1, \ldots, x_k, T_{\mathbf{b}_1}, \ldots, T_{\mathbf{b}_l}), 1 \leq i \leq l)$ of FO^k-formulas that are positive in $T_{\mathbf{b}_1}, \ldots, T_{\mathbf{b}_l}$ and have the property that $\varphi^\infty_{\mathbf{B},\mathbf{b}_i}(x_1, \ldots, x_k)$ defines the complement of the query $Q^k_{\mathbf{B},\mathbf{b}_i}$, $1 \leq i \leq l$. Thus, for every finite σ-structure $\mathbf{A}$ and every k-tuple $\mathbf{a}$ from $\mathbf{A}$,*

$$(\mathbf{A}, \mathbf{a}) \equiv^k_{\infty\omega} (\mathbf{B}, \mathbf{b}) \iff \mathbf{A}, \mathbf{a} \models \neg\varphi^\infty_{\mathbf{B},\mathbf{b}_i}(x_1, \ldots, x_k).$$

Proof. (Outline) For every $i \leq l$, let $\chi_{\mathbf{B},\mathbf{b}_i}(x_1, \ldots, x_k)$ be the conjunction of all atomic or negated atomic formulas $\eta(x_1, \ldots, x_k)$ such that $\mathbf{B}, \mathbf{b}_i \models \eta(x_1, \ldots, x_k)$. Moreover, for every j such that $1 \leq j \leq k$ and every element b from the universe of $\mathbf{B}$, let $\mathbf{b}_i[j/b]$ be the k-tuple obtained from the k-tuple $\mathbf{b}_i = (b^i_1, \ldots, b^i_k)$ by replacing b^i_j by b. We then consider the system $\mathsf{S}_{\mathbf{B}} = (\varphi_{\mathbf{B},\mathbf{b}_i}, 1 \leq i \leq l)$, where $\varphi_{\mathbf{B},\mathbf{b}_i}(x_1, \ldots, x_k, T_{\mathbf{b}_1} \ldots, T_{\mathbf{b}_l})$ is the formula

$$\neg\chi_{\mathbf{B},\mathbf{b}_i}(x_1, \ldots, x_k) \vee \left[\bigvee_{j=1}^k (\exists x_j) \bigwedge_{b \in B} T_{\mathbf{b}_i[j/b]}(x_1, \ldots, x_k)\right] \vee$$

$$\left[\bigvee_{j=1}^k \bigvee_{b \in B} (\forall x_j) T_{\mathbf{b}_i[j/b]}(x_1, \ldots, x_k)\right].$$

By induction on m simultaneously for all $i \leq l$, it can be shown that on every σ-structure $\mathbf{A}$ the component $\Phi^m_{\mathbf{B}, \mathbf{b}_i}$, $1 \leq i \leq l$, of the mth stage of the system $S_{\mathbf{B}}$ consists of all k-tuples $\mathbf{a}$ from $\mathbf{A}$ such that the Spoiler can win the k-pebble game on $(\mathbf{A}, \mathbf{a})$ and $(\mathbf{B}, \mathbf{b})$ within m rounds. $\square$

By combining Theorem 2.7.2 with Proposition 2.7.20, we can now obtain the result of Dawar, Lindell, and Weinstein [15] to the effect that every $\equiv^k_{\infty\omega}$-equivalence class is FO^k-definable.

Theorem 2.7.21. *Let k be a positive integer, $\mathbf{B}$ a finite σ-structure, and $\mathbf{b}$ a k-tuple from $\mathbf{B}$.*

- *The k-ary query $Q^k_{\mathbf{B}, \mathbf{b}}$ is definable by some FO^k-formula $\theta_{\mathbf{B}, \mathbf{b}}(x_1, \ldots, x_k)$.*
- *The Boolean query $Q^k_{\mathbf{B}}$ is definable by some FO^k-sentence $\theta_{\mathbf{B}}$ of FO^k. In other words, for each fixed positive integer k and each fixed finite σ-structure $\mathbf{B}$, the following query is FO^k-definable: "Given a finite σ-structure $\mathbf{A}$, does the Duplicator win the k-pebble game on $\mathbf{A}$ and $\mathbf{B}$?"*

Proof. (Outline) Let $\mathbf{b}_1, \ldots, \mathbf{b}_l$ be an enumeration of all k-tuples from the universe of $\mathbf{B}$ and let $S_{\mathbf{B}} = (\varphi_{\mathbf{B}, \mathbf{b}_i}, 1 \leq i \leq l)$, be the system of positive FO^k-formulas used in the proof of Theorem 2.7.20. Theorem 2.7.2 implies that for every $i \leq l$ and every $m \geq 1$, there is an FO^k-formula $\varphi^m_{\mathbf{B}, \mathbf{b}_i}(x_1, \ldots, x_k)$ that defines the component $\Phi^m_{\mathbf{B}, \mathbf{b}_i}$ of the mth stage of this system.

Let us now apply the system $S_{\mathbf{B}}$ to the structure $\mathbf{B}$ itself. There is then a positive integer m_0 such that on $\mathbf{B}$, the least fixed point of this system is equal to its m_0th stage, that is, for every $i \leq l$,

$$\mathbf{B} \models (\forall x_1 \ldots \forall x_k)[\varphi^{m_0}_{\mathbf{B}, \mathbf{b}_i}(x_1, \ldots, x_k) \leftrightarrow \varphi^{m_0+1}_{\mathbf{B}, \mathbf{b}_i}(x_1, \ldots, x_k)].$$

It can then be shown that the query $Q^k_{\mathbf{B}, \mathbf{b}}$ is definable by the following FO^k-formula $\theta_{\mathbf{B}, \mathbf{b}}(x_1, \ldots, x_k)$:

$$\neg\varphi^{m_0}_{\mathbf{B}, \mathbf{b}}(x_1, \ldots, x_k) \wedge [\bigwedge_{i=1}^{l}(\forall x_1 \ldots \forall x_k)(\varphi^{m_0}_{\mathbf{B}, \mathbf{b}_i}(x_1, \ldots, x_k) \leftrightarrow \varphi^{m_0+1}_{\mathbf{B}, \mathbf{b}_i}(x_1, \ldots, x_k))].$$

Finally, the query $Q^k_{\mathbf{B}}$ is definable by the FO^k-sentence

$$(\exists x_1 \ldots \exists x_k)(\bigvee_{i=1}^{l} \theta_{\mathbf{B}, \mathbf{b}_i}(x_1, \ldots, x_k)). \quad \square$$

Theorem 2.7.21 yields the following normal form for $L^k_{\infty\omega}$-definability on finite structures, $k \geq 1$, a result due to Dawar, Lindell, and Weinstein [15].

Corollary 2.7.22. *Let σ be a vocabulary and k a positive integer. For every $L^k_{\infty\omega}$-sentence ψ, there are FO^k-sentences ψ_m, $m \geq 1$, such that for every finite σ-structure $\mathbf{A}$, we have that*

$$\mathbf{A} \models \psi \iff \mathbf{A} \models \bigvee_{i=1}^{\infty} \psi_m.$$

Proof. The class of finite σ-structures that satisfy ψ is equal to the union of all $\equiv^k_{\infty\omega}$-equivalence classes of finite σ-structures that satisfy ψ. Thus, the desired sentences ψ_m are the FO^k-sentences $\theta_{\mathbf{B}}$, where $\mathbf{B}$ varies over all finite σ-structures that satisfy ψ. $\square$

Since $L^k_{\infty\omega}$ and FO^k are closed under negations, we also have that on the class of all finite σ-structures, every $L^k_{\infty\omega}$-sentence is equivalent to a countable conjunction of FO^k-sentences. Thus, the expressive power of $L^k_{\infty\omega}$ on finite structures reduces to a single application of infinitary disjunction or infinitary conjunction to a countable set of FO^k-sentences.

2.7.5 Least Fixed-Point Logic vs. Partial Fixed-Point Logic on Finite Structures

We now take a closer look at the relationship between least fixed-point logic LFP and partial fixed-point logic PFP on finite structures. Since every LFP-formula is also a PFP-formula, we have that on the class $\mathcal{F}$ of all finite σ-structures, $\mathrm{LFP}(\mathcal{F}) \subseteq \mathrm{PFP}(\mathcal{F})$. Recall that Theorem 2.6.11 asserts that on the class $\mathcal{O}$ of all ordered finite σ-structures, we have that $\mathrm{LFP}(\mathcal{O}) = \mathrm{P}(\mathcal{O})$; moreover, Theorem 2.6.38 asserts that $\mathrm{PFP}(\mathcal{O}) = \mathrm{PSPACE}(\mathcal{O})$. Consequently, $\mathrm{LFP}(\mathcal{O}) \neq \mathrm{PFP}(\mathcal{O})$ if and only if $\mathrm{P} \neq \mathrm{PSPACE}$. Thus, showing that PFP has strictly higher expressive power than LFP on the class $\mathcal{O}$ of all ordered finite σ-structures amounts to resolving one of the outstanding open problems in computational complexity. Chandra and Harel [11] raised the question of how LFP and PFP compare in terms of expressive power on $\mathcal{F}$ and conjectured that $\mathrm{LFP}(\mathcal{F}) \neq \mathrm{PFP}(\mathcal{F})$. Initially, researchers in finite model theory speculated that this conjecture was not equivalent to any open problem in complexity theory; moreover, they felt that it would be possible to confirm it using existing techniques. To justify this intuition, recall that, by Fagin's Theorem (Theorem 2.4.7), $\mathrm{ESO} = \mathrm{NP}$ on every class $\mathcal{C}$ of finite σ-structures. Consequently, showing that $\mathrm{LFP}(\mathcal{O}) \neq \mathrm{ESO}(\mathcal{O})$ amounts to establishing that $\mathrm{P} \neq \mathrm{NP}$. In contrast, $\mathrm{LFP}(\mathcal{F}) \neq \mathrm{ESO}(\mathcal{F})$, since, as shown in this section, the EVEN CARDINALITY query is not LFP-definable on $\mathcal{F}$, but, of course, it is ESO-definable on $\mathcal{F}$. Similarly, $\mathrm{PFP}(\mathcal{F}) \neq \mathrm{ESO}(\mathcal{F})$, since the EVEN CARDINALITY query is not PFP-definable on $\mathcal{F}$. So, it seems plausible that one could separate LFP from PFP on $\mathcal{F}$ by introducing suitable combinatorial games that would make it possible to differentiate between these two fixed-point logics on $\mathcal{F}$; of course, these games would have to be different from the k-pebble games, $k \geq 1$, since k-pebble games capture definability in the finite-variable infinitary logic $L^\omega_{\infty\omega}$, which subsumes both LFP and PFP on classes of finite structures. It turned out, however, that this intuition was wrong. Indeed, a decade after Chandra and Harel [11] formulated their conjecture, Abiteboul and Vianu [3] established that the separation of LFP from PFP on the class $\mathcal{F}$ of all finite σ-structures is literally equivalent to the separation of P from PSPACE. In what follows, we shall highlight some of the key ideas that go into the proof of this result. For a complete proof, we refer the reader to the paper by Abiteboul and Vianu [3] and to the subsequent excellent exposition by Dawar, Lindell, and Weinstein [15].

Definition 2.7.23. *Let σ be a vocabulary and k a positive integer.*

- *If $\mathbf{A}$ is a finite σ-structure and $\mathbf{a}$ is a k-tuple of elements of $\mathbf{A}$, then the k-type of $\mathbf{a}$ on $\mathbf{A}$ is the collection of all $L^k_{\infty\omega}$-formulas $\varphi(\mathbf{x})$ such that $\mathbf{A} \models \varphi(\mathbf{a})$.*
- *If $\mathbf{A}$ is a finite σ-structure and $\mathbf{a}, \mathbf{b}$ are two k-tuples of elements of $\mathbf{A}$, then we write $\mathbf{A} \equiv^{k,\mathbf{A}}_{\infty\omega} \mathbf{b}$ to denote that $\mathbf{a}$ and $\mathbf{b}$ have the same k-type on $\mathbf{A}$.*

As we have seen, LFP cannot express the EVEN CARDINALITY query on $\mathcal{F}$, but it can express every polynomial-time-computable query on $\mathcal{O}$. It follows that no LFP-formula $\psi(x,y)$ exists such that for every finite σ-structure $\mathbf{A}$, this formula defines a linear order on the universe A of $\mathbf{A}$. In contrast, Abiteboul and Vianu [3] showed that, for every $k \geq 1$, there is an LFP-formula such that, for every finite σ-structure $\mathbf{A}$, this formula defines (in a sense that has to be made precise) a linear order on the set of the equivalence classes of the equivalence relation $\equiv^{k,\mathbf{A}}_{\infty\omega}$.

By definition, a *linear preorder* on a set B is a binary relation $\preceq$ on B that is reflexive and transitive, and has the property that, for every b_1 and b_2 in B, we have that $b_1 \preceq b_2$ or $b_2 \preceq b_1$. Every linear preorder $\preceq$ gives rise to an equivalence relation $\equiv$ defined by the condition: $b_1 \equiv b_2$ if and only if $b_1 \preceq b_2$ and $b_2 \preceq b_1$. Moreover, $\preceq$ induces a linear order, also denoted by $\preceq$, on the quotient set $B/\equiv$ of the equivalence classes of $\equiv$, where $[b_1]_\equiv \preceq [b_2]_\equiv$ if and only if $b_1 \preceq b_2$. The next theorem is the key technical result in [3]; here, we shall give a hint of a different proof that was presented in [15].

Theorem 2.7.24. *Let σ be a vocabulary and $\mathcal{F}$ the class of all finite σ-structures. For every positive integer k, there is an LFP-definable $2k$-ary query Q_k on $\mathcal{F}$ such that for every finite σ-structure $\mathbf{A}$, the value $Q_k(\mathbf{A})$ of this query on $\mathbf{A}$ is a linear preorder on A^k whose induced equivalence relation coincides with the equivalence relation $\equiv^{k,\mathbf{A}}_{\infty\omega}$ of k-types on $\mathbf{A}$.*

Proof. (Hint) Using the characterization of $L^k_{\infty\omega}$-equivalence in terms of k-pebble games, it is possible to design a *color-refinement* algorithm such that on every finite σ-structure $\mathbf{A}$, it inductively preorders all k-tuples from $\mathbf{A}$ according to their k-type on $\mathbf{A}$. This algorithm is naturally expressed in inflationary fixed point logic IFP, which, as shown by Gurevich and Shelah [35], has the same expressive power as LFP on the class of all finite σ-structures (see also Chap. 3 for additional information on IFP). $\square$

We can finally present Abiteboul and Vianu's surprising resolution of Chandra and Harel's conjecture.

Theorem 2.7.25. [3] *Let σ be a vocabulary and $\mathcal{F}$ the class of all finite σ-structures. The following statements are then equivalent:*

1. $\mathrm{LFP}(\mathcal{F}) = \mathrm{PFP}(\mathcal{F})$.
2. $\mathrm{P} = \mathrm{PSPACE}$.

Proof. (Hint) Assume first that $\mathrm{LFP}(\mathcal{F}) = \mathrm{PFP}(\mathcal{F})$. As seen in Example 2.6.36, PFP can express PSPACE-complete queries on $\mathcal{F}$. Therefore, such queries are LFP-definable on $\mathcal{F}$. Since every LFP-definable query is polynomial-time computable, it follows that $\mathrm{PSPACE} \subseteq \mathrm{P}$.

For the other direction, assume that $\mathrm{P} = \mathrm{PSPACE}$. We have to show that $\mathrm{LFP}(\mathcal{F}) = \mathrm{PFP}(\mathcal{F})$. This will require essentially all the machinery we have developed in this section. Fix a positive integer k. If $\mathbf{A}$ is a finite σ-structure, then the equivalence relation $\equiv_{\infty\omega}^{k,\mathbf{A}}$ induces a quotient structure $\mathbf{A}/ \equiv_{\infty\omega}^{k,\mathbf{A}}$ whose universe consists of the equivalence classes $[\mathbf{a}]_{\equiv_{\infty\omega}^{k,\mathbf{A}}}$ of k-tuples from A. Let

$$\mathcal{F}/ \equiv_{\infty\omega}^{k} = \{\mathbf{A}/ \equiv_{\infty\omega}^{k,\mathbf{A}}: \mathbf{A} \in \mathcal{F}\}$$

be the class of all these quotient structures. Theorem 2.7.24 implies that there is an LFP-definable query that defines a linear order on the universe of every quotient structure $\mathbf{A}/ \equiv_{\infty\omega}^{k,\mathbf{A}}$ in $\mathcal{F}/ \equiv_{\infty\omega}^{k}$. Consequently, $\mathrm{LFP}(\mathcal{F}/ \equiv_{\infty\omega}^{k}) = \mathrm{P}(\mathcal{F}/ \equiv_{\infty\omega}^{k})$. We can now use *transfer properties* between $\mathcal{F}$ and $\mathcal{F}/ \equiv_{\infty\omega}^{k}$ to show that $\mathrm{PFP}(\mathcal{F}) \subseteq \mathrm{LFP}(\mathcal{F})$, as indicated in the diagram below:

$$\varphi \in \mathrm{PFP}(\mathcal{F}) \quad \equiv \quad \psi \in \mathrm{LFP}(\mathcal{F})$$

$$\downarrow \qquad\qquad\qquad \uparrow$$

$$\varphi^* \in \mathrm{PFP}(\mathcal{F}/ \equiv_{\infty\omega}^{k}) \equiv \psi^* \in \mathrm{LFP}(\mathcal{F}/ \equiv_{\infty\omega}^{k})$$

Specifically, assume that Q is a query on $\mathcal{F}$ definable by a PFP-formula φ with k distinct variables. The formula φ can be "transformed" to a PFP-formula φ^* over the vocabulary of the quotient structures, so that φ^* defines the "transformation" of the query Q to a query Q^* on $\mathcal{F}/ \equiv_{\infty\omega}^{k}$. Since Q^* is PFP-definable on $\mathcal{F}/ \equiv_{\infty\omega}^{k}$, it is polynomial-space computable. The hypothesis $\mathrm{PSPACE} = \mathrm{P}$ implies that Q^* is polynomial-time computable, and hence Q^* is LFP-definable on $\mathcal{F}/ \equiv_{\infty\omega}^{k}$. Let ψ^* be an LFP-formula that defines Q^* on $\mathcal{F}/ \equiv_{\infty\omega}^{k}$. We can now "pull back" ψ^* and obtain an LFP-formula ψ that defines the query Q on $\mathcal{F}$. Thus, $\mathrm{PFP}(\mathcal{F}) \subseteq \mathrm{LFP}(\mathcal{F})$. $\square$

Thus, the difference in computational power between polynomial-time and polynomial-space computations, if any, amounts to the difference in expressive power between least fixed points and partial fixed points of first-order formulas on the class of all finite structures.

2.8 Existential Infinitary Logics with Finitely Many Variables

In Sect. 2.7, we saw that the finite-variable infinitary logics $\mathrm{L}_{\infty\omega}^{k}$ and the k-pebble games, $k \geq 1$, provide powerful tools for analyzing the expressive power of least fixed-point logic LFP. Our goal in this section is to develop a similar methodology for analyzing the expressive power of the existential fragment of LFP and, in particular, the expressive power of Datalog and Datalog($\neq$). To this effect, we shall introduce finite-variable existential infinitary logics and certain asymmetric pebble games that turn out to be tailored for the study of Datalog and Datalog($\neq$).

2.8.1 The Infinitary Logics $\exists L_{\infty\omega}^k$ and $\exists L_{\infty\omega}^k(\neq)$

Informally, an existential finite-variable infinitary logic is a fragment of $L_{\infty\omega}^\omega$ in which the rules for constructing formulas do not include applications of universal quantification or negation. These fragments can be further differentiated depending on whether the basic formulas include negated equalities or negated atomic formulas. We now formally define two of these fragments, originally introduced by Kolaitis and Vardi [47].

Definition 2.8.1. *Let σ be a vocabulary.*

- *For every positive integer k, we write $\exists L_{\infty\omega}^k$ to denote the collection of all $L_{\infty\omega}$-formulas that have at most k distinct variables and are obtained from atomic formulas (which may be equality statements) using existential quantification, infinitary conjunction, and infinitary disjunction. We write $\exists FO^k$ to denote the collection of all first-order $\exists L_{\infty\omega}^k$-formulas.*
- *The finite-variable existential infinitary logic $\exists L_{\infty\omega}^\omega$ is the union of all $\exists L_{\infty\omega}^k$'s, that is,*

$$\exists L_{\infty\omega}^\omega = \bigcup_{k=1}^{\infty} \exists L_{\infty\omega}^k.$$

- *For every positive integer k, we write $\exists L_{\infty\omega}^k(\neq)$ to denote the collection of all $L_{\infty\omega}$-formulas that have at most k distinct variables and are obtained from atomic formulas and negated equality statements (that is, formulas of the form $t_1 \neq t_2$, where t_1, t_2 are among the k variables and the constant symbols of σ), using existential quantification, infinitary conjunction, and infinitary disjunction. We write $\exists FO^k(\neq)$ to denote the collection of all first-order $\exists L_{\infty\omega}^k(\neq)$-formulas.*
- *The finite-variable existential infinitary logic $\exists L_{\infty\omega}^\omega(\neq)$ is the union of all $\exists L_{\infty\omega}^k(\neq)$'s, that is,*

$$\exists L_{\infty\omega}^\omega(\neq) = \bigcup_{k=1}^{\infty} \exists L_{\infty\omega}^k(\neq).$$

As an example, the expression

$$(\exists z)(E(x,z) \wedge (\exists x)(x = z \wedge (\exists z)(E(x,z) \wedge E(z,y))))$$

is an $\exists FO^3$-formula that defines the query "there is a path of length 3 from x to y". Actually, for every $m \geq 1$, the query "there is a path of length m from x to y" is $\exists FO^3$-definable. This is a special case of a result concerning the relationship between Datalog and $\exists L_{\infty\omega}^{\omega}$. Before stating this result in precise terms, we need to introduce a parametrization of Datalog programs based on the number of variables occurring in the rules.

For every positive integer k, let k-Datalog be the collection of all Datalog programs in which the body of every rule has at most k distinct variables and also the head of every rule has at most k variables (the variables of the body may be different from the variables of the head). For instance, the NON-2-COLORABILITY query is expressible in 4-Datalog, since, as seen in Example 2.6.20, it is definable by the goal predicate Q of the Datalog program below, which asserts the existence of a cycle of odd length:

$$\begin{vmatrix} O(x,y) : - \; E(x,y) \\ O(x,y) : - \; E(x,z), E(z,w), O(w,y) \\ Q \qquad : - \; O(x,x) \end{vmatrix}$$

A complete proof of the next result can be found in [50].

Theorem 2.8.2. *Let σ be a vocabulary, k a positive integer, and*

$$\phi_1(x_1,\ldots,x_{n_1},S_1,\ldots,S_l),\ldots,\phi_l(x_1,\ldots,x_{n_l},S_1,\ldots,S_l)$$

a system of positive $\exists FO^k$-formulas over the vocabulary $\sigma \cup \{S_1,\ldots,S_l\}$. The following statements are then true for the above system and for the operator Φ associated with it:

- *For every $m \geq 1$, each component Φ_i^m, $1 \leq i \leq l$, of the stage $\Phi^m = (\Phi_1^m,\ldots,\Phi_l^m)$ is $\exists FO^k$-definable on the class $\mathcal{S}$ of all σ-structures.*
- *Each component ϕ_i^{∞}, $1 \leq i \leq l$, of the least fixed point $(\phi_1^{\infty},\ldots,\phi_l^{\infty})$ of the system is $\exists FO^k$-definable on the class of all σ-structures.*

Consequently, every query definable by a k-Datalog program on the class $\mathcal{S}$ of all σ-structures is also $\exists L_{\infty\omega}^k$-definable on $\mathcal{S}$. In symbols,

$$k\text{-Datalog}(\mathcal{S}) \subseteq \exists L_{\infty\omega}^k(\mathcal{S}).$$

Proof. (Hint) This result can be proved by induction on m simultaneously for all $i \leq l$. As was the case with Theorem 2.7.2, the key idea is to reuse variables judiciously. Some additional technical difficulties arise from the limited syntax of $\exists L_{\infty\omega}^k$. These are overcome by using the following closure property of $\exists FO^k$-definable queries, which has to be established separately:

If Q is an $\exists FO^k$-definable query and $\pi : \{1,\ldots,k\} \mapsto \{1,\ldots,k\}$ is a function, then the query Q_π is also $\exists FO^k$-definable, where, for every σ-structure A and every sequence $(a_1,\ldots,a_k)$ of elements from the universe of A,

$$(a_1,\ldots,a_k) \in Q_\pi(A) \iff (a_{\pi(1)},\ldots,a_{\pi(k)}) \in Q(A).$$

By refining the proof of Proposition 2.6.21, it can be shown that every query definable by a k-Datalog program is also definable by the least fixed point of a system of positive $\exists FO^k$-formulas. Consequently, k-Datalog$(\mathcal{S}) \subseteq \exists L^k_{\infty\omega}(\mathcal{S})$. □

A result similar to Theorem 2.8.2 can be established about the relationship between k-Datalog($\neq$) and $\exists L^\omega_{\infty\omega}(\neq)$.

Theorem 2.8.3. *Let k be a positive integer. Every query definable by a k-Datalog($\neq$) program on the class $\mathcal{S}$ of all σ-structures is also $\exists L^k_{\infty\omega}(\neq)$-definable on $\mathcal{S}$.*

It should be pointed out that on the class $\mathcal{F}$ of all finite σ-structures, k-Datalog is properly contained in $\exists L^\omega_{\infty\omega}$, since the latter can express queries that are not computable. Similarly, k-Datalog($\neq$) is properly contained in $\exists L^\omega_{\infty\omega}(\neq)$ on $\mathcal{F}$.

The preservation properties of Datalog and Datalog($\neq$) in Propositions 2.6.23 and 2.6.26 extend to $\exists L^\omega_{\infty\omega}$ and $\exists L^\omega_{\infty\omega}(\neq)$. Specifically, every $\exists L^\omega_{\infty\omega}$-definable query is preserved under homomorphisms and every $\exists L^\omega_{\infty\omega}$-definable query is preserved under one-to-one homomorphisms. These preservation properties give rise to sufficient, but not necessary, conditions for inexpressibility in $\exists L^\omega_{\infty\omega}$ or in $\exists L^\omega_{\infty\omega}(\neq)$. In what follows, we shall introduce a variant of pebble games that can actually characterize definability in these two infinitary logics.

2.8.2 Existential Pebble Games

The k-pebble game is a symmetric game, in the sense that the Duplicator wins the k-pebble game on $\mathbf{A}$ and $\mathbf{B}$ if and only if (s)he wins the k-pebble game on $\mathbf{B}$ and $\mathbf{A}$. This is a consequence of the following two properties of the k-pebble game:

1. In each move of the game, the Spoiler can choose either of the two structures, and place a pebble on or remove a pebble from that structure.
2. The payoff condition is that the substructures generated by the pebbled elements must be isomorphic.

Thus, we can reverse the order of $\mathbf{A}$ and $\mathbf{B}$ without affecting the winner of the k-pebble game. We are interested in games that can characterize definability in the k-variable existential infinitary logics $\exists L^k_{\infty\omega}$, $k \geq 1$. A closer scrutiny of the relationship between k-pebble games and $L^k_{\infty\omega}$ reveals that moves of the Spoiler on the structure $\mathbf{B}$ correspond to universal quantification in $L^k_{\infty\omega}$-formulas. This suggests that games for $\exists L^k_{\infty\omega}$ should be such that the Spoiler is limited to always playing on $\mathbf{A}$ (and the Duplicator is limited to always playing on $\mathbf{B}$). Moreover, the payoff condition should be modified appropriately to take account of the absence of negation and universal quantification in $\exists L^k_{\infty\omega}$. These considerations led to the introduction of *existential k-pebble games* in [50].

Definition 2.8.4. *Let k be a positive integer, σ a vocabulary, and $\mathbf{A}$ and $\mathbf{B}$ two σ-structures. The $(\exists, k)$-pebble game on $\mathbf{A}$ and $\mathbf{B}$ is played between two players, called the* Spoiler *and the* Duplicator, *each of whom has k pebbles that are labeled $1, \ldots, k$. In each move, the Spoiler either places a pebble that is not currently used on an element of $\mathbf{A}$ or removes a pebble from an element of $\mathbf{A}$. The Duplicator responds by either placing the pebble with the same label on an element of $\mathbf{B}$ or by removing the pebble with the same label from an element of $\mathbf{B}$. Assume that at some point in time during the game, r pebbles have been placed on each structure, where $1 \leq r \leq k$, and let $(a_i, b_i) \in A \times B$, $1 \leq i \leq r$, be the pairs of elements of $\mathbf{A}$ and $\mathbf{B}$ such that the label of the pebble on a_i is the same as the label of the pebble on b_i.*

The Spoiler wins the $(\exists, k)$-pebble game on $\mathbf{A}$ and $\mathbf{B}$ at this point in time if the mapping $a_i \mapsto b_i$, $1 \leq i \leq r$, is not a homomorphism between the substructures of $\mathbf{A}$ and $\mathbf{B}$ generated by $\{a_1, \ldots, a_r\}$ and $\{b_1, \ldots, b_r\}$, respectively.

The Duplicator wins the $(\exists, k)$-pebble game on $\mathbf{A}$ and $\mathbf{B}$ if the above never happens, which means that the Duplicator has a winning strategy *that allows him to continue playing "forever" by maintaining a partial homomorphism at every point in time.*

The $(\exists, \neq, k)$-pebble game on $\mathbf{A}$ and $\mathbf{B}$ is defined in an entirely analogous way, with the exception that the payoff condition for the Duplicator is that the mapping $a_i \mapsto b_i$, $1 \leq i \leq r$, is a one-to-one homomorphism between the substructures of $\mathbf{A}$ and $\mathbf{B}$ generated by $\{a_1, \ldots, a_r\}$ and $\{b_1, \ldots, b_r\}$, respectively.

The concept of a winning strategy for the Duplicator in the $(\exists, k)$-pebble game and the $(\exists, \neq, k)$-pebble game can be made precise in terms of families of partial homomorphisms or partial one-to-one homomorphisms with appropriate closure and extension properties.

Definition 2.8.5. *A* winning strategy *for the Duplicator in the $(\exists, k)$-pebble game (or, in the $(\exists, \neq, k)$-pebble game) on $\mathbf{A}$ and $\mathbf{B}$ is a nonempty family $\mathcal{I}$ of partial homomorphisms (or, partial one-to-one homomorphisms) from $\mathbf{A}$ to $\mathbf{B}$ with the following properties:*

1. *If $f \in \mathcal{I}$, then $|f - \{(c_1^{\mathbf{A}}, c_1^{\mathbf{B}}), \ldots, (c_s^{\mathbf{A}}, c_s^{\mathbf{B}})\}| \leq k$.*
2. *$\mathcal{I}$ is* closed under subfunctions: *If $g \in \mathcal{I}$ and f is a function such that $\{(c_1^{\mathbf{A}}, c_1^{\mathbf{B}}), \ldots, (c_s^{\mathbf{A}}, c_s^{\mathbf{B}})\} \subseteq f \subseteq g$, then $f \in \mathcal{I}$.*
3. *$\mathcal{I}$ has the* forth property up to k: *If $f \in \mathcal{I}$ and $|f - \{(c_1^{\mathbf{A}}, c_1^{\mathbf{B}}), \ldots, (c_1^{\mathbf{A}}, c_s^{\mathbf{B}})\}| < k$, then for every $a \in A$, there is a $g \in \mathcal{I}$ such that $f \subseteq g$ and $a \in \mathrm{dom}(g)$.*

$$\text{Spoiler plays on } \mathbf{A}: \quad a_1 \ a_2 \ \ldots \ a_r$$
$$\downarrow \ \downarrow \ \ldots \ \downarrow$$
$$\text{Duplicator plays on } \mathbf{B}: \quad b_1 \ b_2 \ \ldots \ b_r \qquad r \leq k$$

Fig. 2.12. A typical run of the $(\exists, k)$-pebble game on $\mathbf{A}$ and $\mathbf{B}$

It is clear that if the Duplicator wins the k-pebble game on **A** and **B**, then the Duplicator also wins the $(\exists, k)$-pebble game on **A** and **B**. The converse, however, is not always true. Intuitively, it is easier for the Duplicator to win the $(\exists, k)$-pebble game than it is to win the k-pebble game, because the Spoiler cannot switch between the two structures. Note also that, unlike the k-pebble game, the $(\exists, k)$-pebble game is asymmetric. For instance, the Spoiler wins the $(\exists, k+1)$-pebble game on the cliques $\mathbf{K}_{k+1}$ and $\mathbf{K}_k$, but the Duplicator wins the $(\exists, k+1)$-pebble game on the cliques $\mathbf{K}_k$ and $\mathbf{K}_{k+1}$. A similar state of affairs holds for the $(\exists, \neq, k)$-pebble game.

We now present the connection between existential pebble games and definability in the finite-variable existential infinitary logics.

Definition 2.8.6. *Let k be a positive integer, and let* **A** *and* **B** *be two σ-structures.*

- *We write* $\mathbf{A} \preceq_{\infty\omega}^{\exists,k} \mathbf{B}$ *to denote that every $\exists L_{\infty\omega}^k$-sentence that is true on* **A** *is also true on* **B**.
- *We write* $\mathbf{A} \preceq_{\omega\omega}^{\exists,k} \mathbf{B}$ *to denote that every first-order sentence of $\exists L_{\infty\omega}^k$ that is true on* **A** *is also true on* **B**.
- *Let $a_1, \ldots, a_r$ be a sequence of elements from A and let $b_1, \ldots, b_r$ be a sequence of elements from B, for some $r \leq k$. We write $(\mathbf{A}, a_1, \ldots, a_r)$ $\preceq_{\infty\omega}^{\exists,k} (\mathbf{B}, b_1, \ldots, b_r)$ to denote that for every $\exists L_{\infty\omega}^k$-formula $\varphi(v_1, \ldots, v_r)$ with free variables among $v_1, \ldots, v_r$, we have that*

$$\mathbf{A} \models \varphi(v_1/a_1, \ldots, v_r/a_r) \implies \mathbf{B} \models \varphi(v_1/b_1, \ldots, v_r/b_r).$$

The relation $\preceq_{\infty\omega}^{\exists,\neq,k}$ is defined in a similar manner, with $\exists L_{\infty\omega}^k(\neq)$ in place of $\exists L_{\infty\omega}^k$.

Theorem 2.8.7. *[47] Let k be a positive integer, and let* **A** *and* **B** *be two σ-structures. The following statements are then equivalent:*

- $\mathbf{A} \preceq_{\infty\omega}^{\exists,k} \mathbf{B}$.
- *The Duplicator wins the $(\exists, k)$-pebble game on* **A** *and* **B**.

Moreover, if **B** *is finite, then the above statements are also equivalent to*

- $\mathbf{A} \preceq_{\omega\omega}^{\exists,k} \mathbf{B}$.

A similar result holds for $\exists L_{\infty\omega}^k(\neq)$ and the $(\exists, \neq, k)$-pebble game.

As a consequence of Theorem 2.8.7, we obtain a characterization of $\exists L_{\infty\omega}^\omega$-definability on classes of finite structures.

Corollary 2.8.8. *Let σ be a vocabulary, $\mathcal{C}$ a class of finite σ-structures, and Q a Boolean query on $\mathcal{C}$. The following statements are then equivalent:*

1. *Q is $\exists L^\omega_{\infty\omega}$-definable on $\mathcal{C}$.*
2. *There is a positive integer k such that, for every structure $\mathbf{A} \in \mathcal{C}$ and every structure $\mathbf{B} \in \mathcal{C}$, if $Q(\mathbf{A}) = 1$ and the Duplicator wins the $(\exists, k)$-pebble game on $\mathbf{A}$ and $\mathbf{B}$, then $Q(\mathbf{B}) = 1$.*

Thus, we have a sound and complete method for studying $\exists L^\omega_{\infty\omega}$-definability on classes of finite structures.

Method 2.8.9 The Method of $(\exists, k)$-Pebble Games for $\exists L^\omega_{\infty\omega}$. Let σ be a vocabulary, $\mathcal{C}$ a class of finite σ-structures, and Q a Boolean query on $\mathcal{C}$.

Soundness. To show that Q is *not* $\exists L^\omega_{\infty\omega}$-definable on $\mathcal{C}$, it suffices to show that, for every positive integer k, there are structures $\mathbf{A}_k$ and $\mathbf{B}_k$ in $\mathcal{C}$ such that

- $Q(\mathbf{A}_k) = 1$ and $Q(\mathbf{B}_k) = 0$;
- the Duplicator wins the $(\exists, k)$-pebble game on $\mathbf{A}$ and $\mathbf{B}$.

Completeness. This method is also complete, that is, if Q is *not* $\exists L^\omega_{\infty\omega}$-definable on $\mathcal{C}$, then, for every positive integer k, such structures $\mathbf{A}_k$ and $\mathbf{B}_k$ exist.

A similar method can be used for studying $\exists L^\omega_{\infty\omega}(\neq)$-definability on classes of finite structures using $(\exists, \neq, k)$-pebble games, $k \geq 1$.

We now present some results concerning the descriptive and computational complexity of determining the winner in the $(\exists, k)$-pebble game, $k \geq 1$. These results should be compared with the results in Propositions 2.7.18 and 2.7.20 and in Theorem 2.7.21 about the descriptive and computational complexity of determining the winner in the k-pebble game, $k \geq 1$.

Theorem 2.8.10. [50] *Let σ be a vocabulary and let k be a positive integer.*

1. *The query "Given two σ-structures $\mathbf{A}$ and $\mathbf{B}$, does the Spoiler win the $(\exists, k)$-pebble game on $\mathbf{A}$ and $\mathbf{B}$?" is LFP-definable. As a result, there is a polynomial-time algorithm such that, given two finite σ-structures $\mathbf{A}$ and $\mathbf{B}$, it determines whether the Spoiler wins the $(\exists, k)$-pebble game on $\mathbf{A}$ and $\mathbf{B}$.*
2. *For every finite σ-structure $\mathbf{B}$, there is a k-Datalog program $\rho_\mathbf{B}$ that expresses the query "Given a σ-structure $\mathbf{A}$, does the Spoiler win the $(\exists, k)$-pebble game on $\mathbf{A}$ and $\mathbf{B}$?"*

Proof. (Sketch) For notational simplicity, let us assume that the vocabulary σ consists of relation symbols only. Let $\theta(x_1, \ldots, x_k, y_1, \ldots, y_k)$ be a quantifier-free formula over the vocabulary $\sigma_1 + \sigma_2$ asserting that the correspondence $x_i \mapsto y_i$, $1 \leq i \leq k$, is not a mapping or that it is a mapping that is *not* a homomorphism from the substructure generated by $x_1, \ldots, x_k$ over the vocabulary σ_1 to the substructure induced by $y_1, \ldots, y_k$ over the vocabulary σ_2. In particular, θ is the disjunction of the following formulas:

- $x_i = x_j \wedge y_i \neq y_j$, for every $i, j \leq k$ such that $i \neq j$.
- $R_1(x_{i_1}, \ldots, x_{i_m}) \wedge \neg R_2(y_{i_1}, \ldots, y_{i_m})$, for every m-ary relation symbol R in σ and every m-tuple $(i_1, \ldots, i_m)$ of indices from the set $\{1, \ldots, k\}$.

Let T be a $2k$-ary relation symbol not in the vocabulary $\sigma_1 + \sigma_2$ and let $\varphi(x_1, \ldots, x_k, y_1, \ldots, y_k, T)$ be the following positive first-order formula over the vocabulary $\sigma_1 + \sigma_2 \cup \{T\}$:

$$\theta(x_1, \ldots, x_k, y_1, \ldots, y_k) \vee \bigvee_{j=1}^{k} (\exists x_j \in D_1)(\forall y_j \in D_2) T(x_1, \ldots, x_k, y_1, \ldots, y_k).$$

It is easy to verify that if $\mathbf{A}$ and $\mathbf{B}$ are σ-structures, and $(a_1, \ldots, a_k)$ and $(b_1, \ldots, b_k)$ are k-tuples of elements from A and B respectively, then the following statements are equivalent:

1. $\mathbf{A} + \mathbf{B} \models \varphi^\infty(a_1, \ldots, a_k, b_1, \ldots, b_k)$.
2. The Spoiler wins the $(\exists, k)$-pebble game on $(A, a_1, \ldots, a_k)$ and $(B, b_1, \ldots, b_k)$.

Let ψ be the sentence $(\exists x_1) \cdots (\exists x_k)(\forall y_1) \cdots (\forall y_k)\varphi^\infty(x_1, \ldots, x_k, y_1, \ldots, y_k)$ of least fixed point logic LFP. Consequently, for every σ-structure $\mathbf{A}$ and every σ-structure $\mathbf{B}$, the following statements are equivalent:

1. $\mathbf{A} + \mathbf{B} \models \psi$.
2. The Spoiler wins the $(\exists, k)$-pebble game on $\mathbf{A}$ and $\mathbf{B}$.

Note that the positive first-order formula φ above involves existential quantifiers that are interpreted over the elements of $\mathbf{A}$, and universal quantifiers that are interpreted over the elements of $\mathbf{B}$. Consequently, if $\mathbf{B}$ is a fixed finite σ-structure, then the universal quantifiers can be replaced by finitary conjunctions over the elements of the universe B of $\mathbf{B}$, and thus φ can be transformed to a k-Datalog program $\rho_\mathbf{B}$ that expresses the query "Given a finite σ-structure $\mathbf{A}$, does the Spoiler win the existential k-pebble game on $\mathbf{A}$ and $\mathbf{B}$?" In what follows, we describe this k-Datalog program in some detail. The goal of $\rho_\mathbf{B}$ is a 0-ary predicate S. Let $\mathbf{b} = (b_1, \ldots, b_k)$ be a k-tuple of elements of B. For each such k-tuple, we introduce a k-ary relation symbol $T_\mathbf{b}$ and the following rules:

- For every i and j such that $b_i \neq b_j$, we have a rule

$$T_\mathbf{b}(x_1', \ldots, x_k') \; :- \qquad ,$$

with an empty body, where $x_i' = x_j' = x_i$ and $x_s' = x_s$, for $s \neq i, j$. Intuitively, these rules say that the correspondence $x_i \mapsto b_i$, $1 \leq i \leq k$, is not a mapping.
- For every m-ary relation symbol R of σ and every m-ary tuple $(i_1, \ldots, i_m)$ such that

$$B, b_{i_1}, \ldots, b_{i_m} \models \neg R(x_{i_1}, \ldots, x_{i_m}),$$

we have a rule

$$T_{\mathbf{b}}(x_1, \ldots, x_k) \; : - \; R(x_{i_1}, \ldots, x_{i_m}).$$

Intuitively, these rules say that the correspondence $x_i \mapsto b_i$, $1 \leq i \leq k$, is not a partial homomorphism.

- For every j such that $1 \leq j \leq k$, we have a rule

$$T(x_1, \ldots, x_k) \; : - \; \bigwedge_{c \in B} T_{\mathbf{b}[j/c]}(x_1, \ldots, x_{j-1}, y, x_{j+1}, \ldots, x_k),$$

where $\mathbf{b}[j/c] = (b_1, \ldots, b_{j-1}, c, b_{j+1}, \ldots, b_k)$ and y is a new variable (note, however, that the body of the rule has k variables).

- For the goal predicate S, we have the rule

$$S \; : - \; \bigwedge_{\mathbf{b} \in B^k} T_{\mathbf{b}}(x_1, \ldots, x_k). \quad \square$$

As stated in Theorem 2.7.19, Grohe [34] showed that if σ is a vocabulary containing at least one binary relation symbol, then for every $k \geq 2$, the following query is P-complete: "given two finite σ-structures $\mathbf{A}$ and $\mathbf{B}$, does the Duplicator win the k-pebble game on $\mathbf{A}$ and $\mathbf{B}$?" In this query, both structures $\mathbf{A}$ and $\mathbf{B}$ are part of the input. Recall, however, that the complexity drops if the structure $\mathbf{B}$ is kept fixed. Indeed, as shown in Theorem 2.7.21, for each fixed positive integer k and for each fixed finite σ-structure $\mathbf{B}$, the following query is FO^k-definable (and, hence, solvable in logarithmic space): "given a finite σ-structure $\mathbf{A}$, does the Duplicator win the k-pebble game on $\mathbf{A}$ and $\mathbf{B}$?" In contrast, we now show that determining the winner in the $(\exists, k)$-pebble game can be P-complete, even for a fixed k and a fixed $\mathbf{B}$.

Proposition 2.8.11. *There are a vocabulary σ consisting of relation symbols of arity at most 3 and a finite σ-structure $\mathbf{B}$ such that the following query is P-complete: "given a finite σ-structure $\mathbf{A}$, does the Duplicator win the $(\exists, 3)$-pebble game on $\mathbf{A}$ and $\mathbf{B}$?"*

Proof. We shall describe a logarithmic-space reduction from the satisfiability problem HORN 3-SAT for Horn formulas with at most three literals per clause, which is a well-known P-complete problem (see [32])

Let σ be a vocabulary consisting of two unary relation symbols N_1 and P_1, two binary relation symbols N_2 and P_2, and two ternary relation symbols N_3 and P_3. intuition These relation symbols will represent the various types of clauses that may occur in a Horn formula with at most three literals per clause. Specifically, N_1 and P_1 will represent the unit clauses $\neg x$ and x, N_2 and P_2 will represent the binary Horn clauses $\neg x \vee \neg y$ and $\neg x \vee y$, and N_3 and P_3 will represent the ternary Horn clauses $\neg x \vee \neg y \vee \neg z$ and $\neg x \vee \neg y \vee z$. Let $\mathbf{B}$ be the Boolean σ-structure whose relations are the sets of satisfying truth assignments of Horn clauses with at most three literals per clause. More precisely, the universe of $\mathbf{B}$ is the set $\{0, 1\}$ and the relations of $\mathbf{B}$ are as follows:

- $N_1^{\mathbf{B}} = \{0\}$ and $P_1^{\mathbf{B}} = \{1\}$;
- $N_2^{\mathbf{B}} = \{0,1\}^2 - \{(1,1)\}$ and $P_2^{\mathbf{B}} = \{0,1\}^2 - \{(1,0)\}$;
- $N_3^{\mathbf{B}} = \{0,1\}^3 - \{(1,1,1)\}$ and $N_3^{\mathbf{B}} = \{0,1\}^3 - \{(1,1,0)\}$.

If φ is a Horn formula with at most three literals per clause, then φ can be encoded by a finite σ-structure $\mathbf{A}_\varphi$ such that the universe A of $\mathbf{A}$ is the set of all variables occurring in φ and the relations on $\mathbf{A}$ represent the clauses of φ. For instance, $N_2^{\mathbf{A}}$ consists of all pairs (x,y) of variables such that $\neg x \vee \neg y$ is a clause of φ, and $P_3^{\mathbf{A}}$ consists of all triples (x,y,z) of variables such that $\neg x \vee \neg y \vee z$ is a clause of φ. Clearly, $\mathbf{A}_\varphi$ can be constructed in logarithmic space from φ.

We now claim that φ is satisfiable if and only if the Duplicator wins the $(\exists,3)$-pebble game on $\mathbf{A}_\varphi$ and $\mathbf{B}$. If φ is satisfiable, then a satisfying truth assignment is a homomorphism from $\mathbf{A}_\varphi$ to $\mathbf{B}$. Hence, the Duplicator can win the $(\exists,3)$-pebble game on $\mathbf{A}_\varphi$ and $\mathbf{B}$ by using the values of this homomorphism to respond to the moves of the Spoiler. In fact, in this case the Duplicator can win the $(\exists,k)$-pebble game on $\mathbf{A}_\varphi$ and $\mathbf{B}$ for every $k \geq 1$. The other direction requires more work. We start with the observation that the well-known polynomial-time *marking algorithm* for Horn satisfiability is readily expressible in 3-Datalog. More precisely, consider the following 3-Datalog program π with T and P as its IDB predicates and P as its goal predicate:

$$
\begin{aligned}
T(z) &:- P_1(z) \\
T(z) &:- P_2(x,z), T(x) \\
T(z) &:- P_3(x,y,z), T(x), T(y) \\
P &:- N_1(x), T(x) \\
P &:- N_2(x,y), T(x), T(y) \\
P &:- N_3(x,y,z), T(x), T(y), T(z)
\end{aligned}
$$

It is easy to verify that $\mathbf{B}$ does not satisfy the goal predicate P. Moreover, a Horn formula φ with at most three literals per clause is unsatisfiable if and only if the structure $\mathbf{A}_\varphi$ satisfies the goal predicate P. This holds because the first three rules of π mimic the marking algorithm for Horn satisfiability by putting into the predicate T all variables of φ that must take the value "true" in every satisfying truth assignment; the last three rules capture the possible ways in which a Horn formula may be found to be unsatisfiable by this algorithm because all variables occurring in some negative clause are forced to take the value "true". Assume now that the Duplicator wins the $(\exists,3)$-pebble game on $\mathbf{A}_\varphi$ and $\mathbf{B}$. We claim that φ is satisfiable. If this is not the case, then $\mathbf{A}_\varphi$ satisfies the goal predicate P of the above 3-Datalog program π. Since the Duplicator wins the $(\exists,3)$-pebble game on $\mathbf{A}_\varphi$ and $\mathbf{B}$, Theorem 2.8.8 implies that $\mathbf{B}$ satisfies the goal predicate P of π, which is not true. $\square$

Obviously, Proposition 2.8.11 implies that, when both structures $\mathbf{A}$ and $\mathbf{B}$ are part of the input, then determining the winner in the $(\exists,3)$-pebble game is a P-complete problem. In fact, it is known that this holds for every fixed $k \geq 2$ and for vocabularies consisting of a binary relation symbol and a fixed number of unary relation symbols [48]. As stated earlier, it has been conjectured, but remains to be proved, that determining the winner in the k-pebble game when k is part of the input is an EXPTIME-complete problem. In contrast, determining the winner in the $(\exists, k)$-pebble game when k is part of the input has been shown to be EXPTIME-complete.

Theorem 2.8.12. [48] *The following problem is EXPTIME-complete: given a positive integer k, a vocabulary σ consisting of one binary relation symbol and a number of unary relation symbols, and two finite σ-structures $\mathbf{A}$ and $\mathbf{B}$, does the Duplicator win the $(\exists, k)$-pebble game on $\mathbf{A}$ and $\mathbf{B}$?*

We note that some of the results about Datalog and $(\exists, k)$-pebble games that we have presented here have found numerous applications to the study of constraint satisfaction problems, which is the topic of Chap. 6 of this volume.

2.8.3 Descriptive Complexity of Fixed Subgraph Homeomorphism Queries

The original motivation behind the introduction of $(\exists, k)$-pebble games and $(\exists, \neq, k)$-pebble games in [47] was to develop tools for analyzing the expressive power of Datalog and Datalog$(\neq)$. We now close this chapter by presenting a case study of the expressibility of certain important graph-theoretic problems in Datalog$(\neq)$ using $(\exists, \neq, k)$-pebble games.

Definition 2.8.13. *Let $\mathbf{H}$ and $\mathbf{G}$ be two directed graphs.*

A homeomorphism $h : \mathbf{H} \rightsquigarrow \mathbf{G}$ from $\mathbf{H}$ to $\mathbf{G}$ is a one-to-one mapping from the nodes of $\mathbf{H}$ to the nodes of $\mathbf{G}$ such that h maps the edges of $\mathbf{H}$ to pairwise node-disjoint simple paths of $\mathbf{G}$.

The concept of a homeomorphism gives rise to a family of decision problems on directed graphs, one for each fixed finite directed graph $\mathbf{H}$.

Definition 2.8.14. *Let $\mathbf{H}$ be a fixed finite directed graph. The FIXED SUB-GRAPH HOMEOMORPHISM QUERY WITH PATTERN $\mathbf{H}$, denoted by FISH($\mathbf{H}$), asks: given a directed graph $\mathbf{G}$ and a one-to-one mapping from the nodes of H to the nodes of G, is there a homeomorphism $h : H \rightsquigarrow G$ extending this mapping?*

The following examples illustrate some typical members of this family of queries.

Example 2.8.15. Let $\mathbf{H}$ be a directed graph consisting of two parallel directed edges, that is, $\mathbf{H}$ has four nodes s_1, s_2, t_1, t_2 and two edges (s_1, t_1), (s_2, t_2), as depicted in the upper part of Fig. 2.13.

FISH($\mathbf{H}$) is then the 2-DISJOINT PATHS query: given a directed graph $\mathbf{G}$ and four nodes s_1', s_2', t_1', t_2', does $\mathbf{G}$ contain two node-disjoint simple paths from s_1' to t_1' and from s_2' to t_2'? This is depicted in the lower part of Fig. 2.13.

If $\mathbf{H}$ is taken to be a graph consisting of m parallel directed edges, this example generalizes to the m-DISJOINT PATHS query, $m \geq 2$.

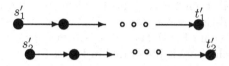

Fig. 2.13. The 2-DISJOINT PATHS query

Example 2.8.16. If $\mathbf{C}_3$ is a directed cycle with three nodes, then FISH($\mathbf{C}_3$) is the following query: given a directed graph $\mathbf{G}$ and three nodes a_1, a_2, a_3, is there a simple cycle in $\mathbf{G}$ containing these nodes?

If $\mathbf{H}$ is taken to be a directed cycle $\mathbf{C}_m$ with m nodes, $m \geq 3$, this example generalizes to the following query: given a directed graph $\mathbf{G}$ and m nodes $a_1, \ldots, a_m$, is there a simple cycle in $\mathbf{G}$ containing these m nodes?

Fortune, Hopcroft, and Wyllie [26] obtained a complete classification of the computational complexity of all FISH($\mathbf{H}$) queries as $\mathbf{H}$ ranges over all finite directed graphs. Before stating this classification result, we need one more concept.

Definition 2.8.17. *A* star *graph is a directed graph that consists either of a single* source *node and edges emanating from this node or of a single* sink *node and edges terminating on this node. Star graphs are depicted in Fig. 2.14.*

Theorem 2.8.18. [26] *The following dichotomy holds for the computational complexity of the* FIXED SUBGRAPH HOMEOMORPHISM QUERY WITH PATTERN $\mathbf{H}$, *where $\mathbf{H}$ ranges over all finite directed graphs:*

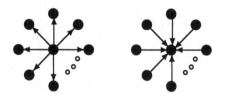

Fig. 2.14. Star graphs

- *If* **H** *is a star graph, then* FISH(**H**) *is in* P.
- *If* **H** *is not a star graph, then* FISH(**H**) *is NP-complete.*

Let us digress for a moment and explain why the preceding result is a dichotomy theorem. Ladner [51] showed that if P $\neq$ NP, then there is a decision problem Q such that

- $Q \in NP - P$;
- Q is *not* NP-complete.

Thus, if P $\neq$ NP, then NP contains problems of intermediate complexity between polynomial-time solvability and NP-completeness. Theorem 2.8.18, however, asserts that no FISH(**H**) query is a problem of such intermediate complexity; this dichotomy is illustrated in Fig. 2.15.

Note that the dichotomy in the computational complexity of FISH(**H**) queries is proper only if P $\neq$ NP. We now present a dichotomy in the descriptive complexity of FISH(**H**) queries that does not depend on any complexity-theoretic assumptions.

Theorem 2.8.19. [47] *The following dichotomy holds for the descriptive complexity of the* FIXED SUBGRAPH HOMEOMORPHISM QUERY WITH PATTERN **H**, *where* **H** *ranges over all finite directed graphs:*

- *If* **H** *is a star graph, then* FISH(**H**) *is* $\exists L^\omega_{\infty\omega}(\neq)$-*definable; in fact, it is definable in* Datalog($\neq$).
- *If* **H** *is not a star graph, then* FISH(**H**) *is not* $\exists L^\omega_{\infty\omega}(\neq)$-*definable.*

Proof. (Hint) If **H** is a star graph, then the FISH(**H**) query is solvable in polynomial time using a max flow algorithm, which can be expressed by a Datalog($\neq$) program.

The 2-DISJOINT PATHS query is the key case of the results concerning the inexpressibility of FISH(**H**) in Datalog($\neq$) when **H** is not a star graph. To this effect, one can show that, for every $k \geq 1$, there are directed graphs $\mathbf{A}_k$ and $\mathbf{B}_k$ such that the following hold:

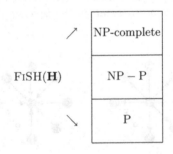

Fig. 2.15. The dichotomy in the computational complexity of FISH(**H**) queries

- $\mathbf{A}_k$ satisfies the 2-DISJOINT PATHS query, but $\mathbf{B}_k$ does not;
- the Duplicator wins the $(\exists, \neq, k)$-pebble game on $\mathbf{A}_k$, $\mathbf{B}_k$.

The graph $\mathbf{A}_k$ consists of two disjoint sufficiently long paths. The graph $\mathbf{B}_k$, however, is much more complicated and so is the description of the Duplicator's winning strategy in the $(\exists, \neq, k)$-pebble game on $\mathbf{A}_k$ and $\mathbf{B}_k$. This graph is extracted from the reduction of 3-SAT to 2-DISJOINT PATHS used by Fortune, Hopcroft, and Wyllie [26] to establish that the 2-DISJOINT PATHS query is NP-hard. □

Several remarks are in order now. The first is that the proof of Theorem 2.8.19 reveals that certain constructions used to prove NP-hardness can also be used to obtain interesting structures on which to play combinatorial games and establish lower bounds for definability. Note that the dichotomy in the descriptive complexity of FISH(**H**) queries cannot be proved using preservation properties of Datalog($\neq$), because these queries are preserved under one-to-one homomorphisms.

It is an open problem to significantly strengthen the lower bound in Theorem 2.8.19 by establishing that if **H** is not a star graph, then the FISH(**H**) query is not $L_{\infty\omega}^\omega$-definable. The critical step would be to show that the 2-DISJOINT PATHS query is not $L_{\infty\omega}^\omega$-definable.

As a by-product of their celebrated work on the graph minor problem, Robertson and Seymour [57, 58] showed that every FISH(**H**) query is solvable in polynomial time when restricted to undirected graphs. It would be interesting to carry out a detailed study of the descriptive complexity of FISH(**H**) queries on undirected graphs. A preliminary investigation by Barland [7] showed that the FISH($\mathbf{C}_3$) query is LFP-definable on the class $\mathcal{G}$ of all finite undirected graphs. This suggests that if there is a dichotomy in the descriptive complexity of FISH(**H**) queries on undirected graphs, then the boundary of that dichotomy is going to be different from the boundary of the dichotomy in Theorem 2.8.19.

Acknowledgments

I am truly grateful to Timos Antonopoulos, Costas D. Koutras, and Scott Weinstein for reading carefully an earlier version of this chapter and offering numerous corrections and suggestions.

References

1. S. Abiteboul, R. Hull, and V. Vianu. *Foundations of Databases*. Addison-Wesley, 1995.
2. S. Abiteboul and V. Vianu. Datalog extensions for database queries and updates. *Journal of Computer and System Sciences*, 43:62–124, 1991.

3. S. Abiteboul and V. Vianu. Generic computation and its complexity. In *Proc. 23rd ACM Symp. on Theory of Computing*, pages 209–219, 1991.
4. M. Ajtai and R. Fagin. Reachability is harder for directed than for undirected finite graphs. *Journal of Symbolic Logic*, 55(1):113–150, 1990.
5. M. Ajtai and Y. Gurevich. Monotone versus positive. *Journal of the ACM*, 34:1004–1015, 1987.
6. S. Arora and R. Fagin. On winning strategies in Ehrenfeucht-Fraïssé games. *Theoretical Computer Science*, 174:97–121, 1997.
7. I. Barland. *Expressing Optimization Problems as Integer Programs, and Undirected Path Problems: a Descriptive Complexity Approach*. PhD thesis, University of California, Santa Cruz, 1996.
8. J. Barwise. On Moschovakis closure ordinals. *Journal of Symbolic Logic*, 42:292–296, 1977.
9. A. Blass, Y. Gurevich, and D. Kozen. A zero–one law for logic with a fixed point operator. *Information and Control*, 67:70–90, 1985.
10. A. Chandra and D. Harel. Computable queries for relational databases. *Journal of Computer and System Sciences*, 21:156–178, 1980.
11. A. Chandra and D. Harel. Structure and complexity of relational queries. *Journal of Computer and System Sciences*, 25:99–128, 1982.
12. A. Chandra and D. Harel. Horn clause queries and generalizations. *Journal of Logic Programming*, 1:1–15, 1985.
13. S. A. Cook. An observation of time–storage trade-off. *Journal of Computer and System Sciences*, 9:308–316, 1974.
14. A. Dawar. A restricted second-order logic for finite structures. *Information and Computation*, 143:154–174, 1998.
15. A. Dawar, S. Lindell, and S. Weinstein. Infinitary logic and inductive definability over finite structures. *Information and Computation*, 119:160–175, 1995.
16. M. de Rougemont. Second-order and inductive definability on finite structures. *Zeitschrift für Mathematische Logik und Grundlagen der Mathematik*, 33:47–63, 1987.
17. M. A. Dickmann. Larger infinitary languages. In J. Barwise and S. Feferman, editors, *Model-Theoretic Logics*, pages 317–363. Springer, 1985.
18. R. Diestel. *Graph Theory*. Springer, 1997.
19. A. Ehrenfeucht. An application of games to the completeness problem for formalized theories. *Fundamenta Mathematicae*, 49:129–141, 1961.
20. H. B. Enderton. *A Mathematical Introduction to Logic*. Academic Press, New York, 1972.
21. R. Fagin. Generalized first-order spectra and polynomial-time recognizable sets. In R. M. Karp, editor, *Complexity of Computation, SIAM-AMS Proceedings*, volume 7, pages 43–73, 1974.
22. R. Fagin. Monadic generalized spectra. *Zeitschrift für Mathematische Logik und Grundlagen der Mathematik*, 21:89–96, 1975.
23. R. Fagin. Probabilities on finite models. *Journal of Symbolic Logic*, 41:50–58, 1976.
24. R. Fagin. Easier ways to win logical games. In N. Immerman and Ph. G. Kolaitis, editors, *Descriptive Complexity and Finite Models, DIMACS Series in Discrete Mathematics and Theoretical Computer Science*, volume 31, pages 1–32. American Mathematical Society, 1997.

25. R. Fagin, L. Stockmeyer, and M. Y. Vardi. On monadic NP vs. monadic co-NP. *Information and Computation*, 120(1):78–92, July 1995.

26. S. Fortune, J. Hopcroft, and J. Wyllie. The directed homeomorphism problem. *Theoretical Computer Science*, 10:111–121, 1980.

27. R. Fraïssé. Sur quelques classifications des systèmes de relations. *Publications Scientifiques de l'Université d' Alger*, Series A, 1:35–182, 1954.

28. H. Gaifman. On local and nonlocal properties. In J. Stern, editor, *Logic Colloquium '81*, pages 105–135. North-Holland, 1982.

29. H. Gaifman and M. Y. Vardi. A simple proof that connectivity is not first-order definable. *Bulletin of the European Association for Theoretical Computer Science*, 26:43–45, June 1985.

30. M. R. Garey and D. S. Johnson. *Computers and Intractability – A Guide to the Theory of NP-Completeness*. W. H. Freeman, 1979.

31. Y. V. Glebskii, D. I. Kogan, M. I. Liogonki, and V. A. Talanov. Range and degree of realizability of formulas in the restricted predicate calculus. *Cybernetics*, 5:142–154, 1969.

32. R. Greenlaw, H. J. Hoover, and W. L. Ruzzo. *Limits to Parallel Computation: P-Completeness Theory*. Oxford University Press, New York, 1995.

33. M. Grohe. Complete problems for fixed-point logics. *Journal of Symbolic Logic*, 60(2):517–527, 1995.

34. M. Grohe. Equivalence in finite-variable logics is complete for polynomial time. *Combinatorica*, 19(4):507–523, 1999.

35. Y. Gurevich and S. Shelah. Fixed point extensions of first-order logic. *Annals of Pure and Applied Logic*, 32:265–280, 1986.

36. W. Hanf. Model-theoretic methods in the study of elementary logic. In J. Addison, L. Henkin, and A. Tarski, editors, *The Theory of Models*, pages 132–145. North-Holland, 1965.

37. J Hartmanis. Turing Award Lecture: On computational complexity and the nature of computer science. *Communications of the ACM*, 37:37–43, 1994.

38. N. Immerman. Upper and lower bounds for first-order expressibility. *Journal of Computer and System Sciences*, 25:76–98, 1982.

39. N. Immerman. Relational queries computable in polynomial time. *Information and Control*, 68:86–104, 1986.

40. N. Immerman. *Descriptive Complexity* Springer, 1999.

41. H. J. Keisler. *Model Theory for Infinitary Logic*. North-Holland, 1971.

42. S. C. Kleene. Arithmetical predicates and function quantifiers. *Transactions of the American Mathematical Society*, 79:312–340, 1955.

43. B. Knaster. Un théorème sur les fonctions d'ensembles. *Annales de la Société Polonaise de Mathematique*, 6:133–134, 1928.

44. Ph. G. Kolaitis and M. Y. Vardi. The decision problem for the probabilities of higher-order properties. In *Proc. 19th ACM Symp. on Theory of Computing*, pages 425–435, 1987.

45. Ph. G. Kolaitis and M. Y. Vardi. Fixpoint logic vs. infinitary logic in finite-model theory. In *Proc. 6th IEEE Symp. on Logic in Computer Science*, pages 46–57, 1992.

46. Ph. G. Kolaitis and M. Y. Vardi. Infinitary logic and 0–1 laws. *Information and Computation*, 98:258–294, 1992. Special issue: Selections from the Fifth Annual IEEE Symposium on Logic in Computer Science.

47. Ph. G. Kolaitis and M. Y. Vardi. On the expressive power of Datalog: tools and a case study. *Journal of Computer and System Sciences*, 51(1):110–134, August 1995. Special Issue: Selections from Ninth Annual ACM SIGACT–SIGMOD–SIGART Symposium on Principles of Database Systems (PODS), Nashville, TN, April 1990.

48. Ph. G. Kolaitis and J. Panttaja. On the complexity of existential pebble games. In *2003 Annual Conference of the European Association for Computer Science Logic, CSL '03, Lecture Notes in Computer Science*, volume 2803, Springer, pages 314–329, 2003.

49. Ph. G. Kolaitis and M. Y. Vardi. On the expressive power of variable-confined logics. In *Proceedings of 11th Annual IEEE Symposium on Logic in Computer Science - LICS '96*, pages 348–59, 1996.

50. Ph. G. Kolaitis and M. Y. Vardi. Conjunctive-query containment and constraint satisfaction. *Journal of Computer and System Sciences*, pages 302–332, 2000. Earlier version in: *Proc. 17th ACM Symp. on Principles of Database Systems* (PODS '98).

51. R. E. Ladner. On the structure of polynomial time reducibility. *Journal of the Association for Computing Machinery*, 22(1):155–171, 1975.

52. M. McArthur. Convergence and 0–1 laws for $L^k_{\infty\omega}$ under arbitrary measures. In *1994 Annual Conference of the European Association for Computer Science Logic, CSL '94, Lecture Notes in Computer Science*, volume 933, pages 228–241. Springer, 1995.

53. R. Milner. Operational and algebraic semantics of concurrent processes. In J. van Leeuwen, editor, *Handbook of Theoretical Computer Science*, volume B, pages 1201–1242. MIT Press/Elsevier, 1990.

54. Y. N. Moschovakis. *Elementary Induction on Abstract Structures*. North-Holland, 1974.

55. C. H. Papadimitriou. *Computational Complexity*. Addison-Wesley, 1994.

56. E. Pezzoli. Computational complexity of Ehrenfeucht–Fraïssé games on finite structures. In *Proc. 12th International Workshop on Computer Science Logic, CSL '98, Lecture Notes in Computer Science*, volume 1584, pages 159–170. Springer, 1999.

57. N. Robertson and P. D. Seymour. Disjoint paths – a survey. *SIAM Journal of Algebraic and Discrete Methods*, 6:300–305, 1985.

58. N. Robertson and P. D. Seymour. Graph Minors. XIII. The disjoint paths problem. *Journal of Combinatorial Theory B*, 63:65–110, 1995.

59. T. Schwentick. Graph connectivity and monadic NP. In *Proc. 35th IEEE Symp. on Foundations of Computer Science*, pages 614–622, 1994.

60. D. Scott. Logic with denumerably long formulas and finite strings of quantifiers. In J. W. Addison, L. Henkin, and A. Tarski, editors, *The Theory of Models*, pages 320–341. North-Holland, 1965.

61. S. Shelah and J. Spencer. Zero–one laws for sparse random graphs. *Journal of the American Mathematical Society*, 1:97–115, 1988.

62. C. Spector. Inductively defined sets of natural numbers. In *Infinitistic Methods*, pages 97–102. Pergamon, 1961.

63. L. J. Stockmeyer. The polynomial-time hierarchy. *Theoretical Computer Science*, 3:1–22, 1977.

64. A. Tarski. A lattice theoretical fixpoint theorem and its applications. *Pacific Journal of Mathematics*, 5:285–309, 1955.

65. J. D. Ullman. *Database and Knowledge-Base Systems*, volumes I and II. Computer Science Press, 1989.

66. J. van Benthem. Correspondence theory. In D. M. Gabbay and F. Guenthner, editors, *Handbook of Philosophical Logic*, volume 2, pages 167–247. Reidel, 1984.

67. M. Y. Vardi. The complexity of relational query languages. In *Proc. 14th ACM Symp. on Theory of Computing*, pages 137–146, 1982.

3

Finite Model Theory and Descriptive Complexity

Erich Grädel

This chapter deals with the relationship between logical definability and computational complexity on finite structures. Particular emphasis is given to *game-based evaluation algorithms* for various logical formalisms and to *logics capturing complexity classes*.

In addition to the most common logical systems such as first-order and second-order logic (and their fragments), this survey focuses on algorithmic questions and complexity results related to fixed-point logics (including fixed-point extensions of first-order logic, the modal μ-calculus, the database query language Datalog, and fixed-point logics with counting).

Finally, it is discussed how the general approach and the methodology of finite model theory can be extended to suitable domains of infinite structures. As an example, some results relating *metafinite model theory* to complexity theory are presented.

3.1 Definability and Complexity

One of the central issues in finite model theory is the relationship between logical definability and computational complexity. We want to understand how the expressive power of a logical system – such as first-order or second-order logic, least fixed-point logic, or a logic-based database query language such as Datalog – is related to its algorithmic properties. Conversely, we want to relate natural levels of computational complexity to the defining power of logical languages, i.e., we want *logics that capture complexity classes*.[1]

The aspects of finite model theory that are related to computational complexity are also referred to as *descriptive complexity theory*. While computational complexity theory is concerned with the computational resources such as time, space, or the amount of hardware that are necessary to decide a property, descriptive complexity theory asks for the logical

---

[1] For a potential application of such results, see Exercise 3.5.32.

resources that are necessary to define it. In this chapter we shall give a survey of descriptive complexity theory. We shall assume that the reader is familiar with fundamental notions of logic and complexity theory. Specifically we assume familiarity with first-order logic and with deterministic and non-deterministic complexity classes. See the appendix to this chapter for a brief survey on alternating complexity classes.

In Sect. 3.1, we discuss some basic issues concerning the relationship between logic and complexity, we introduce model-checking games, and we determine in a detailed way the complexity of first-order model checking.

In Sect. 3.2, we make precise the notion of a logic capturing a complexity class. As our first capturing result, we prove Fagin's Theorem, which says that existential second-order logic captures NP. In a limited scenario, namely for the domain of ordered structures, we then derive capturing results for a number of other complexity classes, including PTIME and LOGSPACE, by use of fragments of second-order logic (such as second-order Horn logic) and by extensions of first-order logic (such as transitive closure logics).

Section 3.3 is devoted to fixed-point logics. These are probably the most important logics for finite model theory and also play an important role in many other fields of logic in computer science. We shall discuss many variants of fixed point logics, including least, inflationary and partial fixed point logic, the modal μ-calculus, and the database query language Datalog. We shall explain model checking issues, capturing results for PTIME and PSPACE, and also discuss structural issues for these logics.

In Sect. 3.4 we introduce logics with counting. One of the limitations of common logics on finite structures is an inability to count. By adding to first-order logic and, in particular, to fixed-point logic an explicit counting mechanism, one obtains powerful logics that come quite close to capturing PTIME.

Section 3.5 is devoted to capturing results on certain specific domains of unordered structures, via a technique called canonization. While the general problem of whether there exists a logic capturing PTIME on all finite structures is still open (and it is widely conjectured that no such logic exists), canonization permits us to find interesting domains of structures where fixed-point logic or fixed-point logic with counting can express all of PTIME.

Finally, in Sect. 3.6 we discuss the extension of the general approach and methods of finite model theory to suitable domains of infinite structures, i.e., the generalization of finite model theory to an *algorithmic model theory*. We discuss several domains of infinite structures for which this approach makes sense, and then treat, as an example, the domain of *metafinite structures*, for which capturing results have been studied in some detail.

3.1.1 Complexity Issues in Logic

One of the central issues in the relationship between complexity theory and logic is the *algorithmic complexity of the common reasoning tasks for a logic*. There are numerous such tasks, but most of them can be easily reduced to two (at least for logics with reasonable closure properties), namely *satisfiability testing* and *model checking*. The **satisfiability problem** for a logic L on a domain $\mathcal{D}$ of structures takes formulae $\psi \in L$ as inputs, and the question to be answered is whether there exists in $\mathcal{D}$ a model for ψ. Although satisfiability problems are of fundamental importance in many areas of logic and its applications, they do not really play a crucial role in finite model theory. Nevertheless, they are considered occasionally and, moreover, some of the central results of finite model theory have interesting connections with satisfiability problems. We shall point out some such relations later.

On the other hand, model-checking problems occupy a central place in finite model theory. For a logic L and a domain $\mathcal{D}$ of (finite) structures, the **model-checking problem** asks, given a structure $\mathfrak{A} \in \mathcal{D}$ and a formula $\psi \in L$, whether it is the case that $\mathfrak{A} \models \psi$. A closely related problem is **formula evaluation** (or query evaluation): given a structure $\mathfrak{A}$ and a formula $\psi(\overline{x})$ (with free variables $\overline{x}$), the problem is to compute the relation defined by ψ on $\mathfrak{A}$, i.e. the set $\psi^{\mathfrak{A}} := \{\overline{a} : \mathfrak{A} \models \psi(\overline{a})\}$. Obviously, the evaluation problem for a formula with k free variables on a structure with n elements reduces to n^k model-checking problems.

Note that a model-checking problem has two inputs: a structure and a formula. We can measure the complexity in terms of both inputs, and this is what is commonly refered to as the **combined complexity** of the model-checking problem (for L and $\mathcal{D}$). However, in many cases, one of the two inputs is fixed, and we measure the complexity only in terms of the other. If we fix the structure $\mathfrak{A}$, then the model-checking problem for L on this structure amounts to deciding $\mathrm{Th}_L(\mathfrak{A}) := \{\psi \in L : \mathfrak{A} \models \psi\}$, the **$L$-theory** of $\mathfrak{A}$. The complexity of this problem is called the **expression complexity** of the model-checking problem (for L on $\mathfrak{A}$). For first-order logic (FO) and for monadic second-order logic (MSO) in particular, such problems have a long tradition in logic and numerous applications in many fields. Of even greater importance for finite model theory are model-checking problems for a fixed formula ψ, which amounts to deciding the **model class** of ψ inside $\mathcal{D}$, $\mathrm{Mod}_{\mathcal{D}}(\psi) := \{\mathfrak{A} \in \mathcal{D} : \mathfrak{A} \models \psi\}$. Its complexity is the **structure complexity** or **data complexity** of the model-checking problem (for ψ on $\mathcal{D}$).

Besides the algorithmic analysis of logic problems, there is another aspect of logic and complexity that has become even more important for finite model theory, and which is really the central programme of descriptive complexity theory. The goal here is to characterize complexity from the point of view of logic (or, more precisely, model theory)[2] by providing, for each important complexity level, logical systems whose expressive power (on finite structures, or on a particular domain of finite structures) coincides precisely with that

---

[2] There also exist other logical approaches to complexity, based for instance on proof theory. Connections to the finite model theory approach exist, but the flavour is quite different.

complexity level. For a detailed definition, see Sect. 3.2. We shall see that there have been important successes in this programme, but that there also remain difficult problems that are still open.

3.1.2 Model Checking for First-Order Logic

We shall now discuss the problem of evaluating first-order formulae on finite structures using a game-based approach. Model-checking problems, for almost any logic, can be cast as strategy problems for appropriate model-checking games (also called Hintikka games).[3] With any formula $\psi(\overline{x})$, any structure $\mathfrak{A}$ (of the same vocabulary as ψ), and any tuple $\overline{a}$ of elements of $\mathfrak{A}$, we associate a **model-checking game** $\mathcal{G}(\mathfrak{A}, \psi(\overline{a}))$. It is played by two players, **Verifier** and **Falsifier**. Verifier (sometimes also called Player 0, or $\exists$, or Eloise) tries to prove that $\mathfrak{A} \models \psi(\overline{a})$, whereas Falsifier (also called Player 1, or $\forall$, or Abelard) tries to establish that the formula is false. For first-order logic, the evaluation games are very simple, in the sense that winning conditions are *positional*, and that the games are *well-founded*, i.e. all possible plays are finite (regardless of whether the input structure is finite or infinite). For more powerful logics, notably fixed-point logics, model checking-games may have infinite plays and more complicated winning conditions (see Sect. 3.3.4).

The Game $\mathcal{G}(\mathcal{A}, \psi(\overline{a}))$

Let $\mathfrak{A}$ be a finite structure and let $\psi(\overline{x})$ be a relational first-order formula, which we assume to be in negation normal form, i.e. built up from atoms and negated atoms by means of the propositional connectives $\wedge, \vee$ and the quantifiers $\exists, \forall$. Obviously, any first-order formula can be converted in linear time into an equivalent one in negation normal form. The model-checking game $\mathcal{G}(\mathcal{A}, \psi(\overline{a}))$ has positions (φ, ρ) such that φ is a subformula of ψ, and $\rho : \text{free}(\varphi) \to A$ is an assignment from the free variables of φ to elements of $\mathfrak{A}$. To simplify the notation we usually write $\varphi(\overline{b})$ for a position (φ, ρ) where ρ assigns the tuple $\overline{b}$ to the free variables of φ. The initial position of the game is the formula $\psi(\overline{a})$.

Verifier (Player 0) moves from positions associated with disjunctions and with formulae starting with an existential quantifier. From a position $\varphi \vee \vartheta$, she moves to either φ or ϑ. From a position $\exists y \varphi(\overline{b}, y)$, Verifier can move to any position $\varphi(\overline{b}, c)$, where $c \in A$. Dually, Falsifier (Player 1) makes corresponding moves from conjunctions and universal quantifications. At atoms or negated atoms, i.e. positions $\varphi(\overline{b})$ of the form $b = b'$, $b \neq b'$, $R\overline{b}$, or $\neg R\overline{b}$, the game is over. Verifier has won the play if $\mathfrak{A} \models \varphi(\overline{b})$; otherwise, Falsifier has won.

Model-checking games are a way of defining the semantics of a logic. The equivalence to the standard definition can be proved by a simple induction.

---

[3] These games should not be confounded with the games used for model comparison (Ehrenfeucht–Fraïssé games) that describe the power of a logic for distinguishing between two structures.

Proposition 3.1.1. *Verifier has a winning strategy for the game* $\mathcal{G}(\mathfrak{A}, \psi(\overline{a}))$ *if, and only if,* $\mathfrak{A} \models \psi(\overline{a})$.

This suggests a game-based approach to model checking: given $\mathfrak{A}$ and ψ, construct the game $\mathcal{G}(\mathfrak{A}, \psi)$ and decide whether Verifier has a winning strategy from the initial position. Let us therefore look a little closer at strategy problems for games.

3.1.3 The Strategy Problem for Finite Games

Abstractly, we can describe a two-player game with positional winning conditions by a directed game graph $\mathcal{G} = (V, V_0, V_1, E)$, with a partioning $V = V_0 \cup V_1$ of the nodes into positions where Player 0 moves and positions where Player 1 moves. The possible moves are described by the edge relation $E \subseteq V \times V$. We call w a successor of v if $(v, w) \in E$, and we denote the set of all successors of v by vE. To describe the winning conditions, we adopt the convention that Player σ loses at positions $v \in V_\sigma$ where no moves are possible. (Alternatively, one could explicitly include in the game description the sets S_0, S_1 of winning terminal positions for each player.)

A **play** of $\mathcal{G}$ is a path $v_0, v_1, \ldots$ formed by the two players starting from a given position v_0. Whenever the current position v_n belongs to V_σ, Player σ chooses a move to a successor $v_{n+1} \in v_n E$; if no move is available, then Player σ has lost the play. If this never occurs, the play goes on infinitely and the winner has to be established by a winning condition on infinite plays. For the moment, let us say that infinite plays are won by neither of the players.[4]

A **strategy** for a player is a function defining a move for each situation in a play where she has to move. Of particular interest are positional strategies, which do not depend on the history of the play, but only on the current position. Hence, a **positional strategy** for Player σ in $\mathcal{G}$ is a (partial) function $f : V_\sigma \to V$ which indicates a choice $(v, f(v)) \in E$ for positions $v \in V_\sigma$. A play $v_0, v_1, \ldots$ is **consistent** with a positional strategy f for Player σ if $v_{n+1} = f(v_n)$ for all $v_n \in V_\sigma$. A strategy for a player is **winning** from position v_0 if she wins every play starting from v_0 that is consistent with that strategy. We say that a strategy is winning on a set W if it is winning from each position in W. The **winning region** W_σ for Player σ is the set of positions from which she has a winning strategy.

A game is **well-founded** if all its plays are finite. Note that a model-checking game $\mathcal{G}(\mathfrak{A}, \psi(\overline{a}))$ for a first-order formula ψ has a finite game graph if, and only if, $\mathfrak{A}$ is finite, but it is well-founded in all cases. In general, however, games with finite game graphs need not be well-founded.

A game is **determined** if, from each position, one of the players has a winning strategy, i.e. if $W_0 \cup W_1 = V$. Well-founded games are always

---

[4] We shall later introduce games with more interesting winning conditions for infinite plays.

determined, and so are large classes of more general games (such as games in the Borel hierarchy; see [82, 96]).

We denote by GAME the strategy problem for games with finite game graphs and positional winning conditions, i.e.

$$\text{GAME} = \{(\mathcal{G}, v) : \text{Player 0 has a winning strategy in } \mathcal{G} \text{ from position } v\}.$$

It is obvious that the GAME problem can be solved in polynomial time. Denote by W_σ^n the set of positions from which Player σ has a strategy to win the game in at most n moves. Then $W_\sigma^0 = \{v \in V_{1-\sigma} : vE = \emptyset\}$ is the set of winning terminal positions for Player σ, and we can compute the sets W_σ^n inductively by using

$$W_\sigma^{n+1} := \{v \in V_0 : vE \cap W_\sigma^n \neq \emptyset\} \cup \{v \in V_1 : vE \subseteq W_\sigma^n\}$$

until $W_\sigma^{n+1} = W_\sigma^n$.

To see that GAME can actually be solved in *linear time*, a little more work is necessary. The following algorithm is a variant of depth-first search, and computes the entire winning sets for both players in time $O(|V| + |E|)$.

Theorem 3.1.2. *Winning regions of finite games can be computed in linear time.*

Proof. We present an algorithm that computes, for each position, which player, if any, has a winning strategy for the game starting at that position. During the computation three arrays are used:

- win[v] contains either 0 or 1, indicating which player wins, or $\bot$ if we do not know yet, or if none of the players has a winning strategy from v;
- $P[v]$ contains the predecessors of v; and
- $n[v]$ is the number of those successors for which win[v] = $\bot$.

A linear-time algorithm for the GAME problem

Input: A game $\mathcal{G} = (V, V_0, V_1, E)$

```
forall  v ∈ V do                    (∗ 1: initialization ∗)
    win[v] := ⊥
    P[v] := ∅
    n[v] := 0
enddo

forall  (u, v) ∈ E do               (∗ 2: calculate P and n ∗)
    P[v] := P[v] ∪ {u}
    n[u] := n[u] + 1
enddo
```

```
forall  v ∈ V₀                    (* 3: calculate win *)
    if n[v] = 0 then  Propagate(v, 1)
forall  v ∈ V₁
    if n[v] = 0 then  Propagate(v, 0)
return win end

procedure Propagate(v, σ)
    if win[v] ≠ ⊥ then  return
    win[v] := σ                   (* 4: mark v as winning for Player σ *)
    forall  u ∈ P[v] do           (* 5: propagate change to predecessors *)
        n[u] := n[u] − 1
        if u ∈ Vσ or n[u] = 0 then  Propagate(u, σ)
    enddo
end
```

The heart of this algorithm is the procedure $\text{Propagate}(v, \sigma)$ which is called any time we have found that Player σ has a winning strategy from position v. $\text{Propagate}(v, \sigma)$ records this fact and investigates whether we are now able to determine the winning player for any of the predecessors of v. This is done by applying the following rules:

- If the predecessor u belongs to Player σ, then this player has a winning strategy from u by moving to position v.
- If the predecessor u belongs to the opponent of Player σ, if $\text{win}[u]$ is undefined, and if the winning player has already been determined for all successors w of u, then $\text{win}[w] = \sigma$ for all of those successors, and hence Player σ wins from u regardless of the choice of her opponent.

Since parts 4 and 5 of the algorithm are reached only once for each position v, the inner part of the loop in part 5 is executed at most $\sum_v |P[v]| = |E|$ times. Therefore the running time of the algorithm is $O(|V| + |E|)$.

The correctness of the value assigned to $\text{win}[v]$ is proved by a straightforward induction on the number of moves in which the corresponding player can ensure that she wins. Note that the positions satisfying $n[v] = 0$ in part 3 are exactly those without outgoing edges even if $n[v]$ is modified by Propagate. □

GAME is known to be a PTIME-complete problem (see [57]). This remains the case for **strictly alternating games**, where $E \subseteq V_0 \times V_1 \cup V_1 \times V_0$. Indeed, any game can be transformed into an equivalent strictly alternating one by introducing for each move $(u, v) \in V_\sigma \times V_\sigma$ a new node $e \in V_{1-\sigma}$ and by replacing the move (u, v) by two moves (u, e) and (e, u).

The GAME problem (sometimes also called the problem of *alternating reachability*) is a general combinatorial problem that reappears in different guises in many areas. To illustrate this by an example, we shall now show that the satisfiability problem for propositional Horn formulae is essentially the same problem as GAME.

Satisfiability for Horn Formulae

It is well known that SAT-HORN, the satisfiability problem for propositional Horn formulae, is

- PTIME-complete [57], and
- solvable in linear time [36, 68].

Using the GAME problem, we can obtain very simple proofs for both results. Indeed, GAME and SAT-HORN are equivalent under log–lin reductions, i.e. reductions that are computable in linear time and logarithmic space. The reductions are so simple that we can say that GAME and SAT-HORN are really the same problem.

Theorem 3.1.3. SAT-HORN *is log–lin equivalent to* GAME.

Proof. GAME $\leq_{\text{log–lin}}$ SAT-HORN. Given a finite game graph $\mathcal{G} = (V, V_0, V_1, E)$, we can construct in time $O(|V| + |E|)$ a propositional Horn formula $\psi_{\mathcal{G}}$ consisting of the clauses $u \leftarrow v$ for all edges $(u, v) \in E$ with $u \in V_0$, and the clauses $u \leftarrow v_1 \wedge \cdots \wedge v_m$ for all nodes $u \in V_1$, where $uE = \{v_1, \ldots, v_m\}$. The minimal model of $\psi_{\mathcal{G}}$ is precisely the winning set W_0 for Player 0. Hence $v \in W_0$ if the Horn formula $\psi_{\mathcal{G}} \wedge (0 \leftarrow v)$ is unsatisfiable.

SAT-HORN $\leq_{\text{log–lin}}$ GAME: Given a Horn formula $\psi(X_1, \ldots, X_n) = \bigwedge_{i \in I} C_i$ with propositional variables $X_1, \ldots, X_n$ and Horn clauses C_i of the form $H_i \leftarrow X_{i_1} \wedge \cdots X_{i_m}$ (where the head of the clause, H_i, is either a propositional variable or the constant 0), we define a game $\mathcal{G}_\psi$ as follows. The positions of Player 0 are the initial position 0 and the propositional variables $X_1, \ldots, X_n$, and the positions of Player 1 are the clauses of ψ. Player 0 can move from a position X to any clause C_i with head X, and Player 1 can move from a clause C_i to any variable occurring in the body of C_i. Formally, $\mathcal{G}_\psi = (V, E)$, $V = V_0 \cup V_1$ with $V_0 = \{0\} \cup \{X_1, \ldots, X_n\}$, $V_1 = \{C_i : i \in I\}$, and

$$E = \{(X, C) \in V_0 \times V_1 : X = \text{head}(C)\} \cup \{(C, X) \in V_1 \times V_0 : X \in \text{body}(C)\}.$$

Player 0 has a winning strategy for $\mathcal{G}_\psi$ from position X if, and only if, $\psi \models X$. In particular, ψ is unsatisfiable if, and only if, Player 0 wins from position 0. □

3.1.4 Complexity of First-Order Model Checking

Roughly, the size of the model-checking game $\mathcal{G}(\mathfrak{A}, \psi)$ is the number of different instantiations of the subformulae of ψ with elements from $\mathfrak{A}$. It is in many cases not efficient to construct the full model-checking game explicitly and then solve the strategy problem, since many positions of the game will not really be needed.

To measure the size of games, and the resulting time and space bounds for the complexity of model checking as precisely as possible, we use, besides the formula length $|\psi|$, the following parameters. The **closure** $\mathrm{cl}(\psi)$ is the set of all subformulae of ψ. Obviously, $|\mathrm{cl}(\psi)| \leq |\psi|$, and in some cases $|\mathrm{cl}(\psi)|$ can be much smaller than $|\psi|$. The **quantifier rank** $\mathrm{qr}(\psi)$ is the maximal nesting depth of quantifiers in ψ, and the **width** of ψ is the maximal number of free variables in subformulae, i.e.

$$\mathrm{width}(\psi) = \max\{|\mathrm{free}(\varphi)| : \varphi \in \mathrm{cl}(\psi)\}.$$

Instead of considering the width, one can also rewrite formulae with as few variables as possible.

Lemma 3.1.4. *A first-order formula ψ has width k if, and only if, it is equivalent, via a renaming of bound variables, to a first-order formula with at most k distinct variable symbols.*

Bounded-variable fragments of logics have received a lot of attention in finite model theory. However, here we state the results in terms of formula width rather than number of variables to avoid the necessity to economize on the number of variables. Given the close connection between games and alternating algorithms, it is not surprising that the good estimates for the complexity of model-checking games are often in terms of alternating complexity classes. We now describe an alternating model-checking algorithm for first-order logic that can be viewed as an on-the-fly construction of the model-checking game while playing it.

Theorem 3.1.5. *There is an alternating model-checking algorithm that, given a finite structure $\mathfrak{A}$ and a first-order sentence ψ, decides whether $\mathfrak{A} \models \psi$ in time $O(|\psi| + \mathrm{qr}(\psi) \log |A|)$ and space $O(\log |\psi| + \mathrm{width}(\psi) \log |A|)$ (assuming that atomic statements are evaluated in constant time).*

Proof. We present a recursive alternating procedure **ModelCheck**$(\mathfrak{A}, \rho, \psi)$ that, given a finite structure $\mathfrak{A}$, a first-order formula ψ that may contain free variables, and an assignment $\rho : \mathrm{free}(\psi) \rightarrow A$, decides whether $\mathfrak{A} \models \psi[\rho]$.

ModelCheck$(\mathfrak{A}, \rho, \psi)$

Input: a first-order formula ψ in negation normal form
        a finite structure $\mathfrak{A}$ (with universe A),
        an assignment $\rho : \mathrm{free}(\psi) \rightarrow A$
if ψ is an atom or negated atom **then**
        if $\mathfrak{A} \models \psi[\rho]$ **accept else reject**
if $\psi = \eta \vee \vartheta$ **then do**
        guess $\varphi \in \{\eta, \vartheta\}$, and let $\rho' := \rho\,|_{\mathrm{free}(\varphi)}$
        ModelCheck$(\mathfrak{A}, \rho', \varphi)$
if $\psi = \eta \wedge \vartheta$ **then do**

> **universally choose** $\varphi \in \{\eta, \vartheta\}$, and let $\rho' := \rho \mid_{\text{free}(\varphi)}$
> **ModelCheck**$(\mathfrak{A}, \rho', \varphi)$

if $\psi = \exists x \varphi$ **then do**
>   **guess** an element a of $\mathfrak{A}$
>   **ModelCheck**$(\mathfrak{A}, \rho[x \mapsto a], \varphi)$

if $\psi = \forall x \varphi$ **then do**
>   **universally choose** an element a of $\mathfrak{A}$
>   **ModelCheck**$(\mathfrak{A}, \rho[x \mapsto a], \varphi)$

A straightforward induction shows that the procedure is correct. The time needed by the procedure is the depth of the syntax tree of ψ plus the time needed to produce the variable assignments. On each computation path, at most $\text{qr}(\psi)$ elements of $\mathfrak{A}$ have to be chosen, and each element needs $\log |A|$ bits. Hence the time complexity is $O(|\psi| + \text{qr}(\psi) \log |A|)$. During the evaluation, the algorithm needs to maintain a pointer to the current position in ψ and to store the current assignment, which needs $\text{free}(\varphi) \log |A|$ bits for the current subformula φ. Hence the space needed by the algorithm is $O(\log |\psi| + \text{width}(\psi) \log |A|)$. □

Theorem 3.1.6. *The model-checking problem for first-order logic is* PSPACE-*complete. For any fixed* $k \geq 2$, *the model-checking problem for first-order formulae of width at most* k *is* PTIME-*complete.*

Proof. Membership of these complexity classes follows immediately from Theorem 3.1.5 via the facts that alternating polynomial time coincides with polynomial space and alternating logarithmic space coincides with polynomial time.

Completeness follows by straightforward reductions from known complete problems. QBF, the evaluation problem for quantified Boolean formulae, is PSPACE-complete. It reduces to first-order model checking on the fixed structure (A, P) with $A = \{0, 1\}$ and $P = \{1\}$. Given a quantified Boolean formula ψ without free propositional variables, we can translate it into a first-order sentence ψ as follows: replace every quantification $\exists X_i$ or $\forall X_i$ over a propositional variable X_i by a corresponding first-order quantification $\exists x_i$ or $\forall x_i$ and replace atomic propositions X_i by atoms $P x_i$. Obviously, ψ evaluates to *true* if, and only if, $(A, P) \models \varphi'$. This proves that the expression complexity and the combined complexity of first-order model checking is PSPACE-complete.

To see that the model-checking problem for first-order formulae of width 2 is PTIME-complete, we reduce to it the GAME problem for strictly alternating games, with Player 0 moving first. Given a strictly alternating game graph $\mathcal{G} = (V, V_0, V_1, E)$, we construct formulae $\psi_i(x)$ of width 2, expressing the fact that Player 0 has a winning strategy from $x \in V_0$ in n rounds. Let

$$\psi_1(x) := \exists y (Exy \wedge \forall z \neg Eyz)$$
$$\psi_{i+1}(x) := \exists y (Exy \wedge \forall z (Eyz \rightarrow \psi_i(z))).$$

Obviously, ψ_n has width 2, and $\mathcal{G} \models \psi_n(v)$ if, and only if, Player 0 can win from position v in at most n rounds. Now, if Player 0 has a winning strategy, then she also has one for winning in at most n rounds, where $n = |V|$, since otherwise the game will be caught in a loop. Hence any instance $\mathcal{G}, v$ of the GAME problem (for strictly alternating games), with $v \in V_0$, can be reduced to the instance $\mathcal{G}, \psi_n(v)$ of the model-checking problem for first-order formulae of width 2. $\square$

Remark. The argument for PTIME-completeness applies also in fact to *propositional modal logic* (ML) [55]. Instead of the formulae $\psi_n(x)$ constructed above, we take the modal formulae

$$\varphi_1 := \Diamond \Box \mathit{false}, \qquad \varphi_{n+1} := \Diamond \Box \varphi_n.$$

Corollary 3.1.7. *The model-checking problem for* ML *is* PTIME-*complete.*

If we consider a fixed formula ψ, Theorem 3.1.5 tells us that the data complexity of first-order logic is much lower than the expression or combined complexity.

Corollary 3.1.8. *Let ψ be a first-order sentence. Then*

$$\{\mathfrak{A} : \mathfrak{A} \ \mathit{finite}, \mathfrak{A} \models \psi\} \in \text{ALOGTIME}.$$

In particular, the evaluation problem for any fixed first-order sentence can be computed deterministically in logarithmic space.

3.1.5 Encoding Finite Structures by Words

Complexity theory, at least in its current form, is based on classical computational models, most notably Turing machines, that take as inputs words over a fixed finite alphabet. If we want to measure the complexity of problems on finite structures in terms of these notions, we have to represent structures by words so that they can be used as inputs for, say, Turing machines. This may seem a trivial issue, and for purely algorithmic questions (say for determining the cost of a model-checking algorithm) it indeed often is. However, the programme of finite model theory is to link complexity with logical definability in a deeper way, and for this purpose the representation of structures by words needs careful consideration. It is also at the source of some major unresolved problems that we shall discuss later.

At least implicitly, an encoding of a finite structure by a word requires that we select *an ordered representation of the structure*. To see this, consider the common encoding of a graph $\mathcal{G} = (V, E)$ by its adjacency matrix. Once we have fixed an enumeration of V, say $V = \{v_0, \dots, v_{n-1}\}$, we can represent the graph by the word $w_0 \cdots w_{n^2-1}$, where $w_{in+j} = 1$ if $(v_i, v_j) \in E$ and $w_{in+j} = 0$ otherwise, i.e. row after row of the adjacency matrix. However, this encoding is not canonic. There are $n!$ possibilities of enumerating V, so there may be up to $n!$ different encodings of the same graph by binary strings. But if the graphs come along with a linear order, we do have a canonic way of enumerating the elements and therefore a canonic encoding. Let us now discuss encodings of arbitrary finite structures (of finite vocabulary) by words.

Definition 3.1.9. For any vocabulary τ, we write $\text{Fin}(\tau)$ for the class of finite τ-structures and $\text{Ord}(\tau)$ for the class of all structures $(\mathfrak{A}, <)$, where $\mathfrak{A} \in \text{Fin}(\tau)$ and $<$ is a linear order on A (the universe of $\mathfrak{A}$).

For any structure $(\mathfrak{A}, <) \in \text{Ord}(\tau)$ of cardinality n and for any k, we can identify A^k with the set $\{0, \ldots, n^k - 1\}$, by associating each k-tuple with its rank in the lexicographical ordering induced by $<$ on A^k. Ordered structures can be encoded as binary strings in many natural ways. The particular choice of an encoding is not important. We only need the following conditions to be satisfied.

Definition 3.1.10. An encoding $code : \text{Ord}(\tau) \rightarrow \Sigma^*$ (over any finite alphabet Σ) is **good** if it identifies isomorphic structures, if its values are polynomially bounded, if it is first-order definable, and if it allows to compute efficiently the values of atomic statements. Formally, this means that the following conditions are satisfied:

(i) $code(\mathfrak{A}, <) = code(\mathfrak{B}, <)$ if and only if $(\mathfrak{A}, <) \cong (\mathfrak{B}, <)$.

(ii) $|code(\mathfrak{A}, <)| \leq p(|A|)$ for some polynomial p.

(iii) For all $k \in \mathbb{N}$ and all symbols $\sigma \in \Sigma$, there exists a first-order formula $\beta_\sigma(x_1, \ldots, x_k)$ of vocabulary $\tau \cup \{<\}$ such that, for all structures $(\mathfrak{A}, <) \in \text{Ord}(\tau)$ and all $\bar{a} \in A^k$, the following equivalence holds:

$$(\mathfrak{A}, <) \models \beta_\sigma(\bar{a}) \text{ iff the } \bar{a}\text{-th symbol of } code(\mathfrak{A}, <) \text{ is } \sigma.$$

(iv) Given $code(\mathfrak{A}, <)$, a relation symbol R of τ, and (a representation of) a tuple $\bar{a}$, one can efficiently decide whether $\mathfrak{A} \models R\bar{a}$.

The precise meaning of 'efficiently' in clause (iv) depends on the context (e.g. the problem that is studied, the machine model considered, and the level of abstraction at which one is studying a given problem). For the analysis of algorithms, one often assumes that atomic statements are evaluated in constant (or even unit) time on a Random Access Machine (RAM). A minimal requirement is that atoms can be evaluated in linear time and logarithmic space.

A convenient encoding is given as follows. Let $<$ be a linear order on A and let $\mathfrak{A} = (A, R_1, \ldots, R_t)$ be a τ-structure of cardinality n. Let ℓ be the maximal arity of $R_1, \ldots, R_t$. With each relation R of arity j, we associate a string $\chi(R) = w_0 \cdots w_{n^j-1} 0^{n^\ell - n^j} \in \{0,1\}^{n^\ell}$, where $w_i = 1$ if the ith tuple of A^j belongs to R, and $w_i = 0$ otherwise. Now, we set $code(\mathfrak{A}, <) = 1^n 0^{n^\ell - n} \chi(R_1) \cdots \chi(R_t)$.

Exercise 3.1.11 Prove that this encoding is good. In fact, this encoding lends itself to a very simple logical description in the following sense: if, besides (or instead of) the linear ordering $<$, the corresponding successor relation S and the constants $0, e$ for the first and last elements with respect to $<$ are available, then the encoding is definable by *quantifier-free* formulae $\beta_\sigma(\overline{x})$.

We can fix any good encoding function and understand ordered structures to be represented by their encodings. With an unordered structure $\mathfrak{A}$, we associate the *set* of all encodings $code(\mathfrak{A}, <)$, where $<$ is a linear order on A. So, when we say that an algorithm M decides a class $\mathcal{K}$ of τ-structures, we actually mean that M decides the set of encodings of structures in $\mathcal{K}$, i.e. the language

$$code(\mathcal{K}) := \{code(\mathfrak{A}, <) : \mathfrak{A} \in \mathcal{K} \text{ and } < \text{ is a linear order on } A\}.$$

It thus makes sense to ask whether such a $\mathcal{K}$ belongs to a complexity class, such as P or NP. In particular, we can ask how complicated it is to decide the class of models of a logical sentence.

Word Structures

We have seen how classes of structures are encoded by languages. On the other hand, any language $L \subseteq \Gamma^*$ can also be considered as a class of structures over the vocabulary $\{<\} \cup \{P_a : a \in \Gamma\}$. Indeed, a word $w = w_0 \ldots w_{m-1} \in \Gamma^*$ is described by the structure $\mathfrak{B}(w)$ with universe $\{0, \ldots, m-1\}$, with the usual interpretation of $<$ and where $P_a = \{i : w_i = a\}$.

Isomorphism Invariance

We have seen that encoding an unordered structure involves selecting an ordering on the universe. In general, different orderings produce different encodings. However, we want to consider properties of structures, not of their encodings, An algorithm that decides whether a structure has a certain property gets encodings $code(\mathfrak{A}, <)$ as inputs and should produce the same answer (yes or no) for all encodings of the same structure. That is, the outcome of the algorithm should not depend on the particular ordered representation of the structure, but only on its isomorphism type. In other words the algorithm should be isomorphism-invariant. For most of the algorithms considered here isomorphism invariance is obvious, but in general it is an undecidable property.

Exercise 3.1.12 A first-order sentence ψ of vocabulary $\tau \cup \{<\}$ is *order-invariant* on a class $\mathcal{K}$ of τ-structures if its truth on any structure in $\mathcal{K}$ does not depend on the choice of the linear ordering $<$. That is, for any $\mathfrak{A} \in \mathcal{K}$ and any pair $<, <'$ of linear orderings on $\mathfrak{A}$ we have that $(\mathfrak{A}, <) \models \psi \iff (\mathfrak{A}, <') \models \psi$.

Prove that it is undecidable whether a given first-order formula is order-invariant on finite structures. *Hint:* use Trakhtenbrot's Theorem. A first-order sentence ψ, in which $<$ and Q do not occur, has a finite model with at least two elements if, and only if, $\psi \to \forall x \exists y (x < y \lor Qx)$ is not order-invariant.

3.2 Capturing Complexity Classes

We have already mentioned that the research programme of descriptive complexity theory links complexity with logic in a deeper way than a complexity analysis of model-checking algorithms can do. We are looking for results saying that, on a certain domain $\mathcal{D}$ of structures, a logic L (such as first-order logic, least fixed-point logic, or a fragment of second-order logic) *captures* a complexity class *Comp*. This means that (1) for every fixed sentence $\psi \in L$, the data complexity of evaluating ψ on structures from $\mathcal{D}$ is a problem in the complexity class *Comp*, and (2) every property of structures in $\mathcal{D}$ that can be decided with complexity *Comp* is definable in the logic L.

Two important examples of such results are Fagin's Theorem, which says that existential second-order logic captures NP on the class of all finite structures, and the Immerman–Vardi Theorem, which says that least fixed-point logic captures PTIME on the class of all ordered finite structures. On *ordered* finite structures, logical characterizations of this kind are known for all major complexity classes. On the other hand, it is not known, and it is one of the major open problems in the area, whether PTIME can be captured by any logic if no ordering is present.

In Sect. 3.2.1, we prove Fagin's Theorem and relate it it to the spectrum problem, which is a classical problem in mathematical logic. In Sect. 3.2.2, we make precise the notion of a logic capturing a complexity class on a domain of finite structures. We then show in Sect. 3.2.3 that on ordered structures, second-order Horn logic captures polynomial time. In Sects. 3.2.4 and 3.2.5, we discuss logics that capture logarithmic space complexity classes.

3.2.1 Capturing NP: Fagin's Theorem

The **spectrum** of a first-order sentence ψ is the set of cardinalities of its finite models, i.e.

$$\text{spectrum}(\psi) := \{k \in \mathbb{N} : \psi \text{ has a model with } k \text{ elements}\}.$$

As early as 1952, Scholz [93] posed the problem of characterizing the class of spectra, i.e. the subsets $S \subseteq \mathbb{N}$ for which there exists a first-order sentence ψ such that $\text{spectrum}(\psi) = S$. A more specific problem is the **complementation problem for spectra,** posed by Asser [7], who asked whether the complement of each spectrum is also a spectrum.

Note that the spectrum of a first-order sentence ψ of relational vocabulary $\tau = \{R_1, \ldots, R_m\}$ can be viewed as the set of finite models of the existential second-order sentence $\exists R_1 \cdots \exists R_m \psi$. Since all relation symbols are quantified, this is a sentence over the empty vocabulary, i.e. its models are just sets. Thus there is a one-to-one correspondence between the spectra of first-order sentences and the classes of finite models of existential second-order sentences *over the empty vocabulary*. If we allow different vocabularies for existential second-order sentences, this naturally leads to the notion of a generalized spectrum [43].

Definition 3.2.1. Existential second-order logic, sometimes denoted by Σ_1^1, is the set of formulae of the form $\exists R_1 \cdots \exists R_m \varphi$, where $m \in \mathbb{N}$, $R_1, \ldots, R_m$ are relation symbols of any finite arity, and φ is a first-order formula. A **generalized spectrum** is the class of finite models of a sentence in existential second-order logic.

Example 3.2.2. The class of bipartite graphs is a generalized spectrum. It is defined by the sentence

$$\exists R \forall x \forall y (Exy \rightarrow (Rx \leftrightarrow \neg Ry)).$$

Exercise 3.2.3 Prove that the class of Hamiltonian graphs, the class of k-colourable graphs (for any fixed k), and the class of graphs that admit a perfect matching are generalized spectra. (A perfect matching in an undirected graph $G = (V, E)$ is a set $M \subseteq E$ of edges such that every node belongs to precisely one edge of M.)

Theorem 3.2.4 (Fagin). *Let $\mathcal{K}$ be an isomorphism-closed class of finite structures of some fixed non-empty finite vocabulary. Then $\mathcal{K}$ is in NP if and only if $\mathcal{K}$ is definable by an existential second-order sentence, i.e. if and only if $\mathcal{K}$ is a generalized spectrum.*

Proof. First, we show how to decide a generalized spectrum. Let $\psi := \exists R_1 \cdots \exists R_m \varphi$ be an existential second-order sentence. We shall describe a non-deterministic polynomial-time algorithm M which, given an encoding $code(\mathfrak{A}, <)$ of a structure $\mathfrak{A}$, decides whether $\mathfrak{A} \models \psi$. First, M non-deterministically guesses relations $R_1, \ldots, R_m$ on A. A relation R_i is determined by a binary string of length n^{r_i}, where r_i is the arity of R_i and $n = |A|$. Then M decides whether $(\mathfrak{A}, R_1, \ldots, R_m) \models \varphi$. Since φ is first-order, this can be done in logarithmic space and therefore in polynomial time.

Hence the computation of M consists of guessing a polynomial number of bits, followed by a deterministic polynomial-time computation. Obviously, M decides the class of finite models of ψ.

Conversely, let $\mathcal{K}$ be an isomorphism-closed class of τ-structures and let M be a non-deterministic one-tape Turing machine which, given an input $code(\mathfrak{A}, <)$, decides in polynomial time whether $\mathfrak{A}$ belongs to $\mathcal{K}$. We shall construct an existential second-order sentence φ whose finite models are precisely the structures in $\mathcal{K}$. The construction given here is not quite the standard one. It is optimized so that it can be easily adapted to other situations, in particular for giving a capturing result for PTIME (see Section 3.2.3).

Let $M = (Q, \Sigma, q_0, F^+, F^-, \delta)$, where Q is the set of states, Σ is the alphabet of M, q_0 is the initial state, F^+ and F^- are the set of accepting and rejecting states, and $\delta : (Q \times \Sigma) \to \mathcal{P}(Q \times \Sigma \times \{-1, 0, 1\})$ is the transition function. Without loss of generality, we can assume that all computations of M for an input $code(\mathfrak{A}, <)$ reach an accepting or rejecting state after at most $n^k - 1$ steps (where n is the cardinality of $\mathfrak{A}$).

We represent a computation of M for an input $code(\mathfrak{A}, <)$ by a tuple $\overline{X}$ of relations on A, and we shall construct a first-order sentence ψ_M of vocabulary $\tau \cup \{<\} \cup \{\overline{X}\}$ such that

$$(\mathfrak{A}, < \overline{X}) \models \psi_M \iff \text{the relations } \overline{X} \text{ represent an accepting}$$
$$\text{computation of } M \text{ on } code(\mathfrak{A}, <).$$

To represent the n^k time and space parameters of the computation we identify numbers up to $n^k - 1$ with tuples in A^k. Given a linear order, the associated successor relation and the least and greatest element are of course definable. Note, further, that if a successor relation S and constants $0, e$ for the first and last elements are available, then the induced successor relation $\overline{y} = \overline{x} + 1$ on k-tuples is definable by a quantifier-free formula

$$\bigvee_{i < k} \left(\bigwedge_{j < i} (x_j = e \wedge y_j = 0) \wedge S x_i y_i \wedge \bigwedge_{j > i} x_j = y_j \right).$$

Hence, for any fixed integer m, the relation $\overline{y} = \overline{x} + m$ is also expressible.

The description $\overline{X}$ of a computation of M on $code(\mathfrak{A}, <)$ consists of the following relations.

(1) For each state $q \in Q$, the predicate

$$X_q := \{\overline{t} \in A^k : \text{at time } \overline{t}, M \text{ is in state } q\}.$$

(2) For each symbol $\sigma \in \Sigma$, the predicate

$$Y_\sigma := \{(\overline{t}, \overline{a}) \in A^k \times A^k : \text{at time } \overline{t}, \text{ cell } \overline{a} \text{ contains the symbol } \sigma\}.$$

(3) The head predicate

$$Z := \{(\overline{t}, \overline{a}) \in A^k \times A^k : \text{at time } \overline{t}, \text{ the head of } M \text{ is on position } \overline{a}\}.$$

The sentence ψ_M is the universal closure of the conjunction

$$\text{START} \wedge \text{COMPUTE} \wedge \text{END}.$$

The subformula START enforces the condition that the configuration of M at time $t = 0$ is $C_0(\mathfrak{A}, <)$, the input configuration on $code(\mathfrak{A}, <)$. Recall that a good encoding is represented by first-order formulae $\beta_\sigma(\overline{x})$ (condition (iii) of the definition of good encodings). We set

$$\text{START} := X_{q_0}(\overline{0}) \wedge Z(\overline{0}, \overline{0}) \wedge \bigwedge_{\sigma \in \Sigma} (\beta_\sigma(\overline{x}) \to Y_\sigma(\overline{0}, \overline{x})).$$

The subformula COMPUTE describes the transitions from one configuration to the next. It is the conjunction of the formulae

$$\text{NOCHANGE} := \bigwedge_{\sigma \in \Sigma} \left(Y_\sigma(\overline{t}, \overline{x}) \wedge (\overline{y} \neq \overline{x}) \wedge (\overline{t}' = \overline{t} + 1) \wedge Z(\overline{t}, \overline{y}) \to Y_\sigma(\overline{t}', \overline{x}) \right)$$

and

$$\text{CHANGE} := \bigwedge_{\substack{q \in Q \\ \sigma \in \Sigma}} \left(\text{PRE}[q, \sigma] \to \bigvee_{(q', \sigma', m) \in \delta(q, \sigma)} \text{POST}[q', \sigma', m] \right)$$

where

$$\text{PRE}[q, \sigma] := X_q(\overline{t}) \wedge Z(\overline{t}, \overline{x}) \wedge Y_\sigma(\overline{t}, \overline{x}) \wedge \overline{t}' = \overline{t} + 1$$
$$\text{POST}[q', \sigma', m] := X_{q'}(\overline{t}') \wedge Y_{\sigma'}(\overline{t}', \overline{x} \wedge \exists \overline{y}(\overline{x} + m = \overline{y} \wedge Z(\overline{t}', \overline{y})).$$

NOCHANGE expresses the fact that the contents of tape cells that are not currently being scanned do not change from one configuration to the next, whereas CHANGE enforces the changes in the relations X_q, Y_σ, and Z imposed by the transition function.

Finally, we have the formula

$$\text{END} := \bigwedge_{q \in F^-} \neg X_q(\overline{t}),$$

which enforces acceptance by forbidding rejection.

Claim 1. *If M accepts $code(\mathfrak{A}, <)$, then $(\mathfrak{A}, <) \models (\exists \overline{X}) \psi_M$.*

This follows immediately from the construction of ψ_M, since for any accepting computation of M on $code(\mathfrak{A}, <)$ the intended meaning of $\overline{X}$ satisfies ψ_M.

Claim 2. *If $(\mathfrak{A}, < \overline{X}) \models \psi_M$, then M accepts $code(\mathfrak{A}, <)$.*

Suppose that $(\mathfrak{A}, < \overline{X}) \models \psi_M$. For any M-configuration C with state q, head position p, and tape content $w_0 \cdots w_{n^k - 1} \in \Sigma^*$, and for any time $j < n^k$, let $\text{CONF}[C, j]$ be the conjunction of the atomic statements that hold for C at time j, i.e.

$$\text{CONF}[C, j] := X_q(\overline{j}) \wedge Z(\overline{j}, \overline{p}) \wedge \bigwedge_{i=0}^{n^k - 1} Y_{w_i}(\overline{j}, \overline{i})$$

where $\overline{j}, \overline{p}$ and $\overline{i}$ are the tuples in A^k representing the numbers j, p, and i.

(a) Let C_0 be the input configuration of M for input $code(\mathfrak{A}, <)$. Since $(\mathfrak{A}, <, \overline{X}) \models \text{START}$, it follows that

$$(\mathfrak{A}, <, \overline{X}) \models \text{CONF}[C_0, 0].$$

(b) Owing to the subformula COMPUTE of ψ_M, we have, for all non-final configurations C and all $j < n^k - 1$, that

$$\psi_M \wedge \text{CONF}[C, j] \models \bigvee_{C' \in \text{Next}(C)} \text{CONF}[C', j + 1],$$

where $\text{Next}(C) = \{C' : C \vdash_M C'\}$ is the set of successor configurations of C. It follows that there exists a computation

$$C_0(\mathfrak{A}, <) = C_0 \vdash_M C_1 \vdash_M \cdots \vdash_M C_{n^k-1} = C_{\text{end}}$$

of M on $code(\mathfrak{A}, <)$ such that, for all $j < n^k$,

$$(\mathfrak{A}, <, \overline{X}) \models \text{CONF}[C_j, j].$$

(c) Since $(\mathfrak{A}, <, \overline{X}) \models \text{END}$, the configuration C_{end} is not rejecting. Thus, M accepts $code(\mathfrak{A}, <)$.

This proves Claim 2. Clearly, one can axiomatize linear orders in first-order logic. Hence

$$\mathfrak{A} \in \mathcal{K} \quad \text{iff} \quad \mathfrak{A} \models (\exists <)(\exists \overline{X})(\text{``$<$ is a linear order''} \wedge \psi_M).$$

This proves that $\mathcal{K}$ is a generalized spectrum. $\square$

Exercise 3.2.5 Prove that every set in NP can be defined by a Σ_1^1-sentence whose first-order part has an $\forall^* \exists^*$-prefix. Furthermore, prove that this cannot be reduced to $\forall^*$. Finally, prove that it can be reduced to $\forall^*$ if

(a) existential second-order quantification over function symbols is allowed, or
(b) if we consider only ordered structures with an explicitly given successor relation and constants 0, e for the first and last elements.

There are several interesting consequences of Fagin's Theorem. First of all, the NP-completeness of SAT (the satisfiability problem for propositional logic) is an easy corollary of Fagin's Theorem.

Theorem 3.2.6 (Cook and Levin). SAT *is* NP-*complete*.

Proof. It is obvious that SAT is an NP-problem. It remains to show that any problem $\mathcal{K}$ in NP can be reduced to SAT. Since, as explained above, words can be viewed as special kinds of finite structures, we can assume that $\mathcal{K} \subseteq \text{Fin}(\tau)$ for some finite vocabulary τ. By Fagin's Theorem, there exists a first-order sentence ψ such that

$$\mathcal{K} = \{\mathfrak{A} \in \text{Fin}(\tau) : \mathfrak{A} \models \exists R_1 \cdots \exists R_m \psi\}.$$

We now present a logspace reduction that associates with every input structure $\mathfrak{A} \in \text{Fin}(\tau)$ a propositional formula $\psi_{\mathfrak{A}}$. Given $\mathfrak{A}$, replace in ψ

- all subformulae $\exists x_i \varphi$ by $\bigvee_{a_i \in A} \varphi[x_i/a_i]$,
- all subformulae $\forall x_i \varphi$ by $\bigwedge_{a_i \in A} \varphi[x_i/a_i]$, and
- all τ-atoms $P\bar{a}$ by their truth values in $\mathfrak{A}$.

Since the τ-atoms can be evaluated efficiently, this translation is computable efficiently. Viewing the atoms $R_i \bar{a}$ as propositional variables, we have obtained a propositional formula $\psi_{\mathfrak{A}}$ such that

$$\mathfrak{A} \in \mathcal{K} \quad \Longleftrightarrow \quad \mathfrak{A} \models \exists R_1 \cdots \exists R_m \psi \quad \Longleftrightarrow \quad \psi_{\mathfrak{A}} \in \text{SAT}.$$

$\square$

Fagin's Theorem is readily extended to the higher levels of the polynomial-time hierarchy, and thus to a correspondance between second-order logic and the polynomial-time hierarchy.

Corollary 3.2.7. *Let $\mathcal{K}$ be an isomorphism-closed class of finite structures of some fixed non-empty vocabulary τ. Then code($\mathcal{K}$) is in the polynomial-time hierarchy* PH *if and only if there exists a second-order sentence ψ such that $\mathcal{K}$ is the class of finite models of ψ.*

In the statement of Fagin's Theorem, we required the vocabulary to be non-empty. The case of the empty vocabulary, i.e. spectra, is different, because the natural way of specifying a finite set is to write down its size n in binary, and so the length of the encoding is logarithmic in n, whereas encodings of structures of non-empty vocabularies have polynomial length. The formula constructed in the proof of Fagin's Theorem talks about computations that are polynomial in n, and hence, in the case of spectra, exponential in the length of the input. As a consequence, Fagin's characterization of generalized spectra in terms of NP implies a characterization of spectra in terms of NEXPTIME. This has also been established in a different way in [71].

Corollary 3.2.8 (Jones and Selman). *A set $S \subseteq \mathbb{N}$ is a spectrum if and only if $S \in$ NEXPTIME.*

Hence the complementation problem for spectra is really a complexity-theoretic problem: spectra are closed under complementation if, and only if, NEXPTIME = Co-NEXPTIME.

Exercise 3.2.9 Prove that a set $S \subseteq \mathbb{N}$ is in EXPTIME if and only if it is a *categorical spectrum*, i.e. the spectrum of a first-order sentence that has, up to isomorphism, at most one model in any finite cardinality.

3.2.2 Logics That Capture Complexity Classes

Fagin's Theorem gives a precise correspondence between a logic and a complexity class: a property of finite structures is decidable in non-deterministic polynomial time exactly when it is definable in existential second-order logic. The same is true for the correspondence between the polynomial-time hierarchy and SO, as given by Corollary 3.2.7.

Note that the results on the model-checking complexity of first-order logic do *not* give such precise correspondences. We know by Theorem 3.1.5 and Corollary 3.1.8 that whenever a property of finite structures is first-order definable, it is decidable in LOGSPACE and in fact even in ALOGTIME. But we do not have a result giving the converse, and in fact the converse is *false*. There are computationally very simple properties of finite structures that are not first-order definable; one of them is the property of having an even number of elements.

Hence the natural question arises of whether complexity classes other than NP and the polynomial-time hierarchy can also be precisely captured by logics. For most of the popular complexity classes, notably PTIME, we do not know whether this is possible on the domain of all finite structures. But we have a lot of interesting capturing results if we do not consider arbitrary finite structures, but certain specific domains. In particular we have close correspondences between logic and complexity for the domain of *ordered finite* structures.

By a **model class** we always mean a class $\mathcal{K}$ of structures of a fixed vocabulary τ that is closed under isomorphism, i.e. if $\mathfrak{A} \in \mathcal{K}$ and $\mathfrak{A} \cong \mathfrak{B}$, then also $\mathfrak{B} \in \mathcal{K}$. We speak of a **domain** of structures instead, if the vocabulary is not fixed. For a domain $\mathcal{D}$ and vocabulary τ, we write $\mathcal{D}(\tau)$ for the class of τ-structures in $\mathcal{D}$.

Intuitively, a logic L captures a complexity class *Comp* on $\mathcal{D}$ if the L-definable properties of structures in $\mathcal{D}$ are precisely those that are decidable in *Comp*. Here is a more detailed definition.

Definition 3.2.10. Let L be a logic, *Comp* a complexity class, and $\mathcal{D}$ a domain of finite structures. We say that L **captures** *Comp* **on** $\mathcal{D}$ if

(1) For every vocabulary τ and every sentence $\psi \in L(\tau)$, the model-checking problem for ψ on $\mathcal{D}(\tau)$ is in the complexity class *Comp*.
(2) For every model class $\mathcal{K} \subseteq \mathcal{D}(\tau)$ whose membership problem is in *Comp*, there exists a sentence $\psi \in L(\tau)$ such that

$$\mathcal{K} = \{\mathfrak{A} \in \mathcal{D}(\tau) : \mathfrak{A} \models \psi\}.$$

By Fagin's Theorem, the logic Σ_1^1 captures NP on the domain of all finite structures, and by Corollary 3.2.7, second-order logic captures the polynomial-time hierarchy.

We sometimes simply write $L \subseteq$ *Comp* to say that condition (1) of Definition 3.2.10 is satisfied for L and *Comp* on the domain of *all* finite structures.

A classical result, from the 'prehistory' of finite model theory, says that a language is regular (i.e. recognizable by a finite automaton) if, and only if, it is definable in monadic second-order logic (MSO). As words can be viewed as a special domain of structures, this is a capturing result in the sense of Definition 3.2.10.

Theorem 3.2.11 (Büchi, Elgot, and Trakhtenbrot). *On the domain of word structures, monadic second-order logic captures the regular languages.*

There are numerous extensions and ramifications of this theorem, most of them established in the context of automata theory. We refer to [95, 97] for a proof and further results. However, the emphasis of most of the work in finite model theory is on structures more complicated structures than words, and concerns complexity levels higher than the regular languages.

3.2.3 Capturing Polynomial Time on Ordered Structures

In this section, we present a logical characterization of polynomial time on ordered structures, in terms of second-order Horn logic. Other such characterizations will follow in subsequent sections.

Definition 3.2.12. Second-order Horn logic, denoted by SO-HORN, is the set of second-order sentences of the form

$$Q_1 R_1 \cdots Q_m R_m \forall y_1 \cdots \forall y_s \bigwedge_{i=1}^{t} C_i$$

where $Q_i \in \{\exists, \forall\}$, the R_i are relation symbols, and the C_i are *Horn clauses with respect to* $R_1, \ldots, R_m$. More precisely, each C_i is an implication of the form

$$H \leftarrow \beta_1 \wedge \cdots \wedge \beta_m$$

where each β_j is either a positive atom $R_k \bar{z}$, or a first-order formula that does not contain $R_1, \ldots, R_m$. The conjunction $\beta_1 \wedge \cdots \wedge \beta_m$ is called the **body** of the clause. H, the **head** of the clause, is either an atom $R_j \bar{z}$ or the Boolean constant 0 (for *false*).

Thus the first-order parts of the sentences in SO-HORN are universal Horn sentences with respect to the quantified predicates $R_1, \ldots, R_m$, but may use arbitrary first-order information about the 'input predicates' from the underlying vocabulary. Σ_1^1-HORN denotes the existential fragment of SO-HORN, i.e. the set of SO-HORN sentences where all second-order quantifiers are existential.

Example 3.2.13. The problem GEN is a well-known P-complete problem [57, 70]. It may be presented as the set of structures (A, S, f, a) in the vocabulary of one unary predicate S, one binary function f, and a constant a, such that a is contained in the closure of S under f. Clearly, the complement of GEN is also P-complete. It is defined by the following sentence of Σ_1^1-HORN:

$$\exists R \forall y \forall z \Big((Ry \leftarrow Sy) \wedge (Rfyz \leftarrow Ry \wedge Rz) \wedge (0 \leftarrow Ra) \Big).$$

Example 3.2.14. The circuit value problem (CVP) is also P-complete [57], even when restricted to circuits with a fan-in of 2 over NAND gates. Such a circuit can be considered as a structure (V, E, I^+, I^-, out), where (V, E) is a directed acyclic graph, I^+ and I^- are monadic predicates, and a is a constant. Here Exy means that node x is one of the two input nodes for y; I^+ and I^- contain the input nodes with values 1 and 0, respectively; and out stands for the output node.

We shall take for granted that E is a connected, acyclic graph with a fan-in of 2, sources $I^+ \cup I^-$, and sink out. The formula $\exists T \exists F \forall x \forall y \forall z \varphi$, where φ is the conjunction of the clauses

$$
\begin{aligned}
Tx &\leftarrow I^+x \\
Fx &\leftarrow I^-x \\
Ty &\leftarrow Fx \wedge Exy \\
Fz &\leftarrow Tx \wedge Exz \wedge Ty \wedge Eyz \wedge y \neq z \\
0 &\leftarrow Tx \wedge Fx \\
Tx &\leftarrow x = out
\end{aligned}
$$

then states that the circuit (V, E, I^+, I^-, out) evaluates to 1.

Exercise 3.2.15 To justify the definition of SO-HORN, show that the admission of quantifiers over functions, or of first-order prefixes of a more general form, would make the restriction to Horn clauses pointless. Any such extension of SO-HORN has the full power of second-order logic.

Theorem 3.2.16. *Every sentence $\psi \in$ SO-HORN is equivalent to some sentence $\psi' \in \Sigma_1^1$-HORN.*

Proof. It suffices to prove the theorem for formulae of the form

$$\psi := \forall P \exists R_1 \cdots \exists R_m \forall \bar{z} \varphi,$$

where φ is a conjunction of Horn clauses. An arbitrary formula in SO-HORN may then be brought to existential form by successively removing the innermost universal second-order quantifier. We first prove the following claim.

Claim. *A formula $\exists \bar{R} \forall \bar{z} \varphi(P, \bar{R}) \in \Sigma_1^1$-HORN is true for all predicates P (on a given structure $\mathfrak{A}$) if it holds for those predicates P that are false at at most one point.*

Let k be the arity of P. For every k-tuple $\bar{a}$, let $P^{\bar{a}} = A^k - \{\bar{a}\}$, i.e. the predicate that is false at $\bar{a}$ and true at all other points. By assumption, there exist predicates $\overline{R}^{\bar{a}}$ such that

$$(\mathfrak{A}, P^{\bar{a}}, \overline{R}^{\bar{a}}) \models \forall \bar{z} \varphi.$$

Now, take any predicate $P \neq A^k$, and let $R_i := \bigcap_{\bar{a} \notin P} R_i^{\bar{a}}$. We claim that $(\mathfrak{A}, P, \overline{R}) \models \forall \bar{z} \varphi$.

Suppose that this is false; there then exists a relation $P \neq A^k$, a clause C of φ, and an assignment $\rho : \{z_1 \ldots, z_s\} \to A$ such that $(\mathfrak{A}, P, \overline{R}) \models \neg C[\rho]$. We now show that there then exists a tuple $\bar{a}$ such that also $(\mathfrak{A}, P^{\bar{a}}, \overline{R}^{\bar{a}}) \models \neg C[\rho]$.

If the head of $C[\rho]$ is $P\bar{u}$, then take $\bar{a} = \bar{u} \notin P$. If the head of $C[\rho]$ is $R_i \bar{u}$, then choose some $\bar{a} \notin P$ such that $\bar{u} \notin R_i^{\bar{a}}$; such an $\bar{a}$ must exist because $\bar{u} \notin R_i$. Finally, if the head is 0, take an arbitrary $\bar{a} \notin P$. The head of $C[\rho]$ is clearly false in $(\mathfrak{A}, P^{\bar{a}}, \overline{R}^{\bar{a}})$. The atom $P\bar{a}$ does not occur in the body of $C[\rho]$, because $\bar{a} \notin P$ and all atoms in the body of $C[\rho]$ are true in $(\mathfrak{A}, P, \overline{R})$; all other atoms of the form $P\bar{v}$ that might occur in the body of the clause remain true for $P^{\bar{a}}$ also. Moreover, every atom $R_i \bar{v}$ in the body remains true if R_i is replaced by $R_i^{\bar{a}}$ (because $R_i \subseteq R_i^{\bar{a}}$). This implies that the clause $(\mathfrak{A}, P^{\bar{a}}, \overline{R}^{\bar{a}}) \models \neg C[\rho]$, and thus

$$(\mathfrak{A}, P^{\bar{a}}, \overline{R}^{\bar{a}}) \models \neg \forall \bar{z} \varphi,$$

which contradicts our assumption.

Thus the claim has been established. This implies that the original formula ψ is equivalent to the conjunction

$$\exists \overline{R} \forall \bar{z} \varphi_0 \wedge \forall \bar{y} (\exists \overline{R}) \forall \bar{z} \varphi_1,$$

where φ_1 and φ_0 are obtained from φ by replacing every atom $P\bar{u}$ by $\bar{u} \neq \bar{y}$ (which is true iff $\bar{u} \in P^{\bar{y}}$), or by $(\bar{u} = \bar{u})$ (which is always true), respectively. It is easy to transform this conjunction into an equivalent formula in Σ_1^1-HORN. □

Theorem 3.2.17. *If $\psi \in$ SO-HORN, then the set of finite models of ψ is in PTIME.*

Proof. We can restrict our attention to sentences $\psi = \exists R_1 \cdots \exists R_m \forall \bar{z} \bigwedge_i C_i$ in Σ_1^1-HORN. Given any finite structure $\mathfrak{A}$ of appropriate vocabulary, we reduce the problem of whether $\mathfrak{A} \models \psi$ to the satisfiability problem for a propositional Horn formula by the same technique as in the proof of Theorem 3.2.6.

Replace the universal quantifiers $\forall z_i$ by conjunctions over the elements $a_i \in A$ and omit the quantifier prefix. Then substitute in the body of each clause the first-order formulae that do not involve $R_1, \ldots, R_m$ by their truth values in $\mathfrak{A}$. If there is any clause that is already made false by this partial interpretation (i.e. the head is false and all atoms in the body are true), then reject ψ. Otherwise, omit all clauses that are already made true (i.e. the head is true or a conjunct of the body is false) and delete the conjuncts already interpreted from the remaining clauses. Consider the atoms $R_i \bar{u}$ as propositional variables. The resulting formula is a propositional Horn formula whose length is polynomially bounded in the cardinality of $\mathfrak{A}$ and which is satisfiable if and only if $\mathfrak{A} \models \psi$. The satisfiability problem for propositional Horn formulae can be solved in linear time. □

Theorem 3.2.18 (Grädel). *On ordered structures,* SO-HORN *and* Σ_1^1-HORN *capture* PTIME.

Proof. This follows from an analysis of our proof of Fagin's Theorem. If the Turing machine M happens to be deterministic, then the sentence $\exists \overline{X} \psi_M$ constructed in that proof can easily be transformed to an equivalent sentence in Σ_1^1-HORN.

To see this, recall that ψ_M is the universal closure of START $\wedge$ NOCHANGE $\wedge$ CHANGE $\wedge$ END. The formulae START, NOCHANGE, and END are already in Horn form. The formula CHANGE has the form

$$\bigwedge_{\substack{q \in Q \\ \sigma \in \Sigma}} \left(\mathrm{PRE}[q,\sigma] \rightarrow \bigvee_{(q',\sigma',m) \in \delta(q,\sigma)} \mathrm{POST}[q',\sigma',m] \right),$$

where

$$\mathrm{PRE}[q,\sigma] := X_q(\bar{t}) \wedge Z(\bar{t},\overline{x}) \wedge Y_\sigma(\bar{t},\overline{x}) \wedge \bar{t}' = \bar{t} + 1$$

$$\mathrm{POST}[q',\sigma',m] := X_{q'}(\bar{t}') \wedge Y_{\sigma'}(\bar{t}',\overline{x}) \wedge \exists \overline{y}(\overline{x} + m = \overline{y} \wedge Z(\bar{t}',\overline{y})).$$

For a deterministic M, we have for each pair (q,σ) a unique value $\delta(q,\sigma) = (q',\sigma',m)$. In this case, the implication $\mathrm{PRE}[q,\sigma] \rightarrow \mathrm{POST}[q',\sigma',m]$ can be replaced by the conjunction of the Horn clauses

$$\mathrm{PRE}[q,\sigma] \rightarrow X_{q'}(\bar{t}')$$

$$\mathrm{PRE}[q,\sigma] \rightarrow Y_{\sigma'}(\bar{t}',\overline{x})$$

$$\mathrm{PRE}[q,\sigma] \wedge \overline{y} = \overline{x} + m \rightarrow Z(\bar{t}',\overline{y}).$$

□

Exercise 3.2.19 Prove that, contrary to the case of Fagin's Theorem, the assumption that a linear order is explicitly available cannot be eliminated, since linear orderings are not axiomatizable by Horn formulae.

Exercise 3.2.20 In [47], where the results of this section were proved, a weaker variant of SO-HORN was used, in which the body may not contain arbitrary first-order formulae of the input vocabulary, but only atoms and negated input atoms. Prove that the two variants of SO-HORN are equivalent on ordered structures with a successor relation and with constants for the first and last elements, but not on ordered structures without a successor relation. *Hint*: sentences in the weak variant of SO-HORN are preserved under substructures, i.e. if $\mathfrak{A} \models \psi$ and $\mathfrak{B} \subseteq \mathfrak{A}$, then also $\mathfrak{B} \models \psi$.

3.2.4 Capturing Logarithmic Space Complexity

In this section and the next, we describe two approaches to defining logics that capture logarithmic space complexity classes on ordered structures. The first approach is based on restrictions of second-order logic, similarly to the definition of SO-HORN, whereas the second technique adds transitive closure operators to first-order logic.

Definition 3.2.21. Second-order Krom logic, denoted by SO-KROM, is the set of second-order formulae

$$Q_1 R_1 \cdots Q_m R_m \forall y_1 \cdots \forall y_s \bigwedge_{i=1}^{t} C_i$$

where every clause C_i is a disjunction of at most two literals of the form $(\neg)R_i\overline{y}$ and of a first-order formula that does not contain $R_1, \ldots, R_m$. Such formulae are Krom (i.e. in 2-CNF) with respect to the quantified predicates. Σ_1^1-KROM is the existential fragment of SO-KROM. The intersection of Σ_1^1-HORN and Σ_1^1-KROM is denoted by Σ_1^1-KROM-HORN.

Example 3.2.22. The reachability problem ('Is there a path in the graph (V, E) from a to b?') is complete for NLOGSPACE via first-order translations. Its complement is expressible by a formula from Σ_1^1-KROM-HORN,

$$\exists T \forall x \forall y \forall z \Big(Txx \wedge (Txz \leftarrow Txy \wedge Eyz) \wedge (0 \leftarrow Tab) \Big).$$

As in the case of SO-HORN, it is also known that every sentence of SO-KROM is equivalent to a sentence of Σ_1^1-KROM (see [47]).

Proposition 3.2.23. *For every sentence* $\psi \in$ SO-KROM, *the set of finite models of* ψ *is in* NLOGSPACE.

The proof is analogous to the proof of Theorem 3.2.17. It uses the fact that 2-SAT, the satisfiability problem for propositional Krom formulae, is in NLOGSPACE. On ordered structures, SO-KROM captures NLOGSPACE. We shall indicate the general idea of the proof here. Suppose that M is an $O(\log n)$-space-bounded non-deterministic Turing machine with an input tape carrying a representation $code(\mathfrak{A}, <)$ of an input structure, and one or more separate work tapes. A *reduced configuration* of M reflects the control state of M, the content of the work tapes, and the positions of the heads on the input tape and the work tapes. Thus a configuration is specified by a reduced configuration together with the input. Given that reduced configurations of M for the input $code(\mathfrak{A}, <)$ have a logarithmic length with respect to $|A|$, we can represent them by tuples $\bar{c} = c_1, \ldots, c_r \in A^r$ for fixed r. The *initial* reduced configuration on any input $code(\mathfrak{A}, <)$ is represented by the tuple $\bar{0}$. Assume that M has a single accepting state, say state 1, and let the first component of the reduced configuration describe the state. The condition that $\bar{y}$ represents an *accepting* configuration is then expressed by $\text{ACCEPT}(\bar{y}) := (y_1 = 1)$. Further, it is not difficult (although it is somewhat lengthy) to write down a quantifier-free formula $\text{NEXT}(\bar{x}, \bar{y})$ such that, for every successor structure $(\mathfrak{A}, S, 0, e)$ and every tuple $\bar{c}$ representing a reduced configuration,

$$(\mathfrak{A}, S, 0, e) \models \text{NEXT}(\bar{c}, \bar{d})$$

if, and only if, $\bar{d}$ represents a reduced successor configuration of $\bar{c}$ for the input $(\mathfrak{A}, <)$. Taking the disjunctive normal form $\text{NEXT}(\bar{x}, \bar{y}) = \bigvee_i \text{NEXT}_i(\bar{x}, \bar{y})$, we can express the staement that M does *not* accept the input $code(\mathfrak{A}, <)$ by the sentence

$$\psi_M := \exists R \forall \bar{x} \forall \bar{y} \big(R\bar{0} \wedge \bigwedge_i (R\bar{y} \leftarrow R\bar{x} \wedge \text{NEXT}_i(\bar{x}, \bar{y}))$$
$$\wedge \, (\square \leftarrow R\bar{y} \wedge \text{ACCEPT}(\bar{y})\big).$$

This proves that, on ordered structures, the complement of every problem in NLOGSPACE is definable in SO-KROM. Since NLOGSPACE is closed under complements, and since the formula ψ_M is in fact in Σ_1^1-KROM-HORN, we have proved the following result.

Theorem 3.2.24 (Grädel). *On ordered structures, the logics SO-KROM, Σ_1^1-KROM, and Σ_1^1-KROM-HORN capture NLOGSPACE.*

Remark. The characterizations of P and NLOGSPACE by second-order Horn and Krom logics can also be reformulated in terms of generalized spectra. The notion of a generalized spectrum can be appropriately modified to the notions of a *generalized Horn spectrum* and a *generalized Krom spectrum*. Let a *model class* be any isomorphism-closed class of structures of some fixed finite signature. Fagin's Theorem and Theorems 3.2.18 and 3.2.24 can then be summarized as follows:

- A model class of finite structures is NP iff it is a generalized spectrum.
- A model class of ordered structures is in P iff it is a generalized Horn spectrum.
- A model class of ordered structures is in NLOGSPACE iff it is a generalized Krom spectrum.

3.2.5 Transitive Closure Logics

One of the limitations of first-order logic is the lack of a mechanism for unbounded iteration or recursion. This has motivated the study of more powerful languages that add recursion in one way or another to first-order logic. A simple but important example of a query that is not first-order expressible is reachability. By adding transitive closure operators to FO, we obtain a natural family of logics with a recursion mechanism.

Definition 3.2.25. Transitive closure logic, denoted by TC, is obtained by augmenting the syntax of first order logic by the following rule for building formulae:

Let $\varphi(\overline{x}, \overline{y})$ be a formula with variables $\overline{x} = x_1, \ldots, x_k$ and $\overline{y} = y_1, \ldots, y_k$, and let $\overline{u}$ and $\overline{v}$ be two k-tuples of terms. Then

$$[\mathbf{tc}_{\overline{x},\overline{y}} \, \varphi(\overline{x}, \overline{y})](\overline{u}, \overline{v})$$

is a formula which says that the pair $(\overline{u}, \overline{v})$ is contained in the transitive closure of the binary relation on k-tuples that is defined by φ. In other words, $\mathfrak{A} \models [\mathbf{tc}_{\overline{x},\overline{y}} \, \varphi(\overline{x}, \overline{y})](\overline{a}, \overline{b})$ if, and only if, there exist an $n \geq 1$ and tuples $\overline{c}_0, \ldots, \overline{c}_n$ in A^k such that $\overline{c}_0 = \overline{a}$, $\overline{c}_n = \overline{b}$, and $\mathfrak{A} \models \varphi(\overline{c}_i, \overline{c}_{i+1})$, for all $i < n$.

Of course, it is understood that φ can contain free variables other than $\overline{x}$ and $\overline{y}$; these will also be free in the new formula. Moreover, transitive closure logic is closed under the usual first-order operations. We can thus build Boolean combinations of TC-formulae, we can nest TC-operators, etc.

Example 3.2.26. A directed graph $G = (V, E)$ is acyclic if, and only if, $G \models \forall z[\mathbf{tc}_{x,y}Exy](z,z)$. It is well known that a graph is bipartite (2-colourable) if, and only if, it does not contain a cycle of odd length. This is expressed by the TC-formula $\forall x \forall y([\mathbf{tc}_{x,y}x \neq y \wedge \exists z Exz \wedge Ezy](x,y) \rightarrow \neg Eyx)$.

Exercise 3.2.27 Show that, for every $\psi \in$ TC, the set of finite models of ψ is decidable in NLOGSPACE.

The same idea as in the proof of Theorem 3.2.24 shows that, on ordered structures, TC captures NLOGSPACE. The condition that an $O(\log n)$-space-bounded Turing machine M accepts $code(\mathfrak{A}, <)$ is expressed by the formula

$$\exists \overline{z}(\mathrm{ACCEPT}(\overline{z}) \wedge [\mathbf{tc}_{\overline{x},\overline{y}} \, \mathrm{NEXT}(\overline{x}, \overline{y})](\overline{0}, \overline{z})).$$

Theorem 3.2.28 (Immerman). *On ordered structures,* TC *captures* NLOGSPACE.

An interesting variant of TC is **deterministic transitive closure logic**, denoted DTC, which makes definable the transitive closure of any *deterministic* definable relation. The syntax of DTC is analogous to TC, allowing us to build formulae of the form $[\mathbf{dtc}_{\overline{x},\overline{y}}\ \varphi(\overline{x},\overline{y})](\overline{u},\overline{v})$, for any formula $\varphi(\overline{x},\overline{y})$. The semantics can be defined by the equivalence

$$[\mathbf{dtc}_{\overline{x},\overline{y}}\ \varphi(\overline{x},\overline{y})](\overline{u},\overline{v}) \equiv [\mathbf{tc}_{\overline{x},\overline{y}}\ \varphi(\overline{x},\overline{y}) \wedge \forall \overline{z}(\varphi(\overline{x},\overline{z}) \rightarrow \overline{y} = \overline{z})](\overline{u},\overline{v}).$$

It is clear that transitive closures of deterministic relations can be checked by deterministic Turing machines using only logarithmic space. Conversely, acceptance by such machines amounts to deciding a reachability problem ('is there an accepting configuration that is reachable from the input configuration?') with respect to the successor relation $\vdash_M$ on configurations. Of course, for deterministic Turing machines, $\vdash_M$ is deterministic. We already know that on ordered structures, $\vdash_M$ is first-order definable, and hence acceptance can be defined in DTC.

Theorem 3.2.29 (Immerman). *On ordered finite structures* DTC *captures* LOGSPACE.

In particular, separating DTC from TC on ordered finite structures would amount to separating the complexity classes LOGSPACE and NLOGSPACE. However, on the domain of arbitrary finite structures, we can actually separate these logics [51].

Given a graph $G = (V, E)$, let $2G$ be the graph with vertex set $V \times \{0, 1\}$ and edges $\langle (u, i), (v, j) \rangle$ for $(u, v) \in E, i, j \in \{0, 1\}$. It is easy to see that on the class of all 'double graphs' $2G$, DTC collapses to FO. Take any tuple $\overline{u} = (u_1, i_1), \ldots, (u_k, i_k)$ of vertices in a double graph $2G$, and let the closure of $\overline{u}$ be the set $\{u_1, \ldots, u_k\} \times \{0, 1\}$. Switching the second component of any node is an automorphism of $2G$, and hence no definable deterministic path from $\overline{u}$ can leave the closure of $\overline{u}$. That is, if $2G \models [\mathbf{dtc}_{\overline{x},\overline{y}}\varphi(\overline{x},\overline{y})](\overline{u},\overline{v})$, then each node of $\overline{v}$ belongs to the closure of $\overline{u}$. Therefore DTC-definable paths are of bounded length, and can thus be defined by first-order formulae. On the other hand the usual argument (based on Ehrenfeucht–Fraïssé games) showing that transitive closures are not first-order definable applies also to the class of double graphs. Hence DTC is strictly less powerful than TC on double graphs. In [51] other graph classes are identified on which TC is more expressive than DTC. An interesting example is the class of all hypercubes.

Theorem 3.2.30. *On finite graphs,* DTC $\subsetneq$ TC.

TC is a much richer and more complicated logic than DTC also in other respects. For instance, DTC has a positive normal form: formulae $\neg[\mathbf{dtc}_{\overline{x}\overline{y}}\varphi(\overline{x},\overline{y})](\overline{u},\overline{v})$ can be rewritten using the $\mathbf{dtc}$ operator only positively. On the other hand, the alternation hierarchy in TC is strict [52].

3.3 Fixed-Point Logics

One of the distinguishing features of finite model theory compared with other branches of logic is the eminent role of various kinds of fixed-point logics. Fixed-point logics extend a basic logical formalism (such as first-order logic, conjunctive queries, or propositional modal logic) by a constructor for forming *fixed points of relational operators*.

What do we mean by a **relational operator**? Note that any formula $\psi(R, \overline{x})$ of vocabulary $\tau \cup \{R\}$ can be viewed as defining, for every τ-structure $\mathfrak{A}$, an update operator $F_\psi : \mathcal{P}(A^k) \to \mathcal{P}(A^k)$ on the class of k-ary relations on A, namely

$$F_\psi : R \mapsto \{\overline{a} : (\mathfrak{A}, R) \models \psi(R, \overline{a})\}.$$

A fixed point of F_ψ is a relation R for which $F_\psi(R) = R$. In general, a fixed point of F_ψ need not exist, or there may exist many of them. However, if R happens to occur only positively in ψ, then the operator F_ψ is monotone, and in that case there exists a *least* relation $R \subseteq A^k$ such that $F_\psi(R) = R$. The most influential fixed-point formalisms in logic are concerned with least (and greatest) fixed points, so we shall discuss these first. In finite model theory, a number of other fixed-point logics are important as well, and the structure, expressive power, and algorithmic properties of these logics have been studied intensively. We shall discuss them later.

3.3.1 Some Fixed-Point Theory

There is a well-developed mathematical theory of fixed points of monotone operators on complete lattices. A **complete lattice** is a partial order $(A, \leq)$ such that each set $X \subseteq A$ has a supremum (a least upper bound) and an infimum (a greatest lower bound). Here we are interested mainly in power set lattices $(\mathcal{P}(A^k), \subseteq)$ (where A is the universe of a structure), and later in product lattices $(\mathcal{P}(B_1) \times \cdots \times \mathcal{P}(B_m), \subseteq)$. For simplicity, we shall describe the basic facts of fixed-point theory for lattices $(\mathcal{P}(B), \subseteq)$, where B is an arbitrary (finite or infinite) set.

Definition 3.3.1. Let $F : \mathcal{P}(B) \to \mathcal{P}(B)$ be a function.

(1) $X \subseteq B$ is a **fixed point** of F if $F(X) = X$.
(2) A **least fixed point** or a **greatest fixed point** of F is a fixed point X of F such that $X \subseteq Y$ or $Y \subseteq X$, respectively, for each fixed point Y of F.
(3) F is **monotone**, if $X \subseteq Y \implies F(X) \subseteq F(Y)$ for all $X, Y \subseteq B$.

Theorem 3.3.2 (Knaster and Tarski). *Every monotone operator $F : \mathcal{P}(B) \to \mathcal{P}(B)$ has a least fixed point $\mathbf{lfp}(F)$ and a greatest fixed point $\mathbf{gfp}(F)$. Further, these fixed points may be written in the form*

$$\mathbf{lfp}(F) = \bigcap \{X : F(X) = X\} = \bigcap \{X : F(X) \subseteq X\}$$
$$\mathbf{gfp}(F) = \bigcup \{X : F(X) = X\} = \bigcup \{X : F(X) \supseteq X\}.$$

Proof. Let $S = \{X \subseteq B : F(X) \subseteq X\}$ and $Y = \bigcap S$. We first show that Y is a fixed point of F.

$F(Y) \subseteq Y$. Clearly, $Y \subseteq X$ for all $X \in S$. As F is monotone, it follows that $F(Y) \subseteq F(X) \subseteq X$. Hence $F(Y) \subseteq \bigcap S = Y$.

$Y \subseteq F(Y)$. As $F(Y) \subseteq Y$, we have $F(F(Y)) \subseteq F(Y)$, and hence $F(Y) \in S$. Thus $Y = \bigcap S \subseteq F(Y)$.

By definition, Y is contained in all X such that $F(X) \subseteq X$. In particular Y is contained in all fixed points of F. Hence Y is the least fixed point of F. The argument for the greatest fixed point is analogous. $\square$

Least fixed points can also be constructed inductively. We call an operator $F : \mathcal{P}(B) \to \mathcal{P}(B)$ **inductive** if the sequence of its **stages** X^α (where α is an ordinal), defined by

$$X^0 := \emptyset,$$
$$X^{\alpha+1} := F(X^\alpha), \text{ and}$$
$$X^\lambda := \bigcup_{\alpha < \lambda} X^\alpha \text{ for limit ordinals } \lambda,$$

is increasing, i.e. if $X^\beta \subseteq X^\alpha$ for all $\beta < \alpha$. Obviously, monotone operators are inductive. The sequence of stages of an inductive operator eventually reaches a fixed point, which we denote by X^∞. The least ordinal β for which $X^\beta = X^{\beta+1} = X^\infty$ is called $\mathrm{cl}(F)$, the **closure ordinal** of F.

Lemma 3.3.3. *For every inductive operator* $F : \mathcal{P}(B) \to \mathcal{P}(B)$, $|\mathrm{cl}(F)| \le |B|$.

Proof. Let $|B|^+$ denote the smallest cardinal greater than $|B|$. Suppose that the claim is false for F. Then for each $\alpha < |B|^+$ there exists an element $x_\alpha \in X^{\alpha+1} - X^\alpha$. The set $\{x_\alpha : \alpha < |B|^+\}$ is a subset of B of cardinality $|B|^+ > |B|$, which is impossible. $\square$

Proposition 3.3.4. *For monotone operators, the inductively constructed fixed point coincides with the least fixed point, i.e.* $X^\infty = \mathbf{lfp}(F)$.

Proof. As X^∞ is a fixed point, $\mathbf{lfp}(X) \subseteq X^\infty$. For the converse, we show by induction that $X^\alpha \subseteq \mathbf{lfp}(F)$ for all α. As $\mathbf{lfp}(F) = \bigcap\{Z : F(Z) \subseteq Z\}$, it suffices to show that X^α is contained in all Z for which $F(Z) \subseteq Z$.

For $\alpha = 0$, this is trivial. By monotonicity and the induction hypothesis, we have $X^{\alpha+1} = F(X^\alpha) \subseteq F(Z) \subseteq Z$. For limit ordinals λ with $X^\alpha \subseteq Z$ for all $\alpha < \lambda$ we also have $X^\lambda = \bigcup_{\alpha < \lambda} \subseteq Z$. $\square$

The greatest fixed point can be constructed by a dual induction, starting with $Y^0 = B$, by setting $Y^{\alpha+1} := F(Y^\alpha)$ and $Y^\lambda = \bigcap_{\alpha < \lambda} Y^\alpha$ for limit ordinals. The *decreasing* sequence of these stages then eventually converges to the greatest fixed point $Y^\infty = \mathbf{gfp}(F)$.

The least and greatest fixed points are dual to each other. For every monotone operator F, the dual operator $F^d : X \mapsto \overline{F(\overline{X})}$ (where $\overline{X}$ denotes the complement of X) is also monotone, and we have that

$$\mathbf{lfp}(F) = \overline{\mathbf{gfp}(F^d)} \text{ and } \mathbf{gfp}(F) = \overline{\mathbf{lfp}(F^d)}.$$

Exercise 3.3.5 Prove this.

Everything said so far holds for operators on arbitrary (finite or infinite) power set lattices. In *finite model theory*, we consider operators $F : \mathcal{P}(A^k) \to \mathcal{P}(A^k)$ for finite A only. In this case the inductive constructions will reach the least or greatest fixed point in a polynomial number of steps. As a consequence, these fixed points can be constructed efficiently.

Lemma 3.3.6. *Let $F : \mathcal{P}(A^k) \to \mathcal{P}(A^k)$ be a monotone operator on a finite set A. If F is computable in polynomial time (with respect to $|A|$), then so are the fixed points $\mathbf{lfp}(F)$ and $\mathbf{gfp}(F)$.*

3.3.2 Least Fixed-Point Logic

LFP is the logic obtained by adding least and greatest fixed points to first-order logic.

Definition 3.3.7. *Least fixed-point logic* (LFP) is defined by adding to the syntax of first-order logic the following *least fixed-point formation rule*: If $\psi(R, \overline{x})$ is a formula of vocabulary $\tau \cup \{R\}$ with only positive occurrences of R, if $\overline{x}$ is a tuple of variables, and if $\overline{t}$ is a tuple of terms (such that the lengths of $\overline{x}$ and $\overline{t}$ match the arity of R), then

$$[\mathbf{lfp}R\overline{x} \cdot \psi](\overline{t}) \text{ and } [\mathbf{gfp}R\overline{x} \cdot \psi](\overline{t})$$

are formulae of vocabulary τ. The free first-order variables of these formulae are those in $(\mathrm{free}(\psi) - \{x : x \text{ in } \overline{x}\}) \cup \mathrm{free}(\overline{t})$.

Semantics. For any τ-structure $\mathfrak{A}$ providing interpetations for all free variables in the formula, we have that $\mathfrak{A} \models [\mathbf{lfp}R\overline{x} \cdot \psi](\overline{t})$ if $\overline{t}^{\mathfrak{A}}$ (the tuple of elements of $\mathfrak{A}$ interpreting $\overline{t}$) is contained in $\mathbf{lfp}(F_{\psi})$, where F_{ψ} is the update operator defined by ψ on $\mathfrak{A}$. Similarly for greatest fixed points.

Example 3.3.8. Here is a fixed-point formula that defines the transitive closure of the binary predicate E:

$$\mathrm{TC}(u, v) := [\mathbf{lfp}Txy \cdot Exy \lor \exists z(Exz \land Tzy)](u, v).$$

Note that in a formula $[\mathbf{lfp}R\overline{x} \cdot \varphi](\overline{t})$, there may be free variables in φ additional to those in $\overline{x}$, and these remain free in the fixed-point formula. They are often called **parameters** of the fixed-point formula. For instance, the transitive closure can also be defined by the formula

$$\varphi(u, v) := [\mathbf{lfp}Ty \cdot Euy \lor \exists x(Tx \land Exy)](v)$$

which has u as a parameter.

Exercise 3.3.9 Show that every LFP-formula is equivalent to one without parameters (at the cost of increasing the arity of the fixed-point variables).

Example 3.3.10. Let $\varphi := \forall y(y < x \to Ry)$ and let $(A, <)$ be a partial order. The formula $[\mathbf{lfp}Rx \ . \ \varphi](x)$ then defines the well-founded part of $<$. The closure ordinal of F_φ on $(A, <)$ is the length of the longest well-founded initial segment of $<$, and $(A, <) \models \forall x[\mathbf{lfp}Rx \ . \ \varphi](x)$ if, and only if, $(A, <)$ is well-founded.

Exercise 3.3.11 Prove that the LFP-sentence

$$\psi := \forall y \exists z Fyz \wedge \forall y[\mathbf{lfp}Ry \ . \ \forall x(Fxy \to Rx)](y)$$

is an infinity axiom, i.e. it is satisfiable but does not have a finite model.

Example 3.3.12. The GAME query asks, given a finite game $\mathcal{G} = (V, V_0, V_1, E)$, to compute the set of winning positions for Player 0 (see Section 3.1.3). The GAME query is LFP-definable, by use of $[\mathbf{lfp}Wx \ . \ \varphi](x)$ with

$$\varphi(W, x) := (V_0 x \wedge \exists y(Exy \wedge Wy)) \vee (V_1 \wedge \forall y(Exy \to Wy)).$$

The GAME query plays an important role for LFP. It can be shown that every LFP-definable property of finite structures can be reduced to GAME by a quantifier-free translation [31]. Hence GAME is complete for LFP via this notion of reduction, and thus a natural candidate if one is trying to separate a weaker logic from LFP.

Exercise 3.3.13 Prove that the problem GEN and the circuit value problem (see Examples 3.2.13 and 3.2.14) are expressible in LFP.

The duality between the least and greatest fixed points implies that for any formula ψ,

$$[\mathbf{gfp}R\overline{x} \ . \ \psi](\overline{t}) \equiv \neg[\mathbf{lfp}R\overline{x} \ . \ \neg\psi[R/\neg R]](\overline{t}),$$

where $\psi[R/\neg R]$ is the formula obtained from ψ by replacing all occurrences of R-atoms by their negations. (As R occurs only positively in ψ, the same is true for $\neg\psi[R/\neg R]$.) Because of this duality, greatest fixed points are often omitted in the definition of LFP. On the other hand, it is sometimes convenient to keep the greatest fixed points, and to use the duality (and de Morgan's laws) to translate LFP-formulae to *negation normal form*, i.e. to push negations all the way to the atoms.

Capturing Polynomial Time

From the fact that first-order operations are polynomial-time computable and from Lemma 3.3.6, we can immediately conclude that every LFP-definable property of finite strucures is computable in polynomial time.

Proposition 3.3.14. *Let ψ be a sentence in LFP. It is decidable in polynomial time whether a given finite structure $\mathfrak{A}$ is a model of ψ. In short,* LFP $\subseteq$ PTIME.

Obviously LFP, is a fragment of second-order logic. Indeed, by the Tarski–Knaster Theorem,

$$[\mathbf{lfp}R\overline{x} \,.\, \psi(R,\overline{x})](\overline{y}) \equiv \forall R((\forall \overline{x}(\psi(R,\overline{x}) \to R\overline{x})) \to R\overline{y}).$$

We next relate LFP to SO-HORN.

Theorem 3.3.15. *Every formula $\psi \in$ SO-HORN is equivalent to some formula $\psi^* \in$ LFP.*

Proof. By Theorem 3.2.16, we can assume that $\psi = (\exists R_1)\cdots(\exists R_m)\varphi \in \Sigma_1^1$-HORN. By combining the predicates $R_1, \ldots, R_m$ into a single predicate R of larger arity and by renaming variables, it is easy to transform ψ into an equivalent formula

$$\psi' := \exists R \forall \overline{x} \forall \overline{y} \bigwedge_i C_i \wedge \bigwedge_j D_j,$$

where the C_i are clauses of the form $R\overline{x} \leftarrow \alpha_i(R,\overline{x},\overline{y})$ (with exactly the same head $R\overline{x}$ for every i) and the D_j are clauses of the form $0 \leftarrow \beta_j(R,\overline{x},\overline{y})$. The clauses C_i define, on every structure $\mathfrak{A}$, a monotone operator $F : R \mapsto \{\overline{x} : \bigvee_i \exists \overline{y} \alpha_i(\overline{x},\overline{y})\}$. Let R^ω be the least fixed point of this operator. Obviously $\mathfrak{A} \models \neg\psi$ if and only if $\mathfrak{A} \models \beta_i(R^\omega, \overline{a}, \overline{b})$ for some i and some tuple $\overline{a}, \overline{b}$. But R^ω is defined by the fixed-point formula

$$\alpha^\omega(\overline{x}) := [\mathbf{lfp}R\overline{x} \,.\, \bigvee_i \exists \overline{y}\alpha_i(\overline{x},\overline{y})](\overline{x}).$$

Hence, for $\beta := \exists \overline{x}\exists \overline{y} \bigvee_j \beta_j(\overline{x},\overline{y})$, ψ is equivalent to the formula $\psi^* := \neg\beta[R\overline{z}/\alpha^\omega(\overline{z})]$ obtained from $\neg\beta$ by substituting all occurrences of atoms $R\overline{z}$ by $\alpha^\omega(\overline{z})$. Clearly, this formula is in LFP. $\square$

Hence SO-HORN $\leq$ LFP $\leq$ SO. As an immediate consequence of Theorems 3.2.18 and 3.3.15 we obain the Immerman–Vardi Theorem.

Theorem 3.3.16 (Immerman and Vardi). *On ordered structures, least fixed-point logic captures polynomial time.*

However, on unordered structures, SO-HORN is strictly weaker than LFP.

3.3.3 The Modal μ-Calculus

A fragment of LFP that is of fundamental importance in many areas of computer science (e.g. controller synthesis, hardware verification, and knowledge representation) is the modal μ-calculus (L_μ). It is obtained by adding least and greatest fixed points to propositional modal logic (ML). In other words L_μ relates to ML in the same way as LFP relates to FO.

Modal logics such as ML and the μ-calculus are evaluated on transition systems (alias Kripke structures, alias coloured graphs) at a particular node.

Given a formula ψ and a transition system G, we write $G, v \models \psi$ to denote that G holds at node v of G. Recall that formulae of ML, for reasoning about **transition systems** $G = (V, (E_a)_{a \in A}, (P_b)_{b \in B})$, are built from atomic propositions P_b by means of the usual propositional connectives and the modal operators $\langle a \rangle$ and $[a]$. That is, if ψ is a formula and $a \in A$ is an action, then we can build the formulae $\langle a \rangle \psi$ and $[a]\psi$, with the following semantics:

$$G, v \models \langle a \rangle \psi \text{ iff } G, w \models \psi \text{ for } \textit{some } w \text{ such that } (v, w) \in E_a,$$
$$G, v \models [a]\psi \text{ iff } G, w \models \psi \text{ for } \textit{all } w \text{ such that } (v, w) \in E_a.$$

If there is only one transition relation, i.e. $A = \{a\}$, then we simply write $\Box$ and $\Diamond$ for $[a]$ and $\langle a \rangle$, respectively.

ML can be viewed as an extension of propositional logic. However, in our context it is more convenient to view it as a simple fragment of first-order logic. A modal formula ψ defines a query on transition systems, associating with G a set of nodes $\psi^G := \{v : G, v \models \psi\}$, and this set can be defined equivalently by a first-order formula $\psi^*(x)$. This translation maps atomic propositions P_b to atoms $P_b x$, it commutes with the Boolean connectives, and it translates the modal operators by use of quantifiers as follows:

$$(\langle a \rangle \psi)^*(x) := \exists y (E_a xy \wedge \psi^*(y))$$
$$([a]\psi)^*(x) := \forall y (E_a xy \rightarrow \psi^*(y)).$$

Note that the resulting formula has width 2 and can thus be written with only two variables. We have proved the following proposition.

Proposition 3.3.17. *For every formula $\psi \in$ ML, there exists a first-order formula $\psi^*(x)$ of width 2, which is equivalent to ψ in the sense that $G, v \models \psi$ iff $G \models \psi^*(v)$.*

The *modal fragment* of first-order logic is the image of propositional modal logic under this translation. It has turned out that the modal fragment has interesting algorithmic and model-theoretic properties (see [3] and the references given there).

Definition 3.3.18. The **modal μ-calculus** L_μ extends ML (including propositional variables $X, Y, \ldots$, which can be be viewed as monadic second-order variables) by the following rule for building fixed point formulae: If ψ is a formula in L_μ and X is a propositional variable that only occurs positively in ψ, then $\mu X.\psi$ and $\nu X.\psi$ are also L_μ-formulae.

The semantics of these fixed-point formulae is completely analogous to that for LFP. The formula ψ defines on G (with universe V, and with interpretations for other free second-order variables that ψ may have besides X) the monotone operator $F_\psi : \mathcal{P}(V) \rightarrow \mathcal{P}(V)$ assigning to every set $X \subseteq V$ the set $\psi^G(X) := \{v \in V : (G, X), v \models \psi\}$. Now,

$$G, v \models \mu X.\psi \text{ iff } v \in \mathbf{lfp}(F_\psi)$$
$$G, v \models \nu X.\psi \text{ iff } v \in \mathbf{gfp}(F_\psi).$$

Example 3.3.19. The formula $\mu X.\varphi \vee \langle a \rangle X$ asserts that there exists a path along a-transitions to a node where φ holds.

The formula $\psi := \nu X.\left(\bigvee_{a \in A} \langle a \rangle \, true \wedge \bigwedge_{a \in A} [a] X \right)$ expresses the assertion that the given transition system is deadlock-free. In other words, $G, v \models \psi$ if no path from v in G reaches a dead end (i.e. a node without outgoing transitions).

Finally, the formula $\nu X.\mu Y.\langle a \rangle ((\varphi \wedge X) \vee Y)$ says that there exists a path from the current node on which φ holds infinitely often.

Exercise 3.3.20 Prove that the formulae in Example 3.3.19 do indeed express the stated properties.

The translation from ML into FO is readily extended to a translation from L_μ into LFP.

Proposition 3.3.21. *Every formula* $\psi \in L_\mu$ *is equivalent to a formula* $\psi^*(x) \in$ LFP.

Proof. By induction. A formula of form $\mu X.\varphi$ is translated to $[\mathbf{lfp} X x \, . \, \varphi^*](x)$, and similarly for greatest fixed points. □

Further the argument proving that LFP can be embedded into SO also shows that L_μ is a fragment of MSO.

Let us turn to algorithmic issues. The complexity of the model-checking problem for L_μ is a major open problem, as far as combined complexity and expression complexity are concerned (see Section 3.3.5). However, the data complexity can be settled easily.

Proposition 3.3.22 (data complexity of L_μ). *Fix any formula* $\psi \in L_\mu$. *Given a finite transition system* G *and a node* v, *it can be decided in polynomial time whether* $G, v \models \psi$. *Further, there exist* $\psi \in L_\mu$ *for which the model checking problem is* PTIME-*complete.*

Proof. As L_μ is a fragment of LFP, the first claim is obvious. For the second claim, recall that the GAME problem for strictly alternating games is PTIME-complete (see Section 3.1.2). Player 0 has a winning strategy from position $v \in V_0$ in the game $G = (V, V_0, V_1, E)$ if, and only if, $G, v \models \mu X.\Diamond \Box X$. □

Despite this result, it is not difficult to see that the μ-calculus does not suffice to capture PTIME, even in very restricted scenarios such as word structures. Indeed, as L_μ is a fragment of MSO, it can only define *regular languages*, and of course, not all PTIME-languages are regular. However, we shall see in Section 3.5.3 that there is a multidimensional variant of L_μ that captures the *bisimulation-invariant* fragment of PTIME.

For more information on the μ-calculus, we refer to [5, 21, 56] and the references therein.

3.3.4 Parity Games

For least fixed-point logics, the appropriate evaluation games are *parity games*. These are games of possibly infinite duration where each position is assigned a natural number, called its priority, and the winner of an infinite play is determined according to whether the least priority seen infinitely often during the play is even or odd. It is open whether winning sets and winning strategies for parity games can be computed in polynomial time. The best algorithms known today are polynomial in the size of the game, but exponential with respect to the number of priorities. Practically competitive model-checking algorithms for the modal μ-calculus work by solving the strategy problem for the associated parity game (see e.g. [73]).

Definition 3.3.23. We describe a **parity game** by a labelled graph $\mathcal{G} = (V, V_0, V_1, E, \Omega)$, where (V, V_0, V_1, E) is a game graph as in Section 3.1.2, and $\Omega : V \to \mathbb{N}$ assigns to each position a **priority**. The set V of positions may be finite or infinite, but the number of different priorities must be finite; it is called the **index** of $\mathcal{G}$. Recall that a finite play of a game is lost by the player who gets stuck, i.e. cannot move. The difference to the games of Section 3.1.2 is that we have different winning conditions for infinite plays $v_0 v_1 v_2 \dots$. If the smallest number appearing infinitely often in the sequence $\Omega(v_0)\Omega(v_1)\dots$ of priorities is even, then Player 0 wins the play; otherwise, Player 1 wins.

Recall that a **positional strategy** of Player σ is a partial function $f : V_\sigma \to V$ with $(v, f(v)) \in E$. A strategy f is said to be winning on a set of positions $W \subseteq V$ if any play that starts at a position in W and is consistent with f is winning for Player σ. Further, W_σ, the **winning region** of Player σ, is the set of positions from which Player σ has a winning strategy (which, a priori, need not be positional).

Exercise 3.3.24 (Combination of positional strategies). Let f and f' be positional strategies for Player σ that are winning on the sets W and W', respectively. Let $f \triangleleft f'$ be the positional strategy defined by

$$(f \triangleleft f')(x) := \begin{cases} f(x) & \text{if } x \in W \\ f'(x) & \text{otherwise.} \end{cases}$$

Prove that $f \triangleleft f'$ is winning on $W \cup W'$.

The Positional Determinacy Theorem for parity games states that parity games are always determined (i.e., from each position, one of the players has a winning strategy) and in fact, positional strategies always suffice. This was proved independently by Emerson and Jutla [40] and by Mostowski [86]. Earlier, Gurevich and Harrington [62] had proved that Muller games (which are more general than parity games) are determined via finite-memory strategies.

Theorem 3.3.25 (Positional Determinacy). *In any parity game, the set of positions can be partitioned into two sets W_0 and W_1 such that Player 0 has a positional strategy that is winning on W_0 and Player 1 has a positional strategy that is winning on W_1.*

Here, we only prove this theorem for the case of finite game graphs. The presentation is inspired by a similar proof due to Ehrenfeucht and Mycielski [39] for mean payoff games; see also [12]. For the general case, we refer the reader to [102] or [97].

Proof. Let $\mathcal{G} = (V, V_0, V_1, E, \Omega)$ be a parity game with a finite set V of positions. We call a position $v \in V$ *live* if it is non-terminal (i.e. if there is at least one possible move from v). The theorem trivially holds for games with at most one live position. We now proceed by induction over the number of live positions.

For every live position v in $\mathcal{G}$ and for $\sigma = 0, 1$, we define the game $\mathcal{G}[v, \sigma]$, which is the same as $\mathcal{G}$ except that we change v to a terminal position where Player σ wins. (Technically this means that we put v into $V_{1-\sigma}$ and delete all outgoing edges from v.) By the induction hypothesis, the Forgetful Determinacy Theorem holds for $\mathcal{G}[v, \sigma]$, and we write $W_0[v, \sigma]$ and $W_1[v, \sigma]$ for the winning regions of $\mathcal{G}[v, \sigma]$.

It suffices to show that for every live position u in $\mathcal{G}$, one of the players has a positional strategy to win $\mathcal{G}$ from u. By Exercise 3.3.24, these strategies can then be combined into positional strategies that win on the entire winning regions.

Clearly,

$$W_0[v, 1] \subseteq W_0 \text{ and } W_1[v, 0] \subseteq W_1.$$

Moreover, any positional strategy f for Player σ that is winning from position u in the game $\mathcal{G}[v, 1-\sigma]$ is also winning from u in the game $\mathcal{G}$ and avoids v (i.e. no play that starts at u and is consistent with f ever hits position v). Now let

$$A_\sigma := \bigcup_{v \text{ live}} W_\sigma[v, 1-\sigma].$$

We call positions $u \in A_\sigma$ *strong winning positions* for Player σ because, informally speaking, Player σ can win $\mathcal{G}$ from u even if she gives away some live positions to her opponent. Similarly, positions outside $A_0 \cup A_1$ are called *weak positions*. It remains to show that from weak positions also, one of the players has a positional winning strategy. In fact, one of the players wins, with a positional winning strategy, from *all* weak positions.

By the induction hypothesis, if u is not in $A_{1-\sigma}$, then, for *all* live positions v of $\mathcal{G}$, we have that $u \in W_\sigma[v, \sigma]$ and, moreover, Player σ has a positional strategy f_v by which, starting at any position $u \notin A_{1-\sigma}$, she either wins or eventually reaches v.

We distinguish two cases, depending on whether or not there exist strong winning positions that are live (terminal positions are, of course, always strong).

Case (i). Suppose that there exists a live position $v \in A_\sigma$. In this case, Player σ also wins from every weak position u.

We already know that Player σ has a positional strategy f to win $\mathcal{G}$ from v, and a positional strategy f_v by which she either wins $\mathcal{G}$ or reaches v from u. We can easily combine f and f_v into a positional winning strategy f^* to win $\mathcal{G}$ from u: we set $f^*(x) := f(x)$ if f is winning from x, and $f^*(x) := f_v(x)$ otherwise.

Case (ii). Suppose now that all live positions are weak. We claim that in this case, Player 0 wins from all live (i.e. all weak) positions if the minimal priority on $\mathcal{G}$ is even, and Player 1 wins from all live positions if the minimal priority is odd.

Since all live positions are weak, we already know that Player σ has, for every live position y, a positional strategy f_y by which she either wins or reaches y from any live position in $\mathcal{G}$.

Take now a live position v of minimal priority, and put $\sigma = 0$ if $\Omega(v)$ is even, and $\sigma = 1$ if $\Omega(v)$ is odd. In addition, pick any live position $w \neq v$. We combine the positional winning strategies f_v and f_w into a new positional strategy f with

$$f(x) := \begin{cases} f_w(x) & \text{if } x = v \\ f_v(x) & \text{otherwise.} \end{cases}$$

We claim that f is a winning strategy for Player σ from all live positions of $\mathcal{G}$. If a play in $\mathcal{G}$ in which Player 0 moves according to f hits v only finitely often, then this play eventually coincides with a play consistent with f_v, and is therefore won by Player σ. But if the play hits v infinitely often, the minimal priority seen infinitely often is $\Omega(v)$, and hence Player σ wins also in this case.   □

Exercise 3.3.26 Let $\mathcal{G}$ be a parity game with winning sets W_0 and W_1. Obviously every positional winning strategy for Player 0 has to remain inside W_0, i.e. $f(V_0 \cap W_0) \subseteq W_0$. However, remaining inside the winning region does not suffice for winning a game! Construct a parity game and a positional strategy f for Player 0 such that all plays consistent with f remain insiside W_0, yet are won by Player 1. *Hint*: a trivial game with two positions suffices.

Exercise 3.3.27 A **future game** is any game on a game graph $\mathcal{G} = (V, V_0, V_1, E)$ where the winning condition does not depend on finite prefixes of plays. This means that whenever $\pi = v_0 v_1 \cdots$ and $\pi' = v_0' v_1' \cdots$ are two infinite plays of $\mathcal{G}$ such that for some n and m $v_m v_{m+1} \cdots = v_n' v_{n+1}' \cdots$, then π and π' are won by the same player. Obviously parity games are a special case of future games.

Prove that for every future game $\mathcal{G}$, the winning region of Player 0 is a fixed point (not necessarily the least one) of the operator F_ψ, defined by the formula $\psi(X) := (V_0 \wedge \Diamond X) \vee (V_1 \wedge \Box X)$. Since F_ψ is monotone, the least and greatest fixed points exist, and $\mathbf{lfp}(F_\psi) \subseteq W_0 \subseteq \mathbf{gfp}(F_\psi)$. Find conditions (on parity games) implying that $W_0 = \mathbf{lfp}(F_\psi)$ or that $W_0 = \mathbf{gfp}(F_\psi)$.

Theorem 3.3.28. *It can be decided in* NP $\cap$ Co-NP *whether a given position in a parity game is a winning position for Player 0.*

Proof. A node v in a parity game $\mathcal{G} = (V, V_0, V_1, E, \Omega)$ is a winning position for Player σ if there exists a positional strategy $f : V_\sigma \to V$ which is winning from position v. It therefore suffices to show that the question of whether a given $f : V_\sigma \to V$ is a winning strategy for Player σ from position v can be decided in polynomial time. We prove this for Player 0; the argument for Player 1 is analogous.

Given $\mathcal{G}$ and $f : V_0 \to V$ we obtain a reduced game graph $\mathcal{G}_f = (V, E_f)$ by keeping only the moves that are consistent with f, i.e.

$$E_f = \{(v, w) : (v \in V_\sigma \wedge w = f(v)) \vee (v \in V_{1-\sigma} \wedge (v, w) \in E\}.$$

In this reduced game, only the opponent, Player 1, makes non-trivial moves. We call a cycle in (V, E_f) odd if the smallest priority of its nodes is odd. Clearly, Player 0 wins $\mathcal{G}$ from position v via strategy f if, and only if, in $\mathcal{G}_f$, no odd cycle and no terminal position $w \in V_0$ are reachable from v. Since the reachability problem is solvable in polynomial time, the claim follows. $\square$

In fact, Jurdziński [72] proved that the problem is in UP $\cap$ Co-UP, where UP denotes the class of NP-problems with unique witnesses. The best known deterministic algorithms to compute winning partitions of parity games have running times that are polynomial with respect to the size of the game graph, but exponential with respect to the index of the game [73].

Theorem 3.3.29. *The winning partition of a parity game* $\mathcal{G} = (V, V_0, V_1, E, \Omega)$ *of index d can be computed in space* $O(d \cdot |E|)$ *and time*

$$O\left(d \cdot |E| \cdot \left(\frac{|V|}{\lfloor d/2 \rfloor}\right)^{\lfloor d/2 \rfloor}\right).$$

The Unfolding of a Parity Game

Let $\mathcal{G} = (V, V_0, V_1, E, \Omega)$ be a parity game. We assume that the minimal priority in the range of Ω is even, and that every node v with minimal priority has a unique successor $s(v)$ (i.e. $vE = \{s(v)\}$). This is no loss of generality. We can always tranform a parity game in such a way that all nodes with non-maximal priority have unique successors (i.e. choices are made only at the least relevant nodes). If the smallest priority in the game is odd, we consider instead the dual game (with the roles of the players switched and priorities decreased by one).

Let T be the set of nodes with minimal priority and let $\mathcal{G}^-$ be the game obtained by deleting from $\mathcal{G}$ all edges $(v, s(v)) \in T \times V$ so that the nodes in

T become terminal positions. We define the **unfolding** of $\mathcal{G}$ as a sequence of games $\mathcal{G}^\alpha$ (where α ranges over the ordinals) which all coincide with $\mathcal{G}^-$ up to the winning conditions for the terminal positions $v \in T$. For every α, we define a decomposition $T = T_0^\alpha \cup T_1^\alpha$, where T_σ^α is the set of $v \in T$ in which we declare, for the game $\mathcal{G}^\alpha$, Player σ to be the winner. Further, for every α, we write W_σ^α for the winning set of Player σ in the game $\mathcal{G}^\alpha$. Note that W_σ^α depends of course on the decomposition $T = T_0^\alpha \cup T_1^\alpha$ (this also applies concerning positions outside T). In turn, the decomposition of T for $\alpha + 1$ depends on the winning sets W_σ^α in $\mathcal{G}^\alpha$. We set

$$T_0^0 := T$$
$$T_0^{\alpha+1} := \{v \in T : s(v) \in W_0^\alpha\}$$
$$T_0^\lambda := \bigcap_{\alpha < \lambda} T_0^\alpha \text{ for limit ordinals } \lambda.$$

By determinacy, $V = W_0^\alpha \cup W_1^\alpha$ for all α, and with increasing α, the winning sets of Player 0 are decreasing and the winning sets of Player 1 are increasing:

$$W_0^0 \supseteq W_0^1 \supseteq \cdots W_0^\alpha \supseteq W_0^{\alpha+1} \supseteq \cdots$$
$$W_1^0 \subseteq W_1^1 \subseteq \cdots W_1^\alpha \subseteq W_1^{\alpha+1} \subseteq \cdots .$$

Hence there exists an ordinal α (whose cardinality is bounded by the cardinality of V) for which $W_0^\alpha = W_0^{\alpha+1} =: W_0^\infty$ and $W_1^\alpha = W_1^{\alpha+1} =: W_1^\infty$. We claim that these fixed points coincide with the winning sets W_0 and W_1 for the original game $\mathcal{G}$.

Lemma 3.3.30 (Unfolding Lemma). $W_0 = W_0^\infty$ *and* $W_1 = W_1^\infty$.

Proof. It suffices to define a strategy f for Player 0 and a strategy g for Player 1 for the game $\mathcal{G}$, by means of which Player σ wins from all positions $v \in W_\sigma^\infty$.

First, we fix a winning strategy f^α for Player 0 in $\mathcal{G}^\alpha$, with winning set $W_0^\alpha = W_0^\infty$. Note that f^α can be trivially extended to a strategy f for the game $\mathcal{G}$, since the nodes in T have unique successors in $\mathcal{G}$. We claim that f is in fact a winning strategy in $\mathcal{G}$ from all positions $v \in W_0^\alpha$.

To see this, consider any play $v_0 v_1 v_2 \ldots$ in $\mathcal{G}$ from position $v_0 \in W_0^\alpha$ against f. Such a play can never leave W_0^α. If $v_i \in W_0^\alpha \setminus T$, then $v_{i+1} \in W_0^\alpha$ because f is a winning strategy for $\mathcal{G}^\alpha$; and if $v_i \in W_0^\alpha \cap T = W_0^{\alpha+1} \cap T$, then $v_i \in T_0^{\alpha+1}$, which implies, by the definition of $T_0^{\alpha+1}$, that $v_{i+1} = s(v_i) \in W_0^\alpha$. But a play that never leaves W_0^α is necessarily won by Player 0: either it goes only finitely often through positions in T, and then coincides from a certain point onwards with a winning play in $\mathcal{G}^\alpha$, or it goes infinitely often through positions in T, in which case Player 0 wins because the minimal priority that is hit infinitely often is even.

To construct a winning strategy for Player 1 in the game $\mathcal{G}$, we define, for every node $v \in W_1^\infty$, the ordinal

$$\rho(v) := \min\{\beta : v \in W_1^\beta\}.$$

We fix, for every ordinal α, a winning strategy g^α for Player 1 with winning set W_1^α in the game $\mathcal{G}^\alpha$, and set

$$g(v) := g^{\sigma(v)}(v) \text{ for all } v \in V_1 \setminus T$$

and $g(v) := s(v)$ for $v \in V_1 \cap T$.

Consider any play $v_0 v_1 v_2 \ldots$ in $\mathcal{G}$ from position $v_0 \in W_1^\infty$ against g. We claim that whenever $v_i \in W_1^\infty$, then

(1) $v_{i+1} \in W_1^\infty$,
(2) $\rho(v_{i+1}) \leq \rho(v_i)$, and
(3) if $v_i \in T$, then $\rho(v_{i+1}) < \rho(v_i)$.

If $v_i \in W_1^\infty \setminus T$ and $\rho(v_i) = \alpha$, then $v_i \in W_1^\alpha$, and therefore (since Player 1 moves locally according to his winning strategy g^α and Player 0 cannot leave winning sets of her opponent) $v_{i+1} \in W_1^\alpha$. But if $v_i \in W_1^\infty \cap T$ and $\rho(v_i) = \alpha$, then $v_i \in T_1^\alpha$, $\alpha = \beta + 1$ is a successor ordinal, and $v_{i+1} = s(v_i) \in W_1^\beta$ (by the definition of T_1^α). Hence $\rho(v_{i+1}) \leq \beta < \rho(v_i)$.

Properties (1), (2), and (3) imply that the play stays inside W_1^∞ and that the values $\rho(v)$ are decreasing. Since there are no infinite strictly descending chains of ordinals, the play eventually remains inside W_1^α, for a fixed α, and outside T (since moves from T would reduce the value of $\sigma(v)$). Hence the play eventually coincides with a play in $\mathcal{G}^\alpha$ in which Player 1 plays according to his winning strategy g^α. Thus, Player 1 wins. $\square$

3.3.5 Model-Checking Games for Least Fixed-Point Logic

For the purpose of defining evaluation games for LFP-formulae and analysing the complexity of model checking, it is convenient to make the following assumptions. First, the fixed-point formulae should not contain parameters (the reason for this will be discussed below). Second, the formula should be in negation normal form, i.e. negations apply to atoms only, and third, it should be **well-named**, i.e. every fixed-point variable is bound only once and the free second-order variables are distinct from the fixed-point variables. We write $D_\psi(T)$ for the unique subformula in ψ of the form $[\mathbf{fp} T\overline{x} \cdot \varphi(T, \overline{x})]$ (where $\mathbf{fp}$ means either $\mathbf{lfp}$ or $\mathbf{gfp}$). For technical reasons, we assume, finally, that each fixed-point variable T occurs in $D_\psi(T)$ only inside the scope of a quantifier. This is a common assumption that does not affect the expressive power. We say that T' **depends** on T if T occurs free in $D_\psi(T')$. The transitive closure of this dependency relation is called the **dependency order**, denoted by $\sqsubseteq_\psi$. The **alternation level** $al_\psi(T)$ of T in ψ is the maximal number of alternations between least and greatest fixed-point variables on the $\sqsubset_\psi$-paths from T. The **alternation depth** $ad(\psi)$ of a fixed-point formula ψ is the maximal alternation level of its fixed point variables.

Consider now a finite structure $\mathfrak{A}$ and an LFP-formula $\psi(\overline{x})$, which we assume to be well-named, in negation normal form, and without parameters. The model-checking game $\mathcal{G}(\mathcal{A}, \psi(\overline{a}))$ is a parity game. As in the case of first-order logic, the positions of the game are expressions $\varphi(\overline{b})$, i.e. subformulae of ψ that are instantiated by elements of $\mathfrak{A}$. The initial position is $\psi(\overline{a})$. The moves are as in the first-order game, except for the positions associated with fixed-point formulae and with fixed-point atoms. At such positions there is a unique move (by Falsifier, say) to the formula defining the fixed point. For a more formal definition, recall that as ψ is well-named, there is, for any fixed-point variable T in ψ, a unique subformula $[\mathbf{fp}\ T\overline{x}\ .\ \varphi(T, \overline{x})](\overline{y})$. From position $[\mathbf{fp}T\overline{x}\ .\ \varphi(T, \overline{x})](\overline{b})$, Falsifier moves to $\varphi(T, \overline{b})$, and from any fixed point atom $T\overline{c}$, she moves to the position $\varphi(T, \overline{c})$.

Hence the case where we do not have fixed points the game is the usual model-checking game for first-order logic. Next, we consider the case of a formula with only one fixed-point operator, which is an **lfp**. The intuition is that from position $[\mathbf{lfp}\ T\overline{x}\ .\ \varphi(T, \overline{x})](\overline{b})$, Verifier tries to establish that $\overline{b}$ enters T at some stage α of the fixed-point induction that is defined by φ on $\mathfrak{A}$. The game goes to $\varphi(T, \overline{b})$ and from there, as φ is a first-order formula, Verifier can either win the φ-game in a finite number of steps, or force it to a position $T\overline{c}$, where $\overline{c}$ enters the fixed point at some stage $\beta < \alpha$. The game then resumes at position $\varphi(\overline{c})$, associated again with φ. As any descending sequence of ordinals is finite, Verifier will win the game in a finite number of steps. If the formula is not true, then Falsifier can either win in a finite number of steps or force the play to go through infinitely many positions of the form $T\overline{c}$. Hence, these positions should be assigned priority 1 (and all other positions higher priorities) so that such a play will be won by Falsifier. For **gfp**-formulae, the situation is reversed. Verifier wants to force an infinite play, going infinitely often through positions $T\overline{c}$, so **gfp**-atoms are assigned priority 0.

In the general case, we have a formula ψ with nested least and greatest fixed points, and in an infinite play of $\mathcal{G}(\mathfrak{A}, \psi(\overline{a}))$ one may see different fixed point variables infinitely often. But one of these variables is then the smallest with respect to the dependency order $\sqsubset_\psi$. It can be shown that $\mathfrak{A} \models \psi$ iff this smallest variable is a **gfp**-variable (provided the players play optimally).

Hence, the priority labelling should assign even priorities to **gfp**-atoms and odd priorities to **lfp**-atoms. Further, if $T \sqsubset_\psi T'$ and T, T' are fixed-point variables of different kinds, then T-atoms should get a lower priority than T'-atoms.

As the index of a parity game is the main source of difficulty in computing winning sets, the number of different priorities should be kept as small as possible. We can avoid the factor of 2 appearing in common constructions of this kind by adjusting the definitions of the alternation level and alternation depth, setting $al^*_\psi(T) := al_\psi(T) + 1$ if $al_\psi(T)$ is even or odd and T is an **lfp**-variable or a **gfp**-variable, respectively. In all other cases, $al_\psi^*(T) = al_\psi(T)$. Finally, let $ad^*(\psi)$ be the maximal value of $ad_\psi^*(T)$ for the fixed-point variables in ψ. The priority labelling Ω on positions of $\mathcal{G}(\mathfrak{A}, \psi)$ is then defined by $\Omega(T\overline{b}) = al_\psi^*(T)$ for fixed-point atoms, and $\Omega(\varphi(\overline{b})) = ad^*(\psi)$ for all other formulae.

This completes the definition of the game $\mathcal{G}(\mathfrak{A}, \psi(\overline{a}))$. Note that the priority labelling has the properties described above, and that the index of $\mathcal{G}(\mathfrak{A}, \psi(\overline{a}))$ is at most $ad(\psi) + 1$.

Theorem 3.3.31. *Let $\psi(\overline{x})$ be a well-named and parameter-free* LFP*-formula in negation normal form, and let $\mathfrak{A}$ be a relational structure. $\mathfrak{A} \models \psi(\overline{a})$ if and only if Player 0 has a winning strategy for the parity game $\mathcal{G}(\mathfrak{A}, \psi(\overline{a}))$.*

Proof. This is proved by induction on ψ. The interesting case concerns fixed-point formulae $\psi(\overline{x}) := [\mathbf{gfp}\, T\overline{x} \,.\, \varphi(\overline{x})](\overline{x})$.

In the game $\mathcal{G}(\mathcal{A}, \psi(\overline{a}))$, the positions of minimal priority are the fixed-point atoms $T\overline{b}$, which have unique successors $\varphi(\overline{b})$. By the induction hypothesis we know that, for every interpretation T_0 of T, $(\mathfrak{A}, T_0) \models \varphi(\overline{a})$ iff Player 0 has a winning strategy for $\mathcal{G}((\mathfrak{A}, T_0), \varphi(\overline{a}))$. By the unfolding of greatest fixed points, we also know that $\mathfrak{A} \models [\mathbf{gfp}\, T\overline{x} \,.\, \varphi(\overline{x})](\overline{a})$ if $(\mathfrak{A}, T^\alpha) \models \varphi(\overline{a})$ for all approximations T^α.

By ordinal induction, one can immediately see that the games $\mathcal{G}((\mathfrak{A}, T^\alpha), \varphi(\overline{a}))$ coincide with the unfolding of the game $\mathcal{G} = \mathcal{G}(\mathfrak{A}, \psi(\overline{a}))$ to the games $\mathcal{G}^\alpha$. By the Unfolding Lemma, we conclude that Player 0 wins the game $\mathcal{G}(\mathfrak{A}, \psi(\overline{a}))$ if, and only if, she wins all games $\mathcal{G}^\alpha$ which is the case if, and only if, $(\mathfrak{A}, T^\alpha) \models \varphi(\overline{a})$ for all α, which is equivalent to $\mathfrak{A} \models \psi(\overline{a})$.

For least fixed-point formulae we proceed by dualization. $\square$

Clearly, the size of the game $\mathcal{G}(\mathfrak{A}, \psi(\overline{a}))$ (and the time complexity of its construction) is bounded by $|\text{cl}(\psi)| \cdot |A|^{\text{width}(\psi)}$. Hence, for LFP-formulae of bounded width, the size of the game is polynomially bounded.

Corollary 3.3.32. *The model-checking problem for* LFP*-formulae of bounded width (and without parameters) is in* $\text{NP} \cap \text{Co-NP}$, *in fact in* $\text{UP} \cap \text{Co-UP}$.

As formulae of the μ-calculus can be viewed as LFP-formulae of width 2, the same bound applies to L_μ. (For a different approach to this problem, which does not mention games explicitly, see [100].) It is a well-known open problem whether the model-checking problem for L_μ can be solved in polynomial time.

Exercise 3.3.33 Prove that if the model-checking problem for L_μ can be solved in polynomial time, then the same is true for (parameter-free) LFP-formulae of width k, for any fixed $k \in \mathbb{N}$. *Hint*: given a finite structure $\mathfrak{A} = (A, R_1, \ldots, R_m)$, with relations of R_i of arities $r_i \leq k$, let $G^k(\mathfrak{A})$ be the transition system with universe A^k, unary relations $R_i^* = \{(a_1, \ldots, a_k) : (a_1, \ldots, a_{r_i}) \in R_i\}$ and $I_{ij} = \{(a_1, \ldots, a_k) : a_i = a_j\}$, and binary relations $E_j = \{(\overline{a}, \overline{b}) : a_i = b_i$

for $i \neq j$} (for $j = 1, \ldots, k$) and $E_\sigma = \{(\bar{a}, \bar{b}) : b_i = a_{\sigma(i)}$ for $i = 1, \ldots, k\}$ for each substitution $\sigma : \{1, \ldots, k\} \rightarrow \{1, \ldots, k\}$. Translate formulae $\psi \in \mathrm{LFP}$ of width k into formulae $\psi^* \in L_\mu$ such that $\mathfrak{A} \models \psi(\bar{a})$ iff $G^k(\mathfrak{A}), \bar{a} \models \psi^*$. (See [55, pp. 110–111] for details.)

By Theorem 3.3.29, we obtain the following deterministic complexity bounds for LFP model checking.

Theorem 3.3.34. *Given a finite structure $\mathfrak{A}$ and a formula $\psi(\bar{a})$ of width k and alternation depth d, it can be decided whether $\mathfrak{A} \models \psi(\bar{a})$ in space $O(d \cdot |\mathrm{cl}(\psi)| \cdot |A|^k)$ and time*

$$O\left(d^2 \cdot \left(\frac{|\mathrm{cl}(\psi)| \cdot |A|^k}{\lfloor (d+1)/2 \rfloor} \right)^{\lfloor (d+3)/2 \rfloor} \right).$$

Corollary 3.3.35. *The model-checking problem for LFP-formulae of bounded width and bounded alternation depth is solvable in polynomial time.*

Fixed-Point Formulae with Parameters

We have imposed the condition that the fixed-point formulae do not contain parameters. If parameters are allowed, then, at least with a naive definition of width, Corollary 3.3.32 is no longer true (unless UP = PSPACE). The intuitive reason is that parameters allow us to 'hide' first-order variables in fixed-point variables. Indeed, Dziembowski [37] proved that QBF, the evaluation problem for quantified Boolean formulae, can be reduced to evaluating LFP-formulae with two first-order variables (but an unbounded number of monadic fixed-point variables) on a fixed structure with three elements. Hence the expression complexity of evaluating such formulae is PSPACE-complete. A similar argument works for the case where also the number of fixed-point variables is bounded, but the structure is not fixed (combined complexity rather than expression complexity). We remark that the collection of all unwindings in infinitary logic of LFP-formulae with k variables, including parameters, is not contained in any bounded width fragment of infinitary logic.

LFP-Formulae of Unbounded Width

For LFP-formulae of unbounded width, Theorem 3.3.34 gives only an exponential time bound. In fact, this cannot be improved, even for very simple LFP-formulae [99].

Theorem 3.3.36 (Vardi). *The model-checking problem for LFP-formulae (of unbounded width) is EXPTIME-complete, even for formulae with only one fixed-point operator, and on a fixed structure with only two elements.*

We defer the hardness proof to Section 3.3.10, where we shall show that the expression complexity is EXPTIME-hard even for Datalog, which is a more restricted formalism than LFP.

3.3.6 Definability of Winning Regions in Parity Games

We have seen that the model-checking problem for the μ-calculus or LFP can be reduced to the problem of computing winning regions in parity games. In fact, there is also a reduction in the reverse direction. We can represent any parity game $\mathcal{G} = (V, V_0, V_1, E, \Omega)$ with a priority function $\Omega : V \to \{0, \ldots d - 1\}$ by a transition system $(V, E, V_0, V_1, P_0, \ldots, P_{d-1})$, where $P_i = \{V : \Omega(v) = i\}$. We can then construct, for every fixed $d \in \mathbb{N}$, a formula Win$_d$ of the μ-calculus that defines the winning region of Player 0 in any parity game with priorities $0, \ldots, d - 1$. We set

$$\text{Win}_d = \nu X_0 \mu X_1 \nu X_2 \ldots \lambda X_{d-1} \bigvee_{j=0}^{d-1} \big((V_0 \wedge P_j \wedge \Diamond X_j) \vee (V_1 \wedge P_j \wedge \Box X_j) \big).$$

In this formula, the fixed-point operators alternate between ν and μ, and hence $\lambda = \nu$ if d is odd, and $\lambda = \mu$ if d is even.

Theorem 3.3.37. *For every $d \in \mathbb{N}$, the formula Win$_d$ defines the winning region of Player 0 in parity games with priorities $0, \ldots, d - 1$.*

Proof. We have to show that, for any parity game $\mathcal{G} = (V, V_0, V_1, P_0, \ldots, P_{d-1})$ and every position $v \in V$,

$$\mathcal{G}, v \models \text{Win}_d \iff \text{Player 0 has a winning strategy for } \mathcal{G} \text{ from } v.$$

To see this, let $\mathcal{G}^*$ be the model-checking game for the formula Win$_d$ on $\mathcal{G}, v$ and identify Verifier with Player 0 and Falsifier with Player 1. Hence, Player 0 has a winning strategy for $\mathcal{G}^*$ if, and only if, $\mathcal{G}, v \models \text{Win}_d$.

By the construction of model-checking games, $\mathcal{G}^*$ has positions of the form (φ, u), where $u \in V$ and φ is a subformula of Win$_d$. The priority of a position (X_i, u) is i, and when φ is not a fixed point variable, the priority of (φ, u) is d.

We claim that the game $\mathcal{G}^*$ is essentially, i.e. up to elimination of stupid moves and contraction of several moves into one, the same as the the original game $\mathcal{G}$. To see this, we compare playing $\mathcal{G}$ from a current position $u \in V_0 \cup P_i$ with playing $\mathcal{G}^*$ from any position (φ_k, u), where φ_k is the subformula of Win$_d$ that starts with νX_k or μX_k.

In $\mathcal{G}$, Player 0 selects at position u a successor $w \in uE$, and the play proceeds from w. In $\mathcal{G}^*$, the play goes from (φ_k, u) through positions $(\varphi_{k+1}, u) \ldots, (\varphi_{d-1}, u)$ to (ϑ, u), where

$$\vartheta = \bigvee_{j=0}^{d-1} \big((V_0 \wedge P_j \wedge \Diamond X_j) \vee (V_1 \wedge P_j \wedge \Box X_j) \big).$$

The only reasonable choice for Verifier (Player 0) at this point is to move to the position $(V_0 \wedge P_i \wedge \Diamond X_i, u)$, since with any other move she would lose immediately. But from there, the only reasonable move of Falsifier (Player 1) is to go to position $(\Diamond X_i, u)$, and it is now the turn of Player 0 to select a successor $w \in vE$ and move to position (X_i, w) from which the play proceeds to (φ_i, w).

Thus one move from u to w in $\mathcal{G}$ corresponds to a sequence of moves in $\mathcal{G}^*$ from (φ_k, u) to (φ_i, w), but the only genuine choice is the move from $(\Diamond X_i, u)$ to (X_i, w), i.e. the choice of a successor $w \in uE$. In $\mathcal{G}$, the position u has priority i, and in $\mathcal{G}^*$ the minimal, and hence relevant, priority that is seen in the sequence of moves from (φ_k, u) to (φ_i, w) is that of (X_i, u) which is also i. The situation for positions $u \in V_1 \cap P_i$ is the same, except that the play in $\mathcal{G}^*$ now goes through $(\Box X_i, u)$ and it is Player 1 who selects a successor $w \in uE$ and moves to (X_i, w).

Hence the (reasonable) choices that have to be made by the players in $\mathcal{G}^*$ and the relevant priorities that are seen are the same as in a corresponding play of $\mathcal{G}$. Thus, Player 0 has a winning strategy for $\mathcal{G}$ from v if, and only if, Player 0 has a winning strategy for $\mathcal{G}^*$ from position (φ_0, v). But since $\mathcal{G}^*$ is the model-checking game for Win_d on $\mathcal{G}$, with initial position (φ_0, v), this is the case if, and only if, $\mathcal{G}, v \models \mathrm{Win}_d$. $\Box$

Corollary 3.3.38. *The following three problems are algorithmically equivalent, in the sense that if one of them admits a polynomial-time algorithm, then all of them do.*

(1) Computing winning regions in parity games.

(2) The model-checking problem for LFP-formulae of width at most k, for any $k \geq 2$.

(3) The model-checking problem for the modal μ-calculus.

The formulae Win_d also play an important role in the study of the alternation hierarchy of the modal μ-calculus. Clearly, Win_d has alternation depth d and it has been shown that there is no formula in the μ-calculus with alternation depth $< d$ can be equivalent to Win_d. Hence the alternation hierarchy of the μ-calculus is strict [4, 20].

3.3.7 Simultaneous Fixed-Point Inductions

A more general variant of LFP permits simultaneous inductions over several formulae. A simultaneous induction is based on on a system of operators of the form

$$F_1 : \mathcal{P}(B_1) \times \cdots \times \mathcal{P}(B_m) \longrightarrow \mathcal{P}(B_1)$$

$$\vdots$$

$$F_m : \mathcal{P}(B_1) \times \cdots \times \mathcal{P}(B_m) \longrightarrow \mathcal{P}(B_m),$$

forming together an operator

$$F = (F_1, \ldots, F_m) : \mathcal{P}(B_1) \times \cdots \times \mathcal{P}(B_m) \longrightarrow \mathcal{P}(B_1) \times \cdots \times \mathcal{P}(B_m).$$

Inclusion on the product lattice $\mathcal{P}(B_1) \times \cdots \times \mathcal{P}(B_m)$ is componentwise. Accordingly, F is monotone if, whenever $X_i \subseteq Y_i$ for all i, then also $F_i(\overline{X}) \subseteq F_i(\overline{Y})$ for all i.

Everything said above about least and greatest fixed points carries over to simultaneous induction. In particular, a monotone operator F has a least fixed point $\mathbf{lfp}(F)$ which can be constructed inductively, starting with $\overline{X}^0 = (\emptyset, \ldots, \emptyset)$ and iterating F until a fixed point $\overline{X}^\infty$ is reached.

One can extend the logic LFP by a simultaneous fixed point formation rule.

Definition 3.3.39. Simultaneous least fixed-point logic, denoted by S-LFP, is the extension of first-order logic by the following rule.

Syntax. Let $\psi_1(\overline{R}, \overline{x}_1), \ldots, \psi_m(\overline{R}, \overline{x}_m)$ be formulae of vocabulary $\tau \cup \{R_1, \ldots, R_m\}$, with only positive occurrences of $R_1, \ldots, R_m$, and, for each $i \leq m$, let $\overline{x}_i$ be a sequence of variables matching the arity of R_i. Then

$$S := \begin{cases} R_1 \overline{x}_1 & := \psi_1 \\ & \vdots \\ R_m \overline{x}_m & := \psi_m \end{cases}$$

is a *system of update rules*, which is used to build formulae $[\mathbf{lfp}\, R_i : S](\overline{t})$ and $[\mathbf{gfp}\, R_i : S](\overline{t})$ (for any tuple $\overline{t}$ of terms whose length matches the arity of R_i).

Semantics. On each structure $\mathfrak{A}$, S defines a monotone operator $S^{\mathfrak{A}} = (S_1, \ldots, S_m)$ mapping tuples $\overline{R} = (R_1, \ldots, R_m)$ of relations on A to $S^{\mathfrak{A}}(\overline{R}) = (S_1(\overline{R}), \ldots, S_m(\overline{R}))$ where $S_i(\overline{R}) := \{\overline{a} : (\mathfrak{A}, \overline{R}) \models \psi_i(\overline{R}, \overline{a})\}$. As the operator is monotone, it has a least fixed point $\mathbf{lfp}(S^{\mathfrak{A}}) = (R_1^\infty, \ldots, R_m^\infty)$. Now $\mathfrak{A} \models [\mathbf{lfp}R_i : S](\overline{a})$ if $\overline{a} \in R_i^\infty$. Similarly for greatest fixed points.

Example 3.3.40. We return to the circuit value problem for circuits with fan-in 2 and NAND gates (see Example 3.2.14). Simultaneous LFP-definitions of the nodes evaluating to true and false in the given circuit (V, E, I^+, I^-) are given by the formulae $[\mathbf{lfp}T : S](z)$ and $[\mathbf{lfp}F : S](z)$, respectively, where S is the system

$$Tz := I^+ z \vee \exists x (Exz \wedge Fx)$$
$$Fz := I^- z \vee \exists x \exists y (Exz \wedge Eyx \wedge x \neq y \wedge Tx \wedge Ty).$$

Elimination of Simultaneous Fixed-Points

The question arises of whether simultaneous fixed points provide more expressive power than simple ones. We shall prove that this is not the case. Simultaneous least fixed points can be simulated by nested simple ones, via a technique that is sometimes called the Bekic principle [5]. We shall consider only the case of two monotone operators

$$F : \mathcal{P}(A) \times \mathcal{P}(B) \to \mathcal{P}(A)$$
$$G : \mathcal{P}(A) \times \mathcal{P}(B) \to \mathcal{P}(B).$$

We write (F^∞, G^∞) for the least fixed point of the combined operator (F, G). For any fixed $X \subseteq A$, the operator $G_X : \mathcal{P}(B) \to \mathcal{P}(B)$ with $G_X(Y) := G(X, Y)$ is also monotone, and therefore has a least fixed point $\mathbf{lfp}(G_X) \subseteq B$.

Lemma 3.3.41. *The operator E on $\mathcal{P}(A)$, defined by $E(X) := F(X, \mathbf{lfp}(G_X))$, is monotone and has the least fixed point $\mathbf{lfp}(E) = F^\infty$.*

Proof. If $X \subseteq X'$, then a trivial induction shows that $G_X^\alpha \subseteq G_{X'}^\alpha$ for all stages G_X^α and $G_{X'}^\alpha$ of the induced operators G_X and $G_{X'}$. As a consequence, $\mathbf{lfp}(G_X) \subseteq \mathbf{lfp}(G_{X'})$ and $E(X) = F(X, \mathbf{lfp}(G_X)) \subseteq F(X', \mathbf{lfp}(G_{X'})) = E(X')$. This shows that E is monotone.

Note that $\mathbf{lfp}(G_{F^\infty}) \subseteq G^\infty$, because $G_{F^\infty}(G^\infty) = G(F^\infty, G^\infty) = G^\infty$. Hence G^∞ is a fixed point of G_{F^∞} and therefore contains the least fixed point $\mathbf{lfp}(G_{F^\infty})$. Further,

$$E(F^\infty) = F(F^\infty, \mathbf{lfp}(G_{F^\infty})) \subseteq F(F^\infty, G^\infty) = F^\infty.$$

As $\mathbf{lfp}(E) = \bigcap \{X : E(X) \subseteq X\}$ it follows that $\mathbf{lfp}(E) \subseteq F^\infty$.

It remains to show that $F^\infty \subseteq \mathbf{lfp}(E)$. We proceed by induction, showing that the stages (F^α, G^α) of the operator (F, G) and the stages E^α of E satisfy

$$(F^\alpha, G^\alpha) \subseteq (\mathbf{lfp}(E), \mathbf{lfp}(G_{\mathbf{lfp}(E)})).$$

For $\alpha = 0$, this is clear. Further,

$$F^{\alpha+1} = F(F^\alpha, G^\alpha) \subseteq F(\mathbf{lfp}(E), \mathbf{lfp}(G_{\mathbf{lfp}(E)})) = E(\mathbf{lfp}(E) = \mathbf{lfp}(E)$$
$$G^{\alpha+1} = G(F^\alpha, G^\alpha) \subseteq G(\mathbf{lfp}(E), \mathbf{lfp}(G_{\mathbf{lfp}(E)})) = G_{\mathbf{lfp}(E)}(\mathbf{lfp}(G_{\mathbf{lfp}(E)}))$$
$$= \mathbf{lfp}(G_{\mathbf{lfp}(E)}).$$

Finally, for limit ordinals the induction argument is trivial. □

We are now ready to show that for any system

$$S := \begin{cases} R_1 \bar{x}_1 := \psi_1 \\ \quad \vdots \\ R_m \bar{x}_m := \psi_m \end{cases}$$

the formulae $[\mathbf{lfp}\, R_i : S](\bar{x})$ are equivalent to simple LFP formulae. Further, the translation does not increase the number and arity of the fixed-point variables $R_1, \ldots, R_m$, nor the alternation depth (i.e. the changes between least and greatest fixed points). It therefore remains valid for interesting fragments of LFP, such as monadic LFP and alternation-free LFP, and also for the modal μ-calculus (see [5]). It does, however, increase the nesting depth of fixed-point operators. (We remark that there are alternative elimination techniques that do not increase the nesting depth, but instead augment the arity of the fixed-point operators.)

Theorem 3.3.42. S-LFP $\equiv$ LFP.

Proof. Obviously LFP is contained in S-LFP. For the converse, we restrict our attention to simultaneous inductions over two formulae. The general case is treated by analogous arguments.

Given a system

$$S := \begin{cases} R\overline{x} := \psi(R,T) \\ T\overline{y} := \varphi(R,T) \end{cases}$$

we claim that

$$[\textbf{lfp } R : S](\overline{u}) \equiv [\textbf{lfp} R\overline{x} . \, \psi(R, [\textbf{lfp} T\overline{y} . \, \varphi])](\overline{u})$$
$$[\textbf{lfp } T : S](\overline{v}) \equiv [\textbf{lfp} T\overline{y} . \, \varphi([\textbf{lfp} R\overline{x} . \, \psi], T)](\overline{v}).$$

We shall prove the first equivalence. We fix a structure $\mathfrak{A}$ and consider the operator $S^{\mathfrak{A}} = (F, G)$ with $F : (R, T) \mapsto \{\overline{a} : \mathfrak{A} \models \psi(R, T, \overline{a})\}$ and $G : (R, T) \mapsto \{\overline{a} : \mathfrak{A} \models \varphi(R, T, \overline{a})\}$. Writing (F^{∞}, G^{∞}) for the least fixed point of (F, G) we have that $\mathfrak{A} \models [\textbf{lfp } R : S](\overline{a})$ iff $\overline{a} \in F^{\infty}$.

The formula $\psi(R, [\textbf{lfp} T\overline{y} \quad . \quad \varphi])$ defines on $\mathfrak{A}$ the operator $E : R \mapsto F(R, \textbf{lfp}(G_R))$ with $G_R : T \mapsto G(R, T)$, and we have that $\mathfrak{A} \models [\textbf{lfp} R\overline{x} . \, \psi(R, [\textbf{lfp} T\overline{y} . \, \varphi])](\overline{a})$ iff $\overline{a} \in \textbf{lfp}(E)$. But, by the previous lemma, $F^{\infty} = \textbf{lfp}(E)$. $\qquad\square$

While we have shown that simultaneous fixed points do not provide more expressive power, they permit us to write formulae in a more modular and more readable form.

Positive LFP

While LFP and the modal μ-calculus allow arbitrary nesting of least and greatest fixed points, and arbitrary interleaving of fixed points with Boolean operations and quantifiers, classical studies of inductive definability over first-order logic (such as [85]) focus on a more restricted logic. Let LFP_1 (sometimes also called positive LFP) be the extension of first-order logic that is obtained by taking least fixed points of positive first-order formulae (without parameters) and closing them under disjunction, conjunction, and existential and universal quantification, but *not* under negation (for a more formal definition, see the Chap. 2. LFP_1 can be conveniently characterized in terms of simultaneous least fixed points. We just state the result; for a proof see Chap. 2 again.

Theorem 3.3.43. *A query is definable in* LFP_1 *if and only if it is definable by a formula of the form* $[\mathbf{lfp}R : S](\overline{x})$, *where* S *is a system of update rules* $R_i\overline{x} := \varphi_i(\overline{R}, \overline{x})$ *with first-order formulae* φ_i. *Moreover, we can require, without diminishing the expressive power, that each of the formulae* φ_i *in the system is either a purely existential formula or a purely universal formula.*

3.3.8 Inflationary Fixed-Point Logic

LFP is only one instance of a logic with an explicit operator for forming fixed points. A number of other fixed-point extensions of first-order logic (or fragments of it) have been extensively studied in finite model theory. These include inflationary, partial, non-deterministic, and alternating fixed point logics. All of these have in common that they allow the construction of fixed points of operators that are not necessarily monotone.

An operator $G : \mathcal{P}(B) \to \mathcal{P}(B)$ is called **inflationary** if $G(X) \supseteq X$ for all $X \subseteq B$. With any operator F one can associate an inflationary operator G, defined by $G(X) := X \cup F(X)$. In particular, inflationary operators are inductive, so iterating G yields a fixed point, called the **inflationary fixed point** of F.

Exercise 3.3.44 Prove the following facts. (1) Monotone operators need not be inflationary, and inflationary operators need not be monotone. (2) An inflationary operator need not have a least fixed point. (3) The least fixed point of an inflationary operator (if it exists) may be different from the inductive fixed point. (4) However, if F is a monotone operator, then its inflationary fixed point and its least fixed point coincide.

The logic IFP is defined with a syntax similar to that of LFP, but without the requirement that the fixed-point variable occurs only positively in the formula, and with a semantics given by the associated inflationary operator.

Definition 3.3.45. IFP is the extension of first-order logic by the following fixed-point formation rule. For every formula $\psi(R, \overline{x})$, every tuple $\overline{x}$ of variables, and every tuple $\overline{t}$ of terms (such that the lengths of $\overline{x}$ and $\overline{t}$ match the arity of R), we can build a formula $[\mathbf{ifp}R\overline{x} . \psi](\overline{t})$.

Semantics. On a given structure $\mathfrak{A}$, we have that $\mathfrak{A} \models [\mathbf{ifp}R\overline{x} . \psi](\overline{t})$ if $\overline{t}^{\mathfrak{A}}$ is contained in the union of the stages R^{α} of the *inflationary operator* G_{ψ} defined by $G_{\psi}(R) := R \cup F_{\psi}(R)$.

By the last item of Exercise 3.3.44, least and inflationary inductions are equivalent for positive formulae, and hence IFP is at least as expressive as LFP. On finite structures, inflationary inductions reach the fixed point after a polynomial number of iterations, hence every IFP-definable class of finite structures is decidable in polynomial time.

Proposition 3.3.46. IFP *captures* PTIME *on ordered finite structures.*

Least Versus Inflationary Fixed-Points

As both logics capture PTIME, IFP and LFP are equivalent on ordered finite structures. What about unordered structures? It was shown by Gurevich and Shelah [63] that the equivalence of IFP and LFP holds on all finite structures. Their proof does not work on infinite structures, and indeed there are some important aspects in which least and inflationary inductions behave differently. For instance, there are first-order operators (on arithmetic, say) whose inflationary fixed point is not definable as the least fixed point of a first-order operator. Further, the alternation hierarchy in LFP is strict, whereas IFP has a positive normal form (see Exercise 3.3.52 below). Hence it was conjectured by many that IFP might be more powerful than LFP. However, Kreutzer [80] showed recently that IFP is equivalent to LFP on arbitrary structures. Both proofs, by Gurevich and Shelah and by Kreutzer, rely on constructions showing that the *stage comparison relations* of inflationary inductions are definable by **lfp** inductions.

Definition 3.3.47. For every inductive operator $F : \mathcal{P}(B) \to \mathcal{P}(B)$, with stages X^α and an inductive fixed point X^∞, the **F-rank** of an element $b \in B$ is $|b|_F := \min\{\alpha : b \in X^\alpha\}$ if $b \in X^\infty$, and $|b|_F = \infty$ otherwise. The **stage comparison relations** of G are defined by

$$a \leq_F b \quad \text{iff} \quad |a|_F \leq |b|_F < \infty$$
$$a \prec_F b \quad \text{iff} \quad |a|_F < |b|_F.$$

Given a formula $\varphi(R, \bar{x})$, we write $\leq_\varphi$ and $\prec_\varphi$ for the stage comparison relations defined by the operator F_φ (assuming that it is indeed inductive), and $\leq_\varphi^{\inf}$ and $\prec_\varphi^{\inf}$ for the stage comparison relations of the associated inflationary operator $G_\varphi : R \mapsto R \cup \{\bar{a} : \mathfrak{A} \models \varphi(R, \bar{a})\}$.

Example 3.3.48. For the formula $\varphi(T, x, y) := Exy \lor \exists z(Exz \land Tyz)$ the relation $\prec_\varphi$ on a graph (V, E) is distance comparison:

$$(a, b) \prec_\varphi (c, d) \text{ iff dist}(a, b) < \text{dist}(c, d).$$

Stage comparison theorems are results about the definability of stage comparison relations. For instance, Moschovakis [85] proved that the stage comparison relations $\leq_\varphi$ and $\prec_\varphi$ of any positive first-order formula φ are definable by a simultaneous induction over positive first-order formulae. For results on the equivalence of IFP and LFP one needs a stage comparison theorem for IFP inductions.

We first observe that the stage comparison relations for IFP inductions are easily definable in IFP. For any formula $\varphi(T, \bar{x})$, the stage comparison relation $\prec_\varphi^{\inf}$ is defined by the formula

$$[\mathbf{ifp}\,\bar{x} \prec \bar{y} \,.\, \varphi[T\bar{u}/\bar{u} \prec \bar{x}](\bar{x}) \land \neg\varphi[T\bar{u}/\bar{u} \prec \bar{x}](\bar{y})](\bar{x}, \bar{y}).$$

However, what we need to show is that the stage comparison relation for IFP inductions is in fact LFP-definable.

Theorem 3.3.49 (Inflationary Stage Comparison). *For any formula* $\varphi(R, \overline{x})$ *in* FO *or* LFP*, the stage comparison relation* $\prec_{\varphi}^{\inf}$ *is definable in* LFP. *On finite structures, it is even definable in positive* LFP.

See [38, 63] for proofs in the case of finite structures and [80] for the more difficult construction in the general case. From this result, the equivalence of LFP on IFP follows easily.

Theorem 3.3.50 (Kreutzer). *For every* IFP*-formula, there is an equivalent* LFP*-formula.*

Proof. For any formula $\varphi(R, \overline{x})$, $[\mathbf{ifp} R \overline{x} \, . \, \varphi](\overline{x}) \equiv \varphi(\{\overline{y} : \overline{y} \prec_{\varphi}^{\inf} \overline{x}\}, \overline{x})$.   □

Stage comparison theorems also have other interesting consequences. For instance, Moschovakis's Theorem implies that on finite structures, greatest fixed points (i.e. negations of least fixed points) can be expressed in positive LFP. This gives a normal form for LFP and IFP (see [67]).

Theorem 3.3.51 (Immerman). *On finite structures, every* LFP*-formula (and hence also every* IFP*-formula) is equivalent to a formula in* LFP_1.

This result fails on infinite structures. On infinite structures, there exist LFP formulae that are not equivalent to positive formulae, and in fact the alternation hierarchy of least and greatest fixed points is strict (see [20, 85]).

Exercise 3.3.52 Prove that every IFP-formula is equivalent to one that uses **ifp**-operators only positively. *Hint*: assuming that structures contain at least two elements and that a constant 0 is available, a formula $\neg[\mathbf{ifp} R \overline{x} \, . \, \psi(R, \overline{x})]$ is equivalent to an inflationary induction on a predicate $T \overline{x} y$ which, for $y \neq 0$, simulates the induction defined by ψ, checks whether the fixed point has been reached, and then makes atoms $T \overline{x} 0$ true if $\overline{x}$ is not contained in the fixed point.

In finite model theory, owing to the Gurevich-Shelah Theorem, the two logics LFP and IFP have often been used interchangeably. However, there are significant differences that are sometimes overlooked. Despite the equivalence of IFP and LFP, inflationary inductions are a more powerful concept than monotone inductions. The translation from IFP-formulae to equivalent LFP-formulae can make the formulae much more complicated, requires an increase in the arity of fixed-point variables and, in the case of infinite structures, introduces alternations between least and greatest fixed points. Therefore it is often more convenient to use inflationary inductions in explicit constructions, the advantage being that one is not restricted to inductions over positive formulae. For an example, see the proof of Theorem 3.5.26 below. Furthermore, IFP is more robust, in the sense that inflationary fixed points remain well defined even when other non-monotone operators (e.g. generalized quantifiers) are added to the language (see, for instance, [35]).

The differences between least and inflationary fixed points are particularly significant in the context of modal logic, i.e. when we compare the modal μ-calculus L_μ with its inflationary counterpart. For instance, L_μ has the finite-model property, the satisfiability problem is decidable (complete for EXPTIME), the model-checking problem is in NP $\cap$ Co-NP (and conjectured by many to be solvable in polynomial time), and there are practical, automata-based techniques for solving the algorithmic problems associated with L_μ. Finally, in terms of expressive power, L_μ can be characterized as the bisimulation-invariant fragment of monadic second-order logic (MSO) [69]. On the other hand, the inflationary counterpart of L_μ, the **model iteration calculus** (MIC) [33], behaves very differently. The finite-model property fails, the satisfiability problem is undecidable (and not even in the arithmetic hierarchy), the model-checking problem is PSPACE-complete, and the expressive power goes beyond monadic second-order logic even on words. The appropriate model-checking games for inflationary fixed-point logics such as IFP and MIC are **backtracking games** [34]. These games are a generalization of parity games with an additional rule allowing players, under certain conditions, to return to an earlier position in the play and revise a choice or to force a countback on the number of moves. This new feature makes backtracking games more powerful so that they can capture inflationary inductions. Accordingly, winning strategies become more complex objects and computationally harder than for parity games.

3.3.9 Partial Fixed-Point Logic

Another fixed-point logic that is relevant to finite structures is the partial fixed-point logic (PFP). Let $\psi(R, \overline{x})$ be an arbitrary formula defining on a finite structure $\mathfrak{A}$ a (not necessarily monotone) operator $F_\psi : R \mapsto \{\overline{a} : \mathfrak{A} \models \psi(R, \overline{a})\}$, and consider the sequence of its finite stages $R^0 := \emptyset$, $R^{m+1} = F_\psi(R^m)$.

This sequence is not necessarily increasing. Nevertheless, as $\mathfrak{A}$ is finite, the sequence either converges to a fixed point, or reaches a cycle with a period greater than one. We define the **partial fixed point** of F_ψ as the fixed point that is reached in the former case, and as the empty relation otherwise. The logic PFP is obtained by adding to first-order logic the **partial-fixed-point formation rule**, which allows us to build from any formula $\psi(R, \overline{x})$ a formula $[\mathbf{pfp}\ R\overline{x} \,.\, \psi(R, \overline{x})](\overline{t})$, saying that $\overline{t}$ is contained in the partial fixed point of the operator F_ψ.

Note that if R occurs only positively in ψ, then

$$[\mathbf{lfp}\ R\overline{x} \,.\, \psi(R, \overline{x})](\overline{t}) \equiv [\mathbf{pfp}\ R\overline{x} \,.\, \psi(R, \overline{x})](\overline{t}),$$

so we have that LFP $\leq$ PFP. However, PFP seems to be much more powerful than LFP. For instance, while a least-fixed-point induction on finite structures always reaches the fixed point in a polynomial number of iterations, a partial-fixed-point induction may need an exponential number of stages.

Example 3.3.53. Consider the sequence of stages R^m defined by the formula

$$\psi(R, x) := \Big(Rx \wedge \exists y(y < x \wedge \neg Ry)\Big) \vee \Big(\neg Rx \wedge \forall y(y < x \to Ry)\Big) \vee \forall y Ry$$

on a finite linear order $(A, <)$. It is easily seen than the fixed point reached by this induction is the set $R = A$, but before this fixed point is reached, the induction goes in lexicographic order through all possible subsets of A. Hence the fixed point is reached at stage $2^n - 1$, where $n = |A|$.

Simultaneous Inductions.

As in the case of LFP, one can also extend IFP and PFP by simultaneous inductions over several formulae, but again, the simultaneous fixed-point logics S-IFP and S-PFP are not more expressive than their simple variants. However, the proof is a little different than in the case of LFP. It requires that one encodes several relations into one and hence increases the arity of the fixed point variables. As a consequence, it seems to be unknown whether simultaneous *monadic* PFP collapses to simple monadic PFP.

Complexity

Although a PFP induction on a finite structure may go through exponentially many stages (with respect to the cardinality of the structure), each stage can be represented with polynomial storage space. As first-order formulae can be evaluated efficiently, it follows by a simple induction that PFP-formulae can be evaluated in polynomial space.

Proposition 3.3.54. *For every formula* $\psi \in$ PFP, *the set of finite models of* ψ *is in* PSPACE; *in short:* PFP $\subseteq$ PSPACE.

On ordered structures, one can use techniques similar to those used in previous capturing results, to simulate polynomial-space-bounded computation by PFP-formulae [2, 99].

Theorem 3.3.55 (Abiteboul, Vianu, and Vardi). *On ordered finite structures, PFP captures* PSPACE.

Proof. It remains to prove that every class $\mathcal{K}$ of finite ordered structures that is recognizable in PSPACE, can be defined by a PFP-formula.

Let M be a polynomially space-bounded deterministic Turing machine with state set Q and alphabet Σ, recognizing (an encoding of) an ordered structure $(\mathfrak{A}, <)$ if and only if $(\mathfrak{A}, <) \in \mathcal{K}$. Without loss of generality, we can make the following assumptions. For input structures of cardinality n, M requires space less than $n^k - 2$, for some fixed k. For any configuration C of M, let Next(C) denote its successor configuration. The transition function of M is adjusted so that Next(C) = C if, and only if, C is an accepting configuration.

We represent any configuration of M with a current state q, tape inscription $w_1 \cdots w_m$, and head position i, by the word $\#w_1 \cdots w_{i-1}(qw_i)w_{i+1} \cdots w_{m-1}\#$ over the alphabet $\Gamma := \Sigma \cup (Q \times \Sigma) \cup \{\#\}$, where $m = n^k$ and $\#$ is merely used as an end marker to make the following description more uniform. When moving from one configuration to the next, Turing machines make only local changes. We can therefore associate with M a function $f : \Gamma^3 \to \Gamma$ such that, for any configuration $C = c_0 \cdots c_m$, the successor configuration $\mathrm{Next}(C) = c_0' \cdots c_m'$ is determined by the rules

$$c_0' = c_m' = \# \quad \text{and} \quad c_i' = f(c_{i-1}, c_i, c_{i+1}) \text{ for } 1 \leq i \leq m-1.$$

Recall that we encode structures so that there exist first-order formulae $\beta_\sigma(\overline{y})$ such that $(\mathfrak{A}, <) \models \beta_\sigma(\overline{a})$ if and only the $\overline{a}$th symbol of the input configuration of M for input $code(\mathfrak{A}, <)$ is σ. We now represent any configuration C in the computation of M by a tuple $\overline{C} = (C_\sigma)_{\sigma \in \Gamma}$ of k-ary relations, where

$$C_\sigma := \{\overline{a} : \text{the } \overline{a}\text{-th symbol of } C \text{ is } \sigma\}.$$

The configuration at time t is the stage $t+1$ of a simultaneous **pfp** induction on $(\mathfrak{A}, <)$, defined by the rules

$$C_\#\overline{y} := \forall z(\overline{y} \leq \overline{z}) \vee \forall \overline{z}(\overline{z} \leq \overline{y})$$

and, for all $\sigma \in \Gamma - \{\#\}$,

$$C_\sigma \overline{y} := \left(\beta_\sigma(\overline{y}) \wedge \bigwedge_{\gamma \in \Gamma} \forall \overline{x} \neg C_\gamma \overline{x} \right) \vee$$
$$\exists \overline{x} \exists \overline{z} \left(\overline{x} + 1 = \overline{y} \wedge \overline{y} + 1 = \overline{z} \wedge \bigvee_{f(\alpha, \beta, \gamma) = \sigma} C_\alpha \overline{x} \wedge C_\beta \overline{y} \wedge C_\gamma \overline{z} \right)$$

The first rule just says that each stage represents a word starting and ending with $\#$. The other rules ensure that (1) if the given sequence $\overline{C}$ contains only empty relations (i.e. if we are at stage 0), then the next stage represents the input configuration, and (2) if the given sequence represents a configuration, then the following stage represents its successor configuration.

By our convention, M accepts its input if and only the sequence of configurations becomes stationary (i.e. reaches a fixed point). Hence M accepts $code(\mathfrak{A}, <)$ if and only if the relations defined by the simultaneous **pfp** induction on $\mathfrak{A}$ of the rules described above are non-empty. Hence $\mathcal{K}$ is PFP-definable. $\square$

An alternative characterization of PSPACE is possible in terms of the database query language *while* consisting essentially of first-order relational updates and while-loops. Vardi [99] proved that *while* captures PSPACE on ordered finite structures and Abiteboul and Vianu proved that *while* and PFP are equivalent on finite structures.

Least Versus Partial Fixed-Point Logic

From the capturing results for PTIME and PSPACE we immediately obtain the result that PTIME = PSPACE if, and only if, LFP = PFP on ordered finite structures. The natural question arises of whether LFP and PFP can be separated on the domain of all finite structures. For a number of logics, separation results on arbitrary finite structures can be established by relatively simple methods, even if the corresponding separation on ordered structures would solve a major open problem in complexity theory. For instance, we have proved by quite a simple argument that DTC $\subsetneq$ TC, and it is also not very difficult to show that TC $\subsetneq$ LFP (indeed, TC is contained in stratified Datalog, which is also strictly contained in LFP; see Sect. 3.3.10). Further, it is trivial that LFP is less expressive than Σ_1^1 on all finite structures. However the situation is different for LFP vs. PFP.

Theorem 3.3.56 (Abiteboul and Vianu). LFP *and* PFP *are equivalent on finite structures if, and only if,* PTIME = PSPACE.

3.3.10 Datalog and Stratified Datalog

Datalog and its extensions are a family of rule-based database query languages that extend the conjunctive queries by a relational recursion mechanism similar to the one used in fixed-point logics. Indeed, as we shall see, Datalog can be seen as a fragment of least fixed point logic. For the purpose of this section we simply identify a relational database with a finite relational structure. This is not adequate for all aspects of database theory, but for the questions considered here it is appropriate. For further information on databases, see [1], for example.

Definition 3.3.57. A **Datalog rule** is an expression of the form $H \leftarrow B_1 \wedge \cdots \wedge B_m$, where H, the **head** of the rule, is an atomic formula $R\overline{u}$, and $B_1 \wedge \cdots \wedge B_m$, the **body** of the rule, is a conjunction of literals (i.e. atoms or negated atoms) of the form $S\overline{v}$ or $\neg S\overline{v}$ where $\overline{u}, \overline{v}$ are tuples of variables or constants. The relation symbol R is called the **head predicate** of the rule. We also allow Boolean head predicates. A Datalog rule is **positive** if it does not contain negative literals.

A **Datalog program** Π is a finite collection of rules such that none of its head predicates occurs negated in the body of any rule. The predicates that appear only in the bodies of the rules are called **input predicates**. The **input vocabulary** of Π is the set of input predicates and constants appearing in Π.

Example 3.3.58. The Datalog program Π_{reach} consists of the three rules

$$Txy \leftarrow Exy, \qquad Txz \leftarrow Txy \wedge Tyz, \qquad Ry \leftarrow Tay.$$

The input vocabulary is $\{E, a\}$, and the head predicates are T and R.

Given a structure $\mathfrak{A}$ over the input vocabulary, the program computes an interpretation of the head predicates, i.e. it defines an expansion $\Pi(\mathfrak{A}) := (\mathfrak{A}, R_1, \ldots, R_k)$ of $\mathfrak{A}$, where the R_i are the values of the head predicates as computed by Π. This interpretation can be defined in several equivalent ways, for instance via *minimal-model semantics* or *fixed-point semantics*. We can read a Datalog rule $\varphi_r := R\overline{x} \leftarrow B_1 \wedge \cdots \wedge B_m$, and associate with the program Π the universal closure of the conjunction over these formulae:

$$\psi[\Pi] := \forall \overline{z} \bigwedge_{\varphi_r \in \Pi} \varphi_r.$$

We can compare expansions of $\mathfrak{A}$ by componentwise inclusion of the additional predicates: $(\mathfrak{A}, R_1, \ldots, R_k) \subseteq (\mathfrak{A}, R_1', \ldots, R_k')$ if $R_i \subseteq R_i'$ for all i. Acording to the **minimal-model semantics**, $\Pi(\mathfrak{A})$ is the minimal expansion $(\mathfrak{A}, R_1^\mu, \ldots, R_k^\mu)$ that satisfies $\psi[\Pi]$.

Example 3.3.59. The formula associated with the program Π_{reach} of Example 3.3.58 is

$$\forall x \forall y \forall z ((Txy \leftarrow Exy) \wedge (Txz \leftarrow Txy \wedge Tyz) \wedge (Ry \leftarrow Tay)).$$

The minimal expansion of a graph $G = (V, E)$ with a distinguished node a is $\Pi_{reach}(G, a) = (G, a, T, R)$ where T is the transitive closure of E and R is the set of points reachable by a path from a.

Exercise 3.3.60 Prove that minimal-model semantics is well-defined: for every Datalog program Π and every input database $\mathfrak{A}$, there is a unique minimal expansion of $\mathfrak{A}$ that is a model of $\psi[\Pi]$.

For the case of **fixed-point semantics**, we read a rule $R\overline{x} \leftarrow \beta(\overline{x}, \overline{y})$ as an update operator: whenever an instantiation $\beta(\overline{a}, \overline{b})$ of the body of the rule is true for the current interpretation of the head predicates, make the corresponding instantiation $R\overline{a}$ of the head true. Initially, let all head predicates be empty. At each stage, apply simultaneously the update operators for all rules of the program to the current interpretation of $(R_1, \ldots, R_k)$. Iterate this operation until a fixed point $(R_1^\infty, \ldots, R_k^\infty)$ is reached. Now let $\Pi(\mathfrak{A}) := (\mathfrak{A}, R_1^\infty, \ldots, R_k^\infty)$.

Exercise 3.3.61 Prove that minimal-model semantics and fixed-point semantics coincide: for all Π and $\mathfrak{A}$, $(R_1^\mu, \ldots, R_k^\mu) = (R_1^\infty, \ldots, R_k^\infty)$.

Definition 3.3.62. A **Datalog query** is a pair (Π, R) consisting of a Datalog program Π and a designated head predicate R of Π. With every structure $\mathfrak{A}$, the query (Π, R) associates the result $(\Pi, R)^{\mathfrak{A}}$, the interpretation of R as computed by Π from the input $\mathfrak{A}$.

We now relate Datalog to LFP. We shall show that each Datalog query (Π, R) is equivalent to a formula $\psi(\overline{x}) \in$ LFP, in fact one of very special form.

Let Π be a Datalog program with input vocabulary τ and head predicates $R_1, \ldots, R_k$. We first normalize the rules such that all rules with head predicate R_i have the same head $R_i x_1 \cdots x_{k_i}$. This can be done by appropriate substitutions in the rule body and by adding equalities. For instance, a rule $Rxyyx \leftarrow \beta(x, y, z)$ can be rewritten as $Rx_1 x_2 x_3 x_4 \leftarrow \beta(x_1, x_2, y) \wedge x_3 = x_2 \wedge x_4 = x_1$. We then have a program containing, for each head predicate R_i, rules r_{ij} of the form $R_i \overline{x} \leftarrow \beta_{ij}(\overline{x}, \overline{y})$, where β_{ij} is a conjunction of literals and equalities. We then combine the update operators associated with the same head predicate and describe the update of R_i by the existential first-order formula $\gamma_i(\overline{x}) := \bigvee_j \exists \overline{y} \beta_{ij}(\overline{x}, \overline{y})$. As a consequence, the fixed-point semantics of Π is described by the system

$$
S := \begin{cases} R_1 \overline{x} := \gamma_1 \\ \quad \vdots \\ R_k \overline{x} := \gamma_k \end{cases}
$$

of first-order update rules, and the query (Π, R_i) is equivalent to the formula $[\mathbf{lfp} R_i : S](\overline{x})$. Hence every Datalog query is equivalent to an LFP-formula, in which fixed-point operators are applied only to existential formulae.

Definition 3.3.63. Existential fixed-point logic, denoted EFP, is the set of (simultaneous) LFP-formulae without universal quantifiers and without **gfp**-operators, and where negations are applied to atomic formulae only.

We have seen that Datalog $\subseteq$ EFP. The converse is also true, which can be established by a straightforward induction: with every formula $\psi \in$ EFP one associates a Datalog program Π_ψ with a distinguished head predicate H_ψ such that the query (Π_ψ, H_ψ) is equivalent to ψ. We leave the details as an exercise.

Proposition 3.3.64. *Datalog is equivalent to* EFP.

We know that LFP captures PTIME on ordered finite structures. The question arises of whether Datalog is sufficiently powerful to do the same. The answer depends on the precise variant of Datalog and on the notion of ordered structures that is used. We distinguish three cases.

(1) A simple monotonicity argument shows that Datalog is weaker than PTIME on structures where only a linear order, but not a successor relation, is given. If $\mathfrak{A}$ is a substructure of $\mathfrak{B}$, then $(\Pi, R)^{\mathfrak{A}} \subseteq (\Pi, R)^{\mathfrak{B}}$ for every Datalog query (Π, R). Of course, there even exist very simple *first-order* queries that are not monotone in this sense. Note that this argument does break down on databases where a successor relation S (rather than just a linear order), and constants 0 and e for the first and last elements are given. Exercise: why?

(2) In the literature, Datalog programs are often required to contain only positive rules, i.e. the input predicates also can be used only positively. This restricted variant is too weak to capture PTIME, even on successor structures. If input predicates can be used only positively, then queries are monotone under extensions of the input relations: if a database $\mathfrak{B}$ is obtained from $\mathfrak{A}$ by augmenting some of the input relations, then again $(\Pi, R)^{\mathfrak{A}} \subseteq (\Pi, R)^{\mathfrak{B}}$.

Exercise 3.3.65 Prove this monotonocity property, and give examples of first-order queries that cannot be defined by Datalog programs.

(3) In the case of programs with negations of input predicates and databases with a successor relation and constants 0 and e for the first and last elements, we can capture PTIME by Datalog. This was originally established in [13, 91] and is implicit also in [67].

Theorem 3.3.66 (Blass, Gurevich, and Papadimitriou). *On successor structures, Datalog (with negations of input predicates) captures PTIME.*

Proof. This result can be established in several ways, for instance by a reduction from Σ_1^1-HORN (making use of the fact that PTIME is closed under complement). Instead, we give a direct proof.

It is clear that Datalog queries are computable in polynomial time. It remains to prove that every class $\mathcal{K}$ of finite successor structures that is recognizable in PTIME can be defined by a Boolean Datalog query.

Let M be a polynomial-time Turing machine with state set Q and alphabet Σ, recognizing (an encoding of) a successor structure $\mathfrak{A}$ if and only if $\mathfrak{A} \in \mathcal{K}$. We denote the cardinality of the input structure $\mathfrak{A}$ by n and assume that the computation time of M on $\mathfrak{A}$ is less than n^k.

The construction is similar to the proof of Theorem 3.3.55. Configurations of M are represented by words $\#w_1 \cdots w_{i-1}(qw_i)w_{i+1} \cdots w_{m-1}\#$ over the alphabet $\Gamma := \Sigma \cup (Q \times \Sigma) \cup \{\#\}$, where $m = n^k$, and we describe the behaviour of M by a function $f : \Gamma^3 \to \Gamma$ such that, for any configuration $C = c_0 \cdots c_m$, the successor configuration $\mathrm{Next}(C) = c'_0 \cdots c'_m$ is determined by the rules

$$c'_0 = c'_m = \# \quad \text{and} \quad c'_i = f(c_{i-1}, c_i, c_{i+1}) \text{ for } 1 \le i \le m-1.$$

Let S be a $2k$-ary relation symbol and let Π_S be a Datalog program with head predicate S, computing the successor relation on k-tuples (associated with the lexicographic order defined by the given successor relation). Recall that we can encode successor structures so that there exist quantifier-free formulae $\beta_\sigma(\bar{y})$ such that $\mathfrak{A} \models \beta_\sigma(\bar{a})$ if, and only if, the $\bar{a}$th symbol of the input configuration of M for $code(\mathfrak{A})$ is σ. Let (Π_σ, H_σ) be a Datalog query equivalent to $\beta_\sigma(\bar{y})$.

We represent the computation of M by a tuple $\overline{C} = (C_\sigma)_{\sigma \in \Gamma}$ of $2k$-ary relations, where

$$C_\sigma := \{(\bar{a}, \bar{t}) : \text{ the } \bar{a}\text{th symbol of the configuration at time } \bar{t} \text{ is } \sigma\}.$$

The Datalog program associated with M consists of

(1) the program Π_S defining the successor relation on k-tuples;
(2) the programs Π_σ for describing the input;

(3) the rules

$$C_\# \overline{0}\,\overline{t}$$

$$C_\# \overline{e}\,\overline{t}$$

$$C_\sigma \overline{y}\,\overline{0} \leftarrow H_\sigma \overline{y} \text{ for all } \sigma \in \Gamma - \{\#\};$$

(4) for all $\alpha, \beta, \gamma, \sigma$ with $f(\alpha, \beta, \gamma) = \sigma$, the rule

$$C_\sigma \overline{y}\,\overline{t}' \leftarrow S\overline{x}\,\overline{y} \wedge S\overline{y}\,\overline{z} \wedge S\overline{t}\,\overline{t}' \wedge C_\alpha \overline{x}\,\overline{t} \wedge C_\beta \overline{y}\,\overline{t} \wedge C_\gamma \overline{z}\,\overline{t};$$

(5) the rule

$$\text{Acc} \leftarrow C_{qw}\overline{x}\,\overline{t} \quad \text{for any } \textit{accepting} \text{ state } q \text{ and any symbol } w.$$

The first two rules in (3) say that each configuration starts and ends with $\#$; the following set of rules ensures that the configuration at time 0 is the input configuration. The rules in (4) imply that from time $\overline{t}$ to time $\overline{t}' = \overline{t} + 1$ the computation proceeds as required by M, and the last rule makes the Boolean predicate Acc true if and only if an accepting state has been reached. Obviously, M accepts the input structure $\mathfrak{A}$ if, and only if, the query (Π_M, Acc) evaluates to true on $\mathfrak{A}$. $\qquad\square$

Almost the same proof shows that the expression complexity of Datalog (and hence of LFP) is EXPTIME-complete (see also Theorem 3.3.36).

Theorem 3.3.67. *The evaluation problem for Datalog programs (with head predicates of unbounded arity) is complete for* EXPTIME, *even for programs with only positive rules, and for a fixed database with only two elements.*

Proof. By the results of Section 3.3.5, LFP-formulae, and hence also Datalog programs, can be evaluated in polynomial time with respect to the size of the input structure and in exponential time with respect to the length of the formula (or program).

To prove completeness, we fix a database $\mathfrak{A}$ with two elements and constant symbols 0, 1 (or, alternatively, two unary relations $P_0 = \{0\}$ and $P_1 = \{1\}$). Let M be a deterministic Turing machine that accepts or rejects input words $w = w_0 \cdots w_{m-1} \in \{0,1\}^*$ in time 2^{m^d} (for some fixed d). For every input x for M, we construct a Datalog program $\Pi_{M,w}$ which evaluates, on the fixed database $\mathfrak{A}$, a Boolean head predicate Acc to true if, and only if, M accepts w.

The construction is similar to that in the proof of Theorem 3.3.66, with the following two differences. Whereas in the previous proof k was fixed and n depended on the input, it is now the other way round, with $n := 2$ and $k := m^d$. Further, the description of the input configuration is now simpler: we just explicitly list the atomic facts defining the input configuration for the given input w. Note that this is the only part of the program that depends on w; the remaining rules depend only on M and the *length* of the input. Finally note that the program contains only positive rules. $\qquad\square$

Stratified Datalog

Datalog defines in a natural way queries that require recursion (such as transitive closure), but is very weak in other respects, mainly because it does not include negation.

There exist various possible ways to add negation to Datalog.

Definition 3.3.68. A **stratified Datalog program** is a sequence $\Pi = (\Pi_0, \ldots, \Pi_r)$ of basic Datalog programs, which are called the **strata** of Π, such that each of the head predicates of Π is a head predicate in precisely one stratum Π_i and is used as an input predicate only in higher strata Π_j, where $j > i$. In particular, this means that

(1) if a head predicate of stratum Π_j occurs *positively* in the body of a rule of stratum Π_i, then $j \leq i$, and

(2) if a head predicate of stratum Π_j occurs *negatively* in the body of a rule of stratum Π_i, then $j < i$.

The semantics of a stratified program is defined stratum by stratum. The input predicates of a stratum Π_i are either input predicates of the entire program Π or are head predicates of a lower stratum. Hence, once the lower strata are evaluated, we can compute the interpretation of the head predicates of Π_i as in the case of basic Datalog programs.

Clearly the power of stratified Datalog is between that of Datalog and LFP, and hence stratified Datalog provides yet another formalism that captures PTIME on ordered structures. On unordered structures stratified Datalog is strictly more expressive than Datalog (as it includes all of first-order logic) but strictly less powerful than LFP. The main example separating LFP from Stratified Datalog is the GAME query, which defines the winning positions of Player 0 in a strictly alternating game. It is defined by the LFP formula $[\mathbf{lfp}Wx \,.\, \exists y(Exy \wedge \forall z(Eyz \to Wz)](x)$. This involves a recursion through a universal quantifier, which in general cannot be done in stratified Datalog [31, 79].

Theorem 3.3.69 (Dahlhaus and Kolaitis). *No stratified Datalog program can express the* GAME *query. Hence* stratified Datalog $\subsetneq$ LFP.

Example 3.3.70. Another interesting class of examples showing the limits of stratified Datalog is that of well-foundedness properties, or statements saying that on all infinite paths one will eventually hit a node with a certain property P. These are typical statements in the field of verification (expressed in CTL by the formula $\mathbf{AF}P$).

In LFP, the well-foundedness of a partial order $\prec$ would be expressed as $\forall y[\mathbf{lfp}Wy \,.\, \forall x(x \prec y \to Wx)](y)$. The CTL-formula $\mathbf{AF}P$ is expressed in L_μ by $\mu X.P \vee \Box X$ and in LFP by $[\mathbf{lfp}Rx \,.\, Px \vee \forall y(Exy \to Ry)](x)$.

On *finite* structures, such properties are definable by stratified Datalog programs, since they are essentially negations of reachability problems for cycles. Indeed, $\mathbf{AF}P$ means that there is no path that eventually cycles and on which P is globally false. This can be expressed by the following stratified program:

$$Txy \leftarrow \neg Px \wedge Exy \wedge \neg Py \qquad\qquad Txz \leftarrow Txy \wedge Eyz \wedge \neg Pz$$
$$Sx \leftarrow Txx \qquad\qquad\qquad\qquad Sx \leftarrow \neg Px \wedge Exy \wedge Sy$$
$$Rx \leftarrow \neg Sx$$

The first stratum computes the set T of all pairs of nodes (u, v) such that there exists a path from u to v on which P is false, and the set S of all nodes from which there exists such a path that eventually cycles. Here the finiteness of the graph is used in an essential way, because only this guarantees that every infinite path eventually reaches a cycle. The second stratum takes the complement of S.

However, it can be shown that no stratified Datalog program can express such statements on *infinite* structures (even countable ones).

Another variant of Datalog, called Datalog LITE, which can express all CTL properties and moreover admits linear-time evaluation algorithms (and which is incomparable with stratified Datalog), has been defined and studied in [45].

A stratified Datalog program is **linear** if in the body of each rule there is at most one occurrence of a head predicate of the same stratum (but there may be arbitrary many occurrences of head predicates from lower strata).

Example 3.3.71. The program Π_{reach} in Example 3.3.58 is not linear, but by replacing the second, non-linear rule $Txz \leftarrow Txy \wedge Tyz$ by the linear rule $Txz \leftarrow Txy \wedge Eyz$ we obtain an equivalent linear program. However, one pays a price for the linearization. The original program reaches the fixed point after $O(\log m)$ iterations, while the linear program needs m iterations, where m is the length of the longest path in the graph.

Linear programs suffice to define transitive closures, so it follows by a straightforward induction that TC $\subseteq$ linear stratified Datalog. The converse is also true (see [38, 46]).

Proposition 3.3.72. *Linear stratified Datalog is equivalent to* TC.

Corollary 3.3.73. *On ordered structures, linear stratified Datalog captures* NLOGSPACE.

3.4 Logics with Counting

From the point of view of expressiveness, first-order logic has two main deficiencies: it lacks the power to express anything that requires recursion (the simplest example is transitive closure) and it cannot count, as witnessed by the impossibility to express that a structure has even cardinality, or, more generally, by the 0-1 law. We have already discussed a number of logics that add recursion in one way or another to FO (or part of it), notably the various forms of fixed-point logic. On ordered finite structures, some of these logics can express precisely the queries that are computable in PTIME or PSPACE. However, on arbitrary finite structures they do not, and almost all known examples showing this involve counting. Whereas in the presence of an ordering, the ability to count is inherent in fixed-point logic, hardly any of this ability is retained in its absence. For instance, as LFP and PFP are fragments of $L_{\infty\omega}^{\omega}$, the 0-1 law also holds for them.

Therefore Immerman proposed that counting quantifiers should be added to logics and asked whether a suitable variant of fixed-point logic with counting would suffice to capture PTIME. Although Cai, Fürer and Immerman [23] eventually answered this question negatively, fixed-point logic with counting has turned out to be an important and robust logic, that defines a natural level of expressiveness and allows one to capture PTIME on interesting classes of structures.

3.4.1 Logics with Counting Terms

There are different ways of adding counting mechanisms to a logic, which are not necessarily equivalent. The most straightforward possibility is the addition of quantifiers of the form $\exists^{\geq 2}$, $\exists^{\geq 3}$, etc., with the obvious meaning. While this is perfectly reasonable for bounded-variable fragments of first-order logic or infinitary logic (see e.g. [58, 89]), it is not general enough for fixed-point logic, because it does not allow for recursion over the counting parameters i in quantifiers $\exists^{\geq i}x$. In fact, if the counting parameters are fixed numbers, then adjoining the quantifiers $\exists^{\geq i}x$ does not give additional power to logics such as FO or LFP, since they are closed under the replacement of $\exists^{\geq i}$ by i existential quantifiers (where as their restrictions to bounded width are not). These counting parameters should therefore be considered as variables that range over natural numbers. To define in a precise way a logic with counting and recursion, one extends the original objects of study, namely finite (one-sorted) structures $\mathfrak{A}$, to two-sorted auxiliary structures $\mathfrak{A}^*$ with a second numerical (but also finite) sort.

Definition 3.4.1. With any one-sorted finite structure $\mathfrak{A}$ with universe A, we associate the two-sorted structure $\mathfrak{A}^* := \mathfrak{A} \,\dot\cup\, \langle\{0,\ldots,|A|\}; \leq, 0, e\rangle$, where $\leq$ is the canonical ordering on $\{0,\ldots,|A|\}$, and 0 and e stand for the first and the last element. Thus, we have taken the disjoint union of $\mathfrak{A}$ with a linear order of length $|A| + 1$.

We start with first-order logic over two-sorted vocabularies $\sigma \cup \{\leq, 0, e\}$, with semantics over structures $\mathfrak{A}^*$ defined in the obvious way. We shall use Latin letters $x, y, z, \ldots$ for the variables over the first sort, and Greek letters $\lambda, \mu, \nu, \ldots$ for variables over the second sort. The two sorts are related by

counting terms, defined by the following rule. Let $\varphi(x)$ be a formula with a variable x (over the first sort) among its free variables. Then $\#_x[\varphi]$ is a term in the second sort, with the set of free variables $\mathrm{free}(\#_x[\varphi]) = \mathrm{free}(\varphi) - \{x\}$. The value of $\#_x[\varphi]$ is the number of elements a that satisfy $\varphi(a)$.

Counting logics of this form were introduced by Grädel and Otto [54] and have been studied in detail in [89]. We start with first-order logic with counting, denoted by (FO + C), which is the closure of two-sorted first-order logic under counting terms. Here are two simple examples that illustrate the use of counting terms.

Example 3.4.2. On a undirected graph $G = (V, E)$, the formula $\forall x \forall y (\#_z[Exz] = \#_z[Eyz])$ expresses the assertion that every node has the same degree, i.e., that G is regular.

Example 3.4.3. We present below a formula $\psi(E_1, E_2) \in$ (FO + C) which expresses the assertion that two equivalence relations E_1 and E_2 are isomorphic; of course a necessary and sufficient condition for this is that for every i, they have the same number of elements in equivalence classes of size i:

$$\psi(E_1, E_2) \equiv (\forall \mu)(\#_x[\#_y[E_1 xy] = \mu] = \#_x[\#_y[E_2 xy] = \mu]).$$

3.4.2 Fixed-Point Logic with Counting

We now define **(inflationary) fixed point logic with counting** (IFP + C) and **partial fixed point logic with counting** (PFP + C) by adding to (FO + C) the usual rules for building inflationary or partial fixed points, ranging over both sorts.

Definition 3.4.4. Inflationary fixed point logic with counting, (IFP + C), is the closure of two-sorted first-order logic under the following rules:

(1) The rule for building counting terms.
(2) The usual rules of first-order logic for building terms and formulae.
(3) The fixed-point formation rule. Suppose that $\psi(R, \overline{x}, \overline{\mu})$ is a formula of vocabulary $\tau \cup \{R\}$ where $\overline{x} = x_1, \ldots, x_k$, $\overline{\mu} = \mu_1, \ldots, \mu_\ell$, and R has mixed arity (k, ℓ), and that $(\overline{u}, \overline{v})$ is a $k + \ell$-tuple of first- and second-sort terms, respectively. Then

$$[\mathbf{ifp}\ R\overline{x}\overline{\mu} \,.\, \psi](\overline{u}, \overline{v})$$

is a formula of vocabulary τ.

The semantics of $[\mathbf{ifp}\ R\overline{x}\overline{\mu} \,.\, \psi]$ on $\mathfrak{A}^*$ is defined in the same way as for the logic IFP, namely as the inflationary fixed point of the operator

$$F_\psi : R \longmapsto R \cup \{(\overline{a}, \overline{\imath}) \mid (\mathfrak{A}^*, R) \models \psi(\overline{a}, \overline{\imath})\}.$$

The definition of (PFP + C) is analogous, where we replace inflationary fixed points by partial ones. In the literature, one also finds different variants of fixed-point logic with counting where the two sorts are related by *counting quantifiers* rather than counting terms. Counting quantifiers have the form $(\exists i\ x)$ for 'there exist at least i x', where i is a second-sort variable. It is obvious that the two definitions are equivalent. In fact, (IFP + C) is a very robust logic. For instance, its expressive power does not change if one permits counting over tuples, even of mixed type, i.e. terms of the form $\#_{\bar{x},\bar{\mu}}\varphi$. One can of course also define least fixed-point logic with counting, (LFP + C), but one has to be careful with the positivity requirement (which is more natural when one uses counting quantifiers rather than counting terms). The equivalence of LFP and IFP readily translates to (LFP + C) $\equiv$ (IFP + C). Further, there are a number of other logical formalizations of the concept of inductive definability with counting that turn out to have the same expressive power as (IFP + C) (see [54] and Sect.3.4.3 below for details).

Example 3.4.5. An interesting example of an (IFP + C)-definable query is the method of *stable colourings* for graph-canonization. Given a graph G with a colouring $f : V \rightarrow 0, \ldots, r$ of its vertices, we define a refinement f' of f, giving to a vertex x the new colour $f'x = (fx, n_1, \ldots, n_r)$ where $n_i = \#y[Exy \wedge (fy = i)]$. The new colours can be sorted lexicographically so that they again form an initial subset of $\mathbb{N}$. Then the process can be iterated until a fixed point, the *stable colouring* of G is reached. It is easy to see that the stable colouring of a graph is polynomial-time computable and uniformly definable in (IFP + C).

On many graphs, the stable colouring uniquely identifies each vertex, i.e. no two distinct vertices get the same stable colour. This is the case, for instance, for all trees. Further, Babai, Erdös, and Selkow [8] proved that the probability that this happens on a random graph with n nodes approaches 1 as n goes to infinity. Thus stable colourings provide a polynomial-time graph canonization algorithm for almost all finite graphs.

We now discuss the expressive power and evaluation complexity of fixed-point logic with counting. We are mainly interested in (IFP + C)-formulae and (PFP + C)-formulae without free variables over the second sort, so that we can compare them with the usual logics without counting.

Exercise 3.4.6 Even without making use of counting terms, IFP over two-sorted structures $\mathfrak{A}^*$ is more expressive than IFP over $\mathfrak{A}$. To prove this, construct a two-sorted IFP-sentence ψ such that $\mathfrak{A}^* \models \psi$ if, and only if, $|A|$ is even.

It is clear that counting terms can be computed in polynomial-time. Hence the data complexity remains in PTIME for (IFP + C) and in PSPACE for (PFP + C). We shall see below that these inclusions are strict.

Theorem 3.4.7. *On finite structures,*

(1) IFP $\subsetneq$ (IFP + C) $\subsetneq$ PTIME.
(2) PFP $\subsetneq$ (PFP + C) $\subsetneq$ PSPACE.

Infinitary Logic with Counting

Let $C^k_{\infty\omega}$ be the infinitary logic with k variables $L^k_{\infty\omega}$, extended by the quantifiers $\exists^{\geq m}$ ('there exist at least m') for all $m \in \mathbb{N}$. Further, let $C^\omega_{\infty\omega} := \bigcup_k C^k_{\infty\omega}$.

Proposition 3.4.8. (IFP + C) $\subseteq C^\omega_{\infty\omega}$.

Due to the two-sorted framework, the proof of this result is a bit more involved than for the corresponding result without counting, but not really difficult. We refer to [54, 89] for details.

The separation of (IFP + C) from PTIME has been established by Cai, Fürer, and Immerman [23]. The proof also provides an analysis of the method of stable colourings for graph canonization. We have deswcribed this method in its simplest form in Example 3.4.5. More sophisticated variants compute and refine colourings of k-tuples of vertices. This is called the *k-dimensional Weisfeiler–Lehman method* and, in logical terms, it amounts to labelling each k-tuple by its type in $k + 1$-variable logic with counting quantifiers. It was conjectured that this method could provide a polynomial-time algorithm for graph isomorphism, at least for graphs of bounded degree. However, Cai, Fürer, and Immerman were able to construct two families $(G_n)_{n\in\mathbb{N}}$ and $(H_n)_{n\in\mathbb{N}}$ of graphs such that on one hand, G_n and H_n have $O(n)$ nodes and degree three, and admit a linear-time canonization algorithm, but on the other hand, in first-order (or infinitary) logic with counting, $\Omega(n)$ variables are necessary to distinguish between G_n and H_n. In particular, this implies Theorem 3.4.7.

Inflationary vs. Partial Fixed-Points

By Theorem 3.3.56, partial fixed-point logic collapses to inflationary fixed-point logic if, and only if, PTIME = PSPACE. The analogous result in the presence of counting is also true [54, 89]: PTIME = PSPACE $\Longleftrightarrow$ (IFP + C) = (PFP + C).

3.4.3 Datalog with Counting

Fixed-point formulae have the reputation of being difficult to read, and many people find formalisms such as Datalog easier to understand. In the presence of a successor relation, Datalog (with negation over input predicates) is sufficient to capture PTIME and hence is equally expressive as LFP. In general, however, Datalog and even its most natural extensions, notably stratified Datalog, are weaker than LFP.

Counting terms can also be added to Datalog. We conclude this section by discussing Datalog with counting. We show that (Datalog + C) is closed under negation and equivalent to (IFP + C). In the presence of counting, the common extensions of Datalog, notably stratified Datalog, are therefore equivalent to Datalog.

Definition 3.4.9. Datalog with counting, denoted by (Datalog + C), extends Datalog by allowing two-sorted head predicates and counting terms. The two-sorted head atoms have the form $R\overline{x}\overline{\mu}$, where $\overline{x}$ ranges over the first sort, i.e. over elements of the input database $\mathfrak{A}$, and $\overline{\mu}$ ranges over the second sort. For any atom $Rx\overline{y}\overline{\mu}$ we have a counting term $\#_x[Rx\overline{y}\overline{\mu}]$. A term over the second sort is called an **arithmetical term**. The arithmetical terms are either 0, e, counting terms, or $t + 1$, where t is also an arithmetical term. Thus, a program in (Datalog + C) is a finite set of clauses of the form

$$H \leftarrow B_1 \wedge \cdots \wedge B_m$$

where the head H is an atomic formula $R(\overline{x}, \overline{\mu})$, and $B_1, \ldots, B_m$ are atomic formulae $Rx\overline{\mu}$ or equalities of terms (over the first or the second sort).

For every input database, the program computes intensional relations via the inflationary fixed-point semantics. Note that for classical Datalog programs, it makes no difference whether the fixed-point semantics is defined to be inflationary or not, since the underlying operator is monotone anyway. However, for programs in (Datalog + C), the semantics has to be inflationary, since otherwise, the equalities of arithmetical terms give rise to non-monotone operators. For the same reason, the minimum-model semantics will no longer be defined. Since inflationary fixed-point semantics is one of the various equivalent ways to define the semantics of Datalog, both the syntax and the semantics of (Datalog + C) generalize Datalog in a natural way.

One could also introduce counting in an (at first sight) more general form, namely by allowing counting terms of the form $\#_{\overline{x},\overline{\mu}}[R\overline{x}\overline{\mu}\overline{y}\overline{\nu}]$. While this may be convenient for writing a program in shorter and more understandable form, it does not affect the power of (Datalog + C).

Exercise 3.4.10 [54] Prove that counting over tuples, even of mixed type, does not increase the expressive power of (Datalog + C).

Hence cardinalities of arbitrary predicates can be equated in a Datalog program: we take the liberty of writing equalities such as $|Q| = |R|$ in the body of a rule, for simplicity. The following technical lemma is essential for reducing (IFP + C) to (Datalog + C).

Lemma 3.4.11. *Let Π be a* (Datalog + C) *program with head predicates $Q_1, \ldots, Q_r$. There exists another* (Datalog + C) *program Π', whose head predicates include $Q_1, \ldots, Q_r$ and a Boolean control predicate C^* such that*

- $(\Pi', Q_i) = (\Pi, Q_i)$ *for all i;*
- (Π', C^*) *is true on all databases and C^* becomes true only at the last stage of the evaluation of Π'.*

Proof. In addition to C^*, we add a unary head predicate C^0 and, for every head predicate Q_i of Π a new head predicate Q_i' of the same arity. Then, Π' is obtained by adding the following clauses to Π:

$$C^0 x$$
$$Q'_i \overline{x} \overline{\mu} \leftarrow Q_i \overline{x} \overline{\mu} \quad \text{for } 1 \leq i \leq r$$
$$C^* \leftarrow C^0 x \wedge (|Q_1| = |Q'_1|) \wedge \cdots \wedge (|Q_r| = |Q'_r|)$$

Observe that Q'_i simply lags one step behind Q_i. The atom $C^0 x$ is necessary to avoid the possibility that C^* is set to true in the first stage. $\qquad \square$

Lemma 3.4.11 essentially says that we can attach to any program a Boolean control predicate which becomes true when the evaluation of the program is terminated. We can then compose two Datalog programs while making sure that the evaluation of the second program starts only after the first has been terminated. As an initial application, we shall show that (Datalog + C) is closed under negation.

Lemma 3.4.12. *The complement of a* (Datalog + C) *query is also a* (Datalog + C) *query.*

Proof. Let (Π, Q) be a (Datalog + C) query, and let Π' be the program specified in Lemma 3.4.11. Take a new variable z, and new head predicates $\tilde{Q}$ and R with arity(R) = arity(Q) and arity$(\tilde{Q})$ = arity(Q) + 1. Construct Π'' by adding to Π' the rules

$$\tilde{Q} \overline{x} \overline{\mu} z \leftarrow Q \overline{x} \overline{\mu}$$
$$R \overline{x} \overline{\mu} \leftarrow C^* \wedge (\#_z [\tilde{Q} \overline{x} \overline{\mu} z] = 0).$$

The query (Π'', R) is the complement of (Π, Q). $\qquad \square$

Difficulties in expressing negation are the reason why, in the absence of counting (or of an ordering), Datalog is weaker than fixed-point logic. Also, the limited form of negation that is available in Stratified Datalog (which does not allow for 'recursion through negation') does not suffice to express all fixed-point queries. (Datalog + C) does not have these limitations, and is equally expressive as (IFP + C).

Theorem 3.4.13 (Grädel and Otto). (Datalog + C) $\equiv$ (IFP + C).

It is obvious that (Datalog + C) $\subseteq$ (IFP + C). For the converse, we can construct by induction, for every formula $\psi \in$ (IFP + C), a (Datalog + C) program Π_ψ with goal predicate Q_ψ such that (Π_ψ, Q_ψ) is equivalent to ψ.

Exercise 3.4.14 For atomic formulae, disjunctions, and existential quantification the construction is obvious, and closure under negation has already been proved. Complete the proof for applications of counting terms, i.e formulae $\psi(\overline{y}, \overline{\mu}, \nu) := \#_x [\varphi(\overline{x}, \overline{y}, \overline{\mu})] = \nu$, and fixed point formulae $\psi := [\mathbf{ifp} R \overline{x} \overline{\mu} . \varphi(R, \overline{x}, \overline{\mu})](\overline{y}, \overline{\nu})$. The construction makes use of Lemma 3.4.11.

Example 3.4.15. To illustrate the expressive power of (Datalog + C) we show below a program for the GAME query (for strictly alternating games). The GAME query is the canonical example that separates LFP from Stratified Datalog [31, 79]. GAME is definable in fixed-point logic, by the formula [**lfp**Wx . $\exists y(Exy \wedge \forall z(Eyz \rightarrow Wz))](x)$ that defines the winning positions for Player 0.

Here is a (Datalog + C) program with goal predicate Z, defining GAME:

$$Wx\lambda \leftarrow Exy \wedge Vy\mu \wedge \lambda = \mu + 1$$
$$Fyz\mu \leftarrow Eyz \wedge Wz\mu$$
$$Vy\mu \leftarrow \#_z[Eyz] = \#_z[Fyz\mu]$$
$$Zx \leftarrow Wx\mu$$

The evaluation of this program on a game graph G assigns to W (or V) a set of pairs $(x, \mu) \in V \times \mathbb{N}$, such that Player 0 has a winning strategy from position x in at most μ moves when she (or Player 1, respectively) begins the game.

3.5 Capturing PTIME via Canonization

We have seen that there are a number of logics that capture polynomial time on ordered finite structures, but none of them suffices to express all of PTIME in the absence of a linear order. Indeed, it has been conjectured that no logic whatsoever can capture PTIME on the domain of all finite structures. We shall discuss this problem further at the end of this section. But, of course, even if this conjecture should turn out to be true, it remains an important issue to capture PTIME on other relevant domains besides ordered structures.

3.5.1 Definable Linear Orders

An obvious approach is to try to *define* linear orders and then apply the known results for capturing complexity classes on ordered structures.

Definition 3.5.1. Let $\mathcal{D}$ be a domain of finite structures and let L a logic. We say that $\mathcal{D}$ admits **L-definable linear orders** if, for every vocabulary τ, there exists a formula $\psi(x, y, \bar{z}) \in L(\tau)$ such that there exists in every structure $\mathfrak{A} \in \mathcal{D}(\tau)$ a tuple $\bar{c}$ for which the relation $\{(a, b) : \mathfrak{A} \models \psi(a, b, \bar{c})\}$ is a linear order on A. The elements in $\bar{c}$ are called the parameters of the order defined by ψ on $\mathfrak{A}$.

Example 3.5.2. Let $\mathcal{D}$ consist of all structures $(A, E, R_1, \ldots,)$ such that (A, E) is an undirected cycle. $\mathcal{D}$ admits LFP-definable linear orders (with two parameters), via the formula

$$\psi(x, y, z_1, z_2) := Ez_1z_2 \wedge [\textbf{lfp}Rxy \, . \, (x = z_1 \wedge y = z_2) \vee \exists u(Rxu \wedge Euy \wedge y \neq z_1)$$
$$\vee \exists u(Ruy \wedge Eux \wedge x \neq y](x, y).$$

Furthermore, straightforward automorphism arguments show that we cannot define linear orders with fewer than two parameters.

Exercise 3.5.3 Let $\mathcal{D}$ be the domain of structures $(A, E, R_1, \ldots,)$ such that (A, E) is isomorphic to a finite rectangular grid. Show that $\mathcal{D}$ admits LFP-definable linear orders.

Exercise 3.5.4 Let $\mathcal{K}$ be a class of τ-structures with the following property. For every $m \in \mathbb{N}$, there exists a structure $\mathfrak{A} \in \mathcal{K}$ such that for every m-tuple $\bar{a}$ in $\mathfrak{A}$ there exists a non-trivial automorphism of $\mathfrak{A}, \bar{a}$. Then $\mathcal{K}$ does not admit definable orders in any logic.

On any domain that admits LFP-definable linear orders, we can capture PTIME by using LFP-formulae that express polynomial-time properties on ordered structures, and modify them appropriately.

Proposition 3.5.5. *If $\mathcal{D}$ admits LFP-definable linear orders, then LFP captures polynomial time on $\mathcal{D}$.*

Proof. It only remains to show that every polynomial-time model class $\mathcal{K} \subseteq \mathcal{D}(\tau)$ is L-definable. Let $\varphi(x, y, \bar{z})$ be a formula defining a linear order on the structures in $\mathcal{D}(\tau)$. As LFP captures PTIME on ordered structures, there exists a formula $\psi \in \mathrm{LFP}(\tau \cup \{<\})$ such that, for every structure $\mathfrak{A} \in \mathcal{D}(\tau)$ and every linear order $<$ on A, we have that $(\mathfrak{A}, <) \models \psi$ iff $\mathfrak{A} \in \mathcal{K}$. It follows that

$$\mathfrak{A} \in \mathcal{K} \iff \mathfrak{A} \models \exists \bar{z} \Big(\text{``}\{(x, y) : \varphi(x, y, \bar{z})\} \text{ is a linear order''} \wedge$$
$$\psi[u < v / \varphi(u, v, \bar{z})] \Big),$$

where $\psi[u < v / \varphi(u, v, \bar{z})]$ is the formula obtained from ψ by replacing every atom of the form $u < v$ by $\varphi(u, v, \bar{z})$. $\qquad\qquad\square$

3.5.2 Canonizations and Interpretations

Let S be any set and let $\sim$ be an equivalence relation on S. A *canonization function* for $(S, \sim)$ is a function $f : S \to S$ associating with every element a canonical member of its equivalence class. That means that $f(s) \sim s$ for all $s \in S$, and $f(s) = f(s')$ whenever $s \sim s'$.

In finite model theory, we are interested in canonization algorithms for finite structures, either up to isomorphism or up to a coarser equivalence relation, such as indistinguishability in some logic or bisimulation. As algorithms take encodings of structures as inputs, and as the encoding of a structure is determined by an ordering of its universe, we can view canonization of structures as an operation that associates with every structure $\mathfrak{A}$ an ordered one, say $(\mathfrak{A}', <)$, such that $\mathfrak{A}'$ is equivalent to $\mathfrak{A}$, and such that equivalent structures are mapped to the same ordered structure (and hence the same encoding).

For a class $\mathcal{K}$ of structures, we write $\mathcal{K}^<$ for the class of expansions $(\mathfrak{A}, <)$ of structures $\mathfrak{A} \in \mathcal{K}$ by some linear order.

Definition 3.5.6. Let $\mathcal{K}$ be a class of finite τ-structures, and let $\sim$ be an equivalence relation on $\mathcal{K}$. A **canonization function** for $\sim$ on $\mathcal{K}$ is a function $f : \mathcal{K} \to \mathcal{K}^<$ that associates with every structure $\mathfrak{A} \in \mathcal{K}$ an ordered structure $f(\mathfrak{A}) = (\mathfrak{A}', <)$ with $\mathfrak{A}' \sim \mathfrak{A}$, such that $f(\mathfrak{A}) \cong f(\mathfrak{B})$ whenever $\mathfrak{A} \sim \mathfrak{B}$.

Interpretations

We are especially interested in canonizations that are defined by interpretations. The notion of an interpretation is very important in mathematical logic, and for model theory in particular. Interpretations are used to define a copy of a structure inside another one, and thus permit us to transfer definability, decidability, and complexity results between theories.

Definition 3.5.7. Let L be a logic, let σ, τ be vocabularies, where $\tau = \{R_1, \ldots, R_m\}$ is relational, and let r_i be the arity of R_i. A (**one-dimensional**) $L[\sigma, \tau]$-**interpretation** is given by a sequence I of formulae in $L(\sigma)$ consisting of

- $\delta(x)$, called the domain formula,
- $\varepsilon(x, y)$, called the equality formula, and,
- for every relation symbol $R \in \tau$ (of arity r), a formula $\varphi_R(x_1, \ldots, x_r)$.

An $L[\sigma, \tau]$-interpretation induces two mappings, one between structures, and the other between formulae. For a τ-structure $\mathfrak{A}$ and a σ-structure $\mathfrak{B}$, we say that I **interprets** $\mathfrak{A}$ in $\mathfrak{B}$ (in short, $I(\mathfrak{B}) = \mathfrak{A}$) if there exists a surjective map $h : \delta^{\mathfrak{B}} \to A$, called the *coordinate map*, such that

- for all $b, c \in \delta^{\mathfrak{B}}$,
$$\mathfrak{B} \models \varepsilon(b, c) \iff h(b) = h(c);$$
- for every relation R of $\mathfrak{A}$ and all $b_1, \ldots, b_r \in \delta^{\mathfrak{B}}$,
$$\mathfrak{B} \models \varphi_R(b_1, \ldots, b_k) \iff (h(b_1), \ldots, h(b_k)) \in R,$$
i.e. $h^{-1}(R) = (\delta^{\mathfrak{B}})^k \cap \varphi_R^{\mathfrak{B}}$.

Hence $I = \langle \delta, \varepsilon, \varphi_{R_1}, \ldots, \varphi_{R_m} \rangle$ defines (together with the function $h : \delta^{\mathfrak{B}} \to A$) an interpretation of $\mathfrak{A} = (A, R_1, \ldots, R_m)$ in $\mathfrak{B}$ if and only if $\varepsilon(x, y)$ defines a congruence on the structure $(\delta^{\mathfrak{B}}, \varphi_{R_1}^{\mathfrak{B}}, \ldots, \varphi_{R_m}^{\mathfrak{B}})$ and h is an isomorphism from the quotient structure $(\delta^{\mathfrak{B}}, \varphi_{R_1}^{\mathfrak{B}}, \ldots, \varphi_{R_m}^{\mathfrak{B}})/\varepsilon^{\mathfrak{B}}$ to $\mathfrak{A}$.

Besides the mapping $\mathfrak{B} \mapsto I(\mathfrak{B})$ from σ-structures to τ-structures, I also defines a mapping from τ-formulae to σ-formulae. With every τ-formula ψ it associates a σ-formula ψ^I, which is obtained by relativizing every quantifier Qx to $\delta(x)$, replacing equalities $u = v$ by $\varepsilon(u, v)$, and replacing every atom $R\overline{u}$ by the corresponding formula $\varphi_R(\overline{u})$.

Lemma 3.5.8 (Interpretation Lemma). *For every interpretation I and every structure $\mathfrak{A}$, we have that*
$$\mathfrak{A} \models \psi^I \iff I(\mathfrak{A}) \models \psi.$$

We shall omit δ or ε from an interpretation if they are trivial, in the sense that $\delta(x)$ holds for all x and that $\varepsilon(x, y)$ is equivalent to $x = y$. The notion of an interpretation can be generalized in various ways. In particular, a k-**dimensional interpretation** is given by a sequence $\delta(\overline{x}), \varepsilon(\overline{x}, \overline{y}), \varphi_{R_1}(\overline{x}_1, \ldots, \overline{x}_{r_1}), \ldots, \varphi_{R_m}(\overline{x}_1, \ldots, \overline{x}_{r_m})$, where $\overline{x}, \overline{y}, \overline{x}_1, \ldots$ are disjoint k-tuples of distinct variables. A k-dimensional interpretation of $\mathfrak{A}$ in $\mathfrak{B}$ represents elements of A by elements or equivalence classes of B^k, rather than B.

Exercise 3.5.9 Show that up to first-order interpretation, all finite structures are graphs (see e.g. [66, Chapter 5] and [38, Chapter 11.2]). More precisely, for every vocabulary τ, construct an $\mathrm{FO}[\{E\}, \tau]$-interpretation I and an $\mathrm{FO}[\tau, \{E\}]$-interpretation J such that, for every finite structure $\mathfrak{A}$ (with at least two elements), $I(\mathfrak{A})$ is a graph and $J(I(\mathfrak{A})) \cong \mathfrak{A}$. It then follows that for every model class $\mathcal{K} \subseteq \mathrm{Fin}(\tau)$, $\mathcal{K}$ is decidable in polynomial time if, and only if, the class of graphs $\{I(\mathfrak{A}) : \mathfrak{A} \in \mathcal{K}\}$ is so.

Definition 3.5.10. Let L be a logic and $\sim$ an equivalence relation on a class $\mathcal{K}$ of τ-structures. We say that $(\mathcal{K}, \sim)$ **admits L-definable canonization** if there exists an $L[\tau, \tau \cup \{<\}]$-interpretation I such that the function $\mathfrak{A} \mapsto I(\mathfrak{A})$ is a canonization function for $\sim$. For any domain $\mathcal{D}$ of structures, we say that $(\mathcal{D}, \sim)$ admits L-definable canonization if $(\mathcal{D}(\tau), \sim)$ does for every vocabulary τ. Finally, we say that $\mathcal{D}$ admits L-definable canonization if $(\mathcal{D}, \cong)$ does.

Example 3.5.11. (**Definable canonization versus definability of order.**) Whenever $\mathcal{D}$ admits L-definable linear orders, and L is closed under first-order operations, $\mathcal{D}$ also admits L-definable canonization. This is obvious if the formula $\varphi_<$ defining the order has no parameters. If it uses parameters, then it may define, for each structure $\mathfrak{A}$, a *family* of ordered expansions $(\mathfrak{A}, <)$. But these expansions can be compared by use of the lexicographic order of their encodings. As L is closed under first-order operations, the minimal expansion with respect to this lexicographical order is L-definable, which gives an L-definable canonization.

Note, however, that there exist definable canonizations even in cases where no order is definable. Consider for instance the class of finite directed paths P_n (for $n \in \mathbb{N}$), and take their 'double graphs' (see Section 3.2.5), i.e. the graphs $2P_n = (V, E)$, where $V = \{0, \ldots, n-1\} \times \{0, 1\}$ and $E = \{\langle (m, i), (m+1, j) \rangle : 0 \leq m < n-1, i, j \in \{0, 1\}\}$. On this class, no order is definable in any logic and with any finite number of parameters (to see this use Exercise 3.5.4). However, the class admits DTC-definable canonization.

We shall explain the construction, which is uniform for all n, informally. The obvious equivalence relation on $2P_n$, where $(m, i) \sim (m', j)$ iff $m = m'$, is first-order definable, and so P_n is interpretable in $2P_n$. Further, the nodes 0 and $n-1$ are definable in P_n, and so $(C_n, 0)$, the directed n-cycle with a distinguished point, is interpretable in $2P_n$ as well. It therefore suffices to show that an ordered copy of $2P_n$ is interpretable in $(C_n, 0)$. We represent nodes of $2P_n$ by edges and inverse edges of C_n: the node $(m, 0)$ is represented in C_n by the pair $(m, m+1)$ and the node $(m, 1)$ by the pair $(m+1, m)$. The order on these pairs is

$$(0,1) < (1,0) < (1,2) < (2,1) < \cdots < (n-2, n-1) < (n-1, n-2).$$

The domain formula for the interpretation (of $2P_n$ in C_n) is $\delta(x, y) := Exy \vee Eyz$. It is not difficult to see that the edge relation and the linear order are definable using DTC operators. The details are left to the reader.

A simple but interesting example of definable canonization is tree canonization via fixed-point logic with counting.

Proposition 3.5.12. *The class of (directed) trees admits* (IFP + C)-*definable canonization.*

Proof. The interpretation I that we construct maps a tree $\mathcal{T} = (V, E)$ (with n nodes) to an ordered tree $I(\mathcal{T}) = (\{1, \ldots, n\}, E', <)$, where $<$ is the natural order. That is, the interpretation is one-dimensional, maps nodes to numbers, and is defined by the formulae $\delta(\mu) := \exists\nu(\nu < \mu)$, $\varphi_<(\mu, \nu) := \mu < \nu$, and a formula $\varphi_{E'}(\mu, \nu)$ that we do not explicitly construct.

The construction of E' is based on an inductively defined ternary relation $F \subseteq V \times \{1, \ldots, n\}^2$ that encodes the sequence of binary relations $F_v := \{(i, j) : (v, i, j) \in F\}$. For each node v of $\mathcal{T}$, let $\mathcal{T}_v$ denote the subtree of $\mathcal{T}$ with root v, and let $\mathcal{S}_v$ be the graph $(\{1, \ldots, |\mathcal{T}_v|\}, F_v)$. The construction will ensure that $\mathcal{S}_v$ is isomorphic to $\mathcal{T}_v$.

If v is a leaf, let $F_v = \emptyset$. Suppose now that v has children $v_1, \ldots, v_m$, and that the graphs $\mathcal{S}_{v_1}, \ldots, \mathcal{S}_{v_m}$ have already been constructed. To define $\mathcal{S}_v$, we compute the code words $w_i = \mathrm{code}(\mathcal{S}_{v_i}, <)$ (where $<$ is the natural order) and arrange them in lexicographic order. Now let $\mathcal{S}_v$ be the graph with nodes $1, \ldots, |\mathcal{T}_v|$, obtained by first taking a copy of the $\mathcal{S}_{v_i}$ with the smallest code word, then taking a copy of the second, and so on, and finally adding another node that is connected to the roots of the copies of the $\mathcal{S}_{v_i}$. Obviously, $\mathcal{S}_v$ determines F_v, and $\mathcal{S}_v \cong \mathcal{T}_v$.

It is clear that the inductive construction of F can be done via an (IFP + C)-formula $\psi_F(x, \mu, \nu)$. Now take $\varphi_{E'}(\mu, \nu) := \exists x \psi_F(x, \mu, \nu)$. $\square$

Theorem 3.5.13. *Let $\mathcal{D}$ be a domain of (finite) structures, and let L be a logic that captures PTIME on $\mathcal{D}^<$. If $\mathcal{D}$ admits L-definable canonization, then L captures PTIME on $\mathcal{D}$ also.*

Proof. Let $\mathcal{K} \in \mathcal{D}(\tau)$ be a model class tht is decidable in polynomial time, and let $\psi \in L(\tau \cup \{<\})$ be a formula defining $\mathcal{K}^<$ inside $\mathcal{D}^<(\tau)$. Further, let I be an $L[\tau, \tau \cup \{<\}]$-interpretation that defines a canonization on $\mathcal{D}(\tau)$. By the Interpretation Lemma,

$$\mathfrak{A} \models \psi^I \iff I(\mathfrak{A}) \models \psi \iff I(\mathfrak{A}) \in \mathcal{K}^< \iff \mathfrak{A} \in \mathcal{K}.$$

Hence L captures PTIME on $\mathcal{D}$. $\square$

This result is important because it has been shown, in particular in the work of Grohe [58–60], that a number of interesting domains admit canonization via fixed-point logic with counting (IFP + C). Among these are

(1) the domain of finite (labelled) trees (see Proposition 3.5.12);
(2) the class of planar graphs [58] and, more generally, any domain of structures, whose Gaifman graphs are embeddable in a fixed surface [59];
(3) any domain of structures of bounded tree width [60].

Corollary 3.5.14. (IFP + C) *captures* PTIME *on any of these domains.*

Further, the results extend to domains that can be reduced to any of the domains mentioned above by simple definable operations such as adding or deleting a vertex or edge. An example is that of nearly planar (or apex) graphs, which become planar when one vertex is removed.

3.5.3 Capturing PTIME up to Bisimulation

In mathematics, we consider isomorphic structures as identical. Indeed, it almost goes without saying that relevant mathematical notions do not distinguish between isomorphic objects. As classical algorithmic devices work on ordered *representations of structures* rather than the structures themselves, our capturing results rely on an ability to reason about canonical ordered representations of isomorphism classes of finite structures.

However, in many application domains of logic, structures are distinguished only up to equivalences coarser than isomorphism. Perhaps the best-known example is the modelling of the computational behaviour of (concurrent) programs by transition systems. The meaning of a program is usually not captured by a unique transition system. Rather, transition systems are distinguished only up to appropriate notions of behavioural equivalence, the most important of these being *bisimulation.*

In such a context, the idea of a logic capturing PTIME gets a new twist. One would like to express in a logic precisely those properties of structures that are

(1) decidable in polynomial time, and
(2) invariant under the notion of equivalence being studied.

Let us look at one specific problem in this context, the problem of bisimulation-invariant properties of transition systems.

Definition 3.5.15. Let $G = (V, (E_a)_{a \in A}, (P_b)_{b \in B})$ and $G' = (V', (E'_a)_{a \in A}, (P'_b)_{b \in B})$ be two transition systems of the same vocabulary. A **bisimulation** between G and G' is a non-empty relation $Z \subseteq V \times V'$, respecting the P_b in the sense that $v \in P_b$ iff $v' \in P'_b$, for all $b \in B$ and $(v, v') \in Z$, and satisfying the following back and forth conditions.

Forth. for all $(v, v') \in Z$, $a \in A$ and every w such that $(v, w) \in E_a$, there exists a w' such that $(v', w') \in E_a'$ and $(w, w') \in Z$.

Back. for all $(v, v') \in Z$, $a \in A$ and every w' such that $(v', w') \in E_a'$, there exists a w such that $(v, w) \in E_a$ and $(w, w') \in Z$.

A **rooted transition system** is a pair (G, u), where G is a transition system G and u is a node of G. Two rooted transition systems (G, u) and (G', u') are **bisimilar**, denoted by $G, u \sim G', u'$, if there is a bisimulation Z between G and G' with $(u, u') \in Z$.

Exercise 3.5.16 Bisimulation is a greatest fixed point. Prove that two nodes u, u' of a transition system G are bisimilar, i.e. $(G, u) \sim (G, u')$ if, and only if,

$$G \models [\mathbf{gfp}Rxy \ . \bigwedge_{b \in B} P_b x \leftrightarrow P_b y \wedge$$

$$\bigwedge_{a \in A} (\forall x' \ . \ E_a xx')(\exists y' \ . \ E_a yy')Rx'y' \wedge$$

$$\bigwedge_{a \in A} (\forall y' \ . \ E_a yy')(\exists x' \ . \ E_a xx')Rx'y'](u, u').$$

A class S of rooted transition systems is **invariant under bisimulation** if, whenever $(G, u) \in S$ and $(G, u) \sim (G', u')$, then also $(G', u') \in S$. We say that a class S of finite rooted transition systems is in **bisimulation-invariant PTIME** if it is invariant under bisimulation, and if there exists a polynomial-time algorithm deciding whether a given pair (G, u) belongs to S. A logic L is invariant under bisimulation if all L-definable properties of rooted transition systems are.

Exercise 3.5.17 Prove that ML, the modal μ-calculus L_μ, and the infinitary modal logic ML^∞ are invariant under bisimulation.

Clearly, $L_\mu \subseteq$ bisimulation-invariant PTIME. However, as pointed out in Section 3.3.3, L_μ is far too weak to *capture* this class, mainly because it is essentially a monadic logic. Instead, we have to consider a *multidimensional* variant L_μ^ω of L_μ.

But before we define this logic, we should explain the main technical step, which relies on definable canonization, but of course with respect to bisimulation rather than isomorphism. For simplicity of notation, we consider only transition systems with a single transition relation E. The extension to the case of several transition relations E_a is completely straightforward.

With a rooted transition system $G = (V, E, (P_b)_{b \in B}), u$, we associate a new transition system

$$G_u^\sim := (V_u^\sim, E^\sim, (P_b^\sim)_{b \in B}),$$

where $V_u^\sim$ is the set of all $\sim$-equivalence classes $[v]$ of nodes $v \in V$ that are reachable from u. More formally, let $[v]$ denote the bisimulation equivalence class of a node $v \in V$. Then

$$V_u^\sim := \{[v] : \text{there is a path in } G \text{ from } u \text{ to } v\}$$
$$P_b^\sim := \{[v] \in V_u^\sim : v \in P_b\}$$
$$E^\sim := \{([v], [w]) : (v, w) \in E\}.$$

As shown in the following exercise, the pair $G_u^\sim, [u]$ is, up to isomorphism, a *canonical representant* of the bisimulation equivalence class of G, u.

Exercise 3.5.18 Prove that (1) $(G, u) \sim (G_u^\sim, [u])$, and (2) if $(G, u) \sim (H, v)$, then $(G_u^\sim, [u]) \cong (H_v^\sim, [v])$.

It follows that a class S of rooted transition systems is bisimulation-invariant if and only if $S = \{(G, u) : (G_u^\sim, [u]) \in S\}$. Let $\mathcal{CR}^\sim$ be the domain of canonical representants of finite transition systems, i.e.

$$\mathcal{CR}^\sim := \{(G, u) : (G_u^\sim, [u]) \cong (G, u)\}.$$

Proposition 3.5.19. $\mathcal{CR}^\sim$ *admits LFP-definable linear orderings.*

Proof. We show that for every vocabulary $\tau = \{E\} \cup \{P_b : b \in B\}$, there exists a formula $\psi(x, y) \in \text{LFP}(\tau)$ which defines a linear order on every transition system in $\mathcal{CR}^\sim(\tau)$.

Recall that bisimulation equivalence on a transition system is a greatest fixed point. Its complement, bisimulation inequivalence, is a least fixed point, which is the limit of an increasing sequence $\not\sim_i$ defined as follows: $u \not\sim_0 v$ if u and v do not have the same atomic type, i.e. if there exists some b such that one of the nodes u, v has the property P_b and the other does not. Further, $u \not\sim_{i+1} v$ if the sets of $\sim_i$-classes that are reachable in one step from u and v are different. The idea is to refine this inductive process, by defining relations $\prec_i$ that order the $\sim_i$-classes. On the transition system itself, these relations are pre-orders. The inductive limit $\prec$ of the pre-orders $\prec_i$ defines a linear order of the bisimulation equivalence classes. But in transition systems in $\mathcal{CR}^\sim$, bisimulation classes have only one element, so $\prec$ actually defines a linear order on the set of nodes.

To make this precise, we choose an order on B and define $\prec_0$ by enumerating the $2^{|B|}$ atomic types with respect to the propositions P_b, i.e.

$$x \prec_0 y := \bigvee_{b \in B} \left(\neg P_b x \wedge P_b y \wedge \bigwedge_{b' < b} P_{b'} x \leftrightarrow P_{b'} y\right).$$

In what follows, $x \sim_i y$ can be taken as an abbreviation for $\neg(x \prec_i y \vee y \prec_i x)$, and similarly for $x \sim y$. We define $x \prec_{i+1} y$ by the condition that either $x \prec_i y$, or $x \sim_i y$ and the set of $\sim_i$-classes reachable from x is lexicographically smaller than the set of $\sim_i$-classes reachable from y. Note that this inductive definition of $\prec$ is not monotone, so it cannot be directly captured by an LFP-formula. However, as we know that LFP $\equiv$ IFP, we can use an IFP-formula instead. Explicitly, $\prec$ is defined by $[\mathbf{ifp}\, x \prec y \,.\, \psi(\prec, x, y)](x, y)$, where

$$\psi(\prec, x, y) := x \prec_0 y \vee \left(x \sim y \wedge \right.$$

$$(\exists y' . Eyy') \left((\forall x' . Exx') x' \not\sim y' \wedge \right.$$

$$(\forall z. z \prec y') (\exists x'' (Exx'' \wedge x'' \sim z) \leftrightarrow$$

$$\left. \left. \left. \exists y'' (Eyy'' \wedge y'' \sim z) \right) \right) \right).$$

$\square$

Exercise 3.5.20 Complete the proof by showing that the formula $[\mathbf{ifp} x \prec y . \psi(\prec, x, y)](x, y)$ indeed defines the order described above.

Corollary 3.5.21. *On the domain* $\mathcal{CR}^{\sim}$, *LFP captures* PTIME.

In fact, this result already suffices to give an *abstract capturing result* for bisimulation-invariant PTIME (in the sense of the following section): by composing the mapping from rooted transition systems to their canonical representants with LFP queries on these representants, we obtain an abstract logic with recursive syntax and polynomial-time semantics that describes precisely the polynomial-time computable, bisimulation-invariant queries on rooted transition systems.

In many situations (such as for polynomial time on arbitrary finite structures), we would actually be quite happy with such an abstract capturing result. However, in the bisimulation-invariant scenario we can do better and capture PTIME in terms of a natural logic, the multidimensional μ-calculus L_μ^ω.

Definition 3.5.22. The syntax of the k-**dimensional** μ-**calculus** L_μ^k (for transition systems $G = (V, E, (P_b)_{b \in B})$) is the same as the syntax of the usual μ-calculus L_μ with modal operators $\langle i \rangle$, $[i]$ for $a \in A, i = 1, \ldots, k$, and $\langle \sigma \rangle, [\sigma]$ for every substitution $\sigma : \{1, \ldots, k\} \to \{1, \ldots, k\}$. Let $S(k)$ be the set of all these substitutions.

The semantics is different, however. A formula ψ of L_μ^k is interpreted on a transition system $G = (V, E, (P_b)_{b \in B})$ at node v by evaluating it as a formula of L_μ on the modified transition system

$$G^k = (V^k, (E_i)_{1 \le i \le k}, (E_\sigma)_{\sigma \in S(k)}, (P_{b,i})_{b \in B, 1 \le i \le k})$$

at node $\underline{v} := (v, v, \ldots, v)$. Here $V^k = V \times \cdots \times V$ and

$$E_i := \{(\overline{v}, \overline{w}) \in V^k \times V^k : (v_i, w_i) \in E \text{ and } v_j = w_j \text{ for } j \ne i\}$$
$$E_\sigma := \{(\overline{v}, \overline{w}) \in V^k \times V^k : w_i = v_{\sigma(i)} \text{ for all } i\}$$
$$P_{b,i} := \{\overline{v} \in V^k : v_i \in P_b\}$$

That is, $G, v \models_{L_\mu^k} \psi$ iff $G^k, (v, \ldots, v) \models_{L_\mu} \psi$. The **multidimensional** μ-**calculus** is $L_\mu^\omega = \bigcup_{k < \omega} L_\mu^k$.

Remark. Instead of evaluating a formula $\psi \in L_\mu^k$ at single nodes v of G, we can also evaluate it at k-tuples of nodes: $G, \overline{v} \models_{L_\mu^k} \psi$ iff $G^k, \overline{v} \models_{L_\mu} \psi$.

Example 3.5.23. Bisimulation is definable in L_μ^2 (in the sense of the remark just made). Let

$$\psi^\sim := \nu X \, . \, \Big(\bigwedge_{b \in B} (P_{b,1} \leftrightarrow P_{b,2}) \wedge [1]\langle 2 \rangle X \wedge [2]\langle 1 \rangle X \Big).$$

For every transition system G, we have that $G, v_1, v_2 \models \psi^\sim$ if, and only if, v_1 and v_2 are bisimilar in G. Further, we have that

$$G, v \models \mu Y \, . \, \langle 2 \rangle (\psi^\sim \vee \langle 2 \rangle Y)$$

if, and only if, there exists in G a point w that is reachable from v (by a path of length ≥ 1) and bisimilar to v.

Exercise 3.5.24 Prove that L_μ^ω is invariant under bisimulation. Further, show that L_μ^ω can be embedded in LFP.

This exercise establishes the easy direction of the desired result: $L_\mu^\omega \subseteq$ bisimulation-invariant PTIME. For the converse, it suffices to show that LFP and L_μ^ω are equivalent on the domain $\mathcal{CR}^\sim$. Let S be a class of rooted transition systems in bisimulation-invariant PTIME. For any (G, u), we have that $(G, u) \in S$ if its canonical representant $(G_u^\sim, [u]) \in S$. If LFP and L_μ^ω are equivalent on $\mathcal{CR}^\sim$, then there exists a formula $\psi \in L_\mu^\omega$ such that $G_u^\sim, [u] \models \psi$ iff $(G_u^\sim, [u]) \in S$. By the bisimulation invariance of ψ, it follows that $G, u \models \psi$ iff $(G, u) \in S$.

Proposition 3.5.25. *On the domain $\mathcal{CR}^\sim$, LFP $\leq L_\mu^\omega$. More precisely, for each formula $\psi(x_1, \ldots, x_{k+1}) \in$ LFP of width $\leq k + 1$, there exists a formula $\psi^* \in L_\mu^{k+1}$ such that for each $(G, u) \in \mathcal{CR}^\sim$, we have that $G \models \psi(u, \overline{v})$ iff $G, u, \overline{v} \models \psi^*$.*

Note that although, ultimately, we are interested only in formulae $\psi(x)$ with just one free variable, we need more general formulae, and evaluation of L_μ^k-formulae over k-tuples of nodes, for the inductive treatment. In all formulae, we shall have at least x_1 as a free variable, and we always interpret x_1 as u (the root of the transition system). We remark that, by an obvious modification of the formula given in Exercise 3.5.23, we can express in L_μ^k the assertion that $x_i \sim x_j$ for any i, j.

Atomic formulae are translated from LFP to L_μ^ω according to

$$(x_i = x_j)^* := x_i \sim x_j$$
$$(P_b x_i)^* := P_{b,i} \overline{x}$$
$$(E x_i x_j)^* := \langle i \rangle x_i \sim x_j$$
$$(X x_{\sigma(1)} \cdots x_{\sigma(r)})^* := \langle \sigma \rangle X.$$

Boolean connectives are treated in the obvious way, and *quantifiers* are translated by use of fixed points. To find a witness x_j satisfying a formula ψ, we start at u (i.e. set $x_j = x_1$), and search along transitions (i.e. use the μ-expression for reachability). That is, let $j/1$ be the substitution that maps j to 1 and fixes the other indices, and translate $\exists x_j \psi(\overline{x})$ into

$$\langle j/1 \rangle \mu Y . \psi^* \vee \langle j \rangle Y.$$

Finally, *fixed points* are first brought into normal form so that variables appear in the right order, and then they are translated literally, i.e. $[\mathbf{lfp} X \overline{x} . \psi](\overline{x})$ translates into $\mu X . \psi^*$.

The proof that the translation has the desired property is a straightforward induction, which we leave as an exercise (see [90] for details). Altogether we have established the following result.

Theorem 3.5.26 (Otto). *The multidimensional μ-calculus captures bisimulation-invariant PTIME.*

Otto has also established capturing results with respect to other equivalences. For finite structures $\mathfrak{A}, \mathfrak{B}$, we say that $\mathfrak{A} \equiv_k \mathfrak{B}$ if no first-order sentence of width k can distinguish between $\mathfrak{A}$ and $\mathfrak{B}$. Similarly, $\mathfrak{A} \equiv_k^C \mathfrak{B}$ if $\mathfrak{A}$ and $\mathfrak{B}$ are indistinguishable by first-order sentences of width k with counting quantifiers of the form $\exists^{\geq i} x$, for any $i \in \mathbb{N}$.

Theorem 3.5.27 (Otto). *There exist logics that effectively capture $\equiv_2$-invariant PTIME and $\equiv_2^C$-invariant PTIME on the class of all finite structures.*

For details, see [89].

3.5.4 Is There a Logic for PTIME?

To discuss the problem of whether PTIME can be captured on the domain of *all* finite structures, we need to make precise the notion of a logic, and to refine the notion of a logic capturing a complexity class, so as to exclude pathological examples such the following, which is due to Gurevich [61].

Example 3.5.28. Let the syntax of our 'logic' consist of all pairs (M, k), where M is a Turing machine, and k a natural number. A finite τ-structure $\mathfrak{A}$ is a model of (M, k) if there exists a model class $\mathcal{K} \subseteq \mathrm{Fin}(\tau)$ such that $\mathfrak{A} \in \mathcal{K}$, and M accepts an encoding $code(\mathfrak{B}, <)$ of a finite τ-structure $\mathfrak{B}$ in time $|B|^k$ if, and only if, $\mathfrak{B} \in \mathcal{K}$. Note that this 'logic' captures PTIME on finite structures. But the example is pathological, not mainly because of its unusual format, but because its semantics is not effective: it is undecidable whether a Turing machine accepts an isomorphism-closed class of structures.

Another example of this kind is *order-invariant* LFP. The τ-sentences of this logic are the LFP-sentences of vocabulary $\tau \cup \{<\}$ such that, for all finite

τ-structures $\mathfrak{A}$ and all linear orders $<$, $<'$ on $\mathfrak{A}$, we have that $(\mathfrak{A}, <) \models \psi$ if and only if $(\mathfrak{A}, <') \models \psi$. This defines the syntax. The semantics is the obvious one: a structure $\mathfrak{A}$ is a model of ψ if, and only if, $(\mathfrak{A}, <) \models \psi$ for some, and hence all, linear orders on $\mathfrak{A}$. This 'logic' also captures PTIME, but again it has an undesirable feature: it is undecidable whether a given sentence $\psi \in$ LFP is order-invariant (compare Exercise 3.1.12), so the 'logic' does not have an effective syntax.

We start by defining a general notion of a logic on finite structures by imposing two requirements: an effective syntax and an isomorphism-invariant semantics.

Definition 3.5.29. A **logic** on a domain $\mathcal{D}$ of finite structures is a pair $(L, \models)$, where L is a function that assigns to each vocabulary τ a decidable set $L(\tau)$ (whose elements are called τ-sentences), and $\models$ is a binary relation between sentences and finite structures, so that for each sentence $\psi \in L(\tau)$, the class $\{\mathfrak{A} \in \mathcal{D}(\tau) : \mathfrak{A} \models \psi\}$ is closed under isomorphism.

Recall that, by Definition 3.2.10, a logic captures PTIME on a domain $\mathcal{D}$ if every polynomial-time decidable model class in $\mathcal{D}$ is definable in that logic, and if, for every sentence of the logic, the model-checking problem on $\mathcal{D}$ can be solved in polynomial time. To exclude pathological examples such the first one above, we impose in addition the condition that for each sentence, a polynomial-time model-checking algorithm can be effectively constructed.

Definition 3.5.30. A logic $(L, \models)$ **effectively captures** PTIME on a domain $\mathcal{D}$ of finite structures if it captures PTIME in the sense of Definition 3.2.10 and, moreover, there exists a computable function, which associates with every sentence $\psi \in L(\tau)$ an algorithm M and a polynomial p, such that M decides $\{\mathfrak{A} \in \mathcal{D}(\tau) : \mathfrak{A} \models \psi\}$ in time $p(n)$. We simply say that $(L, \models)$ effectively captures PTIME if it does so on the class of all finite structures.

This definition can be modified in the obvious way to other complexity classes. All capturing results that we have proved so far are effective in this sense.

Exercise 3.5.31 A complexity class $\mathcal{C}$ is **recursively indexable** on a domain $\mathcal{D}$ if there is a recursive index set I, a computable function f mapping every $i \in I$ to (the code of) a Turing machine M_i, and an appropriate resource bound (e.g. a polynomial bounding the running time of M_i) such that:

(1) The class $\mathcal{K}_i$ of all structures from $\mathcal{D}$ accepted by M_i is in $\mathcal{C}$, and, moreover, M_i together with the given resource bound witnesses the membership of $\mathcal{K}_i$ in the complexity class $\mathcal{C}$.
(2) For each model class $\mathcal{K} \in \mathcal{C}$ on the domain $\mathcal{D}$, there is an $i \in I$ such that M_i decides $\mathcal{K}$.

Prove that there is a logic that effectively captures C on the domain $\mathcal{D}$ if, and only if, C is recursively indexable on $\mathcal{D}$.

The above definition of a logic may seem too abstract for practical purposes. However, it is justified by the equivalence with recursive indexings, as described in the exercise above, and by a result of Dawar [32], which shows that if there is any logic that effectively captures PTIME, then there also exists a natural one. More precisely, Dawar proved that, from any logic effectively capturing PTIME, one could extract a model class $\mathcal{K}$ that is complete for PTIME under first-order reductions. As a consequence, PTIME would also be effectively captured by the logic $\mathrm{FO}[\mathcal{Q}_{\mathcal{K}}^{\omega}]$, which adjoins to FO the vectorized Lindstöm quantifiers associated with $\mathcal{K}$ (see [32, 38] for more information).

Exercise 3.5.32 Many finite-model theorists conjecture that there is no logic that effectively captures PTIME on finite structures. If you are the first to prove this, you may win one million dollars. Why?

3.6 Algorithmic Model Theory

3.6.1 Beyond Finite Structures

For a long time, descriptive complexity theory has been concerned almost exclusively with finite structures. Although important problems remain open, the relationship between definability and complexity on finite structures is now fairly well understood, and there are interesting connections to fields such as databases, knowledge representation, and computer-aided verification.

However, for many applications, the strict limitation to finite structures is too restrictive. In most of the fields mentioned above, there have been considerable efforts to extend the relevant methodology from finite structures to suitable domains of infinite ones. In particular, this is the case for databases and computer-aided verification where infinite structures (like constraint databases or transition systems with infinite state spaces) are of increasing importance.

Finite model theory should therefore be generalized to a more comprehensive *algorithmic model theory* that extends the research programme, the general approach, and the methods of finite model theory to interesting domains of infinite structures. From a more general theoretical point of view, one may ask what domains of infinite structures are suitable for such an extension. More specifically, one may ask what conditions must be satisfied by a domain $\mathcal{D}$ of structures that are not necessarily finite such that the approach and methods of finite model theory make sense. There are two obvious and fundamental conditions:

Finite representations. Every structure $\mathfrak{A} \in \mathcal{D}$ should be representable in a finite way (e.g. by a binary string, an algorithm, a collection of automata, an axiomatization in some logic, an interpretation, ...).

Effective semantics. For the relevant logics (e.g. first-order logic), the model-checking problem on $\mathcal{D}$ should be decidable. That is, given a sentence $\psi \in L$ and a representation of a structure $\mathfrak{A} \in \mathcal{D}$, it should be decidable whether $\mathfrak{A} \models \psi$.

These are just minimal requirements, which may need to be refined according to the context and the questions to be considered. We may, for instance, also require the following:

Closure. For every structure $\mathfrak{A} \in \mathcal{D}$ and every formula $\psi(\overline{x})$, the expansion $(\mathfrak{A}, \psi^{\mathfrak{A}})$ of $\mathfrak{A}$ with the relation defined by ψ, should as well be contained in $\mathcal{D}$.

Effective query evaluation. Suppose that we have fixed a way of representing structures. Given a representation of $\mathfrak{A} \in \mathcal{D}$ and a formula $\psi(\overline{x})$, we should be able to compute a representation of $\psi^{\mathfrak{A}}$ (or of the expanded structure $(\mathfrak{A}, \psi^{\mathfrak{A}})$).

Note that, contrary to the case of finite structures, query evaluation does not necessarily reduce to model checking. Further, instead of just effectiveness of these tasks, it may be required that they can be performed within some complexity bounds.

3.6.2 Finitely Presentable Structures

We briefly survey here some domains of infinite but finitely presentable structures which may be relevant to algorithmic model theory. We shall then discuss in a more detailed way *metafinite structures*, for which descriptive complexity issues have already been studied quite intensively.

Recursive structures are countable structures whose functions and relations are computable and therefore finitely presentable. They have been studied quite intensively in model theory since the 1960s (see e.g. [6, 42]). Although recursive model theory is very different from finite model theory, there have been some papers studying classical issues of finite model theory on recursive structures and recursive databases [50, 64, 65, 94]. However, for most applications, the domain of recursive structures is far too large. In general, only quantifier-free formulae admit effective evaluation algorithms.

Constraint databases provide a database model that admits infinite relations that are finitely presented by quantifier-free formulae (constraints) over some fixed background structure. For example, to store geometrical data, it is useful not just to have a finite set as the universe of the database, but to include all real numbers 'in the background'. Also, the presence of interpreted functions on the real numbers, such as addition and multiplication, is desirable. The constraint database framework introduced by Kanellakis, Kuper, and Revesz [74] meets both requirements. Formally, a constraint database consists of a *context structure* $\mathfrak{A}$, such as $(\mathbb{R}, <, +, \cdot)$, and a set $\{\varphi_1, \ldots, \varphi_m\}$ of quantifier-free formulae defining the database relations. Constraint databases are treated in detail in [81] and in Chap. 5 of this book.

Automatic structures are structures whose functions and relations are represented by finite automata. Informally, a relational structure $\mathfrak{A} = (A, R_1, \ldots, R_m)$ is automatic if we can find a regular language $L_\delta \subseteq \Sigma^*$ (which provides names for the elements of $\mathfrak{A}$) and a function $\nu : L_\delta \to A$ mapping every word $w \in L_\delta$ to the element of $\mathfrak{A}$ that it represents. The function ν must be surjective (every element of $\mathfrak{A}$ must be named) but need not be injective (elements can have more than one name). In addition, it must be recognizable by finite automata (reading their input words synchronously) whether two words in L_δ name the same elements, and, for each relation R_i of $\mathfrak{A}$, whether a given tuple of words in L_δ names a tuple in R_i.

Example 3.6.1. (1) All finite structures are automatic.

(2) Some important examples of automatic structures are Presburger arithmetic $(\mathbb{N}, +)$, and its expansions $\mathfrak{N}_p := (\mathbb{N}, +, |_p)$ by the relation $x \mid_p y$ which says that x is a power of p dividing y. Using p-ary encodings (starting with the least significant digit), it is not difficult to construct automata recognizing equality, addition, and $|_p$.

(3) For $p \in \mathbb{N}$, let $Tree(p) := (\{0, \ldots, p-1\}^*, (\sigma_i)_{i<p}, <, \mathrm{el})$, where $\sigma_i(x) := xi$, $x < y$ means that $xz = y$ for some z, and $\mathrm{el}(x, y)$ means that x and y have equal length. Obviously, these structures are automatic as well.

Automatic structures provide a vast playground for finite-model theorists, with many examples of high relevance to computer science. There are also interesting connections to computational group theory, where *automatic groups* have already been studied quite intensively [41, 44]. The general notion of structures presentable by automata was proposed in [75], and their theory has been developed in [16, 18, 19, 92].

The notion of an automatic structure can be modified and generalized in many directions. By using automata over infinite words, we obtain the notion of ω**-automatic structures** (which, unlike automatic structures, may have uncountable cardinality).

Example 3.6.2. (1) All automatic structures are ω-automatic.

(2) The additive group of reals, $(\mathbb{R}, +)$, and indeed the expanded structure $\mathfrak{R}_p := (\mathbb{R}, +, \leq, |_p, 1)$ are ω-automatic, where

$$x \mid_p y \text{ iff } x = p^n \text{ and } y = kx \text{ for some } n, k \in \mathbb{Z}.$$

(3) The tree structures $Tree(p)$ can be extended in a natural way to the (uncountable) ω-automatic structures $Tree^\omega(p) = (\{0, \ldots, p-1\}^{\leq \omega}, (\sigma_i)_{i<p}, \preceq, \mathrm{el})$.

Unlike the class of recursive structures, automatic structures and ω-automatic structures admit effective (in fact, automatic) evaluation of all first-order queries and possess many other pleasant algorithmic properties.

Theorem 3.6.3. *The model checking problems for first-order logic on the domains of automatic or ω-automatic structures are decidable.*

There are a number of extensions of this result, for instance to the extension of first-order logic by the quantifier 'there exist infinitely many' [19]. There also are model-theoretic characterizations of automatic and ω-automatic structures, in terms of *interpretations* into appropriate expansions of Presburger arithmetic, trees, or the additive group of reals (see Examples 3.6.1 and 3.6.2). We write $\mathfrak{A} \leq_{\mathrm{FO}} \mathfrak{B}$ to denote that there exists a first-order interpretation of $\mathfrak{A}$ in $\mathfrak{B}$. Note that the domains of automatic and ω-automatic structures are closed under fist-order interpretations.

Theorem 3.6.4 (Blumensath and Grädel). *(1) For every structure $\mathfrak{A}$, the following are equivalent:*

(i) $\mathfrak{A}$ is automatic.
(ii) $\mathfrak{A} \leq_{\mathrm{FO}} \mathfrak{N}_p$ for some (and hence all) $p \geq 2$.
(iii) $\mathfrak{A} \leq_{\mathrm{FO}} \mathrm{Tree}(p)$ for some (and hence all) $p \geq 2$.

(2) For every structure $\mathfrak{A}$, the following are equivalent:

(i) $\mathfrak{A}$ is ω-automatic.
(ii) $\mathfrak{A} \leq_{\mathrm{FO}} \mathfrak{R}_p$ for some (and hence all) $p \geq 2$.
(iii) $\mathfrak{A} \leq_{\mathrm{FO}} \mathrm{Tree}^\omega(p)$ for some (and hence all) $p \geq 2$.

For a proof, see [19] There are similar characterizations for tree-automatic structures [16]. For further results on automatic structures, see [10, 16, 18, 19, 75–78, 92].

The model-theoretic characterizations of automatic and ω-automatic structures in terms of interpretability suggest a general way to obtain other domains of infinite structures that may be interesting for algorithmic model theory: fix a structure $\mathfrak{A}$ with 'nice' (algorithmic and/or model-theoretic) properties and an appropriate notion of interpretation, and consider the class of all structures that are interpretable in $\mathfrak{A}$. Obviously, each structure in this class is finitely presentable (by an interpretation). Further, many 'nice' properties are preserved by interpretations, and so every structure in the class inherits them from $\mathfrak{A}$. In particular, every class of queries that is effective on $\mathfrak{A}$ and closed under first-order operations is effective on the closure of $\mathfrak{A}$ under first-order interpretations. This approach is also relevant to the domain of structures that we discuss next.

Tree-interpretable structures are structures that are interpretable in the infinite binary tree $T^2 = (\{0, 1\}^*, \sigma_0, \sigma_1)$ via a (one-dimensional) MSO-interpretation. By Rabin's Theorem, monadic second-order formulae can be effectively evaluated on T^2. Since MSO is closed under one-dimensional interpretations, the Interpretation Lemma implies that tree-interpretable structures admit effective evaluation for MSO. Tree-interpretable structures generalize various notions of infinite graphs that have been studied in logic, automata theory and, verification. Some examples are **context-free graphs** [87, 88], which are the configuration graphs of pushdown automata, **HR-equational** and **VR-equational graphs** [27], which are defined via

certain graph grammars, and **prefix-recognizable graphs** [25], which can
for instance be defined as graphs of the form $(V, (E_a)_{a \in A})$, where V is a regular language and each edge relation E_a is a finite union of sets $X(Y \times Z) =$
$\{(xy, xz) : x \in X, y \in Y, z \in Z\}$, for regular languages X, Y, Z. In fact, some
of these classes coincide with the class of tree-interpretable graphs (see [17]).

Theorem 3.6.5. *For any graph* $G = (V, (E_a)_{a \in A})$, *the following are
equivalent:*

(i) G is tree-interpretable.
(ii) G is VR-equational.
(iii) G is prefix-recognizable.
*(iv) G is the restriction to a regular set of the configuration graph of a
    pushdown automaton with ε-transitions.*

On the other hand, the classes of context-free graphs and of HR-equational
graphs are strictly contained in the class of tree-interpretable graphs.

Exercise 3.6.6 Prove that every tree-interpretable structure is automatic. Is
the converse also true?

Tree-Constructible Structures: the Caucal Hierarchy

The question arises of whether there are even more powerful domains than the
tree-interpretable structures on which monadic second-order logic is effective.
An interesting way to obtain such domains is to use tree constructions that
associate with any structure a kind of tree unravelling. A simple variant is
the **unfolding** of a labelled graph G from a given node v to the tree $T(G, v)$.
Courcelle and Walukiewicz [28, 29] have shown that the MSO-theory of
$T(G, v)$ can be effectively computed from the MSO-theory of (G, v). A more
general operation, applicable to relational structures of any kind, has been
invented by Muchnik. Given a relational structure $\mathfrak{A} = (A, R_1, \ldots, R_m)$,
let its **iteration** $\mathfrak{A}^* = (A^*, R_1^*, \ldots, R_m^*, suc, clone)$ be the structure with
universe A^*, relations $R_i^* = \{(wa_1, \ldots, wa_r) : w \in A^*, (a_1, \ldots, a_r) \in R_i\}$,
the successor relation $suc = \{(w, wa) : w \in A^*, a \in A\}$, and the predicate
clone consisting of all elements of the form waa. It is not difficult to see
that unfoldings of graphs are first-order interpretable in their iterations.
Muchnik's Theorem states that the monadic theory of $\mathfrak{A}^*$ is decidable if the
monadic theory of $\mathfrak{A}$ is so (for proofs, see [11, 101]). We define the domain
of **tree-constructible structures** to be the closure of the domain of finite
structures under (one-dimensional) MSO-interpretations and iterations. By
Muchnik's Theorem, and since effective MSO model checking is preserved
under interpretations, the tree constructible structures are finitely presentable
and admit effective evaluation of MSO-formulae.

The tree-constructible graphs form the **Caucal hierarchy**, which was
defined in [26] in a slighly different way. The definition is easily extended to

arbitrary structures: let $\mathcal{C}_0$ be the class of finite structures, and let $\mathcal{C}_{n+1}$ be the class of structures that are interpretable in the iteration $\mathfrak{A}^*$ of a structure $\mathfrak{A} \in \mathcal{C}_n$. There are a number of different, but equivalent, ways to define the levels of the Caucal hierarchy. For instance, one can use the inverse rational mappings given in [25] rather than monadic interpretations, and simple unfoldings rather than iterations without changing the hierarchy [24]. Equivalently, the hierarchy can be defined via higher-order pushdown automata. It is known that the Caucal hierarchy is strict, and that it does not exhaust the class of all structures with a decidable MSO-theory. We refer to [24, 98] for details and further information.

3.6.3 Metafinite Structures.

The class of infinite structures for which descriptive complexity theory has been studied most intensively is the class of the metafinite structures, proposed by Grädel and Gurevich [48], and studied also in [30, 49, 53, 84]. These structures are somewhat reminiscent of the two-sorted structures that we used to define fixed-point logic with counting, (IFP + C). There, the second sort was a finite linear order ($\{0, \ldots, n\}, <$). Metafinite structures are similar two-sorted structures, with the essential differences that (1) the numerical sort need not be finite, (2) the structures may contain functions from the first to the second sort, and (3) operations more general than counting are considered.

Definition 3.6.7. A (simple) **metafinite structure** is a triple $\mathfrak{D} = (\mathfrak{A}, \mathfrak{R}, W)$ consisting of the following:

(i) A finite structure $\mathfrak{A}$, called the primary part of $\mathfrak{D}$.
(ii) A finite or infinite structure $\mathfrak{R}$, called the secondary (or numerical) part of $\mathfrak{D}$. We always assume that $\mathfrak{R}$ contains two distinguished elements 0 and 1 (or *true* and *false*).
(iii) A finite set W of functions $w : A^k \to R$.

The *vocabulary* of $\mathfrak{D}$ is the triple $\tau(\mathfrak{D}) = (\tau_a, \tau_r, \tau_w)$, where each component of $\tau(\mathfrak{D})$ is the set of relation or function symbols in the corresponding component of $\mathfrak{D}$. (We always consider constants as functions of arity 0.) The two distinguished elements 0, 1 of $\mathfrak{R}$ are named by constants of τ_r.

Example 3.6.8. (ℝ-**structures**) The descriptive complexity theory over the real numbers developed by Grädel and Meer [53] (see Sect. 3.6.5) is based on ℝ-structures, which are simple metafinite structure with a secondary part $\mathfrak{R} = (\mathbb{R}, +, -, \cdot, /, \leq, (c_r)_{r \in \mathbb{R}})$. It is convenient to include subtraction and division as primitive operations and assume that every element $r \in \mathbb{R}$ is named by a constant c_r, so that any rational function $g : \mathbb{R}^k \to \mathbb{R}$ (i.e. any quotient of two polynomials) can be written as a term.

There are many variations of metafinite structures. An important one is **metafinite structures with multiset operations.** Any function $f : A \to R$

defines a multiset $\text{mult}(f) = \{\!\{f(a) : a \in A\}\!\}$ over R (where the notation $\{\!\{\ldots\}\!\}$ indicates that we may have multiple occurrences of the same element). For any set R, let $\text{fm}(R)$ denote the class of all finite multisets over R. In some of the metafinite structures that we consider, the secondary part $\mathfrak{R}$ is not just a (first-order) structure in the usual sense, but instead it comes with a collection of *multiset operations* $\Gamma : \text{fm}(R) \to R$, mapping finite multisets over R to elements of R. Some natural examples on, say, the real numbers are addition, multiplication, counting, mean, maximum, and minimum. The use of multiset operations will become clearer when we introduce logics for metafinite structures. Let us just remark that multiset operations are a natural way to make precise the notion of *aggregates* in database query languages such as SQL.

Example 3.6.9. (Arithmetical structures). Of particular interest to us are metafinite structures, whose secondary part is a structure $\mathfrak{N}$ over the natural numbers such that

- $\mathfrak{N}$ includes at least the constants 0, 1, the functions $+, \cdot$, the ordering relation $<$, and the multiset operations $\max, \min, \sum$ (sum), and $\prod$ (product).
- All functions, relations, and multiset operations of $\mathfrak{N}$ can be evaluated in polynomial time.

We call metafinite structures of this kind **arithmetical structures**. A *simple arithmetical structure* is obtained from an arithmetical structure by omitting the multiset operations.

By itself, the notion of metafinite structures contains nothing revolutionary: they are just a special kind of two-sorted structures. The interesting feature of metafinite model theory is not just the structures themselves, but the logics, which access the primary and the secondary part in different ways and are designed so that the approach and methods of finite model theory remain meaningful and applicable. An important feature of these logics is that they contain, besides formulae and terms in the usual sense, a calculus of *weight terms* from the primary to the secondary part.

Definition 3.6.10. Let L be any of the logics for finite structures, such as FO, LFP, ... as described in the previous sections, and let $\tau = (\tau_a, \tau_r, \tau_w)$ be a vocabulary for metafinite structures (where τ_r may or may not have names for multiset operations). The appropriate modification of L for reasoning about metafinite structures $\mathfrak{D} = (\mathfrak{A}, \mathfrak{R}, W)$ of vocabulary τ is defined as follows. We fix a countable set $V = \{x_0, x_1, \ldots\}$ of variables *ranging over elements of the primary part A only*. The **point terms** (defining functions $f : A^k \to A$), the **weight terms** (defining functions $w : A^k \to R$), and the **formulae** (defining relations $R \subseteq A^k$) of $L[\tau]$ are defined inductively as follows:

(1) Point terms are defined in the usual way, by closing the set of variables V under application of function symbols from τ_a.

(2) Weight terms can be built by applying weight function symbols from τ_w to point terms, and function symbols from τ_r to previously defined weight terms. Note that there are no variables ranging over R.

(3) Atomic formulae are equalities of point terms, equalities of weight terms, expressions $Pt_1 \cdots t_r$ containing relations symbols $P \in \tau_a$ and point terms $t_1, \ldots, t_r$, or expressions $Qf_1 \cdots f_r$ containing predicates $Q \in \tau_r$ and weight terms $f_1, \ldots, f_r$.

(4) All the rules of L for building formulae (via propositional connectives, quantifiers, and other operators) may be applied, taking into account the condition that only variables from V may be used.

(5) In addition, we have the **characteristic function rule**: if $\varphi(\overline{x})$ is a formula, then $\chi[\varphi](\overline{x})$ is a weight term.

(6) If τ_w contains **multiset operations**, these provide additional means for building new weight terms. Let $F(\overline{x}, \overline{y})$ be a weight term, $\varphi(\overline{x}, \overline{y})$ a formula (both with free variables among $\overline{x}, \overline{y}$), and Γ a multiset operation. The expression

$$\Gamma_{\overline{x}}(F(\overline{x}, \overline{y}) : \varphi)$$

is then a weight term with free variables $\overline{y}$. (If $\varphi = true$, we simplify this notation to $\Gamma_{\overline{x}}F(\overline{x}, \overline{y})$.)

The semantics for (1)–(4) is the obvious one. A term $\chi[\varphi](\overline{x})$ evaluates to 1 if $\varphi(\overline{x})$ is true, and to 0 otherwise. Finally, let $G(\overline{y})$ be a weight term $\Gamma_{\overline{x}}(F(\overline{x}, \overline{y}) : \varphi)$ formed by application of a multiset operation. The weight term $F(\overline{x}, \overline{y})$ defines, on a metafinite structure $\mathfrak{D} = (\mathfrak{A}, \mathfrak{R}, W)$, a function $F^{\mathfrak{D}} : A^{k+m} \to R$. For any fixed tuple $\overline{b}$, the collection of values $F^{\mathfrak{D}}(\overline{a}, \overline{b})$, as $\overline{a}$ ranges over those tuples such that $\varphi(\overline{a}, \overline{b})$ is *true*, forms a finite multiset

$$(F : \varphi)^{\mathfrak{D}}(\overline{b}) := \{\!\!\{ F^{\mathfrak{D}}(\overline{a}, \overline{b}) : \overline{a} \in A^k \text{ such that } \mathfrak{D} \models \varphi(\overline{a}, \overline{b}) \}\!\!\}.$$

The interpretation of $G(\overline{b})$ on $\mathfrak{D}$ is obtained by applying Γ to this multiset, i.e.

$$G^{\mathfrak{D}}(\overline{b}) := \Gamma((F : \varphi)^{\mathfrak{D}}(\overline{b})).$$

Example 3.6.11. (Binary representations.) Consider arithmetic structures with a primary part of the form $\mathfrak{A} = (\{0, \ldots, n-1\}, <, P)$ where P is a unary relation. P is interpreted as a bit sequence $u_0 \cdots u_{n-1}$ representing the natural number $\sum_{i=0}^{n-1} u_i 2^i$ (where $u_i = 1$ iff $\mathfrak{A} \models P(i)$). The number represented by P is definable by the term

$$\sum_x \left(\chi[Px] \prod_y (2 : y < x) \right).$$

Example 3.6.12. (Counting elements.) On arithmetic structures, first-order logic can count. For any formula $\varphi(\overline{x})$, there is a weight term $\#_{\overline{x}}[\varphi(\overline{x})]$ counting the number of tuples $\overline{a}$ such that $\varphi(\overline{a})$ is true, namely

$$\#_{\overline{x}}[\varphi(\overline{x})] := \sum_{\overline{x}} \chi[\varphi].$$

3.6.4 Metafinite Spectra

Does descriptive complexity theory generalize in a meaningful way from finite to metafinite structures? To give some evidence that such generalizations are indeed possible and fruitful, we focus here on generalizations of Fagin's Theorem to (1) arithmetical structures, and (2) $\mathbb{R}$-structures (see the examples given above).

Recall that Fagin's Theorem says that generalized spectra (or, equivalently, the properties of finite structures that are definable in existential second-order logic) coincide with the complexity class NP. To discuss possible translations to metafinite structures, we need to make precise two notions:

- The notion of a **metafinite spectrum**, i.e. a generalized spectrum of metafinite structures.
- The notion of complexity (in particular, deterministic and non-deterministic polynomial time) in the context of metafinite structures.

For a fixed structure $\mathfrak{R}$, let $M_\tau[\mathfrak{R}]$ denote the class of metafinite structures with a secondary part $\mathfrak{R}$ and vocabulary $\tau = (\tau_a, \tau_r, \tau_w)$ (where, of course, τ_r is the vocabulary of $\mathfrak{R}$). We start with two notions of metafinite spectra.

Definition 3.6.13. A class $\mathcal{K} \subseteq M_\tau[\mathfrak{R}]$ is a **metafinite spectrum** if there exists a first-order sentence ψ of a vocabulary $\tau' \supseteq \tau$ such that $\mathfrak{D} \in \mathcal{K}$ if and only if there exists an expansion $\mathfrak{D}' \in M_{\tau'}[\mathfrak{R}]$ of $\mathfrak{D}$ with $\mathfrak{D}' \models \psi$. (Note that the secondary part is not expanded.) A **primary metafinite spectrum** is defined in a similar way, except that only the primary part of the structures is expanded, and not the set of weight functions. This means that the expanded structures $\mathfrak{D}'$ have the same set of weight functions as $\mathfrak{D}$.

These two notions of metafinite spectra correspond to two variants of **existential second-order logic**. The more restrictive variant allows second-order quantification over primary relations only, whereas the general one allows quantification over weight functions as well. Thus, a primary metafinite spectrum is the class of structures $\mathfrak{D} \in M_\tau[\mathfrak{R}]$ which are models of an existential second-order sentence of the form $\exists R_1 \cdots \exists R_m \psi$, where $R_1, \ldots, R_m$ are relation variables over the primary part, and ψ is first-order. Since relations over the primary part can be replaced by their characteristic functions, a metafinite spectrum in the more general sense is the class of models of a sentence $\exists F_1 \cdots \exists F_m \psi$, where the F_i are function symbols ranging over weight functions. We shall see that both notions of metafinite spectra capture (suitable variants of) non-deterministic polynomial-time in certain contexts, but fail to do so in others.

In general, the notion of *complexity* for problems on metafinite strucures depends on the computation model used and on the **cost** (or **size**) associated with the elements of the secondary part. For instance, if the secondary part consists of natural numbers or binary strings, then a natural notion of cost is given by the number of bits. On the other hand, below we shall study complexity over real numbers with respect to the Blum–Shub–Smale model, and there every element of $\mathbb{R}$ will be treated as a basic entity of cost one.

Let $\|r\|$ denote the cost of r. For a metafinite structure $\mathfrak{D} = (\mathfrak{A}, \mathfrak{R}, W) \in M_\tau[\mathfrak{R}]$, let $|\mathfrak{D}| := |\mathfrak{A}|$ and let $\max \mathfrak{D} := \max_{w \in W} \max_{\overline{a}} \|w(\overline{a})\|$, the cost of the maximal weight. Assuming $\mathfrak{R}$ and τ to be fixed, then $\|\mathfrak{D}\|$, the cost of representing $\mathfrak{D}$, is polynomially bounded in $|\mathfrak{A}|$ and $\max \mathfrak{D}$ (via a polynomial that depends only on the vocabulary of $\mathfrak{D}$). Since most of the popular complexity classes are invariant under polynomial increase of the relevant input parameters, it therefore makes sense to measure the complexity in terms of $|\mathfrak{D}|$ and $\max \mathfrak{D}$. For instance, an algorithm on a class of metafinite structures runs in polynomial time or in logarithmic space if, for every input $\mathfrak{D}$, the computation terminates in at most $q(|\mathfrak{D}|, \max \mathfrak{D})$ steps, for some polynomial q, or uses at most $O(\log |\mathfrak{D}| + \log \max \mathfrak{D})$ of work space, respectively.

We first discuss arithmetical structures, as described in Example 3.6.9, assuming that the cost of natural numbers is given by the length of their binary representations. So the question is whether, or under what circumstances, NP is captured by the class of metafinite spectra or primary metafinite spectra. The original proof of Fagin's Theorem generalizes to the case of arithmetical structures with weights that are not too large.

Definition 3.6.14. A class $\mathcal{K}$ of metafinite structures has **small weights** if there exists a $k \in \mathbb{N}$ such that $\max \mathfrak{D} \leq |\mathfrak{D}|^k$ for all $\mathfrak{D} \in \mathcal{K}$. As $\max \mathfrak{D}$ stands for the *cost* of the largest weight this means that the values of the weights are bounded by a function $2^{p(|\mathfrak{D}|)}$ for some polynomial p.

We obtain the following first generalization of Fagin's result.

Theorem 3.6.15 (Grädel and Gurevich). *Let $\mathcal{K} \subseteq M_\tau[\mathfrak{N}]$ be a class of arithmetical structures with small weights which is closed under isomorphisms. The following are equivalent:*

(i) $\mathcal{K}$ is in NP.
(ii) $\mathcal{K}$ is a primary generalized spectrum.

Proof. It is obvious that *(ii)* implies *(i)*. The converse can be reduced to Fagin's Theorem as follows. We assume that for every structure $\mathfrak{D} = (\mathfrak{A}, \mathfrak{N}, W)$ in $\mathcal{K}$, we have that $\max \mathfrak{D} \leq n^k$, where $n = |\mathfrak{D}| = |\mathfrak{A}|$; further, we suppose without loss of generality, that an ordering $<$ on A is available (otherwise we expand the vocabulary with a binary relation $<$ and add a conjunct $\beta(<)$ asserting that $<$ is a linear order). We can then identify A^k with the initial subset $\{0, \ldots, n^k - 1\}$ of $\mathbb{N}$, viewed as bit positions of the binary representations of the weights of $\mathfrak{D}$. With every $\mathfrak{D} \in \mathcal{K}$ we associate a finite structure $\mathfrak{D}_f$ by expanding the primary part $\mathfrak{A}$ as follows: for every weight function $w \in W$ of arity j, we add a new relation P_w of arity $j + k$, where

$$P_w := \{(\overline{a}, \overline{t}) : \text{ the } \overline{t}\text{th bit of } w(\overline{a}) \text{ is } 1\}.$$

Then $\mathcal{K}$ is in NP if and only if $\mathcal{K}_f = \{\mathfrak{D}_f : \mathfrak{D} \in \mathcal{K}\}$ is an NP-set of finite structures, and, in fact, we can choose the encodings in such a way that $\mathfrak{D}$ and $\mathfrak{D}_f$ are represented by the same binary string. Thus, if $\mathcal{K}$ is in NP, then, by Fagin's Theorem, $\mathcal{K}_f$ is a generalized spectrum, defined by a first-order sentence ψ.

As in Example 3.6.11, one can construct a first-order sentence α (whose vocabulary consists of the weight functions $w \in \tau_w$ and the corresponding primary relations P_w) which expresses the assertion that the P_w encode the weight functions w in the sense defined above. Then $\psi \wedge \alpha$ is a first-order sentence witnessing that $\mathcal{K}$ is a primary metafinite spectrum. $\qquad\square$

The above result also holds for arithmetical structures without multiset operations. However, without the restriction that the weights are small, it is no longer true that every NP-set is a primary metafinite spectrum. If we have inputs with huge weights compared with the primary part, then relations over the primary part cannot code enough information to describe computations that are bounded by a polynomial in the length of the weights.

It is tempting to use unrestricted metafinite spectra instead. However, metafinite spectra in the general sense capture a much larger class than NP.

Theorem 3.6.16 (Grädel and Gurevich). *On arithmetical structures, metafinite spectra capture the recursively enumerable sets.*

We sketch the proof here. It is not difficult to show that every metafinite spectrum of arithmetical structures is recursively enumerable. For the converse, we first note that any tuple $\bar{a} \in \mathbb{N}^k$ can be viewed as an arithmetical structure with an empty primary vocabulary and k nullary weight functions $a_1, \ldots, a_k$. Thus an arithmetical relation $S \subseteq \mathbb{N}^k$ can be viewed as a special class of arithmetical structures. We show first that every recursively enumerable set $S \subseteq \mathbb{N}^k$ is a metafinite spectrum. In particular, there exist undecidable metafinite spectra.

By Matijasevich's Theorem (see [83]), every recursively enumerable set $S \subseteq \mathbb{N}^k$ is Diophantine, i.e. can be represented as

$$S = \{\bar{a} \in \mathbb{N}^k : \text{ there exists } b_1, \ldots, b_m \in \mathbb{N} \text{ such that } Q(\bar{a}, \bar{b}) = 0\}$$

for some polynomial $Q \in \mathbb{Z}[x_1, \ldots, x_k, y_1, \ldots, y_m]$. Let $P, P' \in \mathbb{N}[\bar{x}, \bar{y}]$ such that $Q(\bar{x}, \bar{y}) = P(\bar{x}, \bar{y}) - P'(\bar{x}, \bar{y})$. Thus S is a metafinite spectrum; the desired first-order sentence uses additional weight functions $b_1, \ldots, b_m$ and asserts that $P(\bar{a}, \bar{b}) = P'(\bar{a}, \bar{b})$.

This can be extended to any recursively enumerable class of arithmetical structures, with an arbitrary vocabulary. To see this, we encode structures $\mathfrak{D} \subseteq M_\tau[\mathfrak{N}]$ by tuples $c(\mathfrak{D}) \in \mathbb{N}^k$, where k depends only on τ. (In fact, it is no problem to reduce k to 1.) Similarly to the case of finite structures, an encoding involves the selection of a linear order on the primary part. In fact, it is often more convenient to have a **ranking** of the primary part rather than just a linear ordering.

Definition 3.6.17. Suppose that $\mathfrak{R}$ contains a copy of $(\mathbb{N}, <)$. A **ranking** of a metafinite structure $\mathfrak{D} = (\mathfrak{A}, \mathfrak{R}, W)$ is a bijection $r : A \to \{0, \dots, n-1\} \subseteq R$. A class $\mathcal{K} \subseteq M_\tau[\mathfrak{R}]$ is **ranked** if τ contains a weight function r whose interpretation on every $\mathfrak{D} \in \mathcal{K}$ is a ranking.

The **Coding Lemma** for arithmetical structures [48] says that for every vocabulary τ there exists an encoding function that associates with every ranked arithmetical τ-structure $\mathfrak{D}$ a tuple $code(\mathfrak{D}) \in \mathbb{N}^k$ with the following properties:

(1) $code$ is definable by first-order terms.
(2) The primary part and the weight functions of $\mathfrak{D}$ can be reconstructed from $code(\mathfrak{D})$ in polynomial time.
(3) There exists a polynomial $p(n, m)$ such that $c_i(\mathfrak{D}) \leq 2^{p(|\mathfrak{D}|, \max \mathfrak{D})}$ for every $i \leq k$.

Now let $\mathcal{K} \subseteq M_\tau[\mathfrak{R}]$ be recursively enumerable. The set

$$code(\mathcal{K}) := \{code(\mathfrak{D}, r) : \mathfrak{D} \in \mathcal{K}, \ r \text{ is a ranking of } \mathfrak{D}\} \subseteq \mathbb{N}^k$$

is then also recursively enumerable and therefore Diophantine. The desired first-order sentence ψ uses, besides the symbols of τ, a unary weight function r and nullary weight functions $b_1, \dots, b_m$ and expresses the assertions (i) that r is a ranking and (ii) that $Q(code(\mathfrak{D}, r), \bar{b})) = 0$ for a suitable polynomial $Q \in \mathbb{Z}[x_1, \dots, x_k, y_1, \dots, y_m]$ defining $code(\mathcal{K})$.

3.6.5 Descriptive Complexity over the Real Numbers

There are other contexts in which metafinite spectra do indeed capture (a suitable notion of) non-deterministic polynomial time. An important example are computations over the real numbers based on the model of Blum, Shub, and Smale.

Computation over $\mathbb{R}$

In 1989 Blum, Shub, and Smale [15] introduced a model for computations over the real numbers (and other rings as well), which is now usually called the BSS machine. The important difference from, say, the Turing model is that real numbers are treated as basic entities and that arithmetic operations on the reals are performed in a single step, independently of the magnitude or complexity of the numbers involved. In particular, the model abstracts from the problems that in actual computers real numbers have to be approximated by bit sequences, that the complexity of arithmetic operations depends on the length of these approximate representations, that rounding errors occur, and that exact testing for 0 is impossible in practice. Similar notions of computations over arbitrary fields or rings had been investigated earlier in *algebraic complexity theory* (see [22] for a comprehensive treatment). A novelty of the approach of Blum, Shub, and Smale is that their model is uniform (for all input lengths) whereas the ideas explored in algebraic complexity (such as straight-line programs, arithmetic circuits, and decision trees) are typically non-uniform. One of the main purposes of the BSS approach was to create a uniform complexity theory dealing with problems that have an analytical and topological background, and to show that certain problems remain hard even if arbitrary reals are treated as basic entities.

Many basic concepts and fundamental results of classical computability and complexity theory reappear in the BSS model: the existence of universal machines, the classes $P_\mathbb{R}$ and $NP_\mathbb{R}$ (real analogues of P and NP), and the existence of $NP_\mathbb{R}$-complete problems. Of course, these ideas appear in a different form, with a strong analytical flavour: typical examples of undecidable, recursively enumerable sets are complements of certain Julia sets, and the first problem that was shown to be $NP_\mathbb{R}$-complete is the question of whether a given multivariate polynomial of degree four has a real root [15]. As in the classical setting, all problems in the class $NP_\mathbb{R}$ are decidable within exponential time (but this is not as trivial as in the classical case), and the $P_\mathbb{R}$ versus $NP_\mathbb{R}$ question is one of the major open problems.

However, there also are many differences between classical and real complexity theory. Just to mention a few, we note that the meaning of space resources seems to be very different, that certain separation results between complexity classes can be established (such as $NC_\mathbb{R} \subsetneq P_\mathbb{R}$ and $NP_\mathbb{R} \subsetneq EXP_\mathbb{R}$) whose analogues in the classical theory are open, and that some discrete problems seem to change their complexity behaviour when considered in the BSS model. For a detailed treatment we refer the interested reader to the book [14].

The BSS Model

Let $\mathbb{R}^* := \bigcup_{k \in \mathbb{N}} \mathbb{R}^k$, or (almost) equivalently, the set of functions $X : \mathbb{N} \to \mathbb{R}$ with $X(n) = 0$ for all but finitely many n. For any $X \in \mathbb{R}^*$, we call $|X| := \max\{n : X(n) \neq 0\}$ the **length** of X. Note that $\mathbb{R}^* \times \mathbb{R}^*$ can be identified with $\mathbb{R}^*$ in a natural way by concatenation. A **Blum–Shub–Smale machine** – in what follows called a BSS machine – is essentially a Random Access Machine over $\mathbb{R}$ which can evaluate rational functions at unit cost and whose registers can store arbitrary real numbers.

Definition 3.6.18. A *BSS machine* M over $\mathbb{R}$ is given by a finite set I of instructions labelled by $0, \ldots, N$. The input and output spaces are subsets of $\mathbb{R}^*$. A configuration is a quadruple $(k, r, w, x) \in I \times \mathbb{N} \times \mathbb{N} \times \mathbb{R}^*$, where k is the instruction currently being executed, r and w are the numbers of the so called 'copy registers' (see below) and x describes the content of the registers of the machine. Given an input $x \in \mathbb{R}^*$, the computation is started with a configuration $(0, 0, 0, x)$. If a configuration (k, r, w, x) with $k = N$ is reached, the computation stops; in that case the value of x is the output computed by the machine. The instructions of M are of the following types:

- Computation. An instruction k of this type performs an update $x_0 \leftarrow g_k(x)$ of the first register, where g_k is a rational function on $\mathbb{R}^m$ (for some m). Simultaneously, the copy registers may be updated by rules $r \leftarrow r + 1$ or $r \leftarrow 0$, and similarly for w. The other registers remain unchanged. The next instruction will be $k + 1$.
- Branch. k: **if** $x_0 \geq 0$ **goto** ℓ **else goto** $k + 1$. The contents of the registers remain unchanged.
- Copy. $k : x_w \leftarrow x_r$, i.e. the content of the 'read register' is copied into the 'write register'. The next instruction is $k + 1$; all other registers remain unchanged.

A set $L \subseteq \mathbb{R}^*$ is in $P_{\mathbb{R}}$ if there exists a BSS machine whose running time on every $X \in \mathbb{R}^*$ is bounded by a polynomial in $|X|$, and which accepts X if and only if $X \in L$. The analogue of NP is the class $NP_{\mathbb{R}}$. A set $L \subseteq \mathbb{R}^*$ is in $NP_{\mathbb{R}}$ if there exists a set $L' \in P_{\mathbb{R}}$ and a constant k such that $L = \{X \in \mathbb{R}^* : (\exists Y \in \mathbb{R}^*)(|Y| \leq |X|^k \wedge (X, Y) \in L')\}$. Equivalently, $NP_{\mathbb{R}}$ can be defined as the class of problems over $\mathbb{R}^*$ that are decidable in polynomial time by a *non-deterministic* BSS machine, i.e. a BSS machine that can non-deterministically guess real numbers $Y \in \mathbb{R}$ at unit cost.

Encodings. Recall that $\mathbb{R}$-structures are metafinite structures $\mathfrak{D} = (\mathfrak{A}, \mathfrak{R}, W)$ with a second sort $\mathfrak{R} = (\mathbb{R}, +, -, \cdot, /, \leq, (c_r)_{r \in \mathbb{R}})$. We want to relate decision problems for $\mathbb{R}$-structures (described by logical formulae) to decision problems on $\mathbb{R}^*$ (decided by BSS-machines). We first consider an example.

Example 3.6.19. (4-Feasibility.) The first problem that was shown to be $NP_{\mathbb{R}}$-complete was the problem of whether a real polynomial of degree at most four in n unknowns (where n varies with the input) has a real zero. This problem can be considered as a decision problem on $\mathbb{R}$-structures as follows. Let $A = \{0, \ldots, n\}$. The coefficients of a *homogeneous* polynomial $g \in \mathbb{R}[X_0, \ldots, X_n]$ can be coded via a function $C : A^4 \to \mathbb{R}$, such that

$$g = \sum_{0 \leq i,j,k,\ell \leq n} C(i, j, k, \ell) X_i X_j X_k X_\ell.$$

We obtain an arbitrary (not necessarily homogeneous) polynomial $f \in \mathbb{R}[X_1, \ldots, X_n]$ of degree four by setting $X_0 = 1$ in g. Thus, every multivariate polynomial f of degree at most four is represented by the $\mathbb{R}$-structure $(\mathfrak{A}, \mathfrak{R}, \{C\})$, where $\mathfrak{A} = (\{0, \ldots, n\}, <, 0, n)$ and C is a function from A^4 into $\mathbb{R}$.

Observe that $\mathbb{R}^*$ can be viewed as the class of all $\mathbb{R}$-structures where the primary part is a finite linear order $(\{0, \ldots, n-1\}, <)$, and W consists of a single unary function $X : \{0, \ldots, n-1\} \to \mathbb{R}$. Hence decision problems on $\mathbb{R}^*$ can be regarded as a special case of decision problems on $\mathbb{R}$-structures (in the same way as words can be considered as special cases of finite structures). Conversely, $\mathbb{R}$-structures $\mathfrak{D} = (\mathfrak{A}, \mathfrak{R}, W)$ can be encoded in $\mathbb{R}^*$. We choose a ranking on A and replace all functions and relations in the primary part by the appropriate characteristic functions $\chi : A^k \to \{0,1\} \subseteq \mathbb{R}$. This gives a structure whose primary part is a plain set A, with functions $X_1, \ldots, X_t$ of the form $X_i : A^k \to \mathbb{R}$ and with the ranking $r : A \to \mathbb{R}$. Each of the functions X_i can be represented by a tuple $x_0, \ldots, x_{m-1} \in \mathbb{R}^m$, where $m = |A|^k$ and $x_i = X(\bar{a}(i))$, and where $\bar{a}(i)$ is the ith tuple in A^k with respect to the lexicographic order induced by r. The concatenation of these tuples gives an encoding $code(\mathfrak{D}, r) \in \mathbb{R}^*$ (which depends on the ranking r that was chosen).

Obviously, for structures $\mathfrak{D}$ of a fixed finite signature, the length of $code(\mathfrak{D}, r)$ is bounded by some polynomial n^ℓ, where $n = |\mathfrak{D}|$ and ℓ depends only on the signature. Thus we can also view $code(\mathfrak{D}, r) = (x_0, \ldots, x_{n^\ell - 1})$ as a single function $X_{\mathfrak{D}} : A^\ell \to \mathbb{R}$, where $X(\bar{a}(i)) = x_i$ for all $i < n^\ell$. Thus, encoding an $\mathbb{R}$-structure in $\mathbb{R}^*$ basically means representing the whole structure by a single function (of appropriate arity) from $\{0, \ldots, n-1\}$ into $\mathbb{R}$.

Furthermore, this encoding is first-order definable in the following sense.

Lemma 3.6.20. *For every signature τ, there is a first-order formula $\beta(X, r)$ of signature $\tau \cup \{X, r\}$ such that, for all $\mathbb{R}$-structures $\mathfrak{D}$ of signature τ, for all rankings r, and for all functions X,*

$$(\mathfrak{D}, X, r) \models \beta(X, r) \quad \text{iff} \quad X = code(\mathfrak{D}, r).$$

As in the case of finite structures, we say that a class $\mathcal{K}$ of $\mathbb{R}$-structures is in the complexity class $P_{\mathbb{R}}$ or $NP_{\mathbb{R}}$ if the set of its encodings is. Recall that a metafinite spectrum of $\mathbb{R}$-structures is a set $\mathcal{K}$ of $\mathbb{R}$-structures that is definable by an existential second-order sentence $\exists Y_1 \cdots \exists Y_r \psi$, where ψ is first-order and the variables Y_i range over weight functions $Y_i : A^k \to \mathbb{R}$. Fagin's Theorem now has the following analogue in the real setting.

Theorem 3.6.21 (Grädel and Meer). *Let $\mathcal{K}$ be a class of $\mathbb{R}$-structures. Then $\mathcal{K} \in NP_{\mathbb{R}}$ if and only if $\mathcal{K}$ is a metafinite spectrum.*

Proof. It is easy to see that metafinite spectra are in $NP_{\mathbb{R}}$. Suppose that $\psi = \exists Y_1 \cdots Y_r \varphi$. Given an input structure $\mathfrak{D}$, we guess assignments for all functions Y_i and evaluate φ on $(\mathfrak{D}, Y_1, \ldots, Y_r)$ in polynomial time.

For the converse, let $\mathcal{K} \in NP_{\mathbb{R}}$ and let $\mathcal{K}'$ be the corresponding problem in $P_{\mathbb{R}}$, with $\mathcal{K} = \{\mathfrak{D} : \exists Y((\mathfrak{D}, Y) \in \mathcal{K}')\}$. Let M be a polynomial-time BSS machine deciding $\mathcal{K}'$, and let m be a natural number such that M stops on encodings of $(\mathfrak{D}, Y)$ after less than n^m steps and uses at most $n^m - 3$ registers, where $n = |\mathfrak{D}|$.

We first suppose that we have a ranking $r : A \to \mathbb{R}$ available. From r, the induced (lexicographic) ranking $r_m : A^m \to R$ is first-order definable: we can identify the element in A of maximal rank and thus have the number term n available; we can then use $r_m(\bar{t})$ as an abbreviation for

$$r(t_1)n^{m-1} + \cdots r(t_{m-1})n + r(t_m).$$

We can then identify A^m with the initial subset $\{0, \ldots, n^m - 1\}$ of $\mathbb{N}$. Thus, in the formulae to be constructed below, m-tuples $\bar{t} = t_1, \ldots, t_m$ of variables are considered to range over natural numbers $t < n^m$. Conditions such as $\bar{t} = 0$ or $\bar{t} = \bar{s} + \bar{s}'$ can then be expressed by first-order formulae of vocabulary $\{r\}$.

The computation of M for a given input $code(\mathfrak{D}, Y)$ can be represented by a function $Z : A^{2m} \to \mathbb{R}$ as follows:

- $Z(0, \bar{t})$ is the instruction executed by M at time $\bar{t}$.
- $Z(1, \bar{t})$ and $Z(2, \bar{t})$ are the indices of the read and write registers of M at time $\bar{t}$.
- $Z(\bar{j} + 3, \bar{t})$ is the content of register $\bar{j}$ at time $\bar{t}$.

We construct a first-order formula ψ with the property that, for all ranked structures $(\mathfrak{D}, Y)$ and all Z, we have that $(\mathfrak{D}, Y, Z) \models \psi$ iff Z represents an accepting computation of M for $code(\mathfrak{D}, Y)$.

We first have to express the assertion that at time $t = 0$, the function Z encodes the input configuration of M on $(\mathfrak{D}, Y)$. Thus we need a subformula stating that $Z(i, 0) = 0$ for $i = 0, 1, 2$ and that the values $Z(\bar{j} + 3, 0)$ encode the input $(\mathfrak{D}, Y)$. By Lemma 3.6.20 this can be expressed in first-order logic.

Second, we have to ensure that for every $t < n^m - 1$, if the sequence $\langle Z(\bar{j}, \bar{t}) : \bar{j} = 0, \ldots, n^m - 1 \rangle$ represents a configuration of M, then the sequence of values $Z(\bar{j}, \bar{t} + 1)$ represents the successor configuration. The formula asserting this has the form

$$\forall \bar{t} \bigwedge_{k=0}^{N} (Z(0, \bar{t}) = k \;\rightarrow\; \varphi_k)$$

where φ_k describes transitions performed by the instruction k.

Consider for example a computation instruction $k : x_0 \leftarrow g(x_0, \ldots, x_\ell)$, and assume in addition that it increases the index of the read register by 1 and sets the index of the write register back to 0. The formula φ_k then has to express the following:

- $Z(0, \bar{t} + 1) = k + 1$ (the next instruction is $k + 1$);
- $Z(1, \bar{t} + 1) = Z(1, \bar{t}) + 1$ (the read register index is increased by 1);
- $Z(2, \bar{t} + 1) = 0$ (the write register index is set back to 0);
- $Z(3, \bar{t}+1) = g(Z(3, \bar{t}), Z(4, \bar{t}), \ldots, Z(\ell+3, \bar{t}))$ (into register 0, M writes the result of applying the rational function g to the register contents at time $\bar{t}$).
- $Z(\bar{j}, \bar{t} + 1) = Z(\bar{j}, \bar{t})$ for all $\bar{j} > 3$ (the other registers remain unchanged).

Clearly, these conditions are first-order expressible. It should be noted that whenever $f_0, \ldots, f_\ell$ are number terms and $g : \mathbb{R}^\ell \to \mathbb{R}$ is a rational function, then $g(f_0, \ldots, f_\ell)$ is also a number term.

For another example illustrating the explicit use of the embedding function, consider a copy instruction $k : x_w \leftarrow x_r$. Here the formula has to express (besides the updating of the instruction number, etc. which is done as above), the assertion that the content of the register $Z(2, \bar{t})$ at time $\bar{t}+1$ is the same as the content of the register $Z(1, \bar{t})$ at time $\bar{t}$. This is expressed by the formula

$$\forall \bar{j} \forall \bar{j}' ([Z(1, \bar{t}) = r_m(\bar{j}) \wedge Z(2, \bar{t}) = r_m(\bar{j}')]$$

$$\to Z(\bar{j}' + 3, \bar{t} + 1) = Z(\bar{j} + 3, \bar{t})).$$

To express the assertion that M accepts its input, we just have to say that $Z(3, n^m - 1) = 1$ (by convention, the result of the computation, if it is a single number, is stored in register 0).

Combining all these subformulae in the appropriate way, we obtain the desired formula ψ. It then follows that for all structures $\mathfrak{D}$,

$$\mathfrak{D} \in \mathcal{K} \quad \text{iff} \quad \mathfrak{D} \models (\exists Y)(\exists Z)\psi,$$

which proves the theorem for the case of ranked structures.

Finally, we do away with the assumption that the input structures are ranked. If no ranking is given on the input structures $\mathfrak{D}$, we can introduce one by existentially quantifying over the function r and adding a conjunct $\alpha(r)$ which asserts that r is one–one and that, for all t with $r(t) \neq 0$, there exists an element s such that $r(s) + 1 = r(t)$. It follows that

$$\mathcal{K} = \{\mathfrak{D} : \mathfrak{D} \models (\exists r)(\exists Y)(\exists Z)(\alpha \wedge \psi)\}.$$

$\square$

Example 3.6.22. (Logical description of 4-Feasibility.) An existential second-order sentence for the 4-feasibility problem quantifies two functions $X : A \to \mathbb{R}$ and $Y : A^4 \to \mathbb{R}$ where $X(1), \ldots, X(n)$ describes the zero and $Y(u)$ is the partial sum of all monomials up to $u \in A^4$ in $f(X_1, \ldots, X_n)$ (according to the lexicographical order on A^4). Thus the 4-feasibility problem is described by the sentence

$$\psi := (\exists X)(\exists Y)\Big(Y(\bar{0}) = C(\bar{0}) \wedge Y(\bar{n}) = 0 \wedge \forall \bar{u}(\bar{u} \neq \bar{0} \to$$

$$Y(\bar{u}) = Y(\bar{u} - 1) + C(\bar{u}) \prod_{i=1}^4 X(u_i))\Big).$$

Indeed, $\mathfrak{D} \models \psi$ if and only if the polynomial f of degree four defined by $\mathfrak{D}$ has a real zero.

Capturing Results for Other Complexity Classes

By combining the general ideas of descriptive complexity theory on finite structures with the approach described here, one can find logical characterizations for many other complexity levels, notably for polynomial time, provided that the given $\mathbb{R}$-structures are ranked (i.e. an ordering on the finite part is available). This is carried out in some detail in [30, 53].

Acknowledgements

I am grateful for comments, corrections, and other contributions to Dietmar Berwanger, Achim Blumensath, Anuj Dawar, Phokion Kolaitis, Stephan Kreutzer, Antje Nowack, and Martin Otto.

3.7 Appendix: Alternating Complexity Classes

Alternating algorithms are a generalization of non-deterministic algorithms, based on two-player games. Indeed, one can view non-deterministic algorithms as the restriction of alternating algorithms to solitaire (i.e. one-player) games. Since complexity classes are mostly defined in terms of Turing machines, we focus on the model of alternating Turing machines. But note that alternating algorithms can be defined in terms of other computational models, also.

Definition 3.7.1. An **alternating Turing machine** is a non-deterministic Turing machine whose state set Q is divided into four classes $Q_\exists$, $Q_\forall$, Q_{acc}, and Q_{rej}. This means that there are existential, universal, accepting and rejecting states. States in $Q_{acc} \cup Q_{rej}$ are final states. A configuration of M is called existential, universal, accepting, or rejecting according to its state.

The computation graph $G_{M,x}$ of an alternating Turing machine M for an input x is defined in the same way as for a non-deterministic Turing machine. Nodes are configurations (instantaneous descriptions) of M, there is a distinguished starting node $C_0(x)$ which is the input configuration of M for input x, and there is an edge from configuration C to configuration C' if, and only if, C' is a successor configuration of C. Recall that for *non-deterministic* Turing machines, the acceptance condition is given by the REACHABILITY problem: M accepts x if, and only if, in the graph $G_{M,x}$ some accepting configuration C_a is reachable from $C_0(x)$. For *alternating* Turing machines, acceptance is defined by the GAME problem (see Sect. 3.1.3): the players here are called $\exists$ and $\forall$, where $\exists$ moves from existential configurations and $\forall$ from universal ones. Further, $\exists$ wins at accepting configurations and loses at rejecting ones. By definition, M accepts x if, and only if, Player $\exists$ has a winning strategy from $C_0(x)$ for the game on $G_{M,x}$.

Complexity Classes

Time and space complexity are defined as for nondeterministic Turing machines. For a function $F : \mathbb{N} \to \mathbb{R}$, we say that an alternating Turing machine M is F-time-bounded if for all inputs x, all computation paths from $C_0(x)$ terminate after at most $F(|x|)$ steps. Similarly, M is F-space-bounded if no configuration of M that is reachable from $C_0(x)$ uses more than $F(|x|)$ cells of work space. The complexity classes ATIME(F) and ASPACE(F) contain all problems that are decidable by, respectively, F-time bounded and F-space bounded alternating Turing machines.

The following classes are of particular interest:

- ALOGSPACE = ASPACE($O(\log n)$),
- APTIME = $\bigcup_{d \in \mathbb{N}}$ ATIME(n^d),
- APSPACE = $\bigcup_{d \in \mathbb{N}}$ ASPACE(n^d).

Alternating Versus Deterministic Complexity

There is a general slogan that parallel time complexity coincides with sequential space complexity. Indeed, by standard techniques of complexity theory, one can easily show that, for well-behaved (i.e. space-constructible) functions F, ATIME(F) $\subseteq$ DSPACE(F^2) and DSPACE(F) $\subseteq$ NSPACE(F) $\subseteq$ ATIME(F^2) (see [9] for details). In particular,

- APTIME = PSPACE;
- AEXPTIME = EXPSPACE.

On the other hand, alternating space complexity corresponds to exponential deterministic time complexity.

Theorem 3.7.2. *For any space-constructible function $F(n) \geq \log n$, we have that ASPACE(F) = DTIME($2^{O(F)}$).*

Proof. The proof is closely associated with the GAME problem. For any F-space-bounded alternating Turing machine M, one can, given an input x, construct the computation graph $G_{M,x}$ in time $2^{O(F(|x|))}$ and then solve the GAME problem in order to decide the acceptance of x by M.

For the converse, we shall show that for any $G(n) \geq n$ and any constant c, DTIME(G) $\subseteq$ ASPACE($c \cdot \log G$).

Let $L \in$ DTIME(G). There is then a deterministic one-tape Turing machine M that decides L in time G^2. Let $\Gamma = \Sigma \cup (Q \times \Sigma) \cup \{*\}$ and $t = G^2(n)$. Every configuration $C = (q, i, w)$ (in a computation on some input of length n) can be described by a word

$$\underline{c} = *w_0 \cdots w_{i-1}(qw_i)w_{i+1} \cdots w_t* \in \Gamma^{t+2}.$$

The ith symbol of the successor configuration depends only on the symbols at positions $i - 1$, i, and $i + 1$. Hence, there is a function $f_M : \Gamma^3 \to \Gamma$ such that, whenever symbols a_{-1}, a_0, and a_1 are at positions $i-1, i$ and $i+1$ of some configuration $\underline{c}$, the symbol $f_M(a_{-1}, a_0, a_1)$ will be at position i of the successor configuration $\underline{c}'$.

The following alternating algorithm A decides L:

Input: x
Existential step: guess $s \leq t$,
                   guess $(q^+a) \in Q_{acc} \times \Sigma$, $i \in \{0, \ldots, s\}$
                   $b := (q^+a)$
for $j = 1 \ldots s$ **do**
   Existential step: guess $a_{-1}, a_0, a_1 \in \Gamma^3$
                   verify that $f_M(a_{-1}, a_0, a_1) = b$. If not, reject.
   Universal step: choose $k \in \{-1, 0, 1\}$
                   $b := a_k$
                   $i := i + k$
   od
if ith symbol of input configuration of M on x equals b **then** accept
                                                      else reject.

The algorithm A needs space $O(\log G(n))$. If M accepts the input x, then Player $\exists$ has the following winning strategy for the game on $C_{A,x}$: the value chosen for s is the time at which M accepts x, and $(q^+a), i$ are chosen so that the configuration of M at time s is of the form $*w_0 \cdots w_{i-1}(q^+a)w_{i+1} \cdots w_t*$. At the jth iteration of the loop (that is, at configuration $s - j$), the symbols at positions $i-1, i, i+1$ of the configuration of M at time $s - j$ are chosen for a_{-1}, a_0, a_1.

Conversely, if M does not accept the input x, the ith symbol of the configuration at time s is not (q^+a). The following holds for all j: if, in the jth iteration of the loop, Player $\exists$ chooses a_{-1}, a_0, a_1, then either $f(a_{-1}, a_0, a_1) \neq b$, in which case Player $\exists$ loses immediately, or there is at least one $k \in \{-1, 0, 1\}$ such that the $(i+k)$th symbol of the configuration at time $s - j$ differs from a_k. Player $\forall$ then chooses exactly this k. At the end, a_k will then be different from the ith symbol of the input configuration, so Player $\forall$ wins.

Hence A accepts x if, and only if, M does so. $\square$

In particular, it follows that

- ALOGSPACE = PTIME;
- APSPACE = EXPTIME.

The relationship between the major deterministic and alternating complexity classes is summarized by the following diagram:

$$\begin{array}{ccccccccc}
\text{LOGSPACE} \subseteq & \text{PTIME} & \subseteq \text{PSPACE} \subseteq \text{EXPTIME} \subseteq \text{EXPSPACE} \subseteq \ldots \\
\| & \| & \| & \| \\
& \text{ALOGSPACE} \subseteq \text{APTIME} \subseteq \text{APSPACE} \subseteq \text{AEXPTIME} \subseteq \ldots
\end{array}$$

Alternating Logarithmic Time

For time bounds $F(n) < n$, the standard model of alternating Turing machines needs to be modified a little by an indirect access mechanism. The machine writes down, in binary, an address i on an separate index tape to access the ith symbol of the input. Using this model, it makes sense to define, for instance, the complexity class ALOGTIME = ATIME($O(\log n)$).

Example 3.7.3. Construct an ALOGTIME algorithm for the set of palindromes (i.e., words that are same when read from right to left and from left to right).

Important examples of problems in ALOGTIME are

- the model-checking problem for propositional logic;
- the data complexity of first-order logic.

The results mentioned above relating alternating time and sequential space hold also for logarithmic time and space bounds. Note, however, that these do not imply that ALOGTIME = LOGSPACE, owing to the quadratic overheads. It is known that ALOGTIME $\subseteq$ LOGSPACE, but the converse inclusion is an open problem.

References

1. S. Abiteboul, R. Hull, and V. Vianu. *Foundations of Databases.* Addison-Wesley, 1995.
2. S. Abiteboul and V. Vianu. Datalog extensions for database queries and updates. *Journal of Computer and System Sciences,* 43:62–124, 1991.
3. H. Andréka, J. van Benthem, and I. Németi. Modal languages and bounded fragments of predicate logic. *Journal of Philosophical Logic,* 27:217–274, 1998.
4. A. Arnold. The mu-calculus alternation-depth is strict on binary trees. *RAIRO Informatique Théorique et Applications,* 33:329–339, 1999.
5. A. Arnold and D. Niwiński. *Rudiments of μ-Calculus.* North-Holland, 2001.
6. C. Ash and J. Knight. *Computable Structures and the Hyperarithmetical Hierarchy.* Elsevier, 2000.
7. G. Asser. Das Repräsentantenproblem im Prädikatenkalkül der ersten Stufe mit Identität. *Zeitschrift für Mathematische Logik und Grundlagen der Mathematik,* 1:252–263, 1955.
8. L. Babai, P. Erdös, and S. Selkow. Random graph isomorphism. *SIAM Journal of Computing,* 9:628–635, 1980.
9. J. Balcázar, J. Díaz, and J. Gabarró. *Structural Complexity II.* Springer, 1990.
10. M. Benedikt, L. Libkin, T. Schwentick, and L. Segoufin. Definable relations and first-order query languages over strings. *Journal of the ACM,* 50:694–751, 2003.
11. D. Berwanger and A. Blumensath. The monadic theory of tree-like structures. In E. Grädel, W. Thomas, and T. Wilke, editors, *Automata, Logic, and Infinite Games.* Springer, 2002.

12. H. Björklund, S. Sandberg, and S. Vorobyov. Memoryless determinacy of parity and mean payoff games: A simple proof. *Theoretical Computer Science*, 310:365–378, 2003.

13. A. Blass and Y. Gurevich. Existential fixed point logic. In E. Börger, editor, *Computation Theory and Logic*, Lecture Notes in Computer Science, No. 270, pages 20–36. Springer, 1987.

14. L. Blum, F. Cucker, M. Shub, and S. Smale. *Complexity and Real Computation*. Springer, 1998.

15. L. Blum, M. Shub, and S. Smale. On a theory of computation and complexity over the real numbers. *Bulletin of AMS*, 21:1–46, 1989.

16. A. Blumensath. Automatic structures. Diplomarbeit, RWTH Aachen, 1999.

17. A. Blumensath. Prefix-recognisable graphs and monadic second-order logic. Technical Report AIB-06-2001, RWTH Aachen, 2001.

18. A. Blumensath and E. Grädel. Automatic structures. In *Proc. 15th IEEE Symp. on Logic in Computer Science*, pages 51–62, 2000.

19. A. Blumensath and E. Grädel. Finite presentations of infinite structures: Automata and interpretations. *Theory of Computing Systems*, 37:641–674, 2004.

20. J. Bradfield. The modal μ-calculus alternation hierarchy is strict. *Theoretical Computer Science*, 195:133–153, 1998.

21. J. Bradfield and C. Stirling. Modal logics and mu-calculi. In J. Bergstra, A. Ponse, and S. Smolka, editors, *Handbook of Process Algebra*, pages 293–332. Elsevier, 2001.

22. P. Bürgisser, M. Clausen, and A. Shokrollahi. *Algebraic Complexity Theory*. Springer, 1997.

23. J. Cai, M. Fürer, and N. Immerman. An optimal lower bound on the number of variables for graph identification. *Combinatorica*, 12:389–410, 1992.

24. A. Carayol and S. Wöhrle. The caucal hierarchy of infinite graphs in terms of logic and higher-order pushdown automata. In *Proceedings of FSTTCS*, Lecture Notes in Computer Science, No. 2914, Springer, 2003.

25. D. Caucal. On infinite transition graphs having a decidable monadic theory. In *Automata, Languages and Programming, 23rd International Colloquium, ICALP96*, Lecture Notes in Computer Science, No. 1099, pages 194–205. Springer, 1996.

26. D. Caucal. On infinite terms having a decidable monadic theory. In *Proceedings of 27th International Symposium on Mathematical Foundations of Computer Science MFCS 02*, Lecture Notes in Computer Science, No. 2420, pages 165–176. Springer, 2002.

27. B. Courcelle. The monadic second-order logic of graphs II: Infinite graphs of bounded width. *Mathematical Systems Theory*, 21:187–221, 1989.

28. B. Courcelle. The monadic second-order logic of graphs IX: Machines and their behaviours. *Theoretical Computer Science*, 151:125–162, 1995.

29. B. Courcelle and I. Walukiewicz. Monadic second-order logic, graph coverings and unfoldings of transition systems. *Annals of Pure and Applied Logic*, 92:35–62, 1998.

30. F. Cucker and K. Meer. Logic which capture complexity classes over the reals. *Journal of Symbolic Logic*, 64:363–390, 1999.

31. E. Dahlhaus. Skolem normal forms concerning the least fixed point. In E. Börger, editor, *Computation Theory and Logic*, Lecture Notes in Computer Science, No. 270, pages 101–106, Springer, 1987.

32. A. Dawar. Generalized quantifiers and logical reducibilities. *Journal of Logic and Computation*, 5:213–226, 1995.

33. A. Dawar, E. Grädel, and S. Kreutzer. Inflationary fixed points in modal logic. *ACM Transactions on Computational Logic*, 5:282–315, 2004.

34. A. Dawar, E. Grädel, and S. Kreutzer. Backtracking games and inflationary fixed points. *Theoretical Computer Science*, 350:174–187, 2006.

35. A. Dawar and L. Hella. The expressive power of finitely many generalized quantifiers. *Information and Computation*, 123:172–184, 1995.

36. W. F. Dowling and J. H. Gallier. Linear-time algorithms for testing the satisfiability of propositional horn formulae. *Journal of Logic Programming*, 1(3):267–284, 1984.

37. S. Dziembowski. Bounded-variable fixpoint queries are PSPACE-complete. In *10th Annual Conference on Computer Science Logic CSL 96, Selected papers*, Lecture Notes in Computer Science, No. 1258, pages 89–105. Springer, 1996.

38. H.-D. Ebbinghaus and J. Flum. *Finite Model Theory*, 2nd edition edition. Springer, 1999.

39. A. Ehrenfeucht and J. Mycielski. Positional strategies for mean payoff games. *International Journal of Game Theory*, 8:109–113, 1979.

40. A. Emerson and C. Jutla. Tree automata, mu-calculus and determinacy. In *Proc. 32nd IEEE Symp. on Foundations of Computer Science*, pages 368–377, 1991.

41. D. Epstein, J. Cannon, D. Holt, S. Levy, M. Paterson, and W. Thurston. *Word Processing in Groups*. Jones and Bartlett, Boston, 1992.

42. Yu. L. Ershov, S. S. Goncharov, A. Nerode, and J. B. Remmel. *Handbook of Recursive Mathematics*. North-Holland, 1998.

43. R. Fagin. Generalised first order spectra and polynomial time recognizable sets. In R. Karp, editor, *Complexity of Computation. SIAM-AMS Proceedings* 7, pages 43–73, 1974.

44. B. Farb. Automatic groups: A guided tour. *L'Enseignement Mathématique*, 38:291–313, 1992.

45. G. Gottlob, E. Grädel, and H. Veith. Datalog LITE: A deductive query language with linear time model checking. *ACM Transactions on Computational Logic*, 3:42–79, 2002.

46. E. Grädel. On transitive closure logic. In *Proceedings of 5th Workshop on Computer Science Logic CSL 91*, Lecture Notes in Computer Science, No. 626, pages 149–163, Springer, 1991.

47. E. Grädel. Capturing complexity classes by fragments of second-order logic. *Theoretical Computer Science*, 101:35–57, 1992.

48. E. Grädel and Y. Gurevich. Metafinite model theory. *Information and Computation*, 140:26–81, 1998.

49. E. Grädel, Y. Gurevich, and C. Hirsch. The complexity of query reliability, *17th ACM Symposium on Principles of Database Systems PODS 98*, ACM Press, 1998.

50. E. Grädel and A. Malmström. 0-1 laws for recursive structures. *Archive of Mathematical Logic*, 38:205–215, 1999.

51. E. Grädel and G. McColm. On the power of deterministic transitive closures. *Information and Computation*, 119:129–135, 1995.

52. E. Grädel and G. McColm. Hierarchies in transitive closure logic, stratified datalog and infinitary logic. *Annals of Pure and Applied Logic*, 77:166–199, 1996.

53. E. Grädel and K. Meer. Descriptive complexity theory over the real numbers. In J. Renegar, M. Shub, and S. Smale, editors, *Mathematics of Numerical Analysis: Real Number Algorithms*, Lectures in Applied Mathematics No. 32, pages 381–403. AMS, 1996.

54. E. Grädel and M. Otto. Inductive definability with counting on finite structures. *Computer Science Logic, 6th Workshop, CSL '92, Selected Papers*, Lecture Notes in Computer Science, No. 702, pages 231–247, Springer, 1993.

55. E. Grädel and M. Otto. On logics with two variables. *Theoretical Computer Science*, 224:73–113, 1999.

56. E. Grädel, W. Thomas, and T. Wilke, editors. *Automata, Logics, and Infinite Games*. Lecture Notes in Computer Science No. 2500. Springer, 2002.

57. R. Greenlaw, J. Hoover, and W. Ruzzo. *Limits to Parallel Computation. P-Completeness Theory*. Oxford University Press, 1995.

58. M. Grohe. Fixed-point logics on planar graphs. In *Proc. 13th IEEE Symp. on Logic in Computer Science*, pages 6–15, 1998.

59. M. Grohe. Isomorphism testing for embeddable graphs through definability. In *Proc. 32nd ACM Symp. on Theory of Computing*, pages 63–72, 2000.

60. M. Grohe and J. Mariño. Definability and descriptive complexity on databases of bounded tree-width. In *Proceedings of ICDT 99*, Lecture Notes in Computer Science, No. 1540, pages 70–82, Springer, 1999.

61. Y. Gurevich. Logic and the challenge of computer science. In E. Börger, editor, *Current Trends in Theoretical Computer Science*, pages 1–57. Computer Science Press, 1988.

62. Y. Gurevich and L. Harrington. Trees, automata and games. In *Proceedings of the 14th Annual ACM Symposium on Theory of Computing, STOC '82*, pages 60–65, 1982.

63. Y. Gurevich and S. Shelah. Fixed-point extensions of first-order logic. *Annals of Pure and Applied Logic*, 32:265–280, 1986.

64. D. Harel. Towards a theory of recursive structures. In *Proceedings of 23rd International Symposium on Mathematical Foundations of Computer Science MFCS 98*, Lecture Notes in Computer Science, No. 1450, pages 36–53. Springer, 1998.

65. T. Hirst and D. Harel. More about recursive structures: Descriptive complexity and zero–one laws. In *Proc. 11th IEEE Symp. on Logic in Computer Science*, pages 334–348, 1996.

66. W. Hodges. *Model Theory*. Cambridge University Press, 1993.

67. N. Immerman. Relational queries computable in polynomial time. *Information and Control*, 68:86–104, 1986.

68. A. Itai and J. Makowsky. Unification as a complexity measure for logic programming. *Journal of Logic Programming*, 4:105–117, 1987.

69. D. Janin and I. Walukiewicz. On the expressive completeness of the propositional mu-calculus with respect to monadic second order logic. In *Proceedings of 7th International Conference on Concurrency Theory CONCUR '96*, Lecture Notes in Computer Science, No. 1119, pages 263–277. Springer, 1996.

70. N. Jones and W. Laaser. Complete problems for deterministic polynomial time. *Theoretical Computer Science*, 3:105–117, 1977.

71. N. Jones and A. Selman. Turing machines and the spectra of first-order formulas. *Journal of Symbolic Logic*, 39:139–150, 1974.

72. M. Jurdziński. Deciding the winner in parity games is in UP ∩ Co-UP. *Information Processing Letters*, 68:119–124, 1998.

73. M. Jurdziński. Small progress measures for solving parity games. In *STACS 2000, 17th Annual Symposium on Theoretical Aspects of Computer Science, Proceedings*, Lecture Notes in Computer Science, No. 1770, pages 290–301. Springer, 2000.

74. P. Kanellakis, G. Kuper, and P. Revesz. Constraint query languages. *Journal of Computer and Systems Sciences*, 51:26–52, 1995.

75. B. Khoussainov and A. Nerode. Automatic presentations of structures. In *LCC '94: Selected Papers from the International Workshop on Logical and Computational Complexity*, Lecture Notes in Computer Science, No. 960, pages 367–392. Springer, 1995.

76. B. Khoussainov, S. Rubin, and F. Stephan. On automatic partial orders. *Proceedings of 18th Annual IEEE Symposium on Logic in Computer Science, LICS 03*, pages 168–177, 2003.

77. B. Khoussainov, A. Nies, S. Rubin, and F. Stephan. Automatic structures: Richness and limitations. *Proceedings of 19th Annual IEEE Symposium on Logic in Computer Science, LICS 04*, pages 44–53, 2004.

78. B. Khoussainov, S. Rubin, and F. Stephan. Definability and regularity in automatic structures. In *Proceedings of STACS 04*, pages 440–451, 2004.

79. P. Kolaitis. The expressive power of stratified logic programs. *Information and Computation*, 90:50–66, 1991.

80. S. Kreutzer. Expressive equivalence of least and inflationary fixed point logic. In *Proceedings of 17th IEEE Symp. on Logic in Computer Science LICS02*, pages 403–410, 2002.

81. G. Kuper, L. Libkin, and J. Paredaens, editors. *Constraint Databases*. Springer, 2000.

82. D. Martin. Borel determinacy. *Annals of Mathematics*, 102:336–371, 1975.

83. Y. Matijasevich. *Hilbert's Tenth Problem*. MIT Press, 1993.

84. K. Meer. Query languages for real number databases based on descriptive complexity over R. In *Proc. 24th International Symposium on Mathematical Foundations of Computer Science MFCS 99*, Lecture Notes in Computer Science Nr. 1672, pages 12–22. Springer, 1999.

85. Y. Moschovakis. *Elementary Induction on Abstract Structures*. North-Holland, 1974.

86. A. Mostowski. Games with forbidden positions. Technical Report 78, University of Gdansk, 1991.

87. D. Muller and P. Schupp. Groups, the theory of ends, and context-free languages. *Journal of Computer and System Sciences*, 26:295–310, 1983.

88. D. Muller and P. Schupp. The theory of ends, pushdown automata, and second-order logic. *Theoretical Computer Science*, 37:51–75, 1985.

89. M. Otto. *Bounded Variable Logics and Counting*. Springer, 1997.

90. M. Otto. Bisimulation-invariant Ptime and higher-dimensional mu-calculus. *Theoretical Computer Science*, 224:237–265, 1999.

91. C. Papadimitriou. A note on the expressive power of Prolog. *Bulletin of the EATCS*, 26:21–23, 1985.

92. S. Rubin. *Automatic Structures*. PhD thesis, University of Auckland, New Zealand, 2004.

93. H. Scholz. Ein ungelöstes Problem in der symbolischen Logik. *Journal of Symbolic Logic*, 17:160, 1952.

94. A. Stolboushkin. Towards recursive model theory. In J. Makowsky and E. Ravve, editors, *Logic Colloquium 95*, Lecture Notes in Logic, No. 11, pages 325–338. Springer, 1998.

95. H. Straubing. *Finite Automata, Formal Logic, and Circuit Complexity.* Birkhäuser, Boston, 1994.

96. W. Thomas. On the synthesis of strategies in infinite games. In *Proceedings of STACS 95*, Lecture Notes in Computer Science, No. 900, pages 1–13. Springer, 1995.

97. W. Thomas. Languages, automata, and logic. In G. Rozenberg and A. Salomaa, editors, *Handbook of Formal Languages* Vol. 3, pages 389–455. Springer, 1997.

98. W. Thomas. Constructing infinite graphs with a decidable MSO-theory. In *Proceedings of the 28th International Symposium on Mathematical Foundations of Computer Science MFCS 03*, Lecture Notes in Computer Science, No. 2747, pages 113-124, Springer, 2003.

99. M. Vardi. The complexity of relational query languages. In *Proceedings of the 14th ACM Symposium on the Theory of Computing*, pages 137–146, 1982.

100. M. Vardi. On the complexity of bounded-variable queries. In *Proc. 14th ACM Symp. on Principles of Database Systems*, pages 266–267, 1995.

101. I. Walukiewicz. Monadic second-order logic on tree-like structures. *Theoretical Computer Science*, 275:311–346, 2001.

102. W. Zielonka. Infinite games on finitely coloured graphs with applications to automata on infinite trees. *Theoretical Computer Science*, 200:135–183, 1998.

4

Logic and Random Structures

Joel Spencer

In the world of randomization almost everything seems to be possible.
– Michael Rabin

4.1 An Instructive Example

We begin with a rather easy random model which illustrates many of the concepts we shall deal with. We call it the simple unary predicate with parameters n, p, and denote it by $SU(n, p)$. The model is over a universe Ω of size n, a positive integer. We imagine each $x \in \Omega$ flipping a coin to decide if $U(x)$ holds, and the coin comes up heads with probability p. Here we have p real, $0 \le p \le 1$. Formally we have a probability space on the possible U over Ω defined by the properties $\Pr[U(x)] = p$ for all $x \in \Omega$ and the events $U(x)$ being mutually independent. We consider sentences in a first-order language. In this language, we have only equality (we shall always assume we have equality) and the unary predicate U. (The cognoscenti should note that Ω has no further structure and, in particular, is not considered an ordered set.)

This is a rather spartan language. One thing we can say is

$$YES := \exists_x U(x),$$

that U holds for some $x \in \Omega$. Simple probability gives

$$\Pr[SU(n, p) \models YES] = 1 - (1 - p)^n$$

As p moves from zero to one, $\Pr[YES]$ moves monotonically from zero to one. We are interested in the asymptotics as $n \to \infty$. At first blush this seems trivial: for $p = 0$, $SU(n, p)$ never models YES while for any constant $p > 0$,

$$\lim_{n \to \infty} \Pr[SU(n, p) \models YES] = \lim_{n \to \infty} 1 - (1 - p)^n = 1$$

In an asymptotic sense, YES has already almost surely occurred by the time p reaches any positive constant.

This leads us to a critical notion. *We do not restrict ourselves to p constant but rather consider $p = p(n)$ as a function of n.* What is the parametrization $p = p(n)$ that best enables us to see the transformation of $\Pr[SU(n, p(n)) \models YES]$ from zero to one? Some reflection leads to the parametrization $p(n) = c/n$. If c is a positive constant, then

$$\lim_{n \to \infty} \Pr[SU(n, p(n)) \models YES] = \lim_{n \to \infty} 1 - (1 - \frac{c}{n})^n = 1 - e^{-c}$$

(Technically, as $p \leq 1$ always, this parametrization is not allowable for $n < c$ – but since we are only concerned with limits as $n \to \infty$ this will not concern us.) If we think of c going from zero to infinity, then the limit probability is going from zero to one. We are actually interested less (in this exposition) in the actual limits than in whether the limits are zero or one.

We say that a property A holds *almost always* (with respect to a given $p(n)$) if $\lim_{n \to \infty} \Pr[SU(n, p(n)) \models A] = 1$. We say that A holds *almost never* if the above limit is zero or, equivalently, if $\neg A$ holds almost surely. This notion is extremely general. Whenever we have, for all sufficiently large positive integers n, a probability space over models of size n, we can speak of a property A holding almost surely or almost never. For the particular property YES, the exact results above have the following simple consequences:

- If $p(n) \ll n^{-1}$ then YES holds almost never.
- If $p(n) \gg n^{-1}$ then YES holds almost surely.

Thus, for example, when $p(n) = n^{-1.01}$, YES holds almost never, while when $p(n) = n^{-0.99}$, YES holds almost surely.

We shall say that n^{-1} is a *threshold function* for the property YES. More generally, suppose we have a notion of a random model on n vertices with a probability p of some predicate. We say $p_0(n)$ is a threshold function for a property A if, whenever $p(n) \ll p_0(n)$, the property A holds almost never, and whenever $p(n) \gg p_0(n)$ the property A holds almost surely. This notion, due to Paul Erdős and Alfred Rényi, says roughly that $p_0(n)$ is the "region" around which $\Pr[A]$ is moving from near zero to near one. The threshold function, when it exists, is not totally determined – we could have taken $5/n$ as the threshold function for YES – but is basically determined up to constant factors. In a rough way we think of $p(n)$ increasing through the functions of n – for example from n^{-2} to n^{-1} to $n^{-1} \ln n$ to $\ln^{-5} n$ – and the threshold function is that place where $\Pr[A]$ changes.

A natural problem for probabilists is to determine the threshold function, if one exists, for a given property A. For logicians, the natural question would be to determine all possible threshold functions for all properties A expressible in a given language L. Unfortunately there are technical difficulties (especially with later more complex models) with threshold functions – properties A need not be monotone, threshold functions need not exist, and, worst of all, the limits of probabilities might not exist. Rather, the logician looks for a *zero–one law*, of which the following is prototypical.

Theorem 4.1.1. *Let $p = p(n)$ satisfy $p(n) \gg n^{-1}$ and $1 - p(n) \gg n^{-1}$. Then, for any first-order property A,*

$$\lim_{n \to \infty} \Pr[SU(n,p) \models A] = 0 \ or \ 1$$

Further, the limiting value depends only on A and not on the choice of $p(n)$ within that range.

Our approach to this theorem, which will also be used in later more complex cases, is to find an explicit theory T such that

- every $A \in T$ holds almost surely;
- T is complete.

Will this suffice? When $T \models B$, finiteness of proof gives us the result that B follows from some $A_1, \ldots, A_s \in T$ and hence from $A_1 \wedge \ldots \wedge A_s$. But the finite conjunction of events holding almost surely holds almost surely, so B would hold almost surely. By completeness, either $T \models B$ or $T \models \neg B$, and in the latter case $\neg B$ holds almost surely so that B holds almost never.

In our situation, T is given by two simple schemas.

1. (For $r \geq 1$.) There exist distinct $x_1, \ldots, x_r$ with $U(x_i)$ for $1 \leq i \leq r$.
2. (For $r \geq 1$.) There exist distinct $x_1, \ldots, x_r$ with $\neg U(x_i)$ for $1 \leq i \leq r$.

Note that the number X of x with $U(x)$ has a binomial distribution with parameters $n, p(n)$ – that the event $X \geq r$ holds almost surely follows from basic probabilistic ideas and from the assumption $np(n) \to \infty$. The second schema follows from $n(1 - p(n)) \to \infty$, reversing the roles of U and $\neg U$.

Why is this T complete? Proving completeness of a theory T is bread and butter to the logic community – from the myriad of methods, we choose a combinatorial approach based on the Ehrenfeucht game, as described in Sect. 4.14. Let $t \geq 1$ be arbitrary and let M_1, M_2 be two countable models of T. It suffices to show that Duplicator wins the game $\text{EHR}(M_1, M_2; t)$.

In our case the Duplicator's strategy is simple. A countable model M of T must have an infinite number of $x \in M$ with $U(x)$ (as for all $r \geq 1$ it must have at least r such x) and, similarly, an infinite number of $x \in M$ with $\neg U(x)$. Now when Spoiler selects, say, a new $x \in M_1$ with $U(x)$ Duplicator simply selects a new $x' \in M_2$ with $U(x')$ – as there are only a finite number t of moves, he cannot run out of possible x'.

In this instance the countable models of T were particularly simple – indeed the theory T was $\aleph_0$-categorical; all countable models were isomorphic. In future more complex situations this will generally not be the case, and indeed we find the study of the countable models of the almost sure theory T to be quite intriguing in its own right.

4.2 Random Graphs

A graph G consists of a set of vertices V and an areflexive symmetric binary relation on V. We write the relation $x \sim y$ and say that x, y are adjacent. Pictorially, there is an edge from x to y. For the graph theorists, our graphs are undirected, with neither loops nor multiple edges. The random graph $G(n, p)$ ($n \geq 1$ integral, p real, $0 \leq p \leq 1$) is on a vertex set V of size n, where, for each distinct x, y, $\Pr[x \sim y] = p$ and these events are mutually independent. We may think of each pair x, y of vertices as flipping a coin to decide whether or not to have an edge between them, where the probability that the coin comes up heads is p.

It is a relatively rare area of mathematics that has an explicit starting point. The subject of random graphs began with a monumental paper by Paul Erdős and Alfred Rényi in 1960. The very title of their paper, "On the evolution of random graphs," speaks to a critical vantage point. As the edge probability p increases, the random graph $G(n, p)$ increases in complexity. For many natural properties A, there will be a threshold function $p_0(n)$ for its occurence. As in Sect. 4.1, when $p(n) \ll p_0(n)$ A will hold almost never, while when $p(n) \gg p_0(n)$ A will hold almost always. Finding threshold functions has been a major preoccupation for researchers in random graphs. Let us give some examples, together with some intuitive justification for the threshold functions.

- *Containing a K_4* – i.e. containing four vertices with all six pairs adjacent. The threshold function is $n^{-2/3}$. There are $\binom{n}{4} \sim n^4/24$ possible K_4s and each has six adjacencies with probability p^6, so that the expected number of K_4s is $\sim n^4 p^6/24$. When $p(n) \ll n^{-2/3}$ this expectation goes to zero, so that almost surely there are none of them. When $p(n) \gg n^{-2/3}$ this expectation goes to infinity. By itself, this does not imply that almost surely there is at least one K_4 but more refined methods – in particular, an examination of the variance of the number of K_4s – do show that almost surely there will be a K_4.
- *Containing a triangle.* The threshold function is n^{-1}, for reasons similar to those above.
- *No isolated vertices.* In first-order language $\forall_x \exists_y x \sim y$. Here $n^{-1} \ln n$ is the threshold function. Roughly, a given vertex x has probability $(1-p)^{n-1} \sim e^{-pn}$ of being isolated. When $pn > (1 + \varepsilon) \ln n$, this probability is $o(n^{-1})$, so that the expected number of isolated vertices is $o(1)$ and almost surely there are none. When $pn < (1 - \varepsilon) \ln n$, this probability is $\gg n^{-1}$, so that the expected number of isolated vertices goes to infinity, and more refined techniques show that almost surely there are isolated vertices.
- *Connectivity.* This was one of the most beautiful results in the Erdős–Rényi paper. It turns out that connectivity has the same behavior as no isolated vertices. Their result was amazingly precise. We parametrize $p = (\ln n)/n + c/n$. For c any real (positive or negative) constant,

$$\lim_{n \to \infty} \Pr[G(n,p) \text{ connected}] = e^{-e^{-c}}.$$

- *Every two vertices have a common neighbor.* In first order language $\forall_{x_1} \forall_{x_2} \exists_{y_1} y_1 \sim x_1 \wedge y_1 \sim x_2$. The threshold function is $n^{-1/2} \ln^{1/2} n$. Any x_1, x_2 have an expected number $(n-2)p^2 \sim np^2$ of common neighbors. This would naturally lead us to consider $p = n^{-1/2}$. Indeed, for $p \ll n^{-1/2}$ a randomly chosen x_1, x_2 will not have a common neighbor, while for $p \gg n^{-1/2}$ a randomly chosen x_1, x_2 will have a common neighbor, and indeed many common neighbors. But this does not suffice for *every* pair x_1, x_2 to have a common neighbor; for that one needs the extra polylogarithmic term.
- *Every two vertices are joined by a path of length three.* In first-order language $\forall_{x_1} \forall_{x_2} \exists_{y_1} \exists_{y_2} x_1 \sim y_1 \wedge y_1 \sim y_2 \wedge y_2 \sim x_2$. The threshold function is $n^{-2/3} \ln^{1/3} n$. Any x_1, x_2 have $\binom{n-2}{2} \sim n^2/2$ potential paths (choices of y_1, y_2) of length three, and each potential path has three adjacencies with probability p^3, so that the expected number of paths is $\sim n^2 p^3/2$. This would lead us to consider $p = n^{-2/3}$ as a threshold function but, as above, an extra polylogarithmic term is needed to assure that *every* pair x_1, x_2 has such a path.

These threshold functions, and countless others, seemed to this author to have a common property: the power of n involved was always a rational number. There might be other, generally polylogarithmic, factors but they would be of smaller order than the power of n. Nowhere, so it seemed, was there a natural property with a threshold function, say, $p = n^{-\pi/7}$. In 1988 this author and Saharon Shelah were able to give a formal justification for this observation, and this result is the centerpiece of our discussions.

Theorem 4.2.1. *Let* $0 < \alpha < 1$, α *irrational. Set* $p(n) = n^{-\alpha}$. *Then, for every first-order property* A,

$$\lim_{n \to \infty} \Pr[G(n,p) \models A] = 0 \text{ or } 1.$$

The situation where $\alpha > 1$ has also been studied. It turns out to be considerably simpler than the $0 < \alpha < 1$ case and will not be considered here.

Our approach will be that used in Sect. 4.1. We shall find a theory $T = T_\alpha$ such that each $A \in T_\alpha$ holds almost surely, and T_α will be shown to be complete, using countable models and the Ehrenfeucht game. We shall need several preliminaries.

4.3 Extension Statements

The examples above, "Every vertex has a neighbor," "every two vertices have a common neighbor," and "every two vertices are joined by a path of length three", are all examples of a vital kind of first-order statement that we shall call extension statements. These statements are of the form "For all $x_1, \ldots, x_r$, there exist $y_1, \ldots, y_v$ P", where P is that certain adjacencies between some y_i, y_j and some x_i, y_j must exist. P never considers adjacencies between pairs x_i, x_j and never demands nonadjacency. We allow the case $r = 0$, so that the extension statement reduces to a purely existential statement, but require $v > 0$.

To formalize this, we define a rooted graph to be a pair (R, H), where H is a graph (with $V(H)$ and $E(H)$ denoting its vertex and edge sets, respectively) and R is a proper subset of the vertices. Labeling the roots $x_1, \ldots, x_r$ and the nonroots $y_1, \ldots, y_v$, we define the extension statement $Ext(R, H)$ to be that for all $x_1, \ldots, x_r$ there exist $y_1, \ldots, y_r$ having the edges of H, where we do not examine the edges between the roots and we allow extra edges. A rooted graph (R, H) has three parameters. The number of roots is denoted by r. The number of nonroots is denoted by v. The number of edges (where edges between roots are not counted) is denoted by e. Perhaps surprisingly, r plays a relatively minor role. The key parameter, as the examples below will indicate, is the sign of $v - e\alpha$.

We call (R, H) *dense* if $v - e\alpha < 0$ and *sparse* if $v - e\alpha > 0$. The irrationality of α comes in at this point, making this a strict dichotomy. We further call (R, H) *rigid* if, for all S with $R \subseteq S \subset V(H)$, the rooted graph (S, H) is dense. (As S may be R itself, "rigid" implies "dense".) We call (R, H) *safe* if, for all S with $R \subset S \subseteq V(H)$, the rooted graph $(R, H|_S)$ is sparse. (Here $H|_S$ is the restriction of H to S; we simply throw all other vertices away. As S may be $V(H)$ itself, "safe" implies "sparse".) Very roughly we think of "rigid" as meaning dense through and through, and "safe" as meaning sparse through and through. We call $(R, H|_S)$ a subextension of (R, H), and we call (S, H) a nailextension (we are nailing down some more roots) of (R, H).

Let us look at several examples with $\alpha = \pi/7 = 0.448\cdots$. We have selected this α because it seems to have no special properties whatsoever.

- *Every two vertices have a neighbor.* H has y_1 adjacent to x_1, x_2; $r = 2, v = 1$ and $e = 2$, so $v - e\alpha > 0$ and (R, H) is sparse and safe.
- *Every three vertices have a neighbor.* H has y_1 adjacent to x_1, x_2, x_3; $r = 3, v = 1$ and $e = 3$, so $v - e\alpha < 0$ and (R, H) is dense and rigid.
- *Every vertex lies in a K_5.* H has y_1, y_2, y_3, y_4, x_1 with all ten adjacencies; $r = 1, v = 4$ and $e = 10$, so $v - e\alpha < 0$ and (R, H) is dense and rigid.
- *Every vertex lies in a K_4.* H has y_1, y_2, y_3, x_1 with all six adjacencies; $r = 1, v = 3$ and $e = 10$, so $v - e\alpha > 0$ and (R, H) is dense and rigid.
- *Every two vertices lie in a K_4 except, possibly, they may be nonadjacent.* H has y_1, y_2, x_1, x_2 with five adjacencies (not x_1, x_2): $r = 2, v = 2$ and $e = 5$, so $v - e\alpha < 0$ and (R, H) is dense and rigid.
- *Every three vertices have a common neighbor, which itself has a (different) neighbor.* H has y_1 adjacent to x_1, x_2, x_3, and y_2 adjacent to y_1. Here $r = 3, v = 2, e = 4$ and $v - e\alpha > 0$, so that (R, H) is sparse. But (R, H) is not safe, since the subextension "every three vertices have a common neighbor" ($S = \{x_1, x_2, x_3, y_1\}$) is not sparse.

- *Every four vertices have a common neighbor which itself has a (different)*
  neighbor. H has y_1 adjacent to x_1, x_2, x_3, x_4, and y_2 adjacent to y_1. Here
  $r = 4, v = 2, e = 5$ and $v - e\alpha < 0$, so that (R, H) is dense. But nailing
  down y_1, by setting $S = R \cup \{y_1\}$, gives (S, H) with $r = 5, v = 1, e = 1$
  and $v - e\alpha > 0$, so that y_2 is flapping in the wind and (R, H) is not rigid.

It can be shown that $Ext(R, H)$ holds almost surely if and only if
(R, H) is safe. Let us see the intuitive justification. Given the $x_1, \ldots, x_r$ we
have $\sim cn^v$ choices for $y_1, \ldots, y_v$ and each choice will have the needed e
adjacencies with probability p^e; hence the expected number of extensions is
$\sim cn^v p^e \sim cn^{v - e\alpha}$. When $v - e\alpha < 0$ this expected number goes to zero, so
almost surely a random $x_1, \ldots, x_r$ will not have an extension. If there is a
subextension $(R, H|_S)$ which is not sparse (and hence dense) almost surely a
random $x_1, \ldots, x_r$ cannot be extended to $H|_S$ and hence cannot be extended
to H. The converse requires more work.

What about "rigid"? It is not the case that every three vertices have a
common neighbor; indeed, a random three vertices almost surely will not
have a common neighbor. But *some* sets of three vertices do have a common
neighbor. (Take a vertex y_1, and take three of its neighbors x_1, x_2, x_3 –
those three vertices have the common neighbor y_1.) When x_1, x_2, x_3 have a
common neighbor, that is a special property of the triple. It is not special
when x_1, x_2 have a common neighbor since every pair of vertices have a
common neighbor. It will turn out that all special properties of bounded sets
of vertices are describable in terms of rigid extensions.

4.4 Closure

Fix $\alpha \in (0, 1)$ irrational and $t \geq 1$. Let G be any graph, although we shall be
interested in $G \sim G(n, p)$ with $p = n^{-\alpha}$. Let X be any set of vertices of G.
We define the t-closure of X, denoted by $cl_t(X)$.

Our first definition of $cl_t(X)$ is algorithmic. We say $y_1, \ldots, y_v$ form an
(R, H) extension over $x_1, \ldots, x_r$ if they have the required adjacencies of H
between the y_i, y_j and the x_i, y_j. We say $y_1, \ldots, y_v$ form a rigid extension
over $x_1, \ldots, x_r$ if they form an (R, H) extension for some rigid (R, H). Now
begin with X. If any $y_1, \ldots, y_v$ with (critically) $v \leq t$ form a rigid extension
over X, then add those vertices to X. Iterate until there are no further rigid
extensions. The final set is $cl_t(X)$.

The second definition is that $cl_t(X)$ is the minimal set Z containing X
which does not have any rigid extensions of at most t vertices.

Justifying the assertion that these two definitions are equivalent and
indeed that they are well defined (e. g. that the first does not depend on the
order in which rigid extensions are added on) requires a series of relatively
elementary combinatorial lemmas, which we shall omit here. As an example,
$cl_4(x_1, x_2)$ might consist of x_1, x_2; y_1, y_2 adjacent to each other and to both

$x_1, x_2; y_3, y_4, y_5, y_6$, forming a K_5 with y_2; and y_7 being a common neighbor of x_2, y_1, y_5.

Lemma 4.4.1 (Nonexistence Lemma). *For every* $t \geq 1$ *almost surely* $cl_t(\emptyset) = \emptyset$ *in* $G \sim G(n, n^{-\alpha})$.

Proof When $(\emptyset, H)$ is rigid (or even just dense) it has v vertices and e edges with $v - e\alpha < 0$ so that the expected number of copies of H is $\sim cn^v p^e$, which goes to zero. Hence, almost surely, there is no copy of H. With t fixed, there are only a finite number of such H's to consider, so almost surely none of them exist as subgraphs of G.

Let $x_1, \ldots, x_r \in G, x_1', \ldots, x_r' \in G'$. We see that their t-closures are isomorphic, and write $cl_t(x_1, \ldots, x_r) \cong cl_t(x_1', \ldots, x_r')$ if there is a graph isomorphism φ between the t-closures which preserves both adjacency and nonadjacency and which satisfies $\varphi(x_i) = x_i'$ for $1 \leq i \leq r$. When H is the restriction of G to $cl_t(x_1, \ldots, x_r)$ we write $cl_t(x_1, \ldots, x_r) \cong H$, but with the additional understanding that the roots $x_1, \ldots, x_r$ are in specified positions in H. For completion we include the case $t = 0$: we define the 0-closure of X to be X and say that $cl_0(x_1, \ldots, x_r) \cong cl_0(x_1', \ldots, x_r')$ if the map φ with $\varphi(x_i) = x_i'$ for $1 \leq i \leq r$ is a graph isomorphism on these sets of r vertices. Observe that stating $cl_t(x_1, \ldots, x_r) \cong H$ is a first-order predicate. In the example of the preceding paragraph, it would consist of stating the existence of the $y_1, \ldots, y_7$ with their appropriate adjacencies and then, for each of the finite list of possible (R, H) rigid extensions with $v \leq 4$, the nonexistence of $z_1, \ldots, z_v$ having those adjacencies over $x_1, \ldots, y_7$. A priori, the t-closure might be arbitrarily large, and the following lemma plays an important role in limiting its possibilities.

Lemma 4.4.2 (Finite Closure Lemma). *For all* $\alpha \in (0, 1)$ *and irrational,* $r, t \geq 1$ *integers, there exists* K *such that, in* $G \sim G(n, n^{-\alpha})$, *almost surely*

$$|cl_t(x_1, \ldots, x_r)| < r + K \text{ for all } x_1, \ldots, x_r.$$

Proof: We set $\varepsilon = \min(e\alpha - v)/v$ over all integers v, e with $v \leq t$ and $v - e\alpha \leq 0$. Note, critically, that the restriction $v \leq t$ allows us to restrict to a finite number of cases, and thus the min does exist and (as α is irrational) is positive. We set $K = \lceil r/\varepsilon \rceil$.

Suppose that the result was false and there was $R = \{x_1, \ldots, x_r\}$ with a larger t-closure. Then there would be a sequence $R = R_0 \subset R_1 \subset \ldots \subset R_l$ where each R_{i+1} was rigid over R_i with fewer than t nonroots and R_j having a size in $[r+K, r+K+t)$. (That is, we continue taking rigid extensions and stop when at least $r+K$ vertices are in the set.) Let H_i be the restriction of G to R_i and set H equal to the final H_l. Let (R_{i-1}, H_i) have parameters v_i, e_i. Then H has $V = r + \sum_{i=1}^{l} v_i$ vertices and at least $E = \sum_{i=1}^{l} e_i$ edges. Roughly, the r roots are our capital and each extension costs us $e\alpha - v$. Formally,

$$V - E\alpha \leq r + \sum_{i=1}^{l} (v_i - e_i)\alpha \leq r - \varepsilon \sum_{i=1}^{l} v_i \leq r - K\varepsilon < 0.$$

The existence of such an H would then violate the Nonexistence Lemma.

4.5 The Almost Sure Theory

To describe the almost sure theory $T = T_\alpha$, we require one more somewhat technical point. When (R, H) is safe, we want every $x_1, \ldots, x_r$ to have an (R, H) extension $y_1, \ldots, y_v$. But we further need that these y's have no additional properties relative to the x's. We define this in the first-order world via rigid extensions. Roughly we want to say that any rigid extension over the x's and y's is really just over the xs.

Definition. We say that $y_1, \ldots, y_v$ is t-generic over $x_1, \ldots, x_r$ if the following holds. Consider any $z_1, \ldots, z_w$ distinct from the x's and y's with (critically) $w \le t$, which forms a rigid extension over $x_1, \ldots, x_r, y_1, \ldots, y_v$. Then there are no edges between any z_i and any y_j.

The almost sure theory T_α consists of two schemas.

- Nonexistence. (For H with v vertices, e edges, and $v - e\alpha < 0$) There does not exist a copy of H. To express it in slicker form – for all $t \ge 1$, $cl_t(\emptyset) = \emptyset$.
- Generic Extension. (For (R, H) safe, $t \ge 0$) For all $x_1, \ldots, x_r$, there exist $y_1, \ldots, y_v$ such that the following apply:
  1. $y_1, \ldots, y_v$ form an (R, H) extension over $x_1, \ldots, x_v$.
  2. There are no additional edges of the form y_i, y_j or y_i, x_j except those mandated by H.
  3. $y_1, \ldots, y_v$ is t-generic over $x_1, \ldots x_v$. (For $t = 0$, exclude this condition.)

We have seen by the Nonexistence Lemma that each A in the Nonexistence schema holds almost surely. We indicate the argument for the Generic Extension schema. Let (R, H) be safe. For any $\mathbf{x} = (x_1, \ldots, x_r)$, let $N(\mathbf{x})$ denote the number of (R, H) extensions $\mathbf{y} = (y_1, \ldots, y_v)$. Let $x_1, \ldots, x_r$ be selected randomly so that $N = N(\mathbf{x})$ becomes a random variable. We have seen that the expectation $\mu := E[N] \sim cn^v p^e$, which goes to infinity like a positive power of n. At the heart of this (and the one fairly technical part of the probability analysis) is a large-deviation result: for any fixed $\varepsilon > 0$,

$$\Pr[|N(\mathbf{x}) - \mu| > \varepsilon\mu] = o(n^{-r}).$$

Actually, the probability can be bounded by $\exp[n^{-\lambda}]$ for a positive λ, but the above suffices for our purposes. Here N counts extensions and so is the sum of $\sim cn^v$ indicator random variables (one for each distinct extension) each of which are one (i.e., the extension is there) with probability p^e. If we could think of N as a binomial distribution with parameters cn^v, p^e, then the above large-deviation result would follow from standard probability results, known as the Chernoff bounds. The difficulty arises from the fact that the indicator random variables are not independent, the potential extensions have a complex overlap pattern. Most of the potential extensions (as v is fixed and $n \to \infty$) do not overlap, and so their indicator random variables are independent. Still, it requires some technical skill, which we omit from this presentation, to show the large-deviation result.

Given the large-deviation result, we can easily deduce a counting theorem: almost surely the number of extensions $N(\mathbf{x})$ lies between $\mu(1 \pm \varepsilon)$ for *all* choices of $\mathbf{x}$. This follows since there are only $O(n^r)$ choices for the roots and the failure probability is $o(n^{-r})$ for any particular choice. Now, modulo some combinatorial work, we can deduce Generic Extension. For each $\mathbf{x}$, the number of (R, H) extensions is $\Theta(n^{v-e\alpha})$. How many of these are not t-generic? There are only a finite number of ways $\mathbf{y}$ can be not t-generic over $\mathbf{x}$. One shows that for each such possibility the number of such extensions is (using the counting theorem upper bound) at most $O(n^{v'-\alpha e'})$ where $v' - \alpha e'$ is smaller than $v - e\alpha$. Roughly, the existence of a rigid extension would add v_1 vertices and e_1 edges with $v_1 - e_1\alpha < 0$ and that would decrease $v - e\alpha$. The total number of non-t-generic extensions over $\mathbf{x}$ is then bounded by a constant times a smaller power of n. For n sufficiently large, this is smaller than the total number of extensions and therefore some (R, H) extension – indeed, almost all such extensions – will be t-generic.

The completeness of T_α can be shown via the Ehrenfeucht game but requires a surprisingly subtle strategy for Duplicator. Let G, G' be models of T_α, fix the number of rounds $u \geq 1$, and consider the Ehrenfeucht game $\text{EHR}(G_1, G_2; u)$.

Define integers $t_0, t_1, \ldots, t_u$ as follows. Set $t_0 = 0$ and (for convenience) $t_1 = 1$. Given t_i, select t_{i+1}, where the following apply:

1. $t_{i+1} \geq t_i$.
2. Almost surely in $G(n, n^{-\alpha})$, for every X of size $i + 1$, the t_i-closure of X has a size of at most t_{i+1} vertices outside of X.

Of course, the existence of t_{i+1} requires the Finite Closure Lemma. Now we describe Duplicator's strategy. Let x_j, x'_j denote the vertices of G, G' respectively selected in the jth round. Let $0 \leq i \leq u$ and set $s = u - i$ for convenience. Duplicator plays so that after the sth round (or, equivalently, with i rounds remaining) the t_i-closure of $(x_1, \ldots, x_s)$ and the t_i-closure of $(x'_1, \ldots, x'_i)$ are isomorphic, the isomorphism sending x_i to x'_i.

At the start of the game, setting $t = t_u$, the Nonexistence Schema assures that $cl_t(\emptyset)$ is the same in G and G', so Duplicator is fine. At the end of the game, the 0-closures are isomorphic, which is precisely the condition for Duplicator to have won. It thus suffices to show (the hard part) that if this condition is satisfied for i, then regardless of Spoiler's move Duplicator has a response that preserves the condition for $i - 1$.

To avoid subscripts, let us fix i and write $BIG := t_i$, $SMALL := t_{i-1}$, $\mathbf{x} = (x_1, \ldots, x_s)$ and $\mathbf{x}' = (x'_1, \ldots, x'_s)$. By symmetry, we can assume that Spoiler plays next in G. Let y denote his next move. There are two basic cases which we dub Inside and Outside.

We say y is Inside if $y \in cl_{BIG}(\mathbf{x})$. As $SMALL \leq BIG$, this then determines $cl_{SMALL}(\mathbf{x}, y)$ which lies entirely inside $cl_{BIG}(\mathbf{x})$. Duplicator checks the isomorphism φ between the BIG-closures of $\mathbf{x}, \mathbf{x}'$ and selects $y' = \varphi(y)$, the vertex corresponding to y under the isomorphism.

Otherwise, y is Outside. Let OLD denote the BIG-closure of $\mathbf{x}$. Duplicator calculates $cl_{SMALL}(\mathbf{x}, y)$ and sets NEW equal to those vertices of it which are not already in OLD. Our definition of BIG, which in turn depends on the Finite Closure Lemma, assures us that NEW has at most BIG vertices. Say NEW over OLD forms an (R, H) extension. We need now a combinatorial lemma (proof omitted) that any nonsafe extension contains a rigid subextension. From this it follows that (R, H) must be safe, since otherwise there would be a nonempty NEW^-, rigid over OLD, but then it would be in OLD by the closure definition. Duplicator then goes over to G', and by t-generic extension ($t = SMALL$) finds a NEW' over $OLD' = cl_{BIG}(\mathbf{x}')$ with precisely the same edges and selects y' as the vertex of NEW' corresponding to y. This immediately gives the result that the $SMALL$-closure of $\mathbf{x}', y'$ contains a copy of the $SMALL$-closure of $\mathbf{x}, y$ and some combinatorial lemmas involving t-genericity ensure that it contains nothing more and that the two $SMALL$-closures are isomorphic.

This shows that T_α is complete, and hence the zero-one law.

4.6 The Case p Constant

One of the original motivations for considering this area was a beautiful result shown independently by Glebskii et al. and by Fagin. Let $0 < p < 1$ be constant. They showed a Zero-One Law for this $G(n, p)$, that every first-order A holds either almost surely or almost never.

With our machinery the proof is quite quick. The theory T is given by one schema. (For all $r, s \geq 0$) For all distinct $x_1, \ldots, x_r, y_1, \ldots, y_s$ there exists a distinct z adjacent to all of the x_i and to none of the y_j.

Fix r, s, p. We call z a witness (relative to the x's and y's) if it has precisely the desired adjacencies. Each z has a probability $\varepsilon := p^r(1 - p)^s$ of being a witness. The events of being a witness are independent (involving disjoint edge sets) so the probability is $(1 - \varepsilon)^{n-r-s}$ that there is no witness. There are $\binom{n}{r}\binom{n-r}{s} \leq n^{r+s}$ choices for the x's and y's. Hence the probability that any such choice produces no witness is $\leq n^{r+s}(1 - \varepsilon)^{n-r-s}$. Fixing r, s, p fixes $\varepsilon > 0$ and exponential decay kills off polynomial growth, so the failure probability goes to zero.

The graphs G modeling T are said by Peter Winkler to have the Alice's Restaurant property. Members of a certain generation may remember the refrain, "You can get anything you want at Alice's Restaurant." All possible witnesses are there.

Let G, G' model T. Duplicator's stategy is simplicity itself. Staying alive. When x_i is played in G, Duplicator looks for $x'_i \in G'$ with the appropriate adjacencies to the previously selected vertices. By the Alice's Restaurant property, she never gets stuck.

4.7 Countable Models

Whenever we have a zero-one law, we have the complete theory T of those sentences holding almost surely. By the Gödel Completeness Theorem, such a theory must have a finite or countable model. The models cannot be finite, since for every $r \geq 1$ the sentence "There exist distinct $x_1, \ldots, x_r$" is in the almost sure theory since it holds for all $n \geq r$. Thus T must have a countable model – in our case a countable graph G. What does G look like? The first question is whether G is unique – that is, whether T is $\aleph_0$-categorical.

Consider first the Alice's Restaurant theory T for p constant. This is $\aleph_0$-categorical by an elegant argument. Let G, G' be two countable models of T, both labeled by the positive integers. We build up an isomorphism $\Phi : G \to G'$ by alternating left stages and right stages. After n steps the map Φ will map n elements of G into n elements of G', preserving adjacency and nonadjacency. For a left stage, let x be the least element of G for which $\Phi(x)$ is not defined. We require of $\Phi(x)$ that, for any $a \in G$ for which $\Phi(a)$ has been defined, $\Phi(x)$ must be either adjacent or nonadjacent to $\Phi(a)$ depending on whether x is adjacent or nonadjacent to a. By Alice's Restaurant, we can find such an x'. In the right stage we reverse the roles of G, G'. Let x' be the least element of G' for which $\Phi^{-1}(x')$ is not defined, and find $x = \Phi^{-1}(x')$ with the appropriate adjacencies. By step $2n$, vertices $1, \ldots, n$ have been used up in both G and G' so that at the end of this infinite process all vertices have been used up and Φ is a bijection giving the desired isomorphism. The countable graph G satisfying Alice's Restaurant is sometimes called the Rado graph in honor of the late Richard Rado.

What about the theory T_α for $0 < \alpha < 1$ irrational? This is not $\aleph_0$-categorical. We indicate two arguments that create (well, prove the existence of) different countable models.

Consider rigid extensions with $r = 1$, and so of the form $(\{x\}, H)$, with parameters v, e where $(\emptyset, H)$ is safe. (With $\alpha = \pi/7$, an example is $H = K_5$.) For such an H almost surely there exist copies of H but most vertices do not lie in such copies. Suppose $(\{x\}, H_i)$ is a sequence of such extensions with parameters v_i, e_i. For any s, define the graph H^s to be the union of $H_1, \ldots, H_s$. Here, we consider the H_i as disjoint vertex sets except for the common vertex x. Suppose further that there almost surely exists a copy of H^s. Such a sequence can be shown to exist for any α by employing a little number theory. The key is to find v_i, e_i such that $v_i - e_i \alpha$ is only very slightly negative. Now we can create a model in which some element is in a copy of H^s for all s. We add a constant symbol c to our logic and add the infinite schema (for $s \geq 1$) that c is in a copy of H^s. Any finite segment of this system is consistent, since in T itself one has that there exists a copy of H^s. By compactness there exists a model and the element corresponding to c has the desired property.

Now we create a special countable graph G_α that models T_α. The vertices will be the positive integers. For every safe rooted graph (R, H) and every $r = |R|$ distinct integers $\mathbf{x} = (x_1, \ldots, x_r)$ consider the *witness demand* that there must exist a $\mathbf{y} = (y_1, \ldots, y_v)$ forming an (R, H) extension over $\mathbf{x}$. Witness demands would include, continuing with our standard $\alpha = \pi/7$ example, that there exists a y_1 adjacent to $167, 233$ or that there exist y_1, y_2, y_3 forming a K_4 with 26. We include the case $R = \emptyset$ so that one demand is that there exist y_1, y_2 forming an edge. We turn the witness demands into a countable list. Now satisfy them one by one using new points in a minimal way. That is, when we need a y_1 adjacent to $167, 233$ pick a vertex, say 23801, that has not been touched before (at any stage, only a finite number of points have been touched) and join it to $167, 233$ and nothing else. There are two very nice properties of this construction. First, G_α is a model of T_α. (As you might expect, these minimal extensions are t-generic for all t.) Second, and quite surprisingly, G_α is unique. That is, it does not depend on the ordering of the witness demands nor on the choice of new points to satisfy them. These graphs G_α seem quite intriguing objects worthy of study simply as countable graphs. For any finite set X of vertices, let us define the closure $cl(X)$ as the union of the t-closures of X over all t, noting this is not a first-order concept. In this procedure at some finite time all vertices of X have been touched. Let Y be the value of $cl(X)$ at that moment. After this time, all extensions of Y are via safe extensions and one can show that $cl(X)$ remains the same. That is, in G_α all finite sets have finite closure.

The two models created are different, since in the first there is an x with $cl(\{x\})$ infinite, while in the second there is no such x.

4.8 A Dynamic View

We have seen that for fixed irrational $\alpha \in (0, 1)$, any first-order A holds almost surely or almost never in $G(n, n^{-\alpha})$. Now we consider A fixed and vary α – thinking roughly of the evolution of the random graph as we consider $p = n^{-\alpha}$ with α decreasing from one to zero. To study that evolution, we define

$$f_A(\alpha) = \lim_{n \to \infty} \Pr[G(n, n^{-\alpha}) \models A]$$

To avoid the problems at rational α, we simply define the domain of f_A to be the irrational $\alpha \in (0, 1)$. Our goal is to describe the possible functions f_A. Note that $f_A(\alpha) = 1$ when A is in the theory T_α, otherwise $f_A(\alpha) = 0$. We have given an explicit description of the theories T_α. In this sense the function f_A is described independently of probabilistic calculation. We seek to understand the relationships within the continuum of theories T_α.

We begin with a continuity result. Fix A and the irrational α. We claim that $f_A(\beta)$ is constant in some interval $(\alpha - \varepsilon, \alpha + \varepsilon)$ around α. Suppose A is in T_α (otherwise, take $\neg A$). Then A follows from a finite number of axioms of T_α. These in turn depend on notions of dense and sparse rooted graphs, which depend on whether $v - e\alpha$ is positive or negative. For any particular v, e, whatever the sign of $v - e\alpha$, that sign remains constant in some interval around α. The finite number of axioms leads to a finite number of pairs v, e and so all signs remain constant in some interval. For β in that interval, T_β has these same axioms and so A is in T_β. (It is known, however, that the theories T_α are all different. Between any two α, α' lies a rational a/b and it is known that there is a graph H such that the existence of a copy of H has a threshold function $n^{-a/b}$.)

The discontinuities of f_A must therefore come at the rational $a/b \in (0,1)$. We define the spectrum $Sp(A)$ to be those rational points of discontinuity. The classical theory of random graphs gives natural examples. Existence of a K_4 has a spectrum $\{2/3\}$. Existence of a K_5 has a spectrum $\{1/2\}$. We can put these together: "There exists a K_4 and there does not exist a K_5" to give a spectrum $\{2/3, 1/2\}$ – here as G evolves $\Pr[A]$ starts near zero, jumps to one at $n^{-2/3}$ when K_4's appear, and jumps back down to zero at $n^{-1/2}$ when K_5's appear. With some technical work, it is not difficult to get any finite set of rationals in $(0,1)$ as a spectrum in this way. This author once conjectured that all spectra were such finite sets. That proved not to be the case.

4.9 Infinite Spectra via Almost Sure Encoding

Here we shall describe a first-order A with an infinite spectrum. The central idea will be to take a second-order sentence and give it an almost sure encoding in the first order language.

For definiteness, we shall work near $\alpha = \frac{1}{3}$. By a $K_{3,k}$ is meant a set $x_1, x_2, x_3; y_1, \ldots, y_k$ with all y_j adjacent to all three x's. Basic random graph theory gives that the sentence "There exists a $K_{3,k}$" has a threshold function $n^{-1/3-1/k}$. (There are $e = 3k$ edges and $v = 3 + k$ vertices and $(\emptyset, K_{3,k})$ is sparse and safe if and only if $v - e\alpha > 0$.) Let $N(x_1, x_2, x_3)$ denote the set of common neighbors of x_1, x_2, x_3. Then, for $1/3 + 1/k > \alpha > 1/3 + 1/(k+1)$, the maximal size $|N(x_1, x_2, x_3)|$ is k. Consider then the property, call it A^*, that the maximal size $|N(x_1, x_2, x_3)|$ is even. This would have all values $1/3 + 1/k$ as spectral points. It is not possible to write this property in the first-order language. We shall, however, give an almost sure encoding, a first-order sentence that almost surely has the same truth value as A^*.

Let us look in the second-order world. How can we say that a set S (which will be $N(x_1, x_2, x_3)$ in our application) has even size. We write

$$EVEN(S) : \exists_R \forall_x \neg R(x,x) \wedge \forall_{x,y} R(x,y) \leftrightarrow R(y,x) \wedge \forall_{x \in S} \exists!_{y \in S} R(x,y).$$

That is, there exists an areflexive symmetric binary relation on S (i.e. a graph) which is a matching – each vertex has precisely one neighbor. How can we say that S is bigger than or equal in size to T? Similarly, we write $BIGGER(S,T)$, that there exists an areflexive symmetric binary relation R that yields an injection from $T - S$ to $S - T$. For every $y \in T - S$, there is a $x \in S - T$ with $R(y,x)$, and we do not have $R(y_1,x)$ and $R(y_2,x)$ for distinct $y_1, y_2 \in T - S$ and $x \in S - T$. Now we can write A^* in second order:

$$A^* : \exists_{x_1,x_2,x_3} EVEN[N(x_1,x_2,x_3)] \wedge$$

$$\wedge \forall_{z_1,z_2,z_3} BIGGER[N(x_1,x_2,x_3), N(z_1,z_2,z_3)].$$

Now for the almost sure encoding. We define the first-order ternary predicate (considering u as a variable symbol)

$$R_u(x,y) := \exists_v [v \sim x \wedge v \sim y \wedge v \sim u],$$

that u,x,y have a common neighbor. Our basic idea (though it will need modification) is to replace the second-order $\exists_R$ with the first-order $\exists_u$ and then to replace all instances of the binary R with the new binary R_u.

Lemma 4.9.1 (Representation Lemma). *For any s and any symmetric areflexive R on $1,\ldots,s$ that holds for l pairs with $l < k/3$,*

$$\forall_{x_1,\ldots,x_s} \exists_u \bigwedge_{1 \le i < j \le s} (R_u(x_i,x_j) \leftrightarrow R(i,j))$$

is a theorem of $T = T_\alpha$ for all $1/3 + 1/k > \alpha > 1/3 + 1/(k+1)$.

Consider the rooted graph, call it (S,H), with roots $1,\ldots,s$ and nonroot u, and then, for each $1 \le i < j \le s$ a nonroot v_{ij} with edges from v_{ij} to i,j,u. (S,H) has $v = 1 + l$ nonroots and $e = 3l$ edges. Our bound on l assures that $v - e\alpha > 0$ so that (S,H) is sparse, and some easy combinatorial work shows that it is safe as well. In T_α we have the 1-Generic Extension axiom for (S,H). For all $x_1,\ldots,x_s$ there exists a u and v_{ij} having the above edges and no more, so that, when $R(i,j)$ holds, we do have $R_u(x_i,x_j)$. Suppose now that $\neg R(i,j)$; can u, x_i, x_j have a common neighbor? A common neighbor to three vertices is a rigid extension in our range $\alpha > 1/3$ so this would violate 1-genericity.

We outline a second argument more for those readers in the random graph community. Set $p = n^{-1/3-\varepsilon}$ so that $1/k > \varepsilon > 1/(k+1)$. Any particular $R_u(x,y)$ holds with probability roughly $np^3 \sim n^{-3\varepsilon}$, that being the expected number of common neighbors. Say u is a witness if $R_u(x,y)$ holds for the l needed pairs. Then u would be a witness with a probability of roughly $n^{-3l\varepsilon}$. There are n potential witnesses, so the expected number of witnesses would be roughly $n^{1-3l\varepsilon}$. As $3l\varepsilon < 1$, this expected number goes to infinity, and almost surely for every choice of the x's there is one. There are a number of questions here (for one thing, u, u' being witnesses are no longer fully independent events) that need to be fleshed out, but this can be turned into a full proof.

We have a small technical problem. We want to say $EVEN(S)$, where $S = N(x_1,x_2,x_3)$ has at most k elements, by saying that there is a matching R. Such an R would have perhaps $k/2$ edges while our Representation Lemma only gives us R_u with at most $k/3$ edges. We puff up the Representation Lemma by replacing $\exists_R$ with $\exists_{u_1,u_2}$ and replacing R with $R_{u_1} \vee R_{u_2}$. Now we represent all R with up to just fewer than $2k/3$ edges. To write it out in full, "$N(x_1,x_2,x_3)$ is even" is replaced by "there exist u_1,u_2 such that for all y adjacent to x_1, x_2, x_3 there exists a unique $y' \neq y$ adjacent to x_1, x_2, x_3 with either y, y', u_1 or y, y', u_2 having a common neighbor". Similarly, $BIGGER(S, T)$ may require an injection R of k edges. We therefore replace $\exists_R$ with $\exists_{u_1, u_2, u_3, u_4}$ and R with $R_{u_1} \vee R_{u_2} \vee R_{u_3} \vee R_{u_4}$. With this, $BIGGER(N(x_1, x_2, x_3), N(x_1'x_2'x_3'))$ becomes a first-order predicate. We have given an almost sure encoding that transforms the second order A^* into a totally first-order (though hardly natural to those in graph theory!) sentence A which has the desired infinite spectrum.

The notion of an almost sure encoding is an intriguing one and will appear several more times. One is given a property P in some large language L^+ and one wishes to find (or, in one example later, to disprove the existence of) a sentence A in a given smaller language L which is an almost sure encoding of it. By this we mean that the probability of P and A differing in truth value goes to zero as the model size goes to infinity. Of course, one also has to fix the probability measure, in our case $G(n, p(n))$ with some particular $p(n)$. Hella, Kolaitis and Luosto have called two languages L, L' "almost everywhere equivalent" if for every P in one language there is an A in the other where, as above, the probability of P, A differing in truth value goes to zero as the model size goes to infinity. One particularly intriguing problem they give involves $G(n, p)$ with $p = 1/2$: Is monadic existential second-order logic almost everywhere equivalent to monadic universal second-order logic? They conjecture that the answer is no, but it does seem difficult to show negative results about the existence of an almost sure encoding.

4.10 The Jump Condition

We have already mentioned that the theories T_α are all distinct. However, if we fix the quantifier depth u of the sentences we are examining, the values α fall into definite intervals. Let us recall the sequence $t_0, \ldots, t_u$ from Sect. 4.5. We had $t_0 = 0, t_1 = 1$, and $t_{i+1} = \max[t_i, \lceil (u-i)\varepsilon^{-1} \rceil]$ where ε was the minimum value of $v^{-1}(e\alpha - v)$ over all integers v, e with $v \leq t_i$ and $v - e\alpha \leq 0$. We may try to define this sequence for rational α as well. It does not always work. Take, for example, $u = 5$ and $\alpha = 1/3 + 10^{-6}$. With $t_1 = 1$, we take $v = 1$ and $e = 3$ to give $\varepsilon = 3 \cdot 10^{-6}$. This yields a t_2 of roughly $\frac{4}{3} 10^6$, which is bigger than the numerator $10^6 + 1$ of α. Now, in trying to define t_3, we have v, e with $v \leq t_2$ and $v - e\alpha = 0$, so that $\varepsilon = 0$ and the process explodes.

This is not a surprise, the zero-one law is not supposed to hold for rational α. But it will hold on sentences of quantifier depth u if the rational α is not too rational. To be precise, let XPL_u denote the set of rational α for which the sequence $t_0, \ldots, t_u$ is not well defined, together (a technical point) with those α for which the sequence is well defined and α has a numerator of at most t_u. For $\alpha \notin XPL_u$ we do get a zero-one law. It turns out that XPL_u is a well-ordered set under the ordering $>$. (There is a lot of pretty number theory involved in studying XPL_u, which is quite reminiscent of continued fractions. The example above actually shows that $1/3 + 1/m \in EXP_5$ for all large integers m, so that EXP_5 is infinite. Here $1/3$ is an accumulation point of EXP_5 but only from larger values.) That is, for every $a/b \in XPL_u$ (except the smallest) there is an $(a/b)^- \in XPL_u$ which is the biggest element of XPL_u smaller than a/b. Then XPL_u splits the unit interval into intervals I from (going down) a/b to $(a/b)^-$. (We include the I from the smallest value of XPL_u to zero.) Inside each interval, the sequences $t_0, \ldots, t_u$ are the same. Further, the truth value of any A of quantifier depth u remains the same as α ranges over such an I. (Basically, one only needs notions of safe and dense rooted graphs up to $v = t_u$, and these notions are the same for all α in the interval.) To rewrite this as a condition on possible f_A:

Jump Condition. If $f = f_A$ for some first-order A then there is a u such that f is constant on each interval I defined by the splitting set XPL_u.

4.11 The Complexity Condition

For $\alpha \in (0, 1]$ rational, let us define $g_A(\alpha)$ to be the limiting value of $f_A(\alpha - \varepsilon)$ as ε approaches zero from above. Since EXP_u is well ordered under $>$, this is well defined. Indeed, for $\alpha \in EXP_u$ this gives the value of f_A on the interval from α to the next α^-. Since the intervals I defined above partition the unit interval, g_A will determine f_A.

For $\alpha \in (0, 1]$, we define a theory T_α^-. This will be the limiting theory of the $T_{\alpha+\varepsilon}$ as ε approaches zero from above. Recall that the splitting into dense and sparse rooted graphs was not a strict dichotomy for α rational, because of the possibility that $v - e\alpha = 0$. In T_α^-, we simply consider such rooted graphs as sparse, as that is their status in $T_{\alpha+\varepsilon}$ with ε positive. This can be shown to give a complete theory, and $g_A(\alpha) = 1$ precisely when A lies in this theory. We have a most surprising complexity condition on the functions g_A.

Complexity Condition:

$$\{0^a 1^b : A \in T_{a/b}^-\} \in PH.$$

To see this, let us fix the quantifier depth u and consider how difficult it is to find if $A \in T_{a/b}^-$ as a function of the denominator b. We can, as before, define the sequence $t_0, \ldots, t_u$. Here, having defined t_i, we define ε by only looking at those v, e with $v \leq t_i$ and $v - e(a/b)$ strictly negative. But then $v - e(a/b)$ has a denominator of at most $t_i b$ and so $\varepsilon \geq (t_i b)^{-1}$. Other terms (considering u fixed) supply bounded factors; basically t_i goes up by at most a factor of b as i increases. That is, $t_i = O(b^i)$.

We can write any A of quantifier depth u in the form

$$A : Q_{x_1} Q_{x_2} \cdots Q_{x_u} P(x_1, \ldots, x_u)$$

where Q is either $\exists$ or $\forall$, very possibly taking different values at different times, and P is a Boolean expression composed from the atoms $x_i = x_j$ and

$x_i \sim x_j$. The truth value of A in $T^-_{a/b}$ can now be turned into a game between two players. We shall call them Spoiler and Duplicator as before, though this game is not the Ehrenfeucht game. Duplicator's object is to show that A is a consequence of $T^-_{a/b}$, and Spoiler tries to show that it is not.

The Game Board. The game board has levels $0, 1, \ldots, u$. Each level has a finite set of positions. At level 0 are the possible values of $cl_0(x_1, \ldots, x_u)$. (Recall that these are determined by the graph on $\{x_1, \ldots, x_u\}$ and, to be formally correct, the equalities amongst the x_i.) At level i are the possible values of the t_i-closure of $x_1, \ldots, x_{u-i}$. When $i = u$, the top level, there is only one possible t_u-closure of $\emptyset$, namely $\emptyset$, so there is only a single position.

The Initial Position. The top-level position $\emptyset$.

The Winning Final Positions. The 0-position determines the truth value of $P(x_1, \ldots, x_u)$ – we call a 0-position winning if P is true, otherwise we call it losing.

The Permitted Moves. All moves go down one level. Let H and H' be positions on the levels i and $i - 1$ respectively. Moving from H to H' is permitted if and only if, in $T^-_{a/b}$, the following is a theorem: Given any $x_1, \ldots, x_{u-i}$ with t_i-closure H, there exists an x_{u-i+1} such that the t_{i-1}-closure of $x_1, \ldots, x_{u-i}, x_{u-i+1}$ is H'. We have argued that the T_α are complete via the Ehrenfeucht game, but it could have been done syntactically. The key result is that in T_α, for any positions H, H' on the levels $i, i - 1$, either the above is a theorem or there is a theorem that says: Given any $x_1, \ldots, x_{u-i}$ with t_i-closure H there *does not* exist an x_{u-i+1} such that the t_{i-1}-closure of $x_1, \ldots, x_{u-i}, x_{u-i+1}$ is H'.

The Rules of the Game. There are u rounds. In the ith round when x_i is quantified existentially (i.e. $Q = \exists$) it is Duplicator's move, and when it is quantified universally it is Spoiler's move. In either case, the permitted moves are given above so that the position moves through the levels and at the end of the u rounds is on the bottom level. Those positions have been designated winning and losing, and Duplicator wins or loses accordingly.

This game description works for any T_α or $T^-_{a/b}$. But with $T^-_{a/b}$, we can bound the game complexity by noting that each position is given by a graph (together with designated vertices) of size polynomial in b, certainly $O(b^u)$, and hence can be described by a sequence of bits of length $O(b^{2u})$. Therefore winning the game has a complexity in the polynomial hierarchy at level u.

Well, not quite. We also have to examine whether a move H to H' is permissible. To "prove" that the move is permissible, Duplicator draws a picture of H and H'. When the move is Inside she simply designates the new move x_{u-i+1} and the set H' which is the new closure. When the move is Outside, she states which vertices of H are still in H' plus she adds the new vertices (called NEW in the completeness proof) with all edges and a designated vertex x_{u-i+1}. She further lists the sequence of rigid extensions that give the t_{i+1}-closure. All this can be done with a polynomial-length string. Now Spoiler is allowed a polynomial-length string to show that Duplicator has been duplicitous. He can show that one of the rigid extensions is not really rigid by nailing down some vertices so that the extension becomes sparse. He can show (in the Outside case) that NEW is not really safe over H by demonstrating a dense subextension. Finally, he can show that the t_{i+1}-closure is more than H' by exhibiting, inside Duplicator's picture of $H \cup H'$, a dense extension. (There is a theorem that dense extensions must contain rigid subextensions, so he need not show that his extension is rigid.) This shows that the permissibility of a move is in the second level of the polynomial heirarchy.

Remarkably, the Jump Condition and the Complexity Condition characterize the possible functions f_A. We have seen, albeit in outline form, that these conditions are necessary. That they are sufficient is technically quite challenging. In personal communication, an argument for the sufficiency has been outlined by Gábor Tardos.

4.12 Nonconvergence via Almost Sure Encoding

Let us turn to the random *ordered* graph $G_<(n,p)$. The underlying model is still a vertex set Ω of size n and a probability space of graphs on Ω where each pair of vertices is adjacent with independent probability p. In addition, the set Ω is totally ordered by a built-in relation $<$. This relation is part of the language. For convenience, we can assume $\Omega = \{1, \ldots, n\}$. Now 1 is uniquely defined as that element with nothing less than it, and 2 is uniquely defined as that element with only 1 less than it. We can that express $1 \sim 2$ by the first order sentence

$$\exists_x \exists_y (x \neq y) \wedge (x < y) \wedge [\forall_z z < y \to z = x] \wedge x \sim y.$$

This event (for $n \geq 2$) has probability p. We shall write $y = x + 1$ if $x < y$ and there is no z in between them. When $y \neq 1$ we write $x = y - 1$ when $y = x + 1$. Note, however, that addition and subtraction are in general not defined in this language.

We shall restrict our attention to $p = 1/2$. The example above shows that there is no zero-one law, that $\Pr[A]$ need not converge to zero or one. We aim for the following stronger negative result of Compton, Hansen, and Shelah.

Theorem 4.12.1. *There is an A for which $\lim_{n \to \infty} \Pr[G_<(n, 1/2) \models A]$ does not exist.*

The central idea is to encode arithmetic on an ordered set S, first using second-order language and then in first-order with an almost sure encoding. The second-order encoding is standard. We say that on S there exist ternary relations $+(x, y, z)$ and $*(x, y, z)$ (with the interpretations $x + y = z$ and $x \cdot y = z$, respectively) such that the following apply:

1. $+(x, 1, z)$ if and only if $z = x + 1$ as described above.
2. When $y \neq 1$, $+(x, y, z)$ if and only if $+(x, y - 1, z - 1)$
3. $*(x, 1, z)$ if and only if $z = x$
4. When $y \neq 1$, $*(x, y, z)$ if and only if there exists a u with $*(x, y - 1, u)$ and $+(x, u, z)$.

When this occurs, we say S is arithmetizable. Now for the almost sure encoding. For $c \leq d$, we write $R_{c,d}(x, y, z)$ if $x, y \leq z$ and (critically) there exists an e with $c \leq e < d$ such that e is adjacent to x, y, z and no other elements of S. We say S is first-order arithmetizable if there exist c, d and c', d' such that $R_{c,d}, R_{c',d'}$ have the properties of "plus" and "times" enumerated above. For our specific purposes we shall consider only S of the form $\{1, \ldots, u\}$ though one could give similar results for more general S with a little more technical work. We make all logarithms to base 2 in what follows, for definiteness.

Lemma 4.12.2 (Representation Lemma). *Let $u \leq 0.9 \log^{1/3} n$. Then almost surely there exist $c \leq d$ such that $R_{c,d}$ is the ternary relation $+$ on $\{1, \ldots, u\}$ and also $c \leq d$ such that $R_{c,d}$ is $*$.*

Let $+$ have s instances. Observe that $s < u^2$. Consider a pair c, d with $u < c$ and $d = c + s$. We call c a witness if $R_{c,d}$ is indeed $+$ on $\{1, \ldots, u\}$ There is an arrangement (indeed, many such) of the edges between $\{1, \ldots, u\}$ and $\{c, \ldots, d - 1\}$ such that c is a witness. This occurs if us pairs have a particular set of adjacencies (and no more), and so has a probability 2^{-us} of occurring. There are $\sim n$ potential witnesses c so that the expected number of witnesses is bigger than roughly $n2^{-us}$. We have bounded u so that $us < u^3 < (0.9)^3 \log n$, and so this expected number goes to infinity. Some technical work shows that almost surely there is a witness. (Actually, the technical work isn't so difficult here. We can pick $\sim c' n \log^{-1/3} n$ values c so that the intervals $[c, d)$ are disjoint, and so the events that c is a witness are mutually independent over those different c's.) Representing $*$ is the same. Indeed, with further technical work (perhaps modifying the bound on u), one could almost surely represent every ternary, even k-ary, relation R.

Similar arguments, which we exclude, show that when $u > C \log^{1/3} n$ (where C is a computable absolute constant) the Representation Lemma almost surely fails and $\{1, \ldots, u\}$ is not first-order arithmetizable. For definiteness, let us take $C = 900$. Now the maximal u such that $\{1, \ldots, u\}$ is first-order arithmetizable is determined up to a factor of 1000.

Once we have arithmetized $\{1, \ldots, u\}$ we are off to the races. We can say that u is prime, that u is a Fermat prime; there is a large spectrum here. Certainly we can talk about $\log u$.

Now we can give our first-order sentence A: There exists u such that

1. $\{1, \ldots, u\}$ is first-order arithmetizable
2. $\{1, \ldots, u + 1\}$ is not first-order arithmetizable
3. $\log u$ modulo 40 is one of $1, 2, \ldots, 20$.

Why does this work? The size n of the model almost surely determines u up to a factor of 1000 and so $\log u$ is almost surely determined up to an additive term of 10. For some n, this range of $\log u$ will all be in $1, \ldots, 20$ modulo 40, while for other n this range will all be in $21, \ldots, 39, 0$ modulo 40. This gives infinite subsequences of n on which our sentence has a limiting probility of one and zero respectively, the worst kind of nonconvergence.

Almost sure encoding can be used to show nonconvergence by encoding arithmetic in other contexts. We shall examine, in outline form, $G(n, n^{-1/4})$. Note that we do not include $<$ as a built-in predicate here. We arithmetize a set S in the second-order language by saying that there exists a binary $<$ and ternary $+, *$ with the desired first-order properties. For $u \notin S$, we define a ternary R_u on S, letting $R_u(x, y, z)$ be the first order property that u, x, y, z have a common neighbor. Also, for $u, x \notin S$ we have the binary relation $R_{u,x}(y, z) = R_u(x, y, z)$. (We actually need further technical work here in that such relations are symmetric while $<$ is not.) We say that S is first-order arithmetizable if there exist u_1, u_2, u_3, u_4 such that $R_{u_1, u_2}, R_{u_3}, R_{u_4}$ play the role of $<, +, *$. At $p = n^{-1/4}$, any four vertices have probability $(1 - p^4)^{n-4} \sim e^{-1}$ of having no common neighbor. Basically, each R_u acts like an independent (this part takes some technical work) random ternary predicate with a probability of occurance $1 - e^{-1}$. Key here is that both $1 - e^{-1}$ and e^{-1} are bounded away from zero. Letting S have size s, a given u witnesses a particular ternary R with probability at least e^{-t}, where $t = \binom{s}{3}$ is the number of triples. The expected number of witnesses is at least ne^{-t}. For $s \leq \ln^{1/3} n$ this goes to infinity and one can show that almost surely $+, *, <$ are represented. We cannot quantify over all subsets S in the first-order language but instead look at sets $S = N(x_1, x_2, x_3, x_4)$, the set of common neighbors of x_1, x_2, x_3, x_4. One can show that there are such S's of all sizes up to roughly $\ln n / \ln \ln n$. On sets S, T of size $O(\ln^{1/3} n)$ we can say $BIGGER(S, T)$ in the first-order language (as done in Sect. 4.9) by saying there exist u_1, u_2 such that R_{u_1, u_2} gives an injection from T to S. It is then a first-order property of x_1, x_2, x_3, x_4 that $S = N(x_1, x_2, x_3, x_4)$ is arithmetizable but there is no "bigger" arithmetizable $S' = N(x_1', x_2', x_3', x_4')$. Such an S would almost surely have a size $\Theta(\ln^{1/3} n)$. But when S is arithmetizable, we can say a wide variety of things about its size u. In particular, we get a nonconvergent sentence by saying that there exist x_1, x_2, x_3, x_4 such that the size $u = |N(x_1, x_2, x_3, x_4)|$ has $\log u$ between 1 and 20 modulo 40.

4.13 No Almost Sure Representation of Evenness

In this section we restrict ourselves to the random ordered graph $G_<(n, p)$ with $p = 1/2$. We set, for any property A,

$$f_A(n) = \Pr[G_<(n, p) \models A]$$

We shall outline the proof of the following result of Saharon Shelah.

Theorem 4.13.1. *For any first-order A*

$$\lim_{n \to \infty} f_A(n+1) - f_A(n) = 0.$$

This provides an interesting counterpoint to the Compton, Hansen, and Shelah result discussed earlier. There are A's for which $f_A(n)$ does not converge, but it cannot oscillate back and forth too fast. There is a very nice corollary: There is no first-order sentence that provides an almost sure representation for the property that the number n of vertices is even. For such an A would have $f_A(2n) \to 1$ and $f_A(2n+1) \to 0$, which would contradict the slow oscillation of Shelah's Theorem. We find, in general, that it is quite difficult to prove negative results about almost sure representation, and in this context Shelah's result is particularly striking.

We link $G_<(n,p)$ and $G_<(n+1,p)$ by the following procedure. Take a random graph on $2n+1$ ordered vertices, and call it $G \sim G_<(2n+1,p)$. Restricting to a random subset S of size precisely n gives $G^{(n)}$, with a distribution that is that of $G_<(n,p)$. Restricting to a random set S of size precisely $n+1$ similarly gives $G^{(n+1)} \sim G_<(n+1,p)$. We thus have

$$f_A(n+1) - f_A(n) = \sum_G \mu(G) \left[\Pr[G^{(n+1)} \models A] - \Pr[G^{(n)} \models A] \right]$$

where $\mu(G)$ is the probability that $G_<(2n+1,p)$ is G. Shelah actually showed that for *every* G on $2n+1$ ordered vertices

$$\left| \Pr[G^{(n+1)} \models A] - \Pr[G^{(n)} \models A] \right| \to 0$$

Fix G and a property A. Consider the property that G restricted to S satisfies A as a function of S. For example, a sentence such as

$$\exists_x \forall_y \exists_z z \sim y \wedge y \sim x$$

would turn into

$$\exists_x (x \in S) \wedge [\forall_y (y \in S) \to \exists_z (z \in S) \wedge (z \sim x) \wedge (z \sim y)].$$

Such a property A^* is a Boolean function of the variables $x \in S$ for $x = 1, \ldots, 2n+1$. Here we turn to circuit complexity – the function may be represented by a circuit with primitives $x \in S$. Each $\exists_x$ is an OR gate with fan-in $2n+1$ (that is, all x), and each $\forall_x$ is an AND gate also with fan-in $2n+1$. The statements $x \sim y$ and $x < y$ then have definite truth values and so do not appear in the circuit. A^* is then represented by a bounded-depth polynomial-size circuit. It is a deep theorem of circuit complexity (due originally to Razborov) that such a circuit cannot determine majority – that is, cannot be true if and only if at least half of the $2n+1$ inputs are true. Some further technical work shows that no such circuit can distinguish between a random n and $n+1$ inputs being true - that the difference in the probability that the circuit yields true in the two experiments must tend to zero. This gives Shelah's result.

4.14 The Ehrenfeucht Game

The Ehrenfeucht game is a powerful and very general method for showing that two models have (or do not have) the same first-order properties. We consider first the specific example of graphs. Let G, H be two graphs and let t be a positive integer. We describe the Ehrenfeucht game EHR$(G, H; t)$.

The Board A copy of G and a copy of H on disjoint vertex sets.

The Players Spoiler and Duplicator.

The Play There are t rounds. In the i-th round Spoiler goes first. He selects either a vertex from G or a vertex from H. Then Duplicator goes. She selects a vertex from the graph that Spoiler did not select from. We let x_i denote the vertex selected from G in the ith round and y_i the vertex selected from H in the ith round, regardless of who selected them. We note that Spoiler's choice of which graph to choose from can change from round to round.

The Winner Duplicator wins if and only if the map from x_i to y_i preserves adjacency and equality. That is, x_i, x_j are adjacent in G precisely when y_i, y_j are adjacent in H. Further, $x_i = x_j$ precisely when $y_i = y_j$.

We note that when the graphs both have at least t vertices, there is no point in Spoiler selecting an x_j equal to a previous x_i, as then Duplicator would simply select $y_j = y_i$. Hence we could add the requirement that Spoiler always picks a new vertex. Then Duplicator would also always pick a new vertex.

Theorem 4.14.1. *Duplicator wins* EHR$[G, H; t]$ *if and only if G, H have the same truth values on all first-order sentences of quantifier depth t.*

We illustrate this fundamental result with an example. Suppose G has an isolated vertex and H does not. The property $\forall_x \exists_y x \sim y$ has quantifier depth $t = 2$. Spoiler selects the isolated vertex $x_1 \in G$ and Duplicator must select some $y_1 \in H$. As y_1 is not isolated, Spoiler moves over to H and selects a $y_2 \in H$ adjacent to y_1. Now Duplicator is stuck, there is no $x_2 \in G$ adjacent to x_1 for her to select.

As an immediate corollary, G, H are elementarily equivalent if and only if Duplicator wins EHR$[G, H; t]$ for every positive integer t. Note, however, that this is not the same as Duplicator winning a game with an infinite number of moves.

Corollary 4.14.2. *Let T be a consistent theory with no finite models. Then T is complete if and only if, for every two countable models G, H of T and every positive integer t, Duplicator wins* EHR$[G, H; t]$.

If T is complete, the models G, H are necessarily elementarily equivalent so that Duplicator wins. If T is not complete, there is a sentence A such that $T + A$ and $T + \neg A$ are both consistent and so they have countable models G, H. Letting t be the quantifier depth of A, Spoiler would win EHR$[G, H; t]$.

Let us generalize to first-order languages (we could go even further) with a finite number of relation symbols R of varying arity. This would include the ordered graph (with $<$ as well as adjacency) or the simple unary language (with only one unary U and equality) of Sect. 4.1. Let G, H be two models of the language. Then EHR$[G, H; t]$ is played as described above, with Spoiler and Duplicator selecting $x_1, \ldots, x_t \in G$ and $y_1, \ldots, y_t \in H$. For Duplicator to win, she now has to preserve all the relations. That is, let R be any relation symbol of arity l, say. Then $R(x_{i_1}, \ldots, x_{i_l})$ must have the same truth value as $R(y_{i_1}, \ldots, y_{i_l})$ for every choice of $i_1, \ldots, i_l$ from $1, \ldots, t$.

4.15 About the References

Among the other surveys of this area, we recommend those of Compton [3], Winkler [26], Lynch [15], and this author [23]. The Ehrenfeucht game was first given in [5]. (It was essentially found in earlier work by Fraïssé and is sometimes referred to as the Ehrenfeucht–Fraïssé game.) The classic zero-one law for random graphs with $p = 1/2$ (often called the uniform distribution) is due to Glebskii et al. [8] and Fagin [7]. The classic paper that began the theory of random graphs was that by Paul Erdős and Alfred Rényi [6]. The basic text on random graphs is that by Bollobás [2].

The zero-one Law for $p = n^{-\alpha}$ appeared first in [17]. An approach using the Ehrenfeucht game is given in [21]. A syntactic proof of the completeness of the T_α is given in [22]. An examination of the countable models of T_α is given in [20]. The text [1] also includes some of this material.

In this brief chapter we have examined only a few examples of random structures. Among the many others we shall mention [14] on unary functions, [18, 24] on random unary predicates with order (*considerably* different from sect. 4.1!), and [11] on random partially ordered sets. Łuczak and Shelah [12] have considered an interesting random graph model on vertex set $1, \ldots, n$ where the adjacency probability between i and j depends on $|i - j|$.

While we have restricted ourselves here to first-order logic there are a number of papers considering stronger logics. Generally, these give negative results that a zero-one law or convergence does not always hold. A nice example is given by Kaufmann and Shelah [10], giving a nonconvergent second-order sentence on $G(n, p)$ with $p = 1/2$. Many such results, including those on the random ordered graph given in the text above, can be found in [4]. Shelah [16] has shown that, on the random ordered graph, no first order sentence can almost surely encode the evenness of the model. Hella, Kolaitis, and Luosto [9] have considered the general problem of almost sure equivalence.

Spencer [19] has examined the random graph theory of extension statements in some detail. Łuczak and Spencer [13] have used some detailed random graph theory to give a near characterization of those $p = p(n)$ (*not* just those of the form $n^{-\alpha}$) for which the zero-one law holds. Spencer and Tardos [25] have given the necessary conditions on the function $f_A(\alpha)$ defined in the text.

References

1. N. Alon and J. Spencer. *The Probabilistic Method.* Wiley, 1991.
2. B. Bollobás. *Random Graphs.* Academic Press, 1985.
3. K.J. Compton, 0 − 1 laws in logic and combinatorics. In I. Rival, editor, *Algorithms and Order*, pages 353–383, NATO ASI Series, Kluwer Academic, Dordrecht, 1988.
4. K.J. Compton, C.W. Henson, and S. Shelah. Nonconvergence, undecidability and intractability in asymptotics problems. *Annals of Pure and Applied Logic*, 36:207-224, 1987.
5. A. Ehrenfeucht. An application of games to the completeness problem for formalized theories. *Fundamenta Mathematicae*, 49:129–141, 1961.
6. P. Erdős and A. Rényi. On the Evolution of Random Graphs. *Matematikai Kutató Intézet Közleményei*, 5:17-60, 1960.
7. R. Fagin. Probabilities in finite models. *Journal of Symbolic Logic*, 41:50–58, 1976.
8. Y.V. Glebskii, D.I. Kogan, M.I. Liagonkii, and V.A. Talanov. Range and degree of realizability of formulas in the restricted predicate calculua. *Cybernetics*, 5:142–154. (Russian original: *Kibernetica*,5:17-27, 1969.)
9. L. Hella, P.G. Kolaitis, and K. Luosto. Almost everywhere equivalence of logics in finite model theory. *Bulletin of Symbolic Logic*, 2:422–443, 1996.
10. M. Kaufmann and S. Shelah. On random models of finite power and monadic logic. *Discrete Mathematics*, 54:285–293, 1983.
11. T. Łuczak. First order properties of random posets. *Order*, 8:291–297, 1991.
12. T. Łuczak and S. Shelah. Convergence in homogeneous random graphs. *Random Structures & Algorithms*, 6:371–392, 1995.
13. T. Łuczak and J. Spencer. When does the zero-one law hold? *Journal of the American Mathematical Society*, 4:451-468, 1991.
14. J. Lynch. Probabilities of first-order sentences about unary functions. *Transactions of the American Mathematical Society*, 287:543–568, 1985.
15. J. Lynch. Special year on logic and algorithms tutorial notes: Random finite models. DIMACS Technical Report 97-56, 1997.
16. S. Shelah. Very weak zero one law for random graphs with order and random binary functions. *Random Structures & Algorithms*, 9:351–358, 1995.
17. S. Shelah and J. Spencer. Zero–one laws for sparse random graphs. *Journal of the American Mathematical Society*, 1:97–115, 1988.
18. S. Shelah and J. Spencer. Random sparse unary predicates. *Random Structures & Algorithms*, 5:375-394, 1994.
19. J. Spencer. Threshold functions for extension statements. *Journal of Combinatorial Theory Series A*, 53:286–305, 1990.
20. J. Spencer. Countable sparse random graphs. *Random Structures & Algorithms*, 1:205-214, 1990.
21. J. Spencer. Zero-one laws via the Ehrenfeucht game. *Discrete Applied Mathematics*, 30:235-252, 1991.
22. J. Spencer. Sparse random graphs: a continuum of complete theories. In D. Miklos, editor, *Proceedings of the International Conference "Sets, Graphs and Numbers"*, pages 679–690. Colloq. Math. Soc. János Bolyai 60. North-Holland, 1991.
23. J. Spencer. Zero–one laws with variable probability. *Journal of Symbolic Logic*, 58:1-14, 1993.

24. J. Spencer and K. StJohn. Random unary predicates: Almost sure theories and countable models. *Random Structures & Algorithms*, 13:229–248, 1998.
25. J. Spencer and G. Tardos. Ups and downs of first order sentences on random graphs. *Combinatorica*, 20:263-280, 2000.
26. P. Winkler. Random structures and zero–one laws. In N.W. Sauer, R.E. Woodrow and B. Sands, editors, *Finite and Infinite Combinatorics in Sets and Logic*, pages 399–420. NATO Advanced Science Institutes Series, Kluwer Academic, Dordrecht 1993.

5

Embedded Finite Models and Constraint Databases

Leonid Libkin

5.1 Introduction

The goal of this chapter is to answer two questions:

1. How does one store an *infinite* set in a database?
2. And what does it have to do with *finite* model theory?

Clearly, one cannot store an infinite set, but instead one can store a *finite representation* of an infinite set and write queries as if the entire infinite set were stored. This is the key idea behind *constraint databases*, which emerged relatively recently as a very active area of database research. The primary motivation comes from geographical and temporal databases: how does one store a region in a database? More importantly, how does one design a query language that makes the user view a region as if it were an infinite collection of points stored in the database?

Finite representations used in constraint databases are first-order formulae; in geographical applications, one often uses Boolean combinations of linear or polynomial inequalities. One of the most challenging questions in the development of the theory of constraint databases has been that of the expressive power: what are the limitations of query languages for constraint databases? These questions were easily reduced to questions about the expressiveness of query languages over ordinary *finite* relational databases, with the additional condition that databases may store numbers and arithmetic operations may be used in queries. This is exactly the setting of *embedded finite model theory*.

It turned out that the classical techniques for analyzing the expressive power of relational query languages no longer worked in this new setting. In the past several years, however, most questions about the expressive power have been settled, by using new techniques that mix the finite and the infinite, and bring together results from a number of fields such as model theory, algebraic geometry, and symbolic computation.

In this chapter we present a variety of results on embedded finite models and constraint databases. The core part of this chapter deals with new techniques for analyzing expressive power in the mixed setting. These techniques, which come in the form of *collapse results*, reduce many questions over constraint databases or embedded finite models to the classical finite-model-theory setting.

5.1.1 Organization

In Sect. 5.2, we describe the setting of embedded finite models, and explain connections with relational database theory. Sect. 5.3 contains a brief introduction into constraint databases.

Sect. 5.4 gives an overview of collapse results; it also defines various semantics of logical formulae, and introduces the notion of genericity. Sections 5.5 and 5.6 describe collapse results for various semantics and various notions of genericity. In Sect. 5.7 we look into connections between collapse results and various model-theoretic notions, and in Section 5.8 we describe a close relationship between collapse results and the notion of the VC dimension, which is of interest in model theory and machine learning. Sect. 5.9 presents results on the expressive power of query languages over constraint databases that use two different techniques: reduction to the case of embedded finite models, and the analysis of the topological structure of constraint databases.

Sections 5.10 and 5.11 deal with topics motivated by database considerations. Sect. 5.10 studies query safety, which means guaranteeing finite output for relational databases, and some geometric properties for constraint databases. Section 5.11 briefly analyzes the problems of aggregate operators and higher-order features in constraint databases.

5.2 Relational Databases and Embedded Finite Models

In classical finite model theory, we work with finite structures and deal with sentences such as

$$\exists x \exists y \forall z (\neg E(z, x) \vee \neg E(z, y))$$

which says that the diameter of an (undirected) graph with edge-set E is at least 3. In embedded finite model theory, we still work with finite structures but deal with sentences like

$$\exists x \exists y \, (E(x, y) \wedge (y = x \cdot x + 1))$$

which says that there is an edge (x, y) in a graph with $y = x^2 + 1$. It is assumed here that the nodes of a graph come from some domain that is equipped with arithmetic operations such as addition and multiplication; for example, the nodes could be natural, rational, or real numbers.

To illustrate the difference, consider as an example a relational signature of directed graphs, consisting of a single edge-predicate E. Suppose we want to find the composition of E with itself; that is, to find pairs (a, b) in a directed graph that are connected by a path of length at most 2. This is done by writing a formula

$$\varphi(x, y) \equiv \exists z \ (E(x, z) \wedge E(z, y)).$$

This formula gives us a *conjunctive query*; it can be written in a variety of relational database languages: as

$$q(x, y) :\text{-} \ E(x, z), E(z, y)$$

in Datalog, or

$$\pi_{\#1, \#4} \ (\sigma_{\#2=\#3} \ (R \times R) \ )$$

in relational algebra, or

```
SELECT R1.Source, R2.Destination
FROM R R1, R R2
WHERE R1.Destination=R2.Source
```

in SQL.

Now suppose that the nodes of the graph are natural numbers, and we are only willing to consider paths $E(x, z), E(z, y)$ in which x, y, z are related by some condition: for example, $x + y = z$. It is straightforward to rewrite the above query in first-order logic as

$$\varphi'(x, y) \equiv \exists z \ (E(x, z) \wedge E(z, y) \wedge (x + y = z)),$$

or in SQL as

```
SELECT R1.Source, R2.Destination
FROM R R1, R R2
WHERE R1.Destination=R2.Source
      AND R1.Source + R2.Destination = R2.Source
```

But what about relational algebra? The most natural way seems to be

$$\pi_{\#1, \#4} \ (\sigma_{(\#2=\#3) \wedge (\#1+\#4=\#2)} \ (R \times R) \ );$$

however, relational algebra does not allow arithmetic operations in its selection predicates.

At the first glance, this is easy to remedy: just add arithmetic predicates to the selection conditions. While this seems to be easy, there appear to be two serious problems.

Expressive power. We know that first-order logic, and thus relational algebra, cannot express most recursive and counting queries, such as the transitive closure of a relation or the parity of a set. However, this was proved under the assumption that only equality and order comparisons are allowed on nodes of graphs. How does one prove the analogous result (if it is true) if nodes are numbers, and arithmetic operations are used in formulae?

It appears that the standard techniques for proving expressivity bounds are not directly applicable in this case. Tools based on locality cannot tell us anything meaningful, owing to the presence of order; 0-1 laws are inapplicable altogether, and games become unmanageable as the duplicator must maintain partial isomorphism not only for the graph edges but also for all the arithmetic predicates as well. It thus seems that entirely different techniques are needed to solve the problem of the expressive power in this setting.

Query Evaluation. It is clear that the query φ' above can be evaluated by the usual bottom-up technique: we first construct $R \times R$, then select all the tuples (a, b, c, d) with $b = c$ and $a + d = b$, and then project out the first and the last components. However, what if the condition is not $x + y = z$ but that z is a perfect square? The query will then be rewritten as

$$\varphi''(x, y) \equiv \exists z \ (E(x, z) \wedge E(z, y) \wedge (\exists u \ (z = u \cdot u))),$$

and the selection condition will have to evaluate $\exists u \ (z = u \cdot u)$ with u ranging over the infinite set of natural numbers! In this particular case, it appears that the evaluation is possible: one does not have to check all $u \in \mathbb{N}$, but only $u \leq z$. However, one can have more complex conditions, for example $\exists x_1 \ldots \exists x_k \ p(x_1, \ldots, x_k) = 0$, where p is some polynomial with integer coefficients. The truth value of this sentence cannot be determined algorithmically, as this would imply solving Hilbert's tenth problem. Thus, it is not always possible to evaluate queries with arithmetic conditions. In general, one would encounter this problem in dealing with any undecidable theory.

To give another example of potential problems with query evaluation, consider the following query $\psi(x)$, saying that x^2 belongs to S:

$$\exists y \ S(y) \wedge (x \cdot x = y).$$

This query is clearly evaluable, but its output depends on whether one works with real numbers, or integers; for example, over the reals, the output is $\{-\sqrt{a}, \sqrt{a} \mid a \in S\}$, but over the integers one has to select integers from this set. Thus, the output is different depending on the range of the quantifier $\exists y$: whether it is $\mathbb{R}$ or $\mathbb{Z}$. Also, it is not immediately clear how a query processor can look at the query above and transform the declarative specification involving a quantifier over an infinite set into a finite evaluable query such as $\{-\sqrt{a}, \sqrt{a} \mid a \in S\}$.

To deal with these problems, we now have to give a formal definition of the setting. Intuitively, we are dealing with finite relational structures whose elements come from some interpreted domain with some interpreted operations. Formally, the object of our study is the following:

Definition 5.2.1. *Let $\mathfrak{M} = \langle U, \Omega \rangle$ be an infinite structure on a set U, where the signature Ω contains some function, predicate, and constant symbols. Let SC be a relational signature $\{R_1, \ldots, R_l\}$ where each relation symbol R_i has arity $p_i > 0$. Then an embedded finite model (that is, an SC-structure embedded into $\mathfrak{M}$) is a structure*

$$D = \langle A, R_1^D, \ldots, R_l^D \rangle,$$

where each R_i^D is a finite subset of U^{p_i}, and A is the union of all elements that occur in the relations $R_1^D, \ldots, R_l^D$. The set A is called the active domain of D, and is denoted by $adom(D)$.

The examples of structures $\mathfrak{M}$ that will be used most often will be real and natural numbers with various arithmetic operations, for example $\langle \mathbb{N}, +, \cdot \rangle$, the real ordered field $\langle \mathbb{R}, +, \cdot, 0, 1, <, \rangle$, and the real ordered group $\langle \mathbb{R}, +, -, 0, 1, < \rangle$.

The notation SC comes from the database name *schema* for the relational vocabulary of a finite structure.

In the setting where we mix finite and infinite structures, first-order logic (FO) must be defined carefully. Note that we have two different universes that can be quantified over: the universe U of the infinite structure $\mathfrak{M}$, and the active domain A of the finite structure D.

Definition 5.2.2. *Given a structure $\mathfrak{M} = \langle U, \Omega \rangle$ and a relational signature SC, first-order logic (FO) over $\mathfrak{M}$ and SC, denoted by $\mathrm{FO}(SC, \mathfrak{M})$, is defined as follows:*

- *Any atomic FO formula in the language of $\mathfrak{M}$ is an atomic $\mathrm{FO}(SC, \mathfrak{M})$ formula. For any p-ary symbol R from SC and terms $t_1, \ldots, t_p$ in the language of $\mathfrak{M}$, $R(t_1, \ldots, t_p)$ is an atomic $\mathrm{FO}(SC, \mathfrak{M})$ formula.*
- *Formulae of $\mathrm{FO}(SC, \mathfrak{M})$ are closed under the Boolean connectives ($\vee$, $\wedge$, and $\neg$).*
- *If φ is an $\mathrm{FO}(SC, \mathfrak{M})$ formula, then*

$$\exists x \; \varphi, \quad \forall x \; \varphi, \quad \exists x \in adom \; \varphi, \quad and \quad \forall x \in adom \; \varphi$$

are $\mathrm{FO}(SC, \mathfrak{M})$ formulae.

The class of first-order formulae in the language of $\mathfrak{M}$ will be denoted by $\mathrm{FO}(\mathfrak{M})$ (that is, the formulae built up from atomic $\mathfrak{M}$-formulae by Boolean connectives and quantification $\exists, \forall$). The class of formulae not using the symbols from Ω will be denoted by $\mathrm{FO}(SC)$ (in this case all four quantifiers are allowed).

The notions of free and bound variables are standard. For the semantics, given a $\mathrm{FO}(SC, \mathfrak{M})$ formula $\varphi(x_1, \ldots, x_n)$, and $\vec{a} = (a_1, \ldots, a_n) \in U^n$, we define the relation $(\mathfrak{M}, D) \models \varphi(\vec{a})$. When $\mathfrak{M}$ is understood, we usually write just $D \models \varphi(\vec{a})$. The notion of satisfaction is standard, with only the case of quantification requiring explanation. Let $\varphi(x, \vec{y})$ be a formula, and let $\vec{b}$ be a tuple of elements of U, of the same length as $\vec{y}$. Then

$$
\begin{aligned}
(\mathfrak{M}, D) &\models \exists x\ \varphi(x, \vec{b}) &\Leftrightarrow& \quad (\mathfrak{M}, D) \models \varphi(a, \vec{b}) \text{ for some } a \in U \\
(\mathfrak{M}, D) &\models \forall x\ \varphi(x, \vec{b}) &\Leftrightarrow& \quad (\mathfrak{M}, D) \models \varphi(a, \vec{b}) \text{ for all } a \in U \\
(\mathfrak{M}, D) &\models \exists x \in adom\ \varphi(x, \vec{b}) &\Leftrightarrow& \quad (\mathfrak{M}, D) \models \varphi(a, \vec{b}) \text{ for some } a \in adom(D) \\
(\mathfrak{M}, D) &\models \forall x \in adom\ \varphi(x, \vec{b}) &\Leftrightarrow& \quad (\mathfrak{M}, D) \models \varphi(a, \vec{b}) \text{ for all } a \in adom(D).
\end{aligned}
$$

The quantifiers $\exists x \in adom\ \varphi$ and $\forall x \in adom\ \varphi$ are called *active-domain* quantifiers. Note that they are definable with the unrestricted quantifiers $\exists$ and $\forall$, as $adom(D)$ is definable by an FO formula. However, we find it more convenient to have them explicitly in the syntax so that we can use both restricted and unrestricted quantifiers in the same formula.

Definition 5.2.3. *By* $\mathrm{FO}_{\mathrm{act}}(SC, \mathfrak{M})$, *we denote the fragment of* $\mathrm{FO}(SC, \mathfrak{M})$ *that uses only quantifiers* $\exists x \in adom$ *and* $\forall x \in adom$. *Formulae in this fragment are called the* active-domain semantics *formulae.*

Sometimes we shall also refer to the standard interpretation of the unrestricted quantifiers $\exists$ and $\forall$ as the *natural* semantics of first-order formulae, and to the class $\mathrm{FO}(SC, \mathfrak{M})$ as the class of *natural-semantics formulae*.

Our goal is to study $\mathrm{FO}(SC, \mathfrak{M})$. In particular, we shall show that the solutions to the crucial problems of expressive power and query evaluation depend heavily on the model-theoretic properties of $\mathfrak{M}$. In fact, we shall see the full range of expressivity – from all computable properties to just $\mathrm{FO}_{\mathrm{act}}(SC)$-definable properties – for various structures $\mathfrak{M}$. Of course it is highly undesirable to have a query language that expresses all computable queries, since in the database setting we want to keep the complexity low, and we want queries to be optimizable. The latter situation is much more attractive, since essentially one is dealing with the familiar relational calculus on finite databases.

5.3 Constraint Databases

The field of constraint databases (CDB) was initiated in 1990, and since then has become a well-established topic in the database field. It grew out of the research on Datalog and constraint logic programming (CLP). The original motivation was to combine work in these two areas, with the goal of obtaining a database-style, optimizable version of constraint logic programming. The key idea was that the notion of a tuple in a relational database could be replaced by a conjunction of constraints from an appropriate language (for example, linear arithmetic constraints), and that many of the features of the relational model could be extended in an appropriate way. In particular, standard query languages such as those based on first-order logic and Datalog could be extended, at least in principle, to such a model.

The primary motivation for constraint databases comes from the field of spatial and spatio-temporal databases, and geographical information systems (GIS). One wants to store an infinite set – say, a region on the real plane – in a database and query it *as if* all the points (infinitely many) were stored. This is clearly impossible. However, it is possible to store a *finite representation* of an infinite set, and to make this completely transparent to the user, who can still access the data as though infinitely many points were stored.

To illustrate how infinite geometric objects can be represented with various classes of constraints, we use the following examples.

Consider Fig. 5.1. This figure can be described, using polynomial inequalities with integer coefficients as follows:

$$(x^2/25 + y^2/16 = 1) \vee (x^2 + 4x + y^2 - 2y \le 4)$$
$$\vee (x^2 - 4x + y^2 - 2y \le -4) \vee (x^2 + y^2 - 2y = 8 \wedge y < -1) \,.$$

The first equality describes the outer ellipse of the figure, the second and third disjuncts describe the "eyes", and the last disjunct describes the "mouth".

If we restrict ourselves to inequalities involving linear functions, the face in Fig. 5.1 can no longer be defined. It can, however, be approximated as follows (Fig. 5.2):

$$(-5 \le x \le 5 \wedge y = -4) \vee (-5 \le x \le 5 \wedge y = 4)$$
$$\vee (x = 5 \wedge -4 \le y \le 4) \vee (x = -5 \wedge -4 \le y \le 4)$$
$$\vee (-3 \le x \le -1 \wedge 0 \le y \le 2) \vee (1 \le x \le 3 \wedge 0 \le y \le 2)$$
$$\vee (3y = -x - 6 \wedge -2 \le y \le -1) \vee (3y = x - 6 \wedge -2 \le y \le -1) \,.$$

The first four disjuncts describe the outer rectangle. The next two disjuncts describe the "eyes", and the last two describe the "mouth".

Fig. 5.1. An example of two-variable polynomial constraints

Fig. 5.2. An example of two-variable linear arithmetic constraints

What makes the sets depicted in Figs. 5.1 and 5.2 special is that they are *definable* by FO formulae over some structures, in this case the real field and the real ordered group.

Definition 5.3.1. *Given a structure* $\mathfrak{M} = \langle U, \Omega \rangle$, *a set* $X \subseteq U^n$ *is called* $\mathfrak{M}$-*definable (or definable over* $\mathfrak{M}$, *or just definable if* $\mathfrak{M}$ *is understood) if there exists an FO formula* $\varphi(x_1, \ldots, x_n)$ *in the language of* $\mathfrak{M}$ *such that*

$$X = \{(a_1, \ldots, a_n) \in U^n \mid \mathfrak{M} \models \varphi(a_1, \ldots, a_n)\}.$$

We now consider two classes of definable sets that are especially relevant in the context of constraint databases.

Definition 5.3.2. *We use the abbreviations* **R** *for the real field (that is,* $\langle \mathbb{R}, +, \cdot, 0, 1, < \rangle$) *and* $\mathbf{R}_{\text{lin}}$ *for the real ordered group (* $\langle \mathbb{R}, +, -, 0, 1, < \rangle$). *Sets definable over* **R** *are called* semialgebraic *and sets definable over* $\mathbf{R}_{\text{lin}}$ *are called* semilinear.

A remarkable property of both $\mathbf{R}_{\text{lin}}$ and **R** is that they admit *quantifier elimination*; that is, every formula is equivalent to a quantifier-free one. For $\mathbf{R}_{\text{lin}}$ this is a simple consequence of Fourier-Motzkin elimination; for **R**, this is a celebrated result of Tarski.

Thus, every semialgebraic set in $\mathbb{R}^n$ is a Boolean combination of sets given by polynomial equalities and inequalities of the form

$$p(x_1, \ldots, x_n) \ \{=, >, <\} \ 0,$$

where p is a polynomial (with rational or integer coefficients). Similarly, a semilinear set in $\mathbb{R}^n$ is a Boolean combination of sets given by linear equalities and inequalities of the form

$$a_1 \cdot x_1 + \ldots + a_n \cdot x_n \ \{=, >, <\} \ b,$$

where the a_is and b are rational or integer coefficients. That is, a semilinear set is a Boolean combination of half-spaces and hyperplanes in $\mathbb{R}^n$.

The set shown in Fig. 5.1 is semialgebraic, and the set shown in Fig. 5.2 is semilinear. In general, the majority of geographical applications represent regions by linear constraints; that is, regions are semilinear sets. If linear constraints are not sufficient, one can use polynomial constraints instead.

We are now ready to present a mathematical model of constraint databases.

Definition 5.3.3. *Let* $\mathfrak{M} = \langle U, \Omega \rangle$ *be an infinite structure on a set* U, *and let* SC *be a relational signature* $\{R_1, \ldots, R_l\}$, *where each relation* R_i *has arity* $p_i > 0$. *Then a* constraint database *of schema* SC *is a tuple*

$$\mathbf{D} = \langle R_1^{\mathbf{D}}, \ldots, R_l^{\mathbf{D}} \rangle,$$

where each $R_i^{\mathbf{D}}$ *is a definable subset of* U^{p_i}. *The superscript* **D** *is omitted if it is clear from the context.*

Thus, the only difference between the definition of a constraint database and an embedded finite model is that in the former we interpret the SC-predicates by definable sets, and in the latter we interpret them by finite sets.

The definition of FO($SC, \mathfrak{M}$) is the same for constraint databases as it is for embedded finite models, except that we do not use the restricted quantification $\exists x \in adom$ and $\forall x \in adom$. The quantifiers are thus interpreted as ranging over the entire infinite set U. As linear and polynomial constraints play a special role in the theory of constraint databases, we introduce a special notation for them.

Definition 5.3.4. *If $\mathfrak{M}$ is the real field, we write* FO + POLY(SC) *for* FO($SC, \mathbf{R}$), *or just* FO + POLY *if SC is clear from the context. If $\mathfrak{M}$ is the real ordered group, we write* FO + LIN(SC) *(or just* FO + LIN*) for* FO($SC, \mathbf{R}_{\text{lin}}$).

The notation FO + POLY stands for FO with polynomial constraints, and FO + LIN stands for for FO with linear constraints. An example of definability in FO + POLY is the property that all points in a relation S lie on a common circle: $\exists a \exists b \exists r \, (\forall x \forall y \, S(x, y) \rightarrow (x - a)^2 + (y - b)^2 = r^2)$. In general, FO + POLY can define many useful topological concepts, such as closure, interior, and boundary. These are definable in FO + LIN as well. For example, the FO + LIN query $\alpha(x, y)$,

$$\forall \varepsilon > 0 \exists x' \exists y' \big(S(x', y') \wedge (x - \varepsilon < x' < x + \varepsilon) \wedge (y - \varepsilon < y' < y + \varepsilon) \big)$$

tests whether the pair (x, y) is in the closure of a set $S \subseteq \mathbb{R}^2$.

In FO + POLY one can also define the convex hull of a set. To see how this is done in the two-dimensional case, assume that a semialgebraic set $S \in \mathbb{R}^2$ is given. Then $\varphi(x, y)$ given by the formula

$$\exists x_1, y_1, x_2, y_2, x_3, y_3 \; \exists \lambda_1, \lambda_2, \lambda_3 \left(\begin{array}{l} S(x_1, y_1) \wedge S(x_2, y_2) \wedge S(x_3, y_3) \\ \wedge\, \lambda_1 \geq 0 \wedge \lambda_2 \geq 0 \wedge \lambda_3 \geq 0 \\ \wedge\, \lambda_1 + \lambda_2 + \lambda_3 = 1 \\ \wedge\, (x = \lambda_1 \cdot x_1 + \lambda_2 \cdot x_2 + \lambda_3 \cdot x_3) \\ \wedge\, (y = \lambda_1 \cdot y_1 + \lambda_2 \cdot y_2 + \lambda_3 \cdot y_3) \end{array} \right)$$

is true on (x, y) iff $(x, y) \in \text{conv}(S)$. In general, to define the convex hull of a set S in $\mathbb{R}^n$, one uses Carathéodory's Theorem which states that $\vec{x}$ is in the convex hull of $S \subseteq \mathbb{R}^n$ iff $\vec{x}$ is in the convex hull of some $n + 1$ points in S, and one codes this by an FO formula just as we did above for the case of $\mathbb{R}^2$.

We note again that these examples demonstrate the crucial property of constraint databases: query languages based on FO view the database as if it were infinitely many tuples stored in memory. We refer to the database relations in exactly the same way as we do for the usual relational databases.

Now that we have defined constraint databases and have seen some examples of querying, we consider the same issues that we addressed in the context of embedded finite models: expressive power and query evaluation.

Expressive power. We have seen that FO + POLY is a rather expressive language for talking about properties of semialgebraic sets, and that many topological properties of semilinear sets can already be expressed in the weaker language FO + LIN. We next turn to a very basic topological property: *connectivity.* Suppose we are given a semialgebraic or semilinear set S, and we want to test whether it is topologically connected. Can we do this in FO + POLY or FO + LIN?

At first, it seems that the answer is "no". Indeed, it appears that topological connectivity is rather close to graph connectivity. Take an undirected graph G and embed it in $\mathbb{R}^3$ without self-intersections. The embedding is then topologically connected iff G is a connected graph. However, we know only that FO cannot express graph connectivity; there is nothing yet that tells us that similar bounds exist for FO + LIN and FO + POLY.

Query Evaluation. Suppose we are given an FO($SC, \mathfrak{M}$) query $\varphi(\bar{x})$ and a constraint database $\mathbf{D}$ over $\mathfrak{M}$. How does one evaluate φ on $\mathbf{D}$? The answer to this is very simple – one just puts the definition of relations in $\mathbf{D}$ into φ. For example, if $\varphi(x) \equiv \exists y\, (S(x, y) \wedge (p_1(x, y) > 0))$ and S is given by $p_2(x, y) < 0$, where p_1, p_2 are polynomials, then by putting the definition of S into φ we obtain a new formula $\varphi^{\mathbf{D}}(x) \equiv \exists y\, ((p_2(x, y) < 0) \wedge (p_1(x, y) > 0))$. As this is an FO formula, it gives us a constraint database.

This may look a little bit like cheating, and of course it is. For example, how does one check that $\mathbf{D} \models \varphi(1)$? To do so, one must be able to check whether $\varphi^{\mathbf{D}}(1)$ is true in $\mathbf{R}$; in general, one must be able to check whether $\varphi^{\mathbf{D}}(\bar{a})$ is true in a given structure $\mathfrak{M}$, where $\varphi^{\mathbf{D}}$ is the result of substituting definitions of relations in SC in the query φ. This can only be done if the FO theory of the underlying structure $\mathfrak{M}$ is *decidable.* This property certainly holds for $\mathbf{R}_{\text{lin}}$ and $\mathbf{R}$ (in fact, they satisfy a much stronger property of having quantifier elimination); however, for many structures, this property does not hold (for example, $\langle \mathbb{N}, +, \cdot \rangle$).

We shall see in the remainder of this chapter that the correspondence between the problems of topological connectivity of constraint databases and graph connectivity in the embedded setting is not an accident: in fact, the majority of expressivity bounds for constraint databases are obtained by rather simple reductions to embedded finite models.

5.4 Collapse and Genericity: An Overview

The next five sections will deal primarily with the setting of embedded finite models. In this short section, we give an overview of the main results.

Many results on expressive power use the notion of *genericity,* which comes from the classical relational database setting. Informally, this notion is sometimes stated as a *data independence principle:* when one evaluates queries on relational databases, the exact values of elements stored in the database are not important. For example, the answer to the query "Does the graph have diameter 2?" is the same for the graph $\{(1,2),(1,3),(1,4)\}$ and the graph $\{(a,b),(a,c),(a,d)\}$, which is obtained by the mapping $1 \mapsto a, 2 \mapsto b, 3 \mapsto c, 4 \mapsto d$.

In general, generic queries commute with permutations of the domain. Queries expressible in $\mathrm{FO}(SC, \mathfrak{M})$ need not be generic: for example, the query given by $\exists x\ S(x) \wedge x > 1$ is true on $S = \{2\}$ but false on $S = \{0\}$. However, as all queries definable in standard relational languages – relational calculus, Datalog, etc. – are generic, to reduce questions about $\mathrm{FO}(SC, \mathfrak{M})$ to questions in ordinary finite-model theory, it suffices to restrict one's attention to generic queries.

We now define genericity of *Boolean queries* (which are just classes of SC-structures) and *non-Boolean queries* (which map a finite SC-structure to a finite subset of U^m, $m > 0$). We also define genericity in the ordered and unordered settings. The reason for considering the ordered setting separately is twofold: first, most structures of interest in applications are ordered, and second, in several proofs we need to introduce the order relation to obtain the desired results.

Given a function $\pi : U \to U$, we extend it to finite SC-structures D by replacing each occurrence of $a \in adom(D)$ with $\pi(a)$.

Definition 5.4.1. • *A Boolean query Q is* totally generic *(or* order-generic*) if for every partial injective function (or partial monotone injective function, respectively) π defined on $adom(D)$, we have $Q(D) = Q(\pi(D))$.*

• *A non-Boolean query Q is* totally generic *(or* order-generic*) if for every partial injective function (or partial monotone injective function, respectively) π defined on $adom(D) \cup adom(Q(D))$, we have $\pi(Q(D)) = Q(\pi(D))$.*

Order-genericity of course assumes that U is linearly ordered. Clearly, total genericity is stronger than order-genericity. Some examples of totally generic queries are all queries definable in relational algebra, Datalog, the *While* language, and in fact in almost every language studied in relational database theory. As a concrete example, consider the parity query. Since for any injective $\pi : U \to U$ it is the case that $card(X) = card(\pi(X))$, parity is totally generic.

Examples of order-generic queries include queries definable in relational calculus and Datalog with order (that is, order comparisons are allowed in selection predicates and Datalog rules).

5.4.1 Approaches to Proving Expressivity Bounds

How can one prove bounds on $\mathrm{FO}(SC, \mathfrak{M})$? Probably by reducing the problem to something we know about. And we know a lot about FO over finite structures, ordered or unordered. In our terms, this is either $\mathrm{FO}_{\mathrm{act}}(SC, \langle U, \emptyset \rangle)$, which we denote by $\mathrm{FO}_{\mathrm{act}}(SC)$ (that is, there are no operations on U, and everything is restricted to the active domain), or $FO_{act}(SC, \langle U, < \rangle)$, which will be denoted by $FO_{act}(SC, <)$ (that is, the only predicate on U is the order $<$).

To reduce the expressivity of $FO(SC, \mathfrak{M})$ to $FO_{act}(SC, <)$ or $FO_{act}(SC)$, we have to deal with two problems: unrestricted quantification over U, and the presence of $\mathfrak{M}$-definable constraints in formulae. Fig. 5.3 illustrates possible approaches to the problem.

We need to go from the upper right corner to the lower left corner. One possibility is to move left first, and then down. To move left, we must prove that for a given $\mathfrak{M}$, $FO(SC, \mathfrak{M})$ and $FO_{act}(SC, \mathfrak{M})$ have the same power. That is, all unrestricted quantification can be eliminated. This will be called *natural-active collapse*. To move down, we would have liked to prove that $FO_{act}(SC, \mathfrak{M}) = FO_{act}(SC, <)$, but this is impossible for the following reason.

Lemma 5.4.2. $FO_{act}(SC, <)$ *defines only order-generic queries.*

On the other hand, queries definable in $FO_{act}(SC, \mathfrak{M})$ need not be generic. Thus, we attempt to prove the next best thing: that all generic queries in $FO_{act}(SC, \mathfrak{M})$ and $FO_{act}(SC, <)$ are the same. This is called *active generic collapse*.

Another possibility is to go down first from the right upper corner. For the same reasons as before, we have to restrict ourselves to generic queries, and attempt to prove that any generic query in $FO(SC, \mathfrak{M})$ is definable in $FO(SC, <)$. This is called *natural-generic collapse*. Then, to go left, we have to prove the natural-active collapse over a very simple structure $\langle U, < \rangle$.

Let us now summarize the definitions of that collapse results that we shall be proving here.

Definition 5.4.3. *We say that a structure $\mathfrak{M}$ admits:*

- natural-active collapse *if* $FO(SC, \mathfrak{M}) = FO_{act}(SC, \mathfrak{M})$ *for every* SC;
- active-generic collapse *if, for every* SC, *the classes of order-generic queries in* $FO_{act}(SC, \mathfrak{M})$ *and* $FO_{act}(SC, <)$ *are the same (assuming $\mathfrak{M}$ is ordered);*

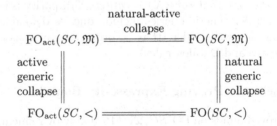

Fig. 5.3. Approaches to proving bounds for $FO(SC, \mathfrak{M})$

- natural-generic collapse *if, for every SC, the classes of order-generic queries in* $\text{FO}(SC, \mathfrak{M})$ *and* $\text{FO}(SC, <)$ *are the same (assuming* $\mathfrak{M}$ *is ordered).*

We shall also consider collapse results for totally generic queries, but they will of lesser importance. The next two sections deal with collapse results: Sect. 5.5 discusses active generic collapse, and Sect. 5.6 discusses natural-active collapse and natural-generic collapse.

5.5 Active-Generic Collapse

Our goal is to prove active-generic collapse over *any* ordered structure. We do this by proving a Ramsey property, defined below, and then showing that it implies this collapse.

We start with a simple example that illustrates the main idea of the proof. Suppose we have a sentence Φ of FO + POLY:

$$\forall x \in adom \; \forall y \in adom \; S(x, y) \rightarrow (\neg(x = y^2) \wedge \neg(y = x^2)).$$

In general, given a sentence, one cannot decide whether it defines a generic query. So assume for the moment that the given sentence happens to express a generic query. How does one show then that this query is definable in FO without polynomial constraints (for example, how does one prove that this query is not parity)? Clearly, one needs a systematic way of finding counterexamples for each non-FO query. This is provided by the following observation. Let $X = \{3^{3^i} \mid i > 0\} \subset \mathbb{N}$. Then, for any $x, y \in X$, we have $x \neq y^2$, because $3^j = 2 \cdot 3^i$ does not hold for any $i, j > 0$. Thus, if $adom(S) \subset X$, then $S \models \Phi$. Now, assume that Φ expresses a generic query Q. Given *any* finite relation S, we can find a monotone embedding π of its active domain into X. Thus, $Q(S) = Q(\pi(S))$ by genericity, and we know that $Q(\pi(S))$ is true. Hence, $Q(S)$ is true for all S, and thus Φ cannot express a non-first-order generic query.

This is the basic idea behind the proof of active-generic collapse: we first show that for each formula, its behavior on some infinite set is described by a first-order formula. This is called the Ramsey property. We then show how genericity and the Ramsey property imply the collapse.

5.5.1 The Ramsey Property

Definition 5.5.1. *Let* $\mathfrak{M} = \langle U, \Omega \rangle$ *be an ordered structure. We say that an* $\text{FO}_{\text{act}}(SC, \mathfrak{M})$ *formula* $\varphi(\vec{x})$ *has the* Ramsey property *if the following is true:*

Let X be an infinite subset of U. Then there exists an infinite set $Y \subseteq X$ and an $\text{FO}_{\text{act}}(SC, <)$ formula $\psi(\vec{x})$ such that for any instance

D of SC with $adom(D) \subset Y$, and for any $\vec{a}$ over Y, it is the case that $D \models \varphi(\vec{a}) \leftrightarrow \psi(\vec{a})$.

We speak of the total Ramsey property if ψ is an $\mathrm{FO}_{\mathrm{act}}$ formula in the language of SC (note the absence of order).

In the rest of this section, we prove the Ramsey property. We fix an ordered structure $\mathfrak{M} = \langle U, \Omega \rangle$ and a schema SC. The following simple lemma will often be used as a first step in proofs of collapse results. Before stating it, note that for any $\mathrm{FO}(SC, \mathfrak{M})$, subformulae $(x = y)$ can be viewed as both atomic $\mathrm{FO}(SC)$ and atomic $\mathrm{FO}(\mathfrak{M})$ formulae. For the rest of the chapter, we choose to view them as atomic $\mathrm{FO}(\mathfrak{M})$ formulae; that is, atomic $\mathrm{FO}(SC)$ formulae are only those of the form $R(\cdots)$ for $R \in SC$.

Lemma 5.5.2. *Let $\varphi(\vec{x})$ be an $\mathrm{FO}(SC, \mathfrak{M})$ formula. Then there exists an equivalent formula $\psi(\vec{x})$ such that every atomic subformula of ψ is either an $\mathrm{FO}(SC)$ formula or an $\mathrm{FO}(\mathfrak{M})$ formula. Furthermore, it can be assumed that none of the variables $\vec{x}$ occurs in an $\mathrm{FO}(SC)$ atomic subformula of $\psi(\vec{x})$. If φ is an $\mathrm{FO}_{\mathrm{act}}(SC, \mathfrak{M})$ formula, then ψ is also an $\mathrm{FO}_{\mathrm{act}}(SC, \mathfrak{M})$ formula.*

Proof. Introduce m fresh variables $z_1, \ldots, z_m$, where m is the maximal arity of a relation in SC, and replace any atomic formula of the form $R(t_1(\vec{y}), \ldots, t_l(\vec{y}))$, where $l \le m$ and the t_is are $\mathfrak{M}$-terms, by $\exists z_1 \in adom \ldots \exists z_l \in adom \; \bigwedge_i (z_i = t_i(\vec{y})) \wedge R(z_1, \ldots, z_l)$. Similarly, use existential quantifiers to eliminate $\vec{x}$-variables from $\mathrm{FO}(SC)$ atomic formulae. $\square$

The key in the inductive proof of the Ramsey property is the case of $\mathrm{FO}(\mathfrak{M})$ subformulae. For this, we first recall the infinite version of Ramsey's Theorem, in the form most convenient for our purposes.

Theorem 5.5.3 (Ramsey). *Given an infinite ordered set X, and any partition of the set of all ordered m-tuples $x_1 < \ldots < x_m$ of elements of X into l classes $A_1, \ldots, A_l$, there exists an infinite subset $Y \subseteq X$ such that all ordered m-tuples of elements of Y belong to the same class A_i.*

Lemma 5.5.4. *Let $\varphi(\vec{x})$ be an $\mathrm{FO}(\mathfrak{M})$ formula. Then φ has the Ramsey property.*

Proof. Consider a (finite) enumeration of all the ways in which the variables $\vec{x}$ may appear in the order of U. For example, if $\vec{x} = (x_1, \ldots, x_4)$, one possibility is $x_1 = x_3, x_2 = x_4$, and $x_1 < x_2$. Let P be such an arrangement, and $\zeta(P)$ a first-order formula that defines it ($x_1 = x_3 \wedge x_2 = x_4 \wedge x_1 < x_3$ in the above example). Note that there are finitely many such arrangements P; let $\mathcal{P}$ be the set of all of these. Each P induces an equivalence relation on $\vec{x}$, for example $\{(x_1, x_3), (x_2, x_4)\}$ for the P above. Let $\vec{x}^P$ be a subtuple of $\vec{x}$ containing a representative of each class (e.g. (x_1, x_4)), and let $\varphi^P(\vec{x}^P)$ be obtained from φ by replacing all variables from an equivalence class by the chosen representative. Then $\varphi(x)$ is equivalent to

$$\bigvee_{P \in \mathcal{P}} \zeta(P) \wedge \varphi^P(\vec{x}^P) .$$

Let $\mathcal{P}' \subseteq \mathcal{P}$ and $P_0 \in \mathcal{P}'$. Let $X \subseteq U$ be an infinite set. Assume that $\psi(\vec{x})$ is given by

$$\bigvee_{P \in \mathcal{P}'} \zeta(P) \wedge \varphi^P(\vec{x}^P).$$

We shall now show that there exists an infinite set $Y \subseteq X$ and a quantifier-free FO($<$) formula $\gamma_{P_0}(\vec{x})$ such that ψ is equivalent to

$$\gamma_{P_0}(\vec{x}) \vee \bigvee_{P \in \mathcal{P}'-\{P_0\}} \zeta(P) \wedge \varphi^P(\vec{x}^P)$$

for tuples $\vec{x}$ of elements of Y.

To see this, suppose that P_0 has m equivalence classes. Consider a partition of tuples of X^m, ordered according to P_0, into two classes: A_1, the class of those tuples for which $\varphi^{P_0}(\vec{x}^{P_0})$ is true, and A_2, the class of those for which $\varphi^{P_0}(\vec{x}^{P_0})$ is false. By Ramsey's Theorem, for some infinite set $Y \subseteq X$, either all ordered tuples over Y^m are in A_1 or all are in A_2. In the first case, ψ is equivalent to $\zeta(P_0) \vee \bigvee_{P \in \mathcal{P}'-\{P_0\}} \zeta(P) \wedge \varphi^P(\vec{x}^P)$, and in the second case ψ is equivalent to $\neg\zeta(P_0) \vee \bigvee_{P \in \mathcal{P}'-\{P_0\}} \zeta(P) \wedge \varphi^P(\vec{x}^P)$, proving the claim.

The lemma now follows by applying this claim inductively to every partition $P \in \mathcal{P}$, passing to smaller infinite sets, while getting rid of all the formulae containing symbols other than $=$ and $<$. At the end, we have an infinite set over which φ is equivalent to a quantifier-free FO($<$) formula.   □

Now a simple inductive argument proves the following.

Proposition 5.5.5. *Let $\mathfrak{M}$ be any ordered structure. Then every* $\mathrm{FO}_{\mathrm{act}}(SC, \mathfrak{M})$ *formula has the Ramsey property.*

Proof. By Lemma 5.5.2, we assume that every atomic subformula is an $\mathrm{FO}_{\mathrm{act}}(SC)$ formula or an FO($\mathfrak{M}$) formula. The base cases for the induction are those of $\mathrm{FO}_{\mathrm{act}}(SC)$ formulae, where there is no need to change the formula or find a subset, and of FO($\mathfrak{M}$) atomic formulae, which is given by Lemma 5.5.4.

Let $\varphi(\vec{x}) = \varphi_1(\vec{x}) \wedge \varphi_2(\vec{x})$, and let $X \subseteq U$ be infinite. First, find ψ_1, $Y_1 \subseteq X$ such that for any D and $\vec{a}$ over Y_1, $D \models \varphi_1(\vec{a}) \leftrightarrow \psi_1(\vec{a})$. Next, by using the hypothesis for φ_2 and Y_1, find an infinite $Y_2 \subseteq Y_1$ such that for any D and $\vec{a}$ over Y_2, $D \models \varphi_2(\vec{a}) \leftrightarrow \psi_2(\vec{a})$. Then take $\psi = \psi_1 \wedge \psi_2$ and $Y = Y_2$.

The case of $\varphi = \neg\varphi'$ is trivial.

For the existential case, let $\varphi(\vec{x}) = \exists y \in adom\ \varphi_1(y, \vec{x})$. By the hypothesis, we find $Y \subseteq X$ and $\psi_1(y, \vec{x})$ such that, for any D and $\vec{a}$ over Y and any $b \in Y$ we have $D \models \varphi_1(b, \vec{a}) \leftrightarrow \psi_1(b, \vec{a})$. Let $\psi(\vec{x}) = \exists y \in adom.\psi_1(y, \vec{x})$. Then, for any D and $\vec{a}$ over Y, $D \models \psi(\vec{a})$ iff $D \models \psi_1(b, \vec{a})$ for some $b \in adom(D)$ iff $D \models \varphi_1(b, \vec{a})$ for some $b \in adom(D)$ iff $D \models \varphi_1(\vec{a})$, thus finishing the proof.   □

It is clear from the proof of Proposition 5.5.5 that only the case of atomic FO($\mathfrak{M}$) formulae requires the introduction of the order relation. Thus, if atomic FO($\mathfrak{M}$) formulae had the total Ramsey property over $\mathfrak{M}$, so would all $\text{FO}_{\text{act}}(SC, \mathfrak{M})$ formulae. In general, this cannot be guaranteed for arbitrary $\mathfrak{M}$ (consider, for example, $\langle U, < \rangle$). However, there is an important class of structures on the reals for which this statement can be shown.

We say that $\mathfrak{M} = \langle \mathbb{R}, \Omega \rangle$ is *analytic* if Ω consists of real analytic functions. For example, $\langle \mathbb{R}, +, \cdot \rangle$ is analytic.

Lemma 5.5.6. *Let $\mathcal{F} = \{f_i(\vec{x})\}_{i \in I}$ be a countable family of real analytic functions, where $\vec{x} = (x_1, \dots, x_l)$. Assume that none of the functions in $\mathcal{F}$ is identically zero. Let $X \subseteq \mathbb{R}$ be a set of cardinality of the continuum. Then there is a set $Y \subseteq X$ of cardinality of the continuum such that, for any tuple $\vec{c}$ of l distinct elements of Y, none of $f_i(\vec{c})$, where $i \in I$, equals zero.*

The proof of this result, which we omit here, is a Zorn's lemma argument based on the fact that a nonzero real analytic function can have at most countably many zeros.

Proposition 5.5.7. *Let $\mathfrak{M} = \langle \mathbb{R}, \Omega \rangle$ be analytic. Then every $\text{FO}_{\text{act}}(SC, \mathfrak{M})$ formula has the total Ramsey property.*

Proof sketch. We only need to modify the proof of Lemma 5.5.4, to show the total Ramsey property of atomic FO($\mathfrak{M}$) formulae. This can be done by using Lemma 5.5.6 in place of Ramsey's Theorem. □

5.5.2 Collapse Results

We now show how the Ramsey property implies active-generic collapse. Recall (see Sect. 5.4) that an m-ary query, $m > 0$, is a mapping from finite SC-structures on U to finite subsets of U^m. We start with the following observation.

Lemma 5.5.8. *If Q is an order-generic query on SC-structures over an infinite set U, then $adom(Q(D)) \subseteq adom(D)$ for every SC-structure D.*

Proof. First note that for any finite subsets $Y \subset X$ of an infinite ordered set U, any $x \in X - Y$, and any number $n > 0$, we can find monotone injective maps $\pi_1, \dots, \pi_n$ defined on X such that for all i, j, $\pi_i(Y) = \pi_j(Y)$, but all $\pi_1(x), \dots, \pi_n(x)$ are distinct. This is true because U has either an infinitely descending or an infinitely ascending chain; in each case it is easy to construct the π_is.

Now suppose that $Z = adom(Q(D)) - adom(D)$ is nonempty for an order-generic query Q. Let $X = adom(Q(D)) \cup adom(D)$, $Y = adom(D)$, and $n = card(Z) + 1$. Construct $\pi_1, \dots, \pi_n$ as above. Now, for every i, j, we have $\pi_i(Q(D)) = Q(\pi_i(D)) = Q(\pi_j(D)) = \pi_j(Q(D))$; hence $\pi_1(Z) = \dots = \pi_n(Z)$. In particular, for every $x \in Z$, $\pi_i(x) \in \pi_1(Z)$, whence $card(\pi_1(Z)) = card(Z) \geq n$. This contradiction proves the lemma. □

Lemma 5.5.9. *Assume that every* $\mathrm{FO}_{\mathrm{act}}(SC, \mathfrak{M})$ *formula has the Ramsey property. Then* $\mathfrak{M}$ *admits active-generic collapse.*

Proof. Let Q be an order-generic query definable in $\mathrm{FO}_{\mathrm{act}}(SC, \mathfrak{M})$. By the Ramsey property, we can find an infinite $X \subseteq U$ and an $\mathrm{FO}_{\mathrm{act}}(SC, <)$-definable Q' that coincides with Q on X. We claim that they coincide everywhere. Let D be an SC-structure. Since X is infinite, there exists a partial monotone injective map π from $adom(D)$ into X. Since Q' is $\mathrm{FO}_{\mathrm{act}}(SC, <)$-definable, it is order-generic, and thus Q and Q' do not extend active domains. Hence, $\pi(Q(D)) = Q(\pi(D)) = Q'(\pi(D)) = \pi(Q'(D))$, from which $Q(D) = Q'(D)$ follows. □

We now put Proposition 5.5.5 and Lemma 5.5.9 together:

Theorem 5.5.10. *Every ordered structure admits active-generic collapse.*

Thus, no matter what functions and predicates there are in $\mathfrak{M}$, first-order logic cannot express more generic active-semantics queries over it than just $\mathrm{FO}_{\mathrm{act}}(SC, <)$. In particular, we have the following.

Corollary 5.5.11. *Let* $\mathfrak{M}$ *be an arbitrary structure. Then queries such as parity, majority, connectivity, transitive closure, and acyclicity are not definable in* $\mathrm{FO}_{\mathrm{act}}(SC, \mathfrak{M})$.

Proof. Assume otherwise, and extend $\mathfrak{M}$ to $\mathfrak{M}^<$ by adding the symbol $<$, to be interpreted as a linear order. Then $\mathrm{FO}_{\mathrm{act}}(SC, \mathfrak{M}^<)$ defines one of the above queries, for an appropriate SC. Since all the queries listed above are order-generic, we obtain from Theorem 5.5.10 that $\mathrm{FO}_{\mathrm{act}}(SC, <)$ defines them, which is not the case. □

We conclude by showing a stronger collapse result over analytic structures.

Corollary 5.5.12. *If* $\mathfrak{M} = \langle \mathbb{R}, \Omega \rangle$ *is analytic, then any totally generic query definable in* $\mathrm{FO}_{\mathrm{act}}(SC, \mathfrak{M})$ *is definable in* $\mathrm{FO}_{\mathrm{act}}(SC)$.

This is indeed a stronger version of collapse, as there exist totally generic queries in $\mathrm{FO}_{\mathrm{act}}(SC, <) - \mathrm{FO}_{\mathrm{act}}(SC)$ (even for very simple vocabularies SC).

5.6 Natural-Active Collapse

So far, we have dealt with formulae that use only the restricted quantification $\forall x \in adom$ and $\exists x \in adom$. We next move to unrestricted quantification, where quantifiers are allowed to range over the infinite universe of a structure $\mathfrak{M}$. Our ultimate goal is to prove natural-active collapse: $\mathrm{FO}(SC, \mathfrak{M}) = \mathrm{FO}_{\mathrm{act}}(SC, \mathfrak{M})$. We start by showing that there is a reason to believe that this may hold for some structures $\mathfrak{M}$, although not for all of them. We then review some notions from model theory that help us distinguish good structures (for which the collapse holds) from bad ones (for which it does not). After that, we give a gentle introduction to the main ideas of the proof of the natural-active collapse, considering a simple case of linear constraints (that is, FO + LIN) and one unrestricted existential quantifier to be eliminated. After that, we present a general proof and an algorithm, and revisit the collapse for generic queries.

5.6.1 Collapse: Failure and Success

We have seen that the active-generic collapse holds for *every* ordered structure Does this extend to the natural-active collapse? To give a negative answer, consider the structure $\mathfrak{N} = \langle \mathbb{N}, +, \cdot \rangle$. (We may include an order relation $<$ as well, but it is definable: $x < y$ iff $\neg(x = y) \wedge \exists z \ (y = x + z)$.) Let SC consist of a single unary predicate S. From the active generic collapse, we know that parity is not definable in $\mathrm{FO}_{\mathrm{act}}(SC, \mathfrak{N})$. However, we have the following proposition.

Proposition 5.6.1. *Parity is definable in* $\mathrm{FO}(SC, \mathfrak{N})$. *Consequently,* $\mathfrak{N}$ *does not admit natural-active collapse.*

Proof. Let $p_1, p_2, \dots$ enumerate the prime numbers. Consider three predicates on $\mathbb{N}$: $P_0(x)$ holds iff x is prime, $P_1(x, y)$ holds iff y equals p_x, and $P_2(x)$ holds iff x is the product of an even number of distinct primes. Note that P_0, P_1, and P_2 are recursive, and thus definable over $\mathfrak{N}$. The way to express parity is then the following: given a set $S = \{x_1, \dots, x_n\}$ with $x_1 < \dots < x_n$, we code it as $c_S = p_{x_1} \cdot \dots \cdot p_{x_n}$. Suppose we have a formula $\varphi(c)$ which holds iff $c = c_S$. Then parity is expressed as

$$\neg \exists x S(x) \ \vee \ \exists c \ (\varphi(c) \wedge P_2(c)).$$

Thus, it remains to show how to express φ. It can be defined by the following formula:

$$\forall p \ P_0(p) \rightarrow \left(\begin{array}{l} (\exists y(c = p \cdot y)) \rightarrow \neg \exists y(c = p \cdot p \cdot y) \\ \wedge \ (\exists y(c = p \cdot y)) \leftrightarrow \exists x \ (S(x) \wedge P_1(x, p)) \end{array} \right).$$

This says that for every prime p that divides c, c is not divisible by p^2, and p is of the form p_x for some $x \in S$, which forces c to be c_S. This completes the proof. □

One may observe that there is nothing specific to parity in the proof above. In particular, the coding scheme can be easily extended to finite SC-structures for any SC, and the fact that every recursive predicate on $\mathbb{N}$ is definable in $\mathfrak{N}$ allows us to state the following proposition.

Proposition 5.6.2. *For any* SC, *every computable property of finite* SC-*structures is definable in* $\mathrm{FO}(SC, \mathfrak{N})$. □

In fact, FO(SC, $\mathfrak{N}$) can even express properties that are *not* computable.

Thus, we have witnessed a rather dramatic failure of natural-active collapse. Is there then something that gives us hope of recovering it for some structures? Let us first look at the simplest possible $\mathfrak{M}$: $\langle U, \emptyset \rangle$. It turns out that in this case the collapse can be proven rather easily.

Theorem 5.6.3. *For every schema,* FO(SC) = FO$_{\text{act}}$(SC).

Proof. We consider the case of nonempty finite structures. If an FO$_{\text{act}}$(SC) formula $\psi(\vec{x})$ equivalent to an FO(SC) formula $\varphi(\vec{x})$ is found in this case, then for arbitrary finite SC-structures, a formula equivalent to φ is given by $(\exists x \in adom(x = x) \wedge \psi(\vec{x})) \vee (\neg \exists x \in adom(x = x) \wedge \varphi_\emptyset(\vec{x}))$, where $\varphi_\emptyset(\vec{x})$ is a quantifier-free formula equivalent to the formula obtained from φ by replacing each occurrence of a predicate from SC by *false*.

Now the proof is by induction on the structure of the formula. The cases of atomic formulae and Boolean connectives are obvious. For the existential case, we define a transformation $[\gamma]^x$ that eliminates all free occurrences of the variable x from quantifier-free formulae:

- If γ is $(x = x)$, then $[\gamma]^x = true$.
- If γ is $(x = y)$ or $R(\ldots, x, \ldots)$, then $[\gamma]^x = false$.
- If γ is any other atomic formula, then $[\gamma]^x = \gamma$.
- If $\gamma = \gamma_1 \vee \gamma_2$, then $[\gamma]^x = [\gamma_1]^x \vee [\gamma_2]^x$.
- If $\gamma = \neg\gamma'$, then $[\gamma]^x = \neg[\gamma']^x$.

Let $\varphi(\vec{z}) = \exists x \alpha(x, \vec{z})$ where $z = (z_1, \ldots, z_n)$. By the hypothesis, α is equivalent to an FO$_{\text{act}}$(SC) formula $\alpha'(x, \vec{z})$. Assume, without loss of generality, that α' is of the form $\mathbf{Q}y_1 \in adom \ldots \mathbf{Q}y_m \in adom \ \beta(x, \vec{y}, \vec{z})$, where β is quantifier-free.

Define $\varphi_0(\vec{z}) \equiv \exists x \in adom \ \alpha'(x, \vec{z})$, $\varphi_i(\vec{z}) \equiv \alpha'(z_i, \vec{z})$ and $\varphi_\infty(\vec{z}) \equiv \mathbf{Q}y_1 \in adom \ldots \mathbf{Q}y_m \in adom \ [\beta(x, \vec{y}, \vec{z})]^x$. Let

$$\varphi'(\vec{z}) \equiv \varphi_0 \vee \left(\bigvee_{i=1}^{n} \varphi_i\right) \vee \varphi_\infty.$$

We now show that $D \models \varphi(\vec{a}) \leftrightarrow \varphi'(\vec{a})$ for every nonempty D and every $\vec{a} \in U^n$. First, note that for every $\vec{b} \in adom(D)^m$, the following three statements are equivalent: (i) $D \models [\beta(x, \vec{b}, \vec{a})]^x$; (ii) for some $c \notin adom(D)$ and not in $\vec{a}$, $D \models \beta(c, \vec{b}, \vec{a})$; (iii) for all $c \notin adom(D)$ and not in $\vec{a}$, $D \models \beta(c, \vec{b}, \vec{a})$. Indeed, these equivalences hold for atomic formulae, and they are preserved under Boolean connectives.

Since all quantified variables y_i range over the active domain, we then obtain that $D \models \varphi_\infty(\vec{a})$ iff for some $c \notin adom(D)$ and not in $\vec{a}$, $D \models \alpha'(c, \vec{a})$. This implies the required equivalence $D \models \varphi(\vec{a}) \leftrightarrow \varphi'(\vec{a})$. $\qquad\square$

Thus, natural-active collapse is a meaningful concept: there are structures that admit it. On the other hand, we know that there are restrictions on structures that admit this collapse. We next discuss such restrictions.

5.6.2 Good Structures vs. Bad Structures: O-minimality

We start with a minimal requirement a structure $\mathfrak{M}$ must satisfy to admit natural-active collapse. Suppose we have an $FO(\mathfrak{M})$ formula, that is, a formula that does not use symbols from SC. What does it mean for it to be equivalent to an $FO_{act}(SC, \mathfrak{M})$ formula? In the absence of a finite structure, this means being equivalent to a quantifier-free $FO(\mathfrak{M})$ formula. Thus, to admit the collapse, a structure $\mathfrak{M}$ must admit *quantifier elimination*: that is, for every formula $\varphi(\vec{x})$ of $FO(\mathfrak{M})$, there is a quantifier-free $FO(\mathfrak{M})$ formula $\psi(\vec{x})$ such that $\mathfrak{M} \models \forall \vec{x}\ \psi(\vec{x}) \leftrightarrow \varphi(\vec{x})$.

Classical model theory provides us with many examples of such structures; some of them have been mentioned already in the introduction, and a few are listed below:

- $\langle U, < \rangle$, where $<$ is a dense order without endpoints on U.
- $\langle \mathbb{R}, +, -, 0, 1, < \rangle$ – this is a consequence of Fourier elimination.
- $\langle \mathbb{R}, +, \cdot, 0, 1, < \rangle$ – this is, of course, Tarski's classical result on quantifier elimination for real closed fields.
- $\langle \mathbb{N}, +, <, 0, 1, (\equiv_k)_{k>0} \rangle$, where $x \equiv_k y$ iff $x = y (\bmod k)$ – this is Presburger arithmetic.

However, quantifier elimination alone is not sufficient to guarantee the collapse. Indeed, any structure $\mathfrak{M}$ admits a definitional expansion to some $\mathfrak{M}'$ that has quantifier elimination (simply by adding new symbols for all definable predicates). Thus, if we take such an expansion $\mathfrak{N}'$ of $\mathfrak{N} = \langle \mathbb{N}, +, \cdot \rangle$, we still have that all computable properties of finite SC-structures are definable in $FO(SC, \mathfrak{N}')$, but $FO_{act}(SC, \mathfrak{N}')$ cannot define parity.

To impose additional restrictions, we consider the model-theoretic notion of o-minimality. An ordered structure $\mathfrak{M} = \langle U, \Omega \rangle$ is *o-minimal* if every definable set is a finite union of points and open intervals. Here, definable sets are those of the form $\{x \in U \mid \mathfrak{M} \models \varphi(x)\}$, where φ is a first-order formula in the language of Ω and constants for elements of U.

An interval is given by its *endpoints*, a and b, and it is either an open interval $(a, b) = \{c \mid a < c < b\}$, a closed interval $[a, b] = \{c \mid a \leq c \leq b\}$, or one of the half-open half-closed versions $[a, b)$ or $(a, b]$; by considering $+\infty$ and $-\infty$ as endpoints, we also have unbounded versions of the above: $\{c \mid c < b\}$, $\{c \mid c \leq b\}$, $\{c \mid c > a\}$, and $\{c \mid c \geq a\}$. Also, an equivalent definition of o-minimality is that every definable set is a finite union of intervals.

Let us list some important examples of o-minimal structures.

- $\langle \mathbb{Q}, <, (q)_{q \in \mathbb{Q}} \rangle$ is o-minimal. Indeed, every first-order formula $\varphi(x)$ is equivalent to a quantifier-free one, which is then a Boolean combination of finitely many formulae of the form $x = q$ or $x < q$. Let $q_1 < \ldots < q_k$ be the finite set of all constants that occur in such formulae. Consider then the intervals $(-\infty, q_1), \{q_1\}, (q_1, q_2), \{q_2\}, \ldots, \{q_k\}, (q_k, \infty)$. It is clear that the set defined by φ is a union of some of those.

- A more complex example is that of the real field, $\langle \mathbb{R}, +, \cdot, 0, 1, < \rangle$. Consider a formula $\varphi(x)$. Since the real field has quantifier elimination, $\varphi(x)$ is equivalent to a Boolean combination of formulae of the form $p(x) > 0$, where p is a polynomial with real coefficients. Consider all such polynomials which are not identically zero, and let $q_1 < \ldots < q_k$ be the finite set of all the roots of these polynomials (each can have only finitely many). We thus again obtain the result that the set defined by $\varphi(x)$ is a union of some intervals among $(-\infty, q_1), \{q_1\}, (q_1, q_2), \{q_2\}, \ldots, \{q_k\}, (q_k, \infty)$, as no polynomial used in the representation of $\varphi(x)$ can change sign on such an interval.
- The same quantifier elimination argument shows that the real ordered group $\langle \mathbb{R}, +, -, 0, 1, < \rangle$ is o-minimal.
- There are other interesting examples of o-minimal structures, where proving o-minimality is very hard. The most notable one is that of the exponential field, $\langle \mathbb{R}, +, \cdot, e^x \rangle$. Others include the expansion of the real field with the Gamma-function or with restricted analytic functions.

We shall present more properties of o-minimal structures before proving natural-active collapse in Section 5.6.5.

5.6.3 Collapse Theorem and Corollaries

Our goal now is to show the following.

Theorem 5.6.4 (Natural-Active Collapse). *Let $\mathfrak{M} = \langle U, \Omega \rangle$ be an o-minimal structure that admits quantifier elimination. Then it admits natural-active collapse.*

Furthermore, if the theory of $\mathfrak{M}$ is decidable and the quantifier elimination procedure is effective, then there is an algorithm that, for every $\mathrm{FO}(SC, \mathfrak{M})$ formula, constructs an equivalent $\mathrm{FO}_{\mathrm{act}}(SC, \mathfrak{M})$ formula. □

The proof of this theorem will be presented in Section 5.6.5, after we present the main ideas in the simpler case of linear constraints, that is, where $\mathfrak{M}$ is $\langle \mathbb{R}, +, -, 0, 1, < \rangle$.

We first state some corollaries of this result. Since the real field and the real-ordered group are o-minimal and admit quantifier elimination, we conclude that they also admit natural-active collapse.

Corollary 5.6.5. *Every natural-semantics* $\mathrm{FO} + \mathrm{LIN}$ *(or* $\mathrm{FO} + \mathrm{POLY}$*) formula is equivalent to an active-domain semantics* $\mathrm{FO} + \mathrm{LIN}$ *(or* $\mathrm{FO} + \mathrm{POLY}$*, respectively) formula.* □

Combining this with active-generic collapse, we obtain the following.

Corollary 5.6.6. *Let Q be an order-generic query expressible in* $\mathrm{FO} + \mathrm{POLY}$ *or* $\mathrm{FO} + \mathrm{LIN}$*. Then Q is expressible in* $\mathrm{FO}_{\mathrm{act}}(SC, <)$*. In particular, queries such as parity, majority, connectivity, transitive closure, and acyclicity are not definable in* $\mathrm{FO} + \mathrm{POLY}$*.* □

Thus, the expressive power of FO + POLY and FO + LIN is remarkably constrained – they cannot express more generic queries than FO queries over ordered finite structures, despite the fact that they possess great expressive power for nongeneric queries, as we saw in Sect. 5.3.

Before we present the proof, we give a simple example of a transformation from $FO(SC, \mathfrak{M})$ to $FO_{act}(SC, \mathfrak{M})$. Let SC contain one binary predicate S, and let $\mathfrak{M}$ be the real field (that is, we are dealing with FO + POLY). Consider the sentence

$$\Phi \equiv \exists a \exists b \forall x \forall y \ (S(x, y) \to a \cdot x + b = y),$$

which says that S lies on a line. Note that this can be reformulated as follows: S lies on a line iff every triple of elements of S is collinear. Given three points $(x_1, y_1), (x_2, y_2), (x_3, y_3)$ in $\mathbb{R}^2$, there is a *quantifier-free* FO + POLY formula $\chi(x_1, x_2, x_3, y_1, y_2, y_3)$ that tests whether these points are collinear. Indeed, such points are collinear iff either $x_1 = x_2 = x_3$, or $y_1 = y_2 = y_3$, or two points coincide, or, in the case when all three points are different, they can be ordered either as $x_{i_1} < x_{i_2} < x_{i_3}$, $y_{i_1} < y_{i_2} < y_{i_3}$ or $x_{i_1} < x_{i_2} < x_{i_3}$, $y_{i_1} > y_{i_2} > y_{i_3}$, and $(x_{i_2} - x_{i_1})(y_{i_3} - y_{i_2}) = (x_{i_3} - x_{i_2})(y_{i_2} - y_{i_1})$. We now express Φ by an equivalent active-domain formula,

$$\forall x_1, x_2, x_3, y_1, y_2, y_3 \in adom \left(\begin{array}{c} S(x_1, y_1) \wedge S(x_2, y_2) \wedge S(x_3, y_3) \to \\ \chi(x_1, x_2, x_3, y_1, y_2, y_3) \end{array} \right).$$

Of course, this transformation is very ad hoc, and takes into account the semantics of the original formula Φ. In what follows, we present a more general transformation.

5.6.4 Collapse Algorithm: the Linear Case

The general proof of natural-active collapse is by induction on the formulae. The cases of atomic formulae and Boolean connectives are simple: for atomic formulae, there is no need to change anything, and one just propagates the connectives. The only hard case is that of the unrestricted quantification $\exists x \varphi$. We now consider an FO + LIN sentence $\Phi \equiv \exists z \varphi(z)$, where

$$\varphi(z) \equiv \mathbf{Q} y_1 \in adom \ldots \mathbf{Q} y_m \in adom \ \alpha(z, \vec{y}),$$

and where each $\mathbf{Q}$ is either $\exists$ or $\forall$. (Of course we could have considered an open formula $\Phi(\vec{x})$ with free variables, as we shall do in the next section. However, our goal here is to present the ideas of the proof, so we make the assumption that there are no free variables. It will turn out that they do not add to the complexity of the proof, but they make notation heavier.)

Using Lemma 5.5.2, we can further assume that α is a Boolean combination of formulae of the following form:

1. atomic SC-formulae $R_j(\vec{u})$, where $R_j \in SC$ and $\vec{u}$ only has variables from $\vec{y}$;
2. linear constraints involving z: $z \vartheta \sum_{i=1}^{m} a_i \cdot y_i + b$, where ϑ is $=$ or $<$;
3. linear constraints not involving z: $\sum_{i=1}^{m} a_i \cdot y_i + b \vartheta 0$.

Let $f_1(\vec{y}), \ldots, f_p(\vec{y})$ enumerate the (finitely many) functions that occur as right-hand sides $\sum_{i=1}^{m} a_i \cdot y_i + b$ of linear constraints in item 2 above (that is, those involving z). We also assume that one of the functions f_i is the function $f(\vec{y}) = y_1$.

Fix an SC-structure D, and let $A = adom(D)$. Let

$$B_0 = \{f_i(\vec{a}) \mid i = 1, \ldots, p, \vec{a} \in A^m\}.$$

Note that $A \subseteq B_0$. Assume that $B_0 = \{b_1, \ldots, b_k\}$ with $b_1 < \ldots < b_k$.

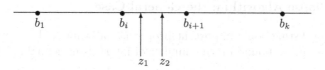

Fig. 5.4. Illustration to the natural-active collapse for the linear case

If $z_1 \in (b_i, b_{i+1})$ satisfies φ, then any other z_2 from this interval satisfies φ, as illustrated in Fig. 5.4. Indeed, the variable z is used only in atomic subformulae of the form of item 2, that is, $z \vartheta f_j(\vec{y})$. Thus, for any instantiation $\vec{a}$ for $\vec{y}$ from the active domain A, we have $D \models \alpha(z_1, \vec{a}) \leftrightarrow \alpha(z_2, \vec{a})$, since the signs of z_1 and z_2 with respect to all $f_j(\vec{a})$ are the same. Since all variables $\vec{y}$ range over A, this implies $D \models \varphi(z_1) \leftrightarrow \varphi(z_2)$. Similarly, we note that for any $z_1, z_2 < b_1$, or for any $z_1, z_2 > b_k$, it is also the case that $D \models \varphi(z_1) \leftrightarrow \varphi(z_2)$.

Thus, if φ is witnessed by an element in an interval (b_i, b_{i+1}), or $(-\infty, b_1)$, or (b_k, ∞), it is witnessed by *every* element of the interval. Hence, if we define

$$B_1 = \{\frac{b+b'}{2} \mid b, b' \in B_0\} \cup \{b - 1 \mid b \in B_0\} \cup \{b + 1 \mid b \in B_0\},$$

we conclude that $D \models \exists z \varphi(z)$ iff $D \models \varphi(b)$ for some $b \in B_1$.

A nice property of B_1 is that it is definable in FO $+$ LIN under the active-domain semantics. In fact, using the definition of B_1, we just rewrite $\exists z \varphi(z)$ as an equivalent active-domain semantics sentence:

$$\exists \vec{u} \in adom \; \exists \vec{v} \in adom \left(\begin{array}{l} \left(\bigvee_{i=1}^{p} \bigvee_{j=1}^{p} (\varphi([\frac{f_i(\vec{u})+f_j(\vec{v})}{2} \; / \; z])) \right) \\[2mm] \vee \left(\bigvee_{i=1}^{p} \varphi([(f_i(\vec{u}) - 1) \; / \; z]) \right) \\[2mm] \vee \left(\bigvee_{i=1}^{p} \varphi([(f_i(\vec{u}) + 1) \; / \; z]) \right) \end{array} \right)$$

where $f_1, \ldots, f_p$ are all the linear functions used in constraints of the form $z = f_i(\vec{y})$ or $z < f_i(\vec{y})$ in the formula φ and the function $f(\vec{y}) = y_1$.

Note that the proof of the existence of a sentence equivalent to Φ is constructive. Furthermore, the simple proof sketched in this section contains the main ingredients of the general proof. To eliminate an unrestricted quantifier from $\varphi(\vec{x}) \equiv \exists z \alpha(z, \vec{x})$, we define some partition of U into a finite union of intervals $\bigcup_i I_i(\vec{x})$, such that:

- if $\varphi(\vec{a})$ is witnessed by $c \in I_i(\vec{a})$, then it is witnessed by any $c' \in I_i(\vec{a})$;
- each interval $I_i(\vec{x})$ is definable by an FO$(SC, \mathfrak{M})$ formula, parametrically in $\vec{x}$, and so is a representative of each such interval; and
- the maximum number of intervals $I_i(\vec{x})$ is uniformly bounded for all $\vec{x}$.

5.6.5 Collapse Algorithm: the General Case

We start by listing some important properties of o-minimal structures. The key is the uniform bound on the number of intervals in definable sets.

Theorem 5.6.7 (Uniform Bounds). *If $\mathfrak{M}$ is o-minimal, and $\gamma(\vec{y}, x)$ is a first-order formula in the language of $\mathfrak{M}$, then there is an integer K_γ such that, for each tuple $\vec{a}$ from U, the set $\{x \mid \mathfrak{M} \models \gamma(\vec{a}, x)\}$ is composed of fewer than K_γ intervals.*

This is a very strong and deep result. O-minimality simply tells us that for every $\gamma(\vec{y}, x)$ and every $\vec{a}$, the set $\gamma(\mathfrak{M}, \vec{a}) = \{x \mid \mathfrak{M} \models \gamma(\vec{a}, x)\}$ is a finite union of intervals. It is conceivable that the number of intervals in $\gamma(\mathfrak{M}, \vec{a})$ depends on $\vec{a}$ in such a way that there is no bound on this number when $\vec{a}$ ranges over U. The Uniform Bounds Theorem tells us that such a situation is impossible: there is an an upper bound on the number of intervals that depends only on γ, and not on $\vec{a}$. As a side remark, the Uniform Bounds Theorem also implies that a structure elementarily equivalent to an o-minimal one is o-minimal itself.

We note, however, that for many familiar o-minimal structures, such as the real field or the real ordered group, the Uniform Bounds Theorem is trivial. Indeed, for the real field, the proof of o-minimality based on quantifier elimination (given in Sect. 5.6.2) immediately yields uniform bounds, as the number of intervals is determined by the number of polynomials used in the formula, and by their degrees (recall that the number of intervals is determined by the total number of roots of all nonzero polynomials used in the formula).

For every $\gamma(\vec{y}, x)$ in the language of $\mathfrak{M}$ and constants, and every $\vec{a}$ over $\mathfrak{M}$, by the ith interval of $\gamma(\vec{a}, \cdot)$ we shall mean the ith interval of $\gamma(\mathfrak{M}, \vec{a})$, in the usual ordering on U. We shall use the following simple facts:

- For every formula $\gamma(\vec{y}, x)$, and every i, there exists a first-order formula denoted by $\hat{\gamma}_i(\vec{y}, x)$ such that $\mathfrak{M} \models \hat{\gamma}_i(\vec{a}, c)$ iff c is in the ith interval of $\gamma(\vec{a}, \cdot)$. In what follows, we always assume that the distinguished variable x is the last one.

- If the quantifier elimination procedure is effective, and atomic sentences of $\mathfrak{M}$ are decidable, then K_γ is computable for each γ. Indeed, for each i, we can write a sentence $\Gamma_i \equiv \exists x \exists \vec{y} \; \hat{\gamma}_i(\vec{y}, x)$ and check whether it is true in $\mathfrak{M}$, using quantifier elimination and recursiveness of $\mathfrak{M}$. Eventually, we find an i such that Γ_i is false; this follows from Theorem 5.6.7. Thus, K_γ can be taken to be this i.

- Since intervals are first-order definable, we can use them in formulae. For example, given a formula $\gamma(\vec{y}, x)$, a number i, and another formula $\beta(\vec{z}, x)$, we can write a first-order formula $\alpha(\vec{y}, \vec{z}, x)$ saying that every x from the ith interval of $\gamma(\vec{y}, \cdot)$ satisfies $\beta(\vec{z}, x)$. This of course is just $\forall x \; (\hat{\gamma}_i(\vec{y}, x) \rightarrow \beta(\vec{z}, x))$, but we shall occasionally use the interval notation in formulae, to simplify the presentation.

Natural-Active Collapse: Eliminating One Existential Quantifier

This is the key case in proving the collapse, as the proof is by induction on the formulae, and this is the only case where there is a need to do something. We consider an $\text{FO}_{\text{act}}(SC, \mathfrak{M})$ formula

$$\alpha(\vec{x}, z) \;\equiv\; \mathbf{Q} y_1 \in adom \ldots \mathbf{Q} y_m \in adom \; \beta(\vec{x}, \vec{y}, z) \,,$$

where $\beta(\vec{x}, \vec{y}, \vec{z})$ is quantifier-free, and has the following properties:

- every atomic subformula of β is either an $\text{FO}(SC)$ formula or an $\text{FO}(\mathfrak{M})$ formula (where equalities are considered to be $\text{FO}(\mathfrak{M})$ formulae);
- there exists at least one $\text{FO}(\mathfrak{M})$ atomic subformula of β, and at least one $\vec{y}$-variable (that is, $m > 0$); and
- z does not occur in atomic $\text{FO}(SC)$ subformulae.

Let $\mathcal{F}$ be the collection of all $\text{FO}(\mathfrak{M})$ atomic subformulae of β, and their negations.

For formulae $\sigma(\vec{x}, \vec{y}, z)$, $\rho(\vec{x}, \vec{y}, z)$, and $\tau(\vec{x}, \vec{y}, z)$ from $\mathcal{F}$, for $i \leq K_\rho$ and $j \leq K_\tau$, we let $\sigma_{ij}^{\rho\tau}(\vec{x}, \vec{y}, \vec{s}, \vec{t})$, where $card(\vec{s}) = card(\vec{t}) = card(\vec{y})$, be the formula defined as follows:

$$\sigma_{ij}^{\rho\tau}(\vec{x}, \vec{y}, \vec{s}, \vec{t}) \;\equiv\; \forall u \; \left((\hat{\rho}_i(\vec{x}, \vec{s}, u) \wedge \hat{\tau}_j(\vec{x}, \vec{t}, u)) \rightarrow \sigma(\vec{x}, \vec{y}, u) \right) \,.$$

Let $\varphi(\vec{x})$ be $\exists z \, \alpha(\vec{x}, z)$.

Lemma 5.6.8. *Let D be a nonempty finite SC-structure over $\mathfrak{M}$. Let $\varphi, \alpha, \beta, \mathcal{F}$ be as above. Let $\vec{a}$ be a tuple over U. Then $D \models \varphi(\vec{a})$ if and only*

*if there exist $\vec{b}, \vec{c} \in adom(D)^m$, two formulae $\rho(\vec{x}, \vec{y}, z)$ and $\tau(\vec{x}, \vec{y}, z)$ in $\mathcal{F}$
and $i \leq K_\rho$, and $j \leq K_\tau$ such that for the ith interval of $\rho(\vec{a}, \vec{b}, \cdot)$ and the
jth interval of $\tau(\vec{a}, \vec{c}, \cdot)$, denoted by I_0 and I_1, respectively, the following three
conditions hold:*

1. *$I_0 \cap I_1 \neq \emptyset$.*
2. *For all $\vec{e} \in adom(D)^m$, and all $c, c' \in I_0 \cap I_1$, we have $\mathfrak{M} \models \sigma(\vec{a}, \vec{e}, c) \leftrightarrow$
   $\sigma(\vec{a}, \vec{e}, c')$ for all $\sigma \in \mathcal{F}$.*
3. *$D \models \alpha'(\vec{b}, \vec{c}, \vec{a})$, where $\alpha'(\vec{s}, \vec{t}, \vec{x})$ is obtained from $\alpha(\vec{x}, z)$ by replacing
   each subformula $\sigma(\vec{x}, \vec{y}, z)$ from $\mathcal{F}$ by $\sigma_{ij}^{\rho\tau}(\vec{x}, \vec{y}, \vec{s}, \vec{t})$.*

Proof. For the *only if* part, assume that $D \models \varphi(\vec{a})$. That is, $D \models \exists z \alpha(\vec{a}, z)$.
Let d witness this; that is, $D \models \alpha(\vec{a}, d)$. For every $\vec{e}$ over $adom(D)$ of the
same length as $\vec{y}$, and every atomic $FO(\mathfrak{M})$ subformula $\rho(\vec{x}, \vec{y}, z)$ of β, we
define $I_d(\vec{e}, \rho)$ to be the maximal interval of $\rho(\mathfrak{M}, \vec{a}, \vec{e}) = \{c \mid \mathfrak{M} \models \rho(\vec{a}, \vec{e}, c)\}$
containing d, in the case when $\mathfrak{M} \models \rho(\vec{a}, \vec{e}, d)$, or the the maximal interval
of $\neg\rho(\mathfrak{M}, \vec{a}, \vec{e})$ containing d, in the case when $\mathfrak{M} \models \neg\rho(\vec{a}, \vec{e}, d)$. Let $\mathcal{I}_d$ be the
collection $\{I_d(\vec{e}, \rho) \mid \vec{e} \in adom(D)^{|\vec{y}|}, \rho \in \mathcal{F}\}$. Since for each $\vec{e}$ and ρ we have
$d \in I_d(\vec{e}, \rho)$, we obtain that $\bigcap \mathcal{I}_d \neq \emptyset$.

Now note that for any finite collection of intervals $I_1, \ldots, I_p$, there are two
indices i and j such that $\bigcap_{l=1}^p I_l = I_i \cap I_j$. Then there are two intervals I_0
and I_1 in $\mathcal{I}_d$ such that $I_0 \cap I_1 = \bigcap \mathcal{I}_d$. Let $\vec{b}$ be such that I_0 is the ith interval
of $\rho(\vec{a}, \vec{b}, \mathfrak{M})$, and let $\vec{c}$ be such that I_1 is the jth interval of $\tau(\vec{a}, \vec{c}, \mathfrak{M})$, where
$\rho, \tau \in \mathcal{F}$ (that is, ρ, τ are either atomic $FO(\mathfrak{M})$ subformulae of φ or negations
of such atomic subformulae).

Let $\vec{e} \in adom(D)^{|\vec{y}|}$. Pick any $\sigma \in \mathcal{F}$ and any $c, c' \in I_0 \cap I_1$. Since
$I_0 \cap I_1 = \bigcap \mathcal{I}_d$, we obtain that $c, c' \in I_0 \cap I_1 \subseteq I_d(\vec{e}, \sigma)$, which implies
$\mathfrak{M} \models \sigma(\vec{a}, \vec{e}, c) \leftrightarrow \sigma(\vec{a}, \vec{e}, c')$. This proves conditions 1 and 2 in the lemma.

To prove condition 3, notice that, for every $FO(\mathfrak{M})$ atomic subformula
$\sigma(\vec{x}, \vec{y}, z)$ of φ and every $\vec{e} \in adom(D)^{|\vec{y}|}$, we have

$$\sigma(\vec{a}, \vec{e}, d) \quad \leftrightarrow \quad \forall u \in I_0 \cap I_1 \ \sigma(\vec{a}, \vec{e}, u) \,,$$

since $I_0 \cap I_1 = \bigcap \mathcal{I}_d$.

Now, for any subformula $\gamma(\vec{x}, \vec{y}, z)$ of $\alpha(\vec{x}, z)$, let $\gamma'(\vec{s}, \vec{t}, \vec{x}, \vec{y})$ be the result
of replacing each $\sigma(\vec{x}, \vec{y}, z)$ from $\mathcal{F}$ by $\sigma_{ij}^{\rho\tau}(\vec{x}, \vec{y}, \vec{s}, \vec{t})$.

We can now restate the above equivalence as

$$(*) \qquad\qquad D \models \sigma(\vec{a}, \vec{e}, d) \leftrightarrow \sigma'(\vec{a}, \vec{e}, \vec{b}, \vec{c})$$

for every $\vec{e} \in adom(D)^{|\vec{y}|}$ (where $\vec{b}$ and $\vec{c}$ are the tuples necessary to define
$I_0 \cap I_1$ above), where $\sigma(\vec{x}, \vec{y}, z)$ is atomic or negated atomic (i.e. $\sigma \in \mathcal{F}$).

The above equivalence is preserved under Boolean combinations and
active quantification over variables from $\vec{y}$ in σ. Hence we obtain $(*)$ for every
σ that is a subformula of α. Finally, this gives us

$$D \models \alpha(\vec{a}, d) \leftrightarrow \alpha'(\vec{a}, \vec{b}, \vec{c}) \,.$$

Since $D \models \alpha(\vec{a}, d)$, we conclude that $D \models \alpha'(\vec{a}, \vec{b}, \vec{c})$, proving condition 3.

To prove the *if* part, assume that there exist $\vec{b}, \vec{c} \in adom(D)^m$, $\rho, \tau \in \mathcal{F}$, and $i \leq K_\rho, j \leq K_\tau$ such that for I_0, I_1 defined as in the statement of the lemma, conditions 1, 2, and 3 hold. Let d be an arbitrary element of $I_0 \cap I_1$. We claim that $D \models \alpha(\vec{a}, d)$, thus proving $D \models \varphi(\vec{a})$.

Indeed, for every $\mathrm{FO}(\mathfrak{M})$ atomic subformula $\sigma(\vec{x}, \vec{y}, z)$ of α, we have

$$\sigma(\vec{a}, \vec{e}, d) \quad \leftrightarrow \quad \forall u \in I_0 \cap I_1 \; \sigma(\vec{a}, \vec{e}, u) \, ,$$

for every $\vec{e}$ over $adom(D)$ – this follows from condition 2. That is, $\sigma(\vec{a}, \vec{e}, d) \leftrightarrow \sigma_{ij}^{\rho\tau}(\vec{a}, \vec{e}, \vec{b}, \vec{c})$. As before, since this equivalence is preserved under Boolean combinations with $\mathrm{FO}(SC)$ atomic formulae, and under active-domain quantification over variables from $\vec{y}$, we obtain

$$D \models \alpha(\vec{a}, d) \leftrightarrow \alpha'(\vec{b}, \vec{c}, a) \, ,$$

thus proving $D \models \alpha(\vec{a}, d)$. The lemma is proved. $\qquad\square$

The Transformation Algorithm

The algorithm that converts natural-semantics formulae into active-semantics formulae works by induction on the structure of the formulae. In the case of atomic formulae, there is no need to change anything. For Boolean connectives, suppose that $\varphi \equiv \chi \vee \psi$. Let χ_{act} and ψ_{act} be $\mathrm{FO}_{\mathrm{act}}(SC, \mathfrak{M})$ formulae equivalent to χ and γ. Then $\chi_{\mathrm{act}} \vee \psi_{\mathrm{act}}$ is an $\mathrm{FO}_{\mathrm{act}}(SC, \mathfrak{M})$ formula equivalent to φ. We deal with negation and conjunction similarly.

The only nontrivial case is that of an existential quantifier $\exists z \alpha(\vec{x}, z)$. To handle it, we use Lemma 5.6.8. For now, assume that we are dealing with nonempty SC-structures. By the induction hypothesis, we assume that α is an $\mathrm{FO}_{\mathrm{act}}(SC, \mathfrak{M})$ formula. We first put α in the form required by Lemma 5.6.8 by taking the conjunction with a true sentence $\exists y \in adom(y = y)$ (since $adom$ is nonempty) to ensure that there are quantifiers and atomic $\mathrm{FO}(\mathfrak{M})$ formulae, then using Lemma 5.5.2 to separate $\mathrm{FO}(\mathfrak{M})$ and $\mathrm{FO}(SC)$ formulae, and finally putting α into prenex form. Once α is in the right form, we apply Lemma 5.6.8, noticing that it translates into a first-order description. The step-by-step process of doing so is described in the algorithm NATURAL-ACTIVE shown on the next page. Note that every occurrence of an unrestricted quantifier $\forall$ or $\exists$ is of the form $\forall y \gamma$ or $\exists x \gamma$, where γ is an $\mathrm{FO}(\mathfrak{M})$ formula. Since $\mathfrak{M}$ has quantifier elimination, this means that every occurrence of unrestricted quantification can be eliminated.

Summing up, we have the following.

Algorithm NATURAL–ACTIVE

INPUT: FO$(SC, \mathfrak{M})$ formula $\varphi(\vec{x})$
OUTPUT: FO$_{\text{act}}(SC, \mathfrak{M})$ formula $\varphi_{\text{act}}(\vec{x})$

1. If φ is an atomic formula, then $\varphi_{\text{act}} = \varphi$.
2. If $\varphi = \psi * \chi$, then $\varphi_{\text{act}} = \psi_{\text{act}} * \chi_{\text{act}}$ where $* \in \{\vee, \wedge\}$; if $\varphi = \neg\psi$, then $\varphi_{\text{act}} = \neg\psi_{\text{act}}$.
3. If $\varphi = \exists x \in adom\ \psi$, then $\varphi_{\text{act}} = \exists x \in adom\ \psi_{\text{act}}$.
4. Let $\varphi(\vec{x}) = \exists z\ \alpha^0(\vec{x}, z)$.

    4.1 Let $\alpha(\vec{x}, z)$ be a formula equivalent to α_{act}^0 which is of the form

    $$\mathbf{Q}y_1 \in adom \dots \mathbf{Q}y_m \in adom\ \beta(\vec{x}, \vec{y}, z),$$

    where $\beta(\vec{x}, \vec{y}, \vec{z})$ is quantifier-free and has the following properties: every atomic subformula of β is either an FO(SC) formula or an FO$(\mathfrak{M})$ formula; there exists at least one FO$(\mathfrak{M})$ atomic subformula of β, $m > 0$, and z does not occur in FO(SC) subformulae.

    4.2 Let $\mathcal{F}$ be the collection of all atomic FO$(\mathfrak{M})$ subformulae of α, and their negations.

    4.3 Let $K = \max_{\gamma \in \mathcal{F}} K_\gamma$.

    4.4 For every pair of formulae $\rho, \sigma \in \mathcal{F}$, and every $i, j < K$, define $\chi_{ij}^{\rho\sigma}(\vec{x}, \vec{s}, \vec{t})$ to be the quantifier-free FO$(\mathfrak{M})$ formula equivalent to $\exists u\ (\hat{\rho}_i(\vec{x}, \vec{s}, u) \wedge \hat{\sigma}_j(\vec{x}, \vec{t}, u))$. Note that $|\vec{s}| = |\vec{t}| = m$.

    4.5 For each $\rho, \sigma \in \mathcal{F}$, each $i, j < K$, and each $\tau \in \mathcal{F}$, define $\tau_{ij}^{\rho\sigma}(\vec{x}, \vec{y}, \vec{s}, \vec{t})$ as a quantifier-free formula equivalent to

    $$\forall u\ \left(\hat{\rho}_i(\vec{x}, \vec{s}, u) \wedge \hat{\sigma}_j(\vec{x}, \vec{t}, u) \rightarrow \tau(\vec{x}, \vec{y}, u) \right)$$

    4.6 For each $\rho, \sigma \in \mathcal{F}$ and each $i, j < K$, define $\alpha_{ij}^{\rho\sigma}(\vec{x}, \vec{s}, \vec{t})$ as α in which every FO$(\mathfrak{M})$ atomic subformula $\tau(\vec{x}, \vec{y}, z) \in \mathcal{F}$ is replaced by $\tau_{ij}^{\rho\sigma}(\vec{x}, \vec{y}, \vec{s}, \vec{t})$.

    4.7 Let same$_\beta(\vec{x}, \vec{r}, u, v)$ be $\bigwedge(\rho(\vec{x}, \vec{r}, u) \leftrightarrow \rho(\vec{x}, \vec{r}, v))$, where the conjunction is taken over all the FO$(\mathfrak{M})$ atomic subformulae ρ of β.

    4.8 For each $\rho, \sigma \in \mathcal{F}$, each $i, j < K$, define $\eta_{ij}^{\rho\sigma}(\vec{x}, \vec{s}, \vec{t}, \vec{r})$ as a quantifier-free formula equivalent to

    $$\forall u, v\ \left((\hat{\rho}_i(\vec{x}, \vec{s}, u) \wedge \hat{\sigma}_j(\vec{x}, \vec{t}, u) \wedge \hat{\rho}_i(\vec{x}, \vec{s}, v) \wedge \hat{\sigma}_j(\vec{x}, \vec{t}, v)) \rightarrow \text{same}_\beta(\vec{x}, \vec{r}, u, v) \right).$$

    4.9 For each $\rho, \sigma \in \mathcal{F}$ and each $i, j < K$, define $\pi_{ij}^{\rho\sigma}(\vec{x}, \vec{s}, \vec{t})$ as $\forall \vec{r} \in adom\ \eta_{ij}^{\rho\sigma}(\vec{x}, \vec{s}, \vec{t}, \vec{r})$.

    4.10 Output, as $\varphi_{\text{act}}(\vec{x})$, the formula

    $$\exists \vec{s} \in adom\ \exists \vec{t} \in adom \bigvee_{\rho, \sigma \in \mathcal{F}} \bigvee_{i, j < K} (\chi_{ij}^{\rho\sigma}(\vec{x}, \vec{s}, \vec{t}) \wedge \pi_{ij}^{\rho\sigma}(\vec{x}, \vec{s}, \vec{t}) \wedge \alpha_{ij}^{\rho\sigma}(\vec{x}, \vec{s}, \vec{t})).$$

Proposition 5.6.9. *Let $\mathfrak{M}$ be o-minimal and admit quantifier elimination. Let $\varphi(\vec{x})$ be any $FO(SC, \mathfrak{M})$ first-order formula, and let φ_{act} be the output of* NATURAL-ACTIVE *on φ. Then, for every nonempty finite SC-structure D, $D \models \forall \vec{x} \; \varphi(\vec{x}) \leftrightarrow \varphi_{\mathrm{act}}(\vec{x})$. Furthermore, if $\mathfrak{M}$ is recursive and the quantifier elimination procedure is effective, then there is an effective procedure yielding such a φ_{act} for an input φ.* □

To conclude the proof of Theorem 5.6.4, we have to deal with the case of $adom(D)$ being empty. Let $\varphi(\vec{x})$ be an $FO(SC, \mathfrak{M})$ formula. Let $\varphi'_\emptyset(\vec{x})$ be obtained from φ by replacing each occurrence of $R(\cdots)$, where $R \in SC$, by *false*. Note that $\varphi'_\emptyset$ is an $FO(\mathfrak{M})$ formula. Let $\varphi_\emptyset$ be a quantifier-free formula equivalent to $\varphi'_\emptyset$. A simple induction on formulae shows that for the empty SC-instance, $\emptyset_{SC}$, it is the case that $\emptyset_{SC} \models \varphi(\vec{a})$ iff $\mathfrak{M} \models \varphi_\emptyset(\vec{a})$, for every $\vec{a}$. Thus, an $FO_{\mathrm{act}}(SC, \mathfrak{M})$ formula

$$\varphi'(\vec{x}) \;\equiv\; [(\exists x \in adom \; (x = x)) \;\wedge\; \varphi_{\mathrm{act}}(\vec{x})]$$
$$\vee[(\neg\exists x \in adom \; (x = x)) \;\wedge\; \varphi_\emptyset(\vec{x})]$$

has the property that $D \models \forall \vec{x} \; \varphi(\vec{x}) \leftrightarrow \varphi'(\vec{x})$, for arbitrary D. This concludes the proof of Theorem 5.6.4. □

5.6.6 Collapse Without O-minimality

We have seen that quantifier elimination is necessary for natural-active collapse. What about o-minimality? It turns out that there are non-o-minimal structures that admit this collapse. Consider the structure $\mathbf{3} = \langle \mathbb{Z}, +, < \rangle$. It is not o-minimal: for example, the formula $\varphi(x)$ given by $\exists y \; (y + y = x)$ defines the set of even numbers. The same example, though, shows that natural-active collapse fails over $\mathbf{3}$: the Boolean query $\exists x \; (S(x) \wedge \varphi(x))$ is not expressible in $FO_{\mathrm{act}}(\{S\}, \mathbf{3})$, since φ cannot be expressed by a quantifier-free formula.

However, it is well known that $\mathbf{3}$ admits quantifier elimination in an extended signature. Let $x \sim_k y$ iff $x = y(\mathrm{mod} \; k)$. These relations are definable over $\mathbf{3}$, and the structure $\mathbf{3}_0 = \langle \mathbb{Z}, +, <, 0, 1, (\sim_k)_{k>0} \rangle$ does admit quantifier elimination. We thus have an example of a structure that has quantifier elimination, is not o-minimal, and admits natural-active collapse.

Proposition 5.6.10. $\mathbf{3}_0$ *admits the natural-active collapse.*

Proof sketch. The proof is again by induction, and we consider the only nontrivial case of existential quantification. To simplify the notation, assume that we have a sentence $\varPhi \equiv \exists z \varphi(z)$, where

$$\varphi(z) \equiv \mathbf{Q} y_1 \in adom \ldots \mathbf{Q} y_m \in adom \; \alpha(z, \vec{y}),$$

and where each $\mathbf{Q}$ is either $\exists$ or $\forall$.

Using Lemma 5.5.2, we can assume that α is a Boolean combination of:

1. atomic SC-formulae with free variables among $\vec{y}$;
2. linear constraints $f(z, \vec{y}) \vartheta 0$, where f is a linear function and ϑ is an $=$, or $<$, or $\leq$ comparison;
3. constraints of the form $f(z, \vec{y}) \sim_c p$ for $c \in \mathbb{N}$ and $0 \leq p < c$, where again f is a linear function.

Let c be the maximum number for which one of the $\sim_c$ relations occurs in α. Let $\chi_i(x)$ enumerate all satisfiable formulae of the form

$$\bigwedge_{1 < b \leq c} x \sim_b p_b,$$

where $p_b < b$, and similarly let $\chi_i^m(\vec{y})$ enumerate all satisfiable conjunctions $\chi_{i_1}(y_1) \wedge \ldots \wedge \chi_{i_m}(y_m)$. Then $\varphi(z)$ is equivalent to

$$\exists z \left(\bigvee_i \chi_i(z) \wedge \mathbf{Q}y_1 \in adom \ldots \mathbf{Q}y_m \in adom \left(\bigvee_j \chi_j^m(\vec{y}) \wedge \alpha(z, \vec{y}) \right) \right).$$

Note that if we know all the residues for z and $\vec{y}$ modulo all the positive integers not exceeding c, then we can infer the truth value of each constraint of the form $f(z, \vec{y}) \sim_b p$ for every $b \leq c$ and $p_b < b$. Thus, we can assume without loss of generality that constraints of the form $f(z, \vec{y}) \sim_b p$ do not appear in α, unless f is identically z or one of the y_is.

To eliminate $\exists z$ from the formula above, we proceed just as in the case of FO + LIN. Let $g_1(\vec{y}), \ldots, g_l(\vec{y})$ enumerate all the linear functions that occur in constraints of the form $z \vartheta g_i(\vec{y})$, and the function $g(\vec{y}) = y_1$. We fix a finite set A, and define a set B_0 as $\{g_i(\vec{a}) \mid i \leq l, \vec{a} \in A^m\}$. Note that $A \subseteq B_0$. Let $b_1 < \ldots < b_k$ list the elements of B_0.

Suppose we have an SC-structure D with $adom(D) = A$, and suppose that $\varphi(z_0)$ holds. Assume that $b_i < z_0 < b_{i+1}$. Then the same argument as in the proof of the collapse for FO + LIN shows that any other $z_0' \in (b_i, b_{i+1})$ that agrees with z_0 on all χ_js also satisfies φ. This shows the following: if there is a z_0 satisfying φ, then there is one such that $|z_0 - b_i| \leq c$ for some b_i. In particular, if $D \models \Phi$, then there exists a $z_0 \in B_1$ such that $D \models \varphi(z_0)$, where $B_1 = \{b + p, b - p \mid b \in B_0, 0 \leq p \leq c\}$. Just as in the case of FO + LIN, this set B_1 is definable in $FO(SC, \mathbf{3}_0)$. Thus, under the assumption that α uses only $\sim_k$ relations to compare a variable with a constant, we can rewrite Φ as

$$\exists \vec{u} \in adom \bigvee_{-c \leq b \leq c} \bigvee_{i=1}^{l} \varphi((g_i(\vec{u}) + b) / z),$$

thus eliminating an unrestricted quantifier $\exists z$. Notice that, unlike the case of FO + LIN, we need m additional active-domain quantifiers (instead of $2m$), as the proof does not require witnesses which are middles of some intervals (b_i, b_{i+1}). $\square$

5.6.7 Natural-Generic Collapse

The natural-generic collapse result says that order-generic queries in $FO(SC, \mathfrak{M})$ can be expressed in $FO(SC, <)$. We now derive this collapse result as a corollary to the two collapse results shown so far.

Corollary 5.6.11 (Natural-Generic Collapse). *Let $\mathfrak{M} = \langle U, \Omega \rangle$ be an o-minimal structure. Then it admits natural-generic collapse.*

Proof. Let Q be an order-generic query definable in $FO(SC, \mathfrak{M})$. Consider a definitional expansion $\mathfrak{M}'$ of $\mathfrak{M}$ obtained by extending Ω with new symbols for all $\mathfrak{M}$-definable predicates. Such an $\mathfrak{M}'$ admits quantifier elimination, and then, by use of natural-active collapse, we obtain that Q is definable in $FO_{act}(SC, \mathfrak{M}')$. From the active-generic collapse, we conclude that Q is definable in $FO_{act}(SC, <)$ (and thus in $FO(SC, <)$). □

While the active-generic collapse holds for all ordered structures, and the bounds of Theorem 5.6.4 are the best currently known for the natural-active collapse, Corollary 5.6.11 has been extended to a larger class of structures. The proof of the result is rather involved, but we shall present a statement of the result below.

The new condition on the structures uses the Vapnik-Chervonenkis (VC) dimension, a central concept in computational learning theory. Suppose that S is an infinite set, and $\mathcal{C} \subseteq 2^S$ is a family of subsets of S. Let $F \subset S$ be finite; we say that $\mathcal{C}$ *shatters* F if the collection $\{F \cap C \mid C \in \mathcal{C}\}$ is 2^F. The *Vapnik-Chervonenkis dimension* of $\mathcal{C}$, $VCdim(\mathcal{C})$, is the maximal cardinality of a finite set shattered by $\mathcal{C}$. If arbitrarily large finite sets are shattered by $\mathcal{C}$, we let $VCdim(\mathcal{C}) = \infty$.

This applies to first-order structures as follows. Let $\mathfrak{M} = \langle U, \Omega \rangle$, and let $\varphi(\vec{x}, \vec{y})$ be a formula in the language of $\mathfrak{M}$ with $|\vec{x}| = n, |\vec{y}| = m$. For each $\vec{a} \in U^n$, we define $\varphi(\vec{a}, \mathfrak{M}) = \{\vec{b} \in U^m \mid \mathfrak{M} \models \varphi(\vec{a}, \vec{b})\}$, and let $F_\varphi(\mathfrak{M})$ be $\{\varphi(\vec{a}, \mathfrak{M}) \mid \vec{a} \in \mathcal{U}^n\}$. Families of sets arising in such a way are called *definable families*.

Definition 5.6.12. $\mathfrak{M}$ *is said to have finite VC dimension if every definable family in $\mathfrak{M}$ has finite VC dimension.* □

Examples of structures that have finite VC dimension include:

- every o-minimal structure;
- $\langle \mathbb{N}, +, < \rangle$ and $\langle \mathbb{Z}, +, < \rangle$;
- every linear order;
- ordered Abelian groups (that is, Abelian groups in which addition is monotone with respect to the order).

In particular, the class is a proper extension of the class of all o-minimal structures. The following is a deep result which we present here without proof:

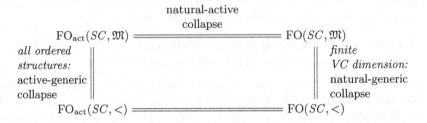

o-minimal and
quantifier elimination:

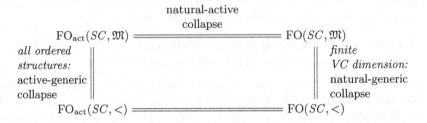

Fig. 5.5. Summary of collapse results

Theorem 5.6.13. *Let $\mathfrak{M}$ be an ordered structure that has finite VC dimension. Then $\mathfrak{M}$ admits natural-generic collapse.*   □

We shall discuss the relationship between the VC dimension and various forms of collapse in Sect. 5.8.

The diagram in Fig. 5.5 summarizes what has been achieved towards proving the collapse results.

5.7 Model Theory and Collapse Results

While most collapse results proved so far apply to o-minimal structures, we have seen a couple of examples outside of the o-minimal world. So it is natural to ask what really causes the natural-active or other forms of collapse: are there some properties of the underlying structure that cause it to happen?

The goal of this section is to give a partial answer to this question. We start by presenting a technical condition, called *pseudo-finite homogeneity*, that ensures a form of collapse that is closely related to natural-active collapse. We then describe a couple of model-theoretic conditions that are often easy to verify, and that imply pseudo-finite homogeneity and thus the collapse. We shall see a number of examples of collapse outside of the o-minimal context that are implied by those conditions.

We start with the following definition.

Definition 5.7.1. *We say that a structure $\mathfrak{M}$ admits restricted quantifier collapse if for every SC, every $FO(SC,\mathfrak{M})$ formula is equivalent to an $FO(SC,\mathfrak{M})$ formula in which SC-relations do not appear in the scope of unrestricted quantifiers.*

For example, in the formula $\exists x \in adom \forall y \in adom \ (S(x,y) \rightarrow \forall z \exists u \ x^2 + y = z^2 + u)$, the SC-relation S appears only in the scope of two active-domain quantifies $\exists x \in adom$ and $\forall y \in adom$. However, for the formula $\exists u \exists v \ (\forall x \in adom \forall y \in adom \ S(x,y) \rightarrow y = u \cdot x + v)$ this is not the case, as S appears in the scope of the quantifiers $\exists u$ and $\exists v$.

Note that if $\mathfrak{M}$ admits restricted quantifier collapse, and if $\mathfrak{M}'$ is the expansion of $\mathfrak{M}$ with all definable predicates, then every $FO(SC, \mathfrak{M})$ formula is equivalent to an $FO_{act}(SC, \mathfrak{M}')$ formula. In particular, if $\mathfrak{M}$ admits quantifier elimination, then restricted quantifier collapse implies natural-active collapse. Furthermore, restricted quantifier collapse always implies natural-generic collapse. Thus:

restricted quantifier + QE collapse	=	natural-active collapse	$\Rightarrow$	restricted quantifier collapse	$\Rightarrow$	natural generic collapse

Remark. Although we shall provide all the necessary model-theoretic definitions here, the reader needs some infinite model theory background to understand the proofs in this section. In particular, many proofs using techniques from classical infinite model theory are only sketched. We nevertheless encourage the reader without such a background to read this section (perhaps skipping the proofs) to see many new examples of collapse results.

We shall also assume that we are dealing with structures in a finite or countable language; this assumption can easily be avoided at the expense of some additional arguments involving infinite cardinals, which we prefer not to deal with here.

5.7.1 Pseudo-finite Homogeneity

We start with a few definitions from model theory. For a structure $\mathfrak{M}$, its theory is denoted by $Th(\mathfrak{M})$. Two structures $\mathfrak{M}_1$ and $\mathfrak{M}_2$ of the same language are elementarily equivalent (written $\mathfrak{M}_1 \equiv \mathfrak{M}_2$) if their theories are the same; that is, if they satisfy the same FO-sentences. For a subset A of $\mathfrak{M}$, and an n-tuple $\vec{a}$, the n-type of $\vec{a}$ over A (or just the type, if n is understood), $tp_{\mathfrak{M}}(\vec{a}/A)$, is the set of all formulae in n free variables, in the language of $\mathfrak{M}$ plus constants for the elements of A, that are satisfied by $\vec{a}$.

A model $\mathfrak{M}$ is called ω-saturated if every consistent 1-type over a finite subset of $\mathfrak{M}$ is realized in $\mathfrak{M}$. It is known that, for every $\mathfrak{M}$, there exists an ω-saturated elementary extension $\mathfrak{M}'$.

Let $L(SC, \mathfrak{M})$ be the language that is the expansion of $L(\mathfrak{M})$, the language of $\mathfrak{M}$, with all the relation symbols in SC. A structure in this language is a pair $(\mathfrak{M}', D)$, where $\mathfrak{M}'$ is a structure in the language of $\mathfrak{M}$ and D is an interpretation of SC symbols over $\mathfrak{M}'$ (not necessarily finite). Let $\mathcal{F}(SC, \mathfrak{M})$ be the theory of all $L(SC, \mathfrak{M})$ structures $(\mathfrak{M}', D)$, where $\mathfrak{M}' \models Th(\mathfrak{M})$ and D is finite. We now call an SC-structure D on $\mathfrak{M}$ *pseudo-finite* if $(\mathfrak{M}, D) \models \mathcal{F}(SC, \mathfrak{M})$.

Definition 5.7.2. *We say that $\mathfrak{M}$ has ω-pseudo-finite homogeneity property, or ω-PFH for short, if for any model $\mathfrak{M}'$ of $\mathrm{Th}(\mathfrak{M})$, any two pseudo-finite SC-structures D_1, D_2 on $\mathfrak{M}'$, and any bijective and $L(\mathfrak{M})$-elementary map $h : D_1 \to D_2$ such that $(\mathfrak{M}', D_1, D_2, h)$ is ω-saturated, it is the case that for every $a \in \mathfrak{M}'$ there exists $b \in \mathfrak{M}'$ such that $h \cup \{(a, b)\}$ is elementary.*

Theorem 5.7.3. *If $\mathfrak{M}$ has ω-PFH, then it admits restricted quantifier collapse.*

Proof sketch. Let φ be an $\mathrm{FO}(SC, \mathfrak{M})$ sentence. Assume that φ is not equivalent to any restricted quantifier sentence. Let α_i enumerate all restricted quantifier $\mathrm{FO}(SC, \mathfrak{M})$ sentences; then, for every α_i, we can find a model $(\mathfrak{M}_i, D_i^1, D_i^2)$ such that $\mathfrak{M}_i \equiv \mathfrak{M}$, $D_i^1 \models \varphi$, $D_i^2 \models \neg\varphi$, and D_i^1, D_i^2 agree on α_i. By compactness, we have a model $(\mathfrak{M}', D_1, D_2)$ such that D_1, D_2 agree on all $\mathrm{FO}_{\mathrm{act}}(SC, \mathfrak{M})$ sentences, and $D_1 \models \varphi$ and $D_2 \models \neg\varphi$.

A standard model-theoretic argument shows that we can further assume that there is a partial $L(SC, \mathfrak{M})$-isomorphism $h : D_1 \to D_2$ that is also an elementary map in the language of $\mathfrak{M}$, and, furthermore, that $(\mathfrak{M}, D_1, D_2, h)$ is ω-saturated. By ω-PFH, for any $k > 0$, h can be extended k times back and forth to an $L(\mathfrak{M})$-elementary map, which is a partial $L(SC, \mathfrak{M})$-isomorphism, since its domain includes $adom(D_1)$ and its range includes $adom(D_2)$. Thus, h is an $L(SC, \mathfrak{M})$-elementary map, which contradicts the statement that $D_1 \models \varphi$ and $D_2 \models \neg\varphi$. □

The notion of pseudo-finite homogeneity may not be a very easy one to check for a given structure; however, other model-theoretic properties imply it, and thus they imply restricted quantifier collapse. We shall see two examples below.

5.7.2 Finite Cover Property and Collapse

Similarly to the definition of ω-saturation, we can define ω_1-saturated structures by requiring that types over countable sets (rather than just finite sets) be realized. By requiring that the structure $(\mathfrak{M}', D_1, D_2, h)$ in the definition of PFH be ω_1-saturated, we obtain a stronger notion of ω_1-PFH.

We now say that $\mathfrak{M}$ has the *pseudo-finite saturation property*, or PFS for short, if for any model $\mathfrak{M}'$ of the theory of $\mathfrak{M}$ and any pseudo-finite set A in $\mathfrak{M}'$ such that $(\mathfrak{M}', A)$ is ω_1-saturated, every consistent 1-type over A is realized in $(\mathfrak{M}', (a)_{a \in A})$. This property is easier to connect to other model-theoretic properties, and, furthermore, we can state the following proposition.

Proposition 5.7.4. *Pseudo-finite saturation implies ω_1-PFH, and thus it implies restricted quantifier collapse.*

Proof. Let $(\mathfrak{M}', D_1, D_2, h)$ be ω_1-saturated, where D_1, D_2 are pseudo-finite. Let $a \in \mathfrak{M}'$, $A = adom(D_1)$, and $p = \mathrm{tp}_{\mathfrak{M}'}(a/A)$. Let $h(p) = \{\varphi(x, h(\vec{a})) \mid \varphi(x, \vec{a}) \in p\}$. Then $h(p)$ is a type over $adom(D_2)$; by pseudo-finite saturation, it is realized by some $b \in \mathfrak{M}'$, and thus $h \cup \{(a, b)\}$ is elementary. □

One known result about pseudo-finite saturation is that it holds for structures that do not have the finite cover property. Recall that a structure $\mathfrak{M}$ has the *finite cover property* if there is a formula $\varphi(x, \vec{y})$ such that, for every $n > 0$, one can find tuples $\vec{a}_1, \ldots, \vec{a}_n$ such that $\exists x \bigwedge_{j \neq i} \varphi(x, \vec{a}_j)$ holds for each $i \leq n$, but $\exists x \bigwedge_{j \leq n} \varphi(x, \vec{a}_j)$ does not hold. Since every $\mathfrak{M}$ that does not have the cover property has pseudo-finite saturation, it also admits restricted quantifier collapse.

In model theory, a number of examples of structures without the finite cover property have been collected; for example, every structure whose theory is categorical in every uncountable power is such a structure. Some of the best known examples are:

- The field of complex numbers $\langle \mathbb{C}, +, \cdot \rangle$ (in fact, any algebraically closed field of characteristic p, where p is zero or prime).
- $\langle \mathbb{N}, \pi \rangle$, where $\pi : \mathbb{N} \to \mathbb{N}$ is a permutation without finite cycles.
- $\langle \mathbb{N}, succ \rangle$.

Corollary 5.7.5. *The three structures above admit restricted quantifier collapse.*

As another example, we consider the first-order theory of finitely many successor relations. This is a decidable theory (in fact, even the monadic second-order theory is decidable, by a classical result by Büchi) with many applications in computer science. Let Σ be a finite alphabet, and let Σ^* be the set of all finite strings over Σ, with ε being the empty string. For each $a \in \Sigma$, let f_a be the unary function that appends a at the end of its argument: $f_a(x) = x \cdot a$. We now have the following.

Proposition 5.7.6. *For any finite Σ, the structure $\langle \Sigma^*, \varepsilon, (f_a)_{a \in \Sigma} \rangle$ admits restricted quantifier collapse.*

Proof sketch. We show that $\mathfrak{M} = \langle \Sigma^*, \varepsilon, (f_a)_{a \in \Sigma} \rangle$ does not have the finite cover property. We need a little preparation. Our proof will use the following known result: $\mathfrak{M}$ does not have the finite cover property if (a) no formula $\alpha(\vec{x}, \vec{y})$ defines an infinite linear order on $\mathfrak{M}$, and (b) for every $\alpha(\vec{x}, \vec{y})$, there is a formula $\beta(\vec{x})$ such that $\beta(\vec{x})$ holds iff the number of $\vec{y}$ for which $\alpha(\vec{x}, \vec{y})$ holds is infinite.[1]

Let $g_a(x)$ be the following definable function: if the last symbol of x is a, then g removes it; otherwise $g_a(x) = x$. Then it is easy to see that

---

[1] The reader familiar with this subject will notice that our condition (b) is not sufficient to conclude that $\mathfrak{M}$ does not have the finite cover property: instead, one would need to show a stronger property (b'): namely, for any formula $\alpha(\vec{x}, \vec{y}, \vec{z})$ such that $\alpha(\mathfrak{M}, \vec{z})$ is an equivalence relation $E_{\vec{z}}$ for every $\vec{z}$, there is a formula $\beta(\vec{z})$ such that $\beta(\vec{z})$ holds iff $E_{\vec{z}}$ has finitely many equivalence classes. However, using quantifier elimination for $\mathfrak{M}$, one can show that $\mathfrak{M}$ eliminates imaginaries and thus each equivalence relation is of the form $\{(\vec{u}, \vec{w}) \mid f(\vec{u}) = f(\vec{v})\}$ for some definable function f. Therefore, (b) implies (b').

$\langle \Sigma^*, \varepsilon, (f_a)_{a\in\Sigma} \rangle$ has quantifier elimination in the language $\langle (f_a, g_a)_{a\in\Sigma}, \varepsilon \rangle$. Using this, one easily concludes (a).

To show (b), we define the distance between two strings x and y, $d(x,y)$, as the minimal length of a term t built from f_a, g_a, ε such that $t(x) = y$. If one thinks of Σ^* as an infinite $|\Sigma|$-ary tree, then $d(u,v)$ is simply the distance in this tree. We define $d(\vec{x}, \vec{y})$ as the minimal distance between a component of $\vec{x}$ and a component of $\vec{y}$. Note that for each fixed i, $d(\vec{x}, \vec{y}) < i$ is definable.

Given a formula $\alpha(\vec{x}, \vec{y})$, assume without loss of generality that it is a Boolean combination of formulae $v = t(u)$, where v, u are variables among $\vec{x}, \vec{y}$ and the ts are terms. Let k be the maximum length of a term in α. We define $\gamma(\vec{x})$ as

$$\forall \vec{y} \; \alpha(\vec{x}, \vec{y}) \rightarrow \bigwedge_i (d(y_i, \vec{x}) < m(k+2)) \wedge (d(y_i, \varepsilon) < m(k+2)),$$

where m is the length of $\vec{y}$. We claim that $\gamma(\vec{x})$ holds iff the number of $\vec{y}$ such that $\alpha(\vec{x}, \vec{y})$ holds is finite. Then we take $\beta \equiv \neg\gamma$.

One direction is trivial. Assume that $\gamma(\vec{x})$ does not hold; then one can find $\vec{y}$ for which $\alpha(\vec{x}, \vec{y})$ holds, and divide $\vec{y}$ into two parts, $\vec{y}_1$ and $\vec{y}_2$, such that $d(\vec{y}_2, (\vec{y}_1, \vec{x}, \varepsilon)) > k + 1$. Now let s be a sufficiently long string; define $s \cdot \vec{y}_2$ as the result of adding s as a prefix to all strings in $\vec{y}_2$. It is clear that $\alpha(\vec{x}, (\vec{y}_1, s \cdot \vec{y}_2))$ still holds, which completes the proof, since s is arbitrary. $\square$

The results of this section have some limitations; in particular, all structures with the pseudo-finite saturation property are stable, which means that one cannot define infinite linear orders in them. To deal with ordered structures (which are the ones most typically used in applications), we present a different model-theoretic notion that implies ω-PFS.

5.7.3 Isolation and Collapse

Let $\mathfrak{M}$ be a structure, let A be a subset of it, and let p be a 1-type over A. Let p' be a subset of p. We say that p' *isolates* p if p is the only type over A that contains p'.

Definition 5.7.7. *We say that $\mathfrak{M}$ has the* isolation property *if, for every model $\mathfrak{M}'$ of the theory of $\mathfrak{M}$, any pseudo-finite set A in $\mathfrak{M}'$, and any element a, there is a finite set $A' \subseteq A$ such that $\text{tp}_{\mathfrak{M}'}(a/A')$ isolates $\text{tp}_{\mathfrak{M}'}(a/A)$.*

This gives us a number of new examples of structures that admit restricted quantifier collapse, thanks to the following proposition.

Proposition 5.7.8. *If $\mathfrak{M}$ has the isolation property, then it has ω-PFH (and thus admits restricted quantifier collapse).*

Proof. Assume that we have an ω-saturated $(\mathfrak{M}', D_1, D_2, h)$, where D_1, D_2 are two pseudo-finite SC-structures, and h is elementary. Let $a \in \mathfrak{M}'$. Let

$A_i = adom(D_i)$; then A_1, A_2 are pseudo-finite sets. Let $p = \text{tp}_{\mathfrak{M}'}(a/A_1)$; by isolation, there is a finite set $A_1' \subseteq A_1$ such that $p' = \text{tp}_{\mathfrak{M}'}(a/A_1')$ isolates p.

For each $\varphi \in p$, let φ_h be φ in which every $c \in A_1$ is replaced by $h(c)$. Since h is elementary, any finite conjunction of formulae φ_h, $\varphi \in p$, is satisfiable in $\mathfrak{M}'$, and thus, by compactness, $h(p) = \{\varphi_h \mid \varphi \in p\}$ is consistent. Furthermore, a straightforward compactness argument shows that $h(p')$ isolates $h(p)$. Since A_1' is finite, $h(p')$ is countable, and thus, by saturation, it is realized by an element $b \in \mathfrak{M}'$. Since $h(p')$ isolates $h(p)$, b is of type $h(p)$, which shows that $h \cup \{(a, b)\}$ is elementary. □

As the simplest example of the isolation property, consider the theory of linear order, whose models are ordered sets $\langle U, < \rangle$. Let $\mathfrak{M}$ be such a structure, and let A be a pseudo-finite set. For every $a \in U$ and every finite set A_0, either there are two consecutive elements of A_0, say $b < c$, such that $(b, c) \cap A_0 = \emptyset$ and $b \leq a \leq c$, or $a > m$, where m is the maximal element of A_0, or $a < m'$, where m' is the minimal element of A_0. As this condition is FO-definable, it must be true for the pseudo-finite set A. We claim that $\text{tp}_{\mathfrak{M}}(a/A)$ is isolated by $\text{tp}_{\mathfrak{M}}(a/A')$, where $A' = \{b, c\}$, or $A' = \{m\}$, or $A' = \{m'\}$, depending on which of the three cases is true. We prove this for the case of $b \leq a \leq c$; the other cases are similar.

To show that $\text{tp}_{\mathfrak{M}}(a/A')$ isolates $\text{tp}_{\mathfrak{M}}(a/A)$, we must prove that for any a', $(\mathfrak{M}, a, b, c) \equiv (\mathfrak{M}, a', b, c)$ implies $(\mathfrak{M}', a, (d)_{d \in A}) \equiv (\mathfrak{M}', a', (d)_{d \in A})$. This is easy to see by an Ehrenfeucht–Fraïssé game argument. By the assumption, the duplicator has a winning strategy on $([b, c], a)$ and $([b, c], a')$. For the winning strategy on $(\mathfrak{M}', a, (d)_{d \in A})$ and $(\mathfrak{M}', a', (d)_{d \in A})$, the duplicator uses the above strategy for moves in the interval $[b, c]$, and copies the spoiler's moves elsewhere.

What about more complex examples? First, it is easy to extend the example above to the case of ordered sets with some additional unary relations. That is:

Corollary 5.7.9. *Let $\mathfrak{M}$ be a structure with one binary relation, interpreted as a linear ordering, and finitely many unary relations. Then $\mathfrak{M}$ admits restricted quantifier collapse.* □

As our next example, we revisit the theory of k successor relations, that is, $\langle \Sigma^*, \varepsilon, (f_a)_{a \in \Sigma} \rangle$. This structure is the infinite k-ary tree in which we have only successor relations available. It is considered most often in the context of monadic second-order logic, which can define the *prefix* relation in addition to the successor relations. So we now consider an extension, $\langle \Sigma^*, \varepsilon, (f_a)_{a \in \Sigma}, \prec \rangle$, where $x \prec y$ means that x is a prefix of y. The question is: does this structure admit the collapse?

The technique of Sect. 5.7.2 does not work here, since $\langle \Sigma^*, \varepsilon, (f_a)_{a \in \Sigma}, \prec \rangle$ does have the finite cover property: structures that do not have it cannot define an infinite linear order; on the other hand, it is easy to define the lexicographic ordering in the presence of $\prec$. This turns out to be one of the examples where isolation does the job.

Proposition 5.7.10. $\mathfrak{M} = \langle \Sigma^*, \varepsilon, (f_a)_{a \in \Sigma}, \prec \rangle$ *admits restricted quantifier collapse.*

Proof. Let $x \preceq y$ mean $x \prec y$ or $x = y$. Let $x \sqcap y$ be the longest common prefix of the strings x and y, and let $x - y$ be defined as follows: if $x = y \cdot z$, then $x - y = z$; if $y \not\preceq x$, then $x - y = \varepsilon$. Let $L \subseteq \Sigma^*$ be a star-free language. Define P_L to be the set of pairs of strings (x, y) such that $y \preceq x$ and $x - y \in L$. It is not hard to show that P_L is definable in $\langle \Sigma^*, \varepsilon, (f_a)_{a \in \Sigma}, \prec \rangle$ (using the fact that star-free languages are exactly those definable over strings considered as finite models).

Before we prove the collapse, we must collect a few more properties of $\mathfrak{M}$. The following is true for any finite (and hence pseudo-finite) set A in any structure $\mathfrak{M}'$ elementarily equivalent to $\mathfrak{M}$. The meet of all elements of A equals the meet of some pair of elements of A. Moreover, for any $c \in \mathfrak{M}'$, $c \sqcap A$, the longest prefix of c that is also a prefix of some element of A, equals $c \sqcap a$ for some $a \in A$. Furthermore, there exist four not necessarily distinct elements $a_1, a_2, a_3, a_4 \in A$ such that $a_1 \sqcap a_2 \preceq c \sqcap A \preceq a_3 \sqcap a_4$, and there are no a', a'' such that $a_1 \sqcap a_2 \prec a' \sqcap a'' \prec a_3 \sqcap a_4$.

We shall use the following known result on definability in $\mathfrak{M}$. Every formula $\varphi(\vec{x})$ is equivalent to a disjunction of the formulae $\alpha_i(\vec{x}) \wedge \beta_i(\vec{x})$ such that the following is true. Each $\alpha_i(\vec{x})$ is a quantifier-free formula that specifies, for each x_i, x_j, x_k, x_l, whether $x_i \sqcap x_j = \varepsilon$ and whether $x_i \sqcap x_j \prec x_k \sqcap x_l$. Each $\beta_i(\vec{x})$ is a conjunction of the formulae $P_L(x_i \sqcap x_j, x_k \sqcap x_l)$ where $\alpha_i(\vec{x})$ implies that there are no elements of the form $x_p \sqcap x_q$ such that $x_i \sqcap x_j \prec x_p \sqcap x_q \prec x_k \sqcap x_l$.

We now show that $\mathfrak{M}$ has the isolation property, and thus admits restricted quantifier collapse. Let $\mathfrak{M}'$ be elementarily equivalent to $\mathfrak{M}$, let A be a pseudo-finite set, and let $c \in \mathfrak{M}'$. Find (at most) four elements $a_1, a_2, a_3, a_4 \in A$ such that $a_1 \sqcap a_2 \preceq c \sqcap A \preceq a_3 \sqcap a_4$, and there are no a', a'' such that $a_1 \sqcap a_2 \prec a' \sqcap a'' \prec a_3 \sqcap a_4$. Then the above result characterizing definability in $\mathfrak{M}$ easily implies that $\mathrm{tp}_{\mathfrak{M}'}(c/\{a_1, a_2, a_3, a_4\})$ isolates $\mathrm{tp}_{\mathfrak{M}}(c/A)$.   □

The notion of isolation could just as well be called ω-isolation: a type over a set is isolated by a type of a subset of cardinality $< \omega$. We could then introduce a notion of λ-isolation for any cardinal λ. The cardinal λ of interest to us here is ω_1; the notion of ω_1-isolation says that $\mathrm{tp}_{\mathfrak{M}}(a/A)$, for A pseudo-finite, is isolated by $\mathrm{tp}_{\mathfrak{M}}(a/A')$, where $A' \subseteq A$ is finite or countable. Just as ω-isolation implies ω-PFH and restricted quantifier collapse, ω_1-isolation implies ω_1-PFH, and thus the same collapse. We shall now use ω_1-isolation to give an alternative proof of restricted quantifier collapse for $\mathbf{3} = \langle \mathbb{Z}, +, < \rangle$. We already know this result: Proposition 5.6.10 showed natural-active collapse for $\mathbf{3}_0$, which is an expansion of $\mathbf{3}$ that has quantifier elimination. But we provide the proof below to illustrate the power of model-theoretic techniques.

Proposition 5.7.11. $\mathbf{3}$ *admits restricted quantifier collapse.*

Proof. Let $\mathfrak{M}$ be a model of $\mathrm{Th}(\mathbf{3})$, and A a pseudo-finite set in $\mathfrak{M}$. Since A is pseudo-finite, for any a, either there exist $a_1 < a_2 \in A$ such that $a_1 \leq a \leq a_2$ and $(a_1, a_2) \cap A = \emptyset$, or $a > m$, where m is the maximal element of A, or

$a < m'$, where m' is the minimal element of A. We assume, without loss of generality, that we are dealing with the first case.

Let $f(\vec{y})$ be a linear function with integer coefficients. For any finite set A and an element a, we have a uniquely defined tuple $\vec{b}_-^{A,f}$ of elements of A such that $f(\vec{b}_-^{A,f}) \leq a$, and for any other tuple $\vec{c}$ of elements of A, either $f(\vec{c}) > a$, or $f(\vec{c}) < f(\vec{b}_-^{A,f})$, or $f(\vec{c}) = f(\vec{b}_-^{A,f})$ and $\vec{c}$ is above $\vec{b}_-^{A,f}$ in the lexicographic ordering. In other words, $\vec{b}_-^{A,f}$ is the lexicographically smallest tuple of elements of A on which f reaches its maximum value which does not exceed a. Since the above can be stated in FO, such a tuple $\vec{b}_-^{A,f}$ is uniquely determined for a pseudo-finite set A.

Similarly, we define $\vec{b}_+^{A,f}$ to be the lexicographically smallest tuple of elements of A on which f reaches its minimum value which lies above a. Again, this is well defined for a pseudo-finite set A.

We now let A' be the set that has a_1, a_2 and all the components of all $\vec{b}_-^{A,f}$ and $\vec{b}_+^{A,f}$ as f ranges over all linear functions with integer coefficients. Since such tuples are unique for each f, the set A' is countable. We claim that $\mathrm{tp}_3(a/A')$ isolates $\mathrm{tp}_3(a/A)$.

For this purpose, it is convenient to use 3_0, the expansion of 3 with $\sim_k, k > 1$, which admits quantifier elimination. Suppose $\mathrm{tp}_3(a/A') = \mathrm{tp}_3(a'/A')$; it then suffices to show that the 3_0-atomic types of a and a' over A are the same. As $\mathrm{tp}_3(a/A')$ specifies all $a - a_1 \sim_k n_k$ and $a_2 - a \sim_k n'_k$ relations for all $k > 1$, and all constants $a_1, a_2 \in A'$, a and a' agree on all the formulae $f(x, \vec{y}) - g(x, \vec{y}) \sim_k n_k$, where f, g are linear functions, $\vec{y}$ takes values in A, and $0 \leq n_k < k$. By quantifier elimination for 3_0, we may assume that other atomic formulae are of the form $x\vartheta f(\vec{y})$, where f is a linear function with integer coefficients, and ϑ is one of $<, >, =$. Suppose that $a > f(\vec{b})$ holds for some $\vec{b}$ over A. Then either $f(\vec{b}) < f(\vec{b}_-^{A,f})$, or $f(\vec{b}) = f(\vec{b}_-^{A,f})$ and $\vec{b}_-^{A,f}$ is lexicographically smaller than $\vec{b}$. Since all the components of $\vec{b}_-^{A,f}$ are in A' and the types of a and a' over A' are the same, we conclude that $a' > f(\vec{b}_-^{A,f})$ and thus $a' > f(\vec{b})$. The cases in which ϑ is $>$ or $=$ are similar. Hence, $\mathrm{tp}_{3_0}(a/A) = \mathrm{tp}_{3_0}(a'/A)$, which proves ω_1-isolation. $\square$

In conclusion, we remark that the techniques of the two previous subsections – using the finite cover property or isolation to prove the collapse – are completely disjoint. While every structure that does not have the finite cover property is stable, every structure with the isolation property is unstable; in particular, one can define an infinite linear order on such a structure.

5.8 The VC Dimension and Collapse Results

In this section we consider the relationship between the Vapnik-Chervonenkis dimension, a concept from statistics and learning theory, and collapse results. We have seen one powerful result (Theorem 5.6.13): any structure whose definable families have finite VC dimension admits natural-generic collapse. It turns out that the VC dimension is even more closely related to collapse results: namely,

natural- active collapse	$\Rightarrow$	restricted quantifier collapse	$\Rightarrow$	finite VC dimension	$\Rightarrow$	natural- generic collapse

as the result below demonstrates.

Theorem 5.8.1. *Let $\mathfrak{M}$ admit restricted quantifier collapse. Then $\mathfrak{M}$-definable families have finite VC dimension.*

Proof. In this proof, we shall use a complexity class $AC^0/poly$ defined as follows. (We use a slightly nonstandard definition, in terms of FO-formulae rather than circuits, as it is more convenient for our purposes.) Consider a class of finite SC-structures $\mathcal{C}$, and assume that $adom(D)$ of size n is always of the form $\{0,\ldots,n-1\}$. Such a class belongs to $AC^0/poly$ if there exists a vocabulary SC' disjoint from SC, a function h from $\mathbb{N}$ to SC'-structures, and a sentence $\Phi_{\mathcal{C}}$ of $FO(SC \cup SC')$ such that (a) $adom(h(n)) \subseteq \{0,\ldots,n-1\}$, and (b) for each SC-structure of size n, we have $D \in \mathcal{C}$ iff $(D, h(n)) \models \Phi_{\mathcal{C}}$. In other words, we use $\Phi_{\mathcal{C}}$ to decide whether $D \in \mathcal{C}$, and $\Phi_{\mathcal{C}}$ uses D as well as some polynomial-size "advice" $h(n)$. Some strong lower bounds have been proved for $AC^0/poly$; they imply, for example, that parity, and importantly for us, 3-colorability, are not in $AC^0/poly$.

Now assume that $\mathfrak{M}$ admits restricted quantifier collapse and has infinite VC dimension. We obtain a contradiction by showing that 3-colorability is in $AC^0/poly$.

To proceed, we need the following known (and nontrivial) result: if $\mathfrak{M}$ has infinite VC dimension, then there is a formula $\varphi(\vec{x}, y)$ (where y is a single variable) that defines a family of infinite VC dimension. Take this formula φ; then, for each n, there is a set $Y_n \subset \mathfrak{M}$ of size n that is shattered by $\{\varphi(\vec{a}, \mathfrak{M}) \mid \vec{a}\}$.

Now expand the language of $\mathfrak{M}$ with a binary relation E (to be interpreted as a finite graph), and consider the sentence Ψ:

$$\exists \vec{x}_1 \exists \vec{x}_2 \exists \vec{x}_3 \left[\forall y \in adom \begin{pmatrix} (\varphi(\vec{x}_1, y) \wedge \neg\varphi(\vec{x}_2, y) \wedge \neg\varphi(\vec{x}_3, y)) \\ \vee\, (\neg\varphi(\vec{x}_1, y) \wedge \varphi(\vec{x}_2, y) \wedge \neg\varphi(\vec{x}_3, y)) \\ \vee\, (\neg\varphi(\vec{x}_1, y) \wedge \varphi(\vec{x}_2, y) \wedge \varphi(\vec{x}_3, y)) \end{pmatrix} \wedge \right.$$

$$\left. \forall y_1 \in adom \forall y_2 \in adom\ E(y_1, y_2) \to \neg \begin{pmatrix} (\varphi(\vec{x}_1, y_1) \wedge \varphi(\vec{x}_1, y_2)) \\ \vee\, (\varphi(\vec{x}_2, y_1) \wedge \varphi(\vec{x}_2, y_2)) \\ \vee\, (\varphi(\vec{x}_3, y_1) \wedge \varphi(\vec{x}_3, y_2)) \end{pmatrix} \right].$$

The fact that φ defines a family that shatters each Y_n lets us model second-order quantifiers over Y_n; in particular, for any graph G with $adom(G) \subseteq Y_n$, $G \models \Psi$ iff G is 3-colorable.

Since $\mathfrak{M}$ admits restricted quantifier collapse, we may assume that Ψ is equivalent to a sentence Ψ' of the form

$$\mathbf{Q}z_1 \in adom \dots \mathbf{Q}z_m \in adom\ \alpha(\vec{z}),$$

where α is a Boolean combination of formulae $E(z_i, z_j)$ and formulae $\beta_l(\vec{z})$, $l \leq k$, over $\mathfrak{M}$.

For each β_l which has p free variables, introduce a new p-ary relation symbol R_l. Let $SC' = \{R_l \mid l \leq k\}$. Next, for each n, fix a bijection $\pi_n : \{0, \dots, n-1\} \rightarrow Y_n$. Let $h(n)$ be an SC'-structure on $\{0, \dots, n-1\}$ in which a tuple $(a_1, \dots, a_p)$ belongs to R_l iff $\beta_l(\pi_n(a_1), \dots, \pi_n(a_p))$ holds in $\mathfrak{M}$. Finally, let Ψ'' be Ψ' in which every subformula $\beta_l(\vec{u})$ is replaced by $R_l(\vec{u})$. We then conclude that, for any graph G on nodes $\{0, \dots, n-1\}$, $(G, h(n)) \models \Psi''$ iff G is 3-colorable, which contradicts the fact that 3-colorability is not in $AC^0/poly$. This proves the theorem. $\square$

A natural question, then, is the following: what kind of bounds on $FO(SC, \mathfrak{M})$ can one show for structures $\mathfrak{M}$ of *infinite* VC dimension? Clearly we cannot hope to prove natural-active or restricted quantifier collapse; but is it possible to prove some meaningful bounds, and if so, how?

While our understanding of the limits of collapse results is by no means complete, in the list below we shall give three examples of very different behaviors of FO over finite models embedded into structures with infinite VC dimension.

- In some cases, there is no collapse at all. We have seen that any computable query over finite SC-structures can be expressed in $FO(SC, \mathfrak{N})$, and $\mathfrak{N}$ has infinite VC dimension. (To see this directly, assume as we did before that a set $X = \{x_1, \dots, x_k\}$ with $x_1 < \dots < x_k$ is coded by $2^{x_1} \cdot 3^{x_2} \cdot \dots \cdot p_k^{x_k}$ where p_k is the kth prime. Let $\varphi(x, y)$ say that y is in the set coded by x. Then the family $\{\varphi(n, \mathfrak{N}) \mid n \in \mathbb{N}\}$ has infinite VC dimension.)

- In another example, we get a collapse to a logic which is more powerful than FO. Namely, we shall show in Section 5.8.1 that, over the random graph $\mathcal{RG}$, $FO(SC, \mathcal{RG})$ collapses to active MSO, that is, $MSO_{act}(SC, \mathcal{RG})$. Recall that MSO (monadic second-order logic) extends FO with quantification over sets. In the active version MSO_{act}, this set quantification is over subsets of $adom(D)$.

- In the last example, we do not know whether natural-generic collapse can be proved. Nevertheless, we succeed in showing that generic queries can be evaluated in AC^0. As AC^0 is one of very few complexity classes for which lower bounds have been proved, this suffices to conclude that queries such as parity are not expressible. The structure for which this result is proved (in Section 5.8.2), extends $\langle \Sigma^*, f_a, \prec \rangle$ from the previous section by adding string length comparisons.

5.8.1 Random Graph and Collapse to MSO

In this section, we give an example of a nicely behaved structure, with a decidable theory and quantifier elimination, that does not admit natural-active collapse. This structure, however, admits a collapse to monadic second-order logic.

This structure is the random graph $\mathcal{RG} = \langle U, E \rangle$ on a countably infinite set U: that is, any model that satisfies every sentence that is true in almost all finite undirected graphs. Here "almost all" is with respect to the uniform probability distribution: $E(a, b)$ holds with probability $1/2$, independently for each pair (a, b). It is known that the set of all such sentences forms a complete theory with infinite models, and that this theory is decidable and ω-categorical. The latter means that up to isomorphism, there is only one countable model.

Other, nonprobabilistic descriptions of $\mathcal{RG}$ exist. For example, let $U = \{u_0, u_1, \ldots\}$, and define E as follows: $(u_i, u_j) \in E$ iff either the ith bit of the binary representation of j or the jth bit of the binary representation of i is 1.

The random graph satisfies the following *extension axioms*, for each $n > 0$:

$$\forall x_1, \ldots, x_n \bigwedge_{i \neq j} x_i \neq x_j \rightarrow \left(\bigwedge_{M \subseteq \{1, \ldots, n\}} \exists z \notin \vec{x} \left(\bigwedge_{i \in M} E(z, x_i) \wedge \bigwedge_{j \notin M} \neg E(z, x_j) \right) \right)$$

In other words, let T be a finite subset of U and $S \subseteq T$. Then the extension axioms say that there exists a $z \notin T$ such that for all $x \in S$, $(z, x) \in E$, and for all $x \in T - S$, $(z, x) \notin E$. It is immediately clear from the extension axioms that $\mathcal{RG}$ has infinite VC dimension; in fact, the family definable by the formula $E(x, y)$ shatters arbitrarily large finite sets.

Recall that MSO is a restriction of second-order logic in which second-order variables range over sets. In the active-domain fragment of MSO, they range over subsets of $adom(D)$.

Theorem 5.8.2. $\mathrm{FO}(SC, \mathcal{RG}) = \mathrm{MSO}_{\mathrm{act}}(SC, \mathcal{RG})$.

Proof. The idea is to use the extension axioms to model MSO queries. Consider an $\mathrm{MSO}_{\mathrm{act}}$ formula

$$\varphi(\vec{x}) \equiv \mathbf{Q}X_1 \subseteq adom \ldots \mathbf{Q}X_m \subseteq adom \; \mathbf{Q}y_1 \in adom \ldots \mathbf{Q}y_n \in adom \; \alpha(\vec{X}, \vec{x}, \vec{y}),$$

where the X_is are second-order variables, the y_js are first-order variables, and α is a Boolean combination of SC- and $\mathcal{RG}$-formulae in variables $\vec{x}, \vec{y}$, and formulae $X_i(x_j)$ and $X_i(y_j)$. Construct a new $\mathrm{FO}(SC, \mathcal{RG})$ formula $\varphi'(\vec{x})$ by replacing each $\mathbf{Q}X_i \subseteq adom$ with $\mathbf{Q}z_i \notin adom \cup \vec{x}$ (which is FO-definable), and changing every atomic subformula $X_i(u)$ to $E(z_i, u)$. It is then easy to see, from the extension axioms, that φ' is equivalent to φ.

For the other direction, we proceed by induction on the formulae. The only nontrivial case is that of unrestricted existential quantification. Suppose we have an $\mathrm{MSO}_{\mathrm{act}}(SC, \mathcal{RG})$ formula $\varphi(\vec{x}, z)$, with $\vec{x} = (x_1, \ldots, x_n)$, of the form

$$\mathbf{Q}\vec{X} \subseteq adom \ \mathbf{Q}\vec{y} \in adom \ \alpha(\vec{X}, \vec{x}, \vec{y}, z),$$

where α again is a Boolean combination of atomic SC- and $\mathcal{RG}$-formulae, as well as formulae $X_i(u)$, where u is one of the first-order variables $z, \vec{x}, \vec{y}$. We want to find an $\mathrm{MSO}_{\mathrm{act}}$ formula equivalent to $\exists z \ \varphi$.

Such a formula is a disjunction of $\exists z \in adom \ \varphi \lor \bigvee_i \varphi(\vec{x}, x_i) \lor \exists z \notin adom \ \varphi$. The former is an $\mathrm{MSO}_{\mathrm{act}}(SC, \mathcal{RG})$ formula. To eliminate z from the latter, all we have to know about z is its connections to $\vec{x}$ and to the active domain in the random graph; the former is taken care of by a disjunction listing all subsets of $\{1, \ldots, n\}$, and the latter by a second-order quantifier over the active domain. For $I \subseteq \{1, \ldots, n\}$, let $\chi_I(\vec{x})$ be a quantifier-free formula saying that no x_i, x_j, with $i \in I, j \notin I$, could be equal. Introduce a new second-order variable Z and define an $\mathrm{MSO}_{\mathrm{act}}$ formula $\psi(\vec{x})$ as

$$\exists Z \subseteq adom \bigvee_{I \subseteq \{1, \ldots, n\}} \left(\chi_I(\vec{x}) \land \mathbf{Q}\vec{X} \subseteq adom \ \mathbf{Q}\vec{y} \in adom \ \alpha_I^Z(\vec{X}, Z, \vec{x}, \vec{y}) \right),$$

where $\alpha_I^Z(\vec{X}, Z, \vec{x}, \vec{y})$ is obtained from α by:

1. replacing each $E(z, x_i)$ by *true* for $i \in I$ and *false* for $i \notin I$,
2. replacing each $E(z, y_j)$ by $Z(y_j)$, and
3. replacing each $X_i(z)$ by *false*.

The extension axioms then ensure that ψ is equivalent to $\exists z \notin adom \ \varphi$. $\square$

Thus, $\mathcal{RG}$ provides an example of a structure with quantifier elimination and a decidable first-order theory that does not admit natural-active collapse. At the same time, one can establish meaningful bounds on the expressiveness of queries over $\mathcal{RG}$: for example, each generic query in $\mathrm{FO}(SC, \mathcal{RG})$ is in $\mathrm{MSO}_{\mathrm{act}}(SC)$. (This does not immediately follow from the active-generic collapse, as we do not include any order relation. One can show that the order is not needed, by modifying the proof of Lemma 5.5.4 using some special properties of $\mathcal{RG}$.) Thus, every generic query in $\mathrm{FO}(SC, \mathcal{RG})$ can be evaluated in PSPACE (in fact, even in the polynomial hierarchy).

5.8.2 Complexity Bounds for Generic Queries

We now revisit the structure $\langle \Sigma^*, (f_a)_{a \in \Sigma}, \prec \rangle$ considered in Sect. 5.7.3. Recall that Σ here is a finite alphabet, Σ^* is the set of all finite strings over Σ, f_a is a function that adds a at the end of its argument, and $\prec$ is the prefix relation. We now extend it to a structure $\mathcal{S} = \langle \Sigma^*, (f_a)_{a \in \Sigma}, \prec, \mathrm{el} \rangle$, which adds a binary predicate el, interpreted as follows: $\mathrm{el}(x, y)$ iff $|x| = |y|$, where $|\ |$ stands for the length of a finite string.

Despite looking rather arbitrary, this structure arises naturally in the study of logical properties of formal languages, and has a number of nice properties. For example, the subsets of Σ^* definable in $\mathcal{S}$ are precisely the regular languages. Moreover, in a certain sense, $\mathcal{S}$ is the most general structure whose definable relations are precisely tuples of strings accepted by finite automata. That is, any other structure on Σ^* whose definable relations are tuples accepted by finite automata can be interpreted in $\mathcal{S}$. The characterization of definable relations via automata also implies the decidability of the theory of $\mathcal{S}$.

Using the isolation property, we have proved restricted quantifier collapse for $\langle \Sigma^*, (f_a)_{a \in \Sigma}, \prec \rangle$. However, it is impossible to prove the collapse for $\mathcal{S}$ as its definable families may have infinite VC dimension. To see this, let $\Sigma = \{a, b\}$, and consider a formula $\varphi(x, y)$ saying that there is a prefix of x that has the same length as y and ends with an a:

$$\exists z \exists v \left(z \preceq x \ \wedge \ \mathrm{el}(z, y) \ \wedge \ f_a(v) = z \right)$$

For each n, let $A_n = \{b^i \mid i \leq n\}$, and let A be an arbitrary subset of A_n. Let s_A be a string of length n whose ith position is a iff $b^i \in A$. Then, for each $i \leq n$, $\varphi(s_A, b^i)$ holds iff $b^i \in A$. This shows that arbitrarily large finite sets can be shattered by families definable in $\mathcal{S}$.

This still leaves open the possibility of proving natural-generic collapse for $\mathcal{S}$; however, we do not know if it holds in $\mathcal{S}$. Nevertheless, we can prove reasonably good bounds for $\mathrm{FO}(SC, \mathcal{S})$. For this, we need the complexity class $\mathrm{AC}^0/\mathrm{poly}$ used in Theorem 5.8.1. As this class is a very modest extension of $\mathrm{FO}_{\mathrm{act}}(SC, <)$, some good bounds can be derived.

Proposition 5.8.3. *Every generic query in* $\mathrm{FO}(SC, \mathcal{S})$ *can be evaluated in* $\mathrm{AC}^0/\mathrm{poly}$. *In particular, queries such as parity and connectivity are not expressible in* $\mathrm{FO}(SC, \mathcal{S})$.

Proof sketch. First, we explain the complexity model used here, which is applicable to the evaluation of *generic queries*. Given an SC-structure D with $|adom(D)| = n$, we code elements of the active domain by the numbers $0, \ldots, n - 1$ represented in binary, and then code tuples and relations in a standard fashion, using special delimiter characters. Using this coding, we show that every generic sentence Φ can be evaluated in $\mathrm{AC}^0/\mathrm{poly}$. This is done in three steps:

1. First, we show that it suffices to restrict quantification to strings of length at most m_D, where $m_D = \max\{|x| \mid x \in adom(D)\}$. This is proved by an Ehrenfeucht–Fraïssé game argument. More precisely, one shows the following. Let $\Sigma^{\leq m} = \{x \in \Sigma^* \mid |x| \leq m\}$. Then, for each SC, there is a fixed constant l_{SC} such that if the duplicator can win in $k + l_{SC}$ rounds on the restrictions of $(\mathcal{S}, D_1)$ and $(\mathcal{S}, D_2)$ to $(\Sigma^{\leq m_{D_1}}, D_1)$ and $(\Sigma^{\leq m_{D_1}}, D_2)$, then the duplicator can win in k rounds on $(\mathcal{S}, D_1)$ and $(\mathcal{S}, D_2)$.

2. Second, we define an ordering $<$ on Σ^*: $x < y$ if either $|x| < |y|$, or $|x| = |y|$ and x is lexicographically less than y. Viewing Σ^* as an infinite tree, this amounts to traversing it, level by level, from left to right. Now, by genericity, we may assume that $adom(D)$ is an initial segment of this ordering $<$.

3. Finally, we define an advice function f that, for each n, codes all the relations of $\mathcal{S}$ on the first n' elements of Σ^* in the order $<$. Here n' is the number of all strings of length at most m, where m is the length of the nth string in the $<$-order. For a given SC-structure D with $|adom(D)| = n$, f codes all the relations of $\mathcal{S}$ on $\Sigma^{\leq m_D}$. Assuming that $adom(D)$ is an initial segment of $<$, we conclude that the size of $f(n)$ is polynomial in n. By step 1, we know that quantification over $\Sigma^{\leq m_D}$ suffices. As $f(n)$ provides all the information about $\mathcal{S}$ on $\Sigma^{\leq m_D}$, we conclude that with f, a generic query can be expressed in FO, and thus it belongs to $AC^0/poly$.   □

5.9 Expressiveness of Constraint Query Languages

In this section, we return to constraint databases and study the expressive power of standard query languages such as FO + LIN and FO + POLY. We shall deal mostly with the fundamental topological property of connectivity, which is also important in many applications of constraint databases as spatial databases. That is, we deal with the following problem:

Problem: CONNECTIVITY
Input: an $\mathfrak{M}$-definable set $S \subseteq \mathbb{R}^k$.
Output: true if S is topologically connected, and false otherwise.

The question is whether CONNECTIVITY is definable in $FO(SC, \mathfrak{M})$, where SC consists of just S. We shall deal mostly with the cases where $\mathfrak{M}$ is the real field or the real ordered group (and thus S is semialgebraic or semilinear); then, by definability, we mean definability in FO + POLY and FO + LIN. We remarked in Section 5.3 that the problem looks akin to the problem of finite graph connectivity, simply because any finite graph can be embedded into $\mathbb{R}^3$ without self-intersections, and the result of the embedding is topologically connected iff the original graph is connected. At that point, we did not know whether FO + POLY and FO + LIN define graph connectivity. Now we know that they do not. However, we shall choose a different and less ad hoc way to proceed, as the results we present here give us more than nondefinability of connectivity, and can be used for dimensions 1 and 2 as well.

In the next section, we shall see a reduction from topological connectivity to a definability problem for embedded finite models. In Sect. 5.9.2 we present a different technique, based on the topological structure of definable sets. In Sect. 5.9.3, we study queries that separate FO + POLY from FO + LIN.

5.9.1 Reductions to the Finite Case

Recall that MAJORITY is the following problem: "given two finite sets A and B, is $card(A) > card(B)$?" We now prove the following.

Proposition 5.9.1. *Assume that* FO + POLY *can define* CONNECTIVITY *when the input is restricted to semilinear sets. Then* FO + POLY *can define* MAJORITY.

Proof. Suppose we are given two finite sets A and B. Assume, without loss of generality, that $a, b > 0$ for all $a \in A$ and $b \in B$ (if not, add $\max_{a \in A} |a| + 1$ to all elements of A, and likewise for B; this can be defined in FO + LIN). Let $A = \{a_1, \ldots, a_n\}$ and $B = \{b_1, \ldots, b_m\}$, where $a_1 < \ldots < a_n$ and $b_1 < \ldots < b_m$. This is shown in Fig. 5.6 for $n = 6$ and $m = 4$.

Let $C = B \cup \{0\}$. Assume that $C = \{c_1, \ldots, c_{m+1}\}$, where $c_1 = 0$, and $c_i = b_{i-1}$ for $1 < i \le m + 1$. For each $1 \le i < n$ and $1 \le j < m + 1$, define a semilinear set X_{ij} in $\mathbb{R}^2$ as the union of the following five sets:

$$X_{ij}^1 = \{(x, y) \mid y = a_i, c_j \le x \le (2c_j + c_{j+1})/3\}$$
$$X_{ij}^2 = \{(x, y) \mid x = (2c_j + c_{j+1})/3, a_i \le y \le (a_i + a_{i+1})/2\}$$
$$X_{ij}^3 = \{(x, y) \mid y = (a_i + a_{i+1})/2, (2c_j + c_{j+1})/3 \le x \le (c_j + 2c_{j+1})/3\}$$
$$X_{ij}^4 = \{(x, y) \mid x = (c_j + 2c_{j+1})/3, (a_i + a_{i+1})/2 \le y \le a_{i+1}\}$$
$$X_{ij}^5 = \{(x, y) \mid y = a_{i+1}, (c_j + 2c_{j+1})/3 \le x \le c_{j+1}\}.$$

This is shown in the right picture in Fig. 5.6: the five sets correspond to the five segments of the thick line. We then define a set X as

$$\{(x, 0) \mid a_1 \le x \le a_n\} \cup \{(x, a_n) \mid a_1 \le x \le a_n\} \cup \bigcup_{i=1}^{n-1} \bigcup_{j=1}^{m} X_{ij}.$$

This set is shown in the left picture in Fig. 5.6 (in fact, we show the lines as straight, but it should be kept in mind that in every rectangle $[c_j, c_{j+1}] \times [a_i, a_{i+1}]$ they are given by X_{ij}).

We next observe that X is definable in FO + LIN from A and B. Indeed, C is definable, and then every X_{ij} is definable, as follows from its definition. (The main reason for going from (c_j, a_i) to (c_{j+1}, a_{i+1}) by "steps" rather than a straight line was to achieve definability in FO + LIN.) Secondly, $card(B) \ge card(A)$ iff the set X is connected – this is because the "line" from $(0, 0)$ reaches the ceiling iff $card(B) \ge card(A)$. Thus, X is connected iff MAJORITY is false on A and B, which completes the proof. $\square$

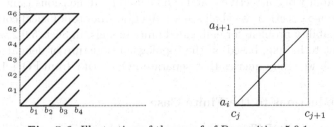

Fig. 5.6. Illustration of the proof of Proposition 5.9.1

We immediately derive the following corollary from this result and the fact that FO + LIN suffices to construct X from A and B:

Corollary 5.9.2. *Neither* FO + LIN *nor* FO + POLY *can define* CONNECTIVITY. *Furthermore,* CONNECTIVITY *is not definable in* FO$(\{S\}, \mathfrak{M})$ *if* $\mathfrak{M}$ *is an o-minimal expansion of the real field* **R**.

The reduction technique is not limited to the CONNECTIVITY problem. We invite the reader to draw simple pictures that give similar reductions for problems such as homeomorphism of two 2-dimensional sets, the existence of exactly one (or at most one, or at least one) hole, or being simply connected.

5.9.2 Topological Properties

In this section, we give a different proof that topological connectivity is not definable in FO + POLY. The proof relies on topological properties of semialgebraic sets, and on a criterion for indistinguishability of two sets in $\mathbb{R}^2$ by certain FO + POLY queries.

Note that connectivity is a query about topological properties of its input. Formally, a Boolean query Q on sets in $\mathbb{R}^k$ is called *topological* if it is invariant under homeomorphisms: for any homeomorphism $h : \mathbb{R}^k \to \mathbb{R}^k$ and any $S \subseteq \mathbb{R}^k$, $Q(S)$ is true iff $Q(h(S))$ is true. Some examples of topological queries are connectivity, having exactly one hole, and having exactly k connected components. Some examples of nontopological queries are properties such as "being a line", "containing the origin" etc.

It turns out that the expressive power of FO + POLY with respect to topological queries on $\mathbb{R}^2$ can be nicely characterized. The characterization is based on the fact that every semialgebraic set S is locally *conic* around any point. This is illustrated in Fig. 5.7: there is a small neighborhood of a point $\vec{x}$ such that the intersection of this neighborhood with the set S is isotopic to the cone with center at $\vec{x}$ and the base that is the intersection of S with the boundary of the neighborhood.

More precisely, let $B_\varepsilon(\vec{x})$ be $\{\vec{y} \in \mathbb{R}^2 \mid \parallel \vec{y} - \vec{x} \parallel \leq \varepsilon\}$ and let $B_\varepsilon^\circ(\vec{x}) = \{\vec{y} \in \mathbb{R}^2 \mid \parallel \vec{y} - \vec{x} \parallel = \varepsilon\}$. Then, for each semialgebraic set S and $\vec{x} \in \mathbb{R}^2$, there is $\varepsilon > 0$ such that $S \cap B_\varepsilon(\vec{x})$ is isotopic to the cone with the center at $\vec{x}$ and the base $B_\varepsilon^\circ(\vec{x}) \cap S$. Furthermore, for any $\varepsilon' < \varepsilon$, $B_{\varepsilon'}(\vec{x}) \cap S$ is isotopic to the same cone, so we can talk about the topological type of a cone of S around $\vec{x}$. We shall use $\mathrm{tp}_S(\vec{x})$ to denote the topological type of such a cone.

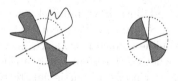

Fig. 5.7. Cones

Fig. 5.8. Four cone types

There are four cone types that are of special interest: the full cone, the half-cone, the line, and the empty cone, shown in Figure 5.8. The first is the cone type of a point in the interior of a set S. The second is the cone type of a point on the boundary of a two-dimensional region. The third is the type of a point in a one-dimensional segment of S. And the last one is the type of a point outside S, or of an isolated point of S. It turns out that for any closed semialgebraic set $S \subseteq \mathbb{R}^2$, these are the only cone types that can be realized by infinitely many points – all other cone types have only finitely many realizers.

We write $S \sim_{\mathsf{tp}} S'$ if, for every topological type T of a cone,

$$card(\{x \in S \mid \mathsf{tp}_S(x) = T\}) \quad = \quad card(\{x \in S' \mid \mathsf{tp}_{S'}(x) = T\}).$$

Note that this condition is somewhat reminiscent of that for Hanf-locality, which says that each local neighborhood must have equally many realizers in two structures.

Cone types characterize the expressive power of FO + POLY with respect to topological queries as follows.

Theorem 5.9.3. *Let Q be a topological FO + POLY query over a schema with one binary relation, and let $S \sim_{\mathsf{tp}} S'$, where S, S' are closed semialgebraic sets in $\mathbb{R}^2$. Then $Q(S)$ is true iff $Q(S')$ is true.*

The proof of this result is rather involved. The main idea is as follows. It is possible to define a set of elementary transformations on closed semialgebraic subsets of $\mathbb{R}^2$ such that these transformations preserve elementary equivalence with respect to topological FO + POLY sentences, and such that every two sets satisfying $S \sim_{\mathsf{tp}} S'$ can be transformed to the same subset of $\mathbb{R}^2$.

Another Proof That Connectivity Is Not in FO + POLY

Suppose that connectivity is tested by a (topological) FO + POLY query Q. Consider S_1 and S_2, shown in Fig. 5.9: S_1 is a disk, and S_2 is a disjoint union of two disks. Both S_1 and S_2 realize the same cone types (the full, the half, and the empty cones), and both have infinitely many realizers for each of these types. Thus, $S_1 \sim_{\mathsf{tp}} S_2$, and by Theorem 5.9.3 we must have $Q(S_1)$ iff $Q(S_2)$. Thus, Q cannot define connectivity, as S_1 is connected and S_2 is not.

It is natural to ask whether Theorem 5.9.3 can be extended to schemas with two or more relation symbols; in particular, to topological queries over multiple regions on the plane. It turns out that the answer is negative.

Fig. 5.9. Proving that connectivity is not in FO + POLY

Suppose that we have two relation symbols, S and T, and assume that S is interpreted as an area shown in light gray, and T as an area shown in dark gray. Fig. 5.10 gives two instances of (S, T): in instance $\mathcal{I}_1$, on the left, T lies inside S, and in instance $\mathcal{I}_2$, on the right, S lies inside T.

We can see that $\mathcal{I}_1 \sim_{\mathsf{tp}} \mathcal{I}_2$, as both instances realize the same cone types. At the same time, $\mathcal{I}_1$ and $\mathcal{I}_2$ can be separated by a topological FO + POLY query. The latter statement is by no means trivial. An obvious way to separate $\mathcal{I}_1$ from $\mathcal{I}_2$ would be to say: "traversing any line from $-\infty$ to $+\infty$, we first enter S and then T". However, it is easy to show that this property, while expressible in FO + POLY, is not topological. Nevertheless, a rather complicated construction yields a topological FO + POLY query that separates $\mathcal{I}_1$ from $\mathcal{I}_2$.

5.9.3 Linear vs. Polynomial Constraints

All expressivity bounds proved so far, in the finite and infinite contexts, apply to both FO + LIN and FO + POLY. In this section we show a few queries that separate the two. As **R** and $\mathbf{R}_{\mathrm{lin}}$ share many model-theoretic properties, in particular most of the properties that were crucial for proving collapse results, new techniques are needed to separate them.

Most separation results are based on the simple observation that multiplication is not definable in $\mathbf{R}_{\mathrm{lin}}$ (indeed, by quantifier elimination, every $\mathbf{R}_{\mathrm{lin}}$-definable function is piecewise linear). To show that an FO + POLY query Q is not expressible in FO + LIN, we then prove that adding Q to FO + LIN would enable us to define multiplication.

We start with two examples, which can be stated for either finite or semilinear sets. For both queries, the input is a set $S \subseteq \mathbb{R}^2$. The queries are:

Fig. 5.10. Topological equivalence for multiple regions

- conv(S), which returns the convex hull of S, and
- collinear(S), which returns the set of triples $s_1, s_2, s_3 \in S$ (that is, a subset of $\mathbb{R}^6$) which are collinear.

We have already seen that conv($\cdot$) is an FO + POLY query. collinear($\cdot$) is expressible in FO + POLY as well, as FO + POLY can test whether any three given points (x_1, y_1), (x_2, y_2), (x_3, y_3), are collinear.

Proposition 5.9.4. *Neither* conv *nor* collinear *is expressible in* FO + LIN, *even if its argument is a finite set.*

Proof sketch. The main idea is illustrated in Figure 5.11. Assume that collinear is definable in FO + LIN. Suppose we are given four distinct points u, v, w, s in $\mathbb{R}^2$. Then, in FO + LIN, we can test whether the lines $l(u, v)$ and $l(w, s)$, passing through u, v and w, s respectively, are parallel. Indeed, such lines are not parallel iff there is a point p such that both collinear(u, v, p) and collinear(w, s, p) hold (Fig. 5.11 (b)).

However, testing whether two lines are parallel is sufficient to define multiplication, as shown in Fig. 5.11 (a). If the lines passing through $(0, 1)$ and $(x, 0)$, and through $(0, y)$ and $(z, 0)$ are parallel, then $z = x \cdot y$. Thus, collinear is not an FO + LIN query.

Finally, conv is not expressible, since three distinct points are collinear iff one of them is in the convex hull of two others.   □

Note that the query convex(S), testing whether an n-dimensional semilinear set $S \subseteq \mathbb{R}^n$ is convex, can be defined in FO + LIN, as S is convex iff for every two points $(x_1, \dots, x_n)$, $(y_1, \dots, y_n) \in S$, the point $(\frac{1}{2}(x_1 + y_1), \dots, \frac{1}{2}(x_n + y_n))$ is in S. Another positive expressibility result is obtained for testing whether a semilinear set $S \subseteq \mathbb{R}^2$ is a line, since S is a line if either it is a vertical line or it is the graph of a function, and for any $\vec{x}, \vec{y}, \vec{z} \in S$, $\vec{x} + (\vec{y} - \vec{z}) \in S$. All these conditions are FO + LIN-expressible.

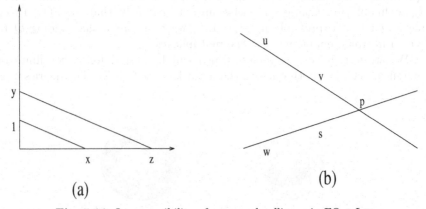

Fig. 5.11. Inexpressibility of conv and collinear in FO + LIN

We now consider one more example: the query ExistsLine(S) is true iff the set $S \subseteq \mathbb{R}^2$ contains the graph of a line, i.e. $\{(x,y) \mid ax + b = y\}$ for some $a, b \in \mathbb{R}$. Along the same lines as the proof of Proposition 5.9.4, we can show that ExistsLine is not definable in FO + LIN. Let $u, w \geq 0$ and $v > 1$, and consider the set $S_{u,v,w} \subseteq \mathbb{R}^2$ defined as follows:

$$S_{u,v,w} = \left\{ (x,y) \;\middle|\; \begin{array}{l} x \leq 0, y \leq 0 \\ \text{or } 0 \leq x \leq 1, 0 \leq y \leq v \\ \text{or } 1 \leq x \leq u, v \leq y \\ \text{or } u \leq x, w \leq y. \end{array} \right\}.$$

This set is shown in Fig. 5.12. It is easy to see that ExistsLine($S_{u,v,w}$) is true iff $w \leq u \cdot v$; thus, in FO + LIN + ExistsLine one can define, for example, the set $\{(x,y) \mid y = x^2, x > 1\}$, which is clearly not FO + LIN-definable. Hence, ExistsLine is not an FO + LIN query.

However, not all results separating FO + LIN and FO + POLY are so simple. Consider the following FO + POLY query $\psi(x_1, x_2, y_1, y_2)$:

$$\forall \lambda \left((0 \leq \lambda \leq 1) \;\to\; S(\lambda \cdot x_1 + (1 - \lambda) \cdot x_2, \; \lambda \cdot y_1 + (1 - \lambda) \cdot y_2) \right),$$

which says that the segment between (x_1, y_1) and (x_2, y_2) is contained in $S \subseteq \mathbb{R}^2$. By the same method as the one we used for ExistsLine, one can show that this is not an FO + LIN query. But now consider a slight modification of this query: suppose we want to know whether the segment connecting two points on the *boundary* of a set S lies entirely in S. It turns out that this query is inexpressible in FO + LIN; the proof of this fact, however, is far from obvious.

5.10 Query Safety

In the previous sections, we worked with two different kinds of objects: arbitrary FO($SC, \mathfrak{M}$) formulae (for which we proved results such as natural-active collapse) and *queries* definable in FO($SC, \mathfrak{M}$) (for which we proved results

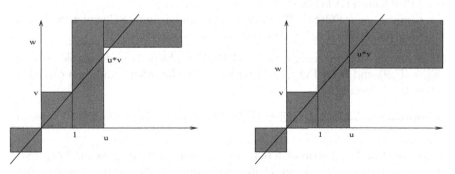

Fig. 5.12. Proving that "contains a line" is not in FO + LIN

such as the active-generic collapse). Queries, unlike arbitrary formulae, are required to have certain *closure* properties: they return finite outputs on embedded finite models.

This notion of closure is well known in classical relational database theory under the name of *safety*: one is often interested in looking at only those formulae in $\text{FO}_{\text{act}}(SC)$ that return finite results. For example, assuming an infinite domain U and one relation S, the formula $\neg S(x)$ produces the infinite set $U - adom(D)$. It is known that for $\text{FO}_{\text{act}}(SC)$, one can identify a recursive subset of safe formulae; that is, the set of formulae that always return finite results on finite SC-structures, and such that every formula with this property is equivalent to one from this set.

In this section we consider the problem of safety in the context of embedded finite models and constraint databases. For the former, we encounter a familiar situation, where the behavior of formulae depends greatly on the properties of the underlying structures. For some structures, most notably $\mathbf{R}_{\text{lin}}$ and $\mathbf{R}$ (linear and polynomial constraints), we can give a nice syntactic characterization. The safety problem also arises in the context of constraint databases. Although the flavor is quite different, we shall show that it reduces to the finite safety problem.

5.10.1 Finite and Infinite Query Safety

Recall that the output of an $\text{FO}(SC, \mathfrak{M})$ formula $\varphi(x_1, \ldots, x_n)$ on a finite SC-structure D is $\varphi(D) \overset{\text{def}}{=} \{\vec{a} \in U^n \mid D \models \varphi(\vec{a})\}$.

Definition 5.10.1. *An* $\text{FO}(SC, \mathfrak{M})$ *formula* $\varphi(\vec{x})$ *is* safe *on a finite SC-structure D if $\varphi(D)$ is finite. A formula is* safe *if it is safe on every finite structure.*

We now define the following problems:

Problem: SAFETY
Input: an $\text{FO}(SC, \mathfrak{M})$ formula $\varphi(\vec{x})$.
Output: true if φ is safe, and false otherwise.
Problem: STATE-SAFETY
Input: an $\text{FO}(SC, \mathfrak{M})$ formula $\varphi(\vec{x})$ and a finite SC-structure D.
Output: true if φ is safe on D, and false otherwise.

It is known that in general the SAFETY problem is undecidable even for $\mathfrak{M} = \langle U, \emptyset \rangle$ and φ an $\text{FO}_{\text{act}}(SC)$ formula. On the other hand, one can easily show the following.

Proposition 5.10.2. *Let* $\mathfrak{M} = \langle U, \emptyset \rangle$. *Then the STATE-SAFETY problem is decidable.*

Proof sketch. By Theorem 5.6.3, we can assume that φ is an $\text{FO}_{\text{act}}(SC)$ formula. Then it is safe on D iff every tuple in the output contains only elements of $adom(D)$ (by genericity, if at least one tuple contains some element $c \notin adom(D)$, then any other $c' \notin adom(D)$ can be substituted for c). This condition can easily be tested by considering a set $c_1, \ldots, c_m$ of distinct elements not in $adom(D)$, where m is the number of free variables in φ, and checking all tuples in $adom(D) \cup \{c_1, \ldots, c_m\}$. □

We now turn to the safety problem for constraint databases. Consider a situation where we have a linear constraint database **D**, but we want to write queries against **D** in FO + POLY. The main reasons for considering this situation are the following. Linear constraints are used to represent spatial data in many applications, and they have several advantages over polynomial constraints: the quantifier elimination procedure is less costly, and numerous algorithms have been developed to deal with figures represented by linear constraints. As FO + LIN is more limited than FO + POLY (for example, it cannot define the convex hull of a set), one may want to use FO + POLY to get extra expressive power.

However, as soon as the class of constraints used in queries is more general than the class used to define constraint database instances, we encounter the safety problem again: the output of an FO + POLY query may fail to be semilinear. More generally, if constraint databases are required to have certain geometric properties, then the safety problem is the problem of whether those geometric properties are preserved by a given query language. Sect. 5.10.4 deals with this problem.

5.10.2 Safe Translations

The main goal of this section is to show that the safety of formulae is greatly affected by the properties of the underlying structure $\mathfrak{M}$. To state these results formally, we use the following concept.

Definition 5.10.3. *We say that there is a* safe translation *of* $\mathrm{FO}_{\mathrm{act}}(SC, \mathfrak{M})$ *formulae if there is a function* $\varphi \to \varphi_{\mathrm{safe}}$ *on* $\mathrm{FO}_{\mathrm{act}}(SC, \mathfrak{M})$ *formulae such that for every* φ,

1. φ_{safe} is safe, and
2. if φ is safe for D, then $\varphi(D) = \varphi_{\mathrm{safe}}(D)$.

A translation is canonical *if* $\varphi_{\mathrm{safe}}(D) = \emptyset$ *whenever φ is not safe on D. A translation is* recursive *if the function* $\varphi \to \varphi_{\mathrm{safe}}$ *is recursive.*

It turns out that recursive safe translations need not exist even for structures with decidable theories.

Proposition 5.10.4. *There exists a structure $\mathfrak{M}$ that is recursive and has a decidable first-order theory, and for which there is no recursive safe translation of* $\mathrm{FO}_{\mathrm{act}}(SC, \mathfrak{M})$ *formulae.*

Proof sketch. Consider a structure $\mathfrak{M}$ whose domain U is the disjoint union of

- the set of Turing machines, appropriately coded as strings;
- the set of input strings to a Turing machine;
- the set of *traces*, i.e. full descriptions of a partial run of a Turing machine on an input word.

The signature of $\mathfrak{M}$ consists of one ternary relation P, which holds for a triple (M, w, t) iff t is a trace for a Turing machine M on an input word w. The key point is that there is no structure or ordering on the traces themselves: hence one cannot determine in first-order logic whether or not a trace is maximal. In fact, using a quantifier elimination argument, one can show that the first-order theory of $\mathfrak{M}$ is decidable.

Let SC contain a single unary relation S. For any Turing machine M, let $\varphi^M(t)$ be the query $\exists! w \in adom(w = w) \wedge \exists w \in adom\, P(M, w, t)$. That is, if $S = \{w\}$, then φ^M checks whether t is a trace of M on w.

Assume that there is a recursive safe translation, and consider $\varphi^M_{\text{safe}}(t)$. Assuming further that we can check the equivalence of φ^M_{safe} and φ^M, we would be able to enumerate all machines that halt on every input, which is clearly impossible.

Thus, to obtain a contradiction, we need to show how to verify the equivalence of φ^M_{safe} and φ^M. For that, we simply turn them into FO($\mathfrak{M}$) formulae $\psi^M(w, t)$ and $\psi^M_{\text{safe}}(w, t)$ by replacing each subformula of the form $S(z)$ by $w = z$. The resulting FO($\mathfrak{M}$) formulae are then true for (w, t) iff t is in the output of the corresponding query on input $\{w\}$. Thus, $\forall w \forall t\, (\psi^M(w, t) \leftrightarrow \psi^M_{\text{safe}}(w, t))$ holds iff φ^M_{safe} and φ^M are equivalent. The result now follows from the decidability of the theory of $\mathfrak{M}$. $\square$

If one drops the condition that the theory of $\mathfrak{M}$ be decidable, but insists on computable functions and predicates in Ω, the situation is even worse: there need not be any safe translations at all (recursive or not).

Proposition 5.10.5. *There is a structure* $\mathfrak{M} = \langle \mathbb{N}, P \rangle$, *where* P *is a computable predicate, such that there is no safe translation of* $\text{FO}_{\text{act}}(SC, \mathfrak{M})$ *formulae.*

Proof. Let P be a ternary predicate defined as follows: $P(i, j, k)$ iff the ith Turing machine on the input j makes at least k moves (assuming some standard encoding of machines and inputs). Consider a schema that consists of a single binary relation S. Assume, contrary to the proposition, that there is a safe translation over $\mathfrak{M}$. Let $\varphi(k) \equiv \exists i, j \in adom\, S(i, j) \wedge P(i, j, k)$, and let $\psi(k)$ be φ_{safe}. Note that ψ is an active-domain formula in the language of S and P. We now show how to use ψ to decide the halting problem.

Suppose we are given the ith machine M_i and the input j. We assume without loss of generality that M_i makes at least one move on j. Define a database D in which S consists of a single tuple (i, j). Since we know that ψ is safe, we then compute the minimum number l such that $D \not\models \psi(l)$. It is computable since (a) it exists, and (b) for each k, it is decidable whether $D \models \psi(k)$.

Assume that $D \models \varphi(l)$. Then M_i does not halt on j. Indeed, if M_i halts, then $\varphi(D)$ is finite, and hence $\varphi(D) = \psi(D)$, but we have $l \in \varphi(D) - \psi(D)$. Assume that $D \not\models \varphi(l)$. Then M_i makes $k < l$ moves on j, and thus halts. Hence, $D \models \varphi(l)$ iff M_i halts on j. Since it is decidable whether $D \models \varphi(l)$, we obtain a contradiction.   □

On the other hand, for some structures $\mathfrak{M}$, recursive safe translations can be obtained.

Proposition 5.10.6. *Let $\mathfrak{M}$ be o-minimal, be based on a dense order, admit effective quantifier elimination, and have a decidable theory (for example, $\mathfrak{M}$ can be $\mathbf{R}_{\mathrm{lin}}$ or $\mathbf{R}$). Then there exists a recursive canonical safe translation of $\mathrm{FO}_{\mathrm{act}}(SC, \mathfrak{M})$ formulae.*

Proof sketch. Given an $\mathrm{FO}_{\mathrm{act}}(SC, \mathfrak{M})$ formula φ, let $\alpha(x)$ be a formula defining the active domain of the output of φ. Let Ψ be an $\mathrm{FO}_{\mathrm{act}}(SC, \mathfrak{M})$ sentence equivalent to

$$\neg \exists x_1, x_2 \left((x_1 < x_2) \wedge (\forall x \; x_1 < x < x_2 \rightarrow \alpha(x)) \right)$$

(which exists, by natural-active collapse). Define φ_{safe} as $\varphi \wedge \Psi$. The proposition then follows from the following easy claim: $D \models \Psi$ iff $\varphi(D)$ is finite.   □

Corollary 5.10.7. *Let $\mathfrak{M}$ be as in Proposition 5.10.6. Then the STATE-SAFETY problem over $\mathfrak{M}$ is decidable.*

Thus, to obtain a nice syntactic characterization of safe queries, we must deal with structures that have good properties (just as in the case of collapse results).

5.10.3 Finite Query Safety: Characterization

To give an idea of the characterization of safety that we are about to provide, let us modify slightly an example that we used in Section 5.2: $\varphi(x) \equiv (x > 1) \wedge \exists y \; S(y) \wedge (x \cdot x = y)$. Assuming that the underlying structure is the real field $\mathbf{R}$, the output of this formula is contained in the output of $\exists y \; S(y) \wedge (x \cdot x = y)$, which is $\{-\sqrt{a}, \sqrt{a} \mid a \in S\}$. Thus, there is an upper bound on the output of φ, which is given by applying certain functions to the active domain. This is the central idea of the *range-restriction* we are about to define. But first we introduce the notion of an effective syntax for safe queries.

Definition 5.10.8. *We say that a class $\mathcal{Q}$ of queries captures the class of safe queries in $\mathrm{FO}(SC, \mathfrak{M})$ if every query in $\mathcal{Q}$ is safe and definable in $\mathrm{FO}(SC, \mathfrak{M})$, and every safe $\mathrm{FO}(SC, \mathfrak{M})$ query is equivalent to a query in $\mathcal{Q}$.*

If there exists a recursively enumerable class $\mathcal{Q}$ of queries that captures safe queries in $\mathrm{FO}(SC, \mathfrak{M})$, we say that the class of safe $\mathrm{FO}(SC, \mathfrak{M})$ queries has an effective syntax.

Proposition 5.10.4 (more precisely, the construction presented in the proof of Proposition 5.10.4) implies that there are structures $\mathfrak{M}$ with a decidable first-order theory but without an effective syntax for safe FO($SC, \mathfrak{M}$). Proposition 5.10.6, on the other hand, shows that there is an effective syntax for FO + LIN and FO + POLY queries, as one can express, in those languages, the question whether the output of a query is finite. This way of guaranteeing effective syntax is quite inelegant, and tells us nothing about the structure of safe queries. Below, we present a much better description, based on the notion of definable functions.

Definition 5.10.9. *Given $\mathfrak{M} = \langle U, \Omega \rangle$, a function $f : U^k \to U$ is $\mathfrak{M}$-definable (or just definable if $\mathfrak{M}$ is understood) if its graph $\{(a_1, \ldots, a_k, a) \in U^{k+1} \mid a = f(a_1, \ldots, a_k)\}$ is an $\mathfrak{M}$-definable set.*

From now on, we assume that $adom(D) \neq \emptyset$. The case of empty SC-structures can be dealt with easily, as in this case an FO($SC, \mathfrak{M}$) formula reduces to a fixed FO($\mathfrak{M}$) formula, whose finiteness can be tested in the o-minimal case.

Definition 5.10.10. *Given $\mathfrak{M} = \langle U, \Omega \rangle$, a query in range-restricted form is a pair $Q = (F, \varphi(x_1, \ldots, x_n))$, where $\varphi(\vec{x})$ is an FO($SC, \mathfrak{M}$) formula, and F is a finite collection of definable functions.*
The semantics is defined as follows. First, for a set X, let

$$F(X) = \{f(\vec{a}) \mid f \in F, \ \vec{a} \in X^{arity(f)}\}.$$

Then, for any finite SC-structure D, define

$$Q(D) = \varphi(D) \cap (F(adom(D)))^n.$$

That is, the finite set $F(adom(D))$ provides an upper bound on the output of Q (every constant in $Q(D)$ must be contained in $F(adom(D))$), and then φ is evaluated within this set. Since F is finite, and every function in F is definable, we obtain the following.

Lemma 5.10.11. *Every query in range-restricted form over $\mathfrak{M}$ is safe and definable in FO($SC, \mathfrak{M}$).*

We now can state the main result of this section.

Theorem 5.10.12. *Let $\mathfrak{M}$ be any o-minimal structure based on a dense linear order. Assume that there is at least one definable constant in $\mathfrak{M}$. Then there is a function Make_Safe that takes as input an FO($SC, \mathfrak{M}$) formula $\varphi(\vec{x})$, and outputs a finite set F of definable functions such that the query $Q = (F, \varphi)$ is equivalent to φ on any finite SC-structure D on which φ is safe. Furthermore, if $\mathfrak{M}$ is decidable and has effective quantifier elimination, then Make_Safe is recursive.*

The proof of this theorem will be given later in this section. But first we shall state some corollaries.

Corollary 5.10.13 (Range-Restricted = Safe). *Let* $\mathfrak{M}$ *be as in Theorem 5.10.12. Then the class of range-restricted queries captures the class of safe* FO$(\mathfrak{M}, SC)$ *queries.*

We now consider specifically the cases of polynomial and linear constraints.

Definition 5.10.14. *(a) A query in the* linear range-restricted form *is a pair* $Q = (F, \varphi)$, *where* φ *is an* FO + LIN *formula and* F *is a finite collection of linear functions (that is, functions of the form* $\langle \vec{a}, \vec{x} \rangle + b$). *The semantics is defined in the same way as for range-restricted queries above.*

(b) A query in the polynomial range-restricted form *is a pair* $Q = (P, \varphi(x_1, \ldots, x_n))$, *where* φ *is an* FO + POLY *formula and* P *is a finite collection of multivariate polynomials with a distinguished variable* z. *The semantics is defined as follows. For a set* X, *and* $p(z, \vec{y})$, *let* $p(X)$ *be the set of all roots of polynomials of the form* $p(z, \vec{a})$, *where* $\vec{a}$ *is a tuple over* X, *provided such a univariate polynomial is not identically zero. Let* $P(X) = \bigcup_{p \in P} p(X)$. *Then* $Q(D)$ *is defined as* $\varphi(D) \cap (P(adom(D)))^n$.

Corollary 5.10.15. *(a) The class of queries in the linear range-restricted form captures the class of safe* FO + LIN *queries.*

(b) The class of queries in the polynomial range-restricted form captures the class of safe FO + POLY *queries.*

Proof. (a) A function definable over $\mathbf{R}_{\text{lin}}$ is piecewise linear. Thus it suffices to apply Theorem 5.10.12, and take all the linear functions of which functions in F are composed.

(b) Similarly, we apply Theorem 5.10.12 and obtain a set F of semialgebraic functions. Each semialgebraic function $f(\vec{y})$ is known to be algebraic. That is, there exists a polynomial $p(z, \vec{y})$ such that $p(z, \vec{y}) = 0$ iff $z = f(\vec{y})$. The result follows from this. $\square$

Algebraic Formulae and the Proof of Theorem 5.10.12

We shall first give an analog of range-restriction using certain FO$(\mathfrak{M})$ formulae, and then show how to derive a set F of definable functions from such a characterization. The FO$(\mathfrak{M})$ that formulae we shall use are *algebraic* formulae. They have distinguished parameters, which we shall always denote by $\vec{y}$ and separate from the single other variable by a semicolon. Assume that $\vec{y}$ is of length m. An FO$(\mathfrak{M})$ formula $\gamma(x; \vec{y})$ is called algebraic if, for each $\vec{b}$ in U^m, there are only finitely many $a \in U$ that satisfy $\gamma(a, \vec{b})$. For example, the formula $\gamma(x; y) \equiv (x^2 = y)$ is algebraic over $\mathbf{R}$.

From the Uniform Bounds Theorem (Theorem 5.6.7), we obtain the following useful fact about algebraic formulae.

Lemma 5.10.16. *Let $\mathfrak{M}$ be o-minimal, and $\gamma(x; \vec{y})$ algebraic. Then there exists a number K such that for any $\vec{b} \in U^m$, the set $\{a \in U \mid \mathfrak{M} \models \gamma(\vec{a}; \vec{b})\}$ has fewer than K elements.*

We now need a syntactic characterization of algebraic formulae over o-minimal structures. Let $\Xi = \{\xi_1(x; \vec{y}), \dots, \xi_k(x; \vec{y})\}$ be a collection of formulae. Let

$$\text{same}_\Xi(x, x'; \vec{y}) \equiv \bigwedge_{i=1}^{k} (\xi_i(x; \vec{y}) \leftrightarrow \xi_i(x'; \vec{y})).$$

Now define

$$\beta_\Xi(x; \vec{y}) \equiv \forall x', x'' \left(x' < x < x'' \rightarrow (\exists z \; x' \leq z \leq x'' \wedge \neg\text{same}_\Xi(x, z; \vec{y})) \right).$$

Proposition 5.10.17. *Let $\mathfrak{M}$ be an o-minimal structure based on a dense order. Then a formula $\gamma(x; \vec{y})$ is algebraic iff there exists a collection of $FO(\mathfrak{M})$ formulae Ξ such that γ is equivalent to β_Ξ.*

Proof. Let Ξ be a collection of formulae, and assume that β_Ξ is not algebraic. That is, for some $\vec{b}$ over U, $\beta_\Xi(\mathfrak{M}; \vec{b}) = \{a \mid \mathfrak{M} \models \beta_\Xi(a; \vec{b})\}$ is infinite. Since $\mathfrak{M}$ is o-minimal, $\beta_\Xi(\mathfrak{M}; \vec{b})$ is a finite union of points and intervals. Since $<$ is dense, this means that there exist $a_0 < b_0 \in U$ such that $[a_0, b_0] \subseteq \beta_\Xi(\mathfrak{M}; \vec{b})$. We now consider the formulae $\xi_i'(x) = \xi_i(x; \vec{b})$ for all $\xi_i \in \Xi$. Since both $\xi_i'(\mathfrak{M}) = \xi_i(\mathfrak{M}; \vec{b})$ and $\neg\xi_i'(\mathfrak{M}) = \neg\xi_i(\mathfrak{M}; \vec{b})$ are finite unions of intervals and $<$ is dense, for every nondegenerate interval J, it is the case that either $J \cap \xi_i'(\mathfrak{M})$ or $J \cap \neg\xi_i'(\mathfrak{M})$ contains an infinite (closed) interval. Using this fact, we construct a sequence of intervals as follows: $I_0 = [a_0, b_0]$, and $I_1 \subseteq I_0$ is an interval that is contained either in $I_0 \cap \xi_1'(\mathfrak{M})$ or in $I_0 \cap \neg\xi_1'(\mathfrak{M})$. At the jth step, $I_j \subseteq I_{j-1}$ is an interval that is contained either in $I_{j-1} \cap \xi_j'(\mathfrak{M})$ or in $I_{j-1} \cap \neg\xi_j'(\mathfrak{M})$. Let $I = I_k$. Then, for any $c, d \in I$, $\mathfrak{M} \models \xi_i(c, \vec{b}) \leftrightarrow \xi_i(d; \vec{b})$.

Since $I = [a', b'] \subseteq [a_0, b_0]$ and $\mathfrak{M} \models \beta_\Xi(c; \vec{b})$ for all $c \in I$, we obtain that, for every $c \in (a', b')$, there exists a $d \in [a', b']$ such that $\mathfrak{M} \models \neg\text{same}_\Xi(c, d; \vec{b})$. That is, for some $\xi_i \in \Xi$, $\mathfrak{M} \models \neg(\xi_i(c; \vec{b}) \leftrightarrow \xi_i(d; \vec{b}))$, which is impossible by the construction of I. This proves that β_Ξ is algebraic.

For the converse, for any $\gamma(x; \vec{y})$, we let Ξ consist of just γ. That is, $\beta_\Xi(x; \vec{y})$ is

$$\forall x', x'' \left(x' < x < x'' \rightarrow (\exists z \; x' \leq z \leq x'' \wedge \neg(\gamma(x; \vec{y}) \leftrightarrow \gamma(z; \vec{y}))) \right).$$

We claim that γ and β_Ξ are equivalent, if γ is algebraic. Fix any $\vec{b}$ of the same length as $\vec{y}$, and assume that $\gamma(a; \vec{b})$ holds. If $\beta_\Xi(a; \vec{b})$ does not hold, then there exist $a' < a < a''$ such that for every $c \in [a', a'']$, $\gamma(c; \vec{b}) \leftrightarrow \gamma(a; \vec{b})$ holds; thus, $\gamma(c; \vec{b})$ holds for infinitely many c, contradicting the algebraicity of γ. Hence $\beta_\Xi(a; \vec{b})$ holds. Conversely, assume that $\beta_\Xi(a; \vec{b})$ holds. If $\gamma(a; \vec{b})$ does not hold, then there is an interval containing a on which $\gamma(\cdot; \vec{b})$ does not hold. Indeed, $\neg\gamma(\mathfrak{M}; \vec{b})$ is a finite union of intervals, whose complement is a finite set of points, so the above observation follows from the density of the ordering. We now pick $a' < a''$ such that $\gamma(\cdot; \vec{b})$ does not hold on $[a', a'']$. Since $\beta_{\Xi}(a; \vec{b})$ holds, we find $c \in [a', a'']$ such that $\neg(\gamma(a; \vec{b}) \leftrightarrow \gamma(c; \vec{b}))$ holds; that is, $\gamma(c; \vec{b})$ holds for $c \in [a', a'']$, which is impossible. Thus, we conclude that $\gamma(a; \vec{b})$ holds, proving that for any $\vec{b}$, $\forall x \ (\gamma(x; \vec{b}) \leftrightarrow \beta_{\Xi}(x; \vec{b}))$. This finishes the proof. □

Given an algebraic formula $\gamma(x; \vec{y})$ and a set $X \subseteq U$, let $\gamma(X)$ be the set of all a that make $\gamma(a; \vec{b})$ true, as $\vec{b}$ ranges over tuples of elements of X. Note that if X is finite, then so is $\gamma(X)$.

We now define a query in the *algebraic range-restricted form* as a pair $Q = (\gamma(x; \vec{y}), \varphi(x_1, \ldots, x_n))$, where φ is an FO$(SC, \mathfrak{M})$ formula, and γ is an algebraic FO$(\mathfrak{M})$ formula. The semantics is defined as $Q(D) = \varphi(D) \cap (\gamma(adom(D)))^n$. Clearly, Q is safe.

Proposition 5.10.18. *Let $\mathfrak{M}$ be any o-minimal structure based on a dense linear order. Then there is a function* Make_Safe$'$ *that takes as input an* FO$(SC, \mathfrak{M})$ *formula* $\varphi(x_1, \ldots, x_n)$, *and outputs an algebraic formula* $\gamma(x; \vec{y})$ *such that the query* $Q = (\gamma, \varphi)$ *is equivalent to* φ *on all structures* D *for which* φ *is safe. Furthermore, if* $\mathfrak{M}$ *has effective quantifier elimination, then* Make_Safe$'$ *is recursive.*

Proof. Let $\psi(z)$ be a one-variable FO$(SC, \mathfrak{M})$ formula that defines the active domain of the output of φ. That is, it is the disjunction of all formulae $\exists \vec{x}^{(i)} \varphi(z, \vec{x}^{(i)})$ where $\vec{x}^{(i)}$ is $\vec{x}$ except for the ith component, and $(z, \vec{x}^{(i)})$ is the tuple in which z is inserted in the ith position. Note that φ is safe on D iff ψ is.

Let $\mathfrak{M}'$ be a definable expansion of $\mathfrak{M}$ that has quantifier elimination, and hence admits natural-active collapse. We can thus assume that ψ is an FO$_{\text{act}}(SC, \mathfrak{M}')$ formula. Let

$$\psi(z) \equiv \mathbf{Q}w_1 \in adom \ldots \mathbf{Q}w_l \in adom \ \alpha(z, \vec{w}),$$

where $\alpha(z, \vec{w})$ is quantifier-free, and all atomic subformulae $R(\cdots)$ contain only variables, excluding z. Let $\Xi = \{\xi_i(z, \vec{w}) \mid i = 1, \ldots, k\}$ be the collection of all FO$(\mathfrak{M}')$ atomic subformulae of α. We may assume without loss of generality that the length of $\vec{w}$ is nonzero, and that Ξ is nonempty (just as we did in the proof of natural-active collapse).

We define same$_{\Xi}(a, b, \vec{w})$, as before, to be $\bigwedge_{i=1}^{k}(\xi_i(a, \vec{w}) \leftrightarrow \xi_i(b, \vec{w}))$, and define $\gamma(x; \vec{w})$ to be $\beta_{\Xi}(x; \vec{w})$. We let Make_Safe(ψ) output γ. Note that γ is actually an FO$(\mathfrak{M})$ formula, since $\mathfrak{M}'$ is a definable expansion.

Since γ is algebraic by Proposition 5.10.17, we must show that $\{a \mid D \models \psi(a)\} = \{a \in \gamma(D) \mid D \models \psi(a)\}$ for every nonempty database for which ψ is safe.

Assume otherwise; that is, for some nonempty D for which ψ is safe, we have $D \models \psi(a)$ but $a \notin \gamma(D)$. Let $\vec{c}_1, \ldots, \vec{c}_M$ be an enumeration of all tuples of of elements of $adom(D)$ of the same length as $\vec{w}$. Note that $M > 0$. Since $a \notin \gamma(D)$, we have that for each $i = 1, \ldots, M$, there exist a_i', a_i'' such that $a_i' < a < a_i''$ and $\mathfrak{M} \models \mathrm{same}_{\Xi}(a, c, \vec{c_i})$ for all $c \in [a_i', a_i'']$.

Let $b' = \max\{a_i'\}$ and $b'' = \min\{a_i''\}$. We have $b' < a < b''$, and for each $\vec{c}$ (of length the same as $\vec{w}$) over the active domain, we have $\xi_i(a; \vec{c}) \leftrightarrow \xi_i(c, \vec{c})$ for every $c \in [b', b'']$. From this, by a simple induction on the structure of the formula (using the fact that z does not appear in any atomic formula $R(\cdots)$), we obtain that $D \models \alpha(a, \vec{c}) \leftrightarrow \alpha(c, \vec{c})$ for every $\vec{c}$ over $adom(D)$ and every $c \in [b', b'']$, and thus $D \models \psi(a) \leftrightarrow \psi(c)$, which implies that ψ is not safe for D. This contradiction proves the correctness of Make_Safe', and the proposition. $\square$

To conclude the proof of Theorem 5.10.12, we have to show how to obtain definable functions from algebraic formulae.

Proposition 5.10.19. *Let $\mathfrak{M}$ be o-minimal, such that there is at least one definable constant. Let $\gamma(x; \vec{y})$ be algebraic. Then there is a finite collection F of definable functions $f(\vec{y})$ such that $\gamma(X) \subseteq F(X)$ for any set $X \subseteq U$. Moreover, if $\mathfrak{M}$ is decidable, then the set F can be found effectively.*

Proof. Let c be a definable constant over $\mathfrak{M}$. Given γ, let K be an integer such that the set $\{a \in U \mid \mathfrak{M} \models \gamma(a, \vec{b})\}$ has fewer than K elements for every $\vec{b}$ (see Lemma 5.10.16). For each $i < K$, define $f_i(\vec{y})$ to be the ith element (in the order $<$) that makes $\gamma(\cdot, \vec{y})$ true, if it exists, and c, if there is no such element. Let $F = \{f_i \mid i < K\}$. Clearly, each f_i is a definable function and $\gamma(X) \subseteq F(X)$. If $\mathfrak{M}$ is decidable, then K can be found, and thus F can be constructed effectively. $\square$

We now finally complete the proof of Theorem 5.10.12. Given an $FO(SC, \mathfrak{M})$ formula $\varphi(\vec{x})$, we first apply Proposition 5.10.18 to obtain an algebraic formula γ giving a bound on the output (if it is finite), and then apply Proposition 5.10.19 to obtain a set of functions F that puts a bound on the output of φ. If $\mathfrak{M}$ is decidable and quantifier elimination is effective, then γ can be effectively found (as the natural-active collapse is effective), and there is an algorithm for constructing F from γ. $\square$

5.10.4 Infinite Query Safety: Reduction

The question of query safety over constraint databases reduces to preserving certain *geometric properties* of regions in $\mathbb{R}^k$. If $\mathfrak{M} = \langle U, \Omega \rangle$ is an infinite structure, let $\mathsf{DS}(\mathfrak{M})$ be the class of definable sets over $\mathfrak{M}$, that is, $\mathsf{DS}(\mathfrak{M}) = \bigcup_{n < \omega} \mathsf{DS}_n(\mathfrak{M})$, and $\mathsf{DS}_n(\mathfrak{M})$ is the collection of definable subsets of U^n. We use SAlg_n for semialgebraic sets in $\mathbb{R}^n$.

Let SC consist of an m-ary relation symbol S, and let $\psi(x_1, \ldots, x_n)$ be an $FO(SC, \mathfrak{M})$ formula. It defines a map from $\mathsf{DS}_m(\mathfrak{M})$ to $\mathsf{DS}_n(\mathfrak{M})$ as follows: for any $X \in \mathsf{DS}_m(\mathfrak{M})$, $\psi(X) = \{\vec{y} \mid (\mathfrak{M}, X) \models \psi(\vec{y})\}$.

Now let $\mathcal{C}$ be a class of objects in $\mathsf{DS}(\mathfrak{M})$. We say that an $FO(SC, \mathfrak{M})$ formula ψ *preserves* $\mathcal{C}$ if for any $X \in \mathcal{C}$, $\psi(X) \in \mathcal{C}$. The safety question for constraint databases is the following. Is there an effective syntax for the class of $\mathcal{C}$-preserving queries?

We now show how this problem can be reduced to finite query safety for embedded finite models.

Definition 5.10.20. *The class $\mathcal{C}$ has a* canonical representation *in* $\mathsf{DS}(\mathfrak{M})$ *if there is a recursive injective function $g : \mathbb{N} \to \mathbb{N}$ with a computable inverse, and for each n, two functions $code_n : 2^{U^n} \to 2^{U^m}$ and $decode_n : 2^{U^m} \to 2^{U^n}$, where $m = g(n)$, such that:*

1. *$decode_n \circ code_n(x) = x$ if $x \in \mathsf{DS}_n(\mathfrak{M})$;*
2. *$|code_n(x)| < \omega$ if $x \in \mathcal{C}$; $decode_n(x) \in \mathcal{C}$ if x is finite;*
3. *$code_n$ is $\mathrm{FO}(\mathfrak{M})$-definable on $\mathsf{DS}_n(\mathfrak{M})$;*
4. *$decode_n$ is $\mathrm{FO}(\mathfrak{M})$-definable on finite sets.*

Intuitively, the canonical representation is a finite representation of $\mathcal{C}$ within $\mathsf{DS}(\mathfrak{M})$ that can be defined in first-order logic over $\mathfrak{M}$. For example, one approach to obtaining a canonical representation of convex polytopes would be to compute their vertices. This suffices to reconstruct the polytope, and the vertices can be defined by a first-order formula.

Similarly to the finite case, we say that there is an effective syntax for $\mathcal{C}$-preserving $\mathrm{FO}(SC, \mathfrak{M})$ formulae if there exists a recursively enumerable set of $\mathcal{C}$-preserving $\mathrm{FO}(SC, \mathfrak{M})$ formulae such that every $\mathcal{C}$-preserving $\mathrm{FO}(SC, \mathfrak{M})$ formula is equivalent to a formula in this set.

Theorem 5.10.21. *Let $\mathfrak{M} = \langle U, \Omega \rangle$ be o-minimal, based on a dense order, and decidable, and have effective quantifier elimination. Suppose $\mathcal{C}$ is a class that has a canonical representation in $\mathsf{DS}(\mathfrak{M})$. Then there is an effective syntax for $\mathcal{C}$-preserving $\mathrm{FO}(SC, \mathfrak{M})$ formulae.*

Proof. Consider an enumeration of all safe $\mathrm{FO}(SC, \mathfrak{M})$ queries $\langle \varphi_i \rangle$ on finite structures (from Proposition 5.10.18, we know that it exists). Let φ use an extra relation symbol of arity m, and assume that n is such that $g(n) = m$ (where g comes from the definition of canonical representations). Let φ_i have l parameters, and again let k be such that $g(k) = l$. If n and k can be found for a given φ_i, we let ψ be

$$decode_k \circ \varphi_i \circ code_n.$$

This produces the required enumeration. We have to check that every query of the form $decode_k \circ \varphi_i \circ code_n$ preserves $\mathcal{C}$, and for every $\mathcal{C}$ preserving ψ, we can get a φ such that $decode \circ \varphi \circ code$ coincides with ψ. It is clear that the first condition is satisfied: if we have $X \in \mathcal{C}$, then $code_n(X)$ is finite, hence $\varphi_i(code_n(X))$ is finite too, and thus the output of $decode_k$ is in $\mathcal{C}$.

For the converse, suppose we have a $\mathcal{C}$-preserving query $\psi : \mathsf{DS}_n(\mathfrak{M}) \to \mathsf{DS}_k(\mathfrak{M})$. Define α as follows: $\alpha = code_k \circ \psi \circ decode_n$. That is, α is a query $\mathsf{DS}_m(\mathfrak{M}) \to \mathsf{DS}_l(\mathfrak{M})$. Given this, we notice that

$$decode_k \circ \alpha \circ code_n = decode_k \circ code_k \circ \psi \circ decode_n \circ code_n = \psi$$

on $\mathsf{DS}_n(\mathfrak{M})$. Thus, it remains to show that α is safe. Let $X \subset U^m$ be finite. Then $decode_n(X) \in \mathcal{C}$, $decode_n(X) \subset U^n$, and $Y = \psi(decode_n(X)) \in \mathsf{DS}_k(\mathfrak{M})$ is in $\mathcal{C}$, too. Hence, $code_k(Y)$ is finite.   □

We now give two applications to semialgebraic sets and FO + POLY. The first one gives an example of a geometric class for which coding is easy.

Proposition 5.10.22. *The class of convex polytopes has a canonical representation in* SAlg. *Consequently, the class of* FO + POLY *queries preserving the property of being a convex polytope has an effective syntax.*

Proof. Given a convex polytope X in $\mathbb{R}^n$, its vertices can be found as $V(X) = \{\vec{x} \in \mathbb{R}^n \mid \vec{x} \in X, \vec{x} \notin \mathrm{conv}(X - \vec{x})\}$, where $\mathrm{conv}(\cdot)$ denotes the convex hull. Thus, $V(X)$ is definable in FO + POLY. We now define $code_n$. To simplify the notation, we let it produce a pair of n-ary relations, but it can be straightforwardly coded by one relation. If $X = \mathrm{conv}(V(X))$, then $code_n(X) = (V(X), \emptyset)$; otherwise, $code_n(X) = (\mathbb{R}^n, X)$. The function $decode_n : 2^{\mathbb{R}^n} \times 2^{\mathbb{R}^n} \to 2^{\mathbb{R}^n}$ is defined as follows:

$$decode_n(Y, Z) = \begin{cases} \bigcup_{(\vec{y}_1, \ldots, \vec{y}_{n+1}) \in Y} \mathrm{conv}(\{\vec{y}_1, \ldots, \vec{y}_{n+1}\}) & \text{if } Y \neq \mathbb{R}^n, \\ Z & \text{otherwise.} \end{cases}$$

Clearly, $decode_n \circ code_n$ is the identity function for any semialgebraic set; these functions are also first-order definable. If X is a polytope, $V(X)$ is finite, and, by Carathéodory's Theorem, each point of X is contained in the convex hull of at most $n + 1$ vertices of X. Hence, $card(code_n(X)) \leq card(V(X))^{n+1}$. If (Y, Z) is finite, then $decode_n(Y)$ is $\mathrm{conv}(Y)$, and thus a convex polytope. This proves the proposition.   □

The second example deals with the case where $\mathcal{C}$ is a class of semilinear sets. We now give two different approaches to showing the following.

Theorem 5.10.23. *There is an effective syntax for the class of* FO + POLY *queries preserving semilinearity.*

One approach to showing this is to prove that the class of semilinear sets has a canonical representation in the class of semialgebraic sets. This is true, although the coding scheme is quite complex and not very intuitive. Another way of showing this theorem is based on the proposition below.

Proposition 5.10.24. *For any $n > 0$, there is an* FO + POLY *sentence over SC containing one n-ary relation symbol, which tests whether the input (which is a semialgebraic set $S \subseteq \mathbb{R}^n$) is semilinear.*   □

An effective syntax for FO + POLY queries preserving semilinearity can then be obtained simply by inserting tests for the input and output being semilinear, and returning the empty set if semilinearity is not preserved. However, the decision procedure is not much simpler than the canonical representation, and we are thus very far from a usable language for FO + POLY-definable queries preserving semilinearity. But the very fact that such a language exists is an interesting and nontrivial property of FO + POLY.

5.10.5 Deciding Safety

The safety of $FO_{act}(SC)$ formulae is already undecidable. However, there are some nice syntactic subclasses of $FO_{act}(SC)$ for which safety is guaranteed. We now consider one such subclass – *conjunctive queries*. The class of conjunctive queries is defined as a $\{\exists, \wedge\}$-fragment of $FO_{act}(SC)$, that is, as the set of formulae built from atomic formulae $S(\cdot)$, where $S \in SC$, using conjunction and existential quantification only. Outputs of such formulae cannot extend the active domain, and hence they are safe. We now consider a natural analog of conjunctive queries over embedded finite models. Although they are no longer guaranteed to produce an output containing only elements of the active domain, their safety remains decidable for underlying structures such as $\mathbf{R}_{lin}$ and $\mathbf{R}$.

A *conjunctive query* (CQ) is an $FO(SC, \mathfrak{M})$ formula of the form

$$\varphi(\vec{x}) \;\equiv\; \exists \vec{y} \in adom \; \alpha_1(\vec{x}, \vec{y}) \wedge \ldots \wedge \alpha_k(\vec{x}, \vec{y}) \wedge \gamma(\vec{x}, \vec{y}),$$

where $\alpha_1(\vec{x}, \vec{y}), \ldots, \alpha_k(\vec{x}, \vec{y}), k \geq 0$ are formulae of the form $S(\vec{u})$, where $S \in SC$ and $\vec{u}$ is a subtuple of $(\vec{x}, \vec{y})$, and γ is an $FO(\mathfrak{M})$ formula.

Theorem 5.10.25. *Let $\mathfrak{M}$ be o-minimal, based on a dense order, and decidable, and admit effective quantifier elimination. Then it is decidable whether a given conjunctive query in $FO(SC, \mathfrak{M})$ is safe.*

Proof. Given two formulae $\varphi(\vec{x})$ and $\psi(\vec{x})$, by the containment $\varphi \subseteq \psi$ we mean $\varphi(D) \subseteq \psi(D)$ for any finite D. From Proposition 5.10.18 we obtain that for any $FO(SC, \mathfrak{M})$ formula $\varphi(\vec{x})$, there exists an active-semantics CQ $\psi(\vec{x})$ such that φ is safe iff $\varphi \subseteq \psi$. The theorem now follows from the lemma below.

Lemma 5.10.26. *Let $\mathfrak{M}$ be as in Theorem 5.10.25. Then containment is decidable for conjunctive queries.*

Proof. Suppose we are given CQs $\varphi(\vec{x})$ and $\psi(\vec{x})$. We claim that one can effectively find a number k such that $\varphi \subseteq \psi$ iff for every D with at most k tuples, $\varphi(D) \subseteq \psi(D)$. This clearly implies the result, as the latter condition can be expressed as an $FO(\mathfrak{M})$ sentence.

To prove the claim, assume that $\varphi(\vec{x})$ is $\exists \vec{y} \in adom \bigwedge_{i=1}^{l} \alpha_i(\vec{u}_i) \wedge \gamma(\vec{x}, \vec{y})$. We claim that k can be taken to be l plus the length of $\vec{y}$. Assume there is an $\vec{a} \in \varphi(D) - \psi(D)$. Let $\vec{b}$ witness $D \models \varphi(\vec{a})$; we then see that there is a structure D' that contains at most k tuples from D such that $D' \models \varphi(\vec{a})$ (it has to contain enough tuples to ensure that all elements of $\vec{b}$ are in $adom(D')$), and that $\bigwedge_{i=1}^{l} \alpha_i(\vec{u}_i)$ holds. But then $D' \models \neg\psi(\vec{a})$, for otherwise we would have $D \models \psi(\vec{a})$. Thus, any counterexample to containment is witnessed by a $\leq k$-element structure. This finishes the proof of Lemma 5.10.26 and of the theorem.   □

The proof can be extended to show a slightly more general result:

Corollary 5.10.27. *It is decidable whether any Boolean combination of* FO + LIN *or* FO + POLY *conjunctive queries is safe.*

Note, however, that the safety of conjunctive queries is not decidable over every structure.

Proposition 5.10.28. *Let* $\mathfrak{N} = \langle \mathbb{N}, +, \cdot \rangle$. *Then the safety of conjunctive queries in* FO($SC, \mathfrak{N}$) *is undecidable, for any* SC.

Proof. Define $\varphi(\vec{x})$ to be $p(\vec{x}) = 0$ for some Diophantine equation. This is a CQ in FO($SC, \mathfrak{M}$), and it is safe iff $p(\vec{x}) = 0$ has finitely many solutions. However, this property of Diophantine equations is undecidable.   □

Some decidability results can be shown for constraint databases as well. We shall give only one example here, for the case of queries preserving the property of being a convex polytope.

Lemma 5.10.29. *Let* $\varphi(x_1, \ldots, x_n)$ *be a union of* FO + POLY *conjunctive queries that mention one m-ary relational symbol S. Then one can effectively find two numbers k and l such that φ preserves the property of being a convex polytope iff, for every convex polytope $\mathbf{D}$ in $\mathbb{R}^m$ with at most k vertices, the output $\varphi(\mathbf{D})$ is a convex polytope with at most l vertices in $\mathbb{R}^n$.*

With this lemma, one can show the following result.

Proposition 5.10.30. *It is decidable whether a union of conjunctive* FO + POLY *queries preserves the property of being a convex polytope.*

Proof. Note that for each i, there is an FO + POLY query ψ_i for each i that tests whether a set $\mathbf{D}$ is a convex polytope with at most i vertices: it checks that the set of vertices $V(\mathbf{D}) = \{x \in \mathbf{D} \mid x \notin \mathrm{conv}(\mathbf{D} - x)\}$ has at most i elements, and that $\mathbf{D} = \mathrm{conv}(V(\mathbf{D}))$. In order to check whether φ in FO + POLY preserves convex polytopes, one applies Lemma 5.10.29 to compute the numbers k and l, and then writes a sentence saying that for every set V in $\mathbb{R}^m$ with at most k elements, applying φ to $\mathrm{conv}(V)$ yields a polytope with at most l vertices. Since conv and ψ_l are definable, this property can be expressed as an FO($\mathbf{R}$) sentence. The proposition now follows from the decidability of the theory of $\mathbf{R}$.   □

5.10.6 Dichotomy Theorem for Embedded Finite Models

We now show a simple but powerful combinatorial structure theorem, saying that over a well-behaved structure, outputs of safe queries cannot grow arbitrarily large in terms of the size of the input. We use the notation $\mathsf{size}(D)$ for the size of a finite structure, measured here as the total number of tuples. It can be measured equivalently as the cardinality of the active domain, or the number of tuples multiplied by their arity, and all the results will still hold.

Theorem 5.10.31 (Dichotomy Theorem). *Let $\mathfrak{M}$ be o-minimal and based on a dense order. Let $\varphi(\vec{x})$ be an $\mathrm{FO}(SC, \mathfrak{M})$ formula. Then there exists a polynomial $p_\varphi : \mathbb{R} \to \mathbb{R}$ such that, for any finite SC-structure D, either $\varphi(D)$ is infinite or $\mathsf{size}(\varphi(D)) \leq p_\varphi(\mathsf{size}(D))$.*

Proof. Expand Ω by one constant (this does not violate o-minimality) and apply Theorem 5.10.12.   □

The Dichotomy Theorem can also be stated in terms of a function measuring the growth of the output size. We define $growth_\varphi : \mathbb{N} \to \mathbb{N} \cup \{\infty\}$ as

$$growth_\varphi(n) = \max\{\mathsf{size}(\varphi(D)) \mid \mathsf{size}(D) = n\}.$$

Corollary 5.10.32. *Let $\varphi(\vec{x})$ be an $\mathrm{FO}(SC, \mathfrak{M})$ formula for $\mathfrak{M}$ as in Theorem 5.10.31. Then there exists a polynomial p_φ such that, for every $n \in \mathbb{N}$, either $growth_\varphi(n) = \infty$ or $growth_\varphi(n) \leq p_\varphi(n)$.*   □

As we have often seen in this chapter, the assumptions about the structure are extremely important. Below, we show that the Dichotomy Theorem fails over some simple decidable structures on the natural numbers.

Proposition 5.10.33. *Let $\mathfrak{M} = \langle \mathbb{N}, +, <, 1 \rangle$. Then there exists an $\mathrm{FO}_{\mathrm{act}}(SC, \mathfrak{M})$ formula $\varphi(x)$ such that $growth_\varphi(n) = 2^n$ for every $n > 0$.*

Proof. Let SC consist of one unary relation S. We show that there exists an $\mathrm{FO}_{\mathrm{act}}(SC, \mathfrak{M})$ sentence Ψ such that $S \models \Psi$ iff S is of the form $S_n = \{2^i \mid 1 \leq i \leq n\}$. This is done by letting Ψ be

$$(\exists x \in adom \ x = 1 + 1 \wedge S(x))$$
$$\wedge \ (\forall x \in adom \ x = 1 + 1 \vee x > 1 + 1)$$
$$\wedge \ (\forall x \in adom \ x = 1 + 1 \vee \exists y \in adom \ y + y = x)$$
$$\wedge \ (\forall x \in adom \ (\forall y \in adom \ y < x \vee y = x) \vee (\exists y \in adom \ y = x + x)).$$

Now define $\varphi(x)$ as $\Psi \wedge \neg(x < 1) \wedge (\exists y \in adom \ x < y \vee x = y)$. Then, for S not of the form S_n, we have $\varphi(S) = \emptyset$, and $\varphi(S_n) = \{1, 2, 3, \ldots, 2^n\}$. Since $card(S_n) = n$, this implies $growth_\varphi(n) = 2^n$ for $n > 0$.   □

The Dichotomy Theorem gives easy expressivity bounds based on the growth of the output size. For example, even if we use exponentiation, we still cannot express any queries with superpolynomial growth, since $\langle \mathbb{R}, +, \cdot, e^x \rangle$ is o-minimal.

To give another application, consider the following problem: given a polyhedron P and $\varepsilon > 0$, find a triangulation of P of mesh $< \varepsilon$. That is, a triangulation such that the diameter of each simplex (a triangle in dimension 2) is less than ε. Every polyhedron admits such a triangulation. The output of such a query can be structured in several ways, for example by storing the information about the face structure of the triangulation. We impose only one requirement, that the vertices of the triangulation be computable.

Proposition 5.10.34. *Let $\mathfrak{M} = \langle \mathbb{R}, \Omega \rangle$ be an o-minimal expansion of the real field $\mathbf{R}$. Then there is no $\mathrm{FO}(SC, \mathfrak{M})$ formula that finds a triangulation of a given polygon with a given mesh. This continues to hold if we restrict ourselves to convex polytopes on a plane.*

Proof. Suppose that such a formula exists; now consider a new query that does the following. Its input is one binary relation containing a set X of points $\vec{x}_1, \ldots, \vec{x}_n$ on the real plane, and one unary relation containing a single real number $\varepsilon > 0$. First, in $\mathrm{FO} + \mathrm{POLY}$, construct $\mathrm{conv}(X)$, and then find vertices of a triangulation with mesh $< \varepsilon$. This is clearly a safe query, so, by the Dichotomy Theorem, there exists a polynomial p such that the number of vertices of the triangulation is at most $m = p(n+1)$ ($n+1$ is the size of the input). Let d be the maximal distance between the points $\vec{x}_i, \vec{x}_j$ (and thus the diameter of $\mathrm{conv}(X)$). Since the segment $[\vec{x}_i, \vec{x}_j]$ with $d(\vec{x}_i, \vec{x}_j) = d$ must be covered by the simplexes of the triangulation, it is possible to find a number ε such that it cannot be covered by fewer than $m+1$ triangles of diameter ε, and hence the number of points in the triangulation is greater than m. This contradiction proves the proposition. $\qquad\qquad \square$

Analogs of the results for growth bounds can be obtained in the constraint database setting as well; we give one example below.

Proposition 5.10.35. *Let $\varphi(\vec{x})$ be an $\mathrm{FO} + \mathrm{POLY}$ formula that preserves the property of being a convex polytope. Then there exists a polynomial p_φ such that, whenever $\mathbf{D}$ is a convex polytope with n vertices, $\varphi(\mathbf{D})$ has at most $p_\varphi(n)$ vertices.*

5.11 Database Considerations

In this section, we consider two aspects of embedded finite models and constraint databases, motivated primarily by database considerations: adding aggregate functions, and higher-order features.

5.11.1 Aggregate Operators

Aggregate operators such as COUNT, SUM, and AVG form an indispensable part of database query languages for the relational data model. How can they be used in the settings of embedded finite models and constraint databases?

We shall now briefly consider two aggregate operators. The *average* operator, present in all commercial database systems, returns the average value of a column of a relation. The *volume* operator, used in geographical information systems, returns the volume (or area) of a set. Here we investigate the possibility of incorporating these operators into languages such as FO + POLY and FO + LIN.

Let $\varphi(\vec{x}, \vec{y})$ be a formula in FO$(SC, \mathfrak{M})$, with $\vec{x}$ and $\vec{y}$ being of length n and m, respectively. For $\vec{a} \in U^n$, we define $\varphi(\vec{a}, D)$ to be $\{\vec{b} \in U^m \mid D \models \varphi(\vec{x}, \vec{y})\}$.

Let AVG(C) be the average value of a finite set $C \subset \mathbb{R}$; we let AVG$(C) = 0$ if C is empty or infinite. We say that the *average operator* AVG is definable over $\mathfrak{M}$ if, for every vocabulary SC and every FO$(SC, \mathfrak{M})$ formula $\varphi(\vec{x}, y)$, there exists an FO$(SC, \mathfrak{M})$ formula $\psi(\vec{x}, z)$ such that for every SC-structure D, $D \models \psi(\vec{a}, c)$ iff $c = $ AVG$(\varphi(\vec{a}, D))$.

An easy application of collapse results shows the following.

Proposition 5.11.1. *Let* $\mathfrak{M} = \langle \mathbb{R}, \Omega \rangle$ *be o-minimal, and such that the expansion* $\mathfrak{M} = \langle \mathbb{R}, \Omega, +, \cdot \rangle$ *is o-minimal as well (for example,* $\mathbf{R}, \mathbf{R}_{\text{lin}}$*). Then the average operator* AVG *is not definable over* $\mathfrak{M}$.

We leave this as an exercise, but we shall soon prove a more general result. Since AVG is not definable, one may consider several ways to overcome this. One possibility is to *approximate* it, rather than define it precisely. What could such an approximation be? Clearly, we cannot hope to define an ε-interval around the value of AVG$(\varphi(\vec{a}, D))$, as then that value would be definable as the center of the interval. Instead, we settle for a little less: we want to produce a formula defining a nonempty set that lies in that ε-interval.

We say that the average operator AVG$^{\varepsilon}$, $\varepsilon > 0$, is definable over $\mathfrak{M}$ if, for every vocabulary SC and every FO$(SC, \mathfrak{M})$ formula $\varphi(\vec{x}, y)$, there exists an FO$(SC, \mathfrak{M})$ formula $\psi(\vec{x}, z)$ such that for every SC-structure D, and every $\vec{a}$, the following two conditions hold:

1. $D \models \exists z \, \psi(\vec{a}, z)$ (that is, $\psi(\vec{a}, D) \neq \emptyset$); and
2. if $D \models \psi(\vec{a}, c)$, then $|c - $ AVG$(\varphi(\vec{a}, D))| < \varepsilon$.

We say that the average operator AVG$^{\varepsilon}_I$, $\varepsilon > 0$, is definable over $\mathfrak{M}$ if the above is true whenever $\varphi(\vec{a}, D) \subseteq I = [0, 1]$.

We shall now show the inexpressibility result for these queries. Recall that all previous inexpressibility results (with the exception of the result on topological queries) were proved by reductions to generic queries. Here we cannot easily find such reductions, as approximating queries are extremely non-generic: they do not say anything about the behavior on the ε-interval, other than that some point of the interval satisfies the formula. The proof below shows a way to circumvent the problem of "extremely nongeneric" queries.

Theorem 5.11.2. *Let $\mathfrak{M} = \langle \mathbb{R}, \Omega \rangle$ be o-minimal, and such that the expansion $\mathfrak{M} = \langle \mathbb{R}, \Omega, +, \cdot \rangle$ is o-minimal as well. Then the average operators AVG^ε (for any $\varepsilon > 0$) and $\mathrm{AVG}_I^\varepsilon$ (for $0 < \varepsilon < 1/2$) are not definable over $\mathfrak{M}$.*

Proof. Let SC consist of two unary relations, U_1 and U_2. Let $c_1, c_2 > 1$ be two real numbers. We say that Φ is a (c_1, c_2)-*separating sentence* if, for any finite instance D of SC, it is the case that $card(U_1) > c_1 \cdot card(U_2)$ implies $D \models \Phi$ and $card(U_2) > c_2 \cdot card(U_1)$ implies $D \models \neg\Phi$. Note that this definition says nothing about the case when $(1/c_2) \cdot card(U_2) \leq card(U_1) \leq c_1 \cdot card(U_2)$, and thus a direct application of bounds on the expressiveness of generic queries is impossible.

Lemma 5.11.3. *Let $\mathfrak{M}$ be as in the theorem, let $c_1, c_2 > 1$, and let SC be as above. Then no (c_1, c_2)-separating sentence is definable in $\mathrm{FO}(SC, \mathfrak{M})$.*

Proof of the lemma. Assume that there is a (c_1, c_2)-separating sentence Φ. From the natural-active collapse, we conclude that there is an $\mathrm{FO}_{\mathrm{act}}(SC, \mathfrak{M}')$ (c_1, c_2)-separating sentence Φ' for some definable expansion $\mathfrak{M}'$ of $\mathfrak{M}$ that has quantifier elimination. From the Ramsey property of active-semantics formulae (Proposition 5.5.5), we obtain that there is an infinite set $Y \subseteq U$ and an $\mathrm{FO}_{\mathrm{act}}(SC, <)$ sentence Ψ such that, for every SC-structure D with $adom(D) \subset Y$, we have $D \models \Phi'$ iff $D \models \Psi$. Thus, it remains to show that $\mathrm{FO}_{\mathrm{act}}(SC, <)$ cannot express a (c_1, c_2)-separating sentence Ψ on instances over an infinite set.

Assume that it can, and let q be the quantifier rank of Ψ. We now consider two instances over Y. In both instances D_1 and D_2, all elements of U_1 precede U_2 in the linear order $<$. In D_1, $card(U_1) = \lceil c_1(2^q + 1) \rceil$ and $card(U_2) = 2^q + 1$; in D_2, $card(U_1) = 2^q + 1$ and $card(U_2) = \lceil c_2(2^q + 1) \rceil$. Since Ψ is a (c_1, c_2)-separating sentence, we must have $D_1 \models \Psi$ and $D_2 \models \neg\Psi$. It is then easy to obtain a contradiction by showing that $D_1 \models \Psi$ iff $D_2 \models \Psi$. This is done by proving that the duplicator can win in a q-round Ehrenfeucht–Fraïssé game on D_1 and D_2. This follows from the fact that for every $n, m > 2^q$, the duplicator can win a q-round game on two ordered sets of cardinalities n and m. Thus, in the case of D_1 and D_2, the duplicator picks separate strategies for U_1 and U_2, and whenever the spoiler plays in U_1, the duplicator forgets about the moves in U_2 and responds in U_1 using the strategy for U_1, and likewise in the case when the spoiler plays in U_2. □

Now assume that $\mathrm{AVG}_I^\varepsilon$ is definable. Again, SC consists of two unary predicates, U_1 and U_2. Let $\Delta = (1 - 2\varepsilon)/16$. Given two finite sets U_1 and U_2, we translate them into intervals $[0, \Delta]$ and $[1 - \Delta, 1]$. By translating a finite set X with $\min X = c, \max X = d > c$ into an interval $[a, b]$, we mean that we map it to the set X' containing exactly the numbers of the form

$$a + \frac{(x-c)(b-a)}{d-c},$$

where $x \in X$; clearly $X' \subset [a,b]$. As the next step, we define $U_1^0 = U_1' \cup \{4\Delta - x \mid x \in U_1'\}$ and $U_2^0 = U_2' \cup \{2 - 4\Delta - x \mid x \in U_2'\}$. We observe that $U_1^0 \subseteq [0, 4\Delta]$ and $U_2^0 \subseteq [1 - 4\Delta, 1]$.

The preceding argument shows that U_1^0 and U_2^0 are FO + POLY-definable. Thus, the set $C = U_1^0 \cup U_2^0 \subset [0,1]$ is definable in FO + POLY. Now easy calculations show that

$$\text{AVG}(C) = \frac{1}{8} - \frac{\varepsilon}{4} + \frac{m}{n+m} \cdot \frac{3 + 2\varepsilon}{4},$$

where n is the cardinality of U_1 and m is the cardinality of U_2.

We now define a sentence Φ by letting $D \models \Phi$ iff $\text{AVG}^\varepsilon(C) = \text{AVG}_I^\varepsilon(C) > 1/2$. Let

$$c_0 = 1 + \frac{16\varepsilon}{3 - 6\varepsilon} > 1.$$

Assume that $m > c_0 \cdot n$. Plugging this into the equation for $\text{AVG}(C)$, we derive $\text{AVG}(C) > 1/2 + \varepsilon$; thus, in this case, $\text{AVG}^\varepsilon(C) > 1/2$ no matter which ε-approximation of the average is picked, and thus $D \models \Phi$. Similarly, if we assume that $n > c_0 \cdot m$, we derive $\text{AVG}(C) < 1/2 - \varepsilon$, and thus $\text{AVG}^\varepsilon(C) < 1/2$ and $D \models \neg\Phi$. Hence, Φ is a (c_0, c_0)-separating sentence, which is definable in $\text{FO}(SC, \langle \mathbb{R}, \Omega, +, \cdot \rangle)$. This contradiction proves the theorem. $\square$

We now briefly consider the spatial aggregate operator *volume*. First, it is easy to see that it is not definable in the languages FO + LIN and FO + POLY. As was mentioned earlier, those languages have the following fundamental closure property: on a semilinear constraint database $\mathbf{D}$, an FO + LIN query returns a semilinear set, and likewise, on a semialgebraic constraint database, an FO + POLY query returns a semialgebraic set.

This closure property can no longer be guaranteed if one allows volume operators, that is, operators VOL that, for every formula $\varphi(\vec{x}, \vec{y})$, produce a formula $\psi(\vec{x}, z) \equiv \text{VOL}\vec{y}\, \varphi(\vec{x}, \vec{y})$ such that $\mathbf{D} \models \psi(\vec{a}, v)$ iff $v = \text{VOL}(\varphi(\vec{a}, \mathbf{D}))$. To see this for the semilinear case, consider a semilinear set $S \subseteq \mathbb{R}^3$ defined by $(x > 0) \wedge (0 < y < x) \wedge (0 < z < x)$. Let $\varphi(x, y, z)$ be $S(x, y, z)$. Then $\text{VOL}(y, z)\, \varphi(x, y, z)$ is true on a pair (a, v) with $a > 0$ iff $v = a^2$, which shows the failure of closure. In the case of semialgebraic sets, one can define functions such as $\ln x$ or $\arctan(x)$ with the help of the volume. These functions are not semialgebraic.

Volume is not definable, but can it be approximated? The reason to think that this may be the case is the following result. Suppose $\varphi(\vec{x}, \vec{y})$ is an $\text{FO}(\mathbf{R})$ formula, defining a semialgebraic set $S \subseteq [0,1]^{n+m}$. Then, for every $\varepsilon > 0$, there is an $\text{FO}(\mathbf{R})$ formula $\psi_\varepsilon(\vec{x}, z)$ such that, for every $\vec{a} \in [0,1]^n$, $\mathbf{R} \models \exists z\, \varphi(\vec{a}, z)$, and for any $0 \leq v \leq 1$ such that $\mathbf{R} \models \varphi(\vec{a}, v)$, we have $|v - V| < \varepsilon$, where V is the volume of the set $\{\vec{b} \in [0,1]^m \mid \mathbf{R} \models \varphi(\vec{a}, \vec{b})\}$.

To achieve approximability of volume in FO + POLY, we only have to replace FO($\mathbf{R}$) formulae by FO($SC, \mathbf{R}$) (that is, FO + POLY) formulae. This motivates the following definition. We say that, for $\varepsilon > 0$, the operator $\mathrm{VOL}_I^\varepsilon$ is definable in FO + POLY if, for every SC and every FO + POLY formula $\varphi(\vec{x}, \vec{y})$, there exists a formula $\psi(\vec{x}, z)$ such that, for any semialgebraic constraint database $\mathbf{D}$, and every $\vec{a} \in [0, 1]^n$, the following holds:

1. $\mathbf{D} \models \exists z \; \psi(\vec{a}, z)$, and
2. if $\mathbf{D} \models \psi(\vec{a}, v)$, then $0 \leq v \leq 1$ and $|v - \mathrm{VOL}(\varphi(\vec{a}, D) \cap [0, 1]^m)| < \varepsilon$.

However, it turns out that this innocent-looking move from FO($\mathbf{R}$) to FO + POLY (that is, FO($SC, \mathbf{R}$)) changes the picture completely.

Theorem 5.11.4. *The operator* $\mathrm{VOL}_I^\varepsilon$ *is not definable in* FO + POLY, *for any* $\varepsilon < 1/2$.

Proof sketch. The proof is again by reduction to separating sentences; however, the reduction is more involved than that for the AVG operator. In particular, the reduction can only be carried out if the input constraint database is finite and has an initial segment of natural numbers as its active domain. To prove that FO + POLY cannot define a separating sentence on such structures, one can no longer use games, and instead has to rely on circuit lower bounds.   □

Note that the bound $1/2$ is tight: for every $\varepsilon > 1/2$, $\mathrm{VOL}_I^\varepsilon$ is definable, as the cases where the volume is 0 or 1 can be tested in FO + POLY, and in all other cases, $1/2$ is an approximation.

5.11.2 Higher-Order Features

So far, we have dealt only with first-order logic over embedded finite models and constraint databases. As we have shown a number of limitations of FO($SC, \mathfrak{M}$) in both contexts, it is natural to ask how to extend it to overcome those shortcomings. The question arises in both the embedded and the constraint setting. In the first case, the solution is rather easy, and essentially follows the standard techniques of (finite) model theory, such as adding fixpoint operators or second-order quantification. Still, one has to be careful to avoid getting undecidable languages over nice structures, such as the real field. In the constraint setting, the answer to this question is a little trickier, but we shall see that nice languages can still be obtained that express properties such as topological connectivity.

In the embedded case, we deal here only with adding second-order quantification, but the reader should see that one can similarly add fixpoint or transitive closure operators, for example. In the case of constraint databases, we specifically consider the case of topological connectivity, although other topological queries inexpressible in FO + POLY could be considered as well.

Second-Order Logic over Embedded Finite Models.

One can define this logic in the general way, as $SO(SC, \mathfrak{M})$, by extending $FO(SC, \mathfrak{M})$ with second-order quantifiers

$$\exists S \; \varphi, \qquad \forall S \; \varphi,$$

where S is a relation symbol not in SC. The semantics is that for some $S \subseteq U^k$, φ holds, where k is the arity of S (or φ holds for all S, in the case of the universal quantifier). Alternatively, we can define an active-semantics version of the above, where the quantifiers are

$$\exists S \in adom \; \varphi, \qquad \forall S \in adom \; \varphi,$$

and the semantics changes in such a way that S must be a subset of $adom(D)^k$. We shall denote the fragment of $SO(SC, \mathfrak{M})$ in which all – first-order and second-order – quantifiers range over the active domain by $SO_{act}(SC, \mathfrak{M})$.

We start by noticing the following:

Proposition 5.11.5. *Active-generic collapse holds over every structure $\mathfrak{M}$ for second-order logic. That is, every order-generic query definable in $SO_{act}(SC, \mathfrak{M})$ is definable in $SO_{act}(SC)$.*

Proof. We expand $\mathfrak{M}$ to $\mathfrak{M}^<$ by adding a symbol $<$, interpreted as a linear order (if it is not there already). The proof now follows the proof for first-order logic, by establishing the Ramsey property (the proof that the Ramsey property implies the collapse does not change). As the proof of the Ramsey property is by induction on the formulae, the only additional case to be considered is that of second-order quantification. It is almost the same as the case of first-order quantification (see the proof of Proposition 5.5.5). Note that the order relation $<$ can be eliminated from $SO_{act}(SC, <)$ formulae, as it is definable in second-order logic. □

Establishing natural-active collapse is harder, as the most naive approach cannot possibly succeed.

Proposition 5.11.6. *Every computable property of finite SC-structures is expressible in $SO(SC, \mathbf{R})$.*

Proof. In second-order logic over $\mathbf{R}$ (in fact, even $\mathbf{R}_{lin}$), one can define the set of natural numbers by the following formula $\varphi(n)$:

$$\exists P \, [P(0) \wedge (\forall x \, (0 < |x| < 1 \rightarrow \neg P(x))) \wedge (\forall x > 0 \, (P(x) \leftrightarrow P(x-1)))] \wedge P(n).$$

Then, for any finite SC-structure over $\mathbb{R}$, one can state in second-order logic that there exists an isomorphic structure over $\mathbb{N}$, and in first-order logic over $\langle \mathbb{N}, +, \cdot \rangle$ one can test an arbitrary computable property of such a structure. □

At the same time, every generic query in $SO_{act}(SC, \mathbf{R})$ is in $SO_{act}(SC)$ and thus its complexity is in the polynomial hierarchy; hence $SO(SC, \mathbf{R}) \neq SO_{act}(SC, \mathbf{R})$.

To overcome this problem, we introduce a *hybrid second-order logic* $HSO(SC, \mathfrak{M})$ as a restriction of $SO(SC, \mathfrak{M})$, in which all second-order quantifiers range over the active domain (but first-order quantifiers can still range over U). Then $HSO_{act}(SC, \mathfrak{M})$ is the restriction of $HSO(SC, \mathfrak{M})$ in which all first-order quantifiers range over the active domain.

Proposition 5.11.7. *Let $\mathfrak{M}$ be o-minimal and admit quantifier elimination. Then hybrid second-order logic has a natural-active collapse over $\mathfrak{M}$: that is, $HSO(SC, \mathfrak{M}) = HSO_{act}(SC, \mathfrak{M})$. Furthermore, if the theory of $\mathfrak{M}$ is decidable and quantifier elimination is effective, then there is an effective transformation of $HSO(SC, \mathfrak{M})$ formulae into equivalent $HSO_{act}(SC, \mathfrak{M})$ formulae.*

The proof of this result is very similar to the proof in the first-order case. It is by induction on the formulae, with only the case of $\exists z \alpha$ being nontrivial. In this case, one proves the exact analog of Lemma 5.6.8, by using essentially the same proof, as the equivalences $(*)$ in that proof are preserved under the addition of active-domain second-order quantifiers.

Thus, every generic query in $HSO(SC, \mathbf{R})$ is definable in $SO_{act}(SC)$; that is, the behavior of hybrid second-order logic is similar to that of first-order logic, as one can apply known bounds from finite model theory in the embedded context.

Connectivity and Constraint Databases

While it has been shown that topological connectivity is not definable in languages such as $FO + LIN$ and $FO + POLY$, it is a very useful query in many applications of spatial databases, and one would want to have a language capable of expressing it. The situation is somewhat similar to that of first-order logic on finite relational structures. As FO cannot express graph connectivity or transitive closure, one enriches the logic by adding fixpoints, transitive closure operators, or second-order quantification, to give it enough power to express some desirable queries.

A similar approach is unlikely to work for constraint databases. If one adds fixpoints straightforwardly to $FO + LIN$ or $FO + POLY$, one loses the crucial closure property. To see this, note that by iterating the semilinear relation $x = 2y$, one obtains relations $x = 4y$, $x = 8y$, ..., $x = 2^n y$, ..., and thus one can define the set of all powers of 2. This set is not semilinear (nor semialgebraic), which shows that $FO + LIN$ and $FO + POLY$ are not closed under fixpoint operators.

To remedy this, we take the simplest possible approach: if we need topological connectivity, we just add it to the language. In this way, we obtain the languages $FO + POLY + C$ and $FO + LIN + C$ by extending the definition of the language by the following: for every formula $\varphi(\vec{x}, \vec{y})$, there is a new formula

$$\psi(\vec{x}) \ \equiv \ \mathsf{C}\vec{y}\,\varphi(\vec{x},\vec{y}).$$

The semantics is as follows. Given a constraint database $\mathbf{D}$, and a tuple $\vec{a}$ of the same length as $\vec{x}$, let $\varphi(\vec{a},\mathbf{D}) = \{\vec{b} \mid \mathbf{D} \models \varphi(\vec{a},\vec{b})\}$. Then

$$\mathbf{D} \models \psi(\vec{a}) \quad \text{iff} \quad \varphi(\vec{a},\mathbf{D}) \text{ is connected.}$$

The main property of these languages is that they are closed; the proofs, however, are quite different for the semialgebraic and the semilinear case.

Proposition 5.11.8. FO + POLY + C *is closed; that is, on a semialgebraic constraint database, an* FO + POLY + C *query produces a semialgebraic set.*

Proof. The proof is by induction on the formulae. The only nontrivial case is that of $\psi(\vec{x}) \equiv \mathsf{C}\vec{y}\,\varphi(\vec{x},\vec{y})$. Assume that on $\mathbf{D}$, φ defines a set $S \subseteq \mathbb{R}^{n+m}$, where n is the length of $\vec{x}$ and m is the length of $\vec{y}$. Let $S_{\vec{a}}$ denote the set $\{\vec{b} \mid (\vec{a},\vec{b}) \in S\} \subseteq \mathbb{R}^m$ for $\vec{a} \in \mathbb{R}^n$. A result in algebraic geometry known as the Local Triviality Theorem states that for any semialgebraic set S as defined above, there is a partition $\mathbb{R}^n = Y_1 \cup \ldots \cup Y_k$ such that each Y_i is semialgebraic, and for $\vec{a}_1, \vec{a}_2 \in Y_i$, the sets $S_{\vec{a}_1}$ and $S_{\vec{a}_2}$ are homeomorphic. In particular, either all sets $S_{\vec{a}}, \vec{a} \in Y_i$ are connected, or none of them is. Hence, the result of ψ on $\mathbf{D}$ is a union of some Y_is, and thus semialgebraic. $\square$

The reason we cannot use the same proof for FO + LIN is that the Local Triviality Theorem fails over $\mathbf{R}_{\mathrm{lin}}$. In the proof above, we used only a part of that theorem, which says that the fibers $S_{\vec{a}}$ have finitely many topological types. But it also asserts that there are semialgebraic homeomorphisms between sets $S_{\vec{a}_1}$ and $S_{\vec{a}_2}$, $\vec{a}_1, \vec{a}_2 \in Y_i$. An analog of this statement does not hold for semilinear sets, and hence the Local Triviality Theorem is not applicable in the semilinear case. (In fact, one can prove local triviality for o-minimal *expansions* of the real field $\mathbf{R}$.)

There are two ways of circumventing the problem. One, quite complex, is to show that the first part of the Local Triviality Theorem still holds for the case of semilinear sets. But we can also give a simple direct proof of closure of FO + LIN + C, which does not require the Local Triviality Theorem.

Proposition 5.11.9. FO + LIN + C *is closed; that is, on a semilinear constraint database, an* FO + LIN + C *query produces a semilinear set.*

Proof. The proof again is by induction on the formulae, and we consider only the case of $\psi(\vec{x}) \equiv \mathsf{C}\vec{y}\,\varphi(\vec{x},\vec{y})$. Assume that on $\mathbf{D}$, φ defines a semilinear set $S \subseteq \mathbb{R}^{n+m}$. Since S is semilinear, it has a representation of the form

$$\bigvee_{i=1}^{k} \psi_i, \quad \psi_i \equiv \bigwedge_{j=1}^{l_i} \langle \vec{a}_{ij}, \vec{x} \rangle \; \vartheta \; \langle \vec{b}_{ij}, \vec{y} \rangle + c_{ij}$$

where $\langle \cdot, \cdot \rangle$ denotes the inner product. Let Z^i be the subset of $\mathbb{R}^{n+m}$ defined by ψ_i. For every $\vec{a} \in \mathbb{R}^n$, the set $Z_{\vec{a}}^i$ is a convex polyhedron, and thus it is connected (unless it is empty).

Let $T_1, \ldots, T_r$ be an arbitrary collection of semilinear sets in $\mathbb{R}^p$. Define a relation $T_i \approx T_j$ if $\mathrm{cl}(T_i) \cap T_j \neq \emptyset$ or $\mathrm{cl}(T_j) \cap T_i \neq \emptyset$, where $\mathrm{cl}(\cdot)$ denotes the closure of a set. Then $T_1 \cup \ldots \cup T_k$ is connected iff the undirected graph with the T_is as vertices and $\approx$ as the edge relation is connected.

Using this fact, we conclude the proof as follows. Given an undirected graph G on nodes $1, \ldots, k$, we write $\vec{a} \to_{\mathbf{D}} G$ if

$$\text{there is an edge } (i, j) \text{ in } G \quad \text{iff} \quad Z^i_{\vec{a}} \approx Z^j_{\vec{a}}.$$

We have seen earlier that closure is FO + LIN-definable. Hence, there is an FO + LIN formula $\alpha_G(\vec{x})$ such that $\mathbf{D} \models \alpha_G(\vec{a})$ iff $\vec{a} \to_{\mathbf{D}} G$. This and the statement in the previous paragraph, imply that

$$\bigvee_{G \text{ connected}} \alpha_G(\vec{x})$$

is equivalent to $\psi(\vec{x})$, where the disjunction is taken over connected undirected graphs on $\{1, \ldots, k\}$. This proves closure, since the above is an FO + LIN formula. $\square$

Note that the formula produced in the proof of Proposition 5.11.9 may be very large, as the number of connected graphs on a k-element set is exponential in k. It turns out that a much more compact formula can always be obtained; the proof of this, however, is much more involved than the simple proof that we provided above. See the bibliographic notes for more detail.

5.12 Bibliographic Notes

Sections 5.2 and 5.3

For a general introduction to finite model theory, see [31, 48, 57] and the previous chapters of this book. A standard reference on database theory is [1], which also covers many topics of finite model theory. Constraint databases were introduced in [49]; for a comprehensive treatment of this topic, see [55]. Mixing the finite and the infinite in the context of databases is discussed in a number of papers; see, for example, [25, 37]. The semialgebraic "face" example is taken from [22], and the semilinear one from [55].

Other approaches to combining the finite and the infinite in model theory include metafinite structures [37] (which, in our terminology, can be described as triples consisting of a finite structure D, an infinite structure $\mathfrak{M}$, and a set of functions from $adom(D)$ to tuples over $\mathfrak{M}$), recursive structures [43] (infinite structures in which every relation is computable, and thus has a finite description by means of a Turing machine), and automatic structures [20, 51] (in which predicates are given by finite automata, as opposed to arbitrary Turing machines).

Section 5.4

The notion of genericity is standard in the field of relational databases, see [1, 46]. Various forms of collapse results were introduced in [11, 45, 61].

Section 5.5

The active-generic collapse was proved independently in [11] and [59]. The Ramsey property is from [11], and the proof given here follows closely the one in [15]. Analytic signatures and total collapse are also discussed in [15]. For a survey of Ramsey theory, see [36]. That there exist properties definable in $FO_{act}(SC, <)$ but not $FO_{act}(SC)$ is shown in [1] (the result is attributed to Gurevich).

Section 5.6

Proposition 5.6.1 is a standard exercise on coding in first-order logic over $\langle \mathbb{N}, +, \cdot \rangle$ (cf. [32]); the result was explicitly stated in this form in [41]. The natural-active collapse without an interpreted structure (Theorem 5.6.3) was proved in [45]. An earlier weaker result [3] showed that unrestricted quantification can always be replaced by quantification over some finite superset of the active domain (the "4 Russians Theorem").

The concept of o-minimality was introduced in [62], and has been extensively studied in the model-theoretic literature; see [75] for an overview. The o-minimality of the exponential field is from [79]; [74] shows that it does not have quantifier elimination. The Uniform Bounds Theorem (Theorem 5.6.7) is from [63]. For general model-theoretic properties of structures, see standard texts such as [26].

The natural-active collapse (Theorem 5.6.4) is from [15]. It was proved earlier by nonconstructive means in [14]. The linear case, sketched in Section 5.6.4, was proved in [61]. (See also [71].) The material of Sect. 5.6.5 is from [15], except for Proposition 5.6.10, which is from [34]. A version of the algorithm for natural-active collapse adapted to FO + POLY was presented in [57].

A different proof of natural-active collapse for FO + POLY was given in [8]. It applies only to finite structures in which all relations are unary, but achieves much better complexity bounds than the general algorithm presented here.

The natural-generic collapse (Sect. 5.6.7) was the first collapse result proved for polynomial constraints, see [11]. That proof used the technique of nonstandard universes; here we derived the result as a corollary of the natural-active collapse. Some extensions of this collapse result are known, for example for quasi-o-minimal structures [9] (which include all o-minimal ones, as well as $\langle \mathbb{N}, +, < \rangle$) and for a larger class of structures with finite VC dimension (Theorem 5.6.13) [7].

More expressivity bounds were proved in [27], which showed that parity is not definable in FO + POLY even if the input is a set of natural numbers such that the distance between two consecutive elements is 1 or 2. That paper also extended some expressivity bounds to algebraically closed fields.

Section 5.7

For the general model-theoretic background, the reader is referred to [26, 44]. The notion of pseudo-finite homogeneity was introduced in [9, 34]. Theorem 5.7.3 is from [34], as are the notion of pseudo-finite saturation and Proposition 5.7.4. The proof of Proposition 5.7.6 uses the fact that term algebras are stable, and some conditions for showing that a structure does not have the finite cover property; these conditions can be found in [44, 64].

The isolation property, Proposition 5.7.8, and Corollary 5.7.9 are from [9]. Proposition 5.7.10 is from [19]. Proposition 5.7.11 is a special case of a more general result (which shows the isolation property for quasi-o-minimal structures) in [9]; see also [34].

Section 5.8

For more on the VC dimension and its applications in learning theory, see [5, 21]. For applications in logic, and for the basic facts used in the proof of Theorem 5.8.1, see [56, 68, 75]. In particular, [56] shows that o-minimal structures have finite VC dimension.

The class $AC^0/poly$ used in the section is a standard complexity class (a.k.a. nonuniform AC^0); see, for example, [48, 57]. Bounds for $AC^0/poly$ implying the inexpressibility of queries such as parity and connectivity can be found in [4, 29, 35].

Theorem 5.8.1 is from [19]. The material of Sect. 5.8.1 is partly from [59] (which showed one direction of Theorem 5.8.2; the other direction is from [18]). In [15] it is shown how to use a random ternary relation to express even more queries (for example, parity), thereby refuting a conjecture in [41] that tied such expressivity results to the decidability of the theory of the underlying structure. For basic information about definability over random graphs (and more generally, random structures), the reader is referred to [31, 44, 57, 69]).

The material of Sect. 5.8.2, including Proposition 5.8.3, is from [19] (which gives a slightly better complexity bound). The structure $\mathcal{S}$ was studied in [23], where the connection with regular languages was shown; in [20], which showed how to interpret automatic structures in it; and in [19], where further model-theoretic properties, including infinite VC dimension, were proved.

Section 5.9

The material on reductions (Sect. 5.9.1) is from [41], which shows many inexpressibility results for FO + POLY by reducing them to parity. Topological properties (Section 5.9.2) of constraint databases were studied in [53, 54, 60, 67]. The conical local structure of semialgebraic sets is described in the texts [10, 22]. Theorem 5.9.3 is from [53]. The failure of Theorem 5.9.3 for multiple regions was shown in [39].

Sect. 5.9.3 is based on [77], which contains many examples of queries that are expressible and inexpressible in FO + LIN. More examples of the power of FO + LIN can be found in [2], where it was also conjectured that ExistsLine is not expressible in FO + LIN. That was first proved in [13], but the proof was very complicated; the simple proof given here is due to [66]. The result for the line segment connecting two boundary points is due to [13].

Section 5.10

Safety is a central notion in relational database theory; see [1]. See [78] for undecidability of safety for first-order logic. Safety with scalar functions was studied in [33]. The STATE-SAFETY problem was introduced in [3, 6], where decidability was proved for some structures (e.g. $\langle \mathbb{N}, < \rangle$).

The concept of safe translation is from [16]. Proposition 5.10.4 is from [70] (where a complete description of the structure and the proof of decidability can be found). Propositions 5.10.5 and 5.10.6 are from [16]. Extensions to Datalog are discussed in [65, 72].

Sect. 5.10.3 follows [16] closely, except that here we have presented range-restriction in terms of definable functions, rather than just algebraic formulae. For the properties of semilinear and semialgebraic functions used in the proof of Corollary 5.10.15, see [58, 75].

The reduction from infinite safety to finite safety (Theorem 5.10.21), as well as the canonical representation for convex polytopes, is from [16]. More examples of canonical representations can be found in [16]. The first proof of Theorem 5.10.23 is based on applying Theorem 5.10.21 to canonical representations for semilinear sets, given in [76]. The other proof uses the decidability of semilinearity, proved in [30].

The decidability result for the safety of conjunctive queries over o-minimal structures is from [16]; it uses the decidability of containment, proved in [47]. (See also Chapter 2 of [55], which discusses some subtle points related to the decidability result of [47].) The undecidability of finiteness of the set of solutions of a Diophantine equation (which proves Proposition 5.10.28) is from [28]. Proposition 5.10.30 is from [16]. All results in the section on the Dichotomy Theorem are from [16].

Section 5.11

Aggregation is a standard feature of database query languages [1, 73]. The results dealing with the average operator are from [17]. How to play a game on ordered sets is described in [42].

That volumes can be approximated for first-order formulae over the real field was shown in [50, 52]. Theorem 5.11.4, showing that these results do not extend to constraint databases, is from [17].

Hybrid logics were introduced in [15], where some collapse results were proved. There exist higher-order logics that capture complexity classes over constraint databases defined with order [38] and with linear constraints [40]. The material on connectivity is from [12]. The Local Triviality Theorem used in the proof of Proposition 5.11.8 can be found in [10, 22, 75]. The proof of Proposition 5.11.9 in [12] is more involved and relies on special properties of cylindric decompositions [24] of semilinear sets; the simple proof presented here is due to [80] (the simplicity is achieved at the expense of exponential-size formulae).

Acknowledgments

Special thanks to Martin Otto who carefully read two early drafts and provided numerous suggestions. The second draft of this chapter was used in a seminar at the University of Freiburg; I would like to thank the participants for their comments, in particular Jörg Flum and Markus Junker. I greatly benefited from comments and suggestions by Michael Benedikt, Martin Grohe, Luc Segoufin, and Mihalis Yannakakis. Partial support was provided by grants from NSERC and CITO, by the European Commission Marie Curie Excellence grant MEXC-CT-2005-024502, and by EPSRC grant E005039.

References

1. S. Abiteboul, R. Hull, and V. Vianu. *Foundations of Databases*. Addison-Wesley, 1995.
2. F. Afrati, T. Andronikos, and T. Kavalieros. On the expressiveness of query languages with linear constraints: capturing desirable spatial properties. In *Constraint Databases and Applications*, Lecture Notes in Computer Science vol. 1191, pages 105–115, Springer 1997.
3. A. K. Ailamazyan, M. M. Gilula, A. P. Stolboushkin and G. F. Shvarts. Reduction of a relational model with infinite domains to the finite-domain case. *Doklady Akademii Nauk SSSR*, 286(1):308–311, 1986. Translation in *Soviet Physics – Doklady*, 31:11–13, 1986.
4. M. Ajtai. Σ_1^1 formulae on finite structures. *Annals of Pure and Applied Logic*, 24:1–48, 1983.
5. M. Anthony and N. Biggs. *Computational Learning Theory*. Cambridge University Press, 1992.
6. A. Avron and J. Hirshfeld. On first order database query languages. In *IEEE Symposium on Logic in Computer Science*, pages 226–231, 1991.
7. J. Baldwin and M. Benedikt. Stability theory, permutations of indiscernibles, and embedded finite models. *Transactions of the American Mathematical Society* 352:4937–4969, 2000.

8. S. Basu. New results on quantifier elimination over real closed fields and applications to constraint databases. *Journal of the ACM*, 46:537–555, 1999.

9. O. Belagradek, A. Stolboushkin, and M. Taitslin. Extended order-generic queries. *Annals of Pure and Applied Logic*, 97:85–125, 1999.

10. R. Benedetti and J.-J. Risler. *Real Algebraic and Semi-algebraic Sets*. Hermann, Paris, 1990.

11. M. Benedikt, G. Dong, L. Libkin and L. Wong. Relational expressive power of constraint query languages. *Journal of the ACM*, 45:1–34, 1998.

12. M. Benedikt, M. Grohe, L. Libkin and L. Segoufin. Reachability and connectivity queries in constraint databases. *Journal of Computer and System Sciences*, 66(1):169–206, 2003.

13. M. Benedikt and H. J. Keisler. Definability with a predicate for a semi-linear set. *Journal of Symbolic Logic* 68(1):319-351, 2003.

14. M. Benedikt and L. Libkin. On the structure of queries in constraint query languages. In *IEEE Symposium on Logic in Computer Science*, pages 25–34, 1996.

15. M. Benedikt and L. Libkin. Relational queries over interpreted structures. *Journal of the ACM*, 47:644–680, 2000.

16. M. Benedikt and L. Libkin. Safe constraint queries. *SIAM Journal on Computing*, 29:1652–1682, 2000.

17. M. Benedikt and L. Libkin. Aggregate operators in constraint query languages. *Journal of Computer and System Sciences*, 64:628–654, 2000.

18. M. Benedikt and L. Libkin. Unpublished notes, 1999.

19. M. Benedikt, L. Libkin, T. Schwentick, and L. Segoufin. Definable relations and first-order query languages over strings. *Journal of the ACM*, 50(5):694-751, 2003.

20. A. Blumensath and E. Grädel. Automatic structures. In *IEEE Symposium on Logic in Computer Science*, pages 51–62, 2000.

21. A. Blumer, A. Ehrenfeucht, D. Haussler, and M. Warmuth. Learnability and the Vapnik-Chervonenkis dimension. *Journal of the ACM*, 36:929–965, 1989.

22. J. Bochnak, M. Coste, and M.-F. Roy. *Real Algebraic Geometry*. Springer, 1998.

23. V. Bruyère, G. Hansel, C. Michaux, and R. Villemaire. Logic and p-recognizable sets of integers. *Bulletin of the Belgian Mathematical Society* 1:191–238, 1994.

24. B. F. Caviness and J. R. Johnson, eds. *Quantifier Elimination and Cylindrical Algebraic Decomposition*. Springer, 1998.

25. A. Chandra and D. Harel. Computable queries for relational databases. *Journal of Computer and System Sciences*, 21(2):156–178, 1980.

26. C. C. Chang and H. J. Keisler. *Model Theory*. North-Holland, 1990.

27. O. Chapuis and P. Koiran. Definability of geometric properties in algebraically closed fields. *Mathematical Logic Quarterly*, 45:533–550, 1999.

28. M. Davis. On the number of solutions of Diophantine equations. *Proceedings of the AMS*, 35:552–554, 1972.

29. L. Denenberg, Y. Gurevich and S. Shelah. Definability by constant-depth polynomial-size circuits. *Information and Control*, 70:216–240, 1986.

30. F. Dumortier, M. Gyssens, L. Vandeurzen, and D. Van Gucht. On the decidability of semi-linearity of semi-algebraic sets, and its implications for spatial databases. *Journal of Computer and System Sciences*, 58:535–571, 1999. Correction in *Journal of Computer and System Sciences*, 59:557–562, 1999.

31. H.-D. Ebbinghaus and J. Flum. *Finite Model Theory*. Springer, 1995.

32. H. B. Enderton. *A Mathematical Introduction to Logic*. Academic Press, New York, 1972.

33. M. Escobar-Molano, R. Hull and D. Jacobs. Safety and translation of calculus queries with scalar functions. In *ACM Symposium on Principles of Database Systems*, pages 253–264, 1993.

34. J. Flum and M. Ziegler. Pseudo-finite homogeneity and saturation. *Journal of Symbolic Logic*, 64:1689–1699, 1999.

35. M. Furst, J. Saxe, and M. Sipser. Parity, circuits, and the polynomial-time hierarchy. *Mathematical Systems Theory*, 17:13–27, 1984.

36. R. L. Graham, B .L. Rothschild, and J .H. Spencer. *Ramsey Theory*. Wiley, New York, 1990.

37. E. Grädel and Y. Gurevich. Metafinite model theory. *Information and Computation*, 140:26–81, 1998.

38. E. Grädel and S. Kreutzer. Descriptive complexity theory for constraint databases. In *Conf. on Computer Science Logic*, pages 67–81, 1999.

39. M. Grohe and L. Segoufin. On first-order topological queries. *ACM Transactions on Computational Logic*, 3:336–358, 2002.

40. S. Grumbach and G. Kuper. Tractable recursion over geometric data. In *Proc. of Constraint Programming*, pages 450–462, 1997.

41. S. Grumbach and J. Su. Queries with arithmetical constraints. *Theoretical Computer Science*, 173:151–181, 1997.

42. Y. Gurevich. Toward logic tailored for computational complexity. In *Computation and Proof Theory*, pages 175–216, Springer 1984.

43. D. Harel. Towards a theory of recursive structures. In *Conference on Mathematical Foundations of Computer Science*, pages 36–53, 1998.

44. W. Hodges. *Model Theory*. Cambridge, 1993.

45. R. Hull and J. Su. Domain independence and the relational calculus. *Acta Informatica*, 31:513–524, 1994.

46. R. Hull and C. K. Yap. The format model: a theory of database organization. *Journal of the ACM*, 31:518–537, 1984.

47. O. H. Ibarra and J. Su. A technique for proving decidability of containment and equivalence of linear constraint queries. *Journal of Computer and System Sciences*, 59:1–28, 1999.

48. N. Immerman. *Descriptive Complexity*. Springer, 1999.

49. P. Kanellakis, G. Kuper, and P. Revesz. Constraint query languages. *Journal of Computer and System Sciences*, 51:26–52, 1995. Extended abstract in *ACM Symposium on Principles of Database Systems*, pages 299–313, 1990.

50. M. Karpinski and A. Macintyre. Approximating the volume of general Pfaffian bodies. In *Structures in Logic and Computer Science: A Selection of Essays in Honor of A. Ehrenfeucht*, Lecture Notes in Computer Science vol. 1261, pages 162–173, Springer 1997.

51. B. Khoussainov and A. Nerode. Automatic presentations of structures. In *Logic and Computational Complexity*, Lecture Notes in Computer Science vol. 960, pages 367–392, Springer 1994.

52. P. Koiran. Approximating the volume of definable sets. In *Symposium on Foundations of Computer Science*, pages 134–141, 1995.

53. B. Kuijpers, J. Paredaens, and J. Van den Bussche. Topological elementary equivalence of closed semi-algebraic sets in the real plane. *Journal of Symbolic Logic*, 65:1530–1555, 2000.

54. B. Kuijpers and J. Van den Bussche. On capturing first-order topological properties of planar spatial databases. In *Int. Conf. on Database Theory*, pages 187–198, 1999.

55. G. Kuper, L. Libkin and J. Paredaens, eds. *Constraint Databases*. Springer, 2000.
56. M. C. Laskowski. Vapnik-Chervonenkis classes of definable sets. *Journal of the London Mathematical Society*, 45:377–384, 1992.
57. L. Libkin. *Elements of Finite Model Theory*. Springer, 2004.
58. D. Marker, M. Messmer, and A. Pillay. *Model Theory of Fields*. Springer, 1996.
59. M. Otto and J. Van den Bussche. First-order queries on databases embedded in an infinite structure. *Information Processing Letters*, 60:37–41, 1996.
60. C. Papadimitriou, D. Suciu, and V. Vianu. Topological queries in spatial databases. *Journal of Computer and System Sciences*, 58:29–53, 1999.
61. J. Paredaens, J. Van den Bussche, and D. Van Gucht. First-order queries on finite structures over the reals. *SIAM Journal on Computing*, 27:1747–1763, 1998.
62. A. Pillay and C. Steinhorn. Definable sets in ordered structures. *Bulletin of the AMS*, 11:159–162, 1984.
63. A. Pillay and C. Steinhorn. Definable sets in ordered structures. III. *Transactions of the American Mathematical Society*, 309:469–476, 1988.
64. B. Poizat. *A Course in Model Theory*. Springer, 2000.
65. P. Revesz. Safe query languages for constraint databases. *ACM Transactions on Database Systems*, 23:58–99, 1998.
66. L. Segoufin. Personal communication, 2001.
67. L. Segoufin and V. Vianu. Querying spatial databases via topological invariants. *Journal of Computer and System Sciences*, 61:270–301, 2000.
68. S. Shelah. Stability, the f.c.p., and superstability. *Annals of Mathematical Logic*, 3:271–362, 1971.
69. J. Spencer. *The Strange Logic of Random Graphs*. Springer, 2001.
70. A. Stolboushkin and M. Taitslin. Finite queries do not have effective syntax. *Information and Computation*, 153:99–116, 1999.
71. A. Stolboushkin and M. Taitslin. Linear vs. order constraint queries over rational databases. In *ACM Symposium on Principles of Database Systems*, pages 17–27, 1999.
72. A. Stolboushkin and M. Taitslin. Safe stratified datalog with integer order does not have syntax. *ACM Transactions on Database Systems*, 23:100–109, 1998.
73. J. D. Ullman and J. Widom. *A First Course in Database Systems*. Prentice-Hall, 1997.
74. L. van den Dries. Remarks on Tarski's problem concerning (R,+,*,exp). In *Logic Colloquium 82*, pages 97–121, North-Holland, 1984.
75. L. van den Dries. *Tame Topology and O-Minimal Structures*. Cambridge University Press, 1998.
76. L. Vandeurzen, M. Gyssens, and D. Van Gucht. An expressive language for linear spatial database queries. In *ACM Symposium on Principles of Database Systems*, pages 109–118, 1998.
77. L. Vandeurzen, M. Gyssens and D. Van Gucht. On the expressiveness of linear-constraint query languages for spatial databases. *Theoretical Computer Science* 254:423–463, 2001.
78. M. Y. Vardi. The decision problem for database dependencies. *Information Processing Letters*, 12:251–254, 1981.
79. A. J. Wilkie. Model completeness results for expansions of the ordered field of real numbers by restricted Pfaffian functions and the exponential function. *Journal of the American Mathematical Society*, 9:1051–1094, 1996.
80. M. Yannakakis. Personal communication, 1999.

6

A Logical Approach to Constraint Satisfaction

Phokion G. Kolaitis and Moshe Y. Vardi

6.1 Introduction

Since the early 1970s, researchers in artificial intelligence (AI) have investigated a class of combinatorial problems that have become known, collectively, as the CONSTRAINT-SATISFACTION problem (CSP). The input to such a problem consists of a set of variables, a set of possible values for the variables, and a set of constraints between the variables; the question is to determine whether there is an assignment of values to the variables that satisfies the given constraints. The study of constraint satisfaction occupies a prominent place in artificial intelligence, because many problems that arise in various areas can be modeled as constraint-satisfaction problems in a natural way; these areas include Boolean satisfiability, temporal reasoning, belief maintenance, machine vision, and scheduling (see [20, 50, 56, 64]). In its full generality, constraint satisfaction is an NP-complete problem. For this reason, researchers in artificial intelligence have pursued both heuristics for constraint-satisfaction problems and tractable cases obtained by imposing various restrictions on the input (see [20, 24, 34, 54, 58]).

Over the past decade, it has become clear that there is an intimate connection between constraint satisfaction and various problems in database theory and finite-model theory. The goal of this chapter is to describe several such connections. We start in Sect. 6.2 by defining the constraint-satisfaction problem and showing how it can be phrased also as a homomorphism problem, a conjunctive-query evaluation problem, or a join-evaluation problem. In Sect. 6.3, we discuss the computational complexity of constraint satisfaction and show that it can be studied from two perspectives, a uniform perspective and a nonuniform perspective. We relate both perspectives to the study of the computational complexity of query evaluation. In Sect. 6.4, we focus on the nonuniform case and describe a Dichotomy Conjecture, asserting that every nonuniform constraint-satisfaction problem is either in PTIME or NP-complete. In Sect. 6.5, we examine the complexity of nonuniform constraint satisfaction from a logical perspective and show that it is related to the data complexity of a fragment of existential second-order logic. We continue in Sect. 6.6, where we offer a logical approach, via definability in Datalog, to establishing the tractability of nonuniform constraint-satisfaction problems. In Sect. 6.7, we leverage the connection between Datalog and certain pebble games, and show how these pebble games offer an algorithmic approach to solving uniform constraint-satisfaction problems. In Sect. 6.8, we relate these pebble games to consistency properties of constraint-satisfaction instances, a well-known approach in constraint solving. Finally, in Sect. 6.9, we show how the same pebble games can be used to identify large "islands of tractability" in the constraint-satisfaction terrain that are based on the concept of bounded treewidth.

Much of the logical machinery used in this chapter is described in detail in Chap. 2. For a book-length treatment of constraint satisfaction from the perspective of graph homomorphism, see [44]. Two books on constraint programming and constraint processing are [3, 23].

6.2 Preliminaries

The standard terminology in AI formalizes an instance $\mathcal{P}$ of constraint satisfaction as a triple $(V, D, \mathcal{C})$, where

- V is a set of variables;
- D is a set of values, referred to as the *domain*;
- $\mathcal{C}$ is a collection of *constraints* $C_1, \ldots, C_q$, where each constraint C_i is a pair $(\mathbf{t}, R)$, and where $\mathbf{t}$ is a k-tuple over V, $k \geq 1$, referred to as the *scope* of the constraint, and R is a k-relation on D.

A *solution* of such an instance is a mapping $h : V \to D$ such that, for each constraint $(\mathbf{t}, R)$ in $\mathcal{C}$, we have that $h(\mathbf{t}) \in R$, where h is defined on tuples componentwise, that is, if $\mathbf{t} = (a_1, \ldots, a_k)$, then $h(\mathbf{t}) = (h(a_1), \ldots, h(a_k))$. The CONSTRAINT-SATISFACTION problem asks whether a given instance is *solvable*, i.e., whether it has a solution. Note that, without loss of generality, we may assume that all constraints $(\mathbf{t}, R_i)$ involving the same scope $\mathbf{t}$ have been consolidated into a single constraint $(\mathbf{t}, R)$, where R is the intersection of all relations R_i constraining $\mathbf{t}$. Thus, we can assume that each tuple $\mathbf{t}$ of variables occurs at most once in the collection $\mathcal{C}$.

Consider the Boolean satisfiability problem 3-SAT: given a 3CNF-formula φ with variables $x_1, \ldots, x_n$ and clauses $c_1, \ldots, c_m$, is φ satisfiable? Such an instance of 3-SAT can be thought of as a CONSTRAINT-SATISFACTION instance in which the set of variables is $V = \{x_1, \ldots, x_n\}$, the domain is $D = \{0, 1\}$, and the constraints are determined by the clauses of φ. For example, a clause of the form $(\neg x \vee \neg y \vee z)$ gives rise to the constraint $((x, y, z), \{0, 1\}^3 - \{(1, 1, 0)\})$. In an analogous manner, 3-COLORABILITY can be modeled as a CONSTRAINT-SATISFACTION problem. Indeed, an instance

$\mathbf{G} = (V, E)$ of 3-COLORABILITY can be thought of as a CONSTRAINT-SATISFACTION instance in which the set of variables is the set V of the nodes of the graph $\mathbf{G}$, the domain is the set $D = \{r, b, g\}$ of three colors, and the constraints are the pairs $((u, v), Q)$, where $(u, v) \in E$ and $Q = \{(r, b)(b, r), (r, g)(g, r), (b, g)(g, b)\}$ is the disequality relation on D.

Let $\mathbf{A}$ and $\mathbf{B}$ be two relational structures[1] over the same vocabulary. A *homomorphism* h from $\mathbf{A}$ to $\mathbf{B}$ is a mapping $h : A \to B$ from the universe A of $\mathbf{A}$ to the universe B of $\mathbf{B}$ such that, for every relation $R^{\mathbf{A}}$ of $\mathbf{A}$ and every tuple $(a_1, \ldots, a_k) \in R^{\mathbf{A}}$, we have that $(h(a_1), \ldots, h(a_k)) \in R^{\mathbf{B}}$. The existence of a homomorphism from $\mathbf{A}$ to $\mathbf{B}$ is denoted by $\mathbf{A} \to \mathbf{B}$, or by $\mathbf{A} \to^h \mathbf{B}$, when we want to name the homomorphism h explicitly. An important observation made in [29][2] is that every such constraint-satisfaction instance $\mathcal{P} = (V, D, \mathcal{C})$ can be viewed as an instance of the HOMOMORPHISM problem, asking whether there is a homomorphism between two structures $\mathbf{A}_{\mathcal{P}}$ and $\mathbf{B}_{\mathcal{P}}$ that are obtained from $\mathcal{P}$ in the following way:

- The universe of $\mathbf{A}_{\mathcal{P}}$ is V and the universe of $\mathbf{B}_{\mathcal{P}}$ is D;
- The relations of $\mathbf{B}_{\mathcal{P}}$ are the distinct relations R occurring in $\mathcal{C}$;
- The relations of $\mathbf{A}_{\mathcal{P}}$ are defined as follows: for each distinct relation R on D occurring in $\mathcal{C}$, we have the relation $R^{\mathbf{A}} = \{\mathbf{t} : (\mathbf{t}, R) \in \mathcal{C}\}$. Thus, $R^{\mathbf{A}}$ consists of all scopes associated with R.

We call $(\mathbf{A}_{\mathcal{P}}, \mathbf{B}_{\mathcal{P}})$ the *homomorphism instance* of $\mathcal{P}$. Conversely, it is also clear that every instance of the homomorphism problem between two structures $\mathbf{A}$ and $\mathbf{B}$ can be viewed as a constraint-satisfaction instance $\mathrm{CSP}(\mathbf{A}, \mathbf{B})$ by simply "breaking up" each relation $R^{\mathbf{A}}$ on $\mathbf{A}$ as follows: we generate a constraint $(\mathbf{t}, R^{\mathbf{B}})$ for each $\mathbf{t} \in R^{\mathbf{A}}$. We call $\mathrm{CSP}(\mathbf{A}, \mathbf{B})$ the *constraint-satisfaction instance* of $(\mathbf{A}, \mathbf{B})$. Thus, as pointed out in [29], the constraint-satisfaction problem can be identified with the homomorphism problem.

To illustrate the passage from the constraint-satisfaction problem to the homomorphism problem, let us consider 3-SAT. A 3CNF-formula φ with variables $x_1, \ldots, x_n$ and clauses $c_1, \ldots, c_m$ gives rise to a homomorphism instance $(\mathbf{A}_{\varphi}, \mathbf{B}_{\varphi})$, defined as follows:

- $\mathbf{A}_{\varphi} = (\{x_1, \ldots, x_n\}, R_0^{\varphi}, R_1^{\varphi}, R_2^{\varphi}, R_3^{\varphi})$, where R_i^{φ} is the ternary relation consisting of all triples (x, y, z) of variables that occur in a clause of φ with i negated literals, $0 \le i \le 3$; for instance, R_2^{φ} consists of all triples (x, y, z) of variables such that $(\neg x \vee \neg y \vee z)$ is a clause of φ (here, we assume without loss of generality that the negated literals precede the positive literals).
- $\mathbf{B}_{\varphi} = (\{0, 1\}, R_0, R_1, R_2, R_3)$, where R_i consists of all triples that satisfy a 3-clause in which the first i literals are negated; for instance, $R_2 = \{0, 1\}^3 - \{1, 1, 0\}$.

Note that $\mathbf{B}_{\varphi}$ does not depend on φ. It is clear that φ is satisfiable if and only if there is a homomorphism from $\mathbf{A}_{\varphi}$ to $\mathbf{B}_{\varphi}$ (in symbols, $\mathbf{A}_{\varphi} \to \mathbf{B}_{\varphi}$).

---

[1] We consider only finite structures in this chapter.

[2] An early version appeared in [30].

As another example, 3-COLORABILITY is equivalent to the problem of deciding whether there is a homomorphism h from a given graph $\mathbf{G}$ to the complete graph $\mathbf{K}_3 = (\{r, b, g\}, \{(r, b)(b, r), (r, g)(g, r), (b, g)(g, b)\})$ with three nodes. More generally, k-COLORABILITY, $k \geq 2$, amounts to the existence of a homomorphism from a given graph $\mathbf{G}$ to the complete graph $\mathbf{K}_k$ with k nodes (also known as the k-clique).

Numerous other important NP-complete problems can be viewed as special cases of the HOMOMORPHISM problem (and, hence, also of the CONSTRAINT-SATISFACTION problem). For example, consider the CLIQUE problem: given a graph $\mathbf{G}$ and an integer k, does $\mathbf{G}$ contain a clique of size k? Considered as a HOMOMORPHISM instance this is equivalent to asking if there is a homomorphism from the complete graph $\mathbf{K}_k$ to $\mathbf{G}$. Considered as a CONSTRAINT-SATISFACTION instance, the set of variables is $\{1, 2, \ldots, k\}$, the domain is the set V of nodes of $\mathbf{G}$, and the constraints are the pairs $((i, j), E)$ such that $i \neq j$, $1 \leq i, j \leq k$, and E is the edge relation of $\mathbf{G}$. For another example, consider the HAMILTONICITY problem: given a graph $\mathbf{G} = (\mathbf{V}, \mathbf{E})$, does it have a Hamiltonian cycle? This is equivalent to asking if there is a homomorphism from the structure $(V, C_V, \neq)$ to the structure $(V, E, \neq)$, where C_V is some cycle on the set V of nodes of $\mathbf{G}$ and $\neq$ is the disequality relation on V. The NP-completeness of the HOMOMORPHISM problem was pointed out explicitly in [53]. In this chapter, we use both the traditional AI formulation of constraint satisfaction and the formulation in terms of the HOMOMORPHISM problem, as each has its own advantages.

It turns out that in both formulations constraint satisfaction can be expressed as a database-theoretic problem. We start with the homomorphism formulation, which is intimately related to *conjunctive-query evaluation* [48]. A *conjunctive query* Q of arity n is a query definable by a positive existential first-order formula $\varphi(X_1, \ldots, X_n)$ that has conjunction as its only propositional connective, that is, by a formula of the form

$$\exists Z_1 \ldots \exists Z_m \psi(X_1, \ldots, X_n, Z_1, \ldots, Z_m),$$

where $\psi(X_1, \ldots, X_n, Z_1, \ldots, Z_m)$ is a conjunction of (positive) atomic formulas. The free variables $X_1, \ldots, X_n$ of the defining formula are called the *distinguished variables* of Q. Such a conjunctive query is usually written as a rule, whose head is $Q(X_1, \ldots, X_n)$ and whose body is $\psi(X_1, \ldots, X_n, Z_1, \ldots, Z_m)$. For example, the formula

$$\exists Z_1 \exists Z_2 (P(X_1, Z_1, Z_2) \wedge R(Z_2, Z_3) \wedge R(Z_3, X_2))$$

defines a binary conjunctive query Q, which becomes, in the form of a rule,

$$Q(X_1, X_2) :\text{-} P(X_1, Z_1, Z_2), R(Z_2, Z_3), R(Z_3, X_2).$$

If a formula defining a conjunctive query Q has no free variables (i.e., if it is a sentence), then Q is a *Boolean* conjunctive query. For example, the sentence

$$\exists Z_1 \exists Z_2 \exists Z_3 (E(Z_1, Z_2) \wedge E(Z_2, Z_3) \wedge E(Z_3, Z_1))$$

defines the Boolean conjunctive query "is there a cycle of length 3?".

If D is a database and Q is a n-ary query, then $Q(D)$ is the n-ary relation on D obtained by evaluating the query Q on D, that is, the collection of all n-tuples from D that satisfy the query (see Chap. 2). The CONJUNCTIVE-QUERY EVALUATION problem asks: given a n-ary query Q, a database D, and an n-tuple $\mathbf{a}$ from D, is $\mathbf{a} \in Q(D)$? Let Q_1 and Q_2 be two n-ary queries that have the same tuple of distinguished variables. We say that Q_1 is *contained in* Q_2, and write $Q_1 \subseteq Q_2$, if $Q_1(D) \subseteq Q_2(D)$ for every database D. The CONJUNCTIVE-QUERY CONTAINMENT problem asks: given two conjunctive queries Q_1 and Q_2, is $Q_1 \subseteq Q_2$? These concepts can be defined for Boolean conjunctive queries in an analogous manner. In particular, if Q is a Boolean query and D is a database, then $Q(D) = 1$ if D satisfies Q; otherwise, $Q(D) = 0$. Moreover, the containment problem for Boolean queries Q_1 and Q_2 is equivalent to asking whether Q_1 logically implies Q_2.

It is well known that conjunctive-query containment can be reformulated both as a CONJUNCTIVE-QUERY EVALUATION problem and as a HOMO-MORPHISM problem. What links these problems together is the *canonical database* D^Q associated with Q. This database is defined as follows. Each variable occurring in Q is considered a distinct element in the universe of D^Q. Every predicate in the body of Q is a predicate of D^Q as well; moreover, for every distinguished variable X_i of Q, there is a distinct monadic predicate P_i (not occurring in Q). Every subgoal in the body of Q gives rise to a tuple in the corresponding predicate of D^Q; moreover, if X_i is a distinguished variable of Q, then $P_i(X_i)$ is also a (monadic) tuple of D^Q. Thus, returning to the preceding example, the canonical database of the conjunctive query $\exists Z_1 \exists Z_2 (P(X_1, Z_1, Z_2) \wedge R(Z_2, Z_3) \wedge R(Z_3, X_2))$ consists of the facts $P(X_1, Z_1, Z_2)$, $R(Z_2, Z_3)$, $R(Z_3, X_2)$, $P_1(X_1)$, $P_2(X_2)$. The relationship between conjunctive-query containment, conjunctive-query evaluation, and homomorphisms is provided by the following classical result, due to Chandra and Merlin.

Theorem 6.2.1. [11] *Let Q_1 and Q_2 be two conjunctive queries that have the same tuple $(X_1, \ldots, X_n)$ of distinguished variables. The following statements are then equivalent:*

- $Q_1 \subseteq Q_2$.
- $(X_1, \ldots, X_n) \in Q_2(D^{Q_1})$.
- *There is a homomorphism $h : D^{Q_2} \to D^{Q_1}$.*

It follows that the HOMOMORPHISM problem can be viewed as a CONJUNCTIVE-QUERY EVALUATION problem or as a CONJUNCTIVE-QUERY CONTAINMENT problem. For this purpose, for a structure $\mathbf{A}$, we view the universe $A = \{X_1, \ldots, X_n\}$ of $\mathbf{A}$ as a set of individual variables and associate with $\mathbf{A}$ the Boolean conjunctive query $\exists X_1 \ldots \exists X_n \wedge_{\mathbf{t} \in R^{\mathbf{A}}} R(\mathbf{t})$; we call this query the *canonical conjunctive query* of $\mathbf{A}$ and denote it by $Q_\mathbf{A}$. It is clear that $\mathbf{A}$ is isomorphic to the canonical database associated with $Q_\mathbf{A}$.

Corollary 6.2.2. *Let $\mathbf{A}$ and $\mathbf{B}$ be two structures over the same vocabulary. The following statements are then equivalent:*

- $\mathbf{A} \to \mathbf{B}$.
- $\mathbf{B} \models Q_\mathbf{A}$.
- $Q_\mathbf{B} \subseteq Q_\mathbf{A}$.

As an illustration, we have that a graph $\mathbf{G}$ is 3-colorable iff $\mathbf{K}_3 \models Q_\mathbf{G}$ iff $Q_{\mathbf{K}_3} \subseteq Q_\mathbf{G}$.

A *relational join*, denoted by the symbol $\bowtie$, is a conjunctive query with no existentially quantified variables. Thus, relational-join evaluation is a special case of conjunctive-query evaluation. For example, $E(Z_1, Z_2) \wedge E(Z_2, Z_3) \wedge E(Z_3, Z_1)$ is a relational join that, when evaluated on a graph $\mathbf{G} = (\mathbf{V}, \mathbf{E})$, returns all triples of nodes forming a 3-cycle. There is a well-known connection between the traditional AI formulation of constraint satisfaction and the formulation in terms of relational-join evaluation that we describe next. Suppose we are given a CONSTRAINT-SATISFACTION instance $(V, D, \mathcal{C})$. We can assume without loss of generality that, in every constraint $(\mathbf{t}, R) \in \mathcal{C}$, the elements in $\mathbf{t}$ are distinct. (Suppose to the contrary that $t_i = t_j$. Then we can delete from R every tuple in which the ith and jth entries disagree, and then project out that j-th column from $\mathbf{t}$ and R.) We can thus view every element of V as a relational *attribute*, every tuple of distinct elements of V as a *relational schema*, and every constraint $(\mathbf{t}, R)$ as a relation R over the schema $\mathbf{t}$ (see [1]). It now follows from the definition of constraint satisfaction that CSP can be viewed as a relational-join evaluation problem.

Proposition 6.2.3. [6, 42] *A constraint-satisfaction instance $(V, D, \mathcal{C})$ is solvable if and only if $\bowtie_{(\mathbf{t}, R) \in \mathcal{C}} R$ is nonempty.*

Note that Proposition 6.2.3 is essentially the same as Corollary 6.2.2. Indeed, the condition $\mathbf{B} \models Q_\mathbf{A}$ amounts to the nonemptiness of the relational join obtained from $Q_\mathbf{A}$ by dropping all existential quantifiers and using the relations from $\mathbf{B}$ as interpretations of the relational symbols in $Q_\mathbf{A}$. Moreover, the homomorphisms from $\mathbf{A}$ to $\mathbf{B}$ are precisely the tuples in the relational join associated with the constraint-satisfaction instance CSP($\mathbf{A}, \mathbf{B}$).

6.3 The Computational Complexity of Constraint Satisfaction

The CONSTRAINT-SATISFACTION problem is NP-complete, because it is clearly in NP and also contains NP-hard problems as special cases, including 3-SAT, 3-COLORABILITY, and CLIQUE. As explained in Garey and Johnson's classic monograph [36], one of the main ways to cope with NP-completeness is to identify polynomial-time solvable cases of the problem at hand that are obtained by imposing restrictions on the possible inputs. For instance, HORN 3-SAT, the restriction of 3-SAT to Horn 3CNF-formulas, is solvable in polynomial-time using a unit-propagation algorithm. Similarly, it is known that 3-COLORABILITY restricted to graphs of bounded treewidth is solvable in polynomial time (see [26]). In the case of constraint satisfaction, the pursuit of tractable cases has evolved over the years from the discovery of isolated cases to the discovery of large "islands of tractability" of constraint satisfaction. In what follows, we give an account of some of the progress made in this area. Using the fact that the CONSTRAINT-SATISFACTION problem can be identified with the HOMOMORPHISM problem, we begin by introducing some terminology and notation that will enable us to formalize the concept of an "island of tractability" of constraint satisfaction.

In general, an instance of the HOMOMORPHISM problem consists of two relational structures **A** and **B**. Thus, all restricted cases of this problem can be obtained by imposing restrictions on the input structures **A** and **B**.

Definition 6.3.1. *Let $\mathcal{A}$, $\mathcal{B}$ be two classes of relational structures. We write* $\mathrm{CSP}(\mathcal{A}, \mathcal{B})$ *to denote the restriction of the* HOMOMORPHISM *problem to input structures from $\mathcal{A}$ and $\mathcal{B}$. In other words,*

$$\mathrm{CSP}(\mathcal{A}, \mathcal{B}) = \{(\mathbf{A}, \mathbf{B}) : \mathbf{A} \in \mathcal{A}, \ \mathbf{B} \in \mathcal{B} \text{ and } \mathbf{A} \to \mathbf{B}\}.$$

An island of tractability *of constraint satisfaction is a pair $(\mathcal{A}, \mathcal{B})$ of classes of relational structures such that* $\mathrm{CSP}(\mathcal{A}, \mathcal{B})$ *is in the complexity class* PTIME *of all decision problems solvable in polynomial time.*

(A more general definition of islands of tractability of constraint satisfaction would consider classes of pairs $(\mathbf{A}, \mathbf{B})$ of structures, see [28]. We do not pursue this more general definition here.)

The ultimate goal in the pursuit of islands of tractability of constraint satisfaction is to identify or characterize classes $\mathcal{A}$ and $\mathcal{B}$ of relational structures such that $\mathrm{CSP}(\mathcal{A}, \mathcal{B})$ is in PTIME. The basic starting point in this investigation is to consider the cases in which one of the two classes $\mathcal{A}$, $\mathcal{B}$ is as small as possible, while the other is as large as possible. This amounts to considering the cases in which one of $\mathcal{A}$, $\mathcal{B}$ is the class *All* of all relational structures over some arbitrary, but fixed, relational vocabulary, while the other is a singleton, consisting of some fixed structure over that vocabulary. Thus, the starting point of the investigation is to determine, for fixed relational structures $\mathbf{A}, \mathbf{B}$, the computational complexity of the decision problems $\mathrm{CSP}(\{\mathbf{A}\}, \mathit{All})$ and $\mathrm{CSP}(\mathit{All}, \{\mathbf{B}\})$.

Clearly, for each fixed **A**, the decision problem $\mathrm{CSP}(\{\mathbf{A}\}, \mathit{All})$ can be solved in polynomial time, because, given a structure **B**, the existence of a homomorphism from **A** to **B** can be checked by testing all functions h from the universe A of **A** to the universe B of **B** (the total number of such functions is $|B|^{|A|}$, which is a polynomial number in the size of the structure $\mathbf{B}$ when $\mathbf{A}$ is fixed). Thus, having a singleton structure "on the left' is of little interest.

At the other extreme, however, the situation is quite different, since the computational complexity of CSP($All, \{\mathbf{B}\}$) may very well depend on the particular structure $\mathbf{B}$. Indeed, CSP($All, \{\mathbf{K}_3\}$) is NP-complete, because it is the 3-COLORABILITY problem; in contrast, CSP($All, \{\mathbf{K}_2\}$) is in P, because it is the 2-COLORABILITY problem. For simplicity, in what follows, for every fixed structure $\mathbf{B}$, we define CSP($\mathbf{B}$) = CSP($All, \{\mathbf{B}\}$) and call this the *nonuniform* CONSTRAINT-SATISFACTION problem associated with $\mathbf{B}$. For such problems, we refer to $\mathbf{B}$ as the *template*. Thus, the first major goal in the study of the computational complexity of constraint satisfaction is to identify those templates $\mathbf{B}$ for which CSP($\mathbf{B}$) is in PTIME. This goal gives rise to an important open decision problem:

The TRACTABILITY-CLASSIFICATION problem: Given a relational structure $\mathbf{B}$, decide whether CSP($\mathbf{B}$) is in PTIME.

In addition to the family of nonuniform constraint-satisfaction problems CSP($\mathbf{B}$), where $\mathbf{B}$ is a relational structure, we also study decision problems of the form CSP($\mathcal{A}, All$), where $\mathcal{A}$ is a class of structures. We refer to such problems as *uniform* CONSTRAINT-SATISFACTION problems.

It is illuminating to consider the complexity of uniform and nonuniform constraint satisfaction from the perspective of query evaluation. As argued in [67] (see Chap. 2), there are three ways to measure the complexity of evaluating queries (we focus here on Boolean queries) expressible in a query language L:

- The *combined complexity* of L is the complexity of the following decision problem: given an L-query Q and a structure $\mathbf{A}$, does $\mathbf{A} \models Q$? In symbols,

$$\{\langle Q, \mathbf{A} \rangle : Q \in L \text{ and } \mathbf{A} \models Q\}.$$

- The *expression complexity* of L is the complexity of the following decision problems, one for each fixed structure $\mathbf{A}$:

$$\{Q : Q \in L \text{ and } \mathbf{A} \models Q\}.$$

- The *data complexity* of L is the complexity of the following decision problems, one for each fixed query $Q \in L$:

$$\{\mathbf{A} : \mathbf{A} \models Q\}.$$

As discussed in Chap. 2, the data complexity of first-order logic is in LOGSPACE, which means that, for each first-order query Q, the problem $\{\mathbf{A} : \mathbf{A} \models Q\}$ is in LOGSPACE. In contrast, the combined complexity for first-order logic is PSPACE-complete. Furthermore, the expression complexity for first-order logic is also PSPACE-complete. In fact, for all but trivial structures $\mathbf{A}$, the problem $\{Q : Q \in FO \text{ and } \mathbf{A} \models Q\}$ is PSPACE-complete. This exponential gap between data complexity, on one hand, and combined and expression complexity, on the other hand, is typical [67]. For conjunctive queries, on the other hand, both the combined complexity and the expression complexity are NP-complete.

Consider now the uniform constraint-satisfaction problem $\mathrm{CSP}(\mathcal{A}, All) = \{(\mathbf{A}, \mathbf{B}) : \mathbf{A} \in \mathcal{A}, \text{ and } \mathbf{A} \rightarrow \mathbf{B}\}$, where $\mathcal{A}$ is a class of structures. By Corollary 6.2.2, we have that

$$\mathrm{CSP}(\mathcal{A}, All) = \{(\mathbf{A}, \mathbf{B}) : \mathbf{A} \in \mathcal{A}, \ \mathbf{B} \text{ is a structure and } \ \mathbf{B} \models Q_{\mathbf{A}}\}.$$

Thus, studying the complexity of uniform constraint satisfaction amounts to studying the combined complexity for a class of conjunctive queries, as considered, for example, in [12, 39, 62]. In contrast, consider the nonuniform CONSTRAINT-SATISFACTION problem $\mathrm{CSP}(\mathbf{B}) = \{\mathbf{A} : \mathbf{A} \rightarrow \mathbf{B}\}$. By Corollary 6.2.2, we have that $\mathrm{CSP}(\mathbf{B}) = \{\mathbf{A} : \mathbf{B} \models Q_{\mathbf{A}}\}$. Thus, studying the complexity of nonuniform constraint satisfaction amounts to studying the expression complexity of conjunctive queries with respect to different structures. This is a problem that has not been studied in the context of database theory.

6.4 Nonuniform Constraint Satisfaction

The first major result in the study of nonuniform constraint-satisfaction problems was obtained by Schaefer [63], who, in effect, classified the computational complexity of all Boolean nonuniform constraint-satisfaction problems. A *Boolean* structure is simply a relational structure with a 2-element universe, that is, a structure of the form $\mathbf{B} = (\{0, 1\}, R_1^{\mathbf{B}}, \ldots, R_m^{\mathbf{B}})$. A *Boolean nonuniform constraint-satisfaction problem* is a problem of the form $\mathrm{CSP}(\mathbf{B})$ with a Boolean template $\mathbf{B}$. These problems are also known as GENERALIZED-SATISFIABILITY problems, because they can be viewed as variants of Boolean-satisfiability problems in which the formulas are conjunctions of generalized connectives [36]. In particular, they contain the well-known problems k-SAT, $k \geq 2$, 1-IN-3-SAT, POSITIVE 1-IN-3-SAT, NOT-ALL-EQUAL 3-SAT, and MONOTONE 3-SAT as special cases. For example, as seen earlier, 3-SAT is $\mathrm{CSP}(\mathbf{B})$, where $\mathbf{B} = (\{0, 1\}, R_0, R_1, R_2, R_3)$ and R_i is the set of all triples that satisfy a 3-clause in which the first i literals are negated, for $i = 0, 1, 2, 3$ (thus, $R_0 = \{0, 1\}^3 - \{(0, 0, 0)\}$). Similarly, MONOTONE 3-SAT is $\mathrm{CSP}(\mathbf{B})$, where $\mathbf{B} = (\{0, 1\}, R_0, R_3)$.

Ladner [51] showed that if PTIME $\neq$ NP, then there are decision problems in NP that neither are NP-complete nor belong to PTIME. Such problems are called *intermediate* problems. Consequently, it is conceivable that a given family of NP-problems contains intermediate problems. Schaefer [63], however, showed that the family of all Boolean nonuniform constraint-satisfaction problems contains no intermediate problems.

Theorem 6.4.1. (Schaefer's Dichotomy Theorem [63])

- *If* $\mathbf{B} = (\{0,1\}, R_1^{\mathbf{B}}, \ldots, R_m^{\mathbf{B}})$ *is a Boolean structure, then either* $\mathrm{CSP}(\mathbf{B})$ *is in* PTIME *or* $\mathrm{CSP}(\mathbf{B})$ *is* NP*-complete.*
- *The* TRACTABILITY-CLASSIFICATION *problem for Boolean structures is decidable; in fact, there is a polynomial-time algorithm to decide, given a Boolean structure* $\mathbf{B}$*, whether* $\mathrm{CSP}(\mathbf{B})$ *is in* PTIME *or is* NP*-complete.*

Schaefer's Dichotomy Theorem can be described pictorially as in Fig. 6.1.

Schaefer [63] actually showed that there are exactly six types of Boolean structures such that $\mathrm{CSP}(\mathbf{B})$ is in PTIME, and provided explicit descriptions of them. Specifically, he showed that $\mathrm{CSP}(\mathbf{B})$ is in PTIME precisely when at least one of the following six conditions is satisfied:

- Every relation $R_i^{\mathbf{B}}$, $1 \leq i \leq m$, of $\mathbf{B}$ is 0-*valid*, that is, $R_i^{\mathbf{B}}$ contains the all-zeros tuple $(0, \ldots, 0)$.
- Every relation $R_i^{\mathbf{B}}$, $1 \leq i \leq m$, of $\mathbf{B}$ is 1-*valid*, that is, $R_i^{\mathbf{B}}$ contains the all-ones tuple $(1, \ldots, 1)$.
- Every relation $R_i^{\mathbf{B}}$, $1 \leq i \leq m$, of $\mathbf{B}$ is *bijunctive*, that is, $R_i^{\mathbf{B}}$ is the set of truth assignments satisfying some 2-CNF formula.
- Every relation $R_i^{\mathbf{B}}$, $1 \leq i \leq m$, of $\mathbf{B}$ is *Horn*, that is, $R_i^{\mathbf{B}}$ is the set of truth assignments satisfying some Horn formula.
- Every relation $R_i^{\mathbf{B}}$, $1 \leq i \leq m$, of $\mathbf{B}$ is *dual Horn*, that is, $R_i^{\mathbf{B}}$ is the set of truth assignments satisfying some dual Horn formula.
- Every relation $R_i^{\mathbf{B}}$, $1 \leq i \leq m$, of $\mathbf{B}$ is *affine*, that is, $R_i^{\mathbf{B}}$ is the set of solutions to a system of linear equations over the two-element field.

Schaefer's Dichotomy Theorem established a dichotomy and a decidable classification of the complexity of $\mathrm{CSP}(\mathbf{B})$ for Boolean templates $\mathbf{B}$. After that result, Hell and Nešetřil [43] established a dichotomy theorem for $\mathrm{CSP}(\mathbf{B})$ problems in which the template $\mathbf{B}$ is an *undirected* graph: if $\mathbf{B}$ is bipartite, then $\mathrm{CSP}(\mathbf{B})$ is solvable in polynomial time; otherwise, $\mathrm{CSP}(\mathbf{B})$ is NP-complete. To illustrate this dichotomy theorem, let $\mathbf{C}_n$, $n \geq 3$, be a cycle with n elements. Then $\mathrm{CSP}(\mathbf{C}_n)$ is in PTIME if n is even, and is NP-complete if n is odd.

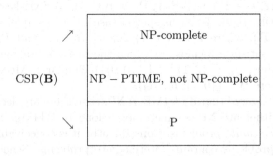

Fig. 6.1. Dichotomy Theorem

The preceding two dichotomy results raise the challenge of classifying the computational complexity of CSP(**B**) for arbitrary relational templates **B**. Addressing this question, Feder and Vardi formulated the following conjecture.

Conjecture 6.4.2. (**Dichotomy Conjecture** [29]) *If* $\mathbf{B} = (B, R_1^{\mathbf{B}}, \ldots, R_m^{\mathbf{B}})$ *is an arbitrary relational structure, then either* CSP(**B**) *is in* PTIME *or* CSP(**B**) *is* NP-complete.

In other words, the Dichotomy Conjecture says that the picture above describes the complexity of nonuniform constraint-satisfaction problems CSP(**B**) for arbitrary structures **B**. The basis for the conjecture is not only the evidence from Boolean constraint satisfaction and undirected constraint satisfaction, but also from our seeming inability to carry out the diagonalization argument of [51] using the constraint-satisfaction machinery [27].

The Dichotomy Conjecture inspired intensive research efforts that significantly advanced our understanding of the complexity of nonuniform constraint satisfaction. In particular, Bulatov confirmed two important cases of this conjecture. We say that a structure $\mathbf{B} = (B, R_1^{\mathbf{B}}, \ldots, R_m^{\mathbf{B}})$ is a *3-element* structure if B contains at most three elements. We say that **B** is *conservative* if all possible monadic relations on the universe are included, that is, every nonempty subset of B is one of the relations $R_i^{\mathbf{B}}$ of **B**.

Theorem 6.4.3. [8, 9] *If* **B** *a 3-element structure or a conservative structure, then either* CSP(**B**) *is in* PTIME *or* CSP(**B**) *is* NP-complete. *Moreover, in both cases the* TRACTABILITY-CLASSIFICATION *problem is decidable in polynomial time.*

In spite of the progress made, the Dichotomy Conjecture remains unresolved in general. The research efforts towards this conjecture, however, have also resulted in the discovery of broad sufficient conditions for tractability and intractability of nonuniform constraint satisfaction that have provided unifying explanations for numerous seemingly disparate tractability and intractability results, and have also led to the discovery of new islands of tractability of CSP(**B**). These broad sufficient conditions are based on concepts and techniques from two different areas: universal algebra and logic.

The approach via universal algebra yields sufficient conditions for tractability of CSP(**B**) in terms of *closure* properties of the relations in **B** under certain functions on its universe B. Let R be a n-ary relation on a set B and let $f : B^k \to B$ a k-ary function. We say that R *is closed under* f, if whenever $\mathbf{t_1} = (t_1^1, t_1^2, \ldots, t_1^n), \ldots, \mathbf{t_k} = (t_k^1, t_k^2, \ldots, t_k^n)$ are k (not necessarily distinct) tuples in R, then the tuple

$$(f(t_1^1, \ldots, t_k^1), f(t_1^2, \ldots, t_k^2), \ldots, f(t_1^n, \ldots, t_k^n))$$

is also in R. We say that $f : B^k \to B$ is a *polymorphism* of a structure $\mathbf{B} = (B, R_1, \ldots, R_m)$ if each of the relations R_j, $1 \leq j \leq m$, is closed under f. It is easy to see that f is a polymorphism of **B** if and only if f is a homomorphism from $\mathbf{B}^k$ to $\mathbf{B}$, where $\mathbf{B}^k$ is the kth *power* of $\mathbf{B}$. By definition, the kth power $\mathbf{B}^k$ is the structure $(B^k, R_1' \ldots, R_m')$ over the same vocabulary as $\mathbf{B}$ with universe B^k and relations R_j', $1 \leq j \leq m$, defined as follows: if R_j is of arity n, then $R_j'(\mathbf{s}_1, \ldots, \mathbf{s}_n)$ holds in $\mathbf{B}^k$ if and only if $R_j(s_1^i, \ldots, s_n^i)$ holds in $\mathbf{B}$ for $1 \leq i \leq n$.

We write $\mathrm{Pol}(\mathbf{B})$ for the set of all polymorphisms of $\mathbf{B}$. As it turns out, the complexity of $\mathrm{CSP}(\mathbf{B})$ is intimately connected to the kinds of functions that $\mathrm{Pol}(\mathbf{B})$ contains. This connection was first unveiled in [29], and explored in depth by Jeavons and his collaborators; for a recent survey, see [10]. In particular, they showed that if $\mathrm{Pol}(\mathbf{B_1}) = \mathrm{Pol}(\mathbf{B_2})$ for two structures $\mathbf{B_1}$ and $\mathbf{B_2}$ (over *finite* vocabularies), then $\mathrm{CSP}(\mathbf{B_1})$ and $\mathrm{CSP}(\mathbf{B_2})$ are polynomially reducible to each other. Thus, the polymorphisms of a template $\mathbf{B}$ characterize the complexity of $\mathrm{CSP}(\mathbf{B})$. The above-mentioned dichotomy results for 3-element and conservative constraint satisfaction are based on a rather deep analysis of the appropriate sets of polymorphisms.

6.5 Monotone Monadic SNP and Nonuniform Constraint Satisfaction

We discussed earlier how nonuniform constraint satisfaction is related to the study of the expression complexity of conjunctive queries. We now show that it can also be viewed as the study of the data complexity of second-order logic. This will suggest a way to identify islands of tractability via logic.

As described in Chaps. 2 and 3, existential second-order logic (ESO) defines, by Fagin's Theorem, precisely the complexity class NP. The class SNP (for *strict* NP) [46, 57] is a fragment of ESO, consisting of all existential second-order sentences with a universal first-order part, namely sentences of the form $(\exists S')(\forall \mathbf{x})\Phi(\mathbf{x}, S, S')$, where Φ is a first-order quantifier-free formula. We refer to the relations over the input vocabulary S as *input relations* and to the relations over the quantified vocabulary S' as *existential relations*. 3-SAT is an example of an SNP problem. The input structure consists of four ternary relations C_0, C_1, C_2, C_3, on the universe $\{0, 1\}$, where C_i corresponds to a clause with three variables, with the first i of them negated. There is a single existential monadic relation T describing a truth assignment. The condition that must be satisfied states that for all x_1, x_2, x_3, if $C_0(x_1, x_2, x_3)$ then $T(x_1)$ or $T(x_2)$ or $T(x_3)$, and similarly for the remaining C_i by negating $T(x_j)$ if $j \leq i$. Formally, we can express 3-SAT with the SNP sentence

$$(\exists T)(\forall x_1, x_2, x_3) \, ((C_0(x_1, x_2, x_3) \to T(x_1) \vee T(x_2) \vee T(x_3)) \wedge$$
$$(C_1(x_1, x_2, x_3) \to \neg T(x_1) \vee T(x_2) \vee T(x_3)) \wedge$$
$$(C_2(x_1, x_2, x_3) \to \neg T(x_1) \vee \neg T(x_2) \vee T(x_3)) \wedge$$
$$(C_3(x_1, x_2, x_3) \to \neg T(x_1) \vee \neg T(x_2) \vee \neg T(x_3))).$$

It is easy to see that $\mathrm{CSP}(\mathbf{B})$ is in SNP for each structure $\mathbf{B}$. For each element a in the universe of $\mathbf{B}$, we introduce an existentially quantified monadic relation T_a; intuitively, $T_a(x)$ indicates that a variable x has been assigned a value a by the homomorphism. The sentence $\varphi_{\mathbf{B}}$ says that the sets T_a cover all elements in the universe,[3] and that the tuples in the input relations satisfy the constraints imposed by the structure $\mathbf{B}$. Thus, if $R(a_1, \ldots, a_n)$ does *not* hold in $\mathbf{B}$, then $\varphi_{\mathbf{B}}$ contains the conjunct $\neg(R(x_1, \ldots, x_n) \wedge \bigwedge_{i=1}^{n} T_{a_i}(x_i))$. For example, 3-COLORABILITY over a binary input relation E can be expressed by the sentence

$$(\exists C_1, C_2, C_3)(\forall x, y) \, ((C_1(x) \vee C_2(x) \vee C_3(x)) \wedge$$
$$\neg(E(x,y) \wedge C_1(x) \wedge C_1(y)) \wedge$$
$$\neg(E(x,y) \wedge C_2(x) \wedge C_2(y)) \wedge$$
$$\neg(E(x,y) \wedge C_3(x) \wedge C_3(y))).$$

It follows that $\mathrm{CSP}(\mathbf{B}) = \{\mathbf{A} : \mathbf{A} \models \varphi_{\mathbf{B}}\}$. Thus, the study of the complexity of nonuniform constraint satisfaction can be viewed as the study of the *data complexity* of certain SNP sentences.

A close examination of $\varphi_{\mathbf{B}}$ above shows that it actually resides in a syntactic fragment of SNP. For *monotone* SNP, we require that all occurrences of an input relation C_i in Φ have the same polarity (the polarity of a relation is positive if it is contained in an even number of subformulas with a negation applied to it, and it is negative otherwise); by convention, we assume that this polarity is negative, so that the C_i can be interpreted as constraints, in the sense that imposing C_i on more elements of the input structure can only make the instance "less satisfiable". For *monadic* SNP, we require that the existential structure S' consist of monadic relations only. Normally we assume that the language contains also the equality relation, so both equalities and inequalities are allowed in Φ, unless we say *without inequality*, which means that the $\neq$ relation cannot be used (note that equalities can always be eliminated here). We refer to the class in which all restrictions hold, that is, monotone monadic SNP without inequality, as MMSNP. It is clear then that nonuniform constraint satisfaction can be expressed in MMSNP.

What is the precise relationship between nonuniform constraint satisfaction and MMSNP? It is easy to see that MMSNP is more expressive than nonuniform constraint satisfaction. The property asserting that the input graph is triangle-free is clearly in MMSNP (in fact, it can be expressed by a universal first-order sentence), but it can be easily shown that there is no graph $\mathbf{G}$ such that $\mathrm{CSP}(\mathbf{G})$ consists of all triangle-free graphs [29]. From a computational point of view, however, MMSNP and nonuniform constraint satisfaction turn out to be equivalent.

Theorem 6.5.1. [29] *Every problem in MMSNP is polynomially equivalent to* $\mathrm{CSP}(\mathbf{B})$ *for some template* $\mathbf{B}$. *The equivalence is obtained by a randomized Turing reduction*[4] *from CSP to MMSNP and by a deterministic Karp reduction from MMSNP to CSP.*

---

[3] It is not necessary to require disjointness.

[4] G. Kun has recently announced a derandomization of this reduction.

An immediate corollary is that the Dichotomy Conjecture holds for CSP if and only if it holds for MMSNP. At the same time, MMSNP seems to be a maximal class with this property. Specifically, any attempt to relax the syntactical restrictions of MMSNP yields a class that is polynomially equivalent to NP, and, consequently, a class for which the dichotomy fails.

Theorem 6.5.2. [29]

- *Every problem in NP has a polynomially equivalent problem in monotone monadic SNP with inequality.*
- *Every problem in NP has a polynomially equivalent problem in monadic SNP without inequality.*
- *Every problem in NP has a polynomially equivalent problem in monotone SNP without inequality.*

By Ladner's Theorem, it follows that if PTIME $\neq$ NP, then there are intermediate problems, which are neither in PTIME nor NP-complete, in each of monotone monadic SNP with inequality, monadic SNP without inequality, and monotone SNP without inequality. This is the sense in which MMSNP is a maximal class for which we would expect a dichotomy theorem to hold.

The fact that each constraint-satisfaction problem CSP($\mathbf{B}$) can be expressed by the MMSNP sentence $\varphi_\mathbf{B}$ suggests a way to identify templates $\mathbf{B}$ for which CSP($\mathbf{B}$) is tractable: characterize those templates $\mathbf{B}$ for which $\varphi_\mathbf{B}$ is equivalent to a sentence in a logic whose data complexity is in PTIME. We discuss this approach in the next section.

6.6 Datalog and Nonuniform Constraint Satisfaction

Consider all tractable problems of the form CSP($\mathbf{B}$). In principle, it is conceivable that every such problem requires a completely different algorithm. In practice, however, there seem to be two basic algorithmic approaches for solving tractable constraint-satisfaction problems: one based on a logical framework and one based on an algebraic framework.[5] Feder and Vardi [29] conjectured that these two algorithmic approaches cover all tractable constraint-satisfaction problems. Their group-theoretic approach, which extended the algorithm used to solve affine Boolean constraint-satisfaction problems [63], has been subsumed recently by a universal-algebraic approach [8, 9]. We discuss the logical approach here.

As described in Chap. 2, a Datalog program is a finite set of rules of the form $t_0 :\text{-} t_1, \ldots, t_m$, where each t_i is an atomic formula $R(x_1, \ldots, x_n)$. The relational predicates that occur in the heads of the rules are the *intensional database* predicates (IDBs), while all the others are the *extensional database*

---

[5] The two approaches, however, are not always cleanly separated; in fact, they can be fruitfully combined to yield new tractable classes; see [17].

predicates (EDBs). One of the IDBs is designated as the *goal* of the program. Note that IDBs may occur in the bodies of rules and, thus, a Datalog program is a recursive specification of the IDBs with a semantics obtained via least fixedpoints of monotone operators. Each Datalog program defines a query which, given a set of EDB predicates, returns the value of the goal predicate. Moreover, this query is computable in polynomial time, since the bottom-up evaluation of the least fixedpoint of the program terminates within a polynomial number of steps (in the size of the given EDBs). It follows that Datalog has data complexity in PTIME. Thus, expressibility in Datalog is a sufficient condition for tractability of a query. This suggests trying to identify those templates $\mathbf{B}$ for which the MMSNP sentence $\varphi_{\mathbf{B}}$ is equivalent to a Boolean Datalog query.

It should be noted, however, that Datalog queries are *preserved under homomorphisms*. This means that if $\mathbf{A} \to^h \mathbf{A}'$ and $t \in P(\mathbf{A})$ for a Datalog program M with goal predicate P, then $h(t) \in P(\mathbf{A}')$. In contrast, constraint-satisfaction problems are not preserved under homomorphisms, though their complements are. If $\mathbf{B}$ is a relational structure, then we write $\overline{\mathrm{CSP}(\mathbf{B})}$ for the *complement* of $\mathrm{CSP}(\mathbf{B})$, that is, the class of all structures $\mathbf{A}$ such that there is no homomorphism $h : \mathbf{A} \to \mathbf{B}$. If $\mathbf{A} \to^h \mathbf{A}'$ and $\mathbf{A} \in \mathrm{CSP}(\mathbf{B})$, then it does not follow that $\mathbf{A}' \in \mathrm{CSP}(\mathbf{B})$. On the other hand, if $\mathbf{A} \to^h \mathbf{A}'$ and $\mathbf{A} \in \overline{\mathrm{CSP}(\mathbf{B})}$, then $\mathbf{A}' \in \overline{\mathrm{CSP}(\mathbf{B})}$, since homomorphisms compose. Thus, rather then try to identify those templates $\mathbf{B}$ for which $\varphi_{\mathbf{B}}$ is equivalent to a Boolean Datalog query, we try to identify those templates $\mathbf{B}$ for which the negated sentence $\neg\varphi_{\mathbf{B}}$ is equivalent to a Boolean Datalog query.

Along this line of investigation, Feder and Vardi [29] provided a unifying explanation for the tractability of many nonuniform $\mathrm{CSP}(\mathbf{B})$ problems by showing that the complement of each of these problems is expressible in Datalog. It should be pointed out, however, that Datalog does not cover all tractable constraint-satisfaction problems. For example, it was shown in [29] that Datalog cannot express the complement of affine Boolean constraint-satisfaction problems; see also [5]. Affine Boolean constraint-satisfaction problems and their generalizations require algebraic techniques to establish their tractability [8, 29]).

For every positive integer k, let k-Datalog be the collection of all Datalog programs in which the body of every rule has at most k distinct variables and also the head of every rule has at most k variables (the variables of the body may be different from the variables of the head). For example, the query NON-2-COLORABILITY is expressible in 3-Datalog, since it is definable by the goal predicate Q of the following Datalog program, which asserts that a cycle of odd length exists:

$$P_1(X, Y) : - E(X, Y)$$
$$P_0(X, Y) : - P_1(X, Z), E(Z, Y)$$
$$P_1(X, Y) : - P_0(X, Z), E(Z, Y)$$
$$Q : - P_1(X, X).$$

The fact that expressibility in Datalog and, more specifically, expressibility in k-Datalog provide sufficient conditions for tractability gives rise to two classification problems:

- THE k-DATALOG-CLASSIFICATION problem: Given a relational structure **B** and $k > 1$, decide whether $\overline{\text{CSP}(\mathbf{B})}$ is expressible in k-Datalog?
- THE DATALOG-CLASSIFICATION problem: Given a relational structure **B**, decide whether $\overline{\text{CSP}(\mathbf{B})}$ is expressible in k-Datalog for some $k > 1$.

The universal-algebraic approach does offer some sufficient conditions for $\overline{\text{CSP}(\mathbf{B})}$ to be expressible in Datalog. We mention two examples here. A k-ary function $f : B^k \to B$ with $k \geq 3$ is a *near-unanimity function* if $f(a_1, \ldots, a_k) = b$, for every k-tuple $(a_1, \ldots, a_k)$ such that at least $k - 1$ of the a_i's are equal to b. Note that the ternary majority function from $\{0, 1\}^3$ to $\{0, 1\}$ is a near-unanimity function.

Theorem 6.6.1. [29] *Let* **B** *be relational structure, and let* $k \geq 3$. *If* Pol(**B**) *contains a k-ary near-unanimity function, then* $\overline{\text{CSP}(\mathbf{B})}$ *is expressible in k-Datalog.*

Since the number of k-ary functions over the universe B of **B** is finite, checking the condition of the preceding theorem for a given k is clearly decidable. It is not known, however, whether it is decidable to check, given **B**, whether Pol(**B**) contains a k-ary near-unanimity function for *some* k.

One special class of Datalog consists of those programs whose IDB predicates are all monadic. We refer to such Datalog programs as *monadic* Datalog programs. It can easily be seen that the Horn case of Boolean constraint satisfaction can be dealt with by monadic programs. Consider, for example, a Boolean template with three relations: H_1 is a monadic relation corresponding to positive Horn clauses ("facts"), H_2 is a ternary relation corresponding to Horn clauses of the form $p \wedge q \to r$, and H_3 is a ternary relation corresponding to negative Horn clauses of the form $\neg p \vee \neg q \vee \neg r$. Unsatisfiability of Horn formulas with at most three literals per clause can then be expressed by the following monadic Datalog program:

$$H(X) : - H_1(X)$$
$$H(X) : - H(X), H_2(Y, Z, X)$$
$$Q : - H(X), H(Y), H(Z), H_2(X, Y, Z)$$

It turns out that we can fully characterize expressibility in monadic Datalog. A k-ary function f is a *set function* if $f(a_1, \ldots, a_k) = f(b_1, \ldots, b_k)$ whenever $\{a_1, \ldots, a_k\} = \{b_1, \ldots, b_k\}$. In other words, a set function depends only the set of its arguments. As a concrete example, the binary Boolean functions $\wedge$ and $\vee$ are set functions.

Theorem 6.6.2. [29] *Let* **B** *be relational structure with universe B. The following two statements are then equivalent:*

- $\overline{\text{CSP}(\mathbf{B})}$ *is expressible in monadic Datalog.*
- $\text{Pol}(\mathbf{B})$ *contains a* $|B|$*-ary set function.*

Since the number of $|B|$-ary functions over the universe B of $\mathbf{B}$ is finite, checking the condition of the theorem is clearly decidable; in fact, it is in NEX-PTIME. Thus, the classification problem for monadic Datalog is decidable.

The main reason for the focus on Datalog as a language to solve constraint-satisfaction problems is that its data complexity is in PTIME. Datalog, however, is not the only logic with this property. We know, for example, that the data complexity of first-order logic is in LOGSPACE. Thus, it would be interesting to characterize the templates $\mathbf{B}$ such that $\text{CSP}(\mathbf{B})$ is expressible in first-order logic. This turns out to have an intimate connection to expressibility in (nonrecursive) Datalog.

Theorem 6.6.3. [5, 60] *Let $\mathbf{B}$ be a relational structure. The following are equivalent:*

- $\text{CSP}(\mathbf{B})$ *is expressible in first-order logic.*
- $\overline{\text{CSP}(\mathbf{B})}$ *is expressible by a finite union of conjunctive queries.*

It is known that a Datalog program is always equivalent to a (possibly infinite) union of conjunctive queries. A Datalog program is *bounded* if it is equivalent to a finite union of conjunctive queries [35]. It is known that a Datalog program is bounded if and only if it is equivalent to a first-order formula [2, 61]. Thus, expressibility of nonuniform CSP in first-order logic is a special case of expressibility in Datalog. Concerning the classification problem, Larose, Loten, and Tardif [52] have shown that there is an algorithm to decide, given a structure $\mathbf{B}$, whether $\text{CSP}(\mathbf{B})$ is expressible in first-order logic; actually, this problem turns out to be NP-complete.

In another direction, we may ask if there are constraint-satisfaction problems that cannot be expressed by Datalog, but can be expressed in least fixedpoint logic (LFP), whose data complexity is also in PTIME. This is an open question. It was conjectured in [29] that if $\overline{\text{CSP}(\mathbf{B})}$ is expressible in LFP, then it is also expressible in Datalog.

6.7 Datalog, Games, and Constraint Satisfaction

So far, we have focused on using Datalog to obtain tractability for nonuniform constraint satisfaction. Kolaitis and Vardi [48] showed how the logical framework also provides a unifying explanation for the tractability of uniform constraint-satisfaction problems. Note that, in general, tractability results for the nonuniform case do not uniformize. Thus, tractability results for each problem in a collection of nonuniform $\text{CSP}(\mathbf{B})$ problems do not necessarily yield a tractable case of the uniform CONSTRAINT-SATISFACTION problem. The reason is that both of the structures $\mathbf{A}$ and $\mathbf{B}$ are part of the input to the uniform CONSTRAINT-SATISFACTION problem, and the running times of the polynomial-time algorithms for CSP($\mathbf{B}$) may very well be exponential in the size of $\mathbf{B}$. We now leverage the intimate connection between Datalog and pebble games to shed new light on expressibility in Datalog, and show how tractability via k-Datalog does uniformize.

As discussed in Chap. 2, Datalog can be viewed as a fragment of least fixedpoint logic (LFP); furthermore, on the class *All* of all finite structures, LFP is subsumed by the finite-variable infinitary logic $L_{\infty\omega}^\omega = \bigcup_{k>0} L_{\infty\omega}^k$ (see Chap. 2). Here we are interested in the existential positive fragments of $\exists L_{\infty\omega}^k$, where k s a positive integer, which are tailored for the study of Datalog

Theorem 6.7.1. [48] *Let k be a positive integer. Every k-Datalog query over finite structures is expressible in $\exists L_{\infty\omega}^k$. Thus, k-Datalog $\subseteq \exists L_{\infty\omega}^k$ on finite structures.*

We make use here of the $(\exists, k)$-pebble games discussed in Chap. 2. We saw there that if k is a positive integer and Q is a Boolean query on a class $\mathcal{C}$ of finite structures, then Q is expressible in $\exists L_{\infty\omega}^k$ on $\mathcal{C}$ iff for all $\mathbf{A}, \mathbf{B} \in \mathcal{C}$ such that $\mathbf{A} \models Q$ and the Duplicator wins the $(\exists, k)$-pebble game on $\mathbf{A}$ and $\mathbf{B}$, we have that $\mathbf{B} \models Q$. The next theorem establishes a connection between expressibility in k-Datalog and $(\exists, k)$-pebble games. (A closely related, but somewhat less precise, such connection was established in [29].) In what follows, if $\mathcal{A}$ is a class of structures and $\mathbf{B}$ is a structure, we write CSP($\mathcal{A}, \mathbf{B}$) to denote the class of structures $\mathbf{A}$ such that $\mathbf{A} \in \mathcal{A}$ and $\mathbf{A} \to \mathbf{B}$.

Theorem 6.7.2. [48] *Let k be a positive integer, $\mathbf{B}$ a relational structure, and $\mathcal{A}$ a class of relational structures such that $\mathbf{B} \in \mathcal{A}$. The following statements are then equivalent:*

- $\overline{\text{CSP}(\mathcal{A}, \mathbf{B})}$ *is expressible in k-Datalog on $\mathcal{A}$.*
- $\overline{\text{CSP}(\mathcal{A}, \mathbf{B})}$ *is expressible in $\exists L_{\infty\omega}^k$ on $\mathcal{A}$.*
- CSP($\mathcal{A}, \mathbf{B}$) *is equal to the class*
  $\{\mathbf{A} \in \mathcal{A} : \text{The Spoiler wins the } (\exists, k)\text{-pebble game on } \mathbf{A} \text{ and } \mathbf{B}\}.$

Recall also from Chap. 2 that the query "Given two structures $\mathbf{A}$ and $\mathbf{B}$, does the Spoiler win the $(\exists, k)$-pebble game on $\mathbf{A}$ and $\mathbf{B}$?" is definable in LFP; as a result, there is a polynomial-time (in fact, $O(n^{2k})$) algorithm that, given two structures $\mathbf{A}$ and $\mathbf{B}$, determines whether the Spoiler wins the $(\exists, k)$-pebble game on $\mathbf{A}$ and $\mathbf{B}$.

By combining Theorem 6.7.2 with the results of Chap. 2, we obtain the following uniform tractability result for classes of constraint-satisfaction problems expressible in Datalog.

Theorem 6.7.3. [48] *Let k be a positive integer, let $\mathcal{A}$ be a class of relational structures, and let $\mathcal{B} = \{\mathbf{B} \in \mathcal{A} : \neg\text{CSP}(\mathcal{A}, \mathbf{B}) \text{ is expressible in } k\text{-Datalog}\}$. Then the uniform CONSTRAINT-SATISFACTION problem CSP($\mathcal{A}, \mathcal{B}$) is solvable in polynomial time. Moreover, the running time of the algorithm is $O(n^{2k})$, where n is the maximum of the sizes of the input structures $\mathbf{A}$ and $\mathbf{B}$.*

Intuitively, if we consider the class of all templates $\mathbf{B}$ for which k-Datalog solves $\mathrm{CSP}(\mathbf{B})$, then computing the winner in the existential k-pebble game offers a *uniform* polynomial-time algorithm. That is, the algorithm determining the winner in the existential k-pebble game is a uniform algorithm for all (nonuniform) constraint-satisfaction problems that can be expressed in k-Datalog.

The characterization in terms of pebble games also sheds light on nonuniform constraint satisfaction. As described in Chap. 2, for every relational structure $\mathbf{B}$ and every positive integer k, there is a k-Datalog program $\rho_{\mathbf{B}}^{k}$ that expresses the query "Given a structure $\mathbf{A}$, does the Spoiler win the $(\exists, k)$ pebble game on $\mathbf{A}$ and $\mathbf{B}$?" As an immediate consequence of this fact, we obtain the result that $\overline{\mathrm{CSP}(\mathbf{B})}$ is expressible in k-Datalog if and only if it is expressible by a *specific* k-Datalog program.

Theorem 6.7.4. [29, 48] $\overline{\mathrm{CSP}(\mathbf{B})}$ *is expressible in k-Datalog if and only if it is expressible by $\rho_{\mathbf{B}}^{k}$.*

It follows that $\overline{\mathrm{CSP}(\mathbf{B})}$ is expressible in k-Datalog if and only if $\neg\varphi_{\mathbf{B}}$ is logically equivalent to $\rho_{\mathbf{B}}^{k}$, where $\varphi_{\mathbf{B}}$ is the MMSNP sentence expressing $\mathrm{CSP}(\mathbf{B})$. Unfortunately, it is not known whether the equivalence of complemented MMSNP to Datalog is decidable.

6.8 Games and Consistency

One of the most fruitful approaches to coping with the intractability of constraint satisfaction has been the introduction and use of various *consistency* concepts that make explicit some additional constraints implied by the original constraints. The connection between consistency properties and tractability was first described in [31, 32]. In a similar vein, the relationship between *local consistency* and *global consistency* was investigated in [21, 65, 66]. Intuitively, local consistency means that any partial solution on a set of variables can be extended to a partial solution containing an additional variable, whereas global consistency means that any partial solution can be extended to a global solution. Note that if the inputs are such that local consistency implies global consistency, then there is a polynomial-time algorithm for constraint satisfaction; moreover, in this case a solution can be constructed via a backtrack-free search. We now describe this approach from the Datalog perspective. The crucial insight is that the key concept of *strong k-consistency* [21] is equivalent to a property of winning strategies for the Duplicator in the $(\exists, k)$-pebble game. Specifically, an instance of a constraint-satisfaction problem is strongly k-consistent if and only if the family of *all* k-partial homomorphisms f is a winning strategy for the Duplicator in the $(\exists, k)$-pebble game on the two relational structures that represent the given instance.

The connection between pebble games and consistency properties, however, is deeper than just a mere reformulation of the concept of strong k-consistency. Indeed, as mentioned earlier, consistency properties underlie the process of making explicit new constraints that are implied by the original constraints. A key technical step in this approach is the procedure known as "establishing strong k-consistency", which propagates the original constraints, adds implied constraints, and transforms a given instance of a constraint-satisfaction problem to a strongly k-consistent instance with the same solution space [15, 21]. In fact, strong k-consistency can be established if and only if the Duplicator wins the $(\exists, k)$-pebble game. Moreover, whenever strong k-consistency can be established, one method for doing this is to first compute the largest winning strategy for the Duplicator in the $(\exists, k)$-pebble game and then modify the original problem by augmenting it with the constraints expressed by the largest winning strategy; this method gives rise to the least constrained instance that establishes strong k-consistency and, in addition, satisfies a natural *coherence* property. By combining this result with known results concerning the definability of the largest winning strategy, it follows that the algorithm for establishing strong k-consistency in this way (with k fixed) is actually expressible in least fixedpoint logic; this strengthens the fact that strong k-consistency can be established in polynomial time when k is fixed. If we consider nonuniform constraint satisfaction, it follows that for every relational structure $\mathbf{B}$, the complement of $\mathrm{CSP}(\mathbf{B})$ is expressible by a Datalog program with k variables if and only if $\mathrm{CSP}(\mathbf{B})$ coincides with the collection of all relational structures $\mathbf{A}$ such that establishing strong k-consistency on $\mathbf{A}$ and $\mathbf{B}$ implies that there is a homomorphism from $\mathbf{A}$ to $\mathbf{B}$.

We start the formal treatment by returning first to $(\exists, k)$-pebble games. Recall from Chap. 2 that a winning strategy for the Duplicator in the $(\exists, k)$-pebble game on $\mathbf{A}$ and $\mathbf{B}$ is a nonempty family of k-partial homomorphisms (that is, partial homomorphisms defined on at most k elements) from $\mathbf{A}$ to $\mathbf{B}$ that is closed under subfunctions and has the forth property up to k. A *configuration* for the $(\exists, k)$-pebble game on $\mathbf{A}$ and $\mathbf{B}$ is a $2k$-tuple $\mathbf{a}, \mathbf{b}$, where $\mathbf{a} = (a_1, \ldots, a_k)$ and $\mathbf{b} = (b_1, \ldots, b_k)$ are elements of A^k and B^k, respectively, such that if $a_i = a_j$, then $b_i = b_j$; this means that the correspondence $a_i \mapsto b_i$, $1 \le i \le k$, is a partial function from A to B, which we denote by $h_{\mathbf{a},\mathbf{b}}$. A *winning configuration* for the Duplicator in the existential k-pebble game on $\mathbf{A}$ and $\mathbf{B}$ is a configuration $\mathbf{a}, \mathbf{b}$ for this game such that $h_{\mathbf{a},\mathbf{b}}$ is a member of some winning strategy for the Duplicator in this game. We denote by $\mathcal{W}^k(\mathbf{A}, \mathbf{B})$ the set of all such configurations. The following results show that expressibility in $\exists \mathrm{L}^k_{\infty\omega}$ can be characterized in terms of the set $\mathcal{W}^k(\mathbf{A}, \mathbf{B})$.

Proposition 6.8.1. [49] *If $\mathcal{F}$ and $\mathcal{F}'$ are two winning strategies for the Duplicator in the $(\exists, k)$-pebble game on two structures $\mathbf{A}$ and $\mathbf{B}$, then the union $\mathcal{F} \cup \mathcal{F}'$ is also a winning strategy for the Duplicator. Consequently, there is a largest winning strategy for the Duplicator in the $(\exists, k)$-pebble*

game, namely the union of all winning strategies, which is precisely the set
$\mathcal{H}^k(\mathbf{A}, \mathbf{B}) = \{h_{\bar{a}, \bar{b}} : (\bar{a}, \bar{b}) \in \mathcal{W}^k(\mathbf{A}, \mathbf{B})\}$.

Corollary 6.8.2. [48] *Let k be a positive integer and Q a k-ary query on a class $\mathcal{C}$ of finite structures. The following two statements are then equivalent:*

- Q *is expressible in* $\exists L_{\infty\omega}^k$ *on* $\mathcal{C}$.
- *If* $\mathbf{A}$, $\mathbf{B}$ *are two structures in* $\mathcal{C}$, $(\mathbf{a}, \mathbf{b}) \in \mathcal{W}^k(\mathbf{A}, \mathbf{B})$, *and* $\mathbf{A} \models Q(\mathbf{a})$, *then* $\mathbf{B} \models Q(\mathbf{b})$.

The following lemma is a crucial definability result.

Lemma 6.8.3. [48] *There is a positive-in-S first-order formula $\varphi(\bar{x}, \bar{y}, S)$, where $\bar{x}$ and $\bar{y}$ are k-tuples of variables, such that the complement of its least fixedpoint on a pair $(\mathbf{A}, \mathbf{B})$ of structures defines the set $\mathcal{W}^k(\mathbf{A}, \mathbf{B})$ of all winning configurations for the Duplicator in the $(\exists, k)$-pebble game on $\mathbf{A}, \mathbf{B}$.*

We now formally define the concepts of *i-consistency* and *strong k-consistency*.

Definition 6.8.4. *Let $\mathcal{P} = (V, D, \mathcal{C})$ be a constraint-satisfaction instance.*

- *A* partial solution *on a set $V' \subset V$ is an assignment $h : V' \to D$ that satisfies all the constraints whose scope is contained in V'.*
- *$\mathcal{P}$ is i-consistent if, for every $i - 1$ variables $v_1, \ldots, v_{i-1}$, for every partial solution on these variables, and for every variable $v_i \notin \{v_1, \ldots, v_{i-1}\}$, there is a partial solution on the variables $v_1, \ldots, v_{i-1}, v_i$ extending the given partial solution on the variables $v_1, \ldots, v_{i-1}$.*
- *$\mathcal{P}$ is strongly k-consistent if it is i-consistent for every $i \leq k$.*

To illustrate these concepts, consider the Boolean formula

$$(\neg x_1 \lor x_3) \land (\neg x_2 \lor x_3) \land (x_2 \lor \neg x_3).$$

It is easy to verify that this formula, viewed as a constraint-satisfaction instance, is strongly 3-consistent. For instance, the partial solution $x_2 = 0$, $x_3 = 0$ can be extended to the solution $x_1 = 0$, $x_2 = 0$, $x_3 = 0$, and the partial solution $x_1 = 1$, $x_3 = 1$ can be extended to the solution $x_1 = 1$, $x_2 = 1$, $x_3 = 1$. In contrast, the Boolean formula

$$(x_1 \lor x_2) \land (\neg x_1 \lor x_3) \land (\neg x_2 \lor x_3) \land (x_2 \lor \neg x_3)$$

is satisfiable and strongly 2-consistent, but not 3-consistent (hence, it is not strongly 3-consistent either). The reason is that the partial solution $x_2 = 0$, $x_3 = 0$ cannot be extended to a solution, since the only solutions of this formula are $x_1 = 0$, $x_2 = 1$, $x_3 = 1$ and $x_1 = 1$, $x_2 = 1$, $x_3 = 1$. Note that the concepts of strong 2-consistency and strong 3-consistency were first studied in the literature under the names of *arc consistency* and *path consistency* (see [23]).

A key insight is that the concepts of *i-consistency* and strong k-consistency can be naturally recast in terms of existential pebble games.

Proposition 6.8.5. [49] *Let $\mathcal{P}$ be a CSP instance, and let $(\mathbf{A}_\mathcal{P}, \mathbf{B}_\mathcal{P})$ be the associated homomorphism instance.*

- *$\mathcal{P}$ is i-consistent if and only if the family of all partial homomorphisms from $\mathbf{A}_\mathcal{P}$ to $\mathbf{B}_\mathcal{P}$ with $i - 1$ elements in their universe has the i-forth property.*
- *$\mathcal{P}$ is strongly k-consistent if and only if the family of all k-partial homomorphisms from $\mathbf{A}_\mathcal{P}$ to $\mathbf{B}_\mathcal{P}$ is a winning strategy for the Duplicator in the $(\exists, k)$-pebble game on $\mathbf{A}_\mathcal{P}$ and $\mathbf{B}_\mathcal{P}$.*

Let us now recall the concept of *establishing strong k-consistency*, as defined, for instance, in [15, 21]. This concept has been defined rather informally in the AI literature to mean that, given a constraint-satisfaction instance $\mathcal{P}$, we associate with it another instance $\mathcal{P}'$ that has the following properties: (1) $\mathcal{P}'$ has the same set of variables and the same set of values as $\mathcal{P}$ (2) $\mathcal{P}'$ is strongly k-consistent; (3) $\mathcal{P}'$ is at least as constrained as $\mathcal{P}$; and (4) $\mathcal{P}$ and $\mathcal{P}'$ have the same space of solutions. The next definition formalizes the above concept in the context of the homomorphism problem (see [19, 49]).

Definition 6.8.6. *Let $\mathbf{A}$ and $\mathbf{B}$ be two relational structures over a k-ary vocabulary σ (i.e., every relation symbol in σ has an arity of at most k). Establishing strong k-consistency for $\mathbf{A}$ and $\mathbf{B}$ means that we associate two relational structures $\mathbf{A}'$ and $\mathbf{B}'$ with them with the following properties:*

- *$\mathbf{A}'$ and $\mathbf{B}'$ are structures over some k-ary vocabulary σ' (in general, different from σ); moreover, the universe of $\mathbf{A}'$ is the universe A of $\mathbf{A}$, and the universe of $\mathbf{B}'$ is the universe B of $\mathbf{B}$.*
- *$\mathrm{CSP}(\mathbf{A}', \mathbf{B}')$ is strongly k-consistent.*
- *If h is a k-partial homomorphism from $\mathbf{A}'$ to $\mathbf{B}'$, then h is a k-partial homomorphism from $\mathbf{A}$ to $\mathbf{B}$.*
- *If h is a function from A to B, then h is a homomorphism from $\mathbf{A}$ to $\mathbf{B}$ if and only if h is a homomorphism from $\mathbf{A}'$ to $\mathbf{B}'$.*

If the structures $\mathbf{A}'$ and $\mathbf{B}'$ have the above properties, then we say that $\mathbf{A}'$ and $\mathbf{B}'$ establish strong k-consistency for $\mathbf{A}$ and $\mathbf{B}$.

A constraint-satisfaction instance $\mathcal{P}$ is *coherent* if every constraint $(\mathbf{t}, R)$ of $\mathcal{P}$ completely determines all constraints $(\mathbf{u}, Q)$ in which all variables occurring in $\mathbf{u}$ are among the variables of $\mathbf{t}$. We formalize this concept as follows.

Definition 6.8.7. *An instance $\mathbf{A}, \mathbf{B}$ of the homomorphism problem is coherent if its associated constraint-satisfaction instance $\mathrm{CSP}(\mathbf{A}, \mathbf{B})$ has the following property: for every constraint $(\mathbf{a}, R)$ of $\mathrm{CSP}(\mathbf{A}, \mathbf{B})$ and every tuple $\mathbf{b} \in R$, the mapping $h_{\mathbf{a}, \mathbf{b}}$ is well defined and is a partial homomorphism from $\mathbf{A}$ to $\mathbf{B}$.*

Note that a constraint-satisfaction instance can be made coherent in polynomial time by constraint propagation.

The main result of this section is that strong k-consistency can be established precisely when the Duplicator wins the $(\exists, k)$-pebble game. Moreover, one method for establishing strong k-consistency is to first compute the largest winning strategy for the Duplicator in this game and then to generate an instance of the constraint-satisfaction problem consisting of all the constraints embodied in the largest winning strategy. Furthermore, this method gives rise to the largest coherent instance that establishes strong k-consistency (and, hence, the least constrained such instance).

Theorem 6.8.8. [49] *Let k be a positive integer, let σ be a k-ary vocabulary, and let $\mathbf{A}$ and $\mathbf{B}$ be two relational structures over σ with universes A and B, respectively. It is possible to establish strong k-consistency for $\mathbf{A}$ and $\mathbf{B}$ if and only if $\mathcal{W}^k(\mathbf{A}, \mathbf{B}) \neq \emptyset$. Furthermore, if $\mathcal{W}^k(\mathbf{A}, \mathbf{B}) \neq \emptyset$, then the following sequence of steps gives rise to two structures $\mathbf{A}'$ and $\mathbf{B}'$ that establish strong k-consistency for $\mathbf{A}$ and $\mathbf{B}$:*

1. *Compute the set $\mathcal{W}^k(\mathbf{A}, \mathbf{B})$.*
2. *For every $i \leq k$ and for every i-tuple $\mathbf{a} \in A^i$, form the set $R_{\mathbf{a}} = \{\mathbf{b} \in B^i : (\mathbf{a}, \mathbf{b}) \in \mathcal{W}^k(\mathbf{A}, \mathbf{B})\}$.*
3. *Form a CONSTRAINT-SATISFACTION instance $\mathcal{P}$ with A as the set of variables, B as the set of values, and $\{(\mathbf{a}, R_{\mathbf{a}}) : \mathbf{a} \in \cup_{i=1}^{k} A^i\}$ as the collection of constraints.*
4. *Let $(\mathbf{A}', \mathbf{B}')$ be the homomorphism instance of $\mathcal{P}$.*

In addition, the structures $\mathbf{A}'$ and $\mathbf{B}'$ obtained above constitute the largest coherent instance establishing strong k-consistency for $\mathbf{A}$ and $\mathbf{B}$, that is, if $(\mathbf{A}'', \mathbf{B}'')$ is another such coherent instance, then for every constraint $(\mathbf{a}, R)$ of $\mathrm{CSP}(\mathbf{A}'', \mathbf{B}'')$, we have that $R \subseteq R_{\mathbf{a}}$.

The key step in the procedure described in Theorem 6.8.8 is the first step, in which the set $\mathcal{W}^k(\mathbf{A}, \mathbf{B})$ is computed. The other steps simply "re-format" $\mathcal{W}^k(\mathbf{A}, \mathbf{B})$. From Lemma 6.8.3 it follows that we can establish strong k-consistency by computing the fixedpoint of a monotone first-order formula. We can now relate the concept of strong k-consistency to the results in [29] regarding Datalog and nonuniform CSP.

Theorem 6.8.9. [49] *Let $\mathbf{B}$ be a relational structure over a vocabulary σ. The following two statements are then equivalent:*

- $\overline{\mathrm{CSP}(\mathbf{B})}$ *is expressible in k-Datalog.*
- *For every structure $\mathbf{A}$ over σ, establishing strong k-consistency for $\mathbf{A}, \mathbf{B}$ implies that there is a homomorphism from $\mathbf{A}$ to $\mathbf{B}$.*

Given the fundamental role that the set $\mathcal{W}^k(\mathbf{A}, \mathbf{B})$ plays here, it is natural to ask about the complexity of computing it. To turn this question into a decision problem, we just ask about the nonemptiness of this set.

Theorem 6.8.10. [45] *The problem* $\{(\mathbf{A}, \mathbf{B}, k) : \mathcal{W}^k(\mathbf{A}, \mathbf{B}) \neq \emptyset\}$, *with* k *encoded in unary, is* EXPTIME-*complete. In words, the following problem is* EXPTIME-*complete: given a positive integer* k *and two structures* $\mathbf{A}$ *and* $\mathbf{B}$, *does the Duplicator win the* $(\exists, k)$-*pebble game on* $\mathbf{A}$ *and* $\mathbf{B}$?

This result is rather surprising. After all, the complexity of constraint satisfaction is "only" NP-complete. In contrast, the complexity of establishing strong k-consistency is provably exponential and not in PTIME. This offers an a posteriori justification of the practice of establishing only a "low degree" of consistency, such as arc consistency or path consistency [3, 23].

6.9 Uniform Constraint Satisfaction and Bounded Treewidth

So far, we have focused on the pursuit of islands of tractability of nonuniform constraint satisfaction, that is, islands of the form $\mathrm{CSP}(\mathbf{B}) = \mathrm{CSP}(All, \{\mathbf{B}\})$, where $\mathbf{B}$ is a fixed template. Even when we discussed uniform constraint satisfaction, it was with respect to tractable templates. In this section we focus on uniform constraint satisfaction of the form $\mathrm{CSP}(\mathcal{A}, All)$, where $\mathcal{A}$ is a class of structures. The goal is to identify conditions on $\mathcal{A}$ that ensure uniform tractability.

As is well known, many algorithmic problems that are "hard" on arbitrary structures become "easy" on trees. This phenomenon has motivated researchers to investigate whether the concept of a tree can be appropriately relaxed while maintaining good computational behavior. As part of their seminal work on graph minors, Robertson and Seymour introduced the concept of *treewidth*, which, intuitively, measures how "tree-like" a structure is; moreover, they showed that graphs of *bounded treewidth* exhibit such good behavior; see [59].

Definition 6.9.1. *A* tree decomposition *of a relational structure* $\mathbf{A}$ *is a labeled tree* T *such that the following conditions hold:*

- *Every node of* T *is labeled by a nonempty subset of the universe* A *of* $\mathbf{A}$,
- *For every relation* R *of* $\mathbf{A}$ *and every tuple* $(a_1, \ldots, a_n)$ *in* R, *there is a node of* T *whose label contains* $\{a_1, \ldots, a_n\}$,
- *For every* $a \in A$, *the set of nodes of* T *whose labels include* a *forms a subtree of* T.

The width *of a tree decomposition* T *is the maximum cardinality of a label of a node in* T *minus 1. The* treewidth *of* $\mathbf{A}$, *denoted* $\mathrm{tw}(\mathbf{A})$, *is the smallest positive integer* k *such that* A *has a tree decomposition of width* k. *We write* $\mathcal{T}(k)$ *to denote the class of all structures* $\mathbf{A}$ *such that* $\mathrm{tw}(\mathbf{A}) < k$.

Clearly, if $\mathbf{T}$ is a tree, then $\mathrm{tw}(\mathbf{T}) = 1$. Similarly, if $n \geq 3$ and $\mathbf{C}_n$ is the n-element (directed) cycle, then $\mathrm{tw}(\mathbf{C}) = 2$. At the other end of the scale,

$\mathrm{tw}(\mathbf{K}_k) = k-1$, for every $k \geq 2$. Computing the treewidth of a structure is an intractable problem. Specifically, the following problem is NP-complete [4]: given a graph $\mathbf{H}$ and an integer $k \geq 1$, is $\mathrm{tw}(\mathbf{H}) \leq k$? Nonetheless, Bodlaender [7] has shown that for every fixed integer $k \geq 1$, there is a linear-time algorithm such that, given a structure $\mathbf{A}$, it determines whether or not $\mathrm{tw}(\mathbf{A}) < k$. In other words, each class $\mathcal{T}(k)$ is recognizable in polynomial time.

Dechter and Pearl [25] and Freuder [33] have shown that the classes of structures of bounded treewidth give rise to large islands of tractability of uniform constraint satisfaction.

Theorem 6.9.2. [25, 33] *If $k \geq 2$ is a positive integer, then $\mathrm{CSP}(\mathcal{T}(k), All)$ is in* PTIME.

The polynomial-time algorithm for $\mathrm{CSP}(\mathcal{T}(k), All)$ in the above theorem is often described as a *bucket-elimination algorithm* [22]. It should be noted that it is not a constraint-propagation algorithm. Instead, this algorithm uses the bound on the treewidth to test whether a solution to the constraint-satisfaction problem exists by solving a join-evaluation problem in which all intermediate relations are of bounded arity.

Kolaitis and Vardi [48], and Dalmau, Kolaitis and Vardi [18] have investigated certain logical aspects of the treewidth of a relational structure and have shown that this combinatorial concept is closely connected to the definability of the canonical conjunctive query of the structure in a fragment of first-order logic with a fixed number of variables. This has made it possible to show that the tractability of $\mathrm{CSP}(\mathcal{T}(k), All)$ can be explained in purely logical terms. Moreover, it led to the discovery of larger islands of tractability of uniform constraint satisfaction.

Definition 6.9.3. *Let $k \geq 2$ be a positive integer.*

- FO^k *is the collection of all first-order formulas with at most k distinct variables.*
- L^k *is the collection of all FO^k-formulas built using atomic formulas, conjunction, and existential first-order quantification only.*

Intuitively, queries expressible in FO^k and L^k are simply first-order queries and conjunctive queries, respectively, with a bound k on the number of distinct variables (each variable, however, may be reused any number of times).

As an example, it is easy to see that if $\mathbf{C}_n$ is the n-element cycle, $n \geq 3$, then the canonical conjunctive query $Q_{\mathbf{C}_n}$ is expressible in L^3. For instance, $Q_{\mathbf{C}_4}$ is logically equivalent to $(\exists x \exists y \exists z)(E(x,y) \wedge E(y,z) \wedge (\exists y)(E(z,y) \wedge E(y,x)))$. As mentioned earlier, for every $n \geq 3$, we have that $\mathrm{tw}(\mathbf{C}_n) = 2$.

The logics FO^k and L^k are referred to as *variable-confined logics* [47]. The complexity of query evaluation for such queries has been studied in [68]. Since in the case of in data complexity the queries are fixed, bounding the number of variables does not change the data complexity. The change in the expression and the combined complexity, however, is quite dramatic, as the combined complexity of FO^k has been shown to be in PTIME [68]. (More generally, the exponential gap between data complexity and expression and combined complexity shrinks when the number of variables is bounded.)

The next result shows that the relationship we have just seen in the example above, between the treewidth and the number of variables needed to express the canonical conjunctive query of a cycle, is not an accident.

Theorem 6.9.4. [48] *Let $k \geq 2$ be a positive integer. If $\mathbf{A} \in \mathcal{T}(k)$, then the canonical conjunctive query $Q_{\mathbf{A}}$ is expressible in L^k.*

Corollary 6.9.5. $\mathrm{CSP}(\mathcal{T}(k), All)$ *can be solved in polynomial time by determining, given a structure $\mathbf{A} \in \mathcal{T}(k)$ and an arbitrary structure $\mathbf{B}$, whether $\mathbf{B} \models Q_{\mathbf{A}}$.*

A precise complexity analysis of $\mathrm{CSP}(\mathcal{T}(k), All)$ is provided in [37], where it is shown that the problem is LOGFCL-complete; by definition, LOGCFL is the class of decision problems that are logspace-reducible to a context-free language. Note that, in contrast, the combined complexity of evaluating FO^k-queries, for $k > 3$, is PTIME-complete [68].

Theorem 6.9.4 can be viewed as a logical recasting of the bucket-elimination algorithm. It derives the tractability of $\mathrm{CSP}(\mathcal{T}(k), All)$ from the fact that the canonical conjunctive query $Q_{\mathbf{A}}$ can be written using at most k variables. Consequently, evaluating this query amounts to solving a join-evaluation problem in which all intermediate relations are of bounded arity. For an investigation of how the ideas underlying Theorem 6.9.4 can be used to solve practical join-evaluation problems, see [55].

It turns out, however, that we can also approach solving $\mathrm{CSP}(\mathcal{T}(k), All)$ from the perspective of k-Datalog and $(\exists, k)$-pebble games. This is because L^k is a fragment of $\exists L^k_{\infty\omega}$, whose expressive power, as seen earlier, can be characterized in terms of such games.

Theorem 6.9.6. [18] *Let $k \geq 2$ be a positive integer.*

- *If $\mathbf{B}$ is an arbitrary, but fixed, structure, then $\mathcal{T}(k) \cap \overline{\mathrm{CSP}(\mathcal{T}(k), \{\mathbf{B}\})}$ is expressible in k-Datalog.[6]*
- *$\mathrm{CSP}(\mathcal{T}(k), All)$ can be solved in polynomial time by determining whether, given a structure $\mathbf{A} \in \mathcal{T}(k)$ and an arbitrary structure $\mathbf{B}$, the Duplicator wins the $(\exists, k)$-pebble on $\mathbf{A}$ and $\mathbf{B}$.*

The situation for bounded-treewidth structures, as described by Theorem 6.9.6, should be contrasted with the situation for bounded-*cliquewidth* structures [16]. Let $\mathcal{C}(k)$ be the class of structures with a cliquewidth bounded by k. It has been shown in [16] that $\mathrm{CSP}(\mathcal{C}(k), \{\mathbf{B}\})$ is in PTIME for each structure $\mathbf{B}$. Since, however, complete graphs have a bounded cliquewidth, it

---

[6] The intersection with $\mathcal{T}(k)$ ensures that only structures with a treewidth bounded by k are considered.

follows that the CLIQUE problem can be reduced to $CSP(\mathcal{C}(k), All)$, implying NP-hardness of the latter.

As a consequence of Theorem 6.9.6, we see that $CSP(\mathcal{T}(k), All)$ can be solved in polynomial time using a constraint-propagation algorithm that is quite different from the bucket-elimination algorithm in Theorem 6.9.2. It should be noted, however, that this requires knowing that we have been given an instance $\mathbf{A}, \mathbf{B}$ where $tw(\mathbf{A}) \leq k$. In contrast, the bucket-elimination algorithm can be used for arbitrary constraint-satisfaction instances (with no tractability guarantee, in general).

The classes $CSP(\mathcal{T}(k), All)$ enjoy also nice tractability properties from the perspective of *Parametrized Complexity Theory* [26], as they are *fixed-parameter tractable*, and, in a precise technical sense, are maximal with this property under a certain complexity-theoretic assumption (see [41]).

The development so far shows that $\mathcal{T}(k)$ provides an island of tractability for uniform constraint satisfaction. We now show that this island can be expanded.

Definition 6.9.7. *Let $\mathbf{A}$ and $\mathbf{B}$ be two relational structures.*

- *We say that $\mathbf{A}$ and $\mathbf{B}$ are* homomorphically equivalent, *denoted by $\mathbf{A} \sim_h \mathbf{B}$, if both $\mathbf{A} \to \mathbf{B}$ and $\mathbf{B} \to \mathbf{A}$ hold.*
- *We say that $\mathbf{B}$ is the* core *of $\mathbf{A}$, and write $core(\mathbf{A}) = \mathbf{B}$, if $\mathbf{B}$ is a substructure of $\mathbf{A}$, $\mathbf{A} \to \mathbf{B}$ holds, and $\mathbf{A} \to \mathbf{B}'$ fails for each proper substructure $\mathbf{B}'$ of $\mathbf{B}$.*

Clearly, $core(\mathbf{K}_k) = \mathbf{K}_k$ and $core(\mathbf{C}_n) = \mathbf{C}_n$. On the other hand, if $\mathbf{H}$ is a 2-colorable graph with at least one edge, then $core(\mathbf{H}) = \mathbf{K}_2$. It should be noted that cores play an important role in database query processing and optimization (see [11]). The next result shows that they can also be used to characterize when the canonical conjunctive query is definable in L^k.

Theorem 6.9.8. [18] *Let $k \geq 2$ be a positive integer and $\mathbf{A}$ a relational structure. The following are then equivalent:*

- *$Q_{\mathbf{A}}$ is definable in L^k.*
- *There is a structure $\mathbf{B} \in \mathcal{T}(k)$ such that $\mathbf{A} \sim_h \mathbf{B}$.*
- *$core(\mathbf{A}) \in \mathcal{T}(k)$.*

The tight connection between definability in L^k and the boundedness of the treewidth of the core suggests a way to expand the "island" $\mathcal{T}(k)$.

Definition 6.9.9. *If $k \geq 2$ is a positive integer, then $\mathcal{H}(\mathcal{T}(k))$ is the class of relational structures $\mathbf{A}$ such that $core(\mathbf{A})$ has a treewidth less than k.*

It should be noted that $\mathcal{T}(k)$ is properly contained in $\mathcal{H}(\mathcal{T}(k))$, for every $k \geq 2$. Indeed, it is known that there are 2-colorable graphs of arbitrarily large treewidth. In particular, *grids* are known to have these properties (see [26]). Yet these graphs are members of $\mathcal{H}(\mathcal{T}(2))$, since their core is $\mathbf{K}_2$.

Theorem 6.9.10. [18] *Let $k \geq 2$ be a positive integer.*

- *If* $\underline{\mathbf{B}}$ *is an arbitrary, but fixed, structure, then* $\mathcal{H}(\mathcal{T}(k)) \cap$ $\mathrm{CSP}(\mathcal{H}(\mathcal{T}(k)), \{\mathbf{B}\})$ *is expressible in k-Datalog.*
- $\mathrm{CSP}(\mathcal{H}(\mathcal{T}(k)), All)$ *is in* PTIME. *Moreover,* $\mathrm{CSP}(\mathcal{H}(\mathcal{T}(k)), All)$ *can be solved in polynomial time by determining whether, given a structure* $\mathbf{A} \in \mathcal{H}(\mathcal{T}(k))$ *and an arbitrary structure* $\mathbf{B}$, *the Spoiler or the Duplicator wins the $(\exists, k)$-pebble on* $\mathbf{A}$ *and* $\mathbf{B}$.

Theorem 6.9.10 yields new islands of tractability for uniform constraint satisfaction, which properly subsume the islands of tractability constituted by the classes of structures of bounded treewidth. This expansion of the tractability landscape comes, however, at a certain price. Specifically, as seen earlier, for every fixed $k \geq 2$, there is a polynomial-time algorithm for determining membership in $\mathcal{T}(k)$ [7]. In contrast, it has been shown that, for every fixed $k \geq 2$, determining membership in $\mathcal{H}(\mathcal{T}(k))$ is an NP-complete problem [18]. Thus, these new islands of tractability are, in some sense, "inaccessible".

Since $\mathcal{H}(\mathcal{T}(k))$ contains structures of arbitrarily large treewidth, the bucket-elimination algorithm cannot be used to solve $\mathrm{CSP}(\mathcal{H}(\mathcal{T}(k)), All)$ in polynomial time. Thus, Theorem 6.9.10 also shows that determining the winner of the $(\exists, k)$-pebble is a polynomial-time algorithm that applies to islands of tractability not covered by the bucket-elimination algorithm.

It is now natural to ask whether there are classes $\mathcal{A}$ of relational structures that are larger than the classes $\mathcal{H}(\mathcal{T}(k))$ such that $\mathrm{CSP}(\mathcal{A}, All)$ is solvable in polynomial time. A remarkable result by Grohe [40] shows essentially that, if we fix the vocabulary, *no* such classes exist, provided a certain complexity-theoretic hypothesis is true.

Theorem 6.9.11. [40] *Assume that* FPT $\neq W[1]$. *If $\mathcal{A}$ is a recursively enumerable class of relational structures over some fixed vocabulary such that* $\mathrm{CSP}(\mathcal{A}, All)$ *is in* PTIME, *then there is a positive integer k such that* $\mathcal{A} \subseteq \mathcal{H}(\mathcal{T}(k))$.

The hypothesis FPT $\neq W[1]$ is a statement in Parametrized Complexity Theory that is analogous to the hypothesis PTIME $\neq$ NP, and it is widely accepted as being true (see [26]). In effect, Theorem 6.9.11 is a converse to Theorem 6.9.10 for fixed vocabularies. Together, these two theorems yield a complete characterization of all islands of tractability of the form $\mathrm{CSP}(\mathcal{A}, All)$, where $\mathcal{A}$ is a class of structures over some fixed vocabulary. Moreover, they reveal that all tractable cases of the form $\mathrm{CSP}(\mathcal{A}, All)$ can be solved by the same polynomial-time algorithm, namely, the algorithm for determining the winner in the $(\exists, k)$-pebble game. In other words, all tractable cases of constraint satisfaction of the form $\mathrm{CSP}(\mathcal{A}, All)$ can be solved in polynomial time using constraint propagation.

It is important to emphasize that the classes $\mathcal{H}(\mathcal{T}(k))$ are the largest islands of tractability for uniform constraint satisfaction only under the assumption in Theorem 6.9.11 of a fixed vocabulary. For variable vocabularies, there has been a long line of research on the impact of the "topology" of conjunctive queries on the complexity of their evaluation; this line of research goes back to the study of *acyclic* joins in [69]. The connection between acyclic joins and acyclic constraints was pointed out in [42]. This is still an active research area. Chekuri and Rajaraman [12] showed that the uniform constraint-satisfaction problem $CSP(\mathcal{Q}(k), All)$ is solvable in polynomial time, where $\mathcal{Q}(k)$ is the class of structures of *querywidth* k. Gottlob, Leone, and Scarcello [39] have defined another notion of width, called *hypertree width*. They have shown that the querywidth of a structure $\mathbf{A}$ provides a strict upper bound on the hypertree width of $\mathbf{A}$, but that the class $\mathcal{H}(k)$ of structures of hypertree width at most k is polynomially recognizable (unlike the class $\mathcal{Q}(k)$), and that $CSP(\mathcal{H}(k), All)$ is tractable. For further discussion of the relative merits of various notions of "width", see [38]. This is an active area of research (see [13, 14]).

Acknowledgments

We are grateful to Benoit Larose and Scott Weinstein for helpful comments on a previous draft of this chapter. This work was supported in part by NSF grants CCR-9988322, CCR-0124077, CCR-0311326, and ANI-0216467, and by a Guggenheim Fellowship. Part of this work was done while the second author was visiting the Isaac Newton Institute for Mathematical Science, as part of a Special Programme on Logic and Algorithms.

References

1. S. Abiteboul, R. Hull, and V. Vianu. *Foundations of Databases*. Addison-Wesley, 1995.
2. M. Ajtai and Y. Gurevich. Datalog vs first-order logic. *Journal of Computer and System Sciences*, 49(3):562–588, 1994.
3. K. Apt. *Principles of Constraint Programming*. Cambridge Univ. Press, 2003.
4. S. Arnborg, D. G. Corneil, and A. Proskurowski. Complexity of finding embeddings in a k-tree. *SIAM Journal of Algebraic and Discrete Methods*, 8:277–284, 1987.
5. A. Atserias. On digraph coloring problems and treewidth duality. In *Proc. 20th IEEE Symp. on Logic in Computer Science*, pages 106–115, 2005.
6. W. Bibel. Constraint satisfaction from a deductive viewpoint. *Artificial Intelligence*, 35:401–413, 1988.
7. H. L. Bodlaender. A linear-time algorithm for finding tree-decompositions of small treewidth. In *Proc. 25th ACM Symp. on Theory of Computing*, pages 226–234, 1993.
8. A. A. Bulatov. A dichotomy theorem for constraints on a three-element set. In *Proc. 43rd Symp. on Foundations of Computer Science*, pages 649–658, 2002.

9. A. A. Bulatov. Tractable conservative constraint satisfaction problems. In *Proc. 18th IEEE Symp. on Logic in Computer Science*, pages 321–330, 2003.

10. A. A. Bulatov, P. Jeavons, and A. A. Krokhin. Classifying the complexity of constraints using finite algebras. *SIAM Journal on Computing*, 34(3):720–742, 2005.

11. A. K. Chandra and P. M. Merlin. Optimal implementation of conjunctive queries in relational databases. In *Proc. 9th ACM Symp. on Theory of Computing*, pages 77–90, 1977.

12. C. Chekuri and A. Rajaraman. Conjunctive query containment revisited. In Ph.G. Kolaitis and F. Afrati, editors, *Proc. 6th Int'l Conf. on Database Theory*, Lecture Notes in Computer Science, volume 1186, pages 56–70. Springer, 1997.

13. H. Chen and V. Dalmau. Beyond hypertree width: Decomposition methods without decompositions. In *Proc. 11th Int'l Conf. on Principles and Practice of Constraint Programming*, Lecture Notes in Computer Science, volume 3709, pages 167–181. Springer, 2005.

14. D. A. Cohen, P. Jeavons, and M. Gyssens. A unified theory of structural tractability for constraint satisfaction and spread cut decomposition. In *Proc. 19th Int'l Joint Conf. on Artificial Intelligence*, pages 72–77, 2005.

15. M. C. Cooper. An optimal k-consistency algorithm. *Artificial Intelligence*, 41(1):89–95, 1989.

16. B. Courcelle, J. A. Makowsky, and U. Rotics. Linear time solvable optimization problems on graphs of bounded cliquewidth. *Theory of Computing Systems*, 33:125–150, 2000.

17. V. Dalmau. Generalized majority–minority operations are tractable. In *Proc. 20th IEEE Symp. on Logic in Computer Science*, pages 438–447, 2005.

18. V. Dalmau, Ph. G. Kolaitis, and M.Y. Vardi. Constraint satisfaction, bounded treewidth, and finite-variable logics. In P. Van Hentenryck, editor, *Proc. 8th Int'l Conf. on Constraint Programming*, Lecture Notes in Computer Science, volume 2470, pages 310–326. Springer, 2002.

19. V. Dalmau and J. Pearson. Closure functions and width 1 problems. In *Proc. 5th Int'l Conf. on Principles and Practice of Constraint Programming*, Lecture Notes in Computer Science, volume 1713, pages 159–173. Springer, 1999.

20. R. Dechter. Constraint networks. In S. C. Shapiro, editor, *Encyclopedia of Artificial Intelligence*, pages 276–185. Wiley, New York, 1992.

21. R. Dechter. From local to global consistency. *Artificial Intelligence*, 55(1): 87–107, May 1992.

22. R. Dechter. Bucket elimination: a unifying framework for reasoning. *Artificial Intelligence*, 113(1–2):41–85, 1999.

23. R. Dechter. *Constraint Processing*. Morgan Kaufmman, 2003.

24. R. Dechter and I. Meiri. Experimental evaluation of preprocessing algorithms for constraint satisfaction problems. *Artificial Intelligence*, 68:211–241, 1994.

25. R. Dechter and J. Pearl. Tree clustering for constraint networks. *Artificial Intelligence*, pages 353–366, 1989.

26. R. G. Downey and M. R. Fellows. *Parametrized Complexity*. Springer, 1999.

27. T. Feder. Constraint satisfaction: A personal perspective. Technical report, Electronic Colloquium on Computational Complexity, 2006. Report TR06-021.

28. T. Feder and D. Ford. Classification of bipartite boolean constraint satisfaction through delta-matroid intersection. Technical report, Electronic Colloquium on Computational Complexity, 2005. Report TR05-016.

29. T. Feder and M. Y. Vardi. The computational structure of monotone monadic SNP and constraint satisfaction: a study through Datalog and group theory. *SIAM J. on Computing*, 28:57–104, 1998.

30. T. A. Feder and M. Y. Vardi. Monotone monadic SNP and constraint satisfaction. In *Proc. 25th ACM Symp. on Theory of Computing*, pages 612–622, 1993.

31. E. C. Freuder. Synthesizing constraint expressions. *Communications of the ACM*, 21(11):958–966, November 1978.

32. E. C. Freuder. A sufficient condition for backtrack-free search. *Journal of the Association for Computing Machinery*, 29(1):24–32, 1982.

33. E. C Freuder. Complexity of k-tree structured constraint satisfaction problems. *Proc. 7th National Conference on Artificial Intelligence*, pages 4–9, 1990.

34. D. H. Frost. *Algorithms and Heuristics for Constraint Satisfaction Problems*. PhD thesis, Department of Computer Science, University of California, Irvine, 1997.

35. H. Gaifman, H. Mairson, Y. Sagiv, and M. Y. Vardi. Undecidable optimization problems for database logic programs. In *Proc. 2nd IEEE Symp. on Logic in Computer Science*, pages 106–115, 1987.

36. M. R. Garey and D. S. Johnson. *Computers and Intractability - A Guide to the Theory of NP-Completeness*. W. H. Freeman and Co., 1979.

37. G. Gottlob, N. Leone, and F. Scarcello. The complexity of acyclic conjunctive queries. In *Proc. 39th IEEE Symp. on Foundation of Computer Science*, pages 706–715, 1998.

38. G. Gottlob, N. Leone, and F. Scarcello. A comparison of structural CSP decomposition methods. In *Proc. 16th Int'l Joint Conf. on Artificial Intelligence*, pages 394–399, 1999.

39. G. Gottlob, N. Leone, and F. Scarcello. Hypertree decompositions and tractable queries. In *Proc. 18th ACM Symp. on Principles of Database Systems*, pages 21–32, 1999.

40. M. Grohe. The complexity of homomorphism and constraint satisfaction problems seen from the other side. In *Proc. 44th IEEE Symp. on Foundations of Computer Science*, pages 552–561, 2003.

41. M. Grohe, T. Schwentick, and L. Segoufin. When is the evaluation of conjunctive queries tractable? In *Proc. 33rd ACM Symp. on Theory of Computing*, pages 657–666, 2001.

42. M. Gyssens, P. G. Jeavons, and D. A. Cohen. Decomposition constraint satisfaction problems using database techniques. *Artificial Intelligence*, 66:57–89, 1994.

43. P. Hell and J. Nešetřil. On the complexity of H-coloring. *Journal of Combinatorial Theory, Series B*, 48:92–110, 1990.

44. P. Hell and J. Nešetřil. *Graphs and Homomorphisms*. Oxford Lecture Series in Mathematics and Its applications, No. 28. Oxford University Press, 2004.

45. Ph. G. Kolaitis and J. Panttaja. On the complexity of existential pebble games. In *Proc. 12th Conf. Computer Science Logic*, Lecture Notes in Computer Science, volume 2803, pages 314–329. Springer, 2003.

46. Ph. G. Kolaitis and M. Y. Vardi. The decision problem for the probabilities of higher-order properties. In *Proc. 19th ACM Symp. on Theory of Computing*, pages 425–435, 1987.

47. Ph. G. Kolaitis and M. Y. Vardi. On the expressive power of variable-confined logics. In *Proc. 11th IEEE Symp. on Logic in Computer Science*, pages 348–359, 1996.

48. Ph.G. Kolaitis and M.Y. Vardi. Conjunctive-query containment and constraint satisfaction. *Journal of Computer and System Sciences*, pages 302–332, 2000.
49. Ph.G. Kolaitis and M.Y. Vardi. A game-theoretic approach to constraint satisfaction. In *Proc. of the 17th National Conference on Artificial Intelligence*, pages 175–181, 2000.
50. V. Kumar. Algorithms for constraint-satisfaction problems. *AI Magazine*, 13:32–44, 1992.
51. R. E.—Ladner. On the structure of polynomial time reducibility. *Journal of The Association for Computing Machinery*, 22:155–171, 1975.
52. B. Larose, C. Loten, and C. Tardif. A characterisation of first-order constraint satisfaction problems. In *Proc. 21st IEEE Symp. on Logic in Computer Science*, pages 201–210, 2006.
53. L. A. Levin. Universal sorting problems. *Problemy Peredaci Informacii*, 9:115–116, 1973. In Russian. English translation in *Problems of Information Transmission* 9:265–266, 1973.
54. A. K. Mackworth and E. C. Freuder. The complexity of constraint satisfaction revisited. *Artificial Intelligence*, 59(1–2):57–62, 1993.
55. B. J. McMahan, G. Pan, P. Porter, and M. Y. Vardi. Projection pushing revisited. In *Proc. 9th Int'l Conf. on Extending Database Technology*, Lecture Notes in Computer Science, volume 2992, pages 441–458. Springer, 2004.
56. P. Meseguer. Constraint satisfaction problems: an overview. *AI Communications*, 2:3–16, 1989.
57. C. Papadimitriou and M. Yannakakis. Optimization, approximation and complexity classes. *Journal of Computer and System Sciences*, 43:425–440, 1991.
58. J. Pearson and P. Jeavons. A survey of tractable constraint satisfaction problems. Technical Report CSD-TR-97-15, Royal Holloway University of London, 1997.
59. N. Robertson and P. D. Seymour. Graph minors IV: Tree-width and well-quasi-ordering. *Journal of Combinatorial Theory, Series B*, 48(2):227–254, 1990.
60. E. Rosen. *Finite Model Theory and Finite Variable Logics*. Ph.D. Thesis, University of Pennsylvania, 1995.
61. B. Rossman. Existential positive types and preservation under homomorphisms. In *Proc. 20th IEEE Symp. on Logic in Computer Science*, pages 467–476, 2005.
62. Y. Saraiya. *Subtree Elimination Algorithms in Deductive Databases*. PhD Thesis, Department of Computer Science, Stanford University, 1991.
63. T. J. Schaefer. The complexity of satisfiability problems. In *Proc. 10th ACM Symp. on Theory of Computing*, pages 216–226, 1978.
64. E. P. K. Tsang. *Foundations of Constraint Satisfaction*. Academic Press, 1993.
65. P. van Beek. On the inherent tightness of local consistency in constraint networks. In *Proc. 11th National Conference on Artificial Intelligence*, pages 368–373, 1994.
66. P. van Beek and R. Dechter. Constraint tightness and looseness versus local and global consistency. *Journal of The Association for Computing Machinery*, 44(4):549–566, 1997.
67. M. Y. Vardi. The complexity of relational query languages. In *Proc. 14th ACM Symp. on Theory of Computing*, pages 137–146, 1982.
68. M. Y. Vardi. On the complexity of bounded-variable queries. In *Proc. 14th ACM Symp. on Principles of Database Systems*, pages 266–76, 1995.
69. M. Yannakakis. Algorithms for acyclic database schemes. In *Proc. 7 Int'l Conf. on Very Large Data Bases*, pages 82–94, 1981.

7

Local Variations on a Loose Theme: Modal Logic and Decidability

Maarten Marx and Yde Venema

7.1 Introduction

This chapter is about decidability and complexity issues in modal logic; more specifically, we confine ourselves to *satisfiability* (and the complementary *validity*) problems. The satisfiability problem is the following: for a fixed class of models, to determine whether a given formula φ is satisfiable in some model of that class (a more precise definition will follow). The general picture is that modal logic behaves quite well in this respect. In fact, many authors follow Vardi [58] in calling modal logic *robustly* decidable on the ground that most of the nice computational properties of modal logic are preserved if one considers extensions or variants of the basic system. The main aim of this chapter is to refine and analyze this picture.

To start with, we should clarify what we are talking about when using the term "modal logic". Traditionally, propositional modal logic would be described as an extension of propositional logic with operators $\Box$ and $\Diamond$ for talking about the necessity and possibility of a formula being true. However, nowadays the term "modal logic" is used for a plethora of formalisms, with applications in various disciplines ranging from linguistics to economics, see [11, 17, 39, 56] for a sample of applications in computer science.

And while (propositional) modal logics will usually still be an extension of classical propositional logic with a number of modal operators, the intended meanings of these operators differ enormously. For instance, the formula $\Box_a \varphi$ could mean "player a knows that φ is the case" in a formalization of game theory, or "after the execution of program a, φ will be the case" in a formal language for program verification. Fortunately, on a technical level, all these formalisms still have a lot in common. That is why this chapter first introduces the notion of a *modal system* as a triple consisting of a (propositional) modal language, a class of models and a truth function. This definition covers most of the systems that appear in the literature under the name "modal logic"; in particular, the familiar system of *basic modal logic*, to be discussed in Sect. 7.3.

Now that we know what modal logic is, can we say what makes it so robustly decidable? If we confine ourselves to *basic modal logic*, the answer seems to be affirmative. As we shall see further on, the fact that the truth of basic modal formulas is invariant under *bisimulations* ensures that basic modal logic has the *tree model property*. That is, every satisfiable modal formula is satisfiable in a special, "loose", model based on a tree. This makes it much easier to check whether a given modal formula is satisfiable: one only needs to worry about these loose models. And since the bisimulation invariance property transfers to many extensions and variants of the basic modal system, so does the decidability of the satisfiability problem.

This analysis, due to Vardi [58], in terms of a *looseness* principle, will form the main theme of our chapter. However, it can only form part of the story. For instance, suppose that we are interested not just in decidability, but also in the computational complexity of the satisfiability problem. Not all loose modal systems are in the same complexity class, so there must be principles besides looseness that determine the computational behavior of a modal system. Or, what if we happen to be working with a modal system that does not allow trees as models? Will this necessarily make the logic undecidable? Answers to such questions cannot be precise and general at the same time — note that the problem of whether a given modal axiom determines a decidable modal logic ("logic" here in the technical sense; see below), is itself undecidable! Nevertheless, we believe that it is possible to provide some rough guidelines, and we shall discuss some of these in this chapter; in particular, at the end of Sect. 7.3, we discuss two *locality principles*.

Thus, it is our aim to act as the reader's travel guide in the landscape of modal logics by pointing out some interesting decidability and complexity theoretic phenomena and by suggesting an interpretation of these phenomena as local variations on a loose theme. On the trip we shall introduce some important modal systems and proof methods — but we have not aimed for a complete or systematic overview in this respect. (For instance, we shall not employ any automata-theoretic methods.) No previous exposure of the reader to modal logic is assumed. Finally, we do not usually provide credits or give references in running text; these are supplied in the "Notes" paragraphs that finish each section.

Overview of chapter In the next section we explain our interpretation of the terms "modal logic" and "modal systems", and we define the notion of bisimulation. Section 7.3 discusses basic modal logic, giving a detailed proof of the decidability of its satisfiability problem; analyzing this proof, we introduce the notions of looseness and locality. In the section after that, we use a number of examples to show what happens if we play around a bit with these principles. Section 7.5 is devoted to a more fine-grained, complexity-theoretic study of the modal satisfiability problem. In the last section, we show how one can use the principles discussed in the earlier parts of the chapter to find large fragments of ordinary first-order logic that have a decidable satisfiability problem.

7.2 Modal Systems and Bisimulations

In this section, we discuss our interpretation of the term "modal logic" by defining and explaining the notion of a modal system. We also introduce the fundamental notion of similarity between two modal models, namely that of a *bisimulation*. The link between modal logic and bisimulation is that modal formulas cannot distinguish bisimilar points.

Modal Systems

A modal system consists of a modal language $\mathcal{L}$, a class of models K, and a function ⊩ interpreting formulas of the language in the models. As *models*, we shall consider only relational structures, that is, structures consisting of a nonempty domain or universe together with a number of relations on it. By the *size* of a model $\mathcal{M}$, we always denote the size of its domain. The elements of the universe of a model will be called *states, points*, or *worlds*. In the modal part of this chapter we shall confine ourselves to models that have a number of *binary* relations (usually just one, which we denote by R) and a countable number of unary relations P_0, P_1, ... See Figure 7.1 for a graphical presentation of these models.

A modal *language* is a simple yet expressive language for talking about such relational structures. In this chapter we consider only *propositional* modal languages; these can be described as extensions of the classical propositional language with a collection of modal connectives such as the unary modal operator ◇. Like the boolean connectives, the modal operators do not bind variables. The *size* of a formula φ (notation $|\varphi|$) in a modal language $\mathcal{L}(\Phi)$ (i.e., with propositional variables from a set Φ) is its length over the alphabet $\Phi \cup \{\neg, \wedge, (,), \nabla_i\}_{i \in I}$, where $\{\nabla_i \mid i \in I\}$ denotes the set of modal connectives of $\mathcal{L}$.

$\mathcal{M}_1$

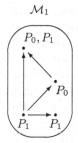

A model $\mathcal{M} = (W, R, P_0, P_1)$ can be seen as a colored directed graph; the edges give the relation R, and the colors show the interpretation of the unary predicates. (Note that points can have more than one color.) The graph part (W, R) of the model is also called a *modal frame*.

Fig. 7.1. Graphical representation of a model

Finally, ⊩ is a function which takes a model $\mathcal{M}$ and a formula φ and returns a subset of the domain of $\mathcal{M}$ that we shall think of as the *meaning* of φ in the model. The standard terminology for stating that $s \in {\Vdash}(\mathcal{M}, \varphi)$ is that φ *is true* or *holds* at s in $\mathcal{M}$, and the standard notation is

$$\mathcal{M}, s \Vdash \varphi.$$

The meaning of the propositional variable p_i is the corresponding set P_i, and thus

$$\mathcal{M}, s \Vdash p_i \leftrightarrow P_i s.$$

For the Boolean connectives we have the standard interpretation in mind, which requires that $\neg\varphi$ is true at a state iff φ is false (i.e., not true) at it, and that $\varphi \wedge \psi$ holds precisely at those states where both φ and ψ hold.

The conditions on modal systems mentioned so far still allow for an enormous freedom in defining the semantics of the modal connectives. But even in this very wide and general setting we can introduce the notions of *satisfiability* and *validity* associated with such a triple: we call a formula *valid* if it is true at every state of every model of the system, and *satisfiable* if it is true at some state of some model of the system. The *validity problem* of a modal system is the problem of deciding whether a given formula of the language is valid or not; the *satisfiability* problem is defined analogously. Given our constraints on the interpretation of Boolean negation, it is obvious that a formula ξ is valid in a class K of models if and only if its negation $\neg\xi$ is not satisfiable in any model in K. Hence, for any class of models K, there are constant-time reductions between the satisfiability problem and the *complement* of the validity problem. We shall use this fact in what follows without explicit mention; also, we shall use the term "complexity of a modal system" when referring to its satisfiability problem.

Each of the three ingredients of a modal system — the language $\mathcal{L}$, the class K of models, and the interpretation function ⊩ — influences the complexity of the satisfiability problem. We shall see that many important and interesting modal systems have a decidable satisfiability problem, but the above definition of a modal system is also wide enough to allow for systems whose satisfiability problem is highly undecidable. Our aim in this chapter is to provide some rough guidelines for determining the complexity of a modal system. For the sake of a simple exposition, we first restrict our attention to a simple yet interesting type of models: those of the signature with one binary relation R and a number of unary relations. Even with this signature fixed, we still have an enormous freedom in defining the modal language $\mathcal{L}$ and the meaning of the modal connectives given by the function ⊩. What, then, the reader will ask, is particularly *modal* about a system? We shall now state a further restriction on modal systems which is very characteristic of modal logic. It concerns the discriminatory power of modal languages.

Bisimulation

An informative way to identify a language is by saying which differences between models it is blind to. In the case of modal logic, the fundamental concept of equivalence between structures involves the notion of *bisimulation*.

Definition 7.2.1. *Given two models* $\mathcal{M} = (W, R, P_i)_{i \in I}$ *and* $\mathcal{M}' = (W', R', P_i')_{i \in I}$, *a nonempty relation* $Z \subseteq W \times W'$ *is a* bisimulation *between* $\mathcal{M}$ *and* $\mathcal{M}'$ *if the following three conditions hold, for all states* $s \in W$ *and* $s' \in W'$ *that are linked by* Z:

(base) *for all* i: $P_i s$ *iff* $P_i' s'$;
(forth) *for all* $t \in W$ *such that* Rst, *there is a* $t' \in W'$ *with* $R's't'$ *and* tZt';
(back) *for all* $t' \in W'$ *such that* $R's't'$, *there is a* $t \in W$ *with* Rst *and* tZt'.

If there is some bisimulation Z *linking* s *and* s', *then we say that* s *and* s' *are* bisimilar; *as notation we use:* $s \leftrightarrow s'$, *or* $\mathcal{M}, s \leftrightarrow \mathcal{M}', s'$ *if we wish to make the models explicit.*

Figure 7.2 contains two simple examples of bisimulating models (the models bisimulate horizontally) in a language with only one unary relation P. Figure 7.3 shows two models which do not bisimulate at the roots. All states in both models satisfy the same unary relations; $\mathcal{M}'$ has all of the finite branches that $\mathcal{M}$ has, but in addition it contains an infinite branch.

We can now make the crucial restriction on $\Vdash$ precise: we want the truth of modal formulas to be invariant under bisimulations. That is, our basic

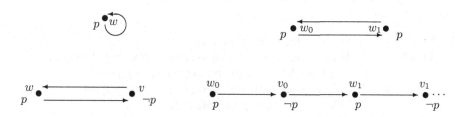

Fig. 7.2. Two examples of bisimulating models

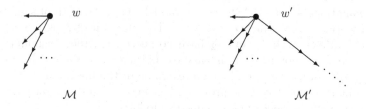

Fig. 7.3. $\mathcal{M}, w$ and $\mathcal{M}', w'$ are not bisimilar

interest is in a truth definition for the modal connectives that makes the semantics satisfy the following constraint:

$$\text{if } \mathcal{M}, s \leftrightharpoons \mathcal{M}', s', \text{ then for all } \varphi: \mathcal{M}, s \Vdash \varphi \text{ iff } \mathcal{M}', s' \Vdash \varphi. \qquad (7.1)$$

We shall call any system in which $\Vdash$ meets this constraint a *modal system in the narrow sense*.

But *why* would we be interested in a language that cannot see the difference between bisimilar states (if not for technical reasons)? Apart from the original logical considerations that we are about to describe, an important reason stems from theoretical computer science. Here, or more specifically in the field of *process theory*, one models processes as *labeled transition systems*; these are relational structures like the one we describe here, though usually with a *collection* of binary relations instead of just one. The idea here is that a state s in a model $\mathcal{M}$ represents some state of the process: the predicates P_i correspond to various direct *observations* that we can make about states, and the relations R_j correspond to the various *transition steps* that the process may take. A pair (s, t) belonging to the relation R_j indicates that at s the process can take an R_j-step, thus reaching the state t, where new direct observations can be made, or new steps can be taken. Now, in this context, states that are bisimilar cannot be distinguished from a process-theoretic point of view and thus represent the *same* state. Thus, bisimulation serves as one of the most fundamental notions of *identity* between process states. This explains why languages designed for expressing properties of processes should indeed be blind to the distinction between bisimilar states.

Let us turn to some concrete examples. We first give some examples of operators which meet this requirement:

$\mathcal{M}, s \Vdash \Diamond\varphi$ if $\mathcal{M}, t \Vdash \varphi$ for some t such that Rst;
$\mathcal{M}, s \Vdash \langle * \rangle\varphi$ if there is some path $s = s_0 R s_1 R s_2 \ldots R s_n = t$ through $\mathcal{M}$
    such that $\mathcal{M}, t \Vdash \varphi$ (including the empty path);
$\mathcal{M}, s \Vdash \overset{\infty}{\Diamond}\varphi$ if there is some path $s = s_0 R s_1 R s_2 \ldots$ through $\mathcal{M}$
    such that $\mathcal{M}, s_i \Vdash \varphi$ for infinitely many i.

We shall show later on that indeed, $\Diamond$ does not break the bisimulation invariance (see (7.2) below; the proofs for the other operators are left to the reader).

The operators $\langle \neq \rangle, \mathsf{E}, \mathsf{P}$, and U defined below are not invariant under bisimulations. Figure 7.4 shows two models $\mathcal{M}_1, \mathcal{M}_2$, both of signature R, P, and worlds s_1, s_2, which bisimulate. The valuation of P is indicated in the models. Since both s_1 and s_2 have no successors, they bisimulate because they are both not in P. It is easy to see that $\langle \neq \rangle p, \mathsf{E}p$ and $\mathsf{P}p$ are all true at s_1 and all false at s_2. A counterexample to the bisimulation invariance of the binary connective U is provided just above Figure 7.7 on page 398. The semantics of the operators is defined as follows:

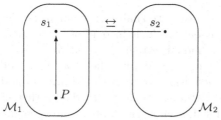

Fig. 7.4. The modal operators $\langle\neq\rangle$, E and P are not invariant under bisimulations

$$\mathcal{M}, s \Vdash \langle\neq\rangle\varphi \quad \text{if } \mathcal{M}, t \Vdash \varphi \text{ for some } t \text{ such that } s \neq t;$$
$$\mathcal{M}, s \Vdash \mathsf{E}\varphi \quad\;\; \text{if } \mathcal{M}, t \Vdash \varphi \text{ for some } t \text{ in } \mathcal{M};$$
$$\mathcal{M}, s \Vdash \mathsf{P}\varphi \quad\;\; \text{if } \mathcal{M}, t \Vdash \varphi \text{ for some } t \text{ such that } Rts;$$
$$\mathcal{M}, s \Vdash U(\varphi, \psi) \text{ if } \mathcal{M}, u \Vdash \varphi \text{ for some } u \text{ such that } Rsu;$$
$$\qquad\qquad\qquad \text{while } \mathcal{M}, t \Vdash \psi \text{ for all } t \text{ satisfying } Rst \text{ and } Rtu.$$

It seems that $\Diamond$ is the simplest nontrivial operator that satisfies the condition of bisimulation invariance. The modal system in which we take $\Diamond$ as the only modal operator, in which we allow every relational structure (of the appropriate signature) as a model, and in which $\Vdash$ has the standard definition, is called the *basic modal logic*. It is discussed in detail in Sect. 7.3.

Some Comments

Before turning to the discussion of the basic modal system, a few comments are in place.

First, it was not our intention to give very rigid definitions. For instance, the question of whether the universal diamond E constitutes a modal system in the narrow sense is really dependent on the perspective that one takes. Earlier on we said that E is not bisimulation-invariant, but what if we take as our *class of models* precisely those in which R is the universal relation on the model (that is, $\forall xy\, Rxy$)? In this case the truth definition for E *does* satisfy the standard, "bisimulation-invariant" clause for the diamond E; the only thing is that now, our class of models is not closed under taking bisimilar models...

Second, in our introductory discussion we avoided the word "logic". In principle, we prefer to use this word in the technical sense only, referring to a *set of formulas* that satisfies certain closure properties. For instance, a *normal modal logic* should be closed under the familiar law of Modus Ponens, and under the rule of Necessitation; the latter means that $\Box\varphi$ belongs to the logic whenever φ does. We can associate such a logic with many modal systems; in particular, when the system's class of models is defined through some property of the binary relation(s) only, the collection of valid formulas will form a logic in the technical sense. Thus the validity problem can often be identified with a membership problem, namely that of a formula in a logic. In a number of cases, we shall forget our principles and follow custom in referring to this associated logic instead of to the modal system.

Finally, the term "modal system *in the narrow sense*" should not be taken too literally; by playing around with the class K of models, the reader will easily see that our definition covers a wide range of modal logics. In fact, if we allow languages with more than one modality, then even various versions of first-order logic itself, such as the finite-variable fragments, can be seen as modal systems in the narrow sense!

7.3 Basic Modal Logic

In this section, we shall introduce the basic system of modal logic and discuss its close connection to the notion of bisimulation. We shall provide a fairly detailed proof of the decidability of the satisfiability problem for basic modal logic and analyze this result in terms of looseness and locality.

Definition 7.3.1. *Given a set Φ of propositional variables, the collection $\mathcal{L}_\Diamond(\Phi)$ of basic modal formulas in Φ is given by the following rule:*

$$\varphi ::= p \mid \neg\varphi \mid \varphi \wedge \psi \mid \Diamond\varphi,$$

where p ranges over elements of Φ. This means that φ is either an atomic formula consisting of a proposition letter in Φ, or a more complex formula obtained from simpler ones by applying one of the connectives $\neg$, $\wedge$, or $\Diamond$. We shall use the standard Boolean abbreviations and also the modal "box" operator $\Box$, where $\Box\varphi$ abbreviates $\neg\Diamond\neg\varphi$.

If the collection Φ of proposition letters is either irrelevant or clear from context, we shall frequently omit it, writing $\mathcal{L}_\Diamond$ instead of $\mathcal{L}_\Diamond(\Phi)$. In order to interpret the formulas of this language in a model of the kind discussed above, we represent such a model as a triple $\mathcal{M} = (W, R, V)$ where W is a nonempty set of states, R is the binary relation of the model, and $V : \Phi \to \mathcal{P}(W)$ is a *valuation* mapping proposition letters to subsets of W. Let M denote the class of all such models.

Definition 7.3.2. *Given a model $\mathcal{M} = (W, R, V)$, a state $s \in W$, and a formula φ, we define the notion of φ being true at s, denoted by $\mathcal{M}, s \Vdash \varphi$, recursively as follows:*

$$
\begin{aligned}
&\mathcal{M}, s \Vdash p && \text{if } s \in V(p); \\
&\mathcal{M}, s \Vdash \neg\varphi && \text{if not } \mathcal{M}, s \Vdash \varphi; \\
&\mathcal{M}, s \Vdash \varphi \wedge \psi && \text{if } \mathcal{M}, s \Vdash \varphi \text{ and } \mathcal{M}, s \Vdash \psi; \\
&\mathcal{M}, s \Vdash \Diamond\varphi && \text{if } \mathcal{M}, t \Vdash \varphi \text{ for some } t \text{ such that } Rst.
\end{aligned}
$$

If φ is true at every state of the model we say that φ holds throughout $\mathcal{M}$, denoted by $\mathcal{M} \Vdash \varphi$; if φ holds at some state in $\mathcal{M}$, we say that φ is satisfiable in $\mathcal{M}$.

The language of the basic modal system *is* $\mathcal{L}_\diamond$, *its class of models is* M, *and* $\Vdash$ *is as in the first part of this definition. Depending on the context, we let* **K** *denote either the basic modal system itself or its logic, that is, the set of valid formulas in this system.*

As the reader can easily verify, it holds that

$$\mathcal{M}, s \Vdash \Box\varphi \text{ if } \mathcal{M}, t \Vdash \varphi \text{ for all } t \text{ such that } Rst.$$

The first thing we should check is whether we have met our design criterion (7.1) with this definition of $\Vdash$. Suppose that $\mathcal{M}$ and $\mathcal{M}'$ are two modal models, and that Z is a bisimulation between $\mathcal{M}$ and $\mathcal{M}'$. We shall prove by a formula induction that every basic modal formula φ satisfies the following:

$$\text{for all } s \in W \text{ and } s' \in W': sZs' \text{ implies that } \mathcal{M}, s \Vdash \varphi \text{ iff } \mathcal{M}', s' \Vdash \varphi. \quad (7.2)$$

We leave the base step and the boolean cases of the inductive step as exercises for the reader, and concentrate on the modal case of the inductive step. Suppose that φ is of the form $\diamond\psi$, and assume that Z links the state s in $\mathcal{M}$ to s' in $\mathcal{M}'$. For reasons of symmetry, it suffices to show that $\mathcal{M}, s \Vdash \varphi$ only if $\mathcal{M}', s' \Vdash \varphi$.

Suppose that $\mathcal{M}, s \Vdash \diamond\psi$. By the truth definition, it follows that there is a state t in W such that Rst and $\mathcal{M}, t \Vdash \psi$. From the fact that s and s' are linked by the bisimulation Z, we may infer that there is some R-successor t' of s' such that $s'Zt'$. The inductive hypothesis gives us that $\mathcal{M}', t' \Vdash \psi$; but we may then conclude from $R's't'$ that $\mathcal{M}', s' \Vdash \diamond\psi$, which is precisely what we were after. This proves (7.2) and shows that basic modal logic indeed constitutes a bisimulation-invariant system.

Invariance Under Bisimulation

So our definition fulfills our design criterion, but how powerful is this modal language precisely? In other words, how many of the bisimulation-invariant properties can we express in this language? It should be obvious from the truth definition of basic modal logic that we can consider $\mathcal{L}_\diamond$ as a fragment of first-order logic. In fact, we have a kind of functional completeness result as long as we consider first-order properties: *every first-order definable bisimulation-invariant property is definable by a modal formula.* In other words, when it comes to expressing bisimulation-invariant properties, modal logic is *just as strong* as first-order logic. In order to state this result formally we need a translation from modal to first-order formulas.

Definition 7.3.3. *Assume that we have an enumeration* $x = x_0, x_1, \ldots$ *of first-order variables. Consider the following translation of* $\mathcal{L}_\diamond$-*formulas to first-order formulas:*

$$ST_{x_i}(p) = Px_i$$
$$ST_{x_i}(\neg\varphi) = \neg ST_{x_i}(\varphi)$$
$$ST_{x_i}(\varphi \wedge \psi) = ST_{x_i}(\varphi) \wedge ST_{x_i}(\psi)$$
$$ST_{x_i}(\Diamond\psi) = \exists x_{i+1}(Rx_ix_{i+1} \wedge ST_{x_{i+1}}(\varphi)).$$

When we speak of "the" standard translation of a modal formula φ, we are usually referring to the formula $ST_{x_0}(\varphi)$.

We can now see modal logic as a fragment of first-order logic because every modal formula is *equivalent* to its standard translation. Formally (but blurring the distinction between a modal and a first-order model a little), we can prove that for every modal formula φ, for every model $\mathcal{M}$, and for every state s in $\mathcal{M}$ we have the following equivalence:

$$\mathcal{M}, s \Vdash \varphi \leftrightarrow \mathcal{M} \models ST_{x_0}(\varphi)[x_0 \mapsto s]. \tag{7.3}$$

Here $[x_0 \mapsto s]$ denotes any assignment which sends x_0 to s. The simple proof of (7.3) is left to the reader.

Observation 1 The map in Definition 7.3.3 has no upper bound on the number of variables used in the first-order translation of a modal formula. However, one could be very parsimonious and define the formulas $ST_x(\varphi)$ and $ST_y(\varphi)$ through a mutual recursion, of which the interesting clauses run as follows:

$$ST_x(\Diamond\psi) = \exists y(Rxy \wedge ST_y(\varphi))$$
$$ST_y(\Diamond\psi) = \exists x(Ryx \wedge ST_x(\varphi)).$$

This shows that, in fact, the translation of modal logic to first-order logic can be carried out within the *two variable fragment* of first-order logic. We shall come back to this observation later on.

Now we are ready to state the celebrated Characterization Theorem for modal logic.

Theorem 7.3.4. *Let $\varphi(x)$ be a first-order formula in the signature consisting of a binary R and a set $\{P_i \mid i \in I\}$ of unary predicates. Then $\varphi(x)$ is invariant under bisimulations if and only if it is equivalent to the standard translation of a modal formula.*

The proof of the functional completeness part of the theorem (the left-to-right direction) falls outside the scope of this book but can be found in any good textbook on modal logic; see the notes. The other direction of the theorem, which just states that the modal language obeys the design criterion (7.1), is the more important one for us here. One way to look at (7.1) is that once we know that a formula is satisfiable at *some* state in *some* model, we know by the invariance result that it is also satisfiable in *any bisimilar* state in *any bisimilar* model. This means that we can *transform* the original model into one that suits our purposes best. Obviously, this method applies to any notion of invariance for any language. The nice thing about bisimulation, however, is that it allows the freedom of completely *unraveling* a model into a tree model.

Definition 7.3.5. *Given a model* $\mathcal{M} = (W, R, V)$ *and a state* s_1 *in* $\mathcal{M}$, *we define the* unraveling *or* unwinding *of* $\mathcal{M}$ *around* s_1 *as the following model* $\mathcal{M}_{s_1}^u = (\vec{W}_{s_1}, \vec{R}, \vec{V})$. *Its universe* $\vec{W}_{s_1}$ *is defined as the set of all finite paths through* $\mathcal{M}$ *starting at* s_1; *formally,* $\vec{W}_{s_1}$ *is the collection of all tuples* $\langle s_1, \ldots, s_n \rangle$ *(with $n \geq 1$) that satisfy* Rs_is_{i+1} *for all* $i < n$. *The relation* $\vec{R}$ *holds of the tuples* $\bar{s} = \langle s_1, \ldots, s_n \rangle$ *and* $\bar{t} = \langle t_1, \ldots, t_m \rangle$ *if and only if* $\bar{t}$ *is obtained from* $\bar{s}$ *by adding an R-successor of* s_n. *Formally, we put* $\vec{R}\bar{s}\bar{t}$ *if* $m = n + 1$ *and* $s_i = t_i$ *for all* $1 \leq i \leq n$. *Finally, the truth of a proposition letter at a tuple is completely determined by its truth in* $\mathcal{M}$ *at the last element of the tuple. Formally, let* $last(\langle s_1, \ldots, s_n \rangle)$ *denote the state* s_n, *and define* $\vec{V}$ *by* $\vec{V}(p) = \{\bar{s} \in \vec{W}_{s_1} \mid last(\bar{s}) \in V(p)\}$.

An example of an unraveling is given in Figure 7.5. Another example can be found in Figure 7.2, in which the model on the lower right-hand side is (an isomorphic copy of) the unraveling of the model on the lower left-hand side.

The operation of unraveling is also well known from process theory: the points of the unravelled model $\mathcal{M}_{s_1}^u$ can be viewed as the process *histories* or *traces* that start at s. From a *technical* perspective, the unraveling of $\mathcal{M}$ around s_1 has certain desirable properties:

- there exists a point with no predecessor, the *root*;
- $\vec{R}$ is acyclic; and
- $\vec{R}$ is injective in the sense that every point except the root has a unique predecessor.

In other words, the graph $(\vec{W}_{s_1}, \vec{R})$ is a *tree*. It is useful to look at this tree as being a *normal form* of the model.

One can easily check that for any model $\mathcal{M}$ and any state s in $\mathcal{M}$, the (graph of the) function $last : \vec{W}_s \to W$ constitutes a bisimulation between $\mathcal{M}_s^u$ and $\mathcal{M}$ that links $\langle s \rangle$ to s. But it immediately follows from this that $\langle s \rangle$ (in $\mathcal{M}_s^u$) satisfies exactly the same formulas as s (in $\mathcal{M}$). Combining this with the observation that unravelings are trees, we find that every satisfiable basic modal formula is also satisfiable in a tree. We say that a modal system $(\mathcal{L}, \mathsf{K}, \Vdash)$ has the *tree model property* if, for every satisfiable formula ξ in $\mathcal{L}$, there exists a tree in K in which ξ is satisfiable. Thus we have established the following.

Theorem 7.3.6. *The basic modal system has the tree model property.*

The following observation is a driving force behind our search for decidable modal fragments of first-order logic.

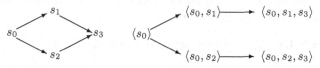

Fig. 7.5. Example of an unraveling

Observation 2. In proving the last theorem we did not use any property of basic modal logic other than its invariance under bisimulation. This means that, in fact, any modal system with a bisimulation-invariant semantics has the tree model property — provided, of course, that tree models are admissible in the system!

Games

In order to facilitate a comparison with the Ehrenfeucht-Fraïssé games often used in first-order logic, it is convenient to rephrase the notion of a bisimulation between two models in game-theoretic terms. Let $\mathcal{M} = (W, R, V)$ and $\mathcal{M}' = (W', R', V')$ be two models, and let s_0 and s_0' be two states in $\mathcal{M}$ and $\mathcal{M}'$, respectively.

We define the bisimulation game as a variant of the familiar Ehrenfeucht-Fraïssé games. In each round of the bisimulation game, $\forall$ selects one of the two models and, inside this model, he chooses a successor of the element played in the previous round (in the first round he chooses a successor of s_0 or s_0'). $\exists$ responds with a successor of the last element played in the other structure. The *length* l of the game is defined as the number of rounds and can be either finite or infinite. A *match* of the game thus gives rise to two sequences: $\bar{s} = s_0, s_1, s_2, \cdots$ and $\bar{s}' = s_0', s_1', s_2', \cdots$, of elements in $\mathcal{M}$ and $\mathcal{M}'$, respectively.

$\exists$ *wins* this match of the game if for each i, s_i and s_i' agree on the truth of all propositional variables; otherwise, $\forall$ wins. We say that $\exists$ has a *winning strategy* in the game $\mathcal{G}_b^l(\mathcal{M}, \mathcal{M}', s, s')$ of l rounds played in $\mathcal{M}, s, \mathcal{M}', s'$ if $\exists$ can win *every* match of length at most l starting in the states s and s'.

It should be fairly clear that $\forall$ is trying to spoil a bisimulation between $\mathcal{M}, s$ and $\mathcal{M}', s'$, while $\exists$ has the opposite intention. Indeed we have a precise game-theoretic characterization of the notion of bisimulation.

Proposition 7.3.7. *There exists a bisimulation between $\mathcal{M}, s$ and $\mathcal{M}', s'$ if and only if $\exists$ has a winning strategy in the game $\mathcal{G}_b^\omega(\mathcal{M}, \mathcal{M}', s, s')$.*

As a corollary, we find that the truth of modal formulas is preserved when $\exists$ has a winning strategy in the game $\mathcal{G}_b^\omega(\mathcal{M}, \mathcal{M}', s, s')$. What is interesting about these games is that they facilitate a more fine-grained perspective on such connections. In particular, if $\exists$ has a winning strategy in a game of fixed finite length n, what can we say about the preservation of modal formulas? Quite a lot, according to the proposition below; in order to formulate it, we need the notion of the *modal depth* of a formula — the straightforward analog of first-order logic's quantifier depth.

Definition 7.3.8. *The modal depth $d_\Diamond(\varphi)$ of a modal formula is inductively defined as follows:*

$$d_\Diamond(p) = 0$$
$$d_\Diamond(\neg\psi) = d_\Diamond(\psi)$$
$$d_\Diamond(\psi_1 \wedge \psi_2) = max(d_\Diamond(\psi_1), d_\Diamond(\psi_2))$$
$$d_\Diamond(\Diamond\psi) = 1 + d_\Diamond(\psi).$$

Proposition 7.3.9. *Let Φ be a finite set of proposition letters, and let n be some natural number. The following are then equivalent:*

1. *$\exists$ has a winning strategy in the game $\mathcal{G}_b^n(\mathcal{M}, \mathcal{M}', s, s')$.*
2. *$\mathcal{M}, s$ and $\mathcal{M}', s'$ satisfy the same $\mathcal{L}_\Diamond(\Phi)$ formulas up to modal depth n.*

We omit the fairly standard proof of this proposition — the notes contain references. The analogous proposition relating $\mathcal{G}_b^\omega(\mathcal{M}, \mathcal{M}', s, s')$ and the full modal language does not hold, as is witnessed by the models in Figure 7.3.

What have we gained from this slightly more fine-grained analysis of modal logic? We have already seen that any satisfiable modal formula ξ can also be satisfied at the root s of a tree model $\mathcal{M}$: take, for instance, some unraveling of the original model. From Proposition 7.3.9 we can conclude that such a ξ can also be satisfied in a *bounded-depth* tree model $\mathcal{M}'$: simply take the tree model $\mathcal{M}$ and throw away all states that are further than d steps away from the root s (where d is the modal depth of ξ). It is obvious that $\exists$ has a winning strategy in the bisimulation game $\mathcal{G}_b^d(\mathcal{M}, \mathcal{M}', s, s)$. From this it follows that ξ holds at the root s of the bounded-depth tree $\mathcal{M}'$.

Finite Trees

We shall now show that the satisfiability problem for the basic modal language (with respect to the class of all models) is indeed *decidable*. We shall do so by establishing the *bounded model property*. A modal language is said to have this property with respect to a class K of models if every formula ξ that is satisfiable in some model in K can in fact be satisfied in a *finite* model in K of *bounded* size (that is, the size of the model is bounded by some computable function on $|\xi|$).

Now, in order to show that the language of basic model logic has this bounded model property, let ξ be an arbitrary satisfiable formula. We have already seen that we may assume that ξ is true at the root of a tree model $\mathcal{M}$ of depth not exceeding the modal depth of ξ. This tree model might still be infinite because of infinite branching, but now we recursively prune the tree as follows. Starting at the root, for every subformula of ξ of the form $\Diamond\varphi$, we choose a successor of the root at which φ is true (if such a successor exists at all). Obviously, at most b successors can be chosen, where b is the number of diamond subformulas of ξ. Hence, by deleting from the model all successors that have not been chosen, together with their descendants, we obtain a tree model whose branching degree at the root is at most b. A simple verification shows that ξ still holds at the root. Now we repeat this process at each of the chosen successors of the root and continue until the leaves of the tree are reached. Obviously, ξ is still satisfied at the root.

Thus we have proved the following.

Proposition 7.3.10. *Any satisfiable modal formula ξ can be satisfied at the root of a finite tree model, of which the depth is bounded by the modal depth of ξ and the branching degree is bounded by the number of diamond subformulas of ξ.*

The decidability of basic modal logic is a straightforward corollary of this. (For instance, we can use the standard translation, the equivalence (7.3), and the fact that first-order model checking is decidable.)

Theorem 7.3.11. *The basic modal system $\mathbf{K}$ has a decidable satisfiability problem.*

We shall now describe a decision procedure which on input ξ systematically tries to build the tree model for ξ described in Proposition 7.3.10. The procedure is based on a simple but powerful idea: it tries to build a model (W, R, V) in which

1. the states are finite sets Δ of "relevant" formulas;
2. we have the following "truth = membership" principle:

$$\varphi \in \Delta \leftrightarrow \mathcal{M}, \Delta \Vdash \varphi, \tag{7.4}$$

for all relevant formulas φ and for all states Δ in the model.

Suppose we can build such a model for an input formula ξ. Then by the *truth lemma* (7.4), ξ is satisfiable if it belongs to some state Δ in our model. Our implementation of the decision procedure is based purely on the proof of the truth lemma; hence, in order to motivate the procedure, we now indicate how to arrive at this proof. Fix a formula ξ.

Let us first confine the collection of relevant formulas. This set will change from state to state but, basically, all relevant formulas will be subformulas of ξ; we need a little extra, though. Given a formula φ, let $\sim\varphi$ denote the formula ψ if φ is of the form $\neg\psi$; otherwise, $\sim\varphi$ is the formula $\neg\varphi$; we say that a set Σ of formulas is closed under taking single negations if $\sim\varphi \in \Sigma$ whenever $\varphi \in \Sigma$. This notion enables us to pretend that a finite set is closed under taking negations by treating $\sim\varphi$ as if it were the real negation of φ. Now, given a set of formulas Σ, let $Cl(\Sigma)$ be the smallest set of formulas that extends Σ and is closed under taking subformulas and single negations. When ξ is a formula, we denote the set $Cl(\{\xi\})$ of relevant ξ formulas as $Cl(\xi)$; it is easy to see that the cardinality of $Cl(\xi)$ is linear in the length of ξ.

Each state of our model $\mathcal{M} = (W, R, V)$ will be a subset of $Cl(\xi)$, but rather than precisely define the universe W now, we assume here that we *have* defined it, and gather sufficient requirements to be placed on this definition to enable a proof of (7.4). First we consider the valuation: the truth lemma prescribes a unique way to define V, at least for the proposition letters occurring in ξ: $V(p) = \{\Delta \mid p \in \Delta\}$. For a definition of the relation R, we shall be rather opportunistic. Again we use the truth lemma as our guideline: it shows that if $R(\Delta, \Delta')$ is to hold, then we should avoid the existence of a relevant formula $\Diamond\varphi$ such that $\varphi \in \Delta'$ but $\Diamond\varphi \notin \Delta$. Now, R is defined by turning this requirement into a definition: we put (Δ, Δ') into R precisely when the above situation does not occur.

Let us now see what requirements we have to impose on the set W; that is, suppose that we want to give an inductive proof of the "truth = membership" principle. Assume that with each state Δ, we have associated a collection $\Sigma \supseteq \Delta$ of relevant formulas.

Obviously, the atomic case of the truth lemma holds by the definition of V. For the inductive boolean cases to go through, it is sufficient to require that Δ is maximal with respect to being a propositionally consistent subset of Σ. That is, Δ and Σ have to satisfy the following condition $Prop\text{-}Max(\Delta, \Sigma)$:
- (for each $\sim\varphi \in \Sigma$): $\sim\varphi \in \Delta \leftrightarrow \varphi \notin \Delta$; and
- (for each $\varphi \wedge \psi \in \Sigma$): $\varphi \wedge \psi \in \Delta \leftrightarrow \varphi \in \Delta$ and $\psi \in \Delta$.

The inductive modal case imposes two further constraints, one for each direction of the truth lemma. We met the first one already when we defined our relation R, but given that $Prop\text{-}Max(\Delta, \Sigma)$ holds, we can reformulate this condition as follows:

- if $R(\Delta, \Delta')$, then for all $\Diamond\psi \in \Sigma$: $\sim\Diamond\psi \in \Delta$ implies $\sim\psi \in \Delta'$.

This formulation clearly brings about the conditions that *each* successor of Δ should satisfy. The other direction of the truth lemma for the case $\varphi = \Diamond\psi$ presents an *existential* requirement:

- if $\Diamond\psi \in \Delta$, then there has to be a Δ' such that $\psi \in \Delta'$ and $R(\Delta, \Delta')$.

Observe that in this last existential requirement we encounter the branch-cutting argument that we saw earlier on. Then we only kept successor states if there was a reason in the form of a $\Diamond\psi$ formula; now, we only create a successor if we need it as a witness for such a formula. The search for suitable successors is the driving force behind our algorithm.

But what about these associated sets of relevant formulas? Will every formula in $Cl(\xi)$ be relevant throughout the procedure? No, and this is precisely what will bound the recursion depth of the algorithm: the set of relevant formulas will decrease as we move away from the root of the model. This is reminiscent of the bounded depth of the tree model in Proposition 7.3.10. In particular, the set of relevant formulas for a state Δ which is m steps away from the root will consist of all formulas from $Cl(\xi)$ of modal depth at most $d_\Diamond(\xi) - m$.

The algorithm presented in Figure 7.6 implements this search for a tree model. We claim that for sets of formulas Δ and Σ such that Σ is closed under taking subformulas and single negations, $K\text{-}World(\Delta, \Sigma)$ will be true iff there exists a tree model $\mathcal{M}$ such that at the root s, for all $\psi \in \Sigma$, $(\mathcal{M}, s \Vdash \psi \leftrightarrow \psi \in \Delta)$. This function can be used to solve the satisfiability

> Assume that Δ and Σ are finite sets of formulas such that $\Delta \subseteq \Sigma$ and Σ is closed under taking subformulas and single negations.
>
> $K\text{-}World(\Delta, \Sigma)$ if and only if
>
> - $Prop\text{-}Max(\Delta, \Sigma)$, and
> - for each formula $\Diamond\psi \in \Delta$ there is a set $\Delta_\psi \subseteq \Sigma$ such that
>   - $\psi \in \Delta_\psi$,
>   - $(\forall \Diamond\varphi \in \Sigma) : {\sim}\Diamond\varphi \in \Delta \Rightarrow {\sim}\varphi \in \Delta_\psi$, and
>   - $K\text{-}World(\Delta_\psi, Cl(\{\varphi \mid \Diamond\varphi \in \Sigma\}))$.

Fig. 7.6. The function $K\text{-}World$ decides **K** satisfiability

problem for the basic modal system, since ξ is satisfiable iff there exists a set $\Delta \subseteq Cl(\xi)$ such that $\xi \in \Delta$ and $K\text{-}World(\Delta, Cl(\xi))$ is true.

Note that with each recursive call of $K\text{-}World$, the size of the set Σ decreases, since we include formulas of smaller modal depth only. Thus the recursion depth is bounded by the modal depth of the input formula ξ. That the function is correct can be proved by induction on the size of Σ; we leave this to the reader. By an appeal to Savitch's Theorem (PSPACE = NPSPACE), it is not hard to see that the procedure runs in PSPACE. We shall come back to this aspect in Section 7.5.

This finishes the proof of Theorem 7.3.11; in the remainder of this chapter we shall analyze this proof and see how much of it can be used for other (modal) logics.

Looseness and Locality

In analyzing this decidability proof, we can distinguish a number of relevant properties of the basic modal system. First of all, bismulation invariance ensures that, in order to check the satisfiability of a modal formula, we only have to worry about "loose" tree models. We shall call this the *looseness* principle of basic modal logic; this property has recently gained status as either the single or at least the crucial property that makes modal logic so robustly decidable.

However, we believe that looseness is not all there is to say in relation to explaining the decidability (or low complexity) of the basic modal system **K**. The semantics of the basic modal language shows that modal formulas only have a limited access to the model. This is what we dub the *locality principle* of modal logic, and one can make this rather vague notion precise in (at least) two ways.

First, in the above proof we used the fact that the effect of a modal formula is bounded by its modal depth. In particular, when working in a tree model we can prune the relevant neighborhood of a state even further by the method of selecting witnesses for $\Diamond$-subformulas. All in all, we find that in order to check whether a modal formula holds at a given state of some tree model, one only has to worry about a bounded, "local" part of the tree model. In particular, what the basic modal language does *not* have is *global expressive power*. We say that a modal system $(\mathcal{L}, \mathsf{K}, \Vdash)$ has global expressive power if it can define the universal diamond E; that is, if there is a formula $\varphi(p)$ such that for every model $\mathcal{M}$ in K and every state s in $\mathcal{M}$, we have

$$\mathcal{M}, s \Vdash \varphi(p) \leftrightarrow \mathcal{M}, t \Vdash p \text{ for some } t \text{ in } \mathcal{M}.$$

By the *first locality principle*, we mean the *lack* of global expressive power. Later on, we shall see that if we add even the tiniest bit of global expressive power to the basic modal system, we destroy its *finite* tree property and lift the complexity of the satisfiability problem from PSPACE to EXPTIME.

We have already met the second locality principle in Observation 1. From the fact that the basic modal language belongs to the two-variable fragment FO_2 of first-order logic, we may conclude that the satisfiability problem for the basic modal system can be reduced to that for FO_2. But, for every modal language in which the connectives have a first-order truth definition, we can come up with a "standard translation", so if the language has only finitely many connectives, this standard translation remains within a fixed finite-variable fragment. Hence, if we consider a modal system $(\mathcal{L}, \mathsf{K}, \Vdash)$ in which $\mathcal{L}$ has only finitely many connectives and in addition, the class of models K allows a definition in some finite-variable fragment, then the satisfiability problem for the modal system can be reduced to that of some finite-variable fragment FO_k. Why are we interested so much in these fixed finite-variable fragments? As we shall see later, one reason is that they have tractable *model checking* problems, whereas the full first-order language does not. To be concrete, given a finite first-order model $\mathcal{M}$ and a first-order sentence ξ, the problem of whether $\mathcal{M} \models \xi$ is decidable in PTIME in $\mathcal{M}$ *and* in ξ, if ξ is from a fixed-variable fragment, whereas it is in PSPACE if ξ is an arbitrary first-order sentence. With the *second locality principle*, we shall mean this reducibility of the satisfiability problem to the satisfiability of some fixed finite-variable fragment of first-order logic (or perhaps of some higher-order formalism, as in the case of $\mathbf{K}^*$ which we shall discuss later on).

It will be useful later to state what we mean by looseness and locality in terms of the bisimulation game. Since it is $\forall$ who tries to spoil a bisimulation, the strength of the bisimulation relation is determined by the moves $\forall$ is allowed to make. Indeed, $\forall$'s powers are limited. First, observe that although a match is made up of long sequences of pairs of states, after every round it is only the last pair which is important. Given such a pair, $\forall$ is allowed to choose a new element, but only if it is a successor of a state in the pair. $\exists$ replies and then the players check whether the match is over because $\forall$ has won or not. If not, the previous pair "is deleted from memory" and the game continues.

We could view the game as being played by moving two windows across the models. These windows completely hide the model from view, except for at most two states. Both players move the windows across the models, and ∀ has the initiative. Now, the principle of looseness means that the states which are visible through the window are always connected by the accessibility relation (this shows we could equally well have dubbed the "looseness principle a "locality" principle as well). The second locality principle is embodied in the fixed finite dimension of the window. (To describe the first locality principle, games do not seem to be the optimal way.)

Summarizing, it seems that these looseness and locality principles in tandem cause the decidability of the basic modal system: looseness means that one only has to check trees, and the first locality principle adds that in fact finite trees suffice. (For the contribution of the second locality principle, the reader will have to wait until we discuss the generalization of the modal language to the guarded and packed fragments of first-order logic in Sect. 7.6.) There can be no doubt that looseness is the most important property for the decidability of a modal system; in fact, if we confine ourselves to the class M of all modal models, it will be hard to *find* a bisimulation-invariant system with an undecidable satisfiability problem! The reason for this is that the modal mu-calculus is decidable, and this modal system can be characterized as the bisimulation-invariant fragment of monadic second-order logic over a signature of binary relations.

7.3.1 Notes

Recent years have seen a proliferation of modern textbooks on modal logics, of which we mention those by Chagrov & Zakharyaschev [14], Popkorn [49] and Blackburn, de Rijke, & Venema [9].

The standard translation, in various forms, can be found in the work of a number of writers on modal and tense logic in the 1960s. Van Benthem [4] first made clear the importance of systematic use of the standard translation to access results and techniques from classical modal theory. The observation that at most two variables are needed to translate basic modal formulas into first-order logic is due to Gabbay [20]. The earliest systematic study of finite-variable fragments seems to be due to Henkin [26] in the setting of algebraic logic, while Immerman & Kozen [34] studied the link with complexity and database theory. See Otto [47] for more on finite-variable logics, or Marx & Venema [43] for a modal perspective on these logics.

Bisimulations were first introduced (under a different name) by van Benthem [4, 5]. The notion was introduced independently in computer science, as an equivalence relation on process graphs; the first reference seems to be Park [48], while the classic computer science paper on the subject is Hennessy & Milner [28]; the latter paper also discusses finitary approximations to bisimulations. The notion of unraveling a modal model stems from Dummett & Lemon [16]. Proposition 7.3.9 is analogous to similar characterizaions of logical equivalence for first-order logic, due to Ehrenfeucht and Fraïssé (see [31]).

Theorem 7.3.4, the Characterization Theorem which identifies modal logic as the bisimulation-invariant fragment of first-order logic, is due to van Benthem [4, 6]. The back-and-forth clauses of a bisimulation can be adapted to analyze the expressivity of a wide range of modal logics, and such analyses are now commonplace. For instance, Janin & Walukiewicz [35] have proved that Kozen's modal mu-calculs is the bisimulation-invariant fragment of a natural monadic second-order logic over process graphs. Related model-theoretic characterizations can be found in Immerman & Kozen [34] (for finite-variable logics). Rosen [51] has presented a version of the Characterization Theorem that also works for the case of finite models.

Finite models have long been used to establish decidability, both in modal logic and elsewhere. Arguments based on *finite* axiomatizability together with the finite model property can be traced back to Harrop [25]. The computational complexity of the satisfiability problem for the basic modal system was established by Ladner [37]: it is PSPACE-complete. The function *K-World* is a slight variation of Ladner's procedure. The presentation given here is taken from Spaan [55].

The problem of whether $\mathcal{M} \models \xi$ for a given a finite first-order model $\mathcal{M}$ and a first-order sentence ξ, is PTIME-complete when ξ is from a fixed finite-variable fragment (see Immerman [33], Vardi [57]), but PSPACE-complete when ξ is an arbitrary first-order sentence (Chandra & Merlin [15]).

7.4 Some Variations

In this section, we shall consider some modal systems that are variations on the basic modal system. Apart from our wish to introduce some new proof techniques for establishing decidability of a modal system, such as the *filtration* and *mosaic* methods, our aim in this section is to clarify the looseness and locality principles that we have just introduced.

We shall first investigate some modal systems that are fairly "tight" in the sense that their class of models is based on grid-like structures; as we shall see, such a lack of looseness brings these systems close to the danger zone of undecidability. Nevertheless, if the locality principles still hold, decidability is still possible. The second system that we consider is obtained by adding just a grain of global expressive power to the basic modal language, while keeping the looseness condition. We shall see that the system is still decidable, but it no longer has the finite-tree property. Finally, we consider a modal system in which the operator is not bisimulation-invariant at all; however, as we shall see, it does have another kind of looseness property, and this enables us to prove its decidability.

7.4.1 Neither Locality nor Looseness: Grid Logics

In this subsection, we consider modal systems that cannot be called loose or local. We shall first meet a simple modal system that is tailored towards encoding the $\mathbb{N} \times \mathbb{N}$-tiling problem, and is undecidable; as a contrast, we shall also discuss a second system with grid-like models which has a decidable satisfiability problem.

A Tiling Logic

In looking for the opposite of looseness one is bound to end up with a *grid*. Grids are well known in complexity theory, since they play an important role in the formulation of a class of complete problems for various complexity classes: *tiling problems*. A tile is a one-by-one square which has a "color" on each of its sides; these colors are given by four functions "right", "left", "up", and "down". Given a set T of tiles, a *tiling* of the grid $\mathbb{N} \times \mathbb{N}$ by T is a map t from $\mathbb{N} \times \mathbb{N}$ to T satisfying, for all $n, m \in \mathbb{N}$,

$$\text{right}(t(n, m)) = \text{left}(t(n + 1, m)),$$
$$\text{up}(t(n, m)) \;\;\; = \text{down}(t(n, m + 1)).$$

Tiles are assumed to be fixed in orientation, so the above conditions say that colors of adjacent tiles match. (We note that it is not necessary to use all tiles of T in a tiling of $\mathbb{N} \times \mathbb{N}$.) If such a tiling exists, we say that T *can tile* $\mathbb{N} \times \mathbb{N}$. The following problem is undecidable:

$\mathbb{N} \times \mathbb{N}$ **tiling**: Given a finite set T of tiles, can T tile $\mathbb{N} \times \mathbb{N}$?

We shall now define a modal system Tile which is tailored to encode the above tiling problem. The language of Tile contains two unary modalities $\Diamond_r$ and $\Diamond_u$ plus the universal modality E. In a model of the form (W, R_r, R_u, V), these modalities receive their meaning in the usual way:

$$\mathcal{M}, s \Vdash \Diamond_r \varphi \;\leftrightarrow\; \mathcal{M}, t \Vdash \varphi \text{ for some } t \text{ with } R_r st,$$
$$\mathcal{M}, x \Vdash \Diamond_u \varphi \;\leftrightarrow\; \mathcal{M}, t \Vdash \varphi \text{ for some } t \text{ with } R_u st,$$
$$\mathcal{M}, x \Vdash E\varphi \;\;\;\leftrightarrow\; \mathcal{M}, t \Vdash \varphi \text{ for some } t.$$

In the intended class of *grid models*, R_r and R_u are (the graphs of) two commuting total functions. In particular, grid models satisfy the following condition:

$$\forall xyz((R_r xy \wedge R_u xz) \rightarrow \exists w(R_r zw \wedge R_u yw)). \tag{7.5}$$

Because of this, the class of grid models is not closed under unraveling; hence, Tile does not satisfy the looseness principle. It is also rather obvious that the first locality principle fails as well, in the presence of the universal modality; we leave it to the reader to verify that the class of grid models can be defined using three variables only, and Tile thus satisfies the second locality principle.

Theorem 7.4.1. *The satisfiability problem of* Tile *is undecidable.*

Proof. Obviously, we reduce the $\mathbb{N} \times \mathbb{N}$-tiling problem to the satisfiability problem for Tile. We present a procedure that outputs, for every instance T of the tiling problem, a formula φ_T such that

$$\text{A}\varphi_T \text{ is Tile-satisfiable iff } T \text{ can tile } \mathbb{N} \times \mathbb{N}. \tag{7.6}$$

(Recall that A is the box version of E; that is, $\text{A}\varphi$ abbreviates $\neg\text{E}\neg\varphi$.)

Take, for any set $T = \{T_1, \ldots, T_k\}$ of tiles, a corresponding set $\{t_1, \ldots, t_k\}$ of propositional variables. Define φ_T as the conjunction of the following formulas (where i ranges over $1, \ldots, k$):

(A1) $\bigvee_{1 \leq i \leq k} t_i$

(A2$_i$) $t_i \rightarrow \bigwedge_{i \neq j} \neg t_j$

(A3$_i$) $t_i \rightarrow \Diamond_r \bigvee\{t_j \mid \text{right}(T_i) = \text{left}(T_j)\}$

(A4$_i$) $t_i \rightarrow \Diamond_u \bigvee\{t_j \mid \text{up}(T_i) = \text{down}(T_j)\}$.

It follows almost immediately that T tiles $\mathbb{N} \times \mathbb{N}$ if and only if there exists a Tile model where φ_T holds throughout. (The reader should verify that in the proof of the left-to-right direction of (7.6) the property (7.5) of grid models is crucial.) This, in turn, is equivalent to the formula $\text{A}\varphi_T$ being satisfiable in some Tile model. Thus (7.6) holds and we have reduced the undecidable tiling problem to the Tile satisfiability problem.   □

We hasten to remark that the undecidability of this system has nothing to do with the fact that we are dealing with more than one modality here; one can easily transform this example into an undecidable modal system in the *basic modal language* extended with the universal modality, or in the basic modal language proper.

It is interesting to note that *without* the universal access to the models provided by A, these grid logics become quite harmless. In fact, their grid-like nature ensures that every satisfiable formula ξ is satisfiable in a model whose size is at most $|\xi|^2 + 1$.

Theorem 7.4.2. *Let* Tile$^-$ *be the modal system* Tile, *but now without the universal modality. Then every* Tile$^-$*-satisfiable formula ξ is satisfiable in a* Tile$^-$ *model of size at most $|\xi|^2 + 1$. As a corollary,* Tile$^-$ *has a decidable satisfiability problem.*

Proof. Let $\mathcal{M}$ satisfy ξ at s. Let k be the modal depth of ξ, we then have that $k \leq |\xi|$. By Proposition 7.3.9, ξ is still satisfiable in the model $\mathcal{M}'$, defined as the substructure of $\mathcal{M}$ with universe s together with all states reachable in at most k (R_r- or R_u-)steps from s. Clearly, the size of the universe of $\mathcal{M}'$ is at most k^2. Unfortunately, $\mathcal{M}'$ is not a Tile model, because not every state has an R_r and R_u successor. In order to mend this, we add one dummy state x to the universe of $\mathcal{M}'$ and put a link from w to x for all states w (including x itself) that do not have a successor yet. That is, we define $W^- = W' \cup \{x\}$

and $R_r^- = R'_r \cup \{(w, x) \mid R'_r wy$ for no y in $\mathcal{M}'\}$, and likewise for R_u^-. Let the valuation stay the same, i.e., we define $V^-(p) = V'(p)$ for all p.

The resulting model $\mathcal{M}^-$ is a Tile model. Clearly, ξ is still satisfied at s in this new model, since x is "too far away" to have any effect on the truth of ξ. This proves the first part of the theorem. Decidability now follows because it is decidable whether a finite model is a Tile model. $\square$

$\mathbf{S5^2}$

The second logic that we consider here is also based on grid-like structures, but here we require only that the models are two-dimensional in nature; there will be no orderings or functions around. The language has two diamonds, $\Diamond_0$ and $\Diamond_1$, with the standard truth definition. The models are of the form $\mathcal{M} = (W, \equiv_0, \equiv_1, V)$, where we require that $(W, \equiv_0, \equiv_1)$ is in fact a *square* over some set U. That is, W consists of the set $U \times U$ of all *pairs* over U, and $s \equiv_i t$ holds if $s_i = t_i$: the ith coordinate of s and the ith coordinate of t should be the same. We denote the resulting system by $\mathbf{S5^2}$.

As a modal system, $\mathbf{S5^2}$ might look rather obscure, but as a logic, it is well known. In fact, it is the exact modal counterpart of a restricted fragment of first-order logic with two variables in a signature that has a binary relation symbol R for every propositional variable r. This can be seen as follows. First, observe that the $\mathbf{S5^2}$ model $\mathcal{M} = (W, \equiv_0, \equiv_1, V)$ with $W = U \times U$ is uniquely determined by the first-order model (U, V) for the signature described. Also observe that we may identify assignments s mapping the two variables x_0 and x_1 to U with pairs $(s(x_1), s(x_0)) \in W$. Thus, viewing the states of the modal models as assignments, we may read the statement "φ holds in (U, V) under assignment s" modally as "in model $(U \times U, \equiv_0, \equiv_1, V)$, φ is true at state s". Because $\mathbf{S5^2}$ models are squares, the truth definition of the diamonds can be rewritten exactly as the definition of the first-order existential quantifiers:

$$\mathcal{M}, (a, b) \Vdash \Diamond_1 \varphi \leftrightarrow \text{ there exists } a' \text{ such that } \mathcal{M}, (a', b) \Vdash \varphi.$$

Thus $\Diamond_i$ is another way of writing $\exists x_i$. In a similar way, one can define modal systems $\mathbf{S5^n}$ corresponding to first-order logic with n variables for any n. See the notes for references.

It will be obvious that this class of models is not closed under unraveling, and that $\mathbf{S5^2}$ will not have the tree model property. Concerning the locality principles, observe that this system has full global expressive power: the "combined" operator $\Diamond_0 \Diamond_1$ behaves just like the universal diamond E. Nevertheless, the system is decidable, and a proof of this uses some kind of finite model property as well.

Here, instead of defining a finite model for ξ by *selecting* points out of the old model, we shall *identify* points in the big model and define the finite model as some sort of quotient structure, which we call a *filtration* of the original model. It will turn out that this filtration will not be a square itself but a square-like structure, which we dub a *pseudo-square* here. That is to say, in the underlying frame (W, R_0, R_1) both R_0 and R_1 are equivalence relations, and their composition should be the universal relation. That is, (W, R_0, R_1) has to validate

$$\forall xy \exists z (R_0 xz \wedge R_1 zy). \tag{7.7}$$

For these kind of structures, we can prove the following proposition, which establishes the bounded finite model property of the language with respect to the class of pseudo-squares. (In fact, the system does have the bounded finite model property, but this is much harder to establish.) As we saw before, decidability follows immediately, because it is decidable whether a finite structure is a pseudo-square.

Proposition 7.4.3. *Any* $\mathbf{S5^2}$*-formula* ξ *is satisfiable in a square iff it is satisfiable in a pseudo-square of size not exceeding* $2^{|\xi|}$*. As a consequence,* $\mathbf{S5^2}$ *has a decidable satisfiability problem.*

Proof. We shall concentrate on the left-to-right direction of this proof, since we are interested only in explaining the notion of filtration at the moment. (For the other direction of the proof, one shows that given a pseudo-square model, one can always find a square that is bisimilar to it — in fact, bisimilar through a *functional* bisimulation; see the notes.)

Suppose ξ is satisfied somewhere in the square model $\mathcal{M} = (W, \equiv_0, \equiv_1, V)$. From this we shall prove that ξ is true somewhere in a *filtration* $\mathcal{M}^f$ of $\mathcal{M}$. As we have mentioned already, filtrating a model means collapsing it. But when will two points in the original model be identified? Generally, taking a quotient of a structure means identifying points without "relevant" differences; in the present context this can be interpreted as "satisfying the same *subformulas* of ξ". Formally, we define $Cl(\xi)$ to be the smallest set of formulas containing ξ which is closed under subformulas. Now, we define the following relation on W:

$$s \sim s' \leftrightarrow \text{ for all } \varphi \text{ in } Cl(\xi) : \mathcal{M}, s \Vdash \varphi \text{ iff } \mathcal{M}, s' \Vdash \varphi.$$

Obviously, $\sim$ is an equivalence relation. Our filtrated model will be based on the equivalence classes of this relation, and so we introduce some notation: by $\bar{s}$ we denote the equivalence class of a point s, and by W^f, the set of these classes. Note that $|W^f| \leq 2^{|\xi|}$ as $|Cl(\xi)|$ is bounded by $|\xi|$.

What would be a good definition for the relations R_0 and R_1 on W^f? In general, this is where the filtration method needs some creative input. Now, if the only requirement were that ξ were to be true somewhere in the resulting model, there would be a whole family of definitions that work (in the sense that they ensure (7.8) below). But the extra constraint, namely that the resulting model should be a pseudo-square, imposes some extra restrictions. Nevertheless, the following definition works:

$$R_i \bar{s}\bar{t} \text{ if for all } \Diamond_i \varphi \in Cl(\xi): \mathcal{M}, s \Vdash \Diamond_i \varphi \text{ iff } \mathcal{M}, s' \Vdash \Diamond_i \varphi.$$

(Observe that this is well defined, by the fact that $\sim$-equivalent points agree about *all* formulas in $Cl(\xi)$.) Finally, the definition of V^f is rather obvious:

$$V^f(p) = \{\bar{s} \in W^f \mid s \in V(p)\}.$$

Note that this is well defined for all proposition letters p occurring in ξ.

We can prove the main claim concerning filtration:

$$\text{for all formulas } \varphi \in Cl(\xi): \mathcal{M}, s \Vdash \varphi \text{ iff } \mathcal{M}^f, \bar{s} \Vdash \varphi. \qquad (7.8)$$

This claim is proved by a formula induction. Leaving the straightforward induction base and the boolean cases of the inductive step to the reader, we concentrate on the case where φ is of the form $\Diamond_0 \psi$. (The case where φ is of the form $\Diamond_1 \psi$ is of course completely analogous.)

First, assume that $\mathcal{M}, s \Vdash \Diamond_0 \psi$. Then, by definition, there is some s' in $\mathcal{M}$ such that $s \equiv_0 s'$ and $\mathcal{M}, s' \Vdash \psi$. By the inductive hypothesis, this gives that $\mathcal{M}^f, \bar{s}' \Vdash \psi$. It easily follows from the definitions that $s \equiv_0 s'$ implies $R_0 \bar{s} \bar{s}'$. But then it follows immediately that $\mathcal{M}^f, \bar{s} \Vdash \Diamond_0 \psi$. For the other direction, suppose that $\mathcal{M}^f, \bar{s} \Vdash \Diamond_0 \psi$. Then, for some $\bar{t}$ in $\mathcal{M}^f$, we have that $R_0 \bar{s} \bar{t}$ and $\mathcal{M}^f, \bar{t} \Vdash \psi$. Hence, by the inductive hypothesis, we have that $\mathcal{M}, t \Vdash \psi$. But then, from reflexivity of $\equiv_0$, it follows that $\mathcal{M}, t \Vdash \Diamond_0 \psi$, and so from $R_0 \bar{s} \bar{t}$ we may infer, using only the definition of R_0, that $\mathcal{M}, s \Vdash \Diamond_0 \psi$.

This proves (7.8), so in order to prove the left-to-right direction of the proposition we have only to show that $\mathcal{M}^f$ is a pseudo-square. We leave it to the reader to verify that both R_0 and R_1 are equivalence relations. In order to check the other condition, let $\bar{s}$ and $\bar{t}$ be points in $\mathcal{M}^f$. Now the fact that $\mathcal{M}$ is a square and that s and t are pairs comes in handy. Let $z = (s_0, t_1)$. Then $s \equiv_0 z \equiv_1 t$. But it then follows that $R_0 \bar{s} \bar{z}$ and $R_1 \bar{z} \bar{t}$, which shows that the composition of R_0 and R_1 is indeed the universal relation on $\mathcal{M}^f$. $\square$

What can we conclude from the examples Tile, Tile$^-$, and S5^2? Not that looseness is a *necessary* condition for a modal system to be decidable: witness Tile$^-$ and S5^2. On the other hand, it should be clear that dropping the looseness principle leads us to the immediate vicinity of the danger zone: adding only a grain of global expressive power will turn the highly decidable logic Tile$^-$ into the undecidable Tile.

Concerning S5^2, it is very interesting to observe what happens if we move to higher dimensions. For instance, there seem to be *two* three-dimensional counterparts of S5^2, according to which relation between two triples one takes to be the accessibility relation for $\Diamond_i$:

$$s \equiv_i t \text{ if } s_j = t_j \text{ for all } j \neq i,$$

$$s \sim_i t \text{ if } s_i = t_i.$$

In the second, relatively loose, interpretation the resulting logic is decidable. In the first interpretation, one obtains a class of rather tight models; the resulting logic is *undecidable*. Since it is *this* logic that corresponds to a *three*-variable fragment of first-order logic (in a way similar to that discussed above for $\mathbf{S5^2}$), this makes an interesting case for the second locality principle.

7.4.2 Universal Access: $\mathbf{K^*}$

We now consider the modal system $\mathbf{K^*}$ obtained by expanding the basic modal language with the modality $\langle * \rangle$, keeping the class of models intact and giving both $\Diamond$ and $\langle * \rangle$ the standard interpretation. Recall that the meaning of $\langle * \rangle$ was defined using the reflexive transitive closure R^* of the relation R.

Let us first see where $\mathbf{K^*}$ stands with respect to the looseness and locality principles. We have seen already that $\langle * \rangle$ is invariant under bisimulations, whence we have an analogue of Theorem 7.3.6: any $\mathbf{K^*}$-satisfiable formula is satisfiable in a tree model. $\mathbf{K^*}$ also meets the second locality principle, at least if we are allowed to include finite-variable fragments of the *infinitary* language $\mathcal{L}_{\omega_1\omega}$ (an extension of first-order logic in which countable conjunctions and disjunctions are allowed). For it is easy to see that $\mathbf{K^*}$-formulas have correspondents in the three-variable fragment of this language: simply add the following clause for $\langle * \rangle$ to the standard translation of $\mathcal{L}_\Diamond$:

$$ST_x(\langle * \rangle\psi) \;=\; \exists y(R^*xy \wedge ST_y(\varphi)), \qquad ST_y(\langle * \rangle\psi) \;=\; \exists x(R^*yx \wedge ST_x(\varphi)).$$

Here we use the fact that the reflexive transitive closure can be expressed using three variables only; for instance, R^*xy could stand for the following abbreviation:

$$x = y \;\vee\; Rxy \;\vee\; \exists y' \, (Rxy' \wedge Ry'y) \;\vee\; \exists y' \, (\exists y \, (Rxy \wedge Ryy') \wedge Ry'y) \;\vee\; \ldots$$

However, $\mathbf{K^*}$ violates the first locality principle in the following way: if r is the root of a tree model $\mathcal{M}$, then we have

$$\mathcal{M}, r \Vdash \langle * \rangle\varphi \leftrightarrow \mathcal{M}, s \Vdash \varphi \text{ for some } s \text{ in } \mathcal{M},$$

as the reader can easily check. In fact, unlike the basic modal system, $\mathbf{K^*}$ does not have the *finite* tree model property; for instance, the following satisfiable formula is not satisfiable on any finite tree:

$$[\,*\,](p \rightarrow \langle * \rangle\neg p) \wedge [\,*\,](\neg p \rightarrow \langle * \rangle p).$$

(It is satisfiable on the natural numbers with successor, with p interpreted as the even numbers.)

Summarizing, the present system is loose, and it satisfies the second but not the first locality principle. What about its decidability, or the finite model property? In fact, both properties hold, as we shall see now. We first prove that $\mathbf{K^*}$ has the bounded model property.

Proposition 7.4.4. *Any satisfiable* **K*** *formula* ξ *is satisfiable on a model of size* $2^{O(|\xi|)}$.

Proof. Suppose that ξ is satisfiable in some model $\mathcal{M} = (W, R, V)$. We again define a collection of relevant formulas. This time, we need a new closure rule: we call a set X of formulas $*$-closed if it contains $\Diamond\langle*\rangle\varphi$ whenever it contains $\langle*\rangle\varphi$. Now let $FL(\xi)$ be the smallest set of formulas containing ξ which is $*$-closed, besides being closed under taking subformulas and single negations. It is not difficult to prove that the cardinality of $FL(\xi)$ is linear in the size of ξ.

The method that we use to construct a finite model for ξ is, just as in the case of **S5**^{2}, that of *filtration*. We define the following relation on points of $\mathcal{M}$:

$$s \sim s' \leftrightarrow \text{ for all } \varphi \text{ in } FL(\xi) : \mathcal{M}, s \Vdash \varphi \text{ iff } \mathcal{M}, s' \Vdash \varphi.$$

Again, it is obvious that $\sim$ is an equivalence relation, and again, our filtrated model will be based on the collection W^f of equivalence classes of this relation; it is convenient to identify the equivalence class of s with the *color* of s, which we define as the set $c(s) = \{\varphi \in FL(\xi) \mid \mathcal{M}, s \Vdash \varphi\}$. Note that $|W^f| \leq 2^{O(|\xi|)}$, as $|FL(\xi)|$ is bounded by $|\xi|$.

To finish the definition of the filtrated model, we define the relation R^f on colors as follows:

$$R^f cd \leftrightarrow \text{ for all } \Diamond\varphi \in FL(\xi): (\varphi \in d \Rightarrow \Diamond\varphi \in c).$$

The valuation V^f is then defined as $V^f(p) = \{c \in W^f \mid p \in c\}$.

The key claim of the filtration proof is the following.

Claim 1. For all formulas $\varphi \in FL(\xi)$ and all colors c, $\varphi \in c$ iff $\mathcal{M}^f \Vdash \varphi$.

PROOF OF CLAIM The proof follows by an induction on the complexity of φ. We treat only the case where φ is of the form $\langle*\rangle\psi$.

First suppose that $\langle*\rangle\psi \in c$. Assume that c is the color of s in $\mathcal{M}$; that is, $\mathcal{M}, s \Vdash \langle*\rangle\psi$. By definition, there is a sequence of states $s_1, \ldots, s_n$ in $\mathcal{M}$ such that $s = s_1$, $Rs_i s_{i+1}$ for all i, and $\mathcal{M}, s_n \Vdash \psi$. By the definition of colors, it follows that $\psi \in c(s_n)$. Also, it is easy to show that $R^f c(s_i) c(s_{i+1})$ for all i. But then it follows immediately that $\mathcal{M}^f, c \Vdash \langle*\rangle\psi$.

For the other direction, suppose that $\mathcal{M}^f, c \Vdash \langle*\rangle\psi$. By the truth definition of $\langle*\rangle$, there must be colors $c_1, \ldots, c_n$ such that $c = c_1$, $R^f c_i c_{i+1}$ for all i, and $\mathcal{M}, c_n \Vdash \psi$. It follows from the inductive hypothesis that $\psi \in c_n$. From this, and the observation that $\varphi \rightarrow \langle*\rangle\varphi$ is valid in any model, it follows that $\langle*\rangle\psi \in c_n$.

We now show that

$$\text{If } R^f dd', \text{ then } \langle*\rangle\chi \in d' \text{ implies } \langle*\rangle\chi \in d. \tag{7.9}$$

Suppose that $R^f dd'$ and $\langle*\rangle\chi \in d'$. It follows that $\langle*\rangle\chi$ belongs to $FL(\xi)$, and so $\Diamond\langle*\rangle\chi$ is in $FL(\xi)$ as well, by $*$-closure. But then, by the definition of R^f, we find that $\Diamond\langle*\rangle\chi$ is in d. Since d is a color, there must be some w in W such that $d = c(w)$. By definition, we have that $\mathcal{M}, w \Vdash \Diamond\langle*\rangle\chi$. From this it is easy to derive that $\mathcal{M}, w \Vdash \langle*\rangle\chi$, and so again, by definition, we have $\langle*\rangle\chi \in d$.

But, from (7.9) and $\langle*\rangle\psi \in c_n$, an easy downward inductive proof shows that $\langle*\rangle\psi \in c_i$ for all i. In particular, we find that $\langle*\rangle\psi$ belongs to $c_1 = c$. This finishes the proof of the claim.

Thus ξ is satisfiable in a model of size $2^{O(|\xi|)}$. $\qquad\qquad\Box$

The last proposition implies decidability, as it is decidable whether a $\mathbf{K}^*$ formula is satisfiable on a finite model. The idea of colors can also be used directly in an algorithm which tries to construct a model like $\mathcal{M}^f$. This construction uses the same idea as the K-World algorithm given earlier: states are identified with subsets of $Cl(\xi)$. Let S_0 consists of all sets $\Delta \subseteq Cl(\xi)$ for which $Prop\text{-}Max(\Delta, Cl(\xi))$ holds and which satisfy $\varphi \in \Delta \Rightarrow \langle*\rangle\varphi \in \Delta$, for all $\langle*\rangle\varphi \in Cl(\xi)$. (For the definition of $Prop\text{-}Max(\Delta, Cl(\xi))$, see Sect. 7.3.) Clearly S_0 can be effectively computed and $|S_0| \leq 2^{O(|\xi|)}$. We now inductively construct a sequence of collections of sets of formulas $S_0 \supsetneq S_1 \supsetneq S_2 \supsetneq S_3 \cdots$. During this construction, just as in the K-World algorithm, we try to find witnesses for diamond formulas. We say that a set $\Delta \in S_i$ is *ready* if S_i contains witnesses for all diamond formulas in Δ:

- for every formula $\Diamond\psi \in \Delta$ there is a $\Delta_\psi \in S_i$ such that $R^f\Delta\Delta_\psi$ and $\psi \in \Delta_\psi$, and
- for every formula $\langle*\rangle\psi \in \Delta$ there are $\Delta_1, \Delta_2, \ldots, \Delta_n \in S_i$ such that $\Delta = \Delta_1$, $R^f\Delta_i\Delta_{i+1}$ and $\psi \in \Delta_n$,

If every set in S_i is ready and S_i contains a set Δ with $\xi \in \Delta$, then the algorithms returns "ξ is satisfiable". If there is no set in S_i containing ξ, then the algorithms returns "ξ is not satisfiable". Otherwise, let S_{i+1} consist of all ready sets in S_i, and we continue the construction. Since $S_i \supsetneq S_{i+1}$, the construction is guaranteed to terminate in at most $2^{O(|\xi|)}$ stages. The correctness of the algorithm can be shown along the lines of the proof of the last proposition. Thus we have established the following.

Theorem 7.4.5. *It is decidable whether a given $\mathbf{K}^*$ formula is satisfiable.*

7.4.3 Generalizing Looseness: the Until Operator

In this subsection, we consider the modal system given by the propositional language expanded with the binary until operator U, the class of all models of the form (W, R, V), and an interpretation of U as given above (recalled below). We have already mentioned that truth in this language is not bisimulation-invariant, and we are thus not dealing with a modal system in the narrow sense; in particular, we shall see that there are satisfiable U-formulas that are not satisfiable in any tree. Nevertheless, we shall show that this system does have some kind of *loose* model property, and we shall use this property for showing that it has a decidable satisfiability problem. In fact, this "looseness property" is the reason why we take a look at this operator: it shows in a relatively simple setting how to generalize the notions of looseness and tree models. These generalizations are made in the section on guarded fragments.

To start with, let $\mathcal{L}_U$ be the language obtained by expanding the classical propositional language with the binary connective U. Recall that M is the class of all models of the form (W, R, V). It is convenient to use the following notation: for s and u elements of W,

$$\mathcal{M}, su \Vdash \psi \text{ iff } \mathcal{M}, t \Vdash \psi, \text{ for all } t \text{ satisfying } Rst \text{ and } Rtu. \tag{7.10}$$

This is because we can now rephrase the truth definition of the until operator as follows:

$$\mathcal{M}, s \Vdash U(\varphi, \psi) \text{ iff } \mathcal{M}, u \Vdash \varphi \text{ and } \mathcal{M}, su \Vdash \psi, \text{ for some } u \text{ such that } Rsu. \tag{7.11}$$

We call the resulting modal system $(\mathcal{L}_U, \text{M}, \Vdash)$ the *until system*. In order to see why truth of $\mathcal{L}_U$-formulas is not invariant under bisimulations, consider the formula $U(p, \top) \wedge \neg U(p, p)$. (Here $\top$ abbreviates $(p \vee \neg p)$.) This formula is satisfiable and its smallest irreflexive model contains three points; see model $\mathcal{M}_1$ in Figure 7.7. Note that in the unraveling $\mathcal{M}_2$ of the model $\mathcal{M}_1$, $U(p, p)$ holds at the root of the tree. This shows that $\mathcal{L}_U$ is really a more expressive language than $\mathcal{L}_\Diamond$. In fact, one can show that the formula $U(p, \top) \rightarrow U(p, p)$ holds throughout any tree model, whence $U(p, \top) \wedge \neg U(p, p)$ is not satisfiable in any tree model. This shows that the until system does not have the tree model property.

Decidability

Unlike our earlier proofs, we shall not use any kind of finite *model* property in order to prove decidability for the until system. This is not because the system does not have the bounded finite model property (it does); our proof

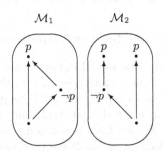

Fig. 7.7. Until formulas are not invariant under bisimulations

method is for didactic purposes. The idea behind the *mosaic method* that we employ is that instead of transforming a model into a finite model, we could just as well "deconstruct" it into a finite "toolkit", which we shall call a linked set of mosaics. One then has to show that a formula is satisfiable if and only if there exists such a linked set of mosaics for it.

What, then, are mosaics? One could best describe them as little pieces of a model that, if linked together in a nice way, contain sufficient information to *reconstruct* another model which looks sufficiently like the original one to preserve the truth of $\mathcal{L}_U$-formulas. In this way we will establish a *loose model property* for the until system: any satisfiable formula is satisfiable in a model consisting of these isomorphic copies of mosaics that hang together only very loosely. (Later on in the chapter, we shall come back to this issue in more technical detail.)

Concerning the notion of a mosaic, the first question is *what information* we are interested in. This question is easy to answer: as in the filtration proof for $\mathbf{S5}^2$, we are interested only in the truth of subformulas of ξ. The second question then should be: *which parts* are we going to cut out of the model? Here we need to define a new concept. We call a subset of the domain of a model $\mathcal{M} = (W, R, V)$ *packed* if every two distinct elements s and t of the subset are R-related (that is, we require that Rst or Rts). Our patchwork pieces will then be packed sets of size at most three.

The number three here derives from the fact that the truth definition of $U(\varphi, \psi)$ employs three variables. In fact, if one were to try to devise a standard translation or a bisimulation game for the $\mathcal{L}_U$-language, the number three would show up as the minimal number of variables needed and as the minimal size of the windows that cover the models during the game. During a game, one would see that these windows would be placed only on packed sets of the models.

Abstracting from the origin of these pieces, we arrive at the following definition. From now on, we let ξ be an arbitrary but fixed $\mathcal{L}_U$ formula; ξ is the formula whose satisfiability needs to be decided. We let $Cl(\xi)$ denote the set of subformulas of ξ.

Definition 7.4.6. *A ξ-type* mosaic *is a quadruple* $\mu = (X, R, A_\varphi, B_\varphi)_{\varphi \in Cl(\xi)}$ *such that X is a set of size at most three; R and every B_φ are binary relations on X; and every A_φ is a unary relation on X. When ξ is clear from the context, we shall use simply the term "mosaic".*

The basic idea underlying this definition is that A_φ holds of a point if we "want" φ to be true at it, while B_φ holds of a pair of points if we "want" φ to be true at every point between them. Obviously, not every such structure is part of a model — we need some further constraints for that. We call a mosaic *coherent* if it satisfies the following conditions (phrased in first-order logic and to be read universally):

(C0) $Rxy \lor Ryx \lor x = y$,

(C1) $A_{\neg\varphi}x \leftrightarrow \neg A_\varphi x$,

(C2) $A_{\varphi\wedge\psi}x \leftrightarrow A_\varphi x \wedge A_\psi x$,

(C3) $B_{\varphi\wedge\psi}xy \leftrightarrow B_\varphi xy \wedge B_\psi xy$,

(C4) $(Rxy \wedge Ryz \wedge B_\varphi xz) \rightarrow A_\varphi y$,

(C5) $(Rxy \wedge A_\varphi y \wedge B_\psi xy) \rightarrow A_{U(\varphi,\psi)}x$.

A few words of explanation: C0 reflects the fact that we have taken only packed subsets of the model as the domain of our mosaic mini-models. C1–C3 are selfexplanatory; note that there is no analog of C1 for the B-predicates, since there is a hidden universal quantifier in the meaning of a predicate B_φ, see (7.10). Finally, C4 and C5 are rather obvious consequences of our intuitive meaning of the A- and B-predicates and the truth definition of the until operator.

The conditions C0–C5 take care of all *universal* constraints on the A- and B-predicates; but of course there are *existential* demands as well, which we shall call *requirements*. A requirement of a mosaic $\mu = (X, R, A_\varphi, B_\varphi)_{\varphi \in Cl(\xi)}$ is one of the two following types of object:

(a) $(A_{U(\varphi,\psi)}, s)$ such that $A_{U(\varphi,\psi)}s$,

(b) $(not\, B_\varphi, s, t)$ such that Rst and $not\, B_\varphi st$.

In order to explain the requirements of type (a), suppose that we want the formula $U(\varphi, \psi)$ to be true at a point s; if there is a point t in the mosaic such that Rst, $A_\varphi t$, and $B_\psi st$, then the mosaic itself *directly fulfills* the requirement. This will rarely be the case, however; the whole point of the mosaic method is that requirements can be fulfilled by *distinct* mosaics as well, as follows. A *link* between two mosaics μ and μ' is simply a partial isomorphism between the two structures. We say that a link $f : \mu \hookrightarrow \mu'$ *fulfills the requirement* $(A_{U(\varphi,\psi)}, s)$ of μ if there is some t in μ' with $Rf(s)t$, $A_\varphi t$, and $B_\psi f(s)t$. Likewise, a link $f : \mu \hookrightarrow \mu'$ *fulfills the requirement* $(notB_\varphi, s, t)$ if there is some u in μ' with $Rf(s)u$, $Ruf(t)$, and $\neg A_\varphi u$.

A collection L of mosaics is called a *linked set of mosaics* if every requirement of every mosaic $\mu \in L$ is fulfilled via some link $f : \mu \hookrightarrow \mu'$ to some μ' also in L. It is a linked set of mosaics *for* ξ if it contains a mosaic with nonempty A_ξ.

The main theorem concerning mosaics is the following. (In order to follow the main line of the chapter, the reader could skip the details of the proof.)

Proposition 7.4.7. *An $\mathcal{L}_U$-formula ξ is satisfiable if and only if there is a linked set of mosaics for ξ.*

Proof. The left-to-right direction of the proof is easy. Suppose that $\mathcal{M} = (W, R, V)$ is a model for ξ. Out of this model, we cut a linked set of mosaics for ξ, as follows. Let X be the collection of triples $\vec{x} = \langle x_1, x_2, x_3 \rangle$ such that Rx_1x_2, Rx_2x_3, and Rx_1x_3. Associate with any such triple a mosaic $\mu_{\vec{x}}$ based on the set $\{x_1, x_2, x_3\}$, with R as in $\mathcal{M}$ and with every A_φ and B_φ defined as given by the truth of φ in $\mathcal{M}$. We leave it as an exercise for the reader to verify that the collection of all these mosaics indeed forms a linked set of mosaics.

The right-to-left direction of the proposition is the hard one, although the key idea underlying its proof is quite intuitive. We construct a model for ξ *step by step*; that is, we approximate our model via a series of finite structures that we call *networks*. A *network* is a structure $\mathcal{N} = (W, R, A_\varphi, B_\varphi)_{\varphi \in Cl(\xi)}$ of the same type as a mosaic but not bounded in size. A network is called *coherent* if it satisfies the conditions C1–C5 above. To ask for C0 would be too much; instead, we require coherent networks to satisfy the following:

(liveness) every packed set X of size at most three *comes from* a mosaic; that is, for each such set $X \subseteq W$ there is a partial isomorphism $f : \mathcal{N} \hookrightarrow \mu$ such that f is defined on X.

Liveness means that, through the mosaics, we are in control of certain small parts of the model: the packed sets of size at most three. Why only these sets? The truth definition of U provides the answer. The meaning of $U(\varphi, \psi)$ depends only on these small packed sets in the model.

A *defect* of a network is a requirement that is not directly fulfilled in the network itself, and a network is called *saturated* if it has no defects. A network is *perfect* if it both coherent and saturated.

This name is well chosen, since perfect networks are the ones that we are after. The reason for this is that with every network $\mathcal{N} = (W, R, A_\varphi, B_\varphi)_{\varphi \in Cl(\xi)}$ we can associate a modal model in an obvious way: it is defined as the structure $\mathcal{N}^\circ = (W, R, V^\circ)$, where $V^\circ(p) = A_p$ for all variables p occurring in ξ. But only for perfect networks can we prove the following *truth lemma*.

Claim 1. If $\mathcal{N}$ is a perfect network, then for all formulas $\varphi \in Cl(\xi)$ and all points s, t in $\mathcal{N}$:

1. $s \in A_\varphi$ iff $\mathcal{M}, s \Vdash \varphi$.
2. If Rst, then $(s, t) \in B_\varphi$ iff $\mathcal{M}, st \Vdash \varphi$.

PROOF OF CLAIM The proof of this claim is by induction on the complexity of φ. We consider only the case where φ is of the form $U(\psi, \chi)$, and only prove part 2 of the claim (the first part is simpler).

By the induction hypothesis and the truth definition of U, in order to prove part 2 it suffices to show that for all pairs of points s and t such that Rst, we have that $(s, t) \notin B_\varphi$ iff $u \notin A_\varphi$ for some u with Rsu and Rut. The left-to-right direction immediately follows from the fact that $\mathcal{N}$ is perfect and thus all requirements of type (b) are fulfilled. For the other direction, suppose that s, t and u are points satisfying Rst, Rsu, Rtu and $u \notin A_\varphi$. Observe that $\{s, t, u\}$ is a packed set of size at most three, so that we may use the liveness condition. This yields a partial isomorphism f from $\mathcal{N}$ to some mosaic μ such that f is defined for each of s, t, and u. It follows that $Rf(s)f(t)$, $Rf(s)f(u)$, $Rf(t)f(u)$, and $f(u) \notin A_\varphi$; but then it follows from condition C4 that $(f(s), f(t)) \notin B_\varphi$. Returning to $\mathcal{N}$, this shows that $(s, t) \notin B_\varphi$, which is what we needed to prove. This finishes the proof of the claim.

It follows from the above claim that in order to show that ξ is satisfiable, it suffices to show that there is a perfect network for it, that is, a perfect network such that A_ξ is not empty.

Claim 2. There is a perfect network for ξ.

PROOF OF CLAIM The proof of this claim falls out into three parts. First we show that there is *some* network for ξ (not necessarily perfect). This is easy, since we are given a linked set of mosaics for ξ: as our network we simply take any mosaic with a nonempty A_ξ.

The second and main part of the proof consists in showing that any defect of any network can be *repaired*; that is, we can find a bigger network in which the defect no longer occurs. Without going into too much technical detail, let us see how to repair a defect of type (b) (defects of type (a) are repaired in a similar way).

Suppose that s and t are points of the network $\mathcal{N}$ such that Rst and *not* $B_\varphi st$ for some subformula φ of ξ, while there is no point u between s and t such that $\neg A_\varphi u$. The idea now is simply to *repair* this defect by adding a *new point* to the network. What kind of point? Well, since we have Rst we know that s and t come from a mosaic; that is, there is a partial isomorphism f from $\mathcal{N}$ to some mosaic μ. Obviously, $(notB_\varphi, f(s), f(t))$ is a requirement of this mosaic. But since we are working with a *linked* set of mosaics, there must be some link g between μ and μ' and some u in μ' such that $Rg(f(s))u$, $Rug(f(t))$, and $\neg A_\varphi u$. Now we simply add an entirely new point r to the network, and make sure that the relations between s, t, and r are such that this part of the model is isomorphic to μ'. It is thus obvious that we have *repaired* the defect, and that the new structure is a network. In order to keep the liveness condition, it is essential *not* to relate r to any *other* point besides s and t: in this way, the only new packed sets are $\{r, s, t\}$ and its subsets.

Finally, these two parts provide the material and the tools for constructing the desired perfect network for ξ. Starting from the mosaic for ξ (which is of course a network), we repair defects, one by one, step by step, thus constructing a sequence $\mathcal{N}_0$, $\mathcal{N}_1$, ... of networks. Using some standard combinatorics, we can ensure that the *limit* of the chain of networks is a network without defects. In particular, if we always take new points from a fixed set, say ω, we can enumerate the set of all (potential) defects of any network in the chain; if at each step of the construction we repair the current network's defect with the lowest number in this enumeration, we can create a perfect network. This finishes the proof of the claim.

□

Theorem 7.4.8. *It is decidable whether a given $\mathcal{L}_U$-formula is satisfiable.*

Proof. We can adjust the "elimination algorithm" given for the system **K*** in order to deal with mosaics. This is done as follows. Let S be the set of all ξ-type mosaics (up to isomorphism). Let $S_0 \subseteq S$ be the subset containing all coherent mosaics. S_0 can be computed effectively, since coherence can be checked effectively. It is not hard to show that $|S| \leq 2^{O(|\xi|)}$. We now inductively construct a sequence of sets of mosaics $S_0 \supsetneq S_1 \supsetneq S_2 \supsetneq S_3 \cdots$, just as in the proof for the system $\mathbf{K}^*$. The idea is that we delete mosaics from S_i if they have a requirement which cannot be fulfilled inside S_i. The details of this construction will be spelled out in the section on guarded fragments.   □

What is important to remember is that the until system has a kind of *loose model property*: if a formula ξ is satisfiable then there is a linked set of mosaics for it, and if there is such a set for ξ, then the proof of Proposition 7.4.7 shows how to construct a *loose model* for ξ. We shall come back to this in Section 7.6

Notes

Tiling problems (or domino problems, as they are sometimes called) were introduced by Wang [61] and have since been used in a variety of forms to prove undecidability and complexity results. An accessible proof of the undecidability of the $\mathbb{N} \times \mathbb{N}$ tiling problem, a result due to Berger [8], can be found in the monograph by Börger, Grädel & Gurevich [10]. Our discussion of the logic Tile was based on Spaan [55], where an example is presented in a language that expands the *basic* modal language with the universal diamond.
    The modal system $\mathbf{S5}^2$ (S5 square) has a long history in the algebraic disguise of the class of diagonal-free cylindric algebras of dimension two, see the monograph [27]. The bounded finite model property of $\mathbf{S5}^2$ was first established by Segerberg [53]. The fact that every pseudo-square bisimulates by a functional bisimulation with a square can be found in Marx & Venema [43]. The higher-dimensional counterparts of $\mathbf{S5}^2$ are studied as modal logics in Venema [59, 60].
    The modal system $\mathbf{K}^*$ can best be seen as a fragment of propositional dynamic logic (PDL) in which there is only one atomic program. For more information on PDL, the reader is referred to the handbook article by Harel [24]. The decidability of PDL was proved by Fischer & Ladner [18]. The elimination algorithm leading to Theorem 7.4.5 is due to Pratt [50].
    The operators "Since" and "Until" were introduced by Hans Kamp in order to prove expressive (in)completeness results for temporal logics over classes of linear flows of time. Nowadays, they belong to the standard repertoire of temporal logics in computer science; see [39]. A bisimulation variant which characterizes this language over arbitrary models was found by Kurtonina & de Rijke [36]; for some decidability results over classes of linear flows of time, see Burgess & Gurevich [12]. Our Theorem 7.4.8 and its proof are based on results and proofs related to the loosely guarded fragment that are due to van Benthem.
    The filtration method has been used extensively as a tool for proving decidability results for modal logics, since Lemmon [38] and Segerberg [52] further developed ideas dating back to McKinsey & Tarski [44]. The mosaic

method for proving decidability of a logic was developed by Németi [45]; it has since been used for a wide range of logics, often related to a multi-dimensional modal setting. With hindsight, even Gödel's proof of the decidability of the satisfiability problem for $\forall^2\exists^*$ prenex sentences can be called a mosaic-style proof as well; see the very clear exposition in [10].

7.5 Modal Complexity

In the previous sections, we have discussed the decidability of the satisfiability problem for several modal systems, gathering various results along the way. For instance, for the basic modal system **K**, we saw that every satisfiable formula can be satisfied in an exponential-size tree model with branches of polynomial depth; for $\mathbf{S5}^2$, we could do no better than finding an exponential-size quasi-model.

In this section, we take a closer look at such differences, examining how they affect the complexity of the modal systems that we present. Our goal is not to give precise reductions and matching algorithms — this is very well documented in the literature. Rather, we shall paint with a broad brush and try to convey once more our earlier message that looseness and locality are key notions in understanding the decidability and complexity of modal systems. To do this we discuss modal systems whose satisfiability problems are complete for the complexity classes NP, PSPACE, EXPTIME, and NEXPTIME, respectively. We believe that these systems, besides being complete for these classes, indeed form very indicative examples.

Our agenda for the section is set out in Table 7.1. We assume that the reader has at least a basic understanding of complexity classes such as NP, PSPACE, EXPTIME, etc. Completeness and hardness are understood in this chapter by means of polynomial-time many-one reductions. (The reader is referred to [3] for basic definitions.) In this section, we concentrate on the satisfiability problem — recall that C-completeness of the satisfiability problem for a modal system implies co-C-completeness of the validity problem.

The layout of this section is summarized in Table 7.1. Every column represents a modal system and the complexity class for which its satisfiability problem is complete. The third row indicates whether satisfiable formulas can be satisfied in tree models for that logic, and the fourth row whether the modal system

Table 7.1. Layout of Section 7.3

modal system/logic	S5	Func	K	K*	$S5^2$
complete for	NP	NP	PSPACE	EXPTIME	NEXPTIME
tree model property	*	yes	yes	yes	no
global expressive power	yes	no	no	yes	yes
subsection	7.5.1	7.5.1	7.5.2	7.5.3	7.5.4

is expressive enough to define the universal modality. We mention these two properties because they correspond to the looseness and first locality principle, respectively (as mentioned before, we shall meet the second locality principle again in the last section). The star in the first column marks the special role of the logic **S5**, which is the logic of the universal modality E by itself.

We shall often use the tractability result concerning model checking that we mentioned earlier on when discussing the second locality principle. In this section, we confine ourselves to modal languages with a finite number of first-order definable modal operators. For modal formulas in such a language, the *model checking* problem (i.e., given as input a (finite) model $\mathcal{M}$, a state s and a formula ξ, to determine whether $\mathcal{M}, s \Vdash \xi$), is solvable in PTIMEin the size of *both* the model *and* the formula. Also, for an elementary (i.e., definable by a single first-order sentence) class of models K, the membership problem (given as input a finite model $\mathcal{M}$, to determine whether $\mathcal{M}$ belongs to K), is also solvable in PTIME. We shall call a modal system *elementary* if it has an elementary class of models and each of its operators has a first-order truth definition.

7.5.1 NP and the Polysize Model Property

The class NP of nondeterministic polynomial-time algorithms is the smallest complexity class that we shall consider for the satisfiability problem for modal systems. The reason for this is that every nontrivial modal logic contains the collection of all valid propositional formulas; hence we can reduce the NP-complete satisfiability problem for propositional logic to that of the modal system. So NP is a nice class to work with since we only have to show an upper bound. Unfortunately, there are not many modal systems with a satisfiability problem in NP.

How can we show that the satisfiability problem is in NP for a given modal system? The easiest route and the one that modal logicians most often take is via the *polysize model property*. A modal system is said to have this property if every satisfiable formula ξ is satisfiable in a model whose size is bounded by $p(|\xi|)$ for a fixed polynomial p. Using the two complexity results mentioned above, namely, PTIME for both the model checking and the membership problem, it is easy to show that for elementary modal systems, the polysize model property implies NP-completeness of the satisfiability problem.

Let us see then, if we can find modal systems with this polysize model property; we shall confine ourselves to the basic modal language. In Sect. 7.3, we showed that every satisfiable formula φ can be satisfied in an at most $|\varphi|$-ary tree of depth at most $|\varphi|$: a model whose size is exponential in $|\varphi|$. Thus, if we want a polysize model, we should restrict either the width or the depth of such trees. This is possible if we consider smaller classes of models.

Restricting the *width* is easy: we consider only models in which R is a total function. The cut-off argument in Section 7.3 yields a linear-sized model. Recall from Definition 7.3.8 that $d_\diamond(\xi)$ denotes the modal depth of ξ.

Proposition 7.5.1. *Let* Func *be the modal system* $(\mathcal{L}_\Diamond, \Vdash, \mathsf{F})$ *such that* $\Vdash$ *is the standard definition and* F *is the class of models in which* R *is a total function. Let* ξ *be a formula in* $\mathcal{L}_\Diamond$. *If* ξ *is* Func-*satisfiable, then it is* Func-*satisfiable in a model containing at most* $d_\Diamond(\xi) + 1$ *states.*

As a corollary, the satisfiability problem for Func *is in NP.*

An extremely simple way of bounding the depth is to make the accessibility relation total; a state at which φ holds is then a witness for $\Diamond\varphi$ at every state in the model.

Note, however, that making the accessibility relation total breaks with the first locality principle! Nevertheless, the resulting modal system, which we shall call **S5** after the name of the logic associated with it, has a satisfiability problem in NP.

Proposition 7.5.2. *Let* **S5** *be the modal system* $(\mathcal{L}_\Diamond, \Vdash, \mathsf{U})$ *such that* $\Vdash$ *is the standard definition and* U *is the class of models in which* R *is the universal relation. Let* ξ *be a formula in the basic modal language. If* ξ *is* **S5**-*satisfiable then it is* **S5**-*satisfiable in a model containing at most* $|\xi|$ *states.*

As a corollary, the satisfiability problem for **S5** *is in NP.*

Proof. Let $\mathcal{M} = (M, R, V)$ be a model such that $R = M \times M$ and $\mathcal{M}, s \Vdash \xi$. Choose, for every subformula $\Diamond\varphi$ of ξ, a state $t \in M$ such that φ holds at t (if such a state exists). Let $\mathcal{M}'$ be the submodel of $\mathcal{M}$ consisting of s plus the selected states. By our pruning argument of Section 7.3, $\mathcal{M}', s \Vdash \xi$, because R is the universal relation. □

This finishes our discussion of NP and the polysize model property. Modal systems with this property are few and far between. In the next subsection, we shall see that for the basic modal system we can get only an exponential upper bound on the size of a model.

7.5.2 PSPACE and Polynomially Deep Paths

In Section 7.3 we showed that every satisfiable formula ξ in the basic modal language is satisfiable in a finite tree model $\mathcal{M}$, with depth and branching degree both bounded by the length $|\xi|$ of the formula. The good news about this argument is that it can be used to show that satisfiability for **K** can be decided in PSPACE. On the other hand, the upper bound that it establishes on the size of $\mathcal{M}$ is no better than exponential — at this stage, the reader might wonder whether this is an optimal bound. Here we show that it is — up to a polynomial. In fact, the satisfiability problem of **K** is *complete* for PSPACE.

We now define, for each natural number n, a satisfiable formula $\xi(n)$ with the following two properties:

- the size of $\xi(n)$ is quadratic in n; and
- when $\xi(n)$ is satisfied in any model $\mathcal{M}$ at state s, then $\mathcal{M}$ contains as a substructure an isomorphic copy of the binary tree of depth n whose root is s.

Thus the size of the smallest model satisfying $\xi(n)$ is exponential in $|\xi(n)|$. The idea underlying the definition of $\xi(n)$ is very simple: take n propositional variables $p_0, \ldots, p_{n-1}$, and write a formula which, when satisfied, forces a binary-branching tree in which every possible valuation on $\{p_0, \ldots, p_{n-1}\}$ occurs at some leaf. Thus the model certainly contains 2^n different states. The formula is constructed using two "macros": $branch(p_i)$ and $store(p_i)$ defined as follows:

$$branch(p_i) := \Diamond(p_i \wedge \Box p_i) \wedge \Diamond(\neg p_i \wedge \Box \neg p_i)$$
$$store(p_i) := (p_i \rightarrow \Box p_i) \wedge (\neg p_i \rightarrow \Box \neg p_i).$$

The formula $\xi(n)$ is then given by

$$branch(p_0) \wedge \bigwedge_{1 \leq i < n} \Box^i (branch(p_i) \wedge \bigwedge_{0 \leq j < i} store(p_j)), \qquad (7.12)$$

in which $\Box^i$ abbreviates a sequence of boxes, of length i. The formula works as follows. Suppose $\mathcal{M}, s \Vdash \xi(n)$. Then the $branch$ part of $\xi(n)$ states that every node t reachable in i R-steps from s has two different successors, one forcing $p_i \wedge \Box p_i$ and the other forcing $\neg p_i \wedge \Box \neg p_i$. The $store$ part of the formula states that successors of t created by the $branch$ part satisfy precisely the same proposition letters $p_0, \ldots, p_{i-1}$ as does t. We leave it to the reader to verify that the interplay of the $branch$ and $store$ macros forces a binary tree of depth n, as desired.

PSPACE lower bound. Of course, failure of the polysize model property for the basic modal system does not in itself imply that its satisfiability problem cannot be decided in NP. However, in fact the lower bound of this problem is known to be PSPACE. This result can be obtained by an interpretation of the validity problem of quantified boolean formulas. This interpretation is based on the same two macros $branch$ and $store$.

In a similar way, one can establish the existence of exponential-sized models and a PSPACE lower bound for the modal system with $\langle * \rangle$ as its *only* modal operator (i.e., the fragment of $\mathbf{K}^*$ of formulas in which the ordinary diamond $\Diamond$ does not occur). To overcome the difficulty that $\langle * \rangle$ has direct one-step access to all states in a tree one has to add additional propositional variables to encode the depth of the tree. See the notes for details.

PSPACE upper bound. The *K-World* algorithm for the basic modal system $\mathbf{K}$ (see Figure 7.6) runs in PSPACE. Recall that for any formula ξ, ξ is $\mathbf{K}$ satisfiable iff there exists a set $\Delta \subseteq Cl(\xi)$ such that $\xi \in \Delta$ and $K\text{-}World(\Delta, Cl(\xi))$ is true. All sets encountered in the execution of $K\text{-}World$ are subsets of $Cl(\xi)$. Each subset of $Cl(\xi)$ can be represented in space $O(|\xi|)$, by using pointers to a copy of the formula. Therefore, at each level of the recursion, $O(|\xi|)$ space is used. After $d_\Diamond(\xi)$ recursive calls ($d_\Diamond(\xi)$ being the modal depth of ξ), there are no more $\Diamond \psi$ formulas in Σ and the recursion stops. Thus the recursion depth is bounded by $d_\Diamond(\xi) \leq |\xi|$, and hence the total amount of space required by the algorithm is $O(|\xi|^2)$. The existential demands in the algorithm (there exists a set Δ with $\xi \in \Delta$ such that $\ldots$, and for all $\Diamond\psi \in \Delta$, there exists ...) make the algorithm nondeterministic. But PSPACE = NPSPACE by Savitch's Theorem.

A crucial point in the PSPACE upper-bound argument is that we can represent a complete branch of the tree model for ξ using only polynomial space. Two factors are important here. First, only a polynomial number of formulas is relevant for each world. And second, the depth of the branches is bounded by the modal depth of the input formula. This is caused by the first locality principle: a lack of global expressive power. In the next subsection we show that adding such expressive power to the basic modal language destroys this polynomial-depth property.

7.5.3 EXPTIME and Exponentially Deep Paths

Now we shall see that global expressive power in combination with another diamond destroys the polynomially bounded deptLh of the satisfying tree models for the basic modal system. In particular, we shall create a satisfiable formula which, when satisfied, forces a branch in the model containing an exponential number of colors. Thus the PSPACE algorithm sketched in the previous subsection will not work anymore. In fact, the additional expressive power will be enough to show that the satisfiability problem is EXPTIME-hard. We again consider the system $\mathbf{K}^*$ of Subsect. 7.4.2. We want to show that its language is strong enough to force the existence of exponentially deep R-paths. A simple way of doing so employs binary counters.

By a binary counter we mean a device that can have a natural number as its value, represented as a binary string of 0s and 1s; it should also be possible to increment this value by one. We use a set $\{p_0, \ldots, p_{n-1}\}$ of propositional variables to implement an n-ary binary counter ("n-ary" means that the counter is reset to zero after reaching the value $2^n - 1$). We use these variables to encode the n bits of the counter, with p_0 encoding the least significant and p_{n-1} the most significant bit. The variable p_i being true in a given state, encodes the fact that the ith bit of the counter is 1 in that state. The key idea of an encoding into the modal language lies in the following characterization of adding 1 to a binary counter. If $a = a_{n-1}\ldots a_0$ and $b = b_{n-1}\ldots b_0$ are two n-bit counters, then $b = a + 1 \,(\mathrm{mod}\ 2^n)$ precisely when the following holds: either $b_i = 0$ and $a_i = 1$ for all i (this is when we start counting at 0 again), or, for some $k \leq n - 1$, we have

(1) $a_k = 0$, and $b_k = 1$,
(2) $a_j = 1$ and $b_j = 0$ for all $j < k$, and
(3) $a_i = b_i$ for all $i > k$.

In a picture:

$$
\begin{array}{l}
10110\ 0\ 1111\ a \\
00000\ 0\ 0001 \\
\hline
10110\ 1\ 0000\ b = a + 1. \\
k
\end{array}
$$

We want to write a formula $\gamma(n)$ which forces a counter to take all values from 0 to $2^n - 1$, in consecutive states, thereby forcing an exponentially deep path. We shall take care that the formula has a length of only $O(n^2)$. The formula $\gamma(n)$ is a conjunction of four formulas. The first conjunct expresses the fact that the counter is initially set to 0:

$$\neg p_0 \wedge \ldots \wedge \neg p_{n-1}.$$

The other conjuncts of $\gamma(n)$ must hold globally in a model. To achieve that aim, we use the dual $[\,*\,]$ of $\langle * \rangle$ ($[\,*\,]\varphi$ abbreviates $\neg\langle * \rangle \neg\varphi$). It is clear that the root s of a tree model has $\mathcal{M}, s \Vdash [\,*\,]\varphi$ if and only if, for all t, $\mathcal{M}, t \Vdash \varphi$.

The second conjunct expresses that every state has a successor:

$$[\,*\,]\Diamond\top.$$

The next two conjuncts take care of addition. They express that whenever an R-transition is made in the model, the binary counter is increased by one. First, we deal with the simple case of resetting the counter:

$$[\,*\,]((p_0 \wedge \ldots \wedge p_{n-1}) \to \Box(\neg p_0 \wedge \ldots \wedge \neg p_{n-1})).$$

Finally, the last conjunct of $\gamma(n)$ covers the case when we have to "carry one". This conjunct is itself a conjunction, having a conjunct of the following form for every k such that $0 \leq k < n$:

$$[\,*\,]((\neg p_k \wedge \bigwedge_{j<k} p_j) \to \Box(p_k \wedge \bigwedge_{j<k} \neg p_j) \wedge \bigwedge_{i>k} store(p_i)),$$

where $store(p_i)$ is defined in the previous subsection and the empty conjunction is set to true.

We leave it to the reader to check the correctness of this formula. Note that the sole use of $[\,*\,]$ was to make statements in the *basic* modal language true *everywhere* in the model. This use is crucial, however: Proposition 7.3.10 states that a formula in the basic modal language can only force models with R-paths of at most its modal depth. Now the modal depth of $\gamma(n)$ is just two (one for $[\,*\,]$, and one for $\Diamond$), *for every n*, while the minimal R-depth of models satisfying $\gamma(n)$ is 2^n.

Complexity bounds. In the previous subsection, we saw that the polynomially bounded depth of models was the key to a PSPACE upper bound. The present result does not yet show that such an upper bound is not possible, but it renders it unlikely (see the notes). And, indeed, the satisfiability problem for $\mathbf{K}^*$ is EXPTIME-*complete*. For the lower bound we refer to the notes. The upper bound follows from the $\mathbf{K}^*$ decision algorithm presented in the previous section. Recall that the algorithm tried to construct a set of ready subsets of $Cl(\xi)$. We remarked that the construction would terminate after $2^{O(|\xi|)}$ stages. Computing which sets in S_i are ready can be done in time polynomial in the size of S_i, which is at most exponential in $|\xi|$. Thus the whole construction can be carried out in deterministic exponential time.

We note that all results carry over to the modal system **K+E** (the basic modal system expanded with the universal modality E). In particular, the formula $\gamma(n)$ with $\neg\langle*\rangle\neg$ substituted by $\neg E\neg$ causes an exponentially deep path. This result will be used in the next section.

7.5.4 NEXPTIME

We now consider a modal system in which matters get even worse: the system **S5²**. For the definitions of **S5²** and its square and pseudo-square models, see Section 7.4.1.

This system does not have the tree model property. In addition, the language has global expressive power: for every φ, if a model $\mathcal{M}$ satisfies $\Box_1\Box_0\varphi$, then $\mathcal{M} \Vdash \varphi$. So we expect that the satisfiability problem will have a high complexity. This is indeed the case. This system is strong enough to interpret the system **K + E** of the previous subsection, inheriting its EXP-TIME lower bound. But **S5²** lacks the tree-like models of **K + E** on which the EXPTIME upper bound is based. We shall sketch an argument that **S5²** is strong enough to force exponential grids, which is the key to a NEXPTIME lower-bound result. A matching upper bound follows from earlier results: every satisfiable formula ξ is satisfiable in a pseudo-square of size at most $2^{|\xi|}$, by Proposition 7.4.3. Being a pseudo-square is a first-order property. As we saw in the subsection on NP, testing whether a modal formula is satisfied in a model takes time polynomial in the formula and the size of the model. Thus for the same reasons as why the polysize model property leads to an NP upper bound, we obtain here a NEXPTIME upper bound.

We start with the interpretation of the **K + E** satisfiability problem. For this purpose, we use a translation reminiscent of the two-variable version of the standard translation (read r as Rxy, $\Diamond_1$ as $\exists y$, and $\Diamond_0$ as $\exists x$, and read w as the assertion expressing that $x = y$). Let $(\cdot)^t$ be a translation function which maps propositional variables to propositional variables, commutes with the booleans, and translates the diamonds as follows:

$$(\Diamond\varphi)^t = \Diamond_1(r \wedge \Diamond_0(w \wedge \varphi^t))$$
$$(E\varphi)^t = \Diamond_1\Diamond_0(w \wedge \varphi^t),$$

where r and w are fixed variables not occurring in the input language. Their function becomes clear in the proof of the next proposition.

Proposition 7.5.3. *Let ξ be a formula in the basic modal language expanded with the universal modality. Then ξ is **K + E**-satisfiable if and only if $w \wedge \xi^t$ is **S5²**-satisfiable.*

Proof. ($\Rightarrow$) Let $\mathcal{M} = (W, R, V)$ be a Kripke model and let $\mathcal{M}, s \Vdash \xi$. We define a square **S5²**-model $\mathcal{M}^* = (W \times W, \equiv_0, \equiv_1, V^*)$, with V^* defined as follows:

$$V^*(w) = \{(x,x) \mid x \in W\}$$
$$V^*(r) = R$$
$$V^*(p) = \{(x,x) \mid x \in V(p)\}.$$

An easy induction shows that $\mathcal{M}^*, (s,s) \Vdash w \wedge \xi^t$.

($\Leftarrow$) Let $\mathcal{M} = (W, \equiv_0, \equiv_1, V)$ be a square **S5²** model and $\mathcal{M}, (s,t) \Vdash w \wedge \xi^t$. Define a Kripke model $\mathcal{M}^\circ$ whose domain consists of all pairs in W where w holds; of which the valuation V° is simply the restriction of V to these w-pairs; and in which the accessibility relation R° holds between (x,y) and (x', y') iff $\mathcal{M}, (x, y') \Vdash r$. A simple induction shows that for all w-pairs (x,y) and for all formulas φ, we have that $\mathcal{M}, (x,y) \Vdash \varphi^t \leftrightarrow \mathcal{M}^\circ, (x,y) \Vdash \varphi$.   □

This result immediately shows that the **S5²** satisfiability problem is EXPTIME-hard. In fact, it is even hard for NEXPTIME. This lower bound can be shown by a reduction to a tiling problem very similar to the one used to show undecidability in Section 7.4. In this case we tile not the grid $\mathbb{N} \times \mathbb{N}$ but the finite grid $2^n \times 2^n$. It is known that this problem is complete for nondeterministic time exponential in n. Here we provide the key idea underlying the reduction, which is that for every n, we can define a satisfiable formula $\xi(n)$ with the properties that

- the length of $\xi(n)$ is quadratic in n, and
- if $\xi(n)$ is satisfied in an **S5²** model $\mathcal{M}$, then $\mathcal{M}$ contains as a substructure an isomorphic copy of the structure $(2^n \times 2^n, S_v, S_h)$, where S_v, S_h are the vertical and horizontal successor functions in the grid $2^n \times 2^n$.

Once we have expressed this, it is straightforward to find a formula saying that a tiling exists, just as in Section 7.4. Because of space limitations we can give only a very rough sketch. The first conjunct of $\xi(n)$ is the translation of the formula $\gamma(2n)$ of the previous subsection. We assume that $\gamma(2n)$ is created from variables $x_0, \ldots, x_{n-1}$ and $y_0, \ldots, y_{n-1}$. So there are two binary counters, that together specify in binary notation a pair $\langle k, l \rangle$ in the grid $2^n \times 2^n$.

Let $\mathcal{M}$ be a Kripke model such that $\mathcal{M}, s \Vdash \gamma(2n)$. Let $\mathcal{M}^*$ be the square **S5²** model as defined in the proof of Proposition 7.5.3. In $\mathcal{M}^*$ we have, besides the tree structure of the Kripke model, also all "grid points": that is, for all worlds $w, w' \in W$, the pair (w, w') exists in the model $\mathcal{M}^*$. We can use these pairs to relate the counter information in w and w'. More concretely, we write formulas ensuring that at (w, w'), a propositional variable S_v holds if and only if w encodes the grid pair $\langle k, l \rangle$ and w' encodes its vertical successor $\langle k, l+1 \rangle$. We again use the characterization of adding one in binary in order to create a formula of the required small size. For the full proof, we refer to the notes.

We have seen in Proposition 7.5.3 how the EXPTIME modal logic $\mathbf{K} + \mathsf{E}$ "lives" inside the NEXPTIME logic **S5²**. Also, we saw that the "extra" points available in the grid models lead to higher complexity. In the next section, we shall do the same but with more variables. We look at first-order logic and find decidable fragments living inside it. In analogy with the last result, we can say that the key feature of these fragments is that they cannot speak about the "extra grid points".

7.5.5 Notes

Most complexity-theoretic classifications of modal satisfiability and validity problems come from the computer science literature. This work can be roughly divided into three groups: temporal logics describing computations, logics for reasoning about knowledge, and description logics. Pointers to this vast literature can be found in the handbook articles by Stirling [56] and Calvanese et alii [13] for temporal logics and description logics, respectively, and in the monograph by Fagin et alii [17] for epistemic logics. Here we provide only the sources for the results in this section.

The NP-completeness of **S5** was proved by Ladner [37]. The results on PSPACE come also from [37]: both the upper and the lower bound for the basic modal system **K** are established there. Ladner's procedure for **K** is like the one given in Figure 7.6, save that he uses "concrete tableaux" (that is, his algorithm specifies how to construct the required atoms) rather than "abstract tableaux" (which factor out the required boolean reasoning). Concrete tableaux were also used by Halpern and Moses [23] to construct PSPACE algorithms for multimodal versions of **K**, **S4**, and indeed **S5**; as these authors show, logics containing two **S5** modalities are PSPACE-hard.

The EXPTIME-hardness of **K*** and **K + E** is due to Fischer & Ladner [18] (who work in the richer setting of propositional dynamic logic). An EXPTIME procedure for **PDL** using an "elimination algorithm" was given by Pratt [50]. We used this idea in the proof of Theorem 7.4.5, and shall do so again in the next section on the guarded fragment. For other applications of the method, see for instance [23], where Halpern & Moses apply it to a multimodal logic equipped with a common knowledge operator.

The modal system Func+E is an example of a modal system in which exponentially deep paths can be forced but which is still decidable in PSPACE, a result due to Sistla & Clarke [54]. We stress that adding the universal modality causes the complexity to go up from NP. Note that in this system there are no models which can be considered to be binary trees. Indeed, Spaan [55] has provided a sufficient condition for EXPTIME-hardness of the satisfiability problem of modal systems. This criterion requires the existence of models which can be considered as finite binary trees, and an expansion of the basic modal language which is powerful enough to make statements which hold everywhere in such a tree model.

The fact that the square tiling problem with a width given in binary is hard for nondeterministic exponential time was established by Fürer [19]. The lower bound for $S5^2$ was established by Marx [40].

7.6 Modal Logic and First-Order Logic

The previous sections were centered around the question of what determines the decidability and complexity of the satisfiability problem for various modal systems. We identified the looseness property of modal logics as the main principle guiding their nice computational properties; we also met two locality principles that influence the complexity of a modal system. It now seems natural to try and see how far we can push these ideas concerning looseness and locality to larger fragments of first-order logic than the modal fragment formed by the range of the standard translation map. The aim of this section is to identify a number of decidable fragments of first-order logic; that is, sets of first-order formulas for which it is decidable whether a given formula in the subset is satisfiable in some first-order model or not.

Convention. We work in a relational first-order language with equality. Thus the language contains neither constants nor function symbols. For a sequence of variables $\bar{x} = x_1, \ldots, x_n$, we shall frequently write $\exists \bar{x} \varphi$, which, as usual, has the same meaning as $\exists x_1 \cdots \exists x_n \varphi$. However, we view $\exists \bar{x}$ not as an abbreviation but as a primitive operator. In particular, this means that the subformulas of $\exists \bar{x} \varphi$ are just $\exists \bar{x} \varphi$ itself, together with the subformulas of φ. By writing $\varphi(\bar{x})$ we indicate that the free variables of φ are among $x_1, \ldots, x_n$.

7.6.1 Guarded Fragments

In order to find larger "loose" fragments of first-order logic, we reconsider the game-theoretic characterization of the modal fragment of first-order logic. Recall that bisimulations can be defined using a certain two-pebble Ehrenfeucht-Fraïssé game in which the universal player's moves are restricted in a certain way. We shall analyze these restrictions and implement them in the standard Ehrenfeucht-Fraïssé games for first-order logic; then we shall be ready to push all modal decidability arguments through for these *guarded fragments*.

Consider once again the bisimulation game from Section 7.3, and the two crucial properties:

Locality The game is played by moving a window of fixed size (two, in this case) across the models.

Looseness The window can only be placed on parts of the model in which all different points are related by the accessibility relation.

How do we generalize this to first-order logic? We implement the locality principle by considering fragments of first-order logic using a fixed finite number of variables. The looseness principle can be generalized in (at least) two different ways, leading to different fragments of first-order logic. To state these generalizations, we need two notions, both of which are well known in finite model theory.

Definition 7.6.1. *Let* $\mathcal{M} = (D, I)$ *be a model for some first-order language. A tuple* $(a_1, \ldots, a_n)$ *of objects in* D *is called* live *in* $\mathcal{M}$ *if either* $a_1 = \cdots = a_n$ *or* $(a_1, \ldots, a_n) \in I(P)$ *for some predicate symbol* P.

A subset A *of* D *is called* guarded *if there is some live tuple* $(a_1, \ldots, a_n)$ *such that* $A \subseteq \{a_1, \ldots, a_n\}$. *In particular, singleton sets are always guarded; note also that guarded sets are always finite.* A *is* packed *or* pairwise guarded *if it is finite and each of its two-element subsets is guarded.*

These notions can help us to incorporate the looseness principle into Ehrenfeucht-Fraïssé games as follows: player ∀ can only move pebbles in such a way that all configurations of pebbles that ever occur on the board are placed on guarded or packed sets.

Definition 7.6.2. *Let* $\mathcal{M} = (D, I)$ *and* $\mathcal{M}' = (D', I')$ *be two models. A* partial isomorphism *between* $\mathcal{M}$ *and* $\mathcal{M}'$ *is a bijection* $f : A \to A'$ *between some subsets* A *of* D *and* A' *of* D' *such that, for all predicate symbols* P *and all tuples* $\overline{a}$ *in* A *(of the appropriate length), we have that* $\overline{a} \in I(P)$ *if and only if* $f(\overline{a}) \in I'(P)$.

Now, for a partial isomorphism $f : A_0 \to A_0'$ *between* $\mathcal{M}'$ *and* $\mathcal{M}'$, *we define the* guarded game $\mathcal{G}_g(\mathcal{M}, \mathcal{M}', f)$ *as a variant of the familiar Ehrenfeucht-Fraïssé game. Here, in each round of the game,* ∀ *selects a structure and a guarded set within that structure;* ∃ *responds with a guarded set in the other structure. A match of the game thus gives rise to two sequences* $A = A_0, A_1, \ldots$ *and* $A' = A_0', A_0', \ldots$ *of subsets of* D *and* D', *respectively.* ∃ *wins this match if there are local isomorphisms* $f_n : A_n \to A_n'$ ($n \in \omega$) *such that* $f_0 = f$ *and, for each* n, f_n *and* f_{n+1} *agree on the intersection* $A_n \cap A_{n+1}$ *while their inverses agree on* $A_n' \cap A_{n+1}'$.

Now let $\overline{a}$ *in* $\mathcal{M}$ *and* $\overline{a}'$ *in* $\mathcal{M}'$ *be (possibly empty) sequences of elements such that* $f(a_i) = a_i'$ *for all* i. *When* ∃ *has a winning strategy in the guarded game* $\mathcal{G}_g(\mathcal{M}, \mathcal{M}', f)$ *we say that* $\overline{a}$ *and* $\overline{a}'$ *are g-bisimilar.*

The packed game $\mathcal{G}_p(\mathcal{M}, \mathcal{M}', f)$ *and the notion of packed bisimilarity are defined in the same way but using packed sets instead of guarded ones.*

These restrictions on the moves of player ∀ have direct syntactical counterparts in the form of restrictions on *quantification*: the idea is that we only allow quantification in the form $\exists \overline{x} \varphi$, where φ has to meet certain criteria.

Definition 7.6.3. *We say that a formula* φ packs *a set of variables* $\{x_1, \ldots, x_k\}$ *if* φ *is a conjunction of formulas of the form* $x_i = x_j$ *or* $R(x_{i_1}, \ldots, x_{i_n})$ *or* $\exists \overline{y} R(x_{i_1}, \ldots, x_{i_n})$ *such that for every* $x_i \neq x_j$, *there is a conjunct in* φ *in which* x_i *and* x_j *both occur free.*

The packed fragment *PF is defined as the smallest set of first-order formulas which contains all atomic formulas and is closed under the boolean connectives and under* packed quantification. *That is, whenever* ψ *is a packed formula,* π *packs* Free(π), *and* Free(ψ) $\subseteq$ Free(π), *then* $\exists \overline{x}(\pi \wedge \psi)$ *is packed as well;* π *is called the* guard *of this formula. The* guarded fragment *GF is the subfragment of PF in which we allow only* guarded quantification; *that is, packed quantification in which the guard* π *is an* atomic *formula.*

PF_n and GF_n denote the restrictions to n variables and at most n-ary predicate symbols of PF and GF, respectively.

When we want to be specific about the free variables occurring in the formulas, we shall often write $\exists \overline{y} \, (\pi(\overline{x}, \overline{y}) \wedge \psi(\overline{x}, \overline{y}))$ for the quantified packed formulas, tacitly assuming that $\overline{x}$ and $\overline{y}$ do not share any variables.

Typical examples of guarded (and thus also packed) sentences are $\forall xy(Rxy \rightarrow Ryx)$, $\exists xy \, (Rxy \wedge Ryx \wedge (Rxx \vee Ryy))$, and the standard translation of a formula in the basic modal language (with R functioning as guard). A typical nonexample is $\forall xyz((Rxy \wedge Ryz) \rightarrow Rxz)$: it is neither guarded nor packed. For an example of a packed formula which is not guarded, consider $\exists xyz((Rxy \wedge Rxz \wedge Ryz) \wedge \neg Cxyz)$.

Note that the notion of packedness only places meaningful restrictions on pairs of *distinct* variables: since the formula $x = x$ packs the set of variables $\{x\}$, the formula $\exists x(x = x \wedge \psi(x))$, (i.e., with a *single* quantification over the variable x) is a packed formula, at least, provided that $\psi(x)$ is packed. When $\psi(x)$ is guarded, then $\exists x(x = x \wedge \psi(x))$ is also guarded. Since this formula is equivalent to $\exists x\psi(x)$, this shows that packedness allows a fairly mild form of ordinary quantification, namely over formulas with one free variable. A nice corollary of this is that we may perform the standard translation of the universal modality E within the two-variable guarded fragment:

$$ST_x(\mathsf{E}\varphi) = ST_y(\mathsf{E}\varphi) = \exists x(ST_x(\varphi)) \equiv \exists x(x = x \wedge ST_x(\varphi)).$$

A similar translation to first-order logic can be defined for the language with the until modality U. Its range is the packed fragment with three variables. The interesting clause here is

$$ST_x(U(\varphi, \psi)) = \exists y(Rxy \wedge ST_y(\varphi) \wedge \forall z((Rxz \wedge Rzy) \rightarrow ST_z(\psi))).$$

This formula is not packed *itself*, because in the subformula $\forall z \, ((Rxz \wedge Rzy) \rightarrow ST_z(\psi)))$ the guard $Rxz \wedge Rzy$ does not pack its own free variables $\{x, y, z\}$. But, of course, the formula is *equivalent* to

$$\exists y \, (Rxy \wedge ST_y(\varphi) \wedge \forall z \, ((Rxz \wedge Rzy \wedge Rxy) \rightarrow ST_z(\psi)))$$

which is packed. It is not hard to convert this example into a proof showing that *every* formula in the Until language is equivalent to a packed formula. The (adjusted) translation is another example of a packed sentence that is not guarded.

We have defined first-order fragments by incorporating restrictions on the moves in an Ehrenfeucht-Fraïssé game into the syntax. It is obvious that packed formulas are preserved when player $\exists$ has a winning strategy. But, in fact, the fragments precisely *characterize* the formulas which are invariant under the corresponding games.

Definition 7.6.4. *A first-order formula* $\varphi(\overline{x})$ *is invariant under guarded (packed) bisimulation if, for all g-bisimilar (p-bisimilar, respectively) tuples* $\overline{a}$ *in* $\mathcal{M}$ *and* $\overline{a}'$ *in* $\mathcal{M}'$ *we have that* $\mathcal{M} \models \varphi[\overline{a}]$ *iff* $\mathcal{M}' \models \varphi[\overline{a}']$.

Theorem 7.6.5. *Let* ξ *be a first-order formula. The following are then equivalent:*
(i) ξ *is equivalent to a formula in the packed (guarded) fragment.*
(ii) ξ *is invariant under packed (guarded) bisimulations.*

This theorem can be relativized in the usual way to n-variable fragments and the corresponding n-pebble games. This is the first analogue of a modal theorem (the Characterization Theorem 7.3.4). In the section on basic modal logic we saw that this theorem allowed us to prove that every satisfiable formula was satisfiable in a tree. These trees were obtained by unraveling or unwinding the model. Analogous notions of unraveling and tree models can be defined for the guarded and packed fragments as well; here, we confine ourselves to the notion of a *loose model*.

Definition 7.6.6. *Let* $\mathcal{M} = (D, I)$ *be a first-order structure. We call* $\mathcal{M}$ *a loose model of degree* $k \in \mathbb{N}$ *if there is some acyclic connected undirected graph* $\mathcal{G} = (G, E)$ *and a function* f *mapping nodes of* $\mathcal{G}$ *to subsets of* D *of size not exceeding* k *such that for every live tuple* $\overline{s}$ *from* $\mathcal{M}$, *the set* $L(\overline{s}) = \{k \in G \mid s_i \in f(k)$ *for all* $s_i\}$, *is a nonempty and connected subset of* $\mathcal{G}$.

In words, we call a model $\mathcal{M} = (D, I)$ loose if we can associate a connected graph $\mathcal{G} = (G, E)$ with it in the following way. Each node t of the graph corresponds to a *small* subset $f(t)$ of the model; a good way of thinking about this is that t "describes" $f(t)$. We then require that the graph "covers" the entire model in the sense that any $a \in D$ belongs to one of these sets (this follows from the fact that for any $a \in D$, the "tuple" a is live). The fact that each set $L(\overline{a})$ is connected whenever $\overline{a}$ is live implies that different nodes of the graph will not give contradictory descriptions of the model. Finally, the *looseness* of the model stems intuitively from the acyclicity of $\mathcal{G}$ and the connectedness of the sets $L(\overline{a})$, because this ensures that when we walk through the graph we may describe different parts of the model, *but we never have to worry about returning to the same part once we have left it.* Summarizing, we may see the graph as a loose, coherent collection of descriptions of local submodels of the model. The loose models are the ones for which we can find such a graph. Note that the degree of a loose model corresponds directly to the second locality principle that we identified at the end of Sect. 7.3.

Now we can announce our second modally flavored theorem: it establishes the *loose model property* for the packed fragment.

Theorem 7.6.7. *Every satisfiable packed formula* ξ *can be satisfied on a loose model of degree not exceeding the number of variables occurring in* ξ.

And, as we shall see later on, this property indeed plays a crucial role in the proof of the following result.

Theorem 7.6.8. *It is decidable whether a packed formula is satisfiable. In fact, the satisfiability problems for both the guarded and the packed fragment are complete for 2EXPTIME.*

The doubly exponential lower bound may raise doubts concerning the relevance of this result. Fortunately, there are some large and very natural fragments for which better bounds may be obtained, and here the second notion of "locality" comes into play. This is because not only does the concept of looseness generalize to these fragments, but we can also give analogous versions for the notion of locality. Recall that we introduced this concept when we saw that the basic modal language could be translated into the *two-variable fragment* of first-order logic. This suggests that we might try to improve on Theorem 7.6.8 by considering finite-variable fragments of *PF* and *GF*. And, indeed, it turns out that "bringing locality into the language" brings down the complexity by one exponent!

In the case of the guarded fragment, we can formulate this result in a nice way, by imposing conditions on the first-order signature rather than on the number of variables used. Recall that the signature of the modal fragment of first-order logic consists of unary relation symbols and one binary symbol. In general, we call a first-order signature L *n-bounded* if all relation symbols in L have arity at most n. It is not very difficult to see that every *guarded sentence* in an n-bounded signature can be rewritten using only n variables. Thus, just as in the basic modal case, the signature determines the number of variables. Note that this property is lost for the full packed fragment, as we can pack arbitrarily large sets with binary relations.

In any case, by implementing both looseness and locality in first-order logic we may obtain the following result.

Theorem 7.6.9. *Fix a natural number n.*

(i) The satisfiability problem for formulas in the packed fragment PF_n is decidable in EXPTIME.

(ii) Hence, the satisfiability problem for sentences in the guarded fragment in the n-bounded signature is decidable in EXPTIME.

Note that for $n \geq 2$ the satisfiability problem for the guarded fragment GF_n is also EXPTIME-hard. This holds by the interpretation of the modal system $\mathbf{K} + \mathsf{E}$ using the standard translation. However, by also implementing the first locality principle (namely no global expressive power) it is even possible to bring the complexity down to PSPACE, see the notes.

Finally, what about finite models? Several subfragments of the packed fragment, including the guarded fragment, are known to have the finite model property. For the *full* packed fragment, this was an open problem at the time of writing this chapter, but recently, a positive solution to this problem has been obtained. For reasons of space limitations, we cannot go into detail here — see the notes for references.

7.6.2 Decidability and Complexity

This subsection provides the proofs of all the results mentioned above. The main idea behind the proofs is given by the *mosaic method* that we met in the decidability proof for the until system. Roughly speaking, this method is based on the idea of deconstructing models into a (modulo isomorphism) finite collection of finite submodels and, conversely, of building up new, "nice", models from such parts.

This subsection is structured as follows. We start with a formal definition of the notion of mosaics and some related concepts. We then state the main result concerning the mosaic method, namely the *Mosaic Theorem*, stating that a packed formula has a model if and only if there is a bounded set of bounded-size mosaics for it. This enables us to define our decision algorithms and establish their complexity. We then continue by proving the Mosaic Theorem. In doing so, we obtain as a by-product the loose model property for the packed fragment.

Linked Sets of Mosaics

Mosaics form the key tools in our proof; for a formal definition we need some syntactic preliminaries. Given a first-order formula ξ, we let $Var(\xi)$ and $Free(\xi)$ denote the sets of variables and free variables, respectively, occurring in ξ. Let V be a set of variables. A *V-substitution* is any partial map $\sigma : V \rightarrow V$. The result of performing a substitution σ on the formula ψ is denoted by ψ^σ. (We can and may assume that if $Var(\psi) \subseteq V$, then $Var(\psi^\sigma) \subseteq V$. For instance, when substituting y for x in $Rxz \wedge \forall y\,(Rzy \rightarrow Qxy)$, we have to rename the *bound* variable y, as in $Ryz \wedge \forall u\,(Rzu \rightarrow Qyu)$. The point is that we do not need to use a *fresh* variable u for this: instead, we may reuse x, giving $Ryz \wedge \forall x\,(Rzx \rightarrow Qyx)$.)

As before, we shall employ a notion of closure to delineate a finite set of *relevant* formulas, i.e., formulas that for some reason critically influence the truth of a given formula ξ. Also, recall that the *single negation* $\sim\varphi$ of a formula φ denotes the formula ψ if φ is of the form $\neg\psi$; otherwise, $\sim\varphi$ is the formula $\neg\varphi$.

Definition 7.6.10. *Let Σ be a set of packed formulas in the set V of variables. We call Σ V-closed if Σ is closed under subformulas, single negations, and V-substitutions (that is, if ψ belongs to Σ, then so does ψ^σ for every V-substitution σ). By $Cl_g(\xi)$, we denote the smallest $Var(\xi)$-closed set of formulas containing ξ.*

For the remainder of this section, we fix a packed formula ξ — all definitions to come should be understood as being relativized to ξ. The number of variables occurring in ξ (free or bound) is denoted by k; that is, k is the size of $Var(\xi)$. It can easily be verified that the sets of guarded and packed formulas are both closed under taking subformulas; hence, the set $Cl_g(\xi)$ consists of guarded (packed, respectively) formulas. An easy calculation shows that the cardinality of $Cl_g(\xi)$ is bounded by $k^k \cdot (2|\xi|)$ (k^k is the number of $Var(\xi)$-substitutions).

The following notion is the counterpart of the maximally propositionally consistent sets that we have met in earlier decidability proofs. The defining conditions again derive from a desire to prove a truth lemma.

Definition 7.6.11. *Let $X \subseteq Var(\xi)$ be a set of variables. An X-type is a set $\Gamma \subseteq Cl_g(\xi)$ with free variables in X satisfying, for all formulas $\varphi \wedge \psi$, $\sim\varphi$, and φ in $Cl_g(\xi)$ with free variables in X, the following conditions:*

(T1) $\varphi \wedge \psi \in \Gamma$ iff $\varphi \in \Gamma$ and $\psi \in \Gamma$;

(T2) $\varphi \notin \Gamma$ iff $\sim\varphi \in \Gamma$;

(T3) $\varphi, x_i = x_j \in \Gamma$ only if $\varphi^\sigma \in \Gamma$ (for any substitution σ mapping x_i to x_j and/or x_j to x_i, while leaving all other variables fixed); and

(T4) if $\psi(\overline{x}, \overline{z})$ and $\pi(\overline{x}, \overline{z})$ are in Γ, then so is $\exists \overline{y} \left(\pi(\overline{x}, \overline{y}) \wedge \psi(\overline{x}, \overline{y}) \right)$ (provided that the latter formula belongs to $Cl_g(\xi)$).

The next definition introduces our key tool for proving the decidability of the packed fragment: mosaics and linked sets of mosaics. Basically, a mosaic consists of a set X of variables in $Var(\xi)$ and a set Γ encoding the relevant information about some small part of a model. Here "small" means that its size is bounded by the number of objects that can be named using variables in X, and "relevant" refers to all formulas in $Cl_g(\xi)$ whose free variables are in X. It turns out that a finite set of such mosaics contains sufficient information to construct a model for ξ, provided that the set links the mosaics together in a nice way. Here is a more formal definition.

Definition 7.6.12. *A mosaic is a pair (X, Γ) such that $X \subseteq Var(\xi)$ and $\Gamma \subseteq Cl_g(\xi)$. A mosaic (X, Γ) is coherent if Γ is an X-type.*

A link between two mosaics (X, Γ) and (X', Γ') is a renaming (that is, an injective substitution) σ with $\mathrm{dom}(\sigma) \subseteq X$ and $\mathrm{ran}(\sigma) \subseteq X'$ which satisfies, for all formulas $\varphi \in Cl_g(\xi)$, $\varphi \in \Gamma$ iff $\varphi^\sigma \in \Gamma'$.

A requirement of a mosaic is a formula of the form $\varphi(\overline{x}) = \exists \overline{y} \left(\pi(\overline{x}, \overline{y}) \wedge \psi(\overline{x}, \overline{y}) \right)$ belonging to Γ. A mosaic (X', Γ') fulfills the requirement $\exists \overline{y} \left(\pi(\overline{x}, \overline{y}) \wedge \psi(\overline{x}, \overline{y}) \right)$ of a mosaic (X, Γ) via the link σ, if, for some variables $\overline{u}, \overline{v}$ in X', we have that $\sigma(\overline{x}) = \overline{u}$ and that $\pi(\overline{u}, \overline{v})$ and $\psi(\overline{u}, \overline{v})$ belong to Γ'. A set S of mosaics is linked if every requirement of every mosaic in S is fulfilled via some link to some mosaic in S. S is a linked set of mosaics for ξ if it is linked and $\xi \in \Gamma$ for some (X, Γ) in S.

Note that a mosaic (X, Γ) may fulfill its own requirements, either via the identity map or via some other map from X to X.

The key result concerning mosaics is the following Mosaic Theorem.

Theorem 7.6.13 (Mosaic Theorem). *Let ξ be a packed formula. Then ξ is satisfiable if and only if there is a linked set of mosaics for ξ.*

Proof. The hard, right-to-left, direction of the theorem is proved in Lemma 7.6.14 below; here we prove only the other direction.

Suppose that ξ is satisfied in the model $\mathcal{M} = (D, I)$. In a straightforward way we can "cut out" from $\mathcal{M}$ a linked set of mosaics for ξ. Consider the set of partial assignments of elements in D to variables in $Var(\xi)$. For each such α, let $(X_\alpha, \Gamma_\alpha)$ be the mosaic given by $X_\alpha = \mathrm{dom}(\alpha)$ and

$$\Gamma_\alpha = \{\varphi \in Cl_g(\xi) \mid \mathcal{M} \models \varphi[\alpha]\}.$$

We leave it to the reader to verify that this collection forms a linked set of mosaics for ξ.   □

In establishing the hard direction of this proposition, we shall in fact prove something stronger: starting from a linked set of mosaics for a formula ξ we shall show that there is a *loose* or *tree-like* model for ξ.

First, however, we want to show that the Mosaic Theorem is the key for proving the decidability of the packed fragment, and also for finding an upper bound for its complexity.

The Decision Algorithm and Its Complexity

The Mosaic Theorem tells us that any packed formula ξ is satisfiable if and only if there is a linked set of mosaics for ξ. Thus in order to decide whether ξ is satisfiable, it suffices to give an algorithm which decides the existence of a linked set of mosaics for ξ. We shall establish the upper complexity bound for the satisfiability problem of packed formulas by implementing such an algorithm. The following observations are easy consequences of our definitions; recall that k denotes the number of variables occurring in ξ.

- We have already observed that the cardinality of $Cl_g(\xi)$ is bounded by $k^k \cdot 2|\xi|$.
- The number of mosaics does not exceed $2^k \cdot 2^{2|\xi| \cdot k^k}$; using the big O notation, this gives at most $2^{O(|\xi|) \cdot k^k}$ mosaics.
- given sets X, Γ with $X \subseteq Var(\xi)$ and $\Gamma \subseteq Cl_g(\xi)$, it is decidable in time $2^{O(|\xi|) \cdot k^k}$ whether (X, Γ) is a coherent mosaic.

Our algorithm is very similar to the one we used for the until system in Subsect. 7.4.3. Let S_0 be the set of all coherent mosaics. By the observations above, S_0 contains fewer than $2^{O(|\xi|) \cdot k^k}$ elements and can be constructed in time $2^{O(|\xi|) \cdot k^k}$. We now inductively construct a sequence of sets of mosaics $S_0 \supsetneq S_1 \supsetneq S_2 \supsetneq S_3 \cdots$, as follows. We call a mosaic μ in a set S_i S_i-*ready* if each of its requirements is fulfilled in (some mosaic of) S_i. Note that one can determine the S_i-readiness of a mosaic (X, Γ) by checking, for each requirement $\varphi(\overline{x}) \in \Gamma$, whether there is a link σ to some mosaic $(X', \Gamma') \in S_i$ which fulfills the requirement. If every mosaic μ in S_i is S_i-ready, then return "YES" if S_i contains a mosaic (X, Γ) with $\xi \in \Gamma$, and "NO" if S_i contains no such mosaic. If, on the other hand, there are mosaics in S_i that are not S_i-ready, then we let S_{i+1} consist of the S_i-ready mosaics and continue the algorithm.

Clearly the algorithm is correct; and since $S_i \supsetneq S_{i+1}$, the construction must halt after at most $|S_0|$ many stages. So let us now see about the complexity. At each stage i, the algorithm determines the S_i-ready mosaics; we claim that this can be done in time exponential in $k^k \cdot O(|\xi|)$.

To check whether a given link between two given mosaics fulfills some given requirement is a task that takes time linear in the size of each mosaic, and so time quadratic in $k^k \cdot 2|\xi|$. In order to find out whether a given mosaic (X, Γ) in a set S_i is S_i-ready, the algorithm has to check, for every requirement $\varphi(\overline{x})$ of the mosaic, for every link σ, and for every mosaic (X', Γ') in S_i, whether σ is a link between the mosaics fulfilling the requirement. Clearly, then, for a given mosaic, this takes time at most $k^k \cdot 2|\xi|$ (for the number of requirements) times k^k (for the number of links) times $|S_i|$ (for the number of mosaics) times $(k^k \cdot 2|\xi|)^2$ (for the checking time). Note that S_i is the only number in this product that is exponential in $k^k \cdot O(|\xi|)$. Hence, in order to compute all the S_i-ready mosaics, the algorithm needs time exponential in $O(|\xi|) \cdot k^k$.

As the size of S_0 is bounded by $2^{O(|\xi|) \cdot k^k}$, the whole computation can be performed in time exponential in $O(|\xi|) \cdot k^k$. Hence, if we consider a formula ξ in a packed fragment with a *fixed number of variables*, $|S_0|$ is singly exponential in $|\xi|$. In general, however, the number of variables k occurring in a formula depends on the formula's length and hence, in general, $|S_0|$ is doubly exponential in $|\xi|$. *Thus, pending the proof of the next lemma, this shows the upper complexity bounds given in Theorems 7.6.8 and 7.6.9.*

Step-by-Step Construction and Loose Models

We now show the hard direction of the Mosaic Theorem and establish, as a by-product, the "loose model property" of Theorem 7.6.7.

Lemma 7.6.14. *Let ξ be a packed formula. If there is a linked set of mosaics for ξ, then ξ is satisfiable in a loose model of degree $|Var(\xi)|$.*

Proof. Assume that S is a linked set of mosaics for ξ. Using a step-by-step construction, we shall build a model for ξ, together with a graph $\mathcal{G}$ and a function f mapping nodes of $\mathcal{G}$ to subsets of the domain of the model. At each stage of the construction, we shall be dealing with some kind of approximation of the final model and graph; these approximations will be called networks and are fairly complex structures.

A *network* is a quintuple $(\mathcal{M}, \mathcal{G}, \mu, \alpha, \sigma)$ such that $\mathcal{M} = (D, I)$ is a model for the first-order language; $\mathcal{G} = (G, E)$ is a connected, adirected, and acyclic graph; $\mu : G \to S$ is a map associating a mosaic $\mu_t = (X_t, \Gamma_t)$ in S with each node t of the graph; and α is a map associating a map $\alpha_t : X_t \to D$ with each node t of the graph. (This map is thus a partial assignment of the variables occurring in ξ.) And, finally, σ is a map associating with each edge (t, t') of the graph a link $\sigma_{tt'}$ from μ_t to $\mu_{t'}$ (we shall usually simplify our notation by writing σ instead of $\sigma_{tt'}$).

The idea is that each mosaic μ_t is supposed to give a complete description of the relevant requirements that we impose on a small part of the model-to-be. Which part? This is given by the assignment α_t. And the word "relevant" refers to the fact that we are interested only in the formulas influencing the truth of ξ; that is, the formulas in $Cl_g(\xi)$. The links between neighboring mosaics are there to ensure that distinct mosaics agree on the part of the model that they both have access to.

Now, obviously, if we want all of this to work properly we have to impose some conditions on the networks. In order to formulate these, we need some auxiliary notation. For a subset $A \subseteq D$, let $L(A)$ denote the set of nodes in $\mathcal{G}$ that have "access" to A; formally, we define $L(A) = \{t \in G \mid A \subseteq \mathrm{ran}(\alpha_t)\}$. For a tuple $\bar{a} = (a_1, \dots, a_n)$ of elements in D we set $L(\bar{a}) = L(\{a_1, \dots, a_n\})$. Now a network is called *coherent* if it satisfies the following conditions (all to be read as universally quantified):

(C1) $P\bar{x} \in \Gamma_t$ iff $\mathcal{M} \models P\bar{x}[\alpha_t]$;
(C2) $x_i = x_j \in \Gamma_t$ iff $\alpha_t(x_i) = \alpha_t(x_j)$;
(C3) $L(A)$ is nonempty for every guarded set $A \subseteq D$;
(C4) $L(A)$ is connected for every guarded set $A \subseteq D$;
(C5) if Ett', then $\sigma_{tt'}(x) = x'$ iff $\alpha_t(x) = \alpha_{t'}(x')$.

A few words of explanation about these conditions: (C1) and (C2) ensure that every mosaic is a complete description of the atomic formulas that hold in the part of the model it refers to. Condition (C3) states that no guarded set in the model remains unseen from the graph, and the conditions (C4) and (C5) are the crucial ones that ensure that remote parts of the graph cannot contain contradictory information about the model — how this works precisely will become clear later on. Note that condition (C5) has two directions: the left-to-right direction states that neighboring mosaics have common access to part of the model, while the other direction makes them agree on their requirements concerning this common part.

The motivation for using these networks is that in the end we want any formula $\varphi(\bar{x}) \in Cl_g(\xi)$ to hold in $\mathcal{M}$ under the assignment α_t if and only if $\varphi(\bar{x})$ belongs to Γ_t. Coherence on its own is not sufficient to make this happen. A *defect* of a network consists of a formula $\exists \bar{y} (\pi(\bar{x}, \bar{y}) \wedge \psi(\bar{x}, \bar{y}))$ which is a requirement of the mosaic μ_t for some node t while there is no neighboring node t' such that $\mu_{t'}$ fulfills $\exists \bar{y} (\pi(\bar{x}, \bar{y}) \wedge \psi(\bar{x}, \bar{y}))$ via the link $\sigma_{tt'}$. A coherent network $\mathcal{N}$ is *perfect* if it has no defects. We say that $\mathcal{N}$ is a network for ξ if for some $t \in G$, $\mu_t = (X_t, \Gamma_t)$ is such that $\xi \in \Gamma_t$.

Claim 1. If $\mathcal{N} = (\mathcal{M}, \mathcal{G}, \mu, \alpha, \sigma)$ is a perfect network, then
(i) $\mathcal{M}$ is a loose model of degree $|Var(\xi)|$, and
(ii) for all formulas $\varphi(\bar{x}) \in Cl_g(\xi)$ and all nodes t of $\mathcal{G}$,

$$\varphi \in \Gamma_t \text{ iff } \mathcal{M} \models \varphi[\alpha_t].$$

PROOF OF CLAIM For part (i) of the claim, let $\mathcal{N} = (\mathcal{M}, \mathcal{G}, \mu, \alpha, \sigma)$ be the perfect network for ξ. Let $\mathcal{M} = (D, I)$. As the function f mapping nodes of $\mathcal{G}$ to *subsets* of D, we simply take the map that assigns the *range* of α_t to the node t. Since the domain of each map α_t is always a subset of $Var(\xi)$, it follows immediately that $f(t)$ will always be a set of size at most $|Var(\xi)|$. Now take an arbitrary live tuple $\overline{s}$ in $\mathcal{M}$; it follows from (C3) and (C4) that $L(\overline{s})$ is a nonempty and connected part of the graph $\mathcal{G}$. Thus $\mathcal{M}$ is a loose model of degree $|Var(\xi)|$.

We prove part (ii) of the claim by induction on the complexity of φ. For atomic formulas, the claim follows by conditions (C1) and (C2), and the boolean case of the induction step is straightforward (since Γ_t is an X-type) and is left to the reader. We concentrate on the case where $\varphi(\overline{x})$ is of the form $\exists \overline{y} \, (\pi(\overline{x}, \overline{y}) \wedge \psi(\overline{x}, \overline{y}))$.

First, assume that $\varphi(\overline{x}) \in \Gamma_t$. Since $\mathcal{N}$ is perfect there is a node t' in G and variables $\overline{u}, \overline{v}$ in $X_{t'}$ such that Ett', $\pi(\overline{u}, \overline{v})$, and $\psi(\overline{u}, \overline{v})$ belong to $\Gamma_{t'}$, while the link σ from μ_t to $\mu_{t'}$ maps $\overline{x}$ to $\overline{u}$. By the induction hypothesis, we find that

$$\mathcal{M} \models \pi(\overline{u}, \overline{v}) \wedge \psi(\overline{u}, \overline{v})[\alpha_{t'}]. \tag{7.13}$$

But, from condition (C5), it follows that $\alpha_{t'}(\overline{x}) = \alpha_t(\overline{u})$; hence (7.13) implies that

$$\mathcal{M} \models \exists \overline{y} \, (\pi(\overline{x}, \overline{y}) \wedge \psi(\overline{x}, \overline{y}))[\alpha_t],$$

which is what we were after.

Now suppose, in order to prove the converse direction, that $\mathcal{M} \models \varphi(\overline{x})[\alpha_t]$. Let $\overline{a}$ denote $\alpha_t(\overline{x})$; there are then $\overline{b}$ in D such that $\mathcal{M} \models \pi(\overline{x}, \overline{y})[\overline{a}\overline{b}]$ and $\mathcal{M} \models \psi(\overline{x}, \overline{y})[\overline{a}\overline{b}]$. Our first aims are to prove that

$$L(\overline{a}\overline{b}) \neq \varnothing \tag{7.14}$$

and

$$L(A) \text{ is connected for every } A \subseteq \{\overline{a}, \overline{b}\}. \tag{7.15}$$

Note that if we are working in the guarded fragment, then $\pi(\overline{x}, \overline{y})$ is an atomic formula, and hence it follows from $\mathcal{M} \models \pi(\overline{x}, \overline{y})[\overline{a}\overline{b}]$ that $\overline{a}\overline{b}$ is live. Thus $\{\overline{a}, \overline{b}\}$ is guarded, and hence (7.14) follows directly by condition (C3). In fact, *every* $A \subseteq \{\overline{a}, \overline{b}\}$ is guarded in this case, and so (7.15) follows immediately by condition (C4).

In the more general case of the packed fragment we have to work a little harder. First, observe that it *does* follow from $\mathcal{M} \models \pi(\overline{x}, \overline{y})[\overline{a}\overline{b}]$ and the conditions on $\pi(\overline{x}, \overline{y})$ in the definition of packed quantification that $\{c, d\}$ is guarded, and thus $L(c, d) \neq \varnothing$, for every *pair* (c, d) of points taken from $\overline{a}\overline{b}$. It follows from (C4) that $\{L(c, d) \mid c, d \text{ taken from } \overline{a}\overline{b}\}$ is a collection of nonempty, connected, pairwise overlapping subgraphs of the acyclic graph $\mathcal{G}$. It is fairly straightforward to prove, for instance by induction on the size of the graph $\mathcal{G}$, that any such collection must have a nonempty intersection. From this, (7.14) and (7.15) follow almost immediately.

We thus may assume the existence of a node t' in $\mathcal{G}$ such that $\{\overline{a}, \overline{b}\} \subseteq \text{ran}\alpha_{t'}$. Let $\overline{u}$ and $\overline{v}$ in $X_{t'}$ be the variables such that $\alpha_{t'}(\overline{u}) = \overline{a}$ and $\alpha_{t'}(\overline{v}) = \overline{b}$. The induction hypothesis implies that $\pi(\overline{u}, \overline{v})$ and $\psi(\overline{u}, \overline{v})$ belong to $\Gamma_{t'}$, and hence $\varphi(\overline{u}) \in \Gamma_{t'}$ by the coherence of $\mu_{t'}$. Since both t and t' belong to $L(\overline{a})$, it follows from (7.15) that there is a path from t to t' *within* $L(\overline{a})$, say $t' = s_0 E s_1 E \ldots E s_n = t$. Let σ_i be the link between the mosaics of s_i and s_{i+1}, and define ρ to be the composition of these maps. It follows by an easy inductive argument on the length of the path that ρ is a link between $\mu_{t'}$ and μ_t such that $\rho(\overline{u}) = \overline{x}$. Hence, by the definition of a link, we have that $\varphi(\overline{x}) \in \Gamma_{t'}$. This finishes the proof of the claim.

By Claim 1, in order to prove the lemma it suffices to construct a perfect network for ξ. This construction uses a step-by-step argument; to start the construction, we need *some* coherent network for ξ.

Claim 2. There is a coherent network for ξ.

PROOF OF CLAIM By our assumption about ξ, there is a coherent mosaic $\mu = (X, \Gamma)$ such that $\xi \in \Gamma$. Without loss of generality we may assume that X is the set $\{x_1, \ldots, x_n\}$ (otherwise, we can take an isomorphic copy of μ in which X does have this form). Let $a_1, \ldots, a_n$ be a list of objects such that, for all i and j, we have that $a_i = a_j$ if and only if the formula $x_i = x_j$ belongs to Γ. Define $D = \{a_1, \ldots, a_n\}$, and put the tuple $(a_{i_1}, \ldots, a_{i_k})$ in the interpretation $I(P)$ of the k-ary predicate symbol P precisely if $Px_{i_1} \ldots x_{i_n} \in \Gamma$. Let $\mathcal{M}$ be the resulting model (D, I), and define $\mathcal{G}$ as the trivial graph with one node 0 and no edges. Let $\mu(0)$ be the mosaic μ; let $\alpha_0 : X \to D$ be given by $\alpha(x_i) = a_i$; and, finally, let σ_{00} be the identity map from X to X.

We leave it for the reader to verify that the quintuple $(\mathcal{M}, \mathcal{G}, \mu, \alpha, \sigma)$ is a coherent network for ξ. This finishes the proof of the claim.

The crucial step of this construction is to show that any defect of a coherent network can be repaired.

Claim 3. For any coherent network $\mathcal{N} = (\mathcal{M}, \mathcal{G}, \mu, \alpha, \sigma)$ and any defect of $\mathcal{N}$ there is a coherent network $\mathcal{N}^+$ that extends $\mathcal{N}$ and lacks this defect.

PROOF OF CLAIM Suppose that $\varphi(\overline{x})$ is a defect of $\mathcal{N}$ because it is a requirement of the mosaic μ_t and not fulfilled by any neighboring mosaic $\mu_{t'}$. We shall define an extension $\mathcal{N}^+$ of $\mathcal{N}$ in which this defect is repaired.

Since S is a linked set of mosaics and μ_t belongs to S, μ_t is linked to a mosaic $(X', \Gamma') \in S$ in which the requirement is fulfilled via some link ρ. Let Y be the set of variables in X' that do not belong to the range of ρ; suppose that $Y = \{y_1, \ldots, y_k\}$ (with all y_i being distinct). For the sake of a smooth presentation, assume that Γ' contains the formulas $\neg x' = y$ for all variables $x' \in X'$ and $y \in Y$ (this is not without loss of generality — we leave the general case as an exercise for the reader). Take a set $\{c_1, \ldots, c_k\}$ of fresh objects (that is, no c_i is an element of the domain D of $\mathcal{M}$), and let γ be the assignment with domain X' defined as follows:

$$\gamma(x') = \begin{cases} \alpha_t(x) \text{ if } x' = \rho(x), \\ c_i \quad \text{ if } x' = y_i. \end{cases}$$

Let t' be an object not belonging to G. Now define the network $\mathcal{N}^+ = (\mathcal{M}^+, \mathcal{G}^+, \mu^+, \alpha^+, \sigma^+)$ as follows:

$$D^+ = D \cup \{c_1, \ldots, c_k\},$$
$$I^+(P) = I(P) \cup \{\bar{d} \mid \text{ for some } \bar{x}, \bar{d} = \gamma(\bar{x}) \text{ and } P\bar{x} \in \Gamma'\},$$
$$G^+ = G \cup \{t'\},$$
$$E^+ = E \cup \{(t, t')\},$$

and μ^+, α^+ and σ^+ are given by the obvious extensions of μ, α, and σ, namely by putting $\mu_{t'}^+ = (X', \Gamma')$, $\alpha_{t'}^+ = \gamma$, and $\sigma_{tt'} = \rho$.

Since the interpretation I^+ agrees with I on "old" tuples, it is a straightforward exercise to verify that the new network $\mathcal{N}^+$ satisfies the conditions (C1 - C3) and (C5).

In order to check that condition (C4) holds, take some guarded subset A from D^+; we shall show that $L^+(A)$ is a connected subgraph of $\mathcal{G}^+$. It is rather easy to see that $L^+(A)$ is identical to either $L(A)$ or $L(A) \cup \{t'\}$; hence by the connectedness of $L(A)$, it suffices to prove, on the assumption that $t' \in L^+(A)$ and $L(A) \neq \varnothing$, that $t \in L(A)$. Hence, suppose that $t' \in L^+(A)$; that is, each $a \in A$ is in the range of γ. But if $L(A) \neq \varnothing$, each such point a must be old; hence, by the definition of γ, each $a \in A$ must belong to $\text{ran}(\alpha_t)$. This gives the result that $t \in L(A)$, as required. This finishes the proof of the claim.

As in the proof for the until system, the previous two claims show that by using some standard combinatorics we can construct a chain of networks such that their *limit* is a perfect network. This finishes the proof of the lemma.   □

7.6.3 Notes

The roots of the decidability proof in this section date back to 1986, when Németi [45] showed that the equational theory of the class Crs of relativized cylindric set algebras is decidable. The first-order counterpart of this result is that a certain subfragment of the guarded fragment is decidable.

The importance of this result for first-order logic was realized in 1994 when Andréka, van Benthem & Németi introduced the guarded fragment and showed that many nice properties of the basic modal system **K** generalize to it. In particular, these authors established a characterization in terms of guarded bisimulations, decidability, and a kind of tree model property. The journal version of their paper is [2]. Some time later, van Benthem [7] generalized some of the results, introducing the loosely guarded fragment. The slightly more general packed fragment was introduced by Marx [41] in order to give a semantic characterization in terms of packed bisimulations (Theorem 7.6.5). (An example of a packed sentence which is not equivalent to a loosely guarded sentence in the same signature is $\exists xyz(\exists wCxyw \wedge \exists wCxzw \wedge \exists wCzyw \wedge \neg Cxyz)$.)

The mosaic-based decision algorithms used by Andréka, van Benthem & Németi were essentially optimal, a result established by Grädel [21]. In that paper, Grädel also defind and established the loose model property for the loosely guarded fragment. Our definition of a loose model is based on the definition of a tree model given there. Grädel & Walukiewicz [22] showed that the same bounds obtain when the guarded fragment is expanded with least and greatest fixed-point operators. Marx, Schlobach & Mikulas [42] defined a PSPACE complete guarded fragment with the finite tree model property. This fragment satisfies both locality principles.

The finite model property for the guarded fragment and several sub-fragments of the packed fragment was established in an algebraic setting by Andréka, Hodkinson & Németi [1]. Grädel [21] provided a direct proof for the guarded fragment. After we finished the writing of this chapter, Hodkinson [32] proved the finite model property of the full packed fragment. All these results are based on variants of a result due to Herwig [29]. The use of Herwig's Theorem to establish the finite model property and to eliminate the need of step-by-step constructions originates with Hirsch et alii [30].

Acknowledgments

We are very grateful to Carlos Areces, Edith Hemaspaandra, and Carla Piazza for scrutinizing earlier versions of this manuscript and for making many suggestions for improvement. We would also like to thank Moshe Vardi and Scott Weinstein for inviting us to participate in this project.

References

1. H. Andréka, I. Hodkinson, and I. Németi. Finite algebras of relations are representable on finite sets. *Journal of Symbolic Logic*, 64(1):243–267, 1999.
2. H. Andréka, J. van Benthem, and I. Németi. Modal languages and bounded fragments of predicate logic. *Journal of Philosophical Logic*, 27(3):217–274, 1998.
3. J. Balcázar, J. Díaz, and J. Gabarró. *Structural Complexity I*. EATCS Monographs on Theoretical Computer Science, No. 11. Springer, 1988.
4. J. van Benthem. *Modal Correspondence Theory*. PhD thesis, Mathematisch Instituut & Instituut voor Grondslagenonderzoek, University of Amsterdam, 1976.
5. J. van Benthem. *Modal Logic and Classical Logic*. Bibliopolis, Naples, 1983.
6. J. van Benthem. *Exploring Logical Dynamics*. Studies in Logic, Language and Information. CSLI Publications, Stanford, 1996.
7. J. van Benthem. Dynamic bits and pieces. Technical Report LP-97-01, Institute for Logic, Language and Computation, University of Amsterdam, 1997.

8. R. Berger. The undecidability of the domino problem. *Memoirs of the American Mathematical Society*, 66: 1–72, 1966.

9. P. Blackburn, M. de Rijke, and Y. Venema. *Modal Logic*. Cambridge University Press, 2001.

10. E. Börger, E. Grädel, and Y. Gurevich. *The Classical Decision Problem*. Springer, 1997.

11. A. Borgida. Description logics in data management. *IEEE Transactions on Knowledge and Data Engineering*, 7:671–682, 1995.

12. J.P. Burgess and Y. Gurevich. The decision problem for linear temporal logic. *Notre Dame Journal of Formal Logic*, 26:115–128, 1985.

13. D. Calvanese, G. De Giacomo, D. Nardi, and M. Lenzerini. Reasoning in expressive description logics. In A. Robinson and A. Voronkov, editors, *Handbook of Automated Reasoning*, pages 1581–1634. Elsevier Science, 1999.

14. A. Chagrov and M. Zakharyaschev. *Modal Logic*. Oxford Logic Guides No. 35. Oxford University Press, Oxford, 1997.

15. A. Chandra and P. Merlin. Optimal implementation of conjunctive queries in relational databases. In *Proceedings of 9th ACM Symposium on Theory of Computing*, pages 77–90, 1977.

16. M.A.E. Dummett and E.J. Lemmon. Modal logics between S4 and S5. *Zeitschrift für mathematische Logik und Grundlagen der Mathematik*, 5:250–264, 1959.

17. R. Fagin, J.Y. Halpern, Y. Moses, and M.Y. Vardi. *Reasoning about Knowledge*. MIT Press, 1995.

18. M. Fischer and R. Ladner. Propositional dynamic logic of regular programs. *Journal of Computer and System Sciences*, 18(2):194–211, 1979.

19. M. Fürer. The computational complexity of the unconstrained limited domino problem (with implications for logical decision problems). In E. Börger, G. Hasenjaeger and D. Rödding, *Logic and Machines: Decision Problems and Complexity*. Lecture Notes in Computer Science No. 171, pages 312–319. Springer, 1981.

20. D.M. Gabbay. An irreflexivity lemma with applications to axiomatizations of conditions on linear frames. In U. Mönnich, editor, *Aspects of Philosophical Logic*, pages 67–89. Reidel, 1981.

21. E. Grädel. On the restraining power of guards. *Journal of Symbolic Logic*, 64(4):1719–1742, 1999.

22. E. Grädel and I. Walukiewicz. Guarded fixed point logic. In *Proceedings of 14th IEEE Symposium on Logic in Computer Science LICS '99, Trento*, 1999.

23. J.Y. Halpern and Y.O. Moses. A guide to completeness and complexity for modal logics of knowledge and belief. *Artificial Intelligence*, 54:319–379, 1992.

24. D. Harel. Dynamic logic. In D.M. Gabbay and F. Guenther, editors, *Handbook of Philosophical Logic*, volume 2, pages 497–604. Reidel, Dordrecht, 1984.

25. R. Harrop. On the existence of finite models and decision procedures for propositional calculi. *Proceedings of the Cambridge Philosophical Society*, 54:1–13, 1958.

26. L. Henkin. *Logical Systems Containing Only a Finite Number of Symbols*. Séminiare de Mathematique Supérieures 21. Les Presses de l'Université de Montréal, Montréal, 1967.

27. L. Henkin, J. D. Monk, and A. Tarski. *Cylindric Algebras, Parts I and II*. North-Holland, 1971 and 1985.

28. M. Hennessy and R. Milner. Algebraic laws for indeterminism and concurrency. *Journal of the ACM*, 32:137–162, 1985.

29. B. Herwig. Extending partial isomorphisms on finite structures. *Combinatorica*, 15:365–371, 1995.

30. R. Hirsch, I. Hodkinson, M. Marx, Sz. Mikulás, and M. Reynolds. Mosaics and step-by-step. Remarks on "A modal logic of relations". In E. Orłowska, editor, *Logic at Work. Essays Dedicated to the Memory of Elena Rasiowa*, Studies in Fuzziness and Soft Computing, pages 158–167. Springer, 1999.

31. W. Hodges. *Model Theory*. Cambridge University Press, 1993.

32. I. Hodkinson. Loosely guarded fragment of first-order logic has the finite model property. *Studia Logica*, 70(2):205–240, 2002.

33. N. Immerman. Upper and lower bounds for first-order expressibility. *Journal of Computer and System Sciences*, 25:76–98, 1982.

34. N. Immerman and D. Kozen. Definability with bounded number of bound variables. In *Proceedings of the Symposium on Logic in Computer Science*, pages 236–244, Washington, 1987. Computer Society Press.

35. D. Janin and I. Walukiewicz. On the expressive completeness of the propositional μ-calculus w.r.t. monadic second-order logic. In *Proceedings of CONCUR '96*, 1996.

36. N. Kurtonina and M. de Rijke. Bisimulations for temporal logic. *Journal of Logic, Language and Information*, 6:403–425, 1997.

37. R. Ladner. The computational complexity of provability in systems of modal propositional logic. *SIAM Journal of computing*, 6(3):467–480, 1977.

38. E.J. Lemmon. Algebraic semantics for modal logics [Parts I and II]. *Journal of Symbolic Logic*, pages 46–65 and 191–218, 1966.

39. Z. Manna and A. Pnueli. *The Temporal Logic of Reactive and Concurrent Systems. Vol. 1, Specification*. Springer, 1992.

40. M. Marx. Complexity of products of modal logics. *Journal of Logic and Computation*, 9(2):221–238, 1999.

41. M. Marx. Tolerance logic. *Journal of Logic, Language and Information* 10:353–373, 2001.

42. M. Marx, S. Schlobach, and Sz. Mikulás. Labelled deduction for the guarded fragment. In D. Basin et al., editors, *Labelled Deduction*, Applied Logic Series, pages 193–214. Kluwer Academic, 2000.

43. M. Marx and Y. Venema. *Multi-dimensional Modal Logic*. Applied Logic Series. Kluwer Academic, 1997.

44. J.C.C. McKinsey and A. Tarski. The algebra of topology. *Annals of Mathematics*, pages 141–191, 1944.

45. I. Németi. Free Algebras and Decidability in Algebraic Logic. DSc. thesis, Mathematical Institute of the Hungararian Academy of Sciences, Budapest, 1986 (in Hungarian; English version in [46]).

46. I. Németi. Decidability of weakened versions of first-order logic. In *Logic Colloquium '92*, pages 177–242, Stanford, 1995. CSLI Publications.

47. M. Otto. *Bounded Variable Logics and Counting. A Study in Finite Models*. Lecture Notes in Logic No. 9. Springer, 1997.

48. D. Park. Concurrency and automata on infinite sequences. In P. Deussen, editor, *Theoretical Computer Science*. Lecture Notes in Computer Science No. 104, pages 167–183. Springer, 1981.

49. S. Popkorn. *First Steps in Modal Logic*. Cambridge University Press, Cambridge, 1992.

50. V. Pratt. Models of program logics. In *Proceedings of the 20th IEEE symposium on Foundations of Computer Science*, pages 115–122, 1979.

51. E. Rosen. Modal logic over finite structures. *Journal of Logic, Language and Information*, 6:427–439, 1997.

52. K. Segerberg. *An Essay in Classical Modal Logic*. Filosofiska Studier 13. University of Uppsala, 1971.

53. K. Segerberg. Two-dimensional modal logic. *Journal of Philosophical Logic*, 2:77–96, 1973.

54. A. Sistla and E. Clarke. Complexity of propositional linear temporal logics. *Journal of the ACM*, 32(3):733–749, 1985.

55. E. Spaan. *Complexity of Modal Logics*. PhD thesis, Institute for Logic, Language and Computation, University of Amsterdam, 1993.

56. C. Stirling. Modal and temporal logics. In S. Abramsky, D.M. Gabbay, and T.S.E. Maibaum, editors, *Handbook of Logic in Computer Science I*, pages 641–761. Clarendon Press, 1992.

57. M. Vardi. On the complexity of bounded-variable queries. In N. Immerman and Ph. G. Kolaitis, editors, *Descriptive Complexity and Finite Models*, volume 31 of *DIMACS Series in Discrete Mathematics and Theoretical Computer Science*, pages 149–184. American Mathematical Society, 1996.

58. M. Vardi. Why is modal logic so robustly decidable? In *DIMACS Series in Discrete Mathematics and Theoretical Computer Science 31*, pages 149–184. American Math. Society, 1997.

59. Y. Venema. *Many-Dimensional Modal Logic*. PhD thesis, Institute for Logic, Language and Computation, University of Amsterdam, 1992.

60. Y. Venema. Cylindric modal logic. *Journal of Symbolic Logic*, 60(2):591–623, 1995.

61. H. Wang. Proving theorems by pattern recognition II. *Bell Systems Techical Journal*, 40:1–41, 1961.

Index

Monographs in Theoretical Computer Science · An EATCS Series

Texts in Theoretical Computer Science · An EATCS Series